W9-BSA-532

The Whole World Book of Quotations

The **Whole World Book** of Quotations

Wisdom from Women and Men
Around the Globe
Throughout the
Centuries

compiled and edited by
Kathryn Petras and Ross Petras

*"Without knowing the force of words,
it is impossible to know men."*
—Confucius

ADDISON-WESLEY PUBLISHING COMPANY

Reading, Massachusetts • Menlo Park, California • New York • Don Mills, Ontario
Wokingham, England • Amsterdam • Bonn • Sydney • Singapore • Tokyo •
Madrid • San Juan • Paris • Seoul • Milan • Mexico City • Taipei

Library of Congress Cataloging-in-Publication Data

The Whole world book of quotations : wisdom from women and men around
   the globe throughout the centuries / compiled and edited by Kathryn
   Petras and Ross Petras.
       p.   cm.
   Includes bibliographical references and index.
   ISBN 0-201-62258-0
   1. Quotations, English.   2. Quotations.   I. Petras, Kathryn.
II. Petras, Ross.
PN6081.W43   1994   94-12465
082—dc20   CIP

Jacket design by Suzanne Heiser
Text design by Wilson Graphics & Design (Kenneth J. Wilson)
Set in 10-point Garamond by Weimer Graphics, Inc.

1 2 3 4 5 6 7 8 9-MA-97969594
First printing, October 1994

Contents

v

Contents

Contents

Acknowledgements

*T*hanks to everyone who make this book a reality, especially Liz Perle McKenna for appreciating—and understanding—our concept, John Bell for expert editorial direction that kept us going even through the rough times, Beth Burleigh for shepherding the project through production against all odds, Kenneth Wilson and Suzanne Heiser for superb book and cover design, and everyone else at Addison-Wesley; and a special thanks to Mitch Kelly for crucial assistance when we needed it most.

Introduction

As we were preparing this book in the fall of 1993, the White House was preparing the ceremony at which Prime Minister Yitzhak Rabin of Israel and Chairman Yasir Arafat of the Palestinian Liberation Organization would sign their recognition pact. President Bill Clinton was to deliver a speech for that historic moment. He asked his speechwriters and advisers to include two quotations on peace: one from the Israeli tradition, the other from Arab culture.

They had little trouble finding a quotation from the Hebrew Bible; it is a basic part of our Western culture, and is quoted and dissected in many reference books. But the White House had trouble obtaining an appropriate saying from the Islamic tradition. Phone calls went out to the State Department, to universities, and even to the Saudi Arabian embassy. Finally, the speech writers were guided to a relevant saying from the Qur'an: "If thine enemy inclines toward peace, do thou also incline toward peace."

This incident told us that we were on the right track in preparing this book, that there is a need for *The Whole World Book of Quotations.* It is a different sort of quotation reference book, and to the best of our knowledge, the first of its type.

It includes some of the best, or at least most interesting, words and thoughts of people most *underrepresented* in all the quotation books on our bookstore and library shelves—women, minorities, and all people outside of Europe and the United States.

As in the more familiar *Bartlett's Familiar Quotations* or *The Oxford Dictionary of Quotations,* there's much that's profound or interesting or sometimes outrageous included here, much that makes you think, much that you can incorporate in your speeches, writings, or thoughts. Although we've included many quotes that will be unfamiliar to many Westerners, many are very familiar to others: quotations that are on the lips of millions of Asians or Africans or Latin Americans, quotations that cap an argument in Teheran or open a speech in Lagos. This may be one of the real virtues of this book. It gives a snapshot view of what many of our neighbors on the planet have said or are saying.

We've included many traditional quotations from the Qur'an and the Hindu and other scriptures, since to a greater degree than in most of the West, religion is truly a part of daily life—the Mahabarata, a sacred epic poem, can be seen as a popular television drama in India. Meanwhile, Lee Kuan Yew operates his highly successful nation-state of Singapore as a virtual justification of Confucianist philosophy. Of course the ideas in the Qur'an are galvanizing an entire generation in the Middle East, toppling governments, and influencing policies to a degree unexpected by most experts.

Such words are powerful and compelling—and they need to be heard. This is why we decided to compile this book. It is designed not as a replacement for such excellent quotation books as *Bartlett's* and *Oxford* but as a complement to them. It starts to fill in the blanks; give us alternative views on topics such as life, love, and work; and highlight both the similarities and the differences among cultures, races, and the sexes.

We were surprised by the impact many of the quotations had on us. We were moved by the beauty of Korean and Vietnamese poetry, the wisdom of the Talmud and the Qur'an. These were the most gratifying aspects of our working on the book, and we hope it is equally gratifying to you.

How to Use This Book

*H*ow to use this book? At first glance the question seems almost tauto-logical. Just as one would use any other standard book of quotation ar-ranged by topic—pick the topic, scan the selections, and pick the appropriate quote. If you don't see your initial topic on the list, look for synonyms, related words, or opposites. For more information on any spe-cific individual quoted, check the alphabetized Biographical Index at the back of the book.

This said, most readers will notice some important differences that are in some cases significant, and which readers should be aware of:

Many of the quotations are in translation.

Obviously, this changes the quotation to some degree. It can weaken the force of the quotation—or, as with the *Rubáiyát of Omar Khayyám,* perhaps artificially strengthen it. We tried to avoid the latter situation, since such words are as much a part of Western tradition as Eastern. In fact, a scholarly survey of the *Rubáiyát* found that the translator, Ed-ward FitzGerald, created some of the English stanzas completely on his own, combined others, and significantly changed the meanings of many more.

But to a great degree, translations of *any* quotation render it artificial. *Any* translator of any selection must take many liberties to not only convey the force and flavor of the original but also make it intelligible to an English-language reader. Idiomatic expressions are the most obvious prob-lem (Mikhail Gorbachev once told an interlocutor not to "hang noodles from his ears"—which sounds ridiculous in English but is simply a verba-tim translation of a common Russian expression). Obviously, a translator can change these idiomatic expressions fairly easily while keeping the true meaning, but what about other aspects? For example, what about the rhyming quality of Arabic poetry? In Arabic, rhymes are extraordinarily easy to compose; in English, they are not. In translating, does one favor rhymes at the cost of meaning? Or does one render a poem in free verse at the expense of the rhyme? Or does one maintain an uneasy truce, alternat-ing between the two as seems expedient? There is no easy answer, and because of this, many quotations taken from great works of poetry often seem forced or artificial because the translators chose from many unac-ceptable alternatives.

The problem is there is *no* solution, let alone an easy one. A reader simply cannot understand the majesty of the language of the Qur'an, nor the subtle beauty of a T'ang dynasty poem, without speaking Arabic or classical Chinese. The power of selections from such great works may be diminished. Which leads to another point—the key role of the translators. Although we, as authors, are familiar with some of the non-Western languages included in this book, only rarely did we translate any passages ourselves, or change an older translation, written in nineteenth-century English, to suit the needs of a modern audience. Translation is difficult enough without amateurs confounding the efforts. In the firm recognition of the translators' efforts, we included their names and the relevant books, whenever possible, in the Bibliography. For more, go to these excellent sources.

Many of the quotations came from different cultures and should be read with this in mind.

If the languages are different in many cases, so is the *context* out of which the quotations arose. Most of us modern North Americans, of whatever race or background, have been schooled in a common Western-oriented tradition, with maybe a survey course on non-Western cultures thrown in. We haven't studied non-Western traditions extensively; we don't instinctively understand their concerns, their environments, their outlooks. In other words, the cultural landscape is different, the cultural signposts are different, and so the quotations are best read with at least a vague understanding of these different contexts. To aid in this, we've included a lengthier than normal Biographical Index with information on the individuals who made the quotations—where they lived, what they represented. And again, we urge readers to use the Bibliography as a guide to more detailed analyses.

The range of this book is far broader than most—it is a cross-section of most of the world—and so inevitably there are omissions.

In this book our aim is to recount quotations from *all* of those groups of people not well represented in other general quotation books. To do this, we emphasize selections from women (who make up over half the human race) and non-Western Europeans or Northern Americans, who historically have made up over 99 percent of all humans. Clearly, in the parameters of three thousand or so quotations, we faced many hard decisions about what and whom to include. Given the surprising difficulty in obtaining many political quotations, we tried to include as many as we could; we tried to cover most major historical periods and most major world cultures; and we tried to include traditional as well as modern wisdom.

Obviously, we omitted much to achieve our goals. Christians and Jews will note that the Bible, so well covered in other books, has been left out; but quotations from the Talmud, so often overlooked, are included. We drew from a broad selection of major contemporary world writers and poets, but we generally included historical writers only from the so-called golden ages of their respective cultures. And some writers, whose words seldom make for epigrammatic "sound bites," are left out or underrepresented: for example, the Egyptian Nobel laureate Naguib Mahfouz is a wonderful narrative writer, but he is underrepresented because much of his writing is extremely contextual and difficult to read in isolated bits.

A cross-section of traditional religious and philosophical texts has been included.

The great traditions of the world's religions and history have been ignored all too often by the secular West. When one of us served with the State Department, he frequently heard talk about the Soviet threat to the Middle East, but next to nothing about the rising tide of Islamic fundamentalism. Communist threats were sexy; obscure mullahs were not, at least not to the policy lords of Washington at that time.

As noted earlier, we in the United States often forget that religion drives many other cultures (and we even forget the role it plays in our own). A first step to understanding others is to understand that their political movements and customs have underpinnings in religions and philosophies outside of our own traditions. Even in Asia, where in many areas religion's impact is waning under the force of modernization, the basic structure of Confucianist or Buddhist thought remains. Lu Xun, among other prominent modern Chinese writers, makes this point very forcefully. All too often, Western commentators focus on China's Communist, or now quasi-capitalist, society as somehow divorced from its four thousand years of history.

As compilers, we chose what moved us.

We tried to follow the basic parameters described thus far, but we also felt free to choose quotes that *we* liked. To some degree we felt luckier than compilers like Justin Kaplan (whose new edition of *Bartlett's Familiar Quotations* we think is the best yet). Kaplan *had* to choose certain quotations since he was working on a book for an audience that shared a culture and would notice if, for example, a John Updike or T. S. Eliot was missing. Our range of possible selections was so broad that we obviously could not include everything, so we had more latitude to omit some selections in favor of particular quotations we liked.

You will notice our own biases: classical Persian poets are well represented, as are modern Chinese and Arab poets. We were especially interested in writers of Pre-Israeli Zionism, as well as in early Islamic legal philosophy and medieval Korean poets. And the words of the Indian philosophers Mahatma Gandhi and Rabindranath Tagore, and modern African writers appear often. All of these writings touched a special nerve for us. And we occasionally put in something that shocked us, such as the national anthem of the Khmer Rouge or a statement by the Ugandan dictator Idi Amin.

Beyond all this, we intended for this book to be read, to be dipped into, as you would any other book of quotations. We hope you enjoy this book for the very reasons we enjoyed compiling it: as a window to other thoughts, other ideas, and other words—words that should be heard today.

The Whole World Book of Quotations

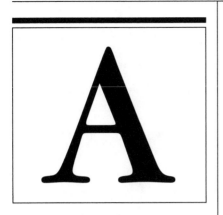

on **ABILITY**

If you cannot accomplish a thing, leave it and pass to another which you can accomplish.

Al Kali (901-967)
Arab philosopher and philologist

Some play the piano well and some badly, and there is a great difference in the melodies they produce.

Mao Zedong (1893-1976)
Chairman of People's Republic of China

He who can do nothing, does nothing.

Wolof proverb

on **ACCEPTANCE**

Accept whatever happens to you,
And be patient in humiliating
vicissitudes.
For gold is tested with fire,
And men who are approved must
be tested in the furnace of
humiliation.

Ben Sira (c. 2nd century B.C.E.)
Hebrew scholar and philosopher, *The Wisdom of Ben Sira*

I try to teach my heart to want nothing it can't have.

Alice Walker (b. 1944)
American writer, *The Color Purple*

on **ACHIEVEMENT**

We must leave our mark on life while we have it in our power; it should close up, when we leave it, without a trace.

Isak Dinesen (1885-1962)
Danish writer

You must do the thing you think you cannot do.

Eleanor Roosevelt (1884-1962)
American humanitarian and First Lady

It is the docile who achieve the most impossible things in this world.

Rabindranath Tagore (1861-1941)
Indian poet and philosopher

on **ACTING AND ACTORS**

There is nothing that gives more assurance than a mask.

Colette (1873-1954)
French writer, *Mes apprentissages*

People often become actresses because of something they dislike about themselves: They pretend they are someone else.

Bette Davis (1908-1989)
American actor

Acting a part is not always synonymous with lying; it is far often the best way of serving the truth. It is more truthful to act what we should feel if the community is to be well served rather than behave

1

as we actually do feel in our selfish private feelings.

> Elizabeth Goudge (1900-1984)
> English writer, *The Bird in the Tree*

We were brought up in the school that teaches: You do what the script tells you. Deliver the goods without comment. Live it—do it—or shut up. After all, the writer is what's important. If the script is good and you don't get in its way, it will come off okay. I never discussed a script with Spence [Spencer Tracy]; we just did it. The same with Hank [Henry Fonda] in *On Golden Pond*. Naturally and unconsciously, we joined into what I call a musical necessity—the chemistry that brings out the essence of the characters and the work.

> Katharine Hepburn (b. 1909)
> American actor

A people without drama is a people without truth.

> Rodolfo Usigli (1905-1979)
> Mexican writer

on **ACTION**

God gives nothing to those who keep their arms crossed.

> Bambara (West African) proverb

On action alone be thy interest, never on its fruits.

> *Bhagavad Gita*
> (c. 4th-3rd century B.C.E.)
> teachings of Krishna from the Hindu
> epic, the *Mahabharata*, 2:47

Taking delight in his own special

kind of action, a man attains perfection.

> *Bhagavad Gita*
> (c. 4th-3rd century B.C.E.)
> teachings of Krishna from the Hindu
> epic, the *Mahabharata*, 18:45

First to know, then to act, then to really know.

> Bishr al Hafifi (767-842)
> Persian Sufi ascetic

Hide your good deeds as well as your evil ones.

> Bishr al Hafifi (767-842)
> Persian Sufi ascetic

The merit of an action lies in finishing it to the end.

> Chingiz (Genghis) Khan
> (c. 1162-1227)
> Mongol conqueror

We couldn't possibly know where it would lead, but we knew it had to be done.

> Betty Friedan (b. 1921)
> American feminist, *It Changed My Life*

Manliness consists not in bluff, bravado, or lordliness. It consists in daring to do the right and facing consequences, whether it is in matters social, political, or other. It consists in deeds, not in words.

> Mohandas K. Gandhi (1869-1948)
> Indian spiritual and political leader

Words that do not match deeds are not important.

> Che Guevara (1928-1967)
> Cuban revolutionary

Action must be taken at once; there is no time to be lost; we shall yet see the oppressors' yoke broken and the fragments scattered on the ground.

> Miguel Hildalgo (1753-1811)
> Mexican revolutionary

Concern should drive us into action and not into a depression.

> Karen Horney (1885-1952)
> American psychoanalyst, *Self-Analysis*

One must scratch that part of the body or mind that itches.

> Aminu Kano (b. 1920)
> Nigerian politician

If you practice inaction, nothing will be left undone: For the way to acquire lordship over society is by invariably not interfering.

> Lao-tzu (c. 604-531 B.C.E.)
> Chinese philosopher and founder of
> Taoism, *Tao-te-ching*

Actions will be judged according to their intentions.

> Muhammad (570-632)
> Prophet of Islam

I don't act; I react.

> Gamel Abdel Nasser (1918-1970)
> Egyptian revolutionary and president

Action, to be effective, must be directed to clearly conceived ends.

> Jawaharlal Nehru (1889-1964)
> Indian prime minister

Our chief defect is that we are more given to talking about things than to doing them.

> Jawaharlal Nehru (1889-1964)
> Indian prime minister

There is only one thing that re-

mains to us, that cannot be taken away: to act with courage and dignity and to stick to the ideals that have given meaning to life.

> Jawaharlal Nehru (1889-1964)
> Indian prime minister

Go! Go! Go! It makes no difference where, just so you go! go! go! Remember, at the first opportunity, go!

> Jeanette Rankin (1880-1973)
> American feminist and politician

Throughout history it has been the inaction of those who could have acted, the indifference of those who should have known better, the silence of the voice of justice when it mattered most, that has made it possible for evil to triumph.

> Haile Selassie (1892-1975)
> Ethiopian emperor

People today distinguish between knowledge and action and pursue them separately, believing that one must know before he can act. . . . They say [they will wait] till they truly know before putting their knowledge into practice. Consequently, to the end of their lives, they will never act and also will never know.

> Wang Yang-ming (1472-1529)
> Chinese philosopher, *Instructions for Practical Living*

In doubt if an action is just, abstain.

> Zoroaster (c. 630-553 B.C.E.)
> Prophet of the ancient Iranian religion of Zoroastrianism

on **ADAPTABILITY**

We are descended from India rubber. . . . That's why our forefathers and the slaves who were sent to America were able to adapt themselves to a situation that was new to them.

> Sylvain Bemba (b. 1932)
> Congolese writer

Each person lives his life in this
  world according to his own
  times;
Whether to come forth and serve,
  or to retire in withdrawal, is not
  a fortuitous decision.

> Chao Meng-fu (1254-1322)
> Chinese painter

A wise man adapts himself to circumstances, as water shapes itself to the vessel that contains it.

> Chinese proverb

Adaptability is imitation. It means power of resistance and assimilation.

> Mohandas K. Gandhi (1869-1948)
> Indian spiritual and political leader

Brothers, I am glad to see so many of you and see you playing the old games. I shall not keep you long, but you have asked for my advice. Our way of life is gone. Your children must travel the white man's roads.

> Geronimo (1829-1909)
> Apache chief

The art of life lies in a constant readjustment to our surroundings.

> Kakuzo Okakura (1862-1913)
> Japanese art critic and philosopher

Man's unique reward . . . is that while animals survive by adjusting themselves to their background, man survives by adjusting his background to himself.

> Ayn Rand (1905-1982)
> American novelist, *For the New Intellectual*

My contemplation of life and human nature in that secluded place [cell 54 of Cairo Central Prison] taught me that he who cannot change the very fabric of his thought will never, therefore, make any progress.

> Anwar Sadat (1918-1981)
> Egyptian military and political leader, *In Search of Identity*

The "Way" of the sage consists neither in imitating the past nor in following the present, but in acting as the times demand.

> *Shang-shu (The Book of Prince Shang)*
> (c. 9th–6th century B.C.E.)
> by followers of Shang Yang, Chinese philosopher and founder of the harsh legalist school

on **ADOLESCENCE**

We are then like some young trees whose branches grow in separate directions, giving the impression that the stem will break apart under opposite pulls.

> Etel Adnan (b. 1925)
> Lebanese writer

To be left alone on the tightrope of youth unknowing is to experience the excruciating beauty of full freedom and the threat of eternal indecision. Few, if any, survive their teens. Most surrender to the vague but murderous pressure of adult conformity. It becomes a constant battle with the superior forces of maturity.

> Maya Angelou (b. 1928)
> American writer, *I Know Why the Caged Bird Sings*

You have started out on the good
  earth;
You have started out with good
  moccasins;
With moccasin strings of the
  rainbow,
  you have started out;
With moccasin strings of the sun's
  rays,
  you have started out;
In the midst of plenty you have
  started out.

> Apache song sung at the "womanhood" rite marking puberty

Adolescence is like cactus.

> Anaïs Nin (1903-1977)
> American writer, *A Spy in the House of Love*

on ADVENTURE

Many would call me an adventurer, and I am one, only one of a different sort, one of those that risks his skin to demonstrate what he believes to be true.

> Che Guevara (1928-1967)
> Cuban revolutionary

The possessor of a sound heart puts to test his power by entering into big adventures.

> Muhammad Iqbal (1873-1938)
> Indian Muslim poet and philosopher

Life is either a daring adventure or nothing. To keep our faces toward change and behave like free spirits in the presence of fate is strength undefeatable.

> Helen Keller (1880-1968)
> American writer and lecturer, *Let Us Have Faith*

We live in a wonderful world that is full of beauty and charm and adventure. There is no end to the adventures that we can have if only we seek them with our eyes open. So many people seem to go about their life's business with their eyes shut. Indeed, they object to other people keeping their eyes open. Unable to play themselves, they dislike the play of others.

> Jawaharlal Nehru (1889-1964)
> Indian prime minister

You can't cross the sea merely by standing and staring at the water.

> Rabindranath Tagore (1861-1941)
> Indian writer and philosopher

on ADVERSITY

We could never learn to be brave and patient, if there were only joy in the world.

> Helen Keller (1880-1968)
> American writer and lecturer

At times of distress, strengthen
  your heart,
Even if you stand at death's door.
The lamp has light before it is
  extinguished.
The wounded lion still knows
  how to roar.

> Samuel ha-Nagid (993-1056)
> Spanish Hebrew poet, "The Wounded Lion"

5

Allah tasketh not a soul beyond its scope.

> *Qur'an* (c. 610–656)
> sacred book of Islam, 2:286

The testing of good and bad is in order that the gold may boil and bring the scum to the top.

> Rumi (1207–1273)
> Persian Sufi poet

He knows not the value of a day of pleasure who has not seen adversity.

> Sa'di of Shiraz (c. 1184–1292)
> Persian poet

Afflictions are the steps to heaven.

> Elizabeth Seton (1774–1821)
> American nun

Adversity is the school of heroism, endurance the majesty of man, and hope the torch of high aspirations.

> Albery A. Whitman (1851–1902)
> American poet

on ADVICE

Be just: the unjust never prosper. Be valiant: die rather than yield. Be merciful: slay neither old men, children, nor women. Destroy neither fruit trees, grain, nor cattle. Keep your word, even to your enemies.

> Abu-Bakr (c. 580–634)
> companion to the Prophet Muhammad
> and first caliph of Islam

When young, beware of fighting; when strong, beware of sex; and when old, beware of possession.

> Confucius (551–479 B.C.E.)
> Chinese philosopher and founder of
> Confucianism, *Analects*

Live and die your own way, unnoticed.

> Ding Ling (c. 1904–1986)
> Chinese writer, "Diary of Miss Sophie"

Those who give advice are amazed that their wisdom does not always affect others; but the real amazement lies in the fact that most great advice does not even reach from the mouth of the advisor to his own ear.

> Muhammad Hijazi (20th century)
> Iranian writer and politician, *Hazar
> Sokhan (A Thousand Sayings)*

Go to bed before 8 P.M. Thieves generally break in between 12 and 2 A.M., so if you spend the evening in useless talk and go to bed late, you are likely to lose your valuables and your reputation as well. Save the firing and the light that will be wasted by staying up late and get up at four in the morning. Have a cold bath and say your prayers, and after you have dressed, give your orders for the day to your wife and children and retainers and so be ready to go on duty before 6 [A.M.]

> Hojo Soun (c. 1519)
> Japanese samurai, "Twenty-one Articles
> of Advice," addressed to his son

Advice is what we ask for when we already know the answer but wish we didn't.

> Erica Jong (b. 1942)
> American writer, *How to Save Your
> Own Life*

Go slow, show not too much concern,

for all our wealth belongs to the surviving heir.

Al-Mumazzaq al-'Abdi (c. 600)
pre-Islamic Arab poet

If you listen to every said-thing in this world, you cannot achieve anything or you the wrong thing will do. If you inside says this is a straight thing, do it. Let not people's said things you inside spoil.

Gabriel Okara (b. 1921)
Nigerian writer, *The Voice*

A hundred sage counsels are lost upon one who cannot take advice.

Panchatantra (c. 5th century)
collection of Hindu tales

Live like a mud-fish: its skin is bright and shiny even though it lives in mud.

Ramakrishna (1836-1886)
Indian mystic

It is not advisable . . . to venture unsolicited opinions. You should spare yourself the embarrassing discovery of their exact value to your listener.

Ayn Rand (1905-1982)
American writer, *Atlas Shrugged*

A man of good sense needs but a suggestion—point the way to him, and that is sufficient.

Ibn Saud (1880-1953)
Saudi Arabian king

Beware of him who gives thee advice according to his own interests.

Talmud
(c. late 4th-early 6th century)
ancient body of Jewish civil and
canonical law, Sanhedrin 76a

Remember that you have only one soul; that you have only one death to die; that you have only one life, which is short and has to be lived by you alone; and there is only one glory, which is eternal. If you do this, there will be many things about which you care nothing.

Teresa of Avila (1515-1582)
Spanish nun, "Maxims for Her Nuns"

on AFRICAN AMERICANS

It is only in his music, which Americans are able to admire because a protective sentimentality limits their understanding of it, that the Negro in America has been able to tell his story.

James Baldwin (1924-1987)
American writer, *Notes of a Native Son*

If we do not now dare everything, the fulfillment of that prophecy, re-created from the Bible in a song by a slave, is upon us: God gave Noah the rainbow sign. Not more water, the fire next time!

James Baldwin (1924-1987)
American writer, *The Fire Next Time*

To be black and conscious in America is to be in a constant state of rage.

James Baldwin (1924-1987)
American writer

If you are black, the only roads into the mainland of American life are through subservience, cowardice, and loss of manhood. These are the white man's roads.

Imamu Amiri Baraka (b. 1934)
American writer, "Black Is a Country,"
Home

7

The drums of Africa beat in my heart. They will not let me rest while there is a single Negro boy or girl without a chance to prove his worth.

> Mary McLeod Bethune
> (1875-1955)
> American educator, *Faith That Moved a Dump Heap*

The destiny of the colored American . . . is the destiny of America.

> Frederick Douglass (1817-1895)
> American abolitionist and writer

Actively we have woven ourselves with the very warp and woof of this nation—we have fought their battles, shared their sorrow, mingled our blood with theirs, and generation after generation have pleaded with a headstrong, careless people to despise not Justice, Mercy and Truth, lest the nation be smitten with a curse. Our song, our toil, our cheer and warning have been given to this nation in blood brotherhood. Are not these gifts worth the giving? Is not this worth the striving? Would America have been America without her Negro People?

> W. E. B. Du Bois (1868-1963)
> American writer and educator, *Souls of Black Folk*

Not only does his Americanism compel the Negro to strive to improve his own status by demanding the rights that are his. It also gives him, as it gives to others committed to the ideals set forth in the American dream, a burning desire to make the system work.

John Hope Franklin (b. 1915)
American educator and historian

We're no longer arguing about riding on the back of the bus, but being the bus driver or the president of the bus company. We're not pushing for the right to buy the hot dog, but selling the hot dog and the right to own the hot dog franchise.

> Benjamin L. Hooks (b. 1925)
> American civil rights activist

I am not tragically colored. There is no great sorrow dammed up in my soul, nor lurking behind my eyes. I do not mind at all. I do not belong to the sobbing school of Negrohood who hold that nature somehow has given them a low-down dirty deal and whose feelings are all hurt about it. Even in the helter-skelter skirmish that is my life, I have seen that the world is to the strong regardless of a little pigmentation more or less. No, I do not weep at the world—I am too busy sharpening my oyster knife.

> Zora Neale Hurston (1903-1960)
> American writer, "How It Feels to Be Colored Me"

To be a Negro in America is to hope against hope.

> Martin Luther King, Jr.
> (1929-1968)
> American civil rights leader, *Where Do We Go from Here: Chaos or Community?*

Lynching is a murder. For the past four hundred years our people have been lynched physically, but now it's done politically. We're lynched politically, we're lynched economically, we're lynched socially, we're lynched in every way that you can imagine.

Malcolm X (1925-1965)
American civil rights activist

After four hundred years of slave labor, we have some back pay coming, a bill owed to us that must be collected.

Malcolm X (1925-1965)
American civil rights activist

You show me a black man who isn't an extremist and I'll show you one who needs psychiatric attention.

Malcolm X (1925-1965)
American civil rights activist,
Autobiography of Malcolm X

The common goal of 22 million Afro-Americans is respect as *human beings*, the God-given right to be a *human being*. Our common goal is to obtain the *human rights* that America has been denying us. We can never get civil rights in America until our *human rights* are first restored. We will never be recognized as citizens there until we are first recognized as *humans*.

Malcolm X (1925-1965)
American civil rights activist, "Racism: The Cancer That Is Destroying America," *Egyptian Gazette*

The American Negro must remake his past in order to make his future.

Arthur A. Schomburg (1874-1938)
American educator

During the next half-century or more, my race must continue passing through the severe American crucible. We are to be tested in our patience, our forbearance, our perseverance, our power to endure wrong, to withstand temptations, to economize, to acquire and use skill; our ability to compete, to succeed in commerce, to disregard the superficial for the real, the appearance for the substance, to be great and yet small, learned and yet simple, high and yet the servant of all. This, this is the passport to all that is best in the life of our Republic, and the Negro must possess it, or be debarred.

Booker T. Washington (1856-1915)
American educator

on AFTERLIFE

Divine wisdom, intending to detain us some time on earth, has done well to cover with a veil the prospect of the life to come; for if our sight could clearly distinguish the opposite bank, who would remain on this tempestuous coast of time?

Madame de Staël (1766-1817)
French writer

Watchfulness is the path to immortality, and thoughtlessness the path to death. The watchful do not die, but the thoughtless are already like the dead.

Dhammapada (c. 3rd century B.C.E.)
collection of ancient Buddhist poems and aphorisms

9

The grave is the first stage of the journey into eternity.

> Muhammad (570-632)
> Prophet of Islam

They say: "There is this life and no other. We live and we die; and nothing but time destroys us." Of this, however, they have no knowledge. They can only guess.

> *Qur'an* (c. 610-656)
> sacred book of Islam, 45:24

I don't know what kind of future life I believe in, but I believe that all that we go through here must have some value.

> Eleanor Roosevelt (1884-1962)
> American humanitarian and First Lady

There is no "next" after you are dead and gone from your own world.

> Rabindranath Tagore (1861-1941)
> Indian writer and philosopher

Perhaps immortality is a gift of heaven rather than the result of some human effort.

> Wang Yang-ming (1472-1529)
> Chinese philosopher, *Wang Wen-ch'eng kung ch'uan-shu*

If you really want to find out something about immortality, you have to live in the mountain forests for 30 years. If you succeed in perfecting your eyes and ears there, if you harmonize the heart and the will so that your mind becomes clear and pure and free of all that is evil, you will be able to discuss the matter.

> Wang Yang-ming (1472-1529)
> Chinese philosopher, *Wang Wen-ch'eng kung ch'uan-shu*

Let us hasten to enjoy our present life. Why bother about what comes after death?

> Yang Tse (420-360 B.C.E.)
> Chinese Taoist philosopher

on AGGRESSION

A man who creates trouble seldom eats it himself.

> Bantu proverb

Fight in the Way of God against those who fight against you, but do not commit aggression.

> *Qur'an* (c. 610-656)
> sacred book of Islam, 2:86

on AGING

Now the swinging bridge
Is quieted with creepers—
Like our tendrilled life.

> Matsuo Basho (1644-1694)
> Japanese poet

For a moment man is a boy, for a moment
a lovesick youth, for a moment
  bereft of wealth,
for a moment in the height of
  prosperity; then at
life's end with limbs worn out by
  old age and
wrinkles adorning his face, like an
  actor he retires
behind the curtain of death.

> Bhartrihari (c. 7th century)
> Indian Hindu poet and philosopher,
> *Sringar Sataka*

O my son, O my grandson. See to it that thou lookest not longingly to thy home, to something within thy home. Do not say: "My mother is

there, my father is there. My neighbors, my protectors, exist, flourish.
. . . I have drink, I have food. I
came to life, I was born, at the place
of abundance, a place of riches." It
is ended; thou goest knowing it.

Florentine Codex (c. 1550)
collection of Aztec writings, words
addressed to boys of seven sent to
priests' training school

Yesterday I fancied I was young;
But already, alas, I am aging.

Ho Nansorhon (1563–1589)
Korean poet, "A Woman's Sorrow"

When young, I knew not the taste
  of sorrow,
But loved to mount the high
  towers;
I loved to mount the high towers
To compose a new song, urging
  myself to talk about sorrow.

Now that I have known all the
  taste of sorrow,
I would like to talk about it, but
  refrain;
I would like to talk about it, but
  refrain,
And say merely: "It is chilly; what
  a fine autumn!"

Hsin Ch'i-chi (1140–1207)
Chinese poet, tz'u song written to the
tune of "The Ugly Slave"

Like a bird in flight
  My life-span seems—

My years its wings,
  Their feathers, days.

In all my years,
  In all their days,

I have reached but a shadow
  Of my desires.

Moses ibn Ezra (1070–1139)
Spanish Hebrew poet, "Wrung with
Anguish," *Songs of Wandering*

A hundred years are no more than
  the dream of a butterfly.
Looking back, how one sighs for
  the things of the past!
Yesterday spring came;
This morning the flowers wither.
Let us hasten with the forfeit cup
Before the night is spent and the
  lamp goes out.

Ma Chih-yuan (1260–1325)
Chinese writer, "Autumn Thoughts"

"Age ain't nothin' but a number."
But age is other things, too. It is
wisdom, if one has lived one's life
properly. It is experience and
knowledge. And it is getting to
know all the ways the world turns,
so that if you cannot turn the
world the way you want, you can
at least get out of the way so you
won't get run over.

Miriam Makeba (b. 1932)
South African singer and political
activist, *Makeba, My Story*

In this country, some people start
being miserable about growing old
while they are still young.

Margaret Mead (1901–1978)
American anthropologist

To be grown up is to sit at the
  table with
people who have died, who
  neither listen
nor speak . . .

Edna St. Vincent Millay
(1892–1950)
American poet, "Childhood Is the
Kingdom Where Nobody Dies," *Wine
from These Grapes*

You and I should have got
  together long ago,
  and shared our feelings
Looking out across these difficult
  times our
  spirits garner strength.
When you see my friends from
  the old days
Tell them I've scrubbed off all that
  old mud.

>   Qiu Jin (1874–1907)
>   Chinese poet and activist

To us vouchsafe to see a hundred
  autumns:
May we attain to lives prolonged
  and happy.

>   *Rig-Veda* (c. 1000 B.C.E.)
>   Hindu sacred literature

age three
there was no past for me

age five
my past went back to yesterday

age seven
my past went back to topknotted
  samurai

age eleven
my past went back to dinosaurs

age fourteen
my past agreed with the texts at
  school

age sixteen
I look at the infinity of my past
  with fear

age eighteen
I know not a thing about time.

>   Tanikawa Shuntaro (b. 1931)
>   Japanese poet

The mountain is silent,
The water without form.
A clear breeze has no price,
The bright moon no lover.
Here, after their fashion,
I will grow old in peace.

>   Song Hon (1535–1598)
>   Korean poet

Aging is a man's destiny, something
that must happen because he is a
human being. For a woman, aging
is not only her destiny . . . it is also
her vulnerability.

>   Susan Sontag (b. 1933)
>   American writer and critic, "The
>   Double Standard of Aging"

The older one grows, the more
one likes indecency.

>   Virginia Woolf (1882–1941)
>   English writer, *Monday or Tuesday*

The body perishes, the heart stays
  young.
The platter wears away with
  serving food.
No log retains its bark when old,
No lover peaceful while the rival
  weeps.

>   Zulu poem

on AMBITION

The trouble with being number
one in the world—at anything—is
that it takes a certain mentality to
attain that position in the first
place, and that is something of a
driving, perfectionist attitude, so
that once you do achieve number
one, you don't relax and enjoy it.

>   Billie Jean King (b. 1943)
>   American athlete, *Billie Jean*

Go for the moon. If you don't get it, you'll still be heading for a star.

> Willis Reed (b. 1942)
> American athlete

Ambition, if it feeds at all, does so on the ambition of others.

> Susan Sontag (b. 1933)
> American writer and critic, *The Benefactor*

on THE AMERICAS

Europe has what we [Americans] do not have yet, a sense of the mysterious and inexorable limits of life, a sense, in a word, of tragedy. And we have what they sorely need: a sense of life's possibilities.

> James Baldwin (1924–1987)
> American writer, *Nobody Knows My Name*

What passes for identity in America is a series of myths about one's heroic ancestors.

> James Baldwin (1924–1987)
> American writer, "A Talk to Harlem Teachers," *Harlem, USA*

The making of an American begins at that point where he himself rejects all other ties, any other history, and himself adopts the vesture of his adopted land.

> James Baldwin (1924–1987)
> American writer, *Notes of a Native Son*

Americans think of themselves as a huge rescue squad on twenty-four-hour call to any spot on the globe where dispute and conflict may erupt.

> Eldridge Cleaver (b. 1935)
> American civil rights activist, *Soul on Ice*

Numerous cities will emerge from the bosom of these immense deserts; our ships will cover the seas, abundance will reign within our walls; and two words only will be seen over our altars and in our tribunals: *humanity* and *liberty.*

> Bernardo De Montegudo (1785–1825)
> Latin American politician

Little of beauty has America given the world save the rude grandeur of God himself stamped on her bosom; the human spirit in this new world has expressed itself in vigor and ingenuity rather than in beauty.

> W. E. B. Du Bois (1868–1963)
> American writer and educator, *The Souls of Black Folk*

When American life is most American it is apt to be most theatrical.

> Ralph Ellison (1914–1994)
> American writer, *Shadow and Act*

In America, with all of its evils and faults, you can still reach through the forest and see the sun. But we don't know yet whether that sun is rising or setting for our country.

> Dick Gregory (b. 1932)
> American civil rights activist, "One Less Door," *Nigger*

On my visits to America, I discovered that the old Marxist dictum, "From each according to his abilities, to each according to his needs," was probably more in force in America—that holy of holies of capitalism—than in any other country in the world.

> Felix Houphouet-Boigny (b. 1905)
> Ivory Coast political leader

America is not like a blanket—one piece of unbroken cloth, the same color, the same texture, the same size. America is more like a quilt—many patches, many pieces, many colors, many sizes, all woven and held together by a common thread.

> Jesse Jackson (b. 1941)
> American civil rights activist and politician

I hear that melting-pot stuff a lot, and all I can say is that we haven't melted.

> Jesse Jackson (b. 1941)
> American civil rights activist and politician

This is America,
This vast confused beauty,
This staring, restless speed of
  loveliness,
Mighty, overwhelming, crude of
  all forms,
Making grandeur out of profusion,
Afraid of no incongruities,
Sublime in its audacity,
Bizarre breaker of molds.

> Amy Lowell (1874-1925)
> American writer, "The Congressional Liberty," *What's O'Clock*

Sitting at the table doesn't make you a diner, unless you eat some of what's on the plate. Being here in America doesn't make you an American. Being born here in America doesn't make you an American.

> Malcolm X (1925-1965)
> American civil rights activist,
> *Malcolm X Speaks*

Uncle Sam has no conscience. They don't know what morals are.

They don't know what morals are. They don't try and eliminate an evil because it's evil, or because it's illegal, or because it's immoral; they eliminate it only when it threatens their existence.

> Malcolm X (1925-1965)
> American civil rights activist,
> *Malcolm X Speaks*

America is a land of creators and rebels.

> José Martí (1853-1895)
> Cuban patriot

America is indeed a revelation, though not quite the one that was planned. Given a clean slate, man, it was hoped, would write the future. Instead, he has written his past.

> Mary McCarthy (1912-1989)
> American writer and critic, "America the Beautiful"

America is not a melting pot. It is a sizzling cauldron.

> Barbara Ann Mikulski (b. 1936)
> American politician

The ideas of the American Revolution are today the most explosive of all forces, more explosive in their capacity to change the world than B-52s or even atomic bombs.

> U Nu (b. 1907)
> Burmese politician and first prime minister of Burma

I think in a country like mine, violence is at the root of all human relations.

> Mario Vargas Llosa (b. 1936)
> Peruvian writer

This country demands that every race measure itself by the American standard.

Booker T. Washington (1856–1915)
American educator

I fear that we have only awakened a sleeping giant, and his reaction will be terrible.

Yamamoto Isoroku (1884–1943)
Japanese admiral, after the attack on Pearl Harbor (December 7, 1941)

on ANCESTORS AND ANCESTRY

If you want to understand me
come, bend over this soul of
 Africa
in the black dock-worker's groans
the Chope's frenzied dances
the Changanas' rebellion
in the strange sadness which
 flows
from an African song, through the
 night.

Noemia de Sousa (b. 1927)
Mozambiquen poet

The pedigree of honey
Does not concern the bee;
A clover, any time to him
Is aristocracy.

Emily Dickinson (1830–1886)
American poet

They were tall; they were larger than the people today.

Florentine Codex (c. 1550)
collection of Aztec writings

I have lived in the redness of the stones that mark a path through my blood; I am the descendant of a

forgotten race, but I carry in my hands the remnants of their fire.

Mohammed Khair-Eddine (b. 1941)
Moroccan writer

When I make my father's face
 with clay,
below the window in twilight
the mysterious lineage of blood
 whispers.

Takamura Kotaro (1883–1956)
Japanese artist and poet

[The] Hopi earth does contain my roots and I am, indeed, from that land. Because the roots are there, I will find them. But when I find them, [my father] said, I must rebuild myself as a Hopi. I am not merely a conduit, but a participant. I am not a victim, but a woman.

Wendy Rose (b. 1948)
American writer

I must hide him in my inmost
 veins
The Ancestor . . .
He is my faithful blood that
 demands fidelity
Protecting my naked pride against
Myself and the scorn of luckier
 races.

Leopold Sedar Senghor (b. 1906)
Senegalese political leader and writer,
"Totem"

Let us listen to the voices of our
Forebears . . .
In the smoky cabin, souls that
 wish us well are murmuring.

Leopold Sedar Senghor (b. 1906)
Senegalese political leader and writer,
"Nuit de Sine"

No man beholds his mother's
 womb—

Yet who denies it's there? Coiled
To the navel of the world is that
Endless cord that links us all
To the great Origin. If I lose my
    way
The trailing cord will bring me to
    the roots.

> Wole Soyinka (b. 1934)
> Nigerian writer, *Death and the King's Horseman*

If today I had a young mind to direct to start on the journey of life and I was faced with the duty of choosing between the natural way of my forefathers and that of the white man's present way of civilization, I would, for its welfare, unhesitatingly set that child's feet in the path of my forefathers. I would raise him to be an Indian!

> Luther Standing Bear (1868–1939)
> Sioux writer, *Land of the Spotted Eagle*

on ANGER

Anger is the foundation of every evil.

> Muhammad Husan Askari
> (d. 1974)
> Pakistani writer

Rage can only with difficulty, and never entirely, be brought under the domination of the intelligence, and therefore is not susceptible to any arguments whatsoever.

> James Baldwin (1924–1987)
> American writer

Unrighteous anger can never be
    excused,
For the weight of a man's anger
    drags him down.

A patient man will control himself
    for a while,
And afterward joy will break out.

> Ben Sira (c. 2nd century B.C.E.)
> Hebrew scholar and philosopher, *The Wisdom of Ben Sira*

If you yield to your anger, you only cease to be civil.

> Abu'l-Fath al-Busti (d. 1009)
> Persian poet

When one is angry, if one can directly forget his anger and examine the right and wrong according to principle, then right and wrong will be clearly seen and desires will naturally be unable to persist.

> Chu Hsi (1130–1200)
> Chinese philosopher

Although I am in great anger, I
    have tempered my words,
    fearing for you.
If I became like thunder, you
    would drown in the waves of
    my wrath.
And in the noise the lightning
    would blind you;
The air would be great black
    waves around you.
You would fly for your life from
    the blast that came forth from
    me.

> Shaykh Muhammad 'Abdille Hasan
> (20th century)
> Somali nationalist

on ANXIETY

Most men, however brave, have some anxiety or fear in them.

> Babur (1483–1530)
> first Mughal emperor of India, *Babur-nama* (his autobiography)

Why worry one's head over a thing that is inevitable? Why die before one's death?

Mohandas K. Gandhi (1869–1948)
Indian spiritual and political leader

Basic anxiety can be roughly described as a feeling of being small, insignificant, helpless, deserted or endangered in a world that is out to abuse, cheat, humiliate, betray, envy. . . . And special in this is the child's feeling that the parents' love, their Christian charity, honesty, generosity . . . may be only a pretense.

Karen Horney (1885–1952)
American psychoanalyst, *The Neurotic Personality of Our Time*

Excessive thinking harms life;
We should go where fate leads,
And ride on the waves of the
 Great Flux
Without joy and without fear.
If life must end, then let it end;
There is no need to be full of
 anxieties.

T'ao Ch'ien (365–427)
Chinese poet, "Shape, Shadow, and Spirit"

on APPEARANCES

A hare is like an ass in the length of its ears, yet it is not its son.

Bambara (West African) proverb

A white bone much resembles ivory; most men fail to distinguish the one from the other. So with men. The specious kind appears to have goodness, but it is not really so.

Huai Nan Tzu (c. 122 B.C.E.)
Chinese scholar

An ox with long horns, even if he does not butt, will be accused of butting.

Malay proverb

Pieces of worthless glass, in splendid settings, look like gems; in the company of the wise, a fool may pass for wise.
 Does not the dog look like a king when he has ascended a royal conveyance?

Sukra Niti (c. 400)
from the *Niti Sastra*, collection of Indian sayings, aphorisms, and moral tales

on ARGUMENT

Never do I argue with a man with a desire to hear him say what is wrong, or to expose him and win a victory over him. . . . Whenever I face an opponent in debate I silently pray, "O Lord, help him so that truth may flow from his heart and on his tongue, and so that if truth is on my side, he may follow me; and if it be on his side, I may follow him."

al-Shafi'i (767–820)
Founder of Sufi school of law

If the object is achieved by quarrel, then quarrel is good.

Vridha Chanakya
from the *Niti Sastra*, collection of Indian sayings, aphorisms, and moral tales

When an arguer argues dispassionately, he thinks only of the argument.

Virginia Woolf (1882–1941)
English writer, *A Room of One's Own*

on ART AND ARTISTS

In art, vitality is the chaotic initial state; beauty is the cosmic final state.

> Chairil Anwar (1922-1949)
> Indonesian poet

Can art be completely invented? It's a matter of shaping reality with the help of imagination.

> Aharon Appelfeld (b. 1932)
> Israeli writer

True revolutions in art restore more than they destroy.

> Louise Bogan (1897-1970)
> American poet, "Reading Contemporary Poetry"

Once form has been smashed, it has been smashed for good, and once a forbidden subject has been released, it has been released for good.

> Louise Bogan (1897-1970)
> American poet, "Experimentalists of a New Generation," *A Poet's Alphabet*

Art is the only thing that can go mattering once as it has stopped hurting.

> Elizabeth Bowen (1899-1973)
> Irish writer, *The Heat of the Day*

What is art
But life upon the larger scale, the higher,
When, graduating up in a spiral line
Of still expanding and ascending gyres,
It pushes toward the intense significance
Of all things, hungry for the Infinite?

Art's life,—and where we live, we suffer and toil.

> Elizabeth Barrett Browning (1806-1861)
> English poet, *Aurora Leigh*

A woman artist must be . . . capable of making the primary sacrifices.

> Mary Cassatt (1844-1926)
> American artist

Art and family life are reconcilable if it's worth it—which is to say, if you act out of conviction and not just convention or a sense of obligation.

> Andree Chedid (b. 1920)
> Egyptian writer

The artist is the only lover; he alone has the pure vision of beauty, and love is the vision of the soul when it is permitted to gaze upon immortal beauty.

> Isadora Duncan (1878-1927)
> American dancer, *My Life*

Art is not necessary at all. All that is necessary to make this world a better place to live in is to love—to love as Christ loved, as Buddha loved.

> Isadora Duncan (1878-1927)
> American dancer

Purity of life is the highest and truest art.

> Mohandas K. Gandhi (1869-1948)
> Indian spiritual and political leader

The world I feel, within the realm of art, is more genuine than the world of matter. Artistic feeling is not tape measures, spectrographs, or flash camera lens.

Gu Cheng (b. 1957)
Chinese poet

In the past, traditional art was based on making manifest what is enduring in man, like love, jealousy, hatred, envy, and greed. . . . Today art has to look again at these unchanging qualities, because society is no longer unchanging. It is up to art today to show us what has become of these unchanging qualities in a world which is moving and changing.

Tawfiq al-Hakim (b. 1902)
Egyptian writer

When the artist . . . intends from the beginning to be obscure and take obscurity as his objective or goal for its own sake and wishes to astonish, shock, and seem mysterious, that is a swindle.

Tawfiq al-Hakim (b. 1902)
Egyptian writer

True artistic renewal does not mean being stripped of fetters. It means moving into new fetters.

Tawfiq al-Hakim (b. 1902)
Egyptian writer

I believe that art is the only way by which an evil man can attain a realm of perfect liberation without becoming an entirely different person. While religion spurns evil men . . . art permits them to enter its realm, as long as they believe in it.

Tanizaki Jun'ichiro (1886–1965)
Japanese writer

The artist's imagination may wander far from nature. But as long as it is a living, moving power in his brain, isn't it just as real as any other natural phenomenon? The artist justifies his existence only when he can transform his imagination into truth.

Tanizaki Jun'ichiro (1886–1965)
Japanese writer

In order to find reality, each must search for his own universe, look for the details that contribute to this reality that one feels under the surface of things. To be an artist means to search, to find and look at these realities. To be an artist means never to look away.

Akira Kurosawa (b. 1910)
Japanese film director

Art is the desire of a man to express himself, to record the reactions of his personality to the world he lives in.

Amy Lowell (1874–1925)
American poet, "Tendencies in Modern American Poetry"

Art is a criticism of society and life, and I believe that if life became perfect, art would be meaningless and cease to exist.

Naguib Mahfouz (b. 1911)
Egyptian writer

The mission of art is to achieve a deeper understanding of nature's beauty. The mission, to put it another way, is to observe nature with an artistic mind, a mind bent on discovering beauty. Therefore, the kind of nature that the average person sees does not make art when it is reproduced.

Shiga Naoya (1883-1971)
Japanese writer

Art, when it is forgetful of nature, degrades itself. Degraded art is, I feel, like the expressionless face of a lovely princess born of a noble family.

Shiga Naoya (1883-1971)
Japanese writer

The artist is the only one who knows that the world is a subjective creation, that there is a choice to be made, a selection of elements.

Anaïs Nin (1903-1977)
American writer, "The New Woman"

To be a friend of the weak—that is the artist's point of departure as well as his ultimate goal.

Dazai Osamu (1909-1948)
Japanese writer

A true artist is an ugly man.

Dazai Osamu (1909-1948)
Japanese writer

What is art?
A violet.
Is that all?
. . . .
What is an artist?
A pig's snout.
I protest!
That snout can smell a violet.

Dazai Osamu (1909-1948)
Japanese writer

Art is a form of catharsis.

Dorothy Parker (1893-1967)
American writer

An artistic style is a living entity, a continuous process of invention. It can never be imposed from without; born of the profoundest tendencies within a society, its direction is to a certain extent unpredictable, in much the same way as the eventual configuration of a tree's branches.

Octavio Paz (b. 1914)
Mexican poet and diplomat

Life and art are so inextricably interwoven that any change in life leads to a new movement in art.

K. Nagieswara Rao (1867-1938)
Indian politician and writer

Art must take reality by surprise. It takes those moments which are for us merely a moment, plus a moment, plus another moment, and arbitrarily transforms them into a special series of moments held together by a major emotion.

Françoise Sagan (b. 1935)
French writer

What is carved should be original, and have life, for whatever may be the subject which is to be made, the form of it should resemble the original and the life of the original. . . . Take great care to penetrate what the animal you wish to imitate is like, and how its character and appearance can best be shown.

Bernardino de Sahagún
(c. 16th century)
Spanish historian

A photograph is not only an image (as a painting is an image), an interpretation of the real; it is also a trace, something directly stenciled off the real, like a footprint or a death mask.

Susan Sontag (b. 1933)
American writer and critic, *On Photography*

The artist, even when he imitates nature, always feels himself to be not a slave but a demigod.

Natsume Soseki (1867–1916)
Japanese writer

The worst thing that can happen to an artist is to be subsidized by the state. It leads to an intellectual and artistic castration.

Mario Vargas Llosa (b. 1936)
Peruvian writer

A work of art has an author and yet, when it is perfect, it has something which is anonymous about it.

Simone Weil (1909–1943)
French philosopher, *Gravity and Grace*

The mind of an artist, in order to achieve the prodigious effort of freeing whole and entire the work that is in him, must be incandescent. . . . There must be no obstacle in it, no foreign matter unconsumed.

Virginia Woolf (1882–1941)
English writer, *A Room of One's Own*

Art must hurt. First, it must hurt the artist himself; the artist must experience pain before he creates. Otherwise, he won't be able to produce tears. A true artist must describe the things he is most afraid of, all that which he wished to avoid.

Itamar Yaoz-Kest (b. 1934)
Israeli writer

on BEAUTY

So fair,
She takes the breath of men away
Who gaze upon her unaware.

Elizabeth Barrett Browning
(1806–1861)
English poet, *Bianca among the Nightingales*

Beauty crowds me till I die,
Beauty, mercy have on me!
Yet if I expire to-day
Let it be in sight of thee!

Emily Dickinson (1830–1886)
American poet

All truths, not merely ideas, but truthful faces, truthful pictures or songs, are highly beautiful.

Mohandas K. Gandhi (1869–1948)
Indian spiritual and political leader

There's nothing moral about beauty.

Nadine Gordimer (b. 1923)
South African writer, *The Late Bourgeois World*

To have reached two noble goals, selflessness and flawlessness, is the highest beauty.

Hsi K'ang (223–262)
Chinese philosopher, "Shih-ssu lun"
("Liberation from the Selfish"), *Hsi Chung-san chi*

Knowing this to be a worthless
  life to live,
why do I keep living on?
Because this life contains
  something called beauty.

Nagai Kafu (1879–1959)
Japanese writer, "Mutterings on a Gloomy Day"

It is because everyone under Heaven recognizes beauty as beauty that the idea of ugliness exists.

Lao-tzu (c. 604–531 B.C.E.)
Chinese philosopher and founder of Taoism, *Tao-te-ching*

You are beautiful and faded
Like an old opera tune
Played upon a harpsichord.

Amy Lowell (1874–1925)
American poet, *A Lady*

Euclid alone
Has looked on Beauty bare.
  Fortunate they
Who, though once only and then
  by far away,
Have heard her massive sandal set
  on stone.

Edna St. Vincent Millay
(1892–1950)
American poet, *Sonnets*

The bloom of my complexion
  made all women jealous;
A glance from my eyes, iridescent
  as autumn pools,
stirred up waves of passion that
  would overthrow fortresses.
The moon strained to catch sight

of me through my window
blinds,
Not even the trees and plants
could stay indifferent to my
beauty.

> Nguyen Gia Thieu (1741–1798)
> Vietnamese poet, "The Complaint of
> the Royal Concubine"

The test of beauty is whether it can
survive close knowledge.

> Marjorie Kinnan Rawlings
> (1896–1953)
> American writer, *Cross Creek*

I am but passionately in love
With beauty, in its myriad shapes
and guises.
I take up the pen of poetry to
portray
And the thousand-fretted lute to
hymn
Beauty—silent, raging or
innocent,
Like the sublime and mighty
beauty
Of mountains and rivers, and
poetry, and thought.

> The Lu (c. 1930s)
> Vietnamese poet, "Cay dan muon dieu"
> ("The Heavenly Flute")

Perhaps scraps of brass may hue
to turquoise,
Peach blossoms flower from
rusting cans,
The greasy scum weave a texture
of gauze
And a tinted haze steam up from
the germs.
. . . .
So this ditch of hopeless dead
water
May well boast a certain splendor;

Then if the frogs can't bear the
silence
Out of dead water a song will
rise.

> Wen Yiduo (1899–1947)
> Chinese writer, "Dead Water"

Anyone who sees beauty and does
not look at it
Will soon be poor.

> Yoruba (West African) oracle poem

on BEGINNINGS

When you forget the beginner's
awe, you start decaying.

> Nobuko Albery (b. 1940)
> Japanese writer

In our beginnings lies our journey's end.

> Kofi Awoonor (b. 1935)
> Ghanaian writer, "Salvation"

All things at first appear difficult.

> Chinese proverb

Is there ever any particular spot
where one can put one's finger and
say, "It all began that day, at such a
time and such a place, with such
an incident?"

> Agatha Christie (1891–1976)
> English writer, *Endless Night*

If you wish to learn the highest
ideals, begin with the alphabet.

> Japanese proverb

The truth is that the beginning of
anything and its end are alike
touching.

> Yoshida Kenko (c. 1283–1352)
> Japanese writer, "Life Frail and
> Fleeting," *Tsure-Zure Gusa (The
> Harvest of Leisure)*

A single spark can start a prairie fire. . . . Our forces, although small at present, will grow rapidly.

> Mao Zedong (1893-1976)
> Chairman of People's Republic of China

The wise man knows at the commencement of a matter what its end will be.

> *Talmud*
> (c. late 4th-early 5th century)
> ancient body of Jewish civil and canonical law, Y. Sotah 5

on BEHAVIOR

A man's behavior is the index of the man, and his discourse is the index of his understanding.

> 'Ali (c. 600-661)
> First Imam of the Sh'ia branch of Islam; fourth caliph

The fruit of timidity is neither gain nor loss.

> Arabic proverb

Learn politeness from the impolite.

> Egyptian proverb

Good behavior is everybody's business, and good taste can be everyone's goal.

> Millicent Fenwick (1910-1992)
> American politician

I used to be very self-conscious. I used to wish I was pretty. My cousin Georgia always taught me that if you *smile*, people will like you. Sometimes people will say something you don't like, and you get angry a bit, but you just smile. You let it go by, even if you really would like to choke 'em. By smiling, I think I've made more friends than if I was the other way.

> Ella Fitzgerald (b. 1918)
> American singer

Blind adoration, in the age of action, is perfectly valueless, is often embarrassing and, equally, often painful.

> Mohandas K. Gandhi (1869-1948)
> Indian spiritual and political leader

You've got to have something to eat and a little love in your life before you can hold still for any damn body's sermon on how to behave.

> Billie Holiday (1915-1959)
> American singer, *Lady Sings the Blues*

Innocence is a desirable thing, a dainty thing, an appealing thing, in its place; but carried too far, it is merely ridiculous.

> Dorothy Parker (1893-1967)
> American writer

on BELIEF

I see myself as a man who is searching for meaning in life. This is rather different from being a staunch believer in something. A believer is someone who senses a consciousness or a direction and believes in it. The one who searches for meaning has not found the direction yet.

> Aharon Appelfeld (b. 1932)
> Israeli writer

Do not believe what your teacher tells you merely out of respect for the teacher. But whatsoever, after due examination and analysis, you find to be conducive to the good, the benefit, the welfare of all beings—that doctrine believe and cling to, and take it as your guide.

> Buddha (c. 563–483 B.C.E.)
> Founder of Buddhism

Remember that it is useless to try to force those to believe who will not, for even the Buddha himself cannot do that.

> Honen (1133–1212)
> Japanese Buddhist leader

If a man hasn't discovered something that he would die for, he isn't fit to live.

> Martin Luther King, Jr.
> (1929–1968)
> American civil rights leader

As for belief, there are things that are as clear as the sky, yet men prefer to sit under an up-turned barrel.

> Ko Hung (283–343)
> Chinese scholar

Beliefs and convictions reach out from the past, and they cannot be altered by fervent desire alone. They possess their own logic and illogic, their own organic existence, their own rhythm of development.

> Raisa Davydovna Orlova
> (1917–1964)
> Soviet/German writer, *Memoirs*

on **BIOGRAPHY**

To the biographer, all lives bar one are dramatic constructions.

> Katherine Anthony (1877–1965)
> American writer, *Writing Biography*

Where I was born, and where and how I lived is unimportant. It is what I have done and where I have been that should be of interest.

> Georgia O'Keeffe (1887–1986)
> American artist, *Georgia O'Keeffe*

Just how difficult it is to write biography can be reckoned by anybody who sits down and considers just how many people know the real truth about his or her love affairs.

> Rebecca West (1892–1983)
> English writer, "The Art of Skepticism"

on **BIRTH**

Let us return to the magic hour of
  our birth
for which we mourn

> Kofi Awoonor (b. 1935)
> Ghanaian writer, "This Earth, My Brother"

Is this not a fatal time for us poor
  women?
This is our kind of war
There our Mother
Cihuacoatl Quilaztli
Takes her tribute of death.

> *Florentine Codex* (c. 1550)
> collection of Aztec writings

Birth and death are not two different states, but they are different aspects of the same state.

> Mohandas K. Gandhi (1869–1948)
> Indian spiritual and political leader

on **BLAME**

They blame him who talks too much; they blame him who is silent; and they also blame him who speaks little; there is not, in fact, a person who is not blamed. Yet there never was, there will never be, nor is there now, a man who is always blamed or a man who is always praised.

> *Dhammapada* (c. 3rd century B.C.E.)
> collection of ancient Buddhist poems
> and aphorisms

Blaming the wolf would not help the sheep much. The sheep must learn not to fall into the clutches of the wolf.

> Mohandas K. Gandhi (1869-1948)
> Indian spiritual and political leader

Do not blame the food because you have no appetite.

> Rabindranath Tagore (1861-1941)
> Indian writer and philosopher

on BLESSINGS

God's gifts put man's best dreams to shame.

> Elizabeth Barrett Browning
> (1806-1861)
> English poet, *Sonnets from the Portuguese*

Great blessings come from Heaven; small blessings come from man.

> Chinese proverb (c. 19th century)

There are two blessings which most people misuse—health and leisure.

> Muhammad (570-632)
> Prophet of Islam

on BOASTING

Those who boast are seldom the great.

> Jawaharlal Nehru (1889-1964)
> Indian prime minister

Had but my deeds been like my words, ah, then
I had been numbered too with holy men.

> Sa'di of Shiraz (c. 1184-1292)
> Persian poet, *Gulistan*

The pretender sees no one but himself,
Because he has the veil of conceit in front;
If he were endowed with a God-discerning eye,
He would see that no one is weaker than himself.

> Sa'di of Shiraz (c. 1184-1292)
> Persian poet, *Gulistan*

Boasting is only a masked shame; it does not truly believe in itself.

> Rabindranath Tagore (1861-1941)
> Indian writer and philosopher

One does not become great by claiming greatness.

> Xhosa (South African) proverb

on BOLDNESS

How can one obtain tiger cubs without entering the tiger's lair?

> Chinese proverb

Men of principle are always bold, but bold men are not always men of principle.

> Confucius (551-479 B.C.E.)
> Chinese philosopher and founder of
> Confucianism, *Analects*

If there is anybody in this land who thoroughly believes that the meek shall inherit the earth, they have not often let their presence be known.

W. E. B. Du Bois (1868–1963)
American writer and educator, *The Gift of Black Folk*

If lordship lies within the lion's
  jaws,
Go, risk it, and from those dread
  portals seize
Such straight-confronting death as
  men desire,
Or riches, greatness, rank, and
  lasting ease.

Handhala of Badghis
(c. 7th century)
Persian poet

If there are still men who really want to live in this world, they should first dare to speak out, to laugh, to cry, to be angry, to accuse, to fight—that they may at least cleanse this accursed place of its accursed atmosphere!

Lu Xun (1881–1936)
Chinese writer

I am known to the horse-troop,
  the night and the desert's
  expanse,
Not more to the paper and pen
  than the sword and lance!

al Mutanabbi (915–965)
Arab poet

Errors and exaggerations do not matter. What matters is boldness in thinking with a strong-pitched voice, in speaking out about things as one feels them in the moment of speaking; in having the temerity to proclaim what one believes to be true without fear of the consequences. If one were to await the possession of the absolute truth, one must be either a fool or a mute. If the creative impulse were muted, the world would then be stayed on its march.

José Clemente Orozco
(1883–1949)
Mexican painter

Plunge into the deep without fear, with the gladness of April in your heart.

Rabindranath Tagore (1861–1941)
Indian writer and philosopher

If we didn't live venturously, plucking the wild goat by the beard, and trembling over precipices, we should never be depressed, I've no doubt; but already should be faded, fatalistic, and aged.

Virginia Woolf (1882–1941)
English writer, *A Writer's Diary*

on BOOKS AND READING

Books succeed,
And lives fail.

Elizabeth Barrett Browning
(1806–1861)
English poet, *Aurora Leigh*

It is better to be without a book than to believe it entirely.

Chinese proverb

Beware that the one who reads is the same as the book, the same as what is read, the same as the speaker and the same as what is spoken without being the word.

Mohammed Dib (b. 1920)
Algerian writer

I can't think of any one film that improved on a good novel, but I can think of many good films that came from very bad novels.

> Gabriel García Márquez (b. 1928)
> Colombian writer

Everywhere I go, kids walk around not with books under their arms, but with radios up against their heads. Children can't read or write, but they can memorize whole albums.

> Jesse Jackson (b. 1941)
> American politician

Reading is actually plunging into one's own identity and, one hopes, emerging stronger than before. You see, unconsciously, we are seeking to find an affirmation to our own world perception and set of values.

> Amalia Kahana-Carmon
> (20th century)
> Israeli poet

Make thy books thy companions. Let thy cases and shelves be thy pleasure grounds and gardens.

> Judah ha-Levi (c. 1075-1141)
> Spanish Hebrew poet and theologian

All books are either dreams or swords.

> Amy Lowell (1874-1925)
> American writer, *Sword Blades and Poppy Seeds*

The great sickness and the grievous evil consist in this: that all the things that man finds written in books, he presumes to think of as true—and all the more so if the books are old.

> Maimonides (1135-1204)
> Spanish Hebrew philosopher, "Letter on Astrology"

My alma mater was books, a good library. . . . I could spend the rest of my life reading, just satisfying my curiosity.

> Malcolm X (1925-1965)
> American civil rights activist,
> *Autobiography of Malcolm X*

Books are . . . funny little portable pieces of thought.

> Susan Sontag (b. 1933)
> American writer and critic

on BRAVERY

A ship in port is safe, but that is not what ships are built for.

> Benazir Bhutto (b. 1953)
> Pakistani politician

Courage is the price that Life exacts for granting peace.

> Amelia Earhart (1898-1937)
> American aviator, *Courage*

Any coward can fight a battle when he's sure of winning; but give me the man who has pluck to fight when he's sure of losing.

> George Eliot (1819-1880)
> English writer, *Janet's Repentance*

Without courage, you cannot practice any other virtue. You have to have courage—courage of different kinds: first, intellectual courage, to sort out different values and make up your mind about which is the one which is right for you to follow. You have to have moral courage to stick up to that—no matter what comes in your way, no matter what the obstacle and the opposition is. Opposition comes not only from your enemies but sometimes from your friends, and the latter is much more difficult to face. You have to have physical courage, because very often going along the path of your choice is full of physical hardship.

Indira Gandhi (1917-1984)
Indian prime minister

If one cannot live the life of the brave, then it is better to die like the brave.

Muhammad Iqbal (1873-1938)
Indian Muslim poet and philosopher

Gut it is will move us from the gutter . . . to the rebirth of real men.

Keorapetse Kgositsile (b. 1938)
South African poet, *My Name Is Afrika*

Courage is the ladder on which all other virtues mount.

Clare Booth Luce (1903-1987)
American diplomat and politician

The brave forget. It is those who fought less bravely, or those who fought without justice and live in fear of their victory, who forget the least.

José Martí (1853-1895)
Cuban patriot, "General Grant"

In the face of danger, worms dig themselves into the earth. Men rise up and fight!

Luis Muñoz Rivera (1859-1916)
Puerto Rican journalist and politician

Bravery ceases to be bravery at a certain point, and becomes mere foolhardiness.

Rabindranath Tagore (1861-1941)
Indian writer and philosopher

on BROTHERHOOD AND SISTERHOOD

Under one roof,
Prostitutes, too, were sleeping;
The hagi flowers and the moon.

Matsuo Basho (1644-1694)
Japanese poet

I am a man, and you are another.

Black Hawk (1767-1838)
Sauk chief, when first meeting President Andrew Jackson

Heaven is my Father, the earth my mother, and even a tiny creature such as myself finds an intimate place in their midst. In everything that moves through the universe, I see my own body, and in everything that governs the universe, my own soul. All men are my brethren, and all things my companions.

Chang Tsai (1021-1077)
Chinese philosopher, "The Western Inscription"

I was born on this earth, so I come from the same womb as humans in all countries, even though our body types may be different. . . . I have drunk deeply of the intellectual heritage of ancient India, Greece, Persia, and Rome, and of modern England, France, Germany, and America. I have pillowed my head upon them, and my soul in dreams has fathomed them. . . . It is as if we were all parts of an electrical force which interconnects all things, or partook of the pure essence that encompasses all things.

K'ang Yu-wei (1858–1927)
Chinese political philosopher,
Datongshu

The good neighbor looks beyond the external accidents and discerns those inner qualities that make all men human and, therefore, brothers.

Martin Luther King, Jr.
(1929–1968)
American civil rights leader, *Strength to Love*

If humanity wishes to strive to exist and if it wishes happiness and prosperity, then it must have mutual friendship and ought not to rely upon force for mutual extermination.

Li Dazhao (1888–1927)
Chinese political theorist

I remember one night at Muzdalifah . . . I lay awake amid sleeping Muslim brothers and I learned that pilgrims from every land—every color and class and rank—all snored in the same language.

Malcolm X (1925–1965)
American civil rights activist,
Autobiography of Malcolm X

Universal love . . . means that one makes no distinction between the state of others and one's own; none between the houses of others and one's own; none between the other person and oneself.

Mo-Tze (c. 5th century B.C.E.)
Chinese philosopher, *Mo-tzu*

Do you love your Creator? Love your fellow-beings first.

Muhammad (570–632)
Prophet of Islam

O ye men! Harken unto my words and take ye them to heart! Know ye that every Muslim is a brother unto every other Muslim, and that ye are now one brotherhood. It is not legitimate for any one of you, therefore, to appropriate unto himself anything that belongs to his brother unless it is willingly given him by that brother.

Muhammad (570–632)
Prophet of Islam, sermon at the
"Farewell Pilgrimage"

All creatures are members of the one family of God.

Qur'an (c. 610–656)
sacred book of Islam

What name, we bilong belly all the same.

Sepik (New Guinea) saying

Wear the Kaftan which consists of plain white material. You will be dressed like everyone else. See the uniformity appear! Be a particle and join the mass; as a drop, enter the ocean.

Ali Shariati (1933–1977)
Iranian scholar, *Hajj*

God told me to look after my people—all are my people.

Smohalla (c. 1815–1907)
Wanapam prophet

A person is a person because he recognizes others as persons.

> Desmond Tutu (b. 1931)
> South African antiapartheid activist and religious leader

My humanity is bound up in yours, for we can only be human together.

> Desmond Tutu (b. 1931)
> South African antiapartheid activist and religious leader

Since we were all born of the same father of souls, why should there be any distinction between you and me or between others and ourselves? When there are clothes, let us wear them together; when there is food, let us enjoy it together.

> Wang Hui-yueh (c. 1850)
> Chinese philosopher

There is no escape—man drags man down, or man lifts man up.

> Booker T. Washington (1856–1915)
> American educator, *The American Standard*

on BUDDHISM

If living on fruits and water is of superior merit, monkeys and fish will go to heaven before men.

> Mira Bai (c. 1520)
> Indian Hindu poet, attacking Buddhist doctrine of simplicity

For no reason it rains,
  whispers of reality.
How lovely it sings,
  drop by drop.
Sitting and lying I listen
  with emptied mind.

I don't need ears,
  I don't need rain.

> Chin 'gak (1178–1234)
> Korean poet, "Night Rain"

Look within! The secret is inside you!

> Hui Neng (638–713)
> Chinese Buddhist leader

The Perfect Way is only difficult
  for those who pick and choose;
Do not like, do not dislike; all will
  then be clear.
Make a hairbreadth difference,
  and Heaven and Earth are set apart.

> Seng-ts'an (c. 520–606)
> Chinese monk

How could sufferings be relieved
  through purification?
To know the Path is to get lost at
  the ford.
Indeed, sickness comes from
  worldly love
And poverty begins with the
  pursuit of greed.

> Wang Wei (699–759)
> Chinese poet, "Two Poems to the Buddhist Scholar Hu, Written When We Were Both Sick"

on BUSINESS

Friendship lasts but for a day, business connections forever.

> Ancient Babylonian proverb

The merchant must be no more pessimist than optimist, since pessimism induces him to hold back his capital but optimism induces him to take such risks that he has more to fear than to hope.

Abu al'Fadl Ja'far al-Dimishqi
(c. 9th century)
Arab writer, *The Beauties of Commerce*

Business pays . . . philanthropy begs.

W. E. B. Du Bois (1868–1963)
American writer and educator,
"Business and Philanthropy," *Crisis*

Profit is profit even in Mecca.

Hausa (Nigerian) proverb

Nothing is illegal if one hundred businessmen decide to do it, and that's true anywhere in the world.

Andrew Young (b. 1932)
American civil rights activist and politician

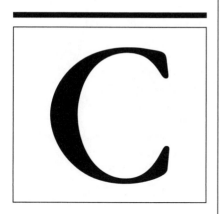

on **CAUSES**

When a just cause reaches its flood tide . . . whatever stands in the way must fall before its overwhelming power.

Carrie Chapman Catt (1859-1947)
American suffragist

The cause is everything. Those even who are dearest to us must be shunted for the sake of the cause.

Mohandas K. Gandhi (1869-1948)
Indian spiritual and political leader

If men refuse to be kindled, sparks can only burn themselves out, just as paper images and carriages burn out on the street during funerals.

Lu Xun (1881-1936)
Chinese writer, *Selected Works*

Never doubt that a small group of thoughtful, committed citizens can change the world. Indeed, it's the only thing that ever has.

Margaret Mead (1901-1978)
American anthropologist

Great causes and little men go ill together.

Jawaharlal Nehru (1889-1964)
Indian prime minister

on **CAUTION**

Take Care
then, mother's son, lest you
   become
a dancer disinherited in mid-dance
hanging a lame foot in air like the
   hen
in a strange unfamiliar compound.
   Pray
protect this patrimony to which
you must return when the song
is finished and the dancers
   disperse.

Chinua Achebe (b. 1930)
Nigerian writer, "Beware, Soul Brothers"

Look twice before you leap.

Charlotte Brontë (1816-1855)
English writer

Chi Wen Tzu always thought three times before taking action. Twice would have been quite enough.

Confucius (551-479 B.C.E.)
Chinese philosopher, founder of Confucianism, *Analects*

Caution is not cowardice; even the ants march armed.

Gandan (Ugandan) proverb

Trust in God—but tie your camel first.

Muhammad (570-632)
Prophet of Islam

33

Take warning in the mischance of others, that others may not take warning of thine.

> Sa'di of Shiraz (c. 1184–1292)
> Persian poet, *Gulistan*

He who does not shave you does not cut you.

> Somali proverb

on CENSORSHIP

Let us be clear: censorship is cowardice. . . . It masks corruption. It is a school of torture: it teaches, and accustoms one to the use of force against an idea, to submit thought to an alien "other." But worst still, censorship destroys criticism, which is the essential ingredient of culture.

> Pablo Antonio Cuadra (b. 1912)
> Nicaraguan poet, "Notes on Culture in the New Nicaragua"

Literature is one of the few areas left where black and white feel some identity of purpose; we all struggle under censorship.

> Nadine Gordimer (b. 1923)
> South African writer

on CHANGE

What was new never came to stay, but to skim the gates of change.

> Osborne Henry Kwesi Brew (b. 1928)
> Ghanaian diplomat and poet

One does not fight to influence change and then leave the change to someone else to bring about.

> Stokely Carmichael (b. 1941)
> American civil rights activist

A boy stopped outside my
  window,
Told me it was the New Year.
So I look out my eastern
  window—
The sun rises as of old,
  unchanged.
Look, boy, it's the same old sun;
Don't bother me now, come back
  some other time.

> Chu Ui-sik (1675–1720)
> Korean poet

It is not the conscious changes made in their lives by men and women—a new job, a new town, a divorce—which really shape them, like the chapter headings in a biography, but a long slow mutation of emotion, hidden, all-penetrative. . . .

> Nadine Gordimer (b. 1923)
> South African writer, *The Lying Days*

Sometimes if something is missing it has to be replaced by something else. It can't be helped.

> Rolando Hinojosa-Smith (b. 1929)
> American writer, *Estampas del Valle y otras obras*

A bowl rotates faster at the top than at the bottom.

> Aminu Kano (b. 1920)
> Nigerian politician

What's wrong with the world, O
  Zaabalawi?
They've turned it upside down
  and made it insipid.

> Egyptian song quoted by Naguib Mahfouz (b. 1911)
> Egyptian writer

Life's picture is constantly under-going change. The spirit beholds a new world every moment.

> Rumi (1207–1273)
> Persian Sufi poet

Whenever they rebuild an old building, they must first of all de-stroy the old one.

> Rumi (1207–1273)
> Persian Sufi poet

The Brahmin . . . had left his fam-ily and came back with his hair turned white. When his neighbors recognized him, they called out: "The man who once left us is still alive?" But the Brahmin answered: "I resemble him, but am no longer the same."

> Seng-chao (384–414)
> Chinese monk and philosopher

The felt unreliability of human ex-perience brought about by the in-human acceleration of historical change has led every sensitive modern mind to the recording of some kind of nausea, of intellectual vertigo.

> Susan Sontag (b. 1933)
> American writer and critic, *Against Interpretation*

We are novices of a new life
. . . .
Maybe we are living the last bad days
Maybe we shall live the first good days too
There is something bitter in this air
Between the past and the future

Between suffering and joy
Between anger and forgiveness.

> Cemal Sureya (b. 1931)
> Turkish poet

Men, without thinking
That they are in fact lies,
Have made promises.
What hurts is this life of mine
Where change is habitual.

> Tenji Shinshi no Ason (c. 1243)
> Japanese poet

on CHARACTER

It will go hard with an obstinate heart at the end,
And the man who loves danger will perish through it.

> Ben Sira (c. 2nd century B.C.E.)
> Hebrew scholar and philosopher, *The Wisdom of Ben Sira*

Distance tests a horse's strength,
Time reveals a man's character.

> Chinese proverb

The superior man is universally minded and no partisan. The infe-rior man is a partisan and not uni-versal.

> Confucius (551–479 B.C.E.)
> Chinese philosopher and founder of Confucianism, *Analects*

The superior man understands what is right; the inferior man un-derstands what will sell.

> Confucius (551–479 B.C.E.)
> Chinese philosopher and founder of Confucianism, *Analects*

What matters in a character is not whether one holds this or that opinion: what matters is how proudly one upholds it.

Madame de Staël (1766–1817)
French writer

Life as it proceeds reveals, coolly and dispassionately, what lies behind the mask that each man wears. It would seem that everyone possesses several faces. Some people use only one all the time, and it then, naturally, becomes soiled and wrinkled. These are the thrifty sort. Others look after their masks in the hope of passing them on to their descendants. Others again are constantly changing their faces. But all of them, when they reach old age, realize one day that the mask they are wearing is their last and that it will soon be worn out, and then, from behind the last mask, the true face appears.

Sadiq Hidayat (1903–1951)
Persian writer, *Buf-i Kur (The Blind Owl)*

Character cannot be developed in ease and quiet. Only through experience of trial and suffering can the soul be strengthened, vision cleared, ambition inspired, and success achieved.

Helen Keller (1880–1968)
American writer and lecturer, *Helen Keller's Journal*

There are complete men and incomplete men. If you would be a complete man, put all of your soul's strength into all of your life's actions.

Eugenio Maria de Hostos
(1839–1903)
Puerto Rican patriot

Listen to a man's words and look at the pupil of his eye. How can a man conceal his character?

Mencius (390–305 B.C.E.)
Chinese philosopher, *Meng-tzu*

Kungfutse asked Mencius, "We are all human beings. Why is it that some are great men and some are small men?"

Mencius replied, "Those who attend to their greater selves become great men, and those who attend to their smaller selves become small men."

"But we are all human beings. Why is it that some people attend to their greater selves and some attend to their smaller selves?"

Mencius replied, "When our senses of sight and hearing are distracted by the things outside, without the participation of thought, then the material things act upon the material senses and lead them astray. That is the explanation. The function of the mind is thinking: when you think, you keep your mind, and when you don't think, you lose your mind. This is what heaven has given to us. One who cultivates his higher self will find that his lower self follows in accord. That is how a man becomes a great man."

Mencius (c. 390–305 B.C.E.)
Chinese philosopher, *Meng-tzu*

If reason dominates in man, he
rises higher than angels.
If lust overpowers man, he
descends lower than the beast.

Rumi (1207–1273)
Persian Sufi poet

The man of good sense is he who strives for himself and profits by the striving.

Ibn Saud (1880–1953)
Saudi Arabian king

on CHARITY

Scatter abroad what you have already amassed rather than pile up new wealth.

'Ali (c. 600–661)
First Imam of Sh'ia branch of Islam; fourth caliph

If someone visits a living man and gets nothing from him to eat, it is as if he had visited the dead.

Nizamuddin Aulia (1234–1325)
Indian religious leader

As water will quench a blazing fire,
So charity will atone for sin.

Ben Sira (c. 2nd century B.C.E.)
Hebrew scholar and philosopher, *The Wisdom of Ben Sira*

Do not . . . be stingy . . . and you will not want for wealth.

Faisal al-Duwish (c. 1930)
Arabian religious leader

He who regards the world as he does the fortune of his own body can govern the world. He who loves the world as he does his own body can be entrusted with the world.

Lao-tzu (c. 604–531 B.C.E.)
Chinese philosopher and founder of Taoism, *Tao-te-ching*

Every good act is charity.

Muhammad (570–632)
Prophet of Islam

Charity is incumbent on each person every day. Charity is assisting anyone, moving and carrying their wares, saying a good word. Every step one takes walking to prayer is charity; showing the way is charity.

Muhammad (570–632)
Prophet of Islam

Better is he who gives little to charity from money honestly earned, than he who gives much from dishonestly gained wealth.

Talmud
(c. late 4th–early 5th century)
ancient body of Jewish civil and canonical law, Kohelet Rabbah 4

Even a poor man who lives on charity should give charity.

Talmud
(c. late 4th–early 5th century)
ancient body of Jewish civil and canonical law, Gittin 7

on CHILDREN AND CHILDHOOD

It's a sad moment, really, when parents first become a bit frightened of their children.

Christina Ama Ata Aidoo (b. 1942)
Ghanaian writer, *No Sweetness Here*

Children have never been very good at listening to their elders, but they have never failed to imitate them.

James Baldwin (1924–1987)
American writer

He who provides for his father atones for his sins,
And he who shows his mother

honor is like a man who lays up treasure.

Ben Sira (c. 2nd century B.C.E.)
Hebrew scholar and philosopher, *The Wisdom of Ben Sira*

There is no end to the violations committed by children on children, quietly talking along.

Elizabeth Bowen (1899-1973)
Irish writer, *The House in Paris*

As I watched her at play . . . it came to me that this child would pass life as the angels live in Heaven. The difficulties of existence would never be hers.

Pearl S. Buck (1892-1973)
American writer, *The Child Who Never Grew*, on her mentally retarded daughter

A good son is repayment of a debt owed you. A bad son is a creditor whose birth should bring no happiness and whose death should cause no sorrow.

Chinese folktale, recorded by P'u Sung-ling (1640-1715)

Who will speak for the bride but her mother?

Egyptian proverb

The greatest lessons in life, if we would but stoop and humble ourselves, we would learn not from the grown-up learned men, but from the so-called ignorant children.

Mohandas K. Gandhi (1869-1948)
Indian spiritual and political leader

Your children are not your children. They are the sons and daughters of Life's longing for itself.

Kahlil Gibran (1883-1931)
Syrian writer, *The Prophet*

Our children, my love
are little ghosts
I hear them laughing in the
    garden
I listen to them playing in the
    empty room

. . . .

the little ghosts
the children we never had
and those we'll never have.

Oscar Hahn (b. 1938)
Chilean poet, "Little Ghosts"

If you can't hold children in your arms, please hold them in your hearts.

Clara Hale (1905-1992)
American social worker

A hare meeting a lioness one day said reproachfully, "I have always a great number of children, while you have but one or two now and then."

The lioness replied, "It is true, but my one child is a lion."

Lokman (c. 1100 B.C.E.)
Ethiopian fabulist

The only form of action open to a child is to break something or strike someone, its mother or another child; it cannot cause things to happen in the world.

Mary McCarthy (1912-1989)
American writer and critic, *On the Contrary*

The period of childhood is a stage on which time and space become entangled.

Yukio Mishima (1925-1970)
Japanese writer, *Confessions of a Mask*

I have all that I lost
and I go carrying my childhood
like a favorite flower
that perfumes my hand.

Gabriela Mistral (1889-1957)
Chilean poet, *Lagar* (*Wine Press*)

I do not love him because he is good,
but because he is my little child.

Rabindranath Tagore (1861-1941)
Indian writer and philosopher, *The Crescent Moon*

The world
For whose sake does it exist?
For the sake of the little ones
Of all places, of all times . . .

Saul Tchernichovsky (1875-1944)
Israeli poet

A father's claim on his child is as high as the mountain-tops lost in the sky;
A mother's right to gratitude is vast as the waters of the Eastern Sea.
The height of the mountains and the vastness of the waters are infinite.

Vietnamese folksong

on CHOICE

You don't get to choose how you're going to die. Or when. You can only decide how you're going to live. Now.

Joan Baez (b. 1941)
American singer and human rights activist

The dog has four feet, but he does not walk them in four roads.

Haitian proverb

To be or not to be is not a question of compromise. Either you be or you don't be.

Golda Meir (1898-1978)
Israeli prime minister

Better hatred than the love of fools; better death than incurable disease; better be killed than be contemptible; better abuse than praise by sycophants.

Naladiyar
Tamil literature

The good is one thing and the pleasant another.
Both with their different ends control a man.
But it is well with him who chooses the good,
While he who chooses the pleasant misses his mark.

Upanishads (c. 600-300 B.C.E.)
sacred philosophical Hindu literature

on CHRISTIANITY

Too often an institution serves to bless the majority opinion. Today when too many move to the rhythmic beat of the status quo, whoever would be a Christian must be a nonconformist.

Martin Luther King, Jr. (1929-1968)
American civil rights leader

39

Men had been living a proud life, having felt no need for the spirit — until Christianity invented it.

> Yukio Mishima (1925–1970)
> Japanese writer

How can we have confidence in the white people? When Jesus Christ came upon the earth, you killed Him and nailed Him to the cross. You thought He was dead, and you were mistaken.

> Tecumseh (c. 1768–1813)
> Shawnee chief, to Indiana Territory
> Governor W. H. Harrison, protesting
> the land sales of 1805–1806

Christianity and Western civilization—what countless crimes have been committed in thy name!

> Ngugi wa Thiong'o (b. 1936)
> Kenyan writer, *Barrel of a Pen:*
> *Resistance to Repression in Neo-*
> *Colonial Kenya*

on CIVIL RIGHTS

The myth of integration as propounded under the banner of the liberal ideology must be cracked because it makes people believe that something is being achieved when in reality the artificially integrated circles are a soporific to the blacks while salving the consciences of the few guilt-stricken whites.

> Steve Biko (1946–1977)
> South African political activist

The white man's happiness cannot be purchased by the black man's misery.

> Frederick Douglass (1817–1895)
> American abolitionist, "The Destiny of
> Colored Americans," *The North Star*

If I have advocated the cause of the Negro, it is not because I am a Negro, but because I am a man.

> Frederick Douglass (1817–1895)
> American abolitionist

The future of American Negroes is in the South. . . . First and greatest of these possible allies are the white working classes about you. The poor whites whom you have been taught to despise and who in turn have learned to fear and hate you. This must not deter you from efforts to make them understand, because in the past, in their ignorance and suffering, they have been led foolishly to look upon you as the cause of most of their distress. You must remember that this attitude is hereditary and that it has been deliberately cultivated ever since emancipation. Slowly but surely the working people of the South, white and black, must come to remember that their emancipation depends upon their mutual cooperation; upon their acquaintanceship with each other; upon their friendship; upon their social intermingling. Unless this happens, each is going to be made the football to break the heads and hearts of the other.

> W. E. B. Du Bois (1868–1963)
> American writer and educator

We are not fighting for the right to be like you. We respect ourselves too much for that. When we advocate freedom, we mean freedom for us to be black, or brown, and you to be white, and yet live together in a free and equal society. This is the only way that integration can bring dignity for both of us.

John Oliver Killens (b. 1916)
American writer, *Black Man's Burden*

I guess it is easy for those who have never felt the stinging darts of segregation to say wait. But when you have seen vicious mobs lynch your mothers and fathers at will and drown your sisters and brothers at whim; when you have seen hate-filled policemen curse, kick, brutalize, and even kill your black brothers and sisters with impunity; when you see the vast majority of your twenty million Negro brothers smothering in an air-tight cage of poverty in the midst of an affluent society; when you suddenly find your tongue twisted and your speech stammering as you seek to explain to your six-year-old daughter why she can't go to the public amusement park that has just been advertised on television, and see tears welling up in her little eyes when she is told that Funtown is closed to colored children, and see the depressing clouds of inferiority begin to form in her little mental sky, and see her begin to distort her little personality by unconsciously developing a bitterness toward white people; when you have to concoct an answer for a five-year-old son asking in agonizing pathos: "Daddy, why do white people treat colored people so mean?"; when you take a cross-country drive and find it necessary to sleep night after night in the uncomfortable corners of your automobile because no motel will accept you . . . when you

are forever fighting a degenerating sense of "nobodiness"—then you will understand why we find it difficult to wait.

Martin Luther King, Jr.
(1929-1968)
American civil rights leader, "Letter from a Birmingham Jail"

There comes a time when the cup of endurance runs over, and men are no longer willing to be plunged into an abyss of injustice where they experience the blackness of corroding despair.

Martin Luther King, Jr.
(1929-1968)
American civil rights leader, "Letter from a Birmingham Jail"

I have a dream that my four little children will one day live in a nation where they will not be judged by the color of their skin but by the content of their character.

Martin Luther King, Jr.
(1929-1968)
American civil rights leader, speech in Washington, D.C., June 15, 1963

We are fighting for the right to live as free humans in this society. In fact, we are actually fighting for rights that are even greater than civil rights and that is human rights.

Malcolm X (1925-1965)
American civil rights activist,
Malcolm X Speaks

All I was trying to do was get home from work.

Rosa Parks (b. 1913)
American civil rights activist, explaining how her refusal to sit in the back of a bus in 1955 led to the Montgomery, Alabama, bus boycott

There is a strong moralistic strain in the civil rights movement that would remind us that power corrupts, forgetting that the absence of power also corrupts.

> Bayard Rustin (1910–1987)
> American civil rights leader, "From Protest to Politics"

We have suffered too many heartaches and shed too many tears and too much blood in fighting the evil of racial segregation to return in 1969 to the lonely and dispiriting confines of its demeaning prison.

> Roy Wilkins (1901–1981)
> American civil rights activist

on CIVILIZATION

Civilization is a method of living, an attitude of equal respect for all men.

> Jane Addams (1860–1935)
> American social worker

Civilization, in the real sense of the term, consists not in the multiplication, but in the deliberate and voluntary reduction of wants.

> Mohandas K. Gandhi (1869–1948)
> Indian spiritual and political leader

It is impossible for a nation to civilize itself; civilization must come from abroad.

> James Africanus Horton
> (1835–1883)
> British physician, *West African Countries and Peoples*

Man's place is higher than the sky. Respect for man is the underlying spirit of civilization.

> Muhammad Iqbal (1873–1938)
> Indian Muslim poet and philosopher

I have no objection to civilization. I object to the fact that civilization should step on what permits us to breathe in the first place.

> Enrique A. Laguerre (b. 1906)
> Puerto Rican writer, *Cauce sin río*

Under every social skin there lurks some barbarism.

> Eugenio Maria de Hostos
> (1839–1903)
> Puerto Rican patriot, *Obras Completas*

If the world suffers from mental deterioration or from moral degradation, then something goes wrong at the very root of civilization or culture. Even though that civilization may drag out for a considerable period, it grows less and less vital and ultimately tumbles down.

> Jawaharlal Nehru (1889–1964)
> Indian prime minister

Do the people of the world not yet realize that by fighting on until the bitter end I am not only performing my sacred duty to my people, but standing guard in the last citadel of collective security? Are they too blind to see that I have my responsibilities to the whole of humanity to face? I must still hold on until my tardy allies appear. And if they never come, then I say prophetically and without bitterness: The West will perish.

> Haile Selassie (1892–1975)
> Ethiopian emperor

It has been a great many years since our white brothers came across the big waters, and a great many of them has not got civilized yet; therefore, we wish to be indulged in our savage state of life until we can have the same time to be civilized. . . . There is some of our white brothers as much savage as the Indian; for that reason we think we might as well enjoy our right as well as our white brothers.

Shullushoma (c. 19th century)
Chickasaw chief, to Secretary of War
John C. Calhoun, December 1824

on THE CLASSES

There is the work of great men and there is the work of little men. Therefore it is said, "Some labor with their minds and some labor with their strength. Those who labor with their minds govern others; those who labor with their strength are governed by others." Those who are governed by others support them; those who govern them are supported by them. This is a universal principle.

Mencius (c. 390–305 B.C.E.)
Chinese philosopher, *Meng-tzu*

An aristocracy in a republic is like a chicken whose head has been cut off: it may run about in a lively way, but in fact it is dead.

Nancy Mitford (1904–1973)
English writer, *Noblesse Oblige*

on CLEVERNESS

Guile excels strength.

Fulfulde (West African) proverb

Cleverness is a wall between hon-
esty and dishonesty; it is not apparent to which side the wall belongs.

Muhammad Hijazi (20th century)
Iranian writer and politician, *Hazar Sokhan* (*A Thousand Sayings*)

on COMMUNISM

The Westerners have lost the
vision of heaven,
they go hunting for the pure spirit
in the belly.
The pure soul takes not color and
scent from the body,
and Communism has nothing to
do save with the body.

Muhammad Iqbal (1873–1938)
Indian Muslim poet and philosopher,
Javidnama

The religion of that prophet [Karl Marx] who knew not the truth, is founded upon equality of the belly.

Muhammad Iqbal (1873–1938)
Indian Muslim poet and philosopher,
Javidnama

Bright red Blood which covers
towns and plains
Of Kampuchea, our motherland.
Sublime Blood of workers and
peasants,
Sublime Blood of revolutionary
men and women fighters!
The Blood changing into
unrelenting hatred . . .

Khmer Rouge anthem for
Democratic Kampuchea, the
Communist name for Cambodia

Between our way of life and communism there can be no peace, no paralyzing coexistence, no gray neutralism. There can only be conflict—total and without reconciliation.

> Ramon Magsaysay (1907-1957)
> Philippine political leader, speaking of
> Huk Communist insurgents

Our principle is that the Party commands the gun, and the gun must never be allowed to command the Party.

> Mao Zedong (1893-1976)
> Chairman of People's Republic of
> China

We are not only good at destroying the old world; we are also good at building the new.

> Mao Zedong (1893-1976)
> Chairman of People's Republic of
> China

Communism is not love. Communism is a hammer which we use to crush the enemy.

> Mao Zedong (1893-1976)
> Chairman of People's Republic of
> China

Be pupils of the masses as well as their teachers.

> Mao Zedong (1893-1976)
> Chairman of People's Republic of
> China

There may be thousands of principles of Marxism, but in the final analysis they can be summed up in one sentence: Rebellion is justified.

> Mao Zedong (1893-1976)
> Chairman of People's Republic of
> China

Many who have read Marxist books have become renegades from the revolution, whereas illiterate workers often grasp Marxism very well.

> Mao Zedong (1893-1976)
> Chairman of People's Republic of
> China

You have never suffered—how can you be a leftist?

> Mao Zedong (1893-1976)
> Chairman of People's Republic of
> China

It [Communism] did not offer an answer to the question: Why should a man be good?

> Jayaprakash Narayan (1902-1979)
> Indian nationalist

I am a good friend to Communists abroad, but I do not like them at home.

> Souvana Phouma (1901-1984)
> Laotian politician, on his country's
> neutrality

The best way to make Communists is to put the Americans into a place where there were no Communists before.

> Norodom Sihanouk (b. 1922)
> Cambodian ruler

I don't like Communism because it hands out wealth through rationing books.

> Omar Torrijos (1929-1981)
> Panamanian soldier and politician

on COMPASSION

If I can stop one Heart from
  breaking
I shall not live in vain.

> Emily Dickinson (1830-1886)
> American poet

Empathy is not merely the basic principle of artistic creation. It is also the only path by which one can reach the truth about life and society.

Nagai Kafu (1879-1959)
Japanese writer

The five kinds of grains are considered good plants, but if the grains are not ripe, they are worse than cockles. It is the same with regard to kindness, which must grow into maturity.

Mencius (c. 390-305 B.C.E.)
Chinese philosopher, *Meng-tzu*

It's much easier to show compassion for animals. They are never wicked.

Haile Selassie (1892-1975)
Ethiopian emperor

He who hath compassion upon others receives compassion from Heaven.

Talmud
(c. late 4th-early 6th century)
ancient body of Jewish civil and
canonical law, Shabbat 151

on COMPETITION

A tiger cannot beat a crowd of monkeys.

Chinese proverb

Rivalry of scholars advances wisdom.

Hebrew proverb

Be second and not the first; if all goes well, the share will be the same; if not, the leader is to blame.

Hitopadesha (c. 3rd-4th century)
Indian moral tales and aphorisms

Those who advocate the theory of competition understand nature but do not understand man.

K'ang Yu-wei (1858-1927)
Chinese political philosopher

Darwin propounded the theory of evolution, considering that what is caused by nature is [therefore] right. [This] leads men to believe that competition is the great principle [of life]. Whereupon competition—which is the greatest evil to the public existing in the world, past or present—is carried on every day and month, and eminent men all pay their respects to it without shame. With this, the earth becomes a jungle, and all is "blood and iron."

K'ang Yu-wei (1858-1927)
Chinese political philosopher

Should we follow the example of natural evolution, then among all mankind throughout the world the strong will oppress the weak, mutually gobbling each other up. . . . In the end, there will remain only the strongest individual, and then he will simply end up being eaten by the birds and beasts.

K'ang Yu-wei (1858-1927)
Chinese political philosopher

If you compete over things, you don't get any more for it; if you yield, neither do you have anything less. The ancients said it very well:

"A person who always makes way for others on the road won't waste one hundred steps in his whole life." He who always gives in on a question of boundaries won't lose even a single section over the course of his life.

> Wang Yu-p'u (c. 18th century)
> Chinese government official

on COMPLAINT

Those who do not complain are never pitied.

> Jane Austen (1775–1817)
> English writer, *Pride and Prejudice*

Petition and complaint are the language of imbecility and cowardice —the evidences of that puerile fear which extinguishes the soul.

> Albery A. Whitman (1851–1902)
> American poet

on CONCENTRATION

The well-resolved mind is single and one-pointed.

> *Bhagavad Gita*
> (c. 4th–3rd century B.C.E.)
> teachings of Krishna from the Hindu
> epic, the *Mahabharata*, 2:41

As the fletcher makes straight his arrow, a wise man makes straight his trembling and unsteady thought, which is difficult to guard, difficult to hold back.

> *Dhammapada* (c. 3rd century B.C.E.)
> collection of ancient Buddhist poems
> and aphorisms

If you wish to see the thousand years, look at today; if you wish to understand the millionfold, then look at the one or the two.

> Hsun-tzu (298–238 B.C.E.)
> Chinese philosopher

At Kugami,
In front of the Otono,
There stands a solitary pine tree,
Surely of many a generation:
How divinely dignified
It stands there!
In the morning
I pass by it:
In the evening
I stand underneath it.
And standing I gaze.
Never tired
Of this solitary pine!

> Ryokan (1758–1831)
> Japanese Zen monk and poet

The bird in a forest can perch but on one bough.
And this should be the wise man's pattern.

> Tso Ssu (c. 3rd century)
> Chinese poet

on CONDUCT

In our actions we should accord with the will of Heaven; in our words we should accord with the hearts of men.

> Chinese proverb

The man of Love follows the path of God—and shows affection to both the believer and the nonbeliever.

> Muhammad Iqbal (1873–1938)
> Indian Muslim poet and philosopher

The man who is kind and who practices righteousness, who remains passive against the affairs of the world, who considers all creatures on earth as his own self, he attains the Immortal Being; the true God is ever with him.

Kabir (1440-1519)
Indian Mughal poet and philosopher

It is in seeing the actions of vicious and wicked people and comparing them with what my conscience tells me regarding such actions that I have learnt what I ought to avoid and what I ought to do. The wise and prudent man will draw a useful lesson even from poison itself.

Lokman (c. 1100 B.C.E.)
Ethiopian fabulist

If men are only shrewd enough, they may even serve kings, eat poison, and dally with women.

Panchatantra (c. 5th century)
collection of Hindu tales

Rabbi Akiba said: "Everything is foreseen, yet freedom is given; the world is judged by grace, yet all is according to the amount of good works."

Talmud
(c. late 4th-early 6th century)
ancient body of Jewish civil and canonical law, Aboth 3:19

Be gentle to all and stern with yourself.

Teresa of Avila (1515-1582)
Spanish nun, "Maxims for Her Nuns"

on CONFORMITY

Unanimity is worse than censorship. Censorship obliges us to hold our own truth silent; unanimity forces us to repeat the truth of others, even though we do not believe it. . . . It dissolves our own personalities into a general, monotonous chorus.

Luis Aguillar (b. 1926)
Cuban educator and writer, "In Defense of Free Speech"

Never say No when the world says Aye.

Elizabeth Barrett Browning (1806-1861)
English poet, *Aurora Leigh*

What a tiresome place America would be if freedom meant we all had to think alike or be the same color or wear the same gray flannel suit! That road leads to the conformity of the graveyard!

John Oliver Killens (b. 1916)
American writer, *Black Man's Burden*

Success, recognition, and conformity are the bywords of the modern world where everyone seems to crave the anesthetizing security of being identified with the majority.

Martin Luther King, Jr. (1929-1968)
American civil rights leader, *Strength to Love*

The simple-minded quickly acquire the color of their companions: The conversations of the parrot make the mirror seem to speak.

Sa'ib of Tabriz (c. 1601-1677)
Persian poet

47

She always says she dislikes the abnormal, it is so obvious. She says the normal is so much more simply complicated and interesting.

Gertrude Stein (1874-1946)
American writer, *The Autobiography of Alice B. Toklas*

Be wise among the wise, but pretend to be dull among fools.

Thiruvalluvar (c. 2nd century)
Indian Tamil writer, *Kural*

Copying everyone else all the time, the monkey one day cut his throat.

Zulu proverb

on CONFUCIANISM

Wealth and honor, benefits and blessings shall enrich my life; poverty and failures, grief and anxiety shall help fulfill it. In my life, I will serve heaven and earth; in death I will find peace.

Chang Tsai (1021-1077)
Chinese philosopher, *The Western Inscription*

If you don't know how to serve men, why worry about serving the gods?

Confucius (551-479 B.C.E.)
Chinese philosopher and founder of Confucianism, *Analects*

The gods should certainly be revered, but kept at a distance. . . . The way is not beyond man; he who creates a way outside of man cannot make it a true way. A good man is content with changing man, and that is enough for him.

Confucius (551-479 B.C.E.)
Chinese philosopher and founder of Confucianism

To be fond of learning is to draw close to wisdom. To practice with vigor is to draw close to benevolence. To know the sense of shame is to draw close to courage. He who knows these three things knows how to cultivate his own character. Knowing how to cultivate his own character, he knows how to govern other men. Knowing how to govern other men, he knows how to govern the world, its states, and its families.

Confucius (551-479 B.C.E.)
Chinese philosopher and founder of Confucianism, *Analects*

What Nature imparts to Man is called human nature. To follow our nature is called the Way. Cultivating the Way is called education.

Chung yung (Doctrine of the Mean)
Confucian text

From the Son of Heaven down to the common people, all must regard cultivation of the personal life as the root or foundation. There is never a case in which the root is in disorder and yet the branches are in order.

Ta hseuh (Great Learning)
Confucian text (c. 500-200 B.C.E.)

on CONQUEST

When an unconquered country is conquered, people are killed. . . . That the beloved of the Gods finds very pitiful and grievous. . . . If anyone does him wrong, it will be forgiven as far as it can be forgiven. . . . The beloved of the Gods considers that the greatest of all victories is the victory of righteousness.

Asoka (273–232 B.C.E.)
Indian king, describing his conversion
to Buddhism and new attitudes

To joy in conquest is to joy in the loss of human life.

Lao-tzu (c. 604–531 B.C.E.)
Chinese philosopher and founder of
Taoism, *Tao-te-ching*, no. 31

The spider is the chamberlain in
the Palace of the Caesars
The owl is the trumpeter on the
battlements of Afrasiyah

Sa'di of Shiraz (c. 1184–1292)
Persian poet

They came, they uprooted, they burned, they slew, they carried off, they departed.

Tarikh-i-Jahan-gusha (c. 1250)
describing the sack of Bukhara by the
invading Mongols

He who, while devouring some,
devoured others,
And as he devoured others, he
devoured some more . . .

Zulu poem (19th century)
in praise of King Shaka

on CONSEQUENCES

The net of Heaven is large and wide, but it lets nothing through.

Chinese proverb

After us, the flood.

Marquise de Pompadour
(1721–1746)
French salonist

Means are not to be distinguished

from ends. If violent means are used, there will be bad results.

Mohandas K. Gandhi (1869–1948)
Indian spiritual and political leader

Like begets like. We gather perfect fruit from perfect trees. . . . Abused soil brings forth stunted growths.

Margaret Sanger (1883–1966)
American social activist, *Women and
the New Race*

Man cuts man with knives and cruel words, never suspecting his turn for being cut will follow. Nature abhors a vacuum. Either love or hatred! Nature likes compensation. Tit for tat! Nature likes a fight. Death or independence!

Natsume Soseki (1867–1916)
Japanese writer

on CONTENTMENT

Chuang-tzu fished in the P'u River. The king of Ch'u sent two grandees to present themselves before him and say: "I wish to trouble you with the administration of my state."

Chuang-tzu held the fishing rod, did not turn his head, and said: "I have heard that there is a sacred tortoise in Ch'u, and that she has been dead for three thousand years. The king keeps her, wrapped in cloth and placed in a box, in the ancestral temple. As regards this tortoise now, would she rather have died and because of that leave behind her bones and be held in honor? Or would she rather have stayed alive and trailed her tail in the mud?"

The two grandees said: "She

would rather have stayed alive and trailed her tail in the mud."

Chuang-tzu said: "Go away. I will trail my tail in the mud."

Chuang-tzu (c. 369-286 B.C.E.)
Chinese Taoist philosopher

When the shoe fits, the foot is forgotten; when the belt fits, the belly is forgotten; when the heart is right, "for" and "against" are forgotten. There is no change in what is inside, no following what is outside, when the adjustment to events is comfortable. One begins with what is comfortable and never experiences what is uncomfortable, when one knows the comfort of forgetting what is comfortable.

Chuang-tzu (c. 369-286 B.C.E.)
Chinese Taoist philosopher

All fortune belongs to him who has a contented mind. Is not the whole earth covered with leather for him whose feet are encased in shoes?

Panchatantra (c. 5th century)
collection of Hindu tales

The secret of contentment is knowing how to enjoy what you have, and to be able to lose all desire for things beyond your reach.

Lin Yutang (1895-1976)
Chinese writer

on CONTRADICTIONS

I don't think that the contradictions between capitalism and socialism can be resolved by war. This is no longer the age of the bow and arrow. It's the nuclear age, and war can annihilate us all. The only way to achieve solutions seems to be for the different social systems to coexist.

Fidel Castro (b. 1927)
Cuban revolutionary and political leader

If there were no contradictions and no struggle, there would be no world, no process, no life, and there would be nothing at all.

Mao Zedong (1893-1976)
Chairman of People's Republic of China

on CONVICTIONS

No one is more dangerous than he who imagines himself pure in heart: for his purity, by definition, is unassailable.

James Baldwin (1924-1987)
American writer, *Nobody Knows My Name*

One needs to be slow to form convictions, but once formed, they must be defended against the heaviest odds.

Mohandas K. Gandhi (1869-1948)
Indian spiritual and political leader

Men who are in earnest are not afraid of the consequences.

Marcus Garvey (1887-1940)
American political leader, *Philosophy and Opinions*

Without fanaticism, one cannot accomplish anything.

Eva Peron (1919-1952)
Argentine politician

Mix a conviction with a man and something happens!

Adam Clayton Powell, Jr.
(1908-1972)

American politician and civil rights leader, "Minimum Living—Minimum Religion," *Keep the Faith, Baby!*

U-turn if you want to. The lady's not for turning.

Margaret Thatcher (b. 1925)
English prime minister, speech in Conservative Conference, 1980

on COOPERATION

I believe that a country's first duty is to set its own house in order; and having set its own house in order, it can contribute better to the community of the world. Instead of being a weak link, it should be a strong link.

George Cable Price (b. 1919)
Belizean politician

We live very close together. So, our prime purpose in this life is to *help* others. And if you can't help them at least don't hurt them.

Dalai Lama (b. 1935)
Tibetan spiritual leader

I am not here on earth for strife,
Love is the mission of my love.
. . . .
Come, let us all be friends for once,
Let us make life easy on us
Let us be lovers and loved ones,
The earth shall be left to no one.

Yunus Emre (c. 1321)
Turkish poet

It is in supporting one another that two hands find strength. A thorny branch can only be cut if left hand is helping. The right hand raised alone could not cut even a morsel of gristle.

'Abdiliaahi Muuse (c. 1890-1966)
Somali sage, in a poem that has become a proverb.

The age of isolation is gone. And gone are the days in which barbed wire served as demarcation lines, separating and isolating countries from one another. No country can escape looking beyond its boundaries to find the source of the currents which influence how it can live with others.

Gamel Abdel Nasser (1918-1970)
Egyptian revolutionary and president, *Falsafat al-Thawrah* (*Philosophy of the Revolution*)

For countless ages the sun rose and set, the moon waxed and waned, the stars shone in the Milky Way; but it was only with the coming of man that these things were understood. Man has unveiled secrets which might have been thought undiscoverable. Much has been achieved in the realm of art, science, literature, and religion. Is all this to end because so few are able to think of man rather than of this or that group of men?

U Thant (1909-1974)
Burmese diplomat

on CORRUPTION

How horribly rapid everything has been, from the days when men were not ashamed to talk of souls and of suffering and of hope to these low days of smiles that will never again be sly enough to hide the knowledge of betrayal and deceit.

Ayi Kwei Armah (b. 1938)
Ghanaian writer, *The Beautyful Ones Are Not Yet Born*

True, I used to see a lot of hope. I saw men tear down the veils behind which the truth had been hidden. But then the same men, when they have power in their hands at last, began to find the veils useful. They made many more. Life has not changed. Only some people have been growing, becoming different, that is all. After a youth spent fighting the white man, why should not the president discover as he grows older that his real desire has been to be like the white governor himself, to live above all the blackness in the big old slave castle?

Ayi Kwei Armah (b. 1938)
Ghanaian writer, *The Beautyful Ones Are Not Yet Born*

When the thinking of a people becomes corrupt, the pure silver becomes impure in its hands.

Muhammad Iqbal (1873–1938)
Indian Muslim poet and philosopher

on COWARDICE

To see what is right and not to do it is want of courage.

Confucius (551–479 B.C.E.)
Chinese philosopher and founder of Confucianism, *Analects*

Nonviolence does not admit of running away from danger. . . . Between violence and cowardly flight

I can only prefer violence to cowardice.

Mohandas K. Gandhi (1869–1948)
Indian spiritual and political leader

Possession of arms implies an element of fear, if not of cowardice.

Mohandas K. Gandhi (1869–1948)
Indian spiritual and political leader

Bullies are always to be found where there are cowards.

Mohandas K. Gandhi (1869–1948)
Indian spiritual and political leader

Cowards can never be moral.

Mohandas K. Gandhi (1869–1948)
Indian spiritual and political leader

Fear has its use, but cowardice has none.

Mohandas K. Gandhi (1869–1948)
Indian spiritual and political leader

A fortress is of no use to cowards.

Thiruvalluvar (c. 2nd century)
Indian Tamil writer, *Kural*

on CREATION

As white and yellow maize I am born,
The many-colored flower of living flesh rises up
and opens its glistening seeds before the face of our mother.
In the moisture of Tlalocan, the quetzal water-plants open their corollas.
I am the work of the only god, his creation.
. . . .
He created you,
he uttered you like a flower,
he painted you like a song:

a Toltec artist.
The book has come to the end;
your heart is now complete.

Aztec poem (c. 1550)

The knowledge of the ancients reached the highest point—the time before anything existed. This is the highest point. It is exhaustive. There is no adding to it.

Chuang-tzu (c. 369-286 B.C.E.)
Chinese Taoist philosopher

When the light of the star which
flows into my eyes as a drop of
gold first pierced the darkness in
space,
there was not a single eye on
earth looking at the sky . . .

Nazim Hikmet (1902-1963)
Turkish poet, "Benerci nicin kendini
oldurdu" ("Why Banerjea Killed
Himself")

Some fools declare that God created the universe. If God created the universe, where was he before creation?
Did God create the universe out of something? If he did, who created the material out of which he created the universe? . . .
. . . Know, therefore, that the universe is not created; it is like time itself without beginning or end. Uncreated and indestructible, the universe is self-sustaining, working by its own inherent power.

Mahapurana (c. 9th century)
Jain sacred text

Wherefrom has this world come?
He who is in the highest heaven has made it; perhaps, He too hasn't

made it. He alone knows; maybe even He doesn't know.

Rig-Veda (c. 1000 B.C.E.)
sacred Hindu literature

But who knows and who can say
Whence it all came, and how
creation happened?
The gods themselves are later
than creation,
so who knows truly whence it
has arisen?

Rig-Veda (c. 1000 B.C.E.)
sacred Hindu literature

From point comes a line, then a
circle:
When the circuit of this circle is
complete,
Then the last is joined to the first.

Sa'di of Shiraz (c. 1184-1292)
Persian poet, *Gulistan*

I was a Hidden Treasure, and I wished to be known, so I created creation that I might be known.

Sufi tradition, of what God said to David

The event of creation did not take place so many kalpas or eons ago, astronomically or biologically speaking. Creation is taking place every moment of our lives.

D.T. Suzuki (1870-1966)
Japanese Buddhist scholar, *The Buddhist Conception of Reality*

Let no man ask what had been before creation of the world.

Talmud
(c. late 4th-early 6th century)
ancient body of Jewish civil and
canonical law, Haggigah 11

on **CREATIVITY**

There is always a state of anxiety, of searching and delving for style.

> Tawfiq al-Hakim (b. 1902)
> Egyptian writer

Our current obsession with creativity is the result of our continued striving for immortality in an era when most people no longer believe in an after-life.

> Arianna Stassinopoulos Huffington (b. 1950)
> Greek writer, "The Working Woman," *The Female Woman*

Human salvation lies in the hands of the creatively maladjusted.

> Martin Luther King, Jr. (1929–1968)
> American civil rights leader, *Strength to Love*

Creation, even when it is a mere outpouring from the heart, wishes to find a public. By definition, creation is sociable. Yet it can be satisfied with merely one single reader: an old friend, a lover.

> Lu Xun (1881–1936)
> Chinese writer

When a man feels the pangs of loneliness, he is able to create. As soon as he reaches detachment, he ceases to create, for he loves no more.
Every creation originates in love.

> Lu Xun (1881–1936)
> Chinese writer

For an artist to do creative work, he needs at once physical health and some physiomental ill health. He needs both serenity and gloom.

> Yukio Mishima (1925–1970)
> Japanese writer

Each time we try to express ourselves
we have to break with ourselves.

> Octavio Paz (b. 1914)
> Mexican writer and diplomat, *Labyrinth of Solitude*

To make a single poem
We need to kill
We must kill many things
Shoot, murder, poison many of the things we love

> Tamura Ryuichi (b. 1923)
> Japanese poet, "Four Thousand Days and Nights"

The profundity of a creative work lies in the degree to which its contents can be summarized in one sentence—a sentence that penetrates human reality.

> Natsume Soseki (1867–1916)
> Japanese writer

on **CRIME**

All crime is a kind of disease and should be treated as such.

> Mohandas K. Gandhi (1869–1948)
> Indian spiritual and political leader

If a man has committed robbery and is caught, that man shall be put to death. If the robber is not caught, the man who has been robbed shall formally declare whatever he has lost before a god, and the city and the mayor in whose territory or district the robbery was committed shall make good to him his lost property.

Hammurapi (1792-1750 B.C.E.)
Babylonian king, law code

When is conduct a crime, and when is a crime not a crime? When Somebody Up There—a monarch, a dictator, a Pope, a legislator—so decrees.

Jessica Mitford (b. 1917)
American writer, *Kind and Unusual Punishment*

Don't tell me there are crimes
  more or less beautiful
because there are no beautiful
  crimes.
There are no degrees in crime.
Don't attempt to convince me
  that every hope
has to be for a time in the hands
  of executioners . . .

Herberto Padilla (20th century)
Cuban poet, "Don't Tell Me"

on CRITICS AND CRITICISM

To arrange a library is to practice
in a quiet and modest way
the art of criticism.

Jorge Luis Borges (1899-1986)
Argentinian writer, "June 1968"

Our civilization has been founded on the notion of criticism: there is nothing sacred or untouchable except the freedom to think. Without criticism, that is to say, without rigor and experimentation, there is no science; without criticism there is no art or literature. I would also say that without criticism there is no healthy society.

Octavio Paz (b. 1914)
Mexican writer and diplomat

Interpretation is the revenge of the intellect upon art.

Susan Sontag (b. 1933)
American writer and critic, *Against Interpretation*

If you don't know what it is, don't mess with it.

Fats Waller (1904-1943)
American musician, about jazz

You cannot lecture on really pure poetry any more than you can talk about the ingredients of pure water—it is adulterated, methylated, sanded poetry that makes the best lectures.

Virginia Woolf (1882-1941)
English writer, *The Second Common Reader*

Literature is strewn with the wreckage of men who have minded beyond reason the opinions of others.

Virginia Woolf (1882-1941)
English writer, *A Room of One's Own*

on CULTURE

Folklore makes one aware of the brotherhood of man.

Augusta Baker (b. 1913)
American librarian

Culture is everything. Culture is the way we dress, the way we carry our heads, the way we walk, the way we tie our ties—it is not only the fact of writing books or building houses.

Aime Cesair (b. 1913)
Martiniquen writer, speaking to the
World Congress of Black Writers and
Artists in Paris

Culture is but the fine flowering of real education, and it is the training of the feeling, the tastes, and the manners that makes it so.

Minnie Kellogg (1880-1949)
Iroquois leader

Culture is the widening of the mind and of the spirit.

Jawaharlal Nehru (1889-1964)
Indian prime minister

Why should there not be "African humanities"? Every language, which means every civilization, can provide material for the humanities, because every civilization is the expression, with its own peculiar emphasis, of certain characteristics of humanity.

Leopold Sedar Senghor (b. 1906)
Senegalese political leader and writer

Culture is an instrument wielded by professors to manufacture professors, who when their turn comes will manufacture professors.

Simone Weil (1909-1943)
French philosopher, *The Need for Roots*

Beyond the refusal of all exterior domination is the urge to reconnect in a deep way with Africa's cultural heritage, which has been for too long misunderstood and rejected. Far from being a superficial or folkloric attempt to bring back to life some of the traditions or practices of our ancestors, it is a matter of constructing a new African society, whose identity is not confused from outside.

Paul Zoungrana (b. 1917)
Upper Voltan religious leader

on CUSTOMS

On entering a country, ask what is
  forbidden,
on entering a village, ask what are
  the customs,
on entering a private house, ask
  what should not be mentioned.

Chinese proverb

You say, "Why do not the Indians till the ground and live as we do?" May we not ask with equal propriety, "Why do not the white people hunt and live as we do?"

Old Tassell (18th century)
Cherokee chief, during a treaty
meeting with U.S. Commissioners
(July 1777)

They are quite different from us, and yet they are human beings! They have their customs and we have ours. Each side thinks his are the only right ones. . . . These customs are not so important after all. It seems that the rules of life a society sets up for itself cannot be the last criterion of "good" and "bad," "beneficial" and "harmful."

Ahmad Faris al-Shidyaq
(1804-1887)
Lebanese writer

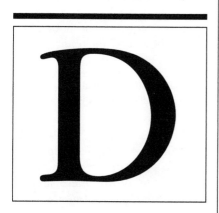

on **DANGER**

In the deadly sweep
Of every wave,
A thousand dangers
lie in wait.

Mirza Ghalib (1797-1869)
Indian Urdu poet

Be ever fearful of trouble when all
  seems fair and clear,
For the easy is soon made
  grievous by the swift-
  transforming sphere.

Nasir-i-Khusraw (c. 1004-1061)
Persian writer, *Diwan*

Paradise lies in the shadow of
swords.

Muhammad (570-632)
Prophet of Islam

We do not run from the troubles
and dangers that are truly ours, and
it is better to learn what they are
earlier than later, and if we don't
run from the others, we are fools.

Katherine Anne Porter
(1894-1980)
American writer

on **DEATH**

Death is a bridge whereby the
lover is joined to the Beloved.

'Abd al-'Aziz b. Sulayman (d. 767)
Sufi poet

Death is a black camel, which
kneels at the gates of all.

Abd-el-Kader (1078-1166)
Persian Sufi leader

Death rides a fast camel.

Arab proverb

If you're afraid to die, you will not
be able to live.

James Baldwin (1924-1987)
American writer

Fear is no obstacle to death.

Bambara (West African) proverb

You are facing the Primary Clear
Light. Be alert and attentive to all
that happens. You can now see
and hear ultimate reality.

Bardo Thodol (c. 760-1300)
popularly called the *Tibetan Book of
the Dead*

Fear not death, for it is your destiny.

Ben Sira (c. 2nd century B.C.E.)
Hebrew scholar and philosopher

Death for an epicure is the
  springtime of calm and peace;
For years his soul smolders like
  incense burning everywhere
While his tomb lies and endures
  under the cool cypresses—
Each dawn a rose blooms and
  each night a nightingale sings
  there.

Yahya Kemal Beyath (1884-1958)
Turkish poet, "Death of the Epicures"

For that which is born, death is certain; and for the dead, birth is certain. Therefore, grieve not over that which is unavoidable.

> *Bhagavad Gita*
> (c. 4th-3rd century B.C.E.)
> teachings of Krishna from the Hindu
> epic, the *Mahabharata*, 2:27

If men but saw the hand of death
Impending over their heads
Even food would give no joy
Much less the deeds that are not
  right.

> Bhoja (995-1055)
> Indian poet

It is good to have a reminder of death before us, for it helps us to understand the impermanence of life on this earth, and this understanding may aid us in preparing for our own death. He who is well prepared is he who knows that he is nothing compared with Wakan-Tanka, who is everything; then he knows that world which is real.

> Black Elk (1863-1950)
> Oglala Sioux holy man

I was born a prince; if princes speak to me I will answer. Since none are present, I am honor bound to keep silent. Oneko, the noble son of Uncas, shall be my executioner. I like it well; for I shall die before my heart is soft, or I have spoken anything unworthy of myself.

> Cannonchet (c. 1630-1676)
> Narragansett chief, upon hearing he
> was sentenced to die

The living all find death unpleasant; men mourn over it. And yet, what is death, but the unbending of the bow and its return to its case?

> Chuang-tzu (c. 369-286 B.C.E.)
> Chinese Taoist philosopher

One day, Chuang-tzu saw a skull. . . . During the night he dreamed that the skull appeared to him and said . . . "In death, there are no rulers above and no subjects below. The course of the four seasons is unknown; our life is eternal. Even a king among men can experience no greater happiness than is ours."

Chuang-tzu . . . asked: "If . . . I could restore your body to you, renew your bones and your flesh and take you back to your parents, your wife, and children and old friends, would you not gladly accept my offers?"

The skull opened its eyes wide, furrowed its brows, and said, "Why should I throw away a happiness greater than a king's to once again thrust myself into the troubles and anxieties of mankind?"

> Chuang-tzu (c. 369-286 B.C.E.)
> Chinese Taoist philosopher

I was given life because it was my time, and now I take leave of it according to the same law. Content with the natural sequence of these events, I am touched neither by joy nor by grief. I am simply hanging in the air . . . incapable of freeing myself, tied by the threads of things.

> Chuang-tzu (c. 369-286 B.C.E.)
> Chinese Taoist philosopher

If you don't know how to live, why wonder about death?

Confucius (551–479 B.C.E.)
Chinese philosopher and founder of Confucianism, *Analects*

In a little while I will be gone from you, my people, and whither I cannot tell. From nowhere we come; into nowhere we go. What is life? It is the flash of a firefly in the night. It is the breath of the buffalo in the wintertime. It is the shadow that runs across the grass and loses itself in the sunset.

Crowfoot (c. 1836–1890)
Blackfoot chief

Clearly death is not a loss.
Regardless the brooks.
Will flow.

With faith
Weeds will turn green and roses
will grow.
Clearly death is not a loss.

Fazil Husnu Daglarca (b. 1914)
Turkish poet, "Sparkle"

I hold the view that death is rather like changing one's clothes when they are torn and old. It is not an end in itself. Yet death is unpredictable—you do not know when and how it will take place.

Dalai Lama (b. 1935)
Tibetan spiritual leader, *Freedom in Exile: The Autobiography of the Dalai Lama*

To my mind, there are two things that, in life, you can do about death. Either you can choose to ignore it, in which case you may have some success in making the idea of it go away for a limited period of time, or you can confront the prospect of your own death and try to analyze it and, in so doing, try to minimize some of the inevitable suffering that it causes. Neither way can you actually overcome it.

Dalai Lama (b. 1935)
Tibetan spiritual leader, *Freedom in Exile: The Autobiography of the Dalai Lama*

We understand death for the first time when he puts his hand upon one whom we love.

Madame de Staël (1766–1817)
French writer

Both the young and the old, both the wise and the foolish, end up in death.

Dhammapada (c. 3rd century B.C.E.)
collection of ancient Buddhist poems and aphorisms

That short, potential stir
That each can make but once,
That bustle so illustrious
'Tis almost consequence,
Is the éclat of death.

Emily Dickinson (1830–1886)
American poet, "Time and Eternity"

Death is the supple Suitor
That wins at last—
It is a stealthy Wooing
Conducted first
By pallid innuendoes
And dim approach
But brave at last with Bugles.

Emily Dickinson (1830–1886)
American poet

Because I have loved so vainly,
And sung with such faltering

breath,
The Master in infinite mercy
  Offers the boon of Death.

> Paul Laurence Dunbar (1872–1906)
> American writer, "Compensation"

We do not know whether it is good to live or to die. Therefore, we should not take delight in living, nor should we tremble at the thought of death. We should be equiminded towards death. This is the ideal. It may be long before we reach it, and only a few of us can attain it. Even then, we must keep it constantly in view, and the more difficult it seems of attainment, the greater should be the effort we put forth.

> Mohandas K. Gandhi (1869–1948)
> Indian spiritual and political leader

You, young fellow,
If you don't want to die,
Die now!
Once dead, you don't have to die
  twice.

> Hakuin (1685–1768)
> Japanese Zen master

Only death does not lie.

> Sadiq Hidayat (1903–1951)
> Persian writer, *Buf-i Kur (The Blind Owl)*

The presence of death annihilates all superstitions. We are the children of death, and it is death that rescues us from the deceptions of life. In the midst of life he calls us and summons us to him.

> Sadiq Hidayat (1903–1951)
> Persian writer, *Buf-i Kur (The Blind Owl)*

[Death is] the best asylum for pains and sorrows and troubles and the injustices of life.

> Sadiq Hidayat (1903–1951)
> Persian writer, *Buf-i Kur (The Blind Owl)*

Death is a reality in which no living creature believes.

> Muhammad Hijazi (20th century)
> Iranian writer and politician, *Hazar Sokhan (A Thousand Sayings)*

In the dim light of my last dawn
I will see my friends and you
and I will only
  take to my grave
the sorrow of an unfinished song.

> Nazim Hikmet (1902–1963)
> Turkish poet, "Letter from Prison"

The sun exactly at noon is exactly beginning to go down. And a creature exactly when he is born is exactly beginning to die.

> Hui Shi (370–290 B.C.E.)
> Chinese philosopher

A certain ascetic said: "Your dwellings are before you, and your life is after your death."
And Samuel, son of Adiya, the Jew, said in verse: "Being dead, I was created, and before that I was not anything that dies; but I died when I came to life."
Hasan, son of Dinar, said: "Hasan [of Basra] saw a man in his death struggle. 'Surely,' he exclaimed, 'a thing of which this is the end ought not to be desired at the first and ought to be feared at the last.'"

> al-Jahiz (c. 778–869)
> Islamic philosopher and writer, *Kitab al-Bayan (The Book of Proof)*

Strange, is it not? that of the
  myriads who
Before us passed the door of
  Darkness through,
Not one returns to tell us of the
  Road,
Which to discover we must travel
  too.

> Omar Khayyám (c. 1048–1122)
> Persian poet and astronomer, *Rubáiyát
> of Omar Khayyám*

I am afraid of dying—but being
dead, oh yes, that to me is often an
appealing prospect.

> Kathe Kollwitz (1867–1945)
> East Prussian artist

Death is a phenomenon like life;
perhaps the dead live.

> Joaquim Maria Machado de Assis
> (1839–1908)
> Brazilian writer, *Esau and Jacob*

I forgot that your light foot
had turned to ash,
and as in happy times
I set out to meet you on the path.
. . . .
I forgot they had made you deaf
to my outcry;
I forgot your silence,
your livid pallor.
. . . .
In vain I kept this appointment
on deserted paths.
I cannot bring to life again
your ghost in my open empty
  arms.

> Gabriela Mistral (1889–1957)
> Chilean poet, "The Useless Wait,"
> *Desolacion (Desolation)*

Die before ye die.

> Muhammad (570–632)
> Prophet of Islam

People sleep, and when they die,
they wake.

> Muhammad (570–632)
> Prophet of Islam

Repeat to a dying person, there is
no god but God.

> Muhammad (570–632)
> Prophet of Islam

One day we must go,
one night we will descend into
  the region of mystery.
Here, we only come to know
  ourselves;
only in passing are we here on
  earth.
In peace and pleasure let us
  spend our lives; come let us
  enjoy ourselves.
Let not the angry do so; the earth
  is vast indeed!
Would that one lived forever;
  would that one were not to die!

> Nahuatl (Aztec) poem (c. 1500)
> *Cantares Mexicanos*

Death is but a new birth of the
spirit into the great unknown.

> Pritish Nandy (b. 1947)
> Indian poet

I postpone death by living, by suffering, by error, by risking, by living, by losing.

> Anaïs Nin (1903–1977)
> American writer, *Diary*

People living deeply have no fear
of death.

> Anaïs Nin (1903–1977)
> American writer, *Diary*

Death knocks at your door, and before you can tell him to come in, he is in the house with you.

> Grace Ogot (b. 1930)
> Kenyan writer

Death is the mother of forms.

> Octavio Paz (b. 1914)
> Mexican writer and diplomat, "Pasado en claro" ("A Draft of Shadows")

You learn something the day you die. You learn how to die.

> Katherine Anne Porter
> (1894–1980)
> American writer

Would that I might die all at once, But mine is a soul that withers day by day.

> Imru' al-Qays (c. 540)
> Arabian poet

Wherever ye be, death will overtake you, though ye be in lofty towers.

> *Qur'an* (c. 610–656)
> sacred book of Islam, 4

The world is a playground, and death is the night.

> Rumi (1207–1273)
> Persian Sufi poet

I died as mineral and became a plant
I died as plant and rose as an animal,
I died as animal and I was a Man.
Why should I fear? When was I less by dying?

> Rumi (1207–1273)
> Persian Sufi poet

Turns his face and heeds them not.
He forgets that day of death Must come inescapably.

> Al-Salib ibn Ruzziq (1101–1161)
> Egyptian poet and politician

To quit this troubled world is better than to enter it: the rosebud enters the garden with straitened heart and departs smiling.

> Sa'ib of Tabriz (1601–1677)
> Persian poet

When poison becomes a habit, it ceases to injure: make your soul gradually acquainted with death.

> Sa'ib of Tabriz (c. 1601–1677)
> Persian poet

The life of this transitory world is the expectation of death: to renounce life is to escape from the expectation of annihilation.

> Sa'ib of Tabriz (1601–1677)
> Persian poet

There is no death, only a change of worlds.

> attributed to Seathl (c. 1788–1866)
> Dwamish chief, to Isaac Stevens, the Washington Territory governor (1854)

To examine the causes of life, we must first have recourse to death.

> Mary Shelley (1797–1851)
> English writer, *Frankenstein*

If it is necessary to die in order to live like men, what harm in dying?

> Rabindranath Tagore (1861–1941)
> Indian writer and philosopher

A man cannot say to the Angel of Death: I wish to arrange my affairs before I die.

> *Talmud*
> (c. late 4th–early 6th century)
> ancient body of Jewish civil and
> canonical law, Debarim Rabbah 9.3

Heaven and Earth exist forever;
Mountains and rivers never
  change.
But herbs and trees in perpetual
  rotation
Are renovated and withered by
  the dews and frosts;
And Man the wise, Man the
  divine—
Shall he alone escape this law?
. . . .
He suddenly departs, never to
  return.
Who will notice there is one
  person less?

> T'ao Ch'ien (365–427)
> Chinese poet, "Substance, Shadow and
> Spirit"

It is sweet to die in one's native land and be buried by the margins of one's native stream.

> Tsali (d. 1838)
> Cherokee warrior

Those who cling to life die, and those who defy death live.

> Uyesugi Kenshin (1530–1578)
> Japanese military leader

It's not true that death is a lump
  like this, or a blow.
So much like a cloth veil, lifted,
like this he comes slowly, even
  like a bride.

The journey is private, it's true,
  listen
to what happens to me, what
  happens to you.

> Yona Wallach (b. 1946)
> Israeli poet, "Death; She Was Always
> Here"

Every man knows that he must die, but no one believes it.

> Yiddish proverb

When wood breaks, it can be
  repaired.
But ivory breaks forever . . .

> Yoruba (West African) funeral song

on DECISIONS

In war and affairs of state, many things seem to be just and reasonable at first sight; yet nothing of the kind ought to be finally decided without being pondered in a hundred different lights.

> Babur (1483–1530)
> First Mughal emperor of India, *Babur-nama*

"Yes," I answered you last night;
"No," this morning, sir, I say;
Colors seen by candle-light
Will not look the same by day.

> Elizabeth Barrett Browning
> (1806–1861)
> English poet, *The Lady's "Yes"*

Be resolved and the thing is done.

> Chinese proverb

There is a magic power in your own hands. Take your vital decisions—they may be grave and momentous and far-reaching in their consequences. Think a hundred times before you take any decision, but once a decision is taken, stand by it as one man.

Fatima Jinna (1893–1967)
Pakistani politician, speech to the All-India Muslim League (October 1937)

One can't realize difficulty arriving at a momentous decision until one comes to do so.

Aminu Kano (b. 1920)
Nigerian politician

It's never the right time to take a particular stand.

Adam Clayton Powell, Jr.
(1908–1972)
American politician and civil rights leader, "One Must Die for Many," *Keep the Faith, Baby*

Standing is still going.

Swahili proverb

To be constantly changing one's plans isn't decision at all—it's indecision.

Rabindranath Tagore (1861–1941)
Indian writer and philosopher

on DEFEAT

Broken spears lie in the roads;
we have torn our hair in grief.
The houses are roofless now, and their walls
are red with blood.

Worms are swarming in the
streets and plazas,
and the walls are splattered with gore.
The water has turned red, as if it were dyed,

and when we drink it,
it has the taste of brine.

Aztec lament at the fall of the capital of Tenochtitlán to the Spanish under Cortés (c. 1525)

You have said to me when I was still young and could hope, that in difficulty I could send a voice four times, once for each quarter of the earth, and you would hear me.
Today I send a voice for a people in despair.
You have given me a sacred pipe, and through this I should make my offering. You see it now!
From the west you have given me the cup of living water and the sacred bow, the power to make life and to destroy it . . . and from the south, the nation's sacred hoop and the tree that was to bloom. . . . At the center of the sacred hoop you have said that I should make the tree to bloom.
With tears running, O Great Spirit, my Grandfather—with running eyes I must say now that the tree has never bloomed. A pitiful old man, you see me here, and I have fallen away and done nothing. Here at the center of the world, where you took me when I was young and taught me; here, old I stand, and the tree is withered, my Grandfather.

Black Elk (1863–1950)
Oglala Sioux holy man, song to Wakan Tanka, the Great Mystery, at Harney Peak, in the Dakota Black Hills (1912)

The nation's hoop is broken and scattered.

There is no center any longer, and the sacred tree is dead.

Black Elk (1863-1950)
Oglala Sioux holy man

I fought hard. But your guns were well aimed. The bullets flew like birds in the air, and whizzed by our ears like the wind through the trees in winter. My warriors fell around me; it began to look dismal. I saw my evil day at hand. The sun rose dim on us in the morning, and at night it sunk in a dark cloud, and it looked like a ball of fire. That was the last sun that shone on Black Hawk. His heart is dead and no longer beats quick in his bosom. He is now a prisoner to the white man; they will do with him as they wish. But he can stand torture, and is not afraid of death. He is no coward. Black Hawk is an Indian.

Black Hawk (1767-1838)
Sauk chief, on a battle with U.S. forces

I once thought that I could conquer the whites; my heart grew bitter and my hands grew strong. But the white men were mighty. I and my people failed. I see the strength of the white men. I will be the white man's friend. I will go to my people and speak good of the white men. I will tell them that they are like the leaves of the forest—very many, very strong—and that I will fight no more against them.

Black Hawk (1767-1838)
Sauk chief

Defeats are always pitiful. Victories are always last resources.

Indira Gandhi (1917-1984)
Indian prime minister

Once I moved about like the wind. Now I surrender to you, and that is all.

Geronimo (1829-1909)
Apache chief, to General George Crook (1886)

How long will it be until it is said there are no Apaches?

Geronimo (1829-1909)
Apache chief, *Geronimo: His Own Story*

That's how it goes, my friend.
The problem is not falling a captive,
it's how to avoid surrender.

Nazim Hikmet (1902-1963)
Turkish poet, "That's How It Goes"

Hear me, my chiefs: I am tired; my heart is sick and sad. From where the sun now stands, I will fight no more forever.

Chief Joseph (c. 1840-1904)
Nez Percé chief, when surrendering to U.S. troops thirty miles from the Canadian border

We are ordinary people,
we are subject to death and destruction,
we are mortals;
allow us to die,
let us perish now,
since our gods are already dead.

Nahuatl (Aztec) passage
from the *Colloquies of 1524*,
transcribed by Fray Bernardino de Sahagun

I see as in a vision the dying spark of our council fires, the ashes cold and white. I see no longer the curling smoke rising from our lodge poles. I hear no longer the songs of the women as they prepare the meal. The antelope have gone; the buffalo wallows are empty. Only the wail of the coyote is heard. . . . We are like birds with a broken wing. My heart is cold within me. My eyes are growing dim—I am old.

> Plenty Coups (1848-1932)
> Crow chief, farewell address at the Little Bighorn, Montana council grounds (1909)

A warrior
I have been.
Now
it is all over.
A hard time
I have.

> Sitting Bull (c. 1834-1890)
> Dakota Sioux chief, "Song of Sitting Bull"

The white man has the country which we loved, and we only wish to wander on the prairie until we die.

> Ten Bears (c. 1800-1872)
> Yamparika Comanche spokesperson

on DELUSION

The Giver of Life deceives!
Only dreams do you follow,
You, our friends!
As truly as our hearts believe,
As truly as they are deceived.

> Aztec song

When the cockroach hides itself in a basket of beans, it thinks it is safe; but one day that basket will be opened and the cockroach will reveal itself.

> Peter Enahoro (b. 1935)
> Nigerian journalist

How curious that a man who closes his hand upon air so often thinks that he has a ruby within his grasp.

> Idries Shah (b. 1924)
> Indian Sufi mystic and writer, *Caravan of Dreams*

on DEMOCRACY

The continuation of authority has frequently proved the undoing of democratic governments. Repeated elections are essential to the system of popular governments, because there is nothing so dangerous as to suffer power to be vested for a long time in one citizen. The people become accustomed to obeying him, and he becomes accustomed to commanding, hence the origin of usurpation and tyranny.

> Simón Bolívar (1783-1830)
> South American revolutionary leader, address at the opening of the Second National Congress of Venezuela (February 15, 1819)

There can be no perfect democracy curtailed by color, race, or poverty. But with all we accomplish all, even peace.

> W. E. B. Du Bois (1868-1963)
> American writer and educator

I swear to the Lord
I still can't see

Why Democracy means
Everybody but me.

> Langston Hughes (1902–1967)
> American writer, "The Black Man
> Speaks," *Jim Crow's Last Stand*

Keep away from Democracy;
follow the Perfect Man,
For the intellect of two hundred
asses cannot bring forth a single
man's thought.

> Muhammad Iqbal (1873–1938)
> Indian Muslim poet and philosopher

Democracy without education is
hypocrisy without limitation.

> Iskander Mirza (b. 1899)
> Pakistani politician

Our military offensive is indispens-
able, since force must be met by
force. But our social offensive is
the extra weapon which the enemy cannot produce. Here the enemy meets democracy's strongest
element—the ability to realize and
satisfy the needs of its people without taking from them their freedom and dignity as human beings.

> Ramon Magsaysay (1907–1957)
> Philippine politician

In the so-called Western secular democracy . . . a divorce has been ef-
fected between politics and
religion, and as a result of this sec-
ularization, the society and particularly its politically active elements
have ceased to attach much or any
importance to morality or ethics.

> Abu'l A'la Mawdudi (1903–1979)
> Pakistani Islamic leader, *Islamic Law
> and Constitution*

Let no one stop you from voting.

With your votes you are working
for your future. It is not a holiday;
it is the most serious day of work
since you were born. Better to
come in clothing dirty from work
than with your soul filthy from having sold your right to justice.

> Luis Muñoz Marín (b. 1898)
> Puerto Rican politician

Democracy is good. I say this because other systems are worse.

> Jawaharlal Nehru (1889–1964)
> Indian prime minister

Changes are inseparable from democracy. To defend democracy is
to defend the possibility of change;
in turn, changes alone can
strengthen democracy.

> Octavio Paz (b. 1914)
> Mexican writer and diplomat, "Latin
> America and Democracy," *One Earth,
> Four or Five Worlds: Reflections on
> Contemporary History*

Democracy cannot be static. Whatever is static is dead.

> Eleanor Roosevelt (1884–1962)
> American humanitarian and First Lady,
> *Let Us Have Faith in Democracy*

It is democracy I am really suffering from as much as I am suffering
from the opposition.

> Anwar Sadat (1918–1981)
> Egyptian military and political leader,
> speaking to foreign journalists about
> unrest in Egypt (September 9, 1981)

No democracy is born perfect, and
none ever gets to be perfect. Yet
democracy is superior to authoritarian and totalitarian regimes be-

cause, unlike them, democracy is perfectible.

> Mario Vargas Llosa (b. 1936)
> Peruvian writer, "Latin America: The Democratic Option," speech to the Trilateral Commission, San Francisco, California (March 1990)

Democracy is not a mere consequence, a certain stage in the development of society. It is the condition on which the survival of productive forces depends.

> Wei Jingsheng (b. 1950)
> Chinese activist, "The Fifth Modernization"

We want to become masters of our own destiny. We need no gods and no emperors; we believe in no savior; we want to direct our own lives.

> Wei Jingsheng (b. 1950)
> Chinese activist

Look rather at the teachings of history, true history, not the history written by Party hacks: genuine democracy, the only valid democracy, is nourished with the blood of martyrs and with the blood of tyrants.

> Wei Jingsheng (b. 1950)
> Chinese activist

on **DEPARTURES**

Dismounting on the sandbar I
  wait for a boat
A stretch of smoke and waves, an
  endless sorrow.
Only when the hills are worn flat
  and the waters dried up

Will there be no parting in the
  world of man.

> Cho'oe Ch'i-won (c. 857)
> Korean poet and politician, "At the Ugang Station"

If only Life-and-Death
Were a thing
Subject to our wills,
What would be the bitterness of
  parting?

> Lady Eguchi (c. 890)
> Japanese writer

Stay:
Will you go? Must you go?
Is it in weariness you go? From
  disgust?
Who advised you, who persuaded
  you?
Say why you are leaving,
You, who are breaking my heart.

> Songjong (1457–1494)
> Korean king

on **DEPENDENCE**

Nothing is more desirable than to be released from an affliction, but nothing is more frightening than to be divested of a crutch.

> James Baldwin (1924–1987)
> American writer, *Nobody Knows My Name*

It is easier to live through someone else than to become complete yourself.

> Betty Friedan (b. 1921)
> American feminist, *The Feminine Mystique*

Inequality emanates from man being dependent upon and employed by another.

> Liu Shih-p'ei (1884–1919)
> Chinese writer

on DESIRE

You may win your heart's desire, but in the end you're cheated of it by death.

> Jorge Luis Borges (1899–1986)
> Argentinian writer

Just as water that has entered the ear may be removed by water, and just as a thorn may be removed by a thorn, so those who know how, remove passion by means of passion itself. Just as a washerman removes the grime from a garment by means of grime, so the wise man renders himself free of impurity by means of impurity itself.

> *Cittavisuddhiprakarana*
> Buddhist Tantric text

A Ch'i individual stole some money at a crowded bazaar. He was walking away with it when the police asked him why it was that he stole the money in the market. The thief replied that the sight of the money filled his mind to the exclusion of the policeman. So his desires made him forgetful of the nature of his act.

> Huai Nan Tzu (c. 122 B.C.E.)
> Chinese scholar

If thou desirest a glory that never vanishes, then seek not to embrace a glory that vanishes.

> Ibn 'Ata'allah (c. 1252–1309)
> Egyptian Sufi leader

To be constantly without desire is the way to have a vision of the mystery of heaven and earth,

For constantly to have desire is the means by which their limitations are seen.

> Lao-tzu (c. 604–531 B.C.E.)
> Chinese philosopher and founder of Taoism, *Tao-te-Ching*

The truth is that you cannot attain God if you have even a trace of desire. Subtle is the way of dharma. If you are trying to thread a needle, you will not succeed if the thread has even a slight fiber sticking out.

> Ramakrishna (1836–1886)
> Indian Hindu mystic

There cannot be self-restraint in the absence of desire: when there is no adversary, what avails thy courage?

Hark, do not castrate thyself, do not become a monk: chastity depends on the existence of lust.

> Rumi (1207–1273)
> Persian Sufi poet

The whole earth cannot satisfy the lust of the flesh; who can do its will? To him who longs for the impossible come guilt and bafflement of desire; but he who is utterly without desire has a happiness that ages not.

> Santi-deva (7th century)
> Indian Buddhist philosopher

Eager to escape sorrow, men rush into sorrow; from desire of happiness they blindly slay their own happiness, enemies to themselves.

> Santi-deva (7th century)
> Indian Buddhist philosopher

on DESPAIR

There's something so showy about desperation, it takes hard wits to see it's a grandiose form of funk.

> Elizabeth Bowen (1899-1973)
> Irish writer, *The Death of the Heart*

Safe Despair it is that raves—
Agony is frugal.
Puts itself severe away
For its own perusal.

> Emily Dickinson (1830-1886)
> American poet

. . . And here am I, budding
 among the ruins
With only sorrow to bite on,
As if weeping were a seed and I
The earth's only furrow.

> Pablo Neruda (1904-1973)
> Chilean poet and diplomat, "Barrio sin luz" ("Lightless Suburb")

I've already lost all hope
I don't wait for joyful hours
In fact, night and day grieving
I howl my agonies,
And as I suffer, I consume myself
 vilely
And ask for death.

> Kata Szidonia Petroczi (1662-1708)
> Hungarian poet

Despair is the one sin that cannot be forgiven.

> Ngugi wa Thiong'o (b. 1936)
> Kenyan writer

Over our vast land the storm-
 clouds rise,
All of us sunk in gloom, who
 dares speak out?
Now, to intensify our pain,
 autumn's come:
The chirping of crickets is too
 much for my ears.

> Zhou En-lai (1898-1976)
> Chinese revolutionary and prime minister of the People's Republic

on DESTRUCTION

Watching Europe burn with its
 civilization of fire,
Watching America disintegrate
 with its gods of steel,
Watching the persecutors of
 mankind turn into dust,
Was I wrong? Was I wrong?

> Mazisi Kumene (b. 1932)
> South African poet

Dead men, not potsherds,
Covered the approaches,
the walls were gaping,
the high gates, the roads,
were piled with dead . . .
The country's blood now filled its
 holes,
like metal in a mold;
Bodies dissolved—like fat left in
 the sun.

> Sumerian lament on the destruction of Ur (2004 B.C.E.)

. . . famished streams
Snake through desolate lands
Dragging our saltless tears
To the banks of a distant river.

> Obiora Udechukwu (20th century)
> Nigerian poet, on the post-Biafran war desolation, *Nssukka Harvest* 7

on **DIGNITY**

Man is not just a stomach. . . .
Above all he hungers for dignity.

Jacobo Arbenz (1913–1971)
Guatemalan politician

Humiliation, slavery, fear have per-
verted us to the bone; we no longer
look like men. . . . Men must be
granted the respect due to them.

Mohammed Dib (b. 1920)
Algerian writer, *Le Metier a tisser*

The sign of our time is that the dignity of the human personality has
no place: the age is, as are its laws,
impersonal, its heart as of stone.
. . . Yet on arrest, in the name of
these laws, we die like dogs, neither executioner nor victim making a sound. Because he has to
gasp for air all his life, panting for
breath is the man of today's only
way out.

Sadiq Hidayat (1903–1951)
Iranian writer

The real tragedy is that we're all
human beings, and human beings
have a sense of dignity. Any domination by one human over another leads to a loss of some part
of his dignity. Is one's dignity that
big it can be crumbled away like
that?

Yusuf Idris (b. 1927)
Egyptian writer, *Al-Farafir* (*The
Farfurs*)

If we must die, let it not be like
  hogs
Hunted and penned in an
  inglorious spot,

. . . .
If we must die, O let us nobly die

Claude McKay (1890–1948)
American poet, "If We Must Die"

on **DIPLOMACY**

There are times when even the
greatest tactician in diplomatic
cunning is outclassed in his own
game. It is then that he discovers
that all that he thought he had
gained is but loss, and that what is
left of national honor and dignity is
but the shadow of an illustrious
past that is gone forever, or of a
potentially great future that will
never come.

Obafemi Awolowo (b. 1909)
Nigerian politician, *Awo: The
Autobiography of Chief Obafemi
Awolowo*

You cannot shake hands with a
clenched fist.

Indira Gandhi (1917–1984)
Indian prime minister

I know no diplomacy save that of
truth.

Mohandas K. Gandhi (1869–1948)
Indian spiritual and political leader

A little that makes for concord is
better than a great deal that makes
for division.

al-Jahiz (c. 778–869)
Islamic philosopher and writer, *The
Exploits of the Turks and the Army of
the Khalifate in General*

Everyone has pointed out that we
are without a navy and that our
coasts are undefended. Meanwhile,
the Americans will be back next
year. Our policy shall be to evade

71

any definite answer to their request, while at the same time keeping a peaceful demeanor.

> Japanese government decree after Admiral Perry demanded that the country be opened to American trade and commerce (1853)

That expression "positive neutrality" is a contradiction in terms. There can be no more positive neutrality than there can be a vegetarian tiger.

> V. K. Krishna Menon (b. 1897)
> Indian politician

Let every girl, let every woman, let every mother here [in Israel]—and there in my country [Egypt]—know we shall solve all our problems through negotiations around the table rather than starting war.

> Anwar Sadat (1918-1981)
> Egyptian military and political leader

Diplomats make it their business to conceal the facts.

> Margaret Sanger (1883-1966)
> American social activist, *Women and the New Race*

History offers examples of winning in diplomacy after losing in war.

> Yoshida Shigeru (1878-1967)
> Japanese politician

All diplomacy is a continuation of war by other means.

> Zhou En-lai (1898-1976)
> Chinese revolutionary and prime minister of the People's Republic

on DIVERSITY

Communities, like individuals, love and cherish their individuality. . . . When unity is evolved out of diversity, then there is a real and abiding national progress.

> Manhar-ul-Haque (1866-1921)
> Bengali lawyer

If we are to achieve a richer culture, rich in contrasting values, we must recognize the whole gamut of human potentialities, and so weave a less arbitrary social fabric, one in which each diverse human gift will find a fitting place.

> Margaret Mead (1901-1978)
> American anthropologist, *Coming of Age in Samoa*

In this market every head has a different fancy: everyone winds his turban in a different fashion.

> Sa'ib of Tabriz (c. 1601-1677)
> Persian poet

White men seem to have difficulty in realizing that people who live differently from themselves still might be traveling the upward and progressive road of life.

> Luther Standing Bear (1868-1939)
> Sioux writer, *Land of the Spotted Eagle*

There is not one state truly alive if it is not as if a cauldron burns and boils in its representative body, and if there is no clash of convictions in it.

> Achmad Sukarno (1902-1970)
> Indonesian politician

on **DREAMS**

He who dreams . . . does not know he is dreaming. . . . Only when he awakens does he know he has dreamt. But there is also the great awakening (*ta-chiao*), and then we see that [everything] here is nothing but a great dream. Of course, the fools believe that they are already awake—what foolishness! Confucius and you, both of you, are dreams; and I, who tell you this, am also a dream.

> Chuang-tzu (c. 369-286 B.C.E.)
> Chinese Taoist philosopher, *Chuang-tzu* (conversation between Ch'u Ch'iao, a disciple of Confucius, and Chuang-tzu)

We all have the same dreams.

> Joan Didion (b. 1935)
> American writer, *The Book of Common Prayer*

Hold fast to dreams
For when dreams go
Life is a barren field
Frozen with snow.

> Langston Hughes (1902-1967)
> American writer, "Hold Fast to Dreams"

I say to you today, my friends, that in spite of the difficulties and frustrations of the moment, I still have a dream. It is a dream deeply rooted in the American dream.

I have a dream that one day this nation will rise up and live out the true meaning of its creed: "We hold these truths to be self-evident, that all men are created equal."

I have a dream that one day on the red hills of Georgia the sons of former slaves and the sons of former slaveowners will be able to sit down together at the table of brotherhood.

> Martin Luther King, Jr.
> (1929-1968)
> American civil rights leader, speech in Washington, D.C. (August 28, 1963)

The most painful thing in life is to wake up from a dream and find no way out. Dreamers are fortunate people. If no way out can be seen, the important thing is not to awaken the sleepers.

> Lu Xun (1881-1936)
> Chinese writer, "What Happens after Nora Leaves Home?" a lecture on Ibsen's *A Doll's House* (1923)

I placed my dream in a boat
and the boat into the sea;
then I ripped the sea with my
  hands
so that my dream would sink.

> Cecilia Meireles (1901-1964)
> Brazilian poet, "Song"

One should not discuss a dream
In front of a simpleton.

> Mu-mon Gensen (1322-1390)
> Japanese Buddhist monk, *The Gateless Gate*

You cannot harm me,
  you cannot harm
    one who has dreamed a
      dream like mine . . .

> Ojibwa (Native American tribe)
> poem fragment

[These] meetings in dreams,
How sad they are!
When, waking up startled
One gropes about,—

And there is no contact to the hand.

> Yakamochi (717-785)
> Japanese poet, *Manyo Shu* (c. 760)

If my dreams
Left their footprints on the road,
The path beneath my love's
window
Would be worn down, though it
is stone.
Alas, in the country of dream
No roads endure, no traces
remain.

> Yi Myong-han (1595-1645)
> Korean poet

on DRINKING

Drink! for you know not whence
you came, nor why;
Drink! for you know not why you
go, nor where.

> Omar Khayyám (c. 1048-1122)
> Persian poet and astronomer, *Rubáiyát
> of Omar Khayyám*

A pot of wine amidst the flowers,
Alone I drink *sans* company,
The moon I invite as a drinking
friend,
And with my shadow we are
three.
The moon, I see, she does not
drink,
My shadow only follows me:
I'll keep them company a while
For spring's the time for gaiety.

I sing: the moon she swings her
head;
I dance: my shadow swells and
sways.
We sport together while awake,
While drunk, we all go our own
ways.

An eternal, speechless trio then,
Till in the clouds we meet again!

> Li Po (701-762)
> Chinese writer, *Drinking Alone under
> the Moon*

Back in my home I drink a cup of
wine
And need not fear the greed of
the evening wind.

> Lu Yu (1125-1209)
> Chinese poet, *Boating in Autumn*

Whenever I'm drunk
I want to go on the wagon. Really
I want to, but I like it,
I like it, and I can't, really,
I mean I can but
I won't.

> Nguyen Khuyen (1835-1909)
> Vietnamese poet, "Going on the
> Wagon"

Pour out wine till I become a
wanderer from myself;
For in selfhood and existence I
have felt only fatigue.

> Attributed to Rumi (1207-1273)
> Persian Sufi poet, *Divani Shamsi
> Tabriz*

To be drunk is, when you think
about it, very wrong.
Wrong I am quite willing to be;
drunk I wish to stay.
Is not the earth drunk, or why
else does it spin?
Is not the sky drunk, or why else
is its face red?
And who laughs at them.

> Tan Da (c. 1930)
> Vietnamese poet

on DUTY

There is more joy in doing one's
  own duty badly
Than in doing another man's duty
  well.

> *Bhagavad Gita*
> (c. 4th–3rd century B.C.E.)
> teachings of Krishna from the Hindu
> epic, the *Mahabharata*

Perform today the duty of
  tomorrow,
the afternoon's before noon
For death won't wait to see if you
  have done
the duty of the day or not.

> Bhoja (995–1055)
> Indian poet

Service is the rent that you pay for
room on this earth.

> Shirley Chisholm (b. 1924)
> American politician

Let no one forget his own duty for
the sake of another's, however
great; let a man, after he has dis-
cerned his own duty, be always attentive to his duty.

> *Dhammapada* (c. 3rd century B.C.E.)
> collection of ancient Buddhist poems
> and aphorisms

What is the use of such terrible diligence as many tire themselves out
with, if they always postpone their
exchange of smiles with Beauty
and Joy to cling to irksome duties
and relations?

> Helen Keller (1880–1968)
> American writer and lecturer, *My
> Religion*

Do you think I should have succeeded in doing anything if I had
kicked and resisted and resented?
Is it our Master's command? Is it
even common sense? I have been
shut out of hospitals into which I
had been ordered to go by the
Commander-in-Chief—obliged to
stand outside the door in the snow
till night—have been refused ra-
tions for as much as 10 days at a
time for the nurses I had brought
by superior command. And I have
been as good friends the day after
with the officials who did these
things—have resolutely ignored
these things *for the sake of the
work*. . . . Who am I that should
not choose to bear what my Master
chooses to bear?

> Florence Nightingale (1820–1910)
> English nurse, a letter to another nurse
> (April 22, 1869)

on **EFFORT**

The Buddhas do but tell the Way; it is for *you* to swelter at the task.

Dhammapada (c. 3rd century B.C.E.)
collection of ancient Buddhist poems
and aphorisms

The Four Great Vows:
However innumerable beings are,
  I vow to save them.
However inexhaustible the
  passions are, I vow to extinguish
  them.
However immeasurable the
  Dharmas are, I vow to master
  them.
However incomparable the
  Buddha-truth is, I vow
  to attain it.

Zen Gatha
portion of the sutras set in verse

If one were to rely only on those arrows which had grown straight all by themselves—in a hundred generations, one would still not have a single arrow. Or . . . if one were to rely only on pieces of wood growing perfectly round [for making wheels]—in a thousand generations, one still would not have a single wheel.

Han Fei-tzu (c. 280–233 B.C.E.)
Chinese philosopher

If there is no dull and determined effort, there will be no brilliant achievement.

Hsun-tzu (298–238 B.C.E.)
Chinese philosopher

You must make the most strenuous efforts. Throughout this life, you can never be certain of living long enough to take another breath.

Huang Po (c. 850)
Chinese Zen Buddhist leader

No individual or people can achieve anything without industry, suffering, and sacrifice.

Fatima Jinna (1893–1967)
Pakistani politician, in a speech to the
All-India Muslim League, October 1937

When do any of us ever do enough?

Barbara Jordan (b. 1936)
American politician

The lark, fearing that Heaven would fall, lay on her back, holding her feet up towards the sky, thinking she might thus prevent the catastrophe. Some laughed at her and said: "With your spindle legs, you want to become a tree, O bird, with a mind capacious as the sea." The lark replied simply, "I am doing what I can."

Grigor Magistros (990–1058)
Armenian scholar and public official,
recording a peasant fable

We must live like angels and produce like the devil!

> Luis Muñoz Marín (b. 1898)
> Puerto Rican politician

Aiming isn't hitting.

> Swahili proverb

on EMOTIONS

We should feel sorrow, but not sink under its oppression; the heart of a wise man should resemble a mirror, which reflects every object without being sullied by any.

> Confucius (551-479 B.C.E.)
> Chinese philosopher and founder of Confucianism, *Analects*

There is no fire like passion, no shark like hatred, no snare like folly, and no torrent like greed.

> *Dhammapada* (c. 3rd century B.C.E.)
> collection of ancient Buddhist poems and aphorisms

What we feel is beyond words. We should be ashamed of our poems.

> Nizar Qabbani (b. 1932)
> Syrian/Lebanese writer and publisher

Jealousy, passion, vanity drive one out of the world.

> *Talmud*
> (c. late 4th-early 6th century)
> ancient body of Jewish civil and canonical law, Aboth

Anyone who says he is not emotional is not getting what he should out of life.

> Ezer Weizman (b. 1924)
> Israeli military and political leader

Laughter spreads ripples on the surface; tears come from inside.

> Itamar Yaoz-Kest (b. 1934)
> Israeli writer

on ENEMIES

I against my brother
I and my brother against our cousin,
I, my brother, and my cousin against the neighbors,
All of us against the foreigner.

> Bedouin proverb

To bless thine enemy is a good way to satisfy thy vanity.

> Jorge Luis Borges (1899-1986)
> Argentinian writer, *In Praise of Darkness*

How we talked, how we laughed at our contentment,
vowed good faith so intently.
Not thinking it all might be altered,
The change that was not to be thought of
This change has happened.

> poem by an unnamed female Chinese poet,
> from the classic 7th-century B.C.E. collection *Scripture of Poetry*

The most revolutionary statement in history is "Love thine enemy."

> Eldridge Cleaver (b. 1935)
> American civil rights activist

In truth, it is I who have defiled myself, for one is one's own fiercest enemy.

> Ding Ling (c. 1904-1986)
> Chinese writer, "Diary of Miss Sophie"

A powerful friend becomes a powerful enemy.

> Ethiopian proverb

To see your enemy and know him is part of the complete education of man.

> Marcus Garvey (1887–1940)
> American political leader, *Philosophy and Opinions*

The country folks here extended
  their warm hands,
But here there were also the
  gleaming green eyes of wolves.

> Gu Cheng (b. 1957)
> Chinese poet, speaking of his family's exile to the countryside during the Cultural Revolution

I tell the truth: your enemy is also your friend—his presence makes your life fuller and richer.

> Muhammad Iqbal (1873–1938)
> Indian Muslim poet and philosopher

The wolves do not bite themselves. They respect each other.

> Benito Juárez (1806–1872)
> Mexican revolutionary and politician

There is no greater mistake than to make light of an enemy. By making light of an enemy many a kingdom has been lost.

> Lao-tzu (c. 604–531 B.C.E.)
> Chinese philosopher and founder of Taoism, *Tao-te-ching*

I don't have a warm personal enemy left. They've all died off. I miss them terribly because they helped define me.

> Claire Booth Luce (1903–1987)
> American diplomat and politician, in a 1981 interview

Brothers and sisters, friends and enemies: I just can't believe that everyone in here is a friend, and I don't want to leave anyone out.

> Malcolm X (1925–1965)
> American civil rights activist, speaking at a Harlem rally

Those who would hunt a man need to remember that a jungle also contains those who hunt the hunters.

> Malcolm X (1925–1965)
> American civil rights activist, *Autobiography of Malcolm X*

Despise the enemy strategically, but take him seriously tactically.

> Mao Zedong (1893–1976)
> Chairman of People's Republic of China

Man is wise . . . when he recognizes no greater enemy than himself.

> Marguerite of Navarre (1492–1549)
> French writer and religious reformer, "Novel XXX, the Third Day," *The Heptmeron, or Novels of the Queen of Navarre*

Until the enemy comes to attack me in my camp, and I hear the fusillade and I see them with my eyes, not until then shall I send out my army in order of battle.

> Menelik (1849–1913)
> Ethiopian emperor, address to European powers (1891) in defiance of Italian colonization

Our enemies did not cross our
  borders
They crept through our
  weaknesses like ants.

> Nizar Qabbani (b. 1932)
> Syrian/Lebanese writer and publisher

He who forgiveth, and is reconciled unto his enemy, shall receive his reward from God; for he loveth not the unjust doers.

> *Qur'an* (c. 610-656)
> sacred book of Islam

Whoever has his foe at his mercy, and does not kill him, is his own enemy.

> Sa'di of Shiraz (c. 1184-1292)
> Persian poet, *Gulistan*

There is no occasion for our rejoicing at a foe's death, because our own life will also not last forever.

> Sa'di of Shiraz (c. 1184-1292)
> Persian poet, *Gulistan*

Fierce language and pretentious advances are signs that the enemy is about to retreat.

> Sun Tzu (c. 335-288 B.C.E.)
> Chinese military leader, *Art of War*

If your enemy is hungry, give him bread to eat; and if thirsty, give him water to drink. Even if he came to kill you, give him food if he is hungry or water if he is thirsty.

> *Talmud*
> (c. late 4th-early 6th century)
> ancient body of Jewish civil and
> canonical law, Midrash Mishle 27

on ENVY AND JEALOUSY

Jealousy is the sister of love, as the devil is the brother of angels.

> Marie-Françoise de Beauveau
> (1711-1786)
> French courtier

The torment of envy is like a grain of sand in the eye.

> Chinese proverb

Anger and jealousy can no more bear
to lose sight of their objects than love.

> George Eliot (1819-1880)
> English writer, *The Mill on the Floss*

He who envies the happiness of others derives from it only evil, like the spider which, from a flower, derives poison.

> Pachacutec Inca Yupanqui
> (1438-1471)
> Incan ruler

Envy is a worm that gnaws and consumes the entrails of ambitious men.

> Pachacutec Inca Yupanqui
> (1438-1471)
> Incan ruler

Achieve some perfection [excellence] yourself, so that you may not fall into sorrow by seeing the perfection in others.

> Rumi (1207-1273)
> Persian Sufi poet

The eye envies, not the ear.

> Twi (West African) proverb

EPITAPHS

Believe me, a thousand friends suffice thee not; In a single enemy thou hast more than enough.

> 'Ali (c. 600-661)
> First Imam of the Sh'ia branch of Islam;
> fourth caliph

For the light that shone in this country was no ordinary light.

> Jawaharlal Nehru (1889-1964)
> Indian prime minister, speaking to

India, hours after Mahatma Gandhi's death (January 30, 1948)

Come back, come back, even if you have broken your repentance a thousand times.

> lines written on the mausoleum of Rumi (1207-1273)
> Persian Sufi poet

The white man lives in the castle; when he dies, he lies in the ground.

> Ashanti (West African) proverb

on EQUALITY

As a prelude, whites must be made to realize that they are only human, not superior. Same with blacks. They must be made to realize that they are also human, not inferior.

> Steve Biko (1946-1977)
> South African political activist

It's a poor rule that won't work both ways.

> Frederick Douglass (1817-1895)
> American abolitionist

Equality . . . like freedom, exists only where you are now. Only as an egg in the womb are we all equal.

> Oriana Fallaci (b. 1930)
> Italian journalist, *Letter to a Child Never Born*

One must remember equality, yet also be aware of difference, for if the people are allowed to act as it pleases them without coming up against displeasure, if one gives rein to its desires without setting [any] limit, it becomes confused and can no longer take delight in anything.

> Hsun-tzu (298-238 B.C.E.)
> Chinese philosopher, *Hsun-tzu: Basic Writings*

Men of all social stations live together: they are equal in their desires, yet vary in their methods; they are equal in their passions, yet different in their intelligence; that is their nature-given vitality.

> Hsun-tzu (298-238 B.C.E.)
> Chinese philosopher, *Hsun-tzu: Basic Writings*

The revolutionists did not succeed in establishing human freedom; they poured the new wine of belief in equal rights for all men into the old bottle of privilege for some; and it soured.

> Suzanne LaFollette (1893-1983)
> American feminist and writer, "The Beginnings of Emancipation," *Concerning Women*

Unless man is committed to the belief that all of mankind are his brothers, then he labors in vain and hypocritically in the vineyards of equality.

> Adam Clayton Powell, Jr. (1908-1972)
> American politician and civil rights leader, "Black Power: A Form of Godly Power," *Keep the Faith, Baby*

Irrespective of caste and creed, all are equal in the eyes of God and only sinful actions bring bad name and dishonor to man.

> Raidas (15th century)
> Indian mystic and religious leader

Man is like a pillowcase. The color of one may be red, another blue, another black, but all contain the same cotton. So it is with man— one is beautiful, one is black, another is holy, a fourth wicked, but the Divine dwells in them all.

> Ramakrishna (1836-1886)
> Indian Hindu mystic

Nations will rise and fall, but equality remains the ideal. The universal aim is to achieve respect for the entire human race, not for the dominant few.

> Carlos P. Romulo (b. 1899)
> Philippine diplomat and soldier, *I Walked with Heroes*

Oh friend! Exercise humility to a
  stern enemy,
For gentleness makes blunt the
  cutting sword.

> Sa'di of Shiraz (c. 1184-1292)
> Persian poet, *Bustan*

Outside the kingdom of the Lord there is no nation which is greater than any other. God and history will remember your judgement.

> Haile Selassie (1892-1975)
> Ethiopian emperor, speech at the League of Nations (1936)

Everyone speaks of himself with regard to his ownself, "I am above and the others are below," whilst all of them are around the globe like the blossom springing on the branches of a Kadamba tree.

> Varahamihira (505-587)
> Indian astronomer

O roc, don't ridicule the small
  black birds:
You and the little birds both fly
  way up in the clouds,
You're a bird,

They're birds.
Really, I can't see much difference
  between you!

> Yi T'aek (1651-1719)
> Korean poet

on ERROR

To err and not reform, this may indeed be called error.

> Confucius (551-479 B.C.E.)
> Chinese philosopher and founder of Confucianism, *Analects*

To go beyond is as wrong as to fall short.

> Confucius (551-479 B.C.E.)
> Chinese philosopher and founder of Confucianism, *Analects*

Prophecy is the most gratuitous form of error.

> George Eliot (1819-1880)
> English writer, *Middlemarch*

If you shut your door to all errors, truth will be shut out.

> Rabindranath Tagore (1861-1941)
> Indian writer and philosopher, *Stray Birds*

on ETERNITY

Our theories of the eternal are as valuable as are those which a chick which has not broken its way through its shell might form of the outside world.

> Buddha (c. 563-483 B.C.E.)
> Founder of Buddhism

What has been, will forever exist. Death is mere appearance.

> Jacob Kahan (b. 1881)
> Israeli poet, "At the Pyramides"

Heaven is eternal and Earth
everlasting.
They can be eternal and
everlasting because they do not
exist for themselves,
And for this reason can exist
forever.

> Lao-tzu (c. 604-531 B.C.E.)
> Chinese philosopher and founder of
> Taoism, *Tao-te-ching*

on ETHICS AND MORALITY

When morality comes up against
profit, it is seldom that profit loses.

> Shirley Chisholm (b. 1924)
> American politician, *Unbought and
> Unbiased*

A gentleman takes as much trouble
to discover what is right as the
lesser men take to discover what
will pay.

> Confucius (551-479 B.C.E.)
> Chinese philosopher and founder of
> Confucianism, *Analects*

I have yet to meet a man as fond of
high moral conduct as he is of out-
ward appearances.

> Confucius (551-479 B.C.E.)
> Chinese philosopher and founder of
> Confucianism, *Analects*

A man may not transgress the
bounds of major morals, but may
make errors in minor morals.

> Confucius (551-479 B.C.E.)
> Chinese philosopher and founder of
> Confucianism, *Analects*

Morality must guide calculation,
and calculation must guide politics.

> Madame de Staël (1766-1817)
> French writer, *De la littérature
> considerée dons ses rapports avec les
> institutions sociales (The Influence of
> Literature upon Society)*

Kindness and generosity . . . form
the true morality of human actions.

> Madame de Staël (1766-1817)
> French writer, "Reflections of the Moral
> Aim of Delphine," *Delphine*

True morality consists not in following the beaten track, but in
finding out the true path for ourselves and in fearlessly following it.

> Mohandas K. Gandhi (1869-1948)
> Indian spiritual and political leader

Because the ethics of men has
been a powerful social ability since
the most ancient period of human
life, there has developed in the human heart a voice of authority that
down to the present day still echoes in our own hearts. It has a mysterious quality that is not due to
the stimulus of the outside world,
nor is it a matter of advantage or
disadvantage; [rather] it is a naturally produced authority. Its mysterious nature is similar to the
mystery of sex, the mystery of
mother love, and the mystery of
sacrifice.

> Li Dazhao (1888-1927)
> Chinese political theorist

It is not safe to be immoral . . .
Against the rock of moral law,
earth's conquerors and exploiters
hurl themselves eventually to their
own destruction. While yet there is

time . . . we must take steps to prevent the helpless rush of man to his doom.

> Sarvepalli Radhakrishnan
> (1888-1975)
> Indian philosopher and politician,
> *Education, Politics and War*

Wrong is wrong only when you are at liberty to choose.

> Rabindranath Tagore (1861-1941)
> Indian writer and philosopher

on EVIL

Old Satan couldn't get along without plenty of help.

> African American proverb
> (mid-1800s)

People do evil simply because they do not know.

> Cheng Yi (1033-1108)
> Chinese scholar, *I-shu*

He who has no wound may touch poison with his hand, and it will not harm him. There is no evil for one who does no evil.

> *Dhammapada* (c. 3rd century B.C.E.)
> collection of ancient Buddhist poems
> and aphorisms, "Evil," 124

In my humble opinion, noncooperation with evil is as much a duty as is cooperation with good.

> Mohandas K. Gandhi (1869-1948)
> Indian spiritual and political leader

Must I do the evil I can before I learn to shun it? Is it not enough to know the evil to shun it? If not, we should be sincere enough to admit that we love evil too much to give it up.

> Mohandas K. Gandhi (1869-1948)
> Indian spiritual and political leader,
> *Non-Violence in Peace and War*

We deserve punishment for the moral evil that appears to proceed from us as its subject, by which we are guilty of rebellion against God, according to the decrees of His providence, which is justice and truth itself.

> Ibn Hazm (994-1064)
> Arab Spanish poet and philosopher,
> *Fisal*

Evil is only of this world. In the other world there is neither good nor evil; all there is, is beauty.

> Tanizaki Jun'ichiro (1886-1965)
> Japanese writer

He who passively accepts evil is as much involved in it as he who helps to perpetuate it. He who accepts evil without protesting against it is really cooperating with it.

> Martin Luther King, Jr.
> (1929-1968)
> American civil rights leader, *Stride
> toward Freedom*

To ignore evil is to become an accomplice to it.

> Martin Luther King, Jr.
> (1929-1968)
> American civil rights leader, *Where Do
> We Go from Here: Chaos or
> Community?*

Blessed . . . is he who has it in his power to do evil, yet does it not.

> Marguerite of Navarre (1492-1549)
> French writer and religious reformer,

"Novel XLIII, The Fifth Day," *The Heptmeron, or Novels of the Queen of Navarre*

It may be necessary temporarily to accept a lesser evil, but one must never label a necessary evil as good.

Margaret Mead (1901–1978)
American anthropologist

It is hazardous to health to be frequently exposed to the ugliness and folly in human life.

Shiga Naoya (1883–1971)
Japanese writer

Wrong-doing has never brought its undertaking to port.

Ptah-hotep (c. 2300 B.C.E.)
Egyptian vizier, *Instruction of Ptah-hotep*

Those who seek gain in evil, and are girt round by their sins—they are companions of the fire: Therein shall they abide forever.

Qur'an (c. 610–656)
sacred book of Islam, 2:81

You do not see clearly the evil in yourself, else you would hate yourself with all your soul.

Like the lion who sprang at his image in the water, you are only hurting yourself, O foolish man.

When you reach the bottom of the well of your own nature, then you will know that the vileness was from yourself.

Rumi (1207–1273)
Persian Sufi poet

These men are not merely evil, I thought. They are the mindlessness of evil made flesh. One should

never stumble into their hands but seek the power to destroy them. . . . To seek the power to destroy them is to fulfill a moral task.

Wole Soyinka (b. 1934)
Nigerian writer, *The Man Died*

There is no longer any barbarity, they told me! "Who told you that?" I asked,

Who split open the stomachs and dismembered the bodies?
Who spilled blood and assassinated children?
Who swooped down upon our souls and hastened our death?
Did the wind of death drag them behind it?

Munawwar Sumadih
(20th century)
Tunisian poet

Then a serpent who could not be charmed
Made its nest in the roots of the huluppu-tree.
The Anzu-bird set his young in the branches of the tree.
And the dark maid Lilith built her home in the trunk.

The young woman who loved to laugh wept.
How Inanna wept!
(Yet they would not leave her tree.)

Sumerian poem (c. 2000 B.C.E.)
"The Marriage of Inanna"

In Eden who sleeps happiest? The serpent.

Derek Walcott (b. 1930)
West Indian writer, "The Brother"

We cannot contemplate without terror the extent of the evil which man can do and endure.

Simone Weil (1909-1943)
French philosopher, *Gravity and Grace*

on EXISTENCE

Who knows the will of the gods
in heaven?
Who understands the plan of the
underworld gods?
Where have mortals learnt the
way of a god?
He who was alive yesterday is
dead today.
For a minute he was dejected,
suddenly he is exuberant.
One moment people are singing
in exaltation,
Another they groan like
professional mourners . . .
I am appalled at these things;
I do not understand their
significance.

Babylonian poem ("I will praise
the Lord of Wisdom")

Our whole world is nothing but a world of grief and misery, and its inhabitants are nothing but grieving and miserable people. The living beings on this earth are all destined for slaughter. The azure heaven and the round earth are no more than a great slaughter-yard, a great prison.

K'ang Yu-wei (1858-1927)
Chinese political philosopher, *The Book of the Great Community*

No passing away and no origination, no destruction and no everlasting continuance, no unity and no multiplicity, no coming and no

going: I revere . . . him who has thus taught . . . the salutary cessation of the world of phenomena.

Nagarjuna (100-165)
Indian Buddhist philosopher

Today everything exists to end in a photograph.

Susan Sontag (b. 1933)
American writer and critic, *On Photography*

Merely to exist is not enough.

Rabindranath Tagore (1861-1941)
Indian writer and philosopher

on EXPECTATIONS

Nothing is so good as it seems beforehand.

George Eliot (1819-1880)
English writer, *Silas Marner*

He who expects much can expect little.

Gabriel García Márquez (b. 1928)
Colombian writer

Don't look for speed in a cheap horse; be content if it neighs.

Hausa (Nigerian) proverb

on EXPERIENCE

Men have no better guidance than examples and facts proved by experience.

Muhammad 'Abduh (1849-1905)
Egyptian reformer

What you really value is what you miss, not what you have.

Jorge Luis Borges (1899-1986)
Argentinian writer

Experience isn't interesting till it begins to repeat itself—in fact, till it does that, it hardly is experience.

> Elizabeth Bowen (1899–1973)
> Irish writer, *The Death of the Heart*

Those who play the game do not see as clearly as those who watch.

> Chinese proverb

I wanted to be born at the
  farthest limit of the world.
I'll explore it, I said to myself,
biting big chunks from it.
And when I want, I'll go
straight to the core.
This is the way of the world I
  thought in my innocence,
round and around the layers of
  peel
until the taste becomes certain.

> Abba Kovner (b. 1918)
> Israeli poet, "Observations at the End of a Journey"

If you want to know the taste of a pear, you must change the pear by eating it yourself. . . . If you want to know the theory and methods of revolution, you must take part in the revolution. All genuine knowledge originates in direct experience.

> Mao Zedong (1893–1976)
> Chairman of People's Republic of China

These people are like . . . a frog living in a well, who has never seen the outside world. He knows only his well, so he will not believe that there is such a thing as the world. Likewise, people talk so much about the world because they have not known the joy of God.

> Ramakrishna (1836–1886)
> Indian Hindu mystic

He who tastes not, knows not.

> Rumi (1207–1273)
> Persian Sufi poet

Facts of experience are valued in Zen more than representations, symbols, and concepts—that is to say, substance is everything in Zen and form nothing.

> D. T. Suzuki (1870–1966)
> Japanese scholar, *Essays in Zen Buddhism*

Do not believe a thing because you read it in a book! Do not believe a thing because another has said it so! Find out the truth for yourself.

> Vivekananda (1863–1902)
> Indian religious leader

on **FAILURE**

Failure is impossible.

Susan B. Anthony (1820-1906)
American suffragist

I have ploughed the sea.

Simón Bolívar (1783-1830)
South American revolutionary, on his
death bed

Though the courts of earthly
rulers have shut their doors in
my face,
Shall I grieve while I still have
access to the Court of the Lord
of Grace?

Nasir-i-Khusraw (1004-1061)
Persian writer, *Diwan*

Sometimes it is more important to
discover what one cannot do than
what one can do.

Lin Yutang (1895-1976)
Chinese writer

Anyone can take a false step
And fall forever,
Everyone is different.
Where are they now, all those lost
souls?

Nguyen Du (1765-1820)
Vietnamese poet, "Calling the Lost
Souls"

Failure is nothing but the kiss of
Jesus.

Mother Teresa (b. 1910)
Yugoslavian missionary, *Life in the
Spirit*

Better ruined ten times than dead
once.

Yiddish proverb

on **FAITH**

There is no conviction in my heart
which the thorns of doubt have
failed to pierce: there is no faith in
my soul which has not been sub-
jected to all the conspiracies of dis-
belief.

Abu 'I Kalam Azad (1888-1958)
Indian politician and Muslim
theologian, *Tarjuman al Qu'ran*

The man unknowing and without
faith,
His soul full of doubt, perishes.

Bhagavad Gita
(c. 4th-3rd century B.C.E.)
teachings of Krishna from the Hindu
epic, the *Mahabharata*, 4:40

When one has faith, then he
thinks. One who lacks faith does
not think.

Chandogya Upanishad
(c. 600 B.C.E.)
sacred philosophical Hindu literature

Faith is a devout belief in what one
does not understand.

Marie Anne de Vichy-Chamrond
(1697-1780)
French socialite, *Correspondence
inedite*

I never talked with God,
Nor visited in Heaven—

Yet certain am I of the spot
As if the chart were given.

> Emily Dickinson (1830–1886)
> American poet, "I Never Saw a Moor"

Let our first act each morning be
the following resolve: I shall not
fear anyone on Earth. I shall fear
only God.

> Mohandas K. Gandhi (1869–1948)
> Indian spiritual and political leader, *The
> Story of My Experiments with Truth*

Faith does not increase, nor does it
decrease; because a diminution in
it would be unbelief.

> Abu Hanifah (d. 767)
> Arab-Persian Islamic jurist

I ask God's forgiveness for my lack
of faithfulness in asking his forgiveness.

> Jami (1414–1492)
> Persian writer

The external forces conceal from
the eyes the deep meaning of
existence;
True faith resides in the heart.

> Kabir (1440–1519)
> Indian Mughal poet and philosopher

Faith is the belief of the heart in
that knowledge which comes from
the Unseen.

> Muhammad ben Kafif
> (c. 8th century)
> Arab Sufi poet

Kindness is a mark of faith; and
whoever hath not kindness, hath
not faith.

> Muhammad (570–632)
> Prophet of Islam

The world is a prison for the believer and a paradise for the unbe-
liever.

> Muhammad (570–632)
> Prophet of Islam, speaking of Islam

He will not enter hell who hath
faith equal to a single grain of mus-
tard seed in his heart.

> Muhammad (570–632)
> Prophet of Islam

I perceived that God takes in hand
the affairs of them that put their
trust in Him and does not let their
tribulation come to naught.

> dhu-al-Nun al Misri (d. 860)
> Egyptian Sufi leader

Whoso believeth in his Lord, he
feareth neither loss nor oppression.

> *Qur'an* (c. 610–656)
> sacred book of Islam, 72:13

Faith is the wealth here best for
man—by faith the flood is crossed.

> *Suttanipata* (c. 450 B.C.E.)
> Buddhist Pali canon, part of the *Sutta-
> Pitaka*, 182, 184

on FAME

You have brought disgrace on me
in making me so famous, for
the light you shed reveals my
  faults
more clearly, making them stand
out.

> Juana Ines de la Cruz (1651–1695)
> Mexican nun and poet, "En
> reconocimiento a las inimitables
> plumas de la Europa" ("In
> acknowledgment of the praises of
> European writers")

Whatever may be the success of my stories, I shall be resolute in preserving my incognito, having observed that a nom de plume secures all the advantages without the disagreeables of reputation.

George Eliot (1819-1880)
English writer

A man worthy of applause is oftentimes despised during his lifetime. But when he is removed by death, his loss comes to be severely felt.

Fakhir Al-Din Razi (1149-1209)
Central Asian Islamic philosopher

Glory is a heavy burden, a murdering poison, and to bear it is an art.

Oriana Fallaci (b. 1930)
Italian journalist, "Federico Fellini," *The Egotists*

Unfortunately many young writers are more concerned with fame than with their own work . . . . It's much more important to write than to be written about.

Gabriel García Márquez (b. 1928)
Colombian writer

A famous writer who wants to continue writing has to be constantly defending himself against fame.

Gabriel García Márquez (b. 1928)
Colombian writer

It is the mark of many famous people that they cannot part with their brightest hour.

Lillian Hellman (1906-1984)
American writer, *Pentimento*

When a great man has become petrified, and everyone begins to proclaim his greatness, he has already turned into a puppet.

Lu Xun (1881-1936)
Chinese writer

on FAMILIARITY

The sweetness of life lies in dispensing with formalities.

'Ali (c. 600-661)
First Imam of the Sh'ia branch of Islam; fourth caliph

If you step on a stranger's foot in the marketplace, you apologize at length. . . . If you step on your older brother's foot, you give him an affectionate pat; and if you step on your parent's foot, you know you are already forgiven. The great politeness is free of formality; perfect conduct, free of concern.

Chuang-tzu (c. 369-286 B.C.E.)
Chinese Taoist philosopher

You do not notice changes in what is before you.

Colette (1873-1954)
French writer, *Mes apprentissages*

Man indeed hates the one whom he knows, turns against the one whom he sees, opposes the one whom he resembles, and becomes observant of the faults of those with whom he mingles; the greater the love and intimacy, the greater the hatred and estrangement.

al-Jahiz (c. 778-869)
Arab Islamic philosopher and writer, *Al Risala*

89

I like familiarity. In me it does not bring contempt—only more familiarity.

> Gertrude Stein (1874-1946)
> American writer

on FAMILY

Mother is the dead heart of the family, spending father's earnings on consumer goods to enhance the environment in which he eats, sleeps, and watches the television.

> Germaine Greer (b. 1939)
> Australian writer, *The Female Eunuch*

What has made this nation great? Not its heroes but its households.

> Sarah Josepha Hale (1788-1879)
> American writer and editor

Of all the love, kindness and pleasure a man can experience in this world, nothing is more beautiful than the love of a woman. If it is granted him, and the two have a child together, they are fused in a single heart in the child, which is truly the most pleasing thing love and kindness can give, and this will always be a bond between them.

> *T'ai-p'ing-ching* (*Classic of the Highest Peace*)
> (c. 2nd-3rd century)
> Chinese religious book

I have learnt too much of the heart of man not to be certain that it is only in the bosom of my family that I shall find happiness.

> François Dominique Toussaint-L'Ouverture (1743-1803)
> Haitian revolutionary leader

on FAREWELLS

My heart aches, what am I to do?
I wish moments could last an
  eternity.
But fate governs the life of man,
meeting and parting are not his
  decision.

> Chinese poem
> from "Chiu-ko" ("Nine Songs"), *Elegies of Ch'u* (c. 2nd century B.C.E.)

When all through the earth, and
  heaven rise dust storms.
How hard and rough, the road a
  woman walks.
Born to a race of heroes, you, my
  love,
discard brush and ink for tools of
  war.
I saw you off and sorrowed—Oh
  to be your horse on land,
your host upon the stream.

> Doan Thi Diem (c. 1705) and Pahn Huy Ich (c. 1750)
> Vietnamese poets, "The Lament of the Warrior's Wife" ("Tale of Kieu")

Farewell! No sound of idle
  mourning let there be
To shudder this full silence—save
  the voice
Of children—little children, white
  and black,
Whispering the deeds I tried to
  do for them;
While I at last unguided and alone
Pass softly, full softly.

> W. E. B. Du Bois (1868-1963)
> American writer and educator,
> "Farewell"

He climbed his horse, she let go
  of his gown—
autumn was tingling maple woods
  with gloom.

And off he rode as clouds of dust
swirled up,
to vanish past all those green
mulberry groves.
She walked back home to face the
night alone,
and by himself he fared the long,
long way.
Who split the lovers' moon? Half
stayed and slept
by her lone pillow, half lit his
far road.

> Nguyen Du (1765-1820)
> Vietnamese poet, "Kim Can Kieu"
> ("Tale of Kieu")

Peach-tree leaves strew the paths
of Paradise,
The brook's farewells and the
accompaniment of the oriole's
song,
What sorrow and bitterness!
Six months in Paradise,
One step: earth.
Of the dream of yesteryear and
this remnant of love, more than
that!

> Tan Da (c. 1930)
> Vietnamese poet, "Tong biet"
> ("Farewell")

on **FATE**

When God wills that an event will
occur, He sets the causes that will
lead to it.

> Babikir Badri (1861-1954)
> Sudanese scholar, *Memoirs*

Men are in the hands of the Creator like reeds upon the water.
They move to and fro. . . . The
waves bend them into various directions, but they bend back. . . .
They bend back to the position
that was predestined for them.
Such is man. There is no escape
from the road on which he was
told to go.

> Yehuda Burla (1886-1969)
> Israeli writer, "Without a Star"

Fate mocks at wishes.

> Abu'l-Fath al-Busti (d. 1009)
> Persian poet

Every moon, every year, every
day,
Every wind comes and goes
And all blood reaches its final
resting place.

> *Chilam Balam*
> Mayan prophecies

Because men do not like the cold,
Heaven does not cause winter to
cease.

> Chinese proverb

There is no one door through
which fortune or misfortune
comes.

> Chinese proverb

In the life of all men,
Each has his own destiny.
With a steady heart and a broad
mind,
why should I be afraid?

> Ch'u Yuan (c. 300 B.C.E.)
> Chinese writer, "Embracing the Sand"

Our joy has not ended when grief
comes trailing it. We have no way
to bar the arrival of grief and joy,
no way to prevent them from de-
parting. Alas, the men of this world
are no more than travelers, stopping now at this inn, now at that,
all of them run by "things" . . .

[but] from these mankind can never escape. And yet there are people who struggle to escape from the inescapable—can you help but pity them?

> Chuang-tzu (c. 369-286 B.C.E.)
> Chinese Taoist philosopher

If we look on heaven and earth as a single crucible, and on the creator as the founder, would there be any place I could not go? When it is time, I will fall asleep, and when the right time comes, I will wake up again.

> Chuang-tzu (c. 369-286 B.C.E.)
> Chinese Taoist philosopher

Run as hard as a wild beast if you will, but you won't get any reward greater than that destined for you.

> Egyptian proverb

God! I am in your hands!
What you say will happen!
Nothing baffles you!

> Ibo (Nigerian) prayer

Long not for a dwelling in heaven,
  and fear not to dwell in hell;
What will be, will be;
  O my soul, hope not at all.

> Kabir (1440-1519)
> Indian Mughal poet and philosopher

Be not glad at the sight of
  prosperity and
  Grieve not at the sight of
  adversity;
As is prosperity so is adversity;
  What God proposeth shall be
  accomplished.

> Kabir (1440-1519)
> Indian Mughal poet and philosopher

Honor, high posts, power, and profit are like sojourning guests: there is no way of keeping them when they are due to depart.

> Ko Hung (283-343)
> Chinese scholar

Fate does not play jokes.

> Gamel Abdel Nasser (1918-1970)
> Egyptian revolutionary and president,
> *The Philosophy of Revolution*

May I hope for easement from the
  turns of fate
when Time is not unmindful of
  the great silent rocks?

> Imru' al-Qays (c. 540)
> pre-Islamic Arab poet

That which God writes on thy fore-head, thou wilt come to it.

> *Qur'an* (c. 610-656)
> sacred book of Islam

Fate is not altered by a thousand
  sighs,
Complain or render thanks—
  arrive it will.

> Sa'di of Shiraz (c. 1184-1292)
> Persian poet, *Gulistan*

A man does not hurt his finger un-less it is decreed from above.

> *Talmud*
> (c. late 4th-early 6th century)
> ancient body of Jewish civil and
> canonical law, Hullin 7

God can only set in motion;
He cannot control the things he
  has made.

> T'ao Ch'ien (365-427)
> Chinese poet, "Substance, Shadow and
> Spirit"

on FAULT

The real fault is to have faults and not amend them.

Confucius (551–479 B.C.E.)
Chinese philosopher, founder of
Confucianism, *Analects*

The wise man will not look for the faults of others, nor for what they have done or left undone, but will look rather to his own misdeeds.

Dhammapada (c. 3rd century B.C.E.)
collection of ancient Buddhist poems
and aphorisms, "Flowers"

It is easy to see the faults of others, but hard to see one's own. Men point out the faults of others but cover their own as a dishonest gambler hides a losing throw of the dice.

Dhammapada (c. 3rd century B.C.E.)
collection of ancient Buddhist poems
and aphorisms, "Defilement"

If there were no fault, there would be no pardon.

Egyptian proverb

on FEAR

All things fear him who fears God, while he who fears nothing else but God is in fear of all things.

Attar (d. 1229)
Persian poet

Nothing in life is to be feared. It is only to be understood.

Marie Curie (1867-1934)
French scientist

Fear of disease killed more men than disease itself.

Mohandas K. Gandhi (1869-1948)
Indian spiritual and political leader

There would be no one to frighten you if you refused to be afraid.

Mohandas K. Gandhi (1869-1948)
Indian spiritual and political leader

The real malady is fear of life, not death.

Naguib Mahfouz (b. 1911)
Egyptian writer, *Small-talk on the Nile*

You gain strength, courage, and confidence by every experience in which you really stop to look fear in the face.

Eleanor Roosevelt (1884-1962)
American humanitarian and First Lady

We are living in a world of fear. The life of man today is corroded and made bitter by fear—fear of the future, fear of the hydrogen bomb, fear of ideologies. Perhaps this fear is a greater danger than the danger itself, because it is fear which drives men to act foolishly, to act thoughtlessly, to act dangerously.

Achmad Sukarno (1902-1970)
Indonesian politician

The greatest obstacle to love is fear. It has been the source of all defects in human behavior throughout the ages.

Mahmoud Mohammed Taha
(1909-1985)
Sudanese reformer

Give up fearing death; it is at all times foolish to miss life's pleasures for fear of death.

Talmud
(c. late 4th-early 6th century)
ancient body of Jewish civil and
canonical law, Disticha Moralia

He who accuses another of being an evil person says so because he is afraid of him.

> Muhammed Taqi (d. 835)
> Arab religious leader

If I ever felt inclined to be timid as I was going into a room full of people, I would say to myself, "You're the cleverest member of one of the cleverest families in the cleverest class of the cleverest nation in the world—why should you be frightened?"

> Beatrice Webb (1858-1943)
> British economist

on FEMINISM

We are coming down from our pedestal and up from the laundry room. We want an equal share in government and we mean to get it.

> Bella Abzug (b. 1920)
> American politician

If particular care is not paid to the ladies, we are determined to foment a rebellion, and will not hold ourselves bound by any laws in which we have no voice, no representation.

> Abigail Adams (1744-1818)
> American First Lady and feminist, letter to her husband, John Adams (March 31, 1776)

I can not say that I think you are very generous to the Ladies, for whilst you are proclaiming peace and good will to Men, Emancipating all Nations, you insist upon retaining an absolute power over Wives.

> Abigail Adams (1744-1818)
> American First Lady and feminist, letter to her husband, John Adams (May 7, 1776)

The true Republic: men, their rights and nothing more; women, their rights and nothing less.

> Susan B. Anthony (1820-1906)
> American suffragist, caption on the front page of her newspaper, *Revolution*

Disfranchisement means inability to make, shape, or control one's own circumstances. . . . That is exactly the position of women in the world of work today; they cannot choose.

> Susan B. Anthony (1820-1906)
> American suffragist

There will never be complete equality until women themselves help to make laws and elect lawmakers.

> Susan B. Anthony (1820-1906)
> American suffragist

No genuine equality, no real freedom, no true manhood or womanhood can exist on any foundation save that of pecuniary independence.

> Susan B. Anthony (1820-1906)
> American suffragist

Whichever way I turn, whatever phase of social life presents itself, the same conviction comes: Independent bread alone can redeem woman from her curse of subjection to man.

> Susan B. Anthony (1820-1906)
> American suffragist

The fact is, women are in chains, and their servitude is all the more debasing because they do not realize it.

Susan B. Anthony (1820–1906)
American suffragist

It was we, the people; not we, the white male citizens; nor yet we, the male citizens; but we the whole people who formed the Union . . . not to give the blessings of liberty, but to secure them . . . to the whole people—women as well as men.

Susan B. Anthony (1820–1906)
American suffragist, *Woman's Right to Suffrage*

Society, being codified by man, decrees that woman is inferior; she can do away with this inferiority only by destroying the male's superiority.

Simone de Beauvoir (1908–1986)
French writer and philosopher, *The Second Sex*

When will it no longer be necessary to attach special weight to the word *woman* and raise it specially?

Ding Ling (c. 1904–1986)
Chinese writer, "Thoughts on March 8"

In my opinion it is a grave error for women to feel that they must move only in women's interests. . . . What, after all, would we think if men all got together and kept doing things that were supposed to be in the interest of men?

Millicent Fenwick (1910–1992)
American politician

The problem lay buried, unspoken, for many years in the mind of American women. It was a strange stirring, a sense of dissatisfaction, a yearning that women suffered in the middle of the 20th century in the United States. Each suburban wife struggled with it alone. As she made the beds, shopped for groceries, matched slipcover material, ate peanut butter sandwiches with her children, chauffeured Cub Scouts and Brownies, lay beside her husband at night—she was afraid to ask even of herself the silent question—"Is this all?"

Betty Friedan (b. 1921)
American feminist, *The Feminine Mystique*

Who knows what women can be when they are finally free to become themselves?

Betty Friedan (b. 1921)
American feminist

Equal rights for the sexes will be achieved when mediocre women occupy high positions.

Françoise Giroud (b. 1916)
Swiss/French politician and journalist

There is no hope even that woman, with her right to vote, will ever purify politics.

Emma Goldman (1869–1940)
American anarchist

True, the movement for women's rights has broken many old fetters, but it has also forged new ones.

Emma Goldman (1869–1940)
American anarchist, "The Tragedy of Women's Emancipation," *Anarchism and Other Essays*

The surest guide to the correctness of the path that women take is joy in the struggle. Revolution is the festival of the oppressed.

> Germaine Greer (b. 1939)
> Australian writer, *The Female Eunuch*

Man has done all he could to debase and enslave [woman's] mind, and now he looks triumphantly on the ruin he has wrought and says [she] . . . is inferior.

> Sarah Moore Grimké (1792–1873)
> American abolitionist, "Letters on the
> Equality of the Sexes and the Condition
> of Women"

"No matter what your fight," I said, "don't be ladylike! God Almighty made woman, and the Rockefeller gang of thieves made the ladies."

> Mother Jones (1830–1930)
> American labor activist

If we bring about that women seek to gain the rights of independence, to increase their sphere of responsibilities, and to incline toward studies, then human abilities will increase daily.

> K'ang Yu-wei (1858–1927)
> Chinese political philosopher

Most people, no doubt, when they espouse human rights, make their own mental reservations about the proper application of the word "human."

> Suzanne LaFollette (1893–1983)
> American feminist and writer, "The
> Beginnings of Emancipation,"
> *Concerning Women*

By educating women to use all their brains, men will not only be just, but will also ensure the future of a new social order in which women will apply their intelligence and warm feelings to the problems of living. Men are fools to entrust the upbringing of their sons, whom they expect to grow up to love freedom, to women who have never known freedom themselves.

> Eugenio Maria de Hostos
> (1839–1903)
> Puerto Rican patriot

How does it feel to be a woman minister? I don't know; I've never been a man minister.

> Golda Meir (1898–1978)
> Israeli politician

The revolution begins at home.

> Cherrie Moraga (b. 1952) and
> Gloria Anzaldua (20th century)
> American writers and activists, *This
> Bridge Called My Back*

Let woman then go on—not asking favors, but claiming as a right the removal of all hindrances to her elevation in the scale of being. Let her receive encouragement for the proper cultivation of her powers, so that she may enter profitably into the active business of life.

> Lucretia Mott (1793–1880)
> American abolitionist and suffragist

The freer that women become, the freer will men be. Because when you enslave someone—you are enslaved.

> Louise Nevelson (1899–1988)
> American artist

The more education a woman has, the wider the gap between men's and women's earnings for the same work.

Sandra Day O'Connor (b. 1930)
American jurist

Be ready when the hour comes, to show that women are human and have the pride and dignity of human beings. Through such resistance our cause will triumph. But even if it does not, we fight not only for success, but in order that some inward feeling may have satisfaction. We fight that our pride, our self-respect, our dignity may not be sacrificed in the future as they have been in the past.

Christabel Pankhurst (1880-1958)
English suffragist

Better that we should die fighting than be outraged and dishonored. . . . Better to die than to live in slavery.

Emmeline Pankhurst (1858-1928)
English suffragist

Women must get educated and strive for their own independence; they can't just go on asking the men for everything. The young intellectuals are all chanting, "Revolution, Revolution," but I say the revolution will have to start in our homes, by achieving equal rights for women.

Qiu Jin (1874-1907)
Chinese poet and activist, *Qiu Jin ji*

Men and women are like right and left hands: it doesn't make sense not to use both.

Jeanette Rankin (1880-1973)
American feminist and politician

It's a Crime for the Slave to Love her Bonds.

Ghada Samman (b. 1942)
Syrian writer

There is perhaps only one human being in a thousand who is passionately interested in his job for the job's sake. The difference is that if that one person in a thousand is a man, we say, simply, that he is passionately keen on his job; if she is a woman, we say she is a freak.

Dorothy L. Sayers (1893-1957)
English writer, "Are Women Human?"

The prolonged slavery of women is the darkest page in human history.

Elizabeth Cady Stanton
(1815-1902)
American suffragist, *History of Woman Suffrage*

I challenge my destiny, my time
I challenge the human eye.

I will sneer at ridiculous rules and
  people
That is the end of it; I will fill my
  eyes with pure
light, and swim in a sea of
  unbounded feeling.

Aisha al-Taimuriya (1840-1902)
Egyptian poet, *Hilyat al-tiraz*
(Embroidered Ornaments)

Ef woman want any rights more'n dey's got, why don't dey jes' *take 'em*, and not be talkin' about it?

Sojourner Truth (c. 1797-1883)
American abolitionist

That . . . man . . . says women can't have as much rights as man, 'cause Christ wasn't a woman. Where did your Christ come from? . . . From God and a woman. Man had nothing to do with it.

> Sojourner Truth (c. 1797-1883)
> American abolitionist

I grew up believing that there was nothing, literally nothing my mother couldn't do once she set her mind to it. . . . So in a way when . . . the women's movement happened, I was really delighted because I felt they were trying to go where my mother was and where I always assumed I would go.

> Alice Walker (b. 1944)
> American writer

People call me a feminist whenever I express sentiments that differentiate me from a doormat or a prostitute.

> Rebecca West (1892-1983)
> English writer

Would men but generously snap our chains, and be content with rational fellowship instead of slavish obedience, they would find us more observant daughters, more affectionate sisters, more faithful wives, more reasonable mothers,— in a word, better citizens. We should then love them with true affection, because we should learn to respect ourselves.

> Mary Wollstonecraft (1759-1797)
> English feminist, "Of the Pernicious Effects which Arise from the Unnatural Distinctions Established in Society," *Vindication of the Rights of Woman*

I do not wish them [women] to have power over men, but over themselves.

> Mary Wollstonecraft (1759-1797)
> English feminist

When man, governed by reasonable laws, enjoys his natural freedom, let him despise woman, if she do not share it with him.

> Mary Wollstonecraft (1759-1797)
> English feminist, *Vindication of the Rights of Woman*

Make them free . . . or the injustice which one half of the human race are obliged to submit to, retorting on their oppressors, the virtue of men will be worm-eaten by the insects whom he keeps under his feet.

> Mary Wollstonecraft (1759-1797)
> English feminist, *Vindication of the Rights of Woman*

I would venture to guess that Anon, who wrote so many poems without signing them, was often a woman.

> Virginia Woolf (1882-1941)
> English writer, *A Room of One's Own*

on FLATTERY

If you need anything from a dog, call him "Sir."

> Arabic proverb

The flatterer takes us twice for a fool: first, we know he lies but we accept his lie; second, we try to believe that his lie is actually the truth.

> Muhammad Hijazi (20th century)
> Iranian writer and politician, *Hazar Sokhan* (*A Thousand Sayings*)

Flattery's fire is hidden. Its sweet taste is apparent, but the smoke is bound to come out at last.

> Rumi (1207–1273)
> Persian Sufi poet and mystic

Beware! never listen to the
  adulation of the flatterer,
Who has a trifling source of gain
  in you;
Someday, if thou shouldst not
  fulfill his desire,
He'll recount two hundred times
  as many faults of yours.

> Sa'di of Shiraz (c. 1184–1292)
> Persian poet

on FOOLS AND FOOLISHNESS

If you give in to a fool, he will say, "This is because they are afraid of me."

> Arabic proverb

By the time the fool has learned the game, the players have dispersed.

> Ashanti (West African) proverb

There is no medicine to cure a fool!

> Bhartrihari (c. 7th century)
> Indian poet and philosopher

Those who realize their folly are not true fools.

> Chuang-tzu (c. 369–286 B.C.E.)
> Chinese Taoist philosopher

A day's life of a virtuous man is better than a hundred years' life of the fool.

> *Dhammapada* (c. 3rd century B.C.E.)
> collection of ancient Buddhist poems and aphorisms

It is better to live alone than with a fool.

> *Dhammapada* (c. 3rd century B.C.E.)
> collection of ancient Buddhist poems and aphorisms

It is in the nature of foolish reasonings to seem good to the foolish reasoner.

> George Eliot (1819–1880)
> English writer, *Impressions of Theophrastus Such*

The fool is thirsty in the midst of water.

> Ethiopian proverb

A maimed nature and a deficient intelligence are far worse than simplicity. . . . One must use the sword and lances to prevent these people from using dialectic as 'Umar did with a man who asked him about ambiguous verses in the Qur'an. He hit him with a whip.

> Abu Hamid Muhammad al-Ghazali (1058–1111)
> Arab Islamic philosopher and theologian, *The Just Balance*

Silence is all the genius a fool has.

> Zora Neale Hurston (1903–1960)
> American writer, *Moses, Man of the Mountain*

Everybody loves a fool, but nobody wants him for a son.

> Malinke (West African) proverb

He who speaks to termite hills will not get any sense out of them.

> 'Abdiliaahi Muuse (c. 1890–1966)
> Somali sage

He who would misuse the boon of human life is far more stupid than he who would employ a gold vessel inlaid with precious gems as a receptacle for filth.

> Nagarjuna (100–165)
> Indian philosopher

If a fool keeps his mouth shut, there will be no difference of opinion.

> Muhammed Taqi (d. 835)
> Arab religious leader

The biggest fool is he who has learned much, taught much, and is still discontented.

> Thiruvalluvar (c. 2nd century)
> Indian Tamil writer, *Kural*

on FORGIVENESS

He who forgives ends the quarrel.

> African proverb

Learning to forgive is much more useful than merely picking up a stone and throwing it at the object of one's anger, the more so when the provocation is extreme. For it is under the greatest adversity that there exists the greatest potential for doing good, both for oneself and others.

> Dalai Lama (b. 1935)
> Tibetan spiritual and political leader,
> *Freedom in Exile: The Autobiography of the Dalai Lama*

Nobody will be able to forgive me but myself.

> Ding Ling (c. 1904–1986)
> Chinese writer, "Diary of Miss Sophie"

Forgiving the unrepentant is like drawing pictures on water.

> Japanese proverb

A kind speech and forgiveness is better than alms followed by injury.

> *Qur'an* (c. 610–656)
> sacred book of Islam

It is fitting for a great God to forgive great sinners.

> *Talmud*
> (c. late 4th–early 6th century)
> ancient body of Jewish civil and
> canonical law, Wayyikra Rabbah 5

on FREEDOM

On such a day
who would dare think of dying?
So much Freedom means
that we swear we'll postpone
  dying
until the morning after.

> Kofi Awoonor (b. 1935)
> Ghanaian writer, memoir written in
> prison

Freedom is not something that anybody can be given. Freedom is something people take, and people are as free as they want to be.

> James Baldwin (1924–1987)
> American writer, "Notes for a
> Hypothetical Novel," *Nobody Knows
> My Name*

If within my poems
You take out the flower

From the four seasons
One of my seasons will die

. . . .

And if you take away freedom
All four seasons and I will die.

> Sherko Bekas (b. 1940)
> Kurdish poet, "The Roots"

A people that loves freedom will in the end be free.

> Simón Bolívar (1783–1830)
> South American revolutionary, *Letter from Jamaica*

I should not dare to call my soul my own.

> Elizabeth Barrett Browning (1806–1861)
> English poet, *Aurora Leigh*

None who have always been free can understand the terrible fascinating power of the hope of freedom to those who are not free.

> Pearl S. Buck (1892–1973)
> American writer, *What America Means to Me*

Men would rather be starving and free than fed in bonds.

> Pearl S. Buck (1892–1973)
> American writer, *What America Means to Me*

I wish that every human life might be pure transparent freedom.

> Simone de Beauvoir (1908–1986)
> French writer and philosopher, *The Blood of Others*

The misfortune which befalls man from his once having been a child is that his liberty was at first concealed from him, and all his life he will retain the nostalgia for a time when he was ignorant of its exigencies.

> Simone de Beauvoir (1908–1986)
> French writer and philosopher

We have dared to be free. Let us dare to be so by ourselves and for ourselves.

> Jean Hackques Dessalines (1749–1806)
> Haitian revolutionary and ruler

Those who profess to favor freedom, and yet deprecate agitation, are men who want crops without plowing up the ground, they want rain without thunder and lightning. They want the ocean without the awful roar of its many waters.

> Frederick Douglass (1817–1895)
> American abolitionist

He who would be free must strike the first blow.

> Frederick Douglass (1817–1895)
> American abolitionist, *My Bondage and My Freedom*

Freedom always entails danger.

> W. E. B. Du Bois (1868–1963)
> American writer and educator

Freedom is not worth fighting for if it means no more than license for everyone to get as much as he can for himself.

> Dorothy Canfield Fisher (1879–1958)
> American writer, *Seasoned Timber*

Freedom is not worth having if it does not connote freedom to err.

> Mohandas K. Gandhi (1869–1948)
> Indian spiritual and political leader

Political freedom is the life-breath of a nation. To attempt social reform, educational reform, industrial expansion, the moral improvement of the race without aiming, first and foremost, at political freedom is the very height of ignorance and futility.

> Aurobindo Ghose (1872–1950)
> Indian political leader and Hindu philosopher

It is heavy upon the heart of the free to live in a world of others.

> Muhammad Iqbal (1873–1938)
> Indian Muslim poet and philosopher

The word will continue to fly
All over the world.
No power can ban it or stop it
From landing at any airport
For the word is a bird
That needs no entry visa
For freedom
For democracy.

> Nabil Janabi (20th century)
> Iraqi poet

You might as well expect the rivers to run backward as that any man who was born a free man should be contented when penned up and denied liberty to go where he pleases.

> Chief Joseph (c. 1840–1904)
> Nez Percé chief

The road to freedom is full of thorns and fire, yet happy is he who follows it!

> Aminu Kano (b. 1920)
> Nigerian politican

It is necessary to grow accustomed to freedom before one may walk in it sure-footedly.

> Suzanne LaFollette (1893–1983)
> American feminist and writer, "Women and Marriage," *Concerning Women*

I am . . . a realist. The magnitude of what one terms license or civil liberties or personal freedom has got to be adjusted to the circumstances.

> Lee Kuan Yew (b. 1923)
> Singaporean politician

After you get your freedom, your enemy will respect you.

> Malcolm X (1925–1965)
> American civil rights activist

Only free men can negotiate; prisoners cannot enter into contracts.

> Nelson Mandela (b. 1918)
> South African president

I cannot and will not give any undertaking at a time when I and you, the people, are not free. Your freedom and mine cannot be separated.

> Nelson Mandela (b. 1918)
> South African president, message read by his daughter at a rally in Soweto (February 10, 1985)

Freedom to many means immediate betterments, as if by magic. . . . Unless I can meet at least some of these aspirations, my support will wane and my head will roll just as surely as the tickbird follows the rhino.

> Julius K. Nyerere (b. 1922)
> Tanzanian nationalist and political leader

Freedom is a hard-bought thing.

Paul Robeson (1898-1976)
American actor, *Here I Stand*

Freedom and Liberty are not synonyms. Freedom is an essence; Liberty, an accident. Freedom is born with a man; Liberty may be conferred on him. . . . Freedom is the gift of God; Liberty, the creature of society. Liberty may be taken away from a man; but on whatsoever soul Freedom may light, the course of that soul is henceforth onward and upward.

James McCune Smith (1813-1864)
American physician and writer

He only has freedom who ideally loves freedom himself and is glad to extend it to others. He who cares to have slaves must chain himself to them. He who builds walls to create exclusion for others builds walls across his own freedom. He who distrusts freedom in others loses his moral right to it. Sooner or later he is lured into the meshes of physical and moral servility.

Rabindranath Tagore (1861-1941)
Indian writer and philosopher,
Gollancz, From Darkness to Light

Emancipation from the bondage
of the soil
is no freedom for the tree.

Rabindranath Tagore (1861-1941)
Indian writer and philosopher, *Fireflies*

Freedom is the first condition of growth. What you do not make free cannot grow. . . . Let men

have the light of liberty. That is the only condition of growth.

Vivekananda (1863-1902)
Indian religious leader

Freedom belongs to the strong.

Richard Wright (1908-1960)
American writer, *Long Black Song*

The land free, the land free for all, land without overseers and without masters . . .

Emiliano Zapata (1879-1919)
Mexican revolutionary, in a
proclamation

There's no absolute freedom anywhere in the world. Freedom is always relative.

Zhang Jie (b. 1937)
Chinese writer

on FRIENDSHIP

He who has a thousand friends
has not a friend to spare.
And he who has one enemy will
meet him everywhere.

'Ali (c. 600-661)
First Imam of the Sh'ia branch of Islam;
fourth caliph, *Sentences*

If you make a friend, make one
only after testing him,
And do not be in a hurry to
confide in him.
There are friends who are so
when it suits their convenience,
Who will not stand by you when
you are in trouble.

Ben Sira (c. 2nd century B.C.E.)
Hebrew scholar and philosopher, *The
Wisdom of Ben Sira*

A faithful friend is a strong
protection;

103

A man who has found one has found a treasure.
A faithful friend is beyond price,
And his value cannot be weighed.

> Ben Sira (c. 2nd century B.C.E.)
> Hebrew scholar and philosopher, *The Wisdom of Ben Sira*

A new friend is new wine;
When it grows old, you will enjoy drinking it.

> Ben Sira (c. 2nd century B.C.E.)
> Hebrew scholar and philosopher, *The Wisdom of Ben Sira*

So long as there is still a little friendship and a desire to help each other—so long as all that is real . . . that is sufficient for a man's short span of life.

> Nathan Bistritzki (b. 1895)
> Israeli writer, *Days and Nights*

The Soul selects her own Society—
Then—shuts the Door—

> Emily Dickinson (1830-1886)
> American poet

The test of friendship is assistance in adversity—and that, too, unconditional assistance. Cooperation which needs consideration is a commercial contract, and not friendship. Conditional cooperation is like adulterated cement which does not bind.

> Mohandas K. Gandhi (1869-1948)
> Indian spiritual and political leader

The best friend a man can have is reading and writing, and the bad ones to avoid are Go and chess and flute and pipe.

> Hojo Soun (c. 1519)
> Japanese samurai, "Twenty-one Articles of Advice"

The capacity for friendship usually goes with highly developed civilizations. The ability to cultivate people differs by culture and class; but on the whole, educated people have more ways to make friends. . . . In England, for instance, you find everyone in your class has read the same books. Here, people grope for something in common—like a newly engaged girl who came to me and said, "It's absolutely wonderful! His uncle and my cousin were on the same football team."

> Margaret Mead (1901-1978)
> American anthropologist

The touchstone of false friends is the day of need: by way of proof, ask a loan from your friends.

> Sa'ib of Tabriz (c. 1601-1677)
> Persian poet

If friendship is firmly established between two hearts, they do not need the interchange of news.

> Sa'ib of Tabriz (c. 1601-1677)
> Persian poet

In choosing a friend, go up a step.

> *Talmud*
> (c. late 4th–early 6th century)
> ancient body of Jewish civil and canonical law, Yebamot 63a

Friendship with the wise gets better with time, as a good book gets better with age.

> Thiruvalluvar (c. 2nd century)
> Indian Tamil writer, *Kural*

on THE FUTURE

God made the world round so we would never be able to see too far down the road.

> Isak Dinesen (1885-1962)
> Danish writer

Life is to adore, with more
 longing and more faith,
the bird that will come, than the
 bird that has flown.

> Luis Llorens Torres (1878-1944)
> Puerto Rican writer, "Psalms"

Who can say with certainty that one will live to see the morrow?

> *Lodan-Gawai-Roltso (The Ocean of Delight for the Wise)*
> Tibetan maxims, verse 204

I naturally believe there will be a future, but I do not waste my time imagining its radiant beauty. . . . It seems to me that we ought to think first about the present. Even if the present is desperately dark, I do not wish to leave it.

Will tomorrow be free from darkness? We'll talk about that tomorrow.

> Lu Xun (1881-1936)
> Chinese writer

The future has to be lived before it can be written about.

> Jawaharlal Nehru (1889-1964)
> Indian prime minister

Happiness or misfortune are prescribed by law of Heaven, but their source comes from ourselves.

> Nguyen Du (1765-1820)
> Vietnamese poet, *The Tale of Kieu*

"Hey you: are you looking for
 something?"
Fima replied: "Yes. I'm looking for tomorrow."
The policeman politely suggested: "Well, go and look for it somewhere else, sir. Move along please. You can't wait here."

> Amos Oz (b. 1939)
> Israeli writer, *Fima*

Tomorrow is now.

> Eleanor Roosevelt (1884-1962)
> American humanitarian and First Lady

Dread not events unknown, and be not downhearted, for the fountain of the water of life is involved in obscurity.

> Sa'di of Shiraz (c. 1184-1292)
> Persian poet

The future is made of the same stuff as the present.

> Simone Weil (1909-1943)
> French philosopher, *On Science, Necessity and the Love of God*

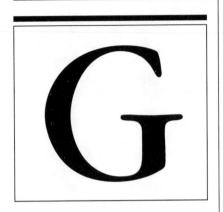

on **GENERATIONS**

It seems to be typical of life in America . . . that the second generation has no time to talk to the first.

James Baldwin (1924–1987)
American writer, *Notes of a Native Son*

Every soul will give something of its own; it will give a thread of love to a naked generation.

Nathan Bistritzki (b. 1895)
Israeli writer, *Days and Nights*

We ignore the generation which has no sense of melancholy.

Ahmet Hasim (1885–1933)
Turkish poet

Out of the sighs of one generation are kneaded the hopes of the next.

Joaquim Maria Machado de Assis (1839–1908)
Brazilian writer, *Education of a Stuffed Shirt*

Old men to their graves, young men to their tasks.

Mañuel Gonzalez Prada (1848–1918)
Peruvian poet and political activist

We need an angry generation,
A generation to plow the horizons

Nizar Qabbani (b. 1932)
Syrian/Lebanese writer and publisher, *What Value Has the People Whose Tongue Is Tied?*

You are a lost generation.

Gertrude Stein (1874–1946)
American writer, as quoted by Ernest Hemingway

Life is not completed in a single life span; it cannot but pass on its impulses. If the chain of life is traced back into the past, one does not come to a beginning, and if one follows it into the future, one generation follows the next, and no end is ever found.

Tsung Ping (375–443)
Chinese philosopher, *Ch'ih-hsien shen-chou*

on **GENIUS**

Talent isn't genius, and no amount of energy can make it so.

Louisa May Alcott (1832–1888)
American writer, *Little Women*

Since when was genius found respectable?

Elizabeth Barrett Browning (1806–1861)
English poet, *Aurora Leigh*

It's no good starting out by thinking one is a heaven-born genius — some people are, but very few. No, one is a tradesman—a tradesman in a good honest trade. You must learn the technical skills, and then, within that trade, you can apply your own creative ideas, but you must submit to the discipline of form.

> Agatha Christie (1891-1976)
> English writer, *An Autobiography*

One is not born a genius; one becomes a genius.

> Simone de Beauvoir (1908-1986)
> French writer and philosopher

Genius has no sex!

> Madame de Staël (1766-1817)
> French writer

on GHETTOS

In the invincible and indescribable squalor of Harlem . . . I was tormented. I felt caged, like an animal. I wanted to escape. I felt if I did not get out I would slowly strangle.

> James Baldwin (1924-1987)
> American writer

The section of the niggers where a nickel costs a dime.

> Langston Hughes (1902-1967)
> American writer

Six blocks of cruelty.

> Ntozake Shange (b. 1949)
> American writer, *For Colored Girls Who Have Considered Suicide*

on GIFTS AND GIVING

Do not be ashamed to give a little; for to deceive is to give still less.

> 'Ali (c. 600-661)
> First Imam of the Sh'ia branch of Islam; fourth caliph

Do not stretch your hand out to receive,
But close it when you should repay.

> Ben Sira (c. 2nd century B.C.E.)
> Hebrew scholar and philosopher, *The Wisdom of Ben Sira*

Everything that you receive
is not measured according to
its actual size, but, rather that
of the receiving vessel.

> Juana Ines de la Cruz (1651-1695)
> Mexican nun and poet, "En reconocimiento a las inimitables plumas de la Europa" ("In acknowledgment of the praises of European writers")

One must be poor to know the luxury of giving.

> George Eliot (1819-1880)
> English writer

One does not give a gift without a motive.

> Malian proverb

on GOALS

If we have not achieved our early dreams, we must either find new ones or see what we can salvage from the old. If we have accomplished what we set out to do in our youth, then we need not weep like Alexander the Great that we have no more worlds to conquer. There is clearly much left to be done, and whatever else we are going to do, we had better get on with it.

> Rosalynn Smith Carter (b. 1927)
> American First Lady and humanitarian, *Something to Gain*

How many cares one loses when one decides not to be something, but to be someone.

> Coco Chanel (1883-1971)
> French designer

One never notices what has been done; one can only see what remains to be done.

> Marie Curie (1867-1934)
> French scientist, *Pierre Curie*

We can only reach our goal amid bloodletting

> Nazim Hikmet (1902-1963)
> Turkish poet

Our children may learn about heroes of the past. Our task is to make ourselves architects of the future.

> Jomo Kenyatta (1891-1978)
> Kenyan politician

Let us not dedicate ourselves to useless battles and the striving after goals impossible to attain. Let us follow the lighted star. Let us seek what is reasonable, not waste our courage on a struggle for dreams.

> Luis Muñoz Rivera (1859-1916)
> Puerto Rican journalist and politician

on GOD

To reflect on the essence of the Creator . . . is forbidden to the human intellect because of the severance of all relation between the two existences.

> Muhammad 'Abduh (1849-1905)
> Egyptian reformer, *Risalat at-Tawhid*

The fear of God makes one secure.

> 'Ali (c. 600-661)
> First Imam of the Sh'ia branch of Islam;
> fourth caliph

All that is in the Qur'an is in the Surat Al Fatiha [the opening chapter], and all that is in the Surat al Fatiha is in the Bism'illah [the opening phrase that is at the head of all except one chapter], and all that is in the Bism'illah is in the *B* of Bism'illah, and all that is in the *B* of Bism'illah is in the point which is under the *B*, and I am the point which is under the *B*.

> attributed to 'Ali (c. 600-661)
> First Imam of the Sh'ia branch of Islam;
> fourth caliph

From a very early period a Hindu was conscious of the fact that the multitudinous deities of his pantheon really illustrate the various ways of describing one single God, the eternally existent One Being with his manifold attributes and manifestations.

> Jatindranath Banerjea (1877-1930)
> Indian nationalist, "The Hindu Concept of God"

God has been replaced, as he has all over the West, with respectability and air conditioning.

> Imamu Amiri Baraka (b. 1934)
> American writer, "What Does Nonviolence Mean?" *Home*

Those who worship Me with devotion, they are in Me and I am in them.

> *Bhagavad Gita*
> (c. 4th-3rd century B.C.E.)
> teachings of Krishna from the Hindu epic, the *Mahabharata*, 9:29

I am the father of this world, the
mother the establisher, the
grandsire,
The object of knowledge, the
purifier, the sacred syllable *om*,
The verse of praise, the chant,
and the sacrificial formula.

Bhagavad Gita
(c. 4th–3rd century B.C.E.)
teachings of Krishna from the Hindu
epic, the *Mahabharata*, 9:17-18

Men's whispers sound like thunder
in Heaven's ears; their secret
thoughts flash like lightning before
Heaven's eyes.

Chinese proverb

Our lord, the lord of the near, of
the nigh, is made to laugh. He is
arbitrary, he is capricious, he
mocketh. . . . He is placing us in
the palm of his hand; he is making
us round. We roll; we become as
pellets. He is casting us from side
to side. We make him laugh; he is
making a mockery of us.

Florentine Codex (c. 1550)
collection of Aztec writings

No one has the capacity to judge
God. We are drops in that limitless
ocean of mercy.

Mohandas K. Gandhi (1869-1948)
Indian spiritual and political leader,
Non-Violence in Peace and War

If the world had two gods, it would
surely go to ruin—this is the first
premise. Now it is known that it
has not gone to ruin—this is the
second premise. From these prem-
ises the conclusion must of necessity follow, that is, the denial of
two gods.

Abu Hamid Muhammad al-Ghazali
(1058-1111)
Arab Islamic philosopher and
theologian, *The Just Balance*

Everyone, whether he is self-deny-
ing or self-indulgent, is seeking after the Beloved. Every place may
be the shrine of love, whether it be
mosque or synagogue.

Hafiz (d. 1389)
Persian poet, *Divan*

We have strayed away from God,
and He is in quest of us;
Like us, He is humble and is a
prisoner of desire:
He is hidden in every atom, and
yet is a stranger to us:
He is revealed in the moonlight,
and in the embrace of houses.

Muhammad Iqbal (1873-1938)
Indian poet and philosopher

Thou are Absolute Being, all else
is naught but a Phantasm,
For in Thy universe all things are
one.
Thy world-captivating Beauty, to
display its perfections,
Appears in thousands of mirrors,
but it is one.

Jami (1414-1492)
Persian writer

You amaze me God you amaze
me,
If I step on a puff-adder it strikes
me
If I disturb a bee it stings me
If I provoke a wasp it stings me
If a bed-bug bites me I crush it
If a snake passes by I kill it.

But when we bite you
You do not push us away, you do
  not smash us
You pet us when we bite you,
You care for all our wounds
  instead.

> Joseph Camillo Kumbirai
> (1922-1986)
> Zimbabwean poet

All attributes ascribed to God are attributes of His acts, and do not imply that God has any qualities.

> Maimonides (1135-1204)
> Spanish Hebrew philosopher, *Guide of the Perplexed*

I believe with perfect faith that the Creator, blessed be his name, is not a body, and that he is free from all accidents of matter, and that he has not any form whatsoever.

> Maimonides (1135-1204)
> Spanish Hebrew philosopher, *Thirteen Principles*

God loves to meet those who love to meet Him and dislikes to meet those who dislike to meet Him.

> Muhammad (570-632)
> Prophet of Islam

The limit of the secret of [God's] heart cannot be known.

> Nanak (1469-1539)
> Indian religious leader and founder of Sikhism

After all, if it comes to all that, there is really neither Ogun or Jesus! There are only mystified forms of our own consciousness.

> Lewis Nkosi (b. 1936)
> South African writer, *Home and Exile and Other Selections*, disputing Nigerian writer Wole Soyinka's espousal of Yoruban theology

Say: He is God—One!
  God—the eternally sought after!
He did not have a son
and was no one's son.
And there is no one equal to Him.

> *Qur'an* (c. 610-656)
> sacred book of Islam, "Unity," 112

In the name of God, Most
  Gracious, Most Merciful.
Praise be to God, the Cherisher
  and Sustainer of the worlds;
Most Gracious, Most Merciful;
Lord of the Day of Judgement.
Thee we do worship, and Thine
  aid we seek.

> *Qur'an* (c. 610-656)
> sacred book of Islam, 1:1-5

To God belong the East and West; wherever you turn, there is the face of God—for God is All pervading, All knowing.

> *Qur'an* (c. 610-656)
> sacred book of Islam, lines cited by Muslims as example of mystical intent in the Qur'an

Thou threwest not when thou didst throw, but God threw.

> *Qur'an* (c. 610-656)
> sacred book of Islam, 8:17

God—there is no god but He, the Living, the Self-subsistent. Slumber seizeth Him not, neither sleep. To Him belongeth whatsoever is in the Heavens and whatsoever is in the Earth. Who is there that shall intercede with Him save by His Will? He knoweth what is present with men and what shall befall them, and nought of His knowledge do they comprehend, save what He willeth. His Throne is wide as the Heavens and the Earth, and the keeping of them wearieth Him not. And He is the High, the Mighty One.

Qur'an (c. 610–656)
sacred book of Islam (famous Throne verse, sura ii, v. 256)

Call not on any other god but God; there is no god but He. Everything shall perish except his Face.

Qur'an (c. 610–656)
sacred book of Islam

God is the Light of the Heavens and of the Earth. The similitude of His light is as it were a niche wherein is a lamp, the lamp within a glass, the glass as though it were a pearly star. It is lit from a blessed Tree, an olive tree neither of the East nor of the West, the oil whereof were like to shine even though no fire were applied to it; Light upon Light; God guideth to His Light whom He will.

Qur'an (c. 610–656)
sacred book of Islam, (famous Light verse, sura xxiv, v. 35)

He who truly fears a thing flees from it, but he who truly fears God flees unto Him.

al-Qushayri (c. 1047)
Sufi leader and writer

Into the bosom of the one great
   sea
Flow streams that come from the
   hills on every side,
Their names are various as their
   springs,

And thus in every land do men
   bow down
To one great God, though known
   by many names.

Sarvepalli Radhakrishnan
(1888–1975)
Indian philosopher and politician,
Hindu View of Life

God is everywhere in you and me.

Raidas (15th century)
Indian mystic and religious leader

You should love everyone because God dwells in all beings.

Ramakrishna (1836–1886)
Indian Hindu mystic, *The Gospel of Ramakrishna*

Brother, the Great Spirit has made us all, but He has made a great difference between His white and His red children. He has given us different complexions and different customs. To you He has given the arts; to these He has not opened our eyes. We know these things to be true. Since He has made so great a difference between us in other things, why may we not conclude that He has given us a different religion according to our understanding? The Great Spirit does right. He knows what is best for His children; we are satisfied.

Red Jacket (c. 1758–1830)
Seneca leader, at a council of chiefs of the Six Nations after a white missionary had addressed them (1805)

The veil between God and you is neither earth nor heaven, nor the throne of the footstool; your selfhood and illusions are the veil, and when you remove these, you have attained God.

> Abu Sa'id (967–1049)
> Persian Sufi leader and poet

God is All-knowing and All-powerful. He does not stand in need of any recommendation or help from any prophet or anyone else; otherwise, where would be the difference between God and man?

> Dayananda Saraswati (b. 1824)
> Indian philosopher

Grasping without eyes, hasting without feet, he sees without eyes, he hears without ears. He knows what can be known, but no one knows him.

> *Upanishads* (c. 600–300 B.C.E.)
> sacred philosophical Hindu literature

on THE GOLDEN RULE

A good deed will make a good neighbor.

> Bantu proverb

He who returns favors is
  remembered afterward,
And when he totters, he will find
  a support.

> Ben Sira (c. 2nd century B.C.E.)
> Hebrew scholar and philosopher, *The Wisdom of Ben Sira*

Tsze-kung asked, saying, "Is there one word which may serve as a rule of practice for all one's life?" The Master said, "Is not Reciprocity such a word? What you do not want done to yourself, do not to others."

> Confucius (551–479 B.C.E.)
> Chinese philosopher and founder of Confucianism, *Analects*

No man is a true believer unless he desireth for his brother that which he desireth for himself.

> Muhammad (570–632)
> Prophet of Islam

Whoever believes in God and the hereafter should not injure his neighbor and should honor his guest.

> Muhammad (570–632)
> Prophet of Islam

It is a fundamental rule of human life that, if the approach is good, the response is good.

> Jawaharlal Nehru (1889–1964)
> Indian politician

I will cease to live as a self and will take as my self my fellow-creatures.

> Santi-deva (7th century)
> Indian Buddhist philosopher

A hurtful act is the transference to others of the degradation which we bear in ourselves.

> Simone Weil (1909–1943)
> French philosopher

on GOOD AND EVIL

According as a man acts and walks in the path of life, so he becomes. He that does good becomes good; he that does evil becomes evil. By pure actions he becomes pure; by evil actions he becomes evil.

> *Brihadaranyaka Upanishad*
> (c. 600–300 B.C.E.)
> sacred philosophical Hindu literature

If a man foolishly does me wrong, I will return to him the protection of my ungrudging love; the more evil comes from him, the more good shall go from me.

> Buddha (c. 563–483 B.C.E.)
> Founder of Buddhism, *The Sutra of Forty-two Sections*

Understand that for every rule which I have mentioned from the Qur'an, the Devil has one to match it, which he puts beside the proper rule to cause error.

> Abu Hamid Muhammad al-Ghazali (1058–1111)
> Arab Islamic philosopher and theologian, *The Just Balance*

When evil men plot, good men must plan. When evil men burn and bomb, good men must build and bind. When evil men shout ugly words of hatred, good men must commit themselves to the glories of love.

> Martin Luther King, Jr. (1929–1968)
> American civil rights leader

Good men are bad men's
  instructors,
And bad men are good men's
  materials.

> Lao-tzu (c. 604–531 B.C.E.)
> Chinese philosopher and founder of Taoism, *Tao-te-ching*

Lend your light to the blind. Why should the wickedness of men irritate you, when it is only blindness?

> Eugenio Maria de Hostos (1839–1903)
> Puerto Rican patriot

God seeks comrades and claims love; the Devil seeks slaves and claims obedience.

> Rabindranath Tagore (1861–1941)
> Indian writer and philosopher, *Fireflies*

God never changes;
Patient endurance
Attains to all things;
Who God possesses
In nothing is wanting;
Alone God suffices.

> Teresa of Avila (1515–1582)
> Spanish nun, "Bookmark"

Man's heart is like a printing block. If the block does not err, then even if one copies ten million papers, there will not be errors. If the block errs, then if one repeatedly copies them on paper there will be none without errors.

> Wang Hsun (c. 13th century)
> Chinese philosopher

on GOSSIP

Whoever listens to slander is himself a slanderer.

> 'Ali (c. 600–661)
> First Imam of the Sh'ia branch of Islam; fourth caliph

For what do we live, but to make sport for our neighbors, and laugh at them in our turn?

> Jane Austen (1775–1817)
> English writer, *Pride and Prejudice*

He who chatters with you will chatter of you.

> Egyptian proverb

Be thou good thyself, and let people speak evil of thee; it is better than to be wicked, and that they should consider thee as good.

> Sa'di of Shiraz (c. 1184–1292)
> Persian poet, *Gulistan*

He who gossips and he who listens to it deserve to be thrown to the dogs.

> *Talmud*
> (c. late 4th–early 6th century)
> ancient body of Jewish civil and
> canonical law, P'sahim 108

The soul that's made by free will
  heal again
Not so the wound by the tongue
  that is made.

> Thiruvalluvar (c. 2nd century)
> Indian Tamil writer, *Kural*

on GOVERNMENT

Let not difference of religion interfere with policy, and be not violent in inflicting retribution. Adorn the confidential council with men who know their work.

> Akbar (1542–1605)
> Mughal Indian emperor

A federal system of government is always full of problems and difficulties, but so is democracy, because the art of persuasion is much more difficult than a dictatorship, though in the long run more rewarding and satisfying.

> Abu Bakar Tafawa Balewa
> (1912–1966)
> Nigerian politician

Recall to mind the nations which have shone most highly on the earth and you will be grieved to see that almost the entire world has been, and still is, a victim of bad government. You will find many systems of governing men, but all are calculated to oppress them; and if the habit of seeing the human race, led by shepherds of peoples, did not dull the horror of such a revolting sight, we would be astonished to see our social species grazing on the surface of the globe, even as lowly herds destined to feed their cruel drivers.

> Simón Bolívar (1783–1830)
> South American revolutionary leader,
> address at the opening of the Second
> National Congress of Venezuela
> (February 15, 1819)

Cliques . . . are like dry rot in the administration. . . . Every clique is a refuge for incompetence. It fosters corruption and disloyalty, it begets cowardice, and consequently is a burden upon and a drawback to the progress of the country. Its instincts and actions are those of the pack.

> Madame Chiang Kai-shek (b. 1897)
> Chinese politician, *China Shall Rise
> Again*

An oppressive government is more to be feared than a tiger.

> Confucius (551–479 B.C.E.)
> Chinese philosopher and founder of
> Confucianism, *Analects*

In a country well governed, poverty is something to be ashamed of. In a country badly governed, wealth is something to be ashamed of.

> Confucius (551–479 B.C.E.)
> Chinese philosopher and founder of
> Confucianism, *Analects*

Good government obtains when those who are near are made happy, and those who are far off are attracted.

> Confucius (551–479 B.C.E.)
> Chinese philosopher and founder of
> Confucianism, *Analects*

Tzu-kung asked about government. The Master said, "Give them enough food, give them enough arms, and the common people will have trust in you."

Confucius (551–479 B.C.E.)
Chinese philosopher and founder of Confucianism, *Analects*

When Tzu-hsia was Warden of Chu-fu, he sought advice about government. The Master said, "Do not try to hurry things. Ignore minor considerations. If you hurry things, your personality will not come into play. If you let yourself be distracted by minor considerations, nothing important will ever get finished."

Confucius (551–479 B.C.E.)
Chinese philosopher and founder of Confucianism, *Analects*

Tzu-lu asked about government. The Master said, "Lead them; encourage them!" Tzu-lu asked for a further maxim. The Master said, "Untiringly."

Confucius (551–479 B.C.E.)
Chinese philosopher and founder of Confucianism, *Analects*

If one leads them with administrative measures and uses punishments to make them conform, the people will be evasive, but if one leads them with virtue, they will come up to expectations.

Confucius (551–479 B.C.E.)
Chinese philosopher and founder of Confucianism, *Analects*

Intelligence dies for want of nourishment under a machinery of government which leaves nothing to the initiative of the citizen.

Mustafa Fazil (1830–1875)
Egyptian prince, "Manifeste de la Jeune Turquie," an open letter to the Sultan Abdul 'Aziz, *Liberté* (March 24, 1867)

You give bureaucrats power over others, and when the others are poor and helpless, nothing matches government. More than any single exploitive tyrannical force, the possibility of what government can do is absolutely terrifying.

Millicent Fenwick (1910–1992)
American politician

Are you a politician asking what your country can do for you, or a zealous one asking what you can do for your country? If you are the first, then you are a parasite; if the second, then you are an oasis in the desert.

Kahlil Gibran (1883–1931)
Syrian writer

The trouble with military rule is that every colonel or general is soon full of ambition. The navy takes over today and the army tomorrow.

Yakuba Gowon (b. 1934)
Nigerian politician

Of all the cases of corruption and disorder in the world, there is none which did not originate in the autocratic form of government. It's like being tied up with dozens of ropes—autocracy being the main rope. If you cut it, the rest will fall away. Otherwise you can't untie yourself in a hundred days.

Han Wenju (c. 1900)
Chinese activist and writer

In the government of a semi-barbarous race . . . a little despotism is absolutely necessary.

James Africanus Horton
(1835-1883)
British physician, *Letters*

The system doesn't have to be pure, but it does have to work.

Aminu Kano (b. 1920)
Nigerian politican

I am more interested in the purpose of government than its mechanics—though the means should at least be good enough to lead to the ends desired.

Aminu Kano (b. 1920)
Nigerian politican

The fundamental difference between Islamic government, on the one hand, and constitutional monarchy and republics, on the other, is this: whereas the representatives of the people or the monarch in such regimes engage in legislation, in Islam the legislative power and competence to establish laws belong exclusively to God Almighty.

Ayatollah Khomeini (1902-1989)
Iranian spiritual and political leader

Treat [the people] as slaves, guard them against brigands, and they will come to regard themselves as slaves and brigands.

Liang Qichao (1808-1883)

Chinese political theorist, "Lun chin-pu" ("On Progress")

No person, class or group, not even the entire population of the state as a whole, can lay claim to sovereignty. God alone is the real sovereign; all others are merely his subjects.

Abu'l A'la Mawdudi (1903-1979)
Pakistani Islamic leader, *Islamic Law and Constitution*

We prefer self-government with danger to servitude with tranquility.

Kwame Nkrumah (1909-1972)
Ghanaian politician and revolutionary leader

To govern is to educate.

Domingo Faustino Sarmiento
(1811-1888)
Argentinian politician

Just as the larger fish in the sea swallow the smaller, so also is it with men. If not for the fear of government, the stronger would swallow the weaker.

Talmud
(c. late 4th-early 6th century)
ancient body of Jewish civil and canonical law, Abodah zarah, 4a

An Islamic state cannot be isolated from society because Islam is a comprehensive, integrated way of life. The division between private and public, the state and society, that is familiar in Western culture, has not been known in Islam.

Hassan al-Turabi (b. 1930)
Sudanese politician, "The Islamic State"

on GRATITUDE

How can you thank a man for giving you what's yours?

Malcolm X (1925-1965)
American civil rights activist

Ingratitude is sooner or later fatal to its author.

Twi (West African) proverb

on GRAVES AND GRAVEYARDS

The serene decision of the tombs
is beautiful,
Their uncompromising
architecture
And the little squares with the
coolness of a patio
And the isolation and eternal
individuation;
Each contemplated his own death,
Unique and personal like a
memory.
The quietude pleases us,
We confuse such peace in life
with dying
And while we believe we desire
not to be
We are praying for a peaceful life.

Jorge Luis Borges (1899-1986)
Argentinian writer, "La Recoleta" ("The
Recoleta")

For each man produced by
Heaven, Earth provides a grave.

Chinese proverb

And where are the graves, so
many graves
Of all who have died on earth
since the beginning?
Grave tunnelling into grave,
Headstone and obelisk crumbed
into one dust,
Bodies heaped upon bodies, in
motionless orgy—
All sleeping together in deep
holes,
Fragments of chalk,
Stained rubies.

Moses ibn Ezra (1070-1139)
Spanish Hebrew poet, "Graves"

What a great number of graves! The land extends with them all the way to the horizon, raising its hands up in surrender though nothing could have threatened it. The city of silence and truth. The meeting place of success and failure, the criminal and the victim. The gathering place of thieves and policemen, where they lie in peace beside each other for the first and last times.

Naguib Mahfouz (b. 1911)
Egyptian writer, *al Liss wa 'Kilab*

Every tombstone is a hand stretched forth from the house of oblivion of the earth to search for thee.

Sa'ib of Tabriz (c. 1601-1677)
Persian poet

on GREATNESS

When the Chinese suspect someone of being a potential troublemaker, they always resort to one of two methods: they crush him, or they hoist him on a pedestal.

Lu Xun (1881-1936)
Chinese writer

117

The great man is one who never loses his child's heart.

> Mencius (c. 390–305 B.C.E.)
> Chinese philosopher, *Meng-tzu*

The ordinary man repents his sins; the elect repent of their heedlessness.

> dhu-al-Nun al Misri (c.795–860)
> Egyptian Sufi leader

Great men can't be ruled.

> Ayn Rand (1905–1982)
> American writer, *The Fountainhead*

We can do no great things—only small things with great love.

> Mother Teresa (b. 1910)
> Yugoslavian missionary, *Life in the Spirit*

on GREED

The beauty was in the waking of the powerless. Is it always to be true that it is impossible to have things strong and at the same time beautiful? The famished men need not stay famished. But to gorge themselves in this heartbreaking way, consuming, utterly destroying the common promise of their greed, was that ever necessary?

> Ayi Kwei Armah (b. 1938)
> Ghanaian writer, *The Beautyful Ones Are Not Yet Born*, speaking of the betrayal of decolonization's ideals by charismatic leader Nkrumah of Ghana

To obtain one leads to wishing for two—enough is always something more than a man possesses.

> Chinese proverb

Earth provides enough to satisfy every man's need, but not every man's greed.

> Mohandas K. Gandhi (1869–1948)
> Indian spiritual and political leader, *Small Is Beautiful*

There is no greater disaster than greed.

> Lao-tzu (c. 604–531 B.C.E.)
> Chinese philosopher and founder of Taoism, *Tao-te ching*

Beware of covetousness, which is a malady, diseaseful, incurable. Intimacy with it is impossible, it makes the sweet friend bitter, it alienates the trusted one from his master, it makes both father and mother mad . . . it divorces a man's wife.

> Ptah-hotep (c. 2300 B.C.E.)
> Egyptian vizier

Greed makes man blind and foolish, and makes him an easy prey for death.

> Rumi (1207–1273)
> Persian Sufi poet

The enjoyments of both worlds will not satisfy the greedy man: Burning fire always has an appetite.

> Sa'ib of Tabriz (c. 1601–1677)
> Persian poet

It is well known that when greed has for its object material gain then it can have no end. It is like the chasing of the horizon by a lunatic. To go on in a competition, multiplying millions becomes a steeplechase of insensate futility that has no obstacles but no goal.

Rabindranath Tagore (1861–1941)
Indian writer and philosopher, *The Religion of Man*

Nothing destroys one's respect in the hearts of others more than greed.

Muhammed Taqi (d. 835)
Arab religious leader

on GRIEVING

They say a man is like a funeral ram which must take whatever beating comes to it without opening its mouth; only the silent tremor of pain down its body tells of its suffering.

Chinua Achebe (b. 1930)
Nigerian writer, *Arrow of God*

You grieve for those beyond grief
and you speak words of insight;
but learned men do not grieve
for the dead or the living.

Bhagavad Gita
(c. 4th–3rd century B.C.E.)
teachings of Krishna from the Hindu epic, the *Mahabharata*

I tell you, hopeless grief is passionless.

Elizabeth Barrett Browning
(1806–1861)
English poet, "Grief," *Poems of 1844*

What piercing cold I feel!
My dead wife's comb, in our
 bedroom,
under my heel. . . .

Taniguchi Buson (1715–1783)
Japanese painter and poet

My eyes have only one job: to cry.

Nur Jahan (c. 1646)
Indian poet

My kinsmen may still be grieving,
While others have started singing.
I am dead and gone—what more
 is there to say?
My body is buried in the
 mountains.

Dai Jian (20th century)
Chinese poet

A person wept the live-long night
 beside a sick man's bed;
When it dawned the sick was
 well, and the mourner—he was
 dead.

Husayn Wa'idh Kashifi
(15th century)
Islamic poet

And forth they went imploring
 God for rain;
"My tears," I said, "could serve
 you for a flood."
"In truth," they cried, "your tears
 might well contain
Sufficiency; but they are dyed
 with blood."

Al-Mu'tamid (d. 1095)
Arab Spanish ruler

Like a child in its cradle
I would that very gentle arms
Might rock my grieving spirit
And be as it were a kindly shelter
For my heart—a traveler lost
On a remote deserted road.

Nguyen Vy (d. 1975)
Vietnamese poet, "Dem sau ve"
("Night-time Depression")

Formerly, people used to grieve over the departed, but in our days they grieve over the survivors.

> Sa'ib of Tabriz (c. 1601–1677)
> Persian poet

on GUESTS

He left us and we rejoiced; then an even more unbearable person came.

> Arabic proverb

Visit rarely, and you will be more loved.

> Arabic proverb

on GUILT

He who is guilty is the one that has much to say.

> Ashanti (West African) proverb

You can get used to anything if you have to, even feeling perpetually guilty.

> Golda Meir (1898–1978)
> Israeli prime minister, *My Life*

Ah! it is well for the unfortunate to be resigned, but for the guilty there is no peace.

> Mary Shelley (1797–1851)
> English writer, *Frankenstein*

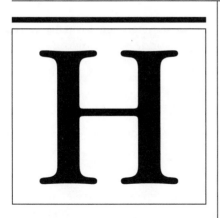

on **HABIT**

Curious things, habits. People themselves never knew they had them.

Agatha Christie (1891-1976)
English writer, *Witness for the Prosecution*

The fool who repeats again and again: "I am bound, I am bound," remains in bondage. He who repeats day and night: "I am a sinner, I am a sinner," becomes a sinner indeed.

Ramakrishna (1836-1886)
Indian Hindu mystic

on **HAPPINESS**

The word "happiness" does have a meaning, doesn't it? I shall go out in search of it.

Mallam Ba (c. 1920)
Malian writer, *So Long a Letter*

It may be that true happiness lies in the conviction that one has irremediably lost happiness. Then we can begin to move through life without hope or fear, capable of finally enjoying all the small pleasures, which are the most lasting.

Maria-Luisa Bombal (1910-1980)
Chilean writer, "The Tree"

When I look at what the world does and where people nowadays believe they can find happiness, I am not sure that that is true happiness. The happiness of these ordinary people seems to consist in slavishly imitating the majority, as if this were their only choice. And yet they all believe they are happy. I cannot decide whether that is happiness or not. Is there such a thing as happiness?

Chuang-tzu (c. 369-286 B.C.E.)
Chinese Taoist philosopher

Be happy. It's one way of being wise.

Colette (1873-1954)
French writer

Having only coarse food to eat, plain water to drink, and a bent arm for a pillow, one can still find happiness therein.

Confucius (551-479 B.C.E.)
Chinese philosopher, founder of Confucianism, *Analects*

The greatest happiness is to transform one's feelings into actions.

Madame de Staël (1766-1817)
French writer

Eden is that old-fashioned House
We dwell in every day;
Without suspecting our abode
Until we drive away.

Emily Dickinson (1830-1886)
American poet

Happiness is to take up the struggle in the midst of the raging storm and not to pluck the lute in the moonlight or recite poetry among the blossoms.

> Ding Ling (c. 1904–1986)
> Chinese writer, "Thoughts on March 8"

Whether happiness may come or not, one should try and prepare one's self to do without it.

> George Eliot (1819–1880)
> English writer

No benefit is more constant than simplicity; no happiness more constant than peace.

> Han Fei-tzu (c. 280–233 B.C.E.)
> Chinese philosopher

The secret of happiness is only a few words; yet we will not accept it from anyone, but must learn it from a lifetime of experience, when it is far too late.

> Muhammad Hijazi (20th century)
> Iranian writer and politician, *Hazar Sokhan (A Thousand Sayings)*

All human happiness is sensuous happiness.

> Lin Yutang (1895–1976)
> Chinese writer

My happiness is not the means to any end. It is the end. It is its own goal. It is its own purpose. Neither am I the means to any end others may wish to accomplish. I am not a tool for their use. I am not a servant of their needs. I am not a bandage for their wounds. I am not a sacrifice on their altars.

> Ayn Rand (1905–1982)
> American writer, *Anthem*

If something makes you happy in this world, you should think of what will happen to you if that thing were taken away.

> Rumi (1207–1273)
> Persian Sufi poet

on **HASTE**

Stumbling is the fruit of haste.

> 'Ali (c. 600–661)
> First Imam of the Sh'ia branch of Islam; fourth caliph

The power of doing anything with quickness is always much prized by the possessor, and often without any attention to the imperfection of the performance.

> Jane Austen (1775–1817)
> English writer, *Pride and Prejudice*

on **HATE**

I imagine one of the reasons people cling to their hates so stubbornly is because they sense, once hate is gone, they will be forced to deal with pain.

> James Baldwin (1924–1987)
> American writer, *Notes of a Native Son*

The price of hating other human beings is loving oneself less.

> Eldridge Cleaver (b. 1935)
> American civil rights activist, *Soul on Ice*

Hatred does not cease by hatred; hatred ceases only by love. This is the eternal law.

> *Dhammapada* (c. 3rd century B.C.E.)
> collection of ancient Buddhist poems and aphorisms, "The Twin Verses"

We compound our suffering by victimizing each other.

Athol Fugard (b. 1932)
South African playwright

Hate has no medicine.

Ghanaian (West African) proverb

Like an unchecked cancer, hate corrodes the personality and eats away its vital unity. Hate destroys a man's sense of values and his objectivity. It causes him to describe the beautiful as ugly and the ugly as beautiful, and to confuse the true with the false, and the false with the true.

Martin Luther King, Jr.
(1929-1968)
American civil rights leader, *Strength to Love*

To the eye of enmity, virtue appears the ugliest blemish.

Sa'di of Shiraz (c. 1184-1292)
Persian poet, *Gulistan*

He who hates, hates himself.

Zulu proverb

on HEAVEN

Like my mother, and my
  grandmother too,
Plus seven generations before
  them,
I also seek admission to heaven,
Which the Moslem Party and the
  Mohammedan Party say has
  rivers of milk
And thousands of houris all over.

But there's a contemplative voice
  inside me,

Stubbornly mocking: Can you ever
Get dry after a soaking in the blue
After the sly temptations in every
  port?
Anyway, who can say for sure
That there really are houris there
With voices as rich and husky as
  Nina's, with eyes that flirt like
  Jati's?

Chairil Anwar (1923-1949)
Indonesian poet

[Heaven is] that moment in which something attains its maximum depth, its maximum reach, its maximum sense, and becomes completely uninteresting.

Julio Cortazar (1914-1984)
Argentinian writer, *Hopscotch*

Heaven sees as the people see.
Heaven hears as the people hear.

Mencius (c. 390-305 B.C.E.)
Chinese philosopher, *Shu ching*

The raven utters no cries,
The ittidu-bird utters not the cry
  of the ittidu-bird,
The lion kills not,
The wolf snatches not the lamb,
Unknown is the kid-devouring
  wild dog . . .

Sumerian folk poem
about Dilumn, a legendary bright, pure
land where death, sorrow, and pain
were unknown

on HELL

Hell has three gates: lust, anger, and greed.

Bhagavad Gita (c. 1st century)
teachings of Krishna from the Hindu
epic, the *Mahabharata*

I have seen a place—
its name is Eternal Hatred
It is built in the deepest abyss
of the stones of mortal sin.
Pride was the first stone—
this was seen in Lucifer.

Mechthild of Magdeburg
(1210-1297)
German mystic

What if this were Hell, this
  absence of sleep, this poet's
  desert,
this pain of living, this dying of
  not dying,
this anguish of shadows, this
  passion over death and light.

Leopold Sedar Senghor (b. 1906)
Senegalese political leader and writer,
"Midnight Elegy," *Ethiopics*

on HELP

He could be helped in a certain
way only because he was hurt in a
certain way; and his help is simply
to be enabled to move from one
conundrum to the next . . . from
one disaster to the next.

James Baldwin (1924-1987)
American writer, *Notes of a Native Son*

God you are no longer awake!
God creator do not permit an evil
  thing!
What have I done?
Come and fight on my side
  against my enemy.

Ibo (Nigerian) prayer

on HEROES

Perhaps the final hour is come
I have left no testament

Only a pen, for my mother
I am no hero
in an age without heroes
I just want to be a man

Bei Dao (b. 1949)
Chinese poet, "Declaration," *The
August Sleepwalker*

Where are now the warriors of the
world of the spirit? Where are
those who raise their voices for
truth, who lead us to goodness,
beauty, strength and health? Where
are those who utter heartwarming
words, who will lead us out of the
wilderness? Our homes are gone
and the nation is destroyed, yet we
have no Jeremiah crying out his
last sad song to the world and to
posterity.

Lu Xun (1881-1936)
Chinese writer, *Lu Xun Quanji*

Within the Arab circle there is a
role wandering aimlessly in search
of a hero. For some reason it seems
to me that this role is beckoning to
us—to move, to take up its lines,
put on its costumes and give it life.
Indeed, we are the only ones who
can play it. The role is to spark the
tremendous latent strengths in the
region surrounding us to create a
great power, which will then rise
up to a level of dignity and undertake a positive part in building the
future of mankind.

Gamel Abdel Nasser (1918-1970)
Egyptian politician, *Realities*

We want religious heroes who will
not wait for the transformation of
the whole world but assert with
their lives, if necessary, the truth of

the conviction "one earth, one family."

Sarvepalli Radhakrishnan
(1888–1975)
Indian philosopher and politician

Kill reverence and you've killed the hero in man.

Ayn Rand (1905–1982)
American writer, *The Fountainhead*

on HISTORY

People are trapped in history and history is trapped in them.

James Baldwin (1924–1987)
American writer, *Notes of a Native Son*

What is not recorded is not remembered.

Benazir Bhutto (b. 1953)
Pakistani politician, *Daughter of Destiny*

If we tried
To sink the past beneath our feet, be sure
The future would not stand.

Elizabeth Barrett Browning
(1806–1861)
English poet, *Casa Guidi Windows*

The term of life of a dynasty does not normally exceed three generations. For in the first generation are still preserved the characteristic features of rough, uncivilized rural life, such as hard conditions of life, courage, ferocity, and partnership in authority. Therefore the strength of the 'Asabiya is maintained . . .

Ibn Khaldun (1332–1406)
Arab historian and philosopher

A community receives light from its history, it becomes aware of itself by remembrance of its history.

Muhammad Iqbal (1873–1938)
Indian Muslim poet and philosopher

Preserve your history and become everlasting; receive new life from the times that have gone by.

Muhammad Iqbal (1873–1938)
Indian Muslim poet and philosopher

It is given to men . . . to attack the rights of others, to take their property, to attempt the lives of those who defend their liberty, and to make of their virtues a crime and of their own vices a virtue; but there is one thing which is beyond the reach of perversity, and that is the tremendous verdict of history. History will judge us.

Benito Juárez (1806–1872)
Mexican revolutionary and political leader

Historical experience is written in blood and iron.

Mao Zedong (1893–1976)
Chairman of People's Republic of China

The people, and the people alone, are the motive force in the making of world history.

Mao Zedong (1893–1976)
Chairman of People's Republic of China

Destiny is history and history is the road laid out before the steps that have not been taken.

Miguel M. Mendez (b. 1930)
American writer, *Peregrinos de Aztlan*

125

You don't change the course of history by turning the face of portraits to the wall.

> Jawaharlal Nehru (1889–1964)
> Indian prime minister

One of the ways of helping to destroy a people is to tell them they don't have a history, that they have no roots.

> Desmond Tutu (b. 1931)
> South African antiapartheid activist and religious leader

It is a great pity that every human being does not, at an early stage of his life, have to write a historical work. He would then realize that the human race is in quite a jam about truth.

> Rebecca West (1892–1983)
> English writer

on HOME

Every beast roars in its own den.

> Bantu proverb

The village is desolate, people
  have changed,
Grass nearly engulfs the leaning
  walls and house.
Only the well in front of the gate
  remains—
Its sweet, cool taste has not
  changed.

> Cho'oe Ch'i-won (c. 857)
> Korean poet and politician, "Upon First Returning Home"

A house should not be built so close to another that a chicken from one can lay an egg in the neighbor's yard, nor so far away that a child cannot shout to the yard of his neighbor.

> Julius K. Nyerere (b. 1922)
> Tanzanian nationalist and political leader

Where shall I go . . . where is my home, that I can call it my own? To the West? No—where I was born. Shall it be my native home and remain inviolate? I hoped it was so, but alas, it is not so. Our people are in the state of a great dilemma—to go or stay—but must go, says the government of the U.S. Humanity speaks: they may stay. They ought to enjoy the home of their fathers.

> Mavis Bryant Pierce (1811–1874)
> Seneca leader, *Book of Memorandum*

My land is a waste land
Its cities are silent;
Even the vultures have abandoned
  it,
Its trees have been uprooted,
Its earth is mud and excrement.
This land is not mine.

. . . .

My land
Is a handful of earth
Which I lost.

> Tawfiq Sayigh (1923–1971)
> Iraqi poet, "Aydan wa Aydan," *Hiwar*

on HOMESICKNESS

O Palm, thou art a stranger in the
  West,
Far from thy Orient home, like
  me unblest,
Weep! But thou canst not, dumb,
  dejected tree,
Thou art not made to sympathize
  with me.

. . . .
But yonder tall groves thou
remembrest not,
As I, in hating foes, have my old
friends forgot.

'Abd-al-Rahman (d. 1709)
Indian Sufi writer

We enjoyed a brief spring
together on Mount Ch'u;
Now you leave and tears soak my
kerchief.
Don't think me strange gazing
windward dispirited,
It's hard to meet a friend this far
from home.

Cho'oe Ch'i-won (c. 857)
Korean poet and politician, "On Seeing
a Fellow Villager Off in Shan-Yang"

That I can live long enough
To obtain one and only one
desire—
That someday I can see again
The mulberry and catalpa trees of
home.

Ts'ai Yen (c. 3rd century)
Chinese poet, "Eighteen Verses Sung to
a Tatar Reed Whistle"

on **HONESTY**

One must be frank to be relevant.

Corazon Aquino (b. 1933)
Philippine politician

Let the world know you as you are,
not as you think you should be, because sooner or later, if you are
posing, you will forget the pose,
and then where are you?

Fanny Brice (1891–1951)
American comedian and singer

Teach thy tongue to say: "I do not
know."

Hebrew proverb

The underlying sickness of human
life is an unwillingness to look
with open eyes at the condition of
the world.

Hu Shih (1891–1962)
Chinese writer, "I-pu-sheng chu'i"
("Ibsenism")

We should face reality and our past
mistakes in an honest adult way.
Boasting of glory does not make
glory, and singing in the dark does
not dispel fear.

Hussein (b. 1935)
Jordanian king, during a conference of
Arab chiefs of state, Khartoum, Sudan
(August 30, 1967)

There is no future for a people
who deny their past.

Adam Clayton Powell, Jr.
(1908–1972)
American politician and civil rights
leader, "Civil War II," *Marching Blacks*

on **HOPE**

He who has help has hope, and he
who has hope has everything.

Arab proverb

When you can see the end of
things even in their beginnings,
there's no more hope, unless you
want to pretend, or forget, or get
drunk or something.

Ayi Kwei Armah (b. 1938)
Ghanaian writer, *The Beautyful Ones
Are Not Yet Born*

After rain comes sunshine;
after darkness comes the glorious
  dawn.
There is no sorrow without its
  alloy of
joy, there is no joy without its
  admixture
of sorrow. Behind the ugly
  terrible mask
of Misfortune lies the beautiful
  soothing
countenance of Prosperity. So,
  tear the mask!

> Obafemi Awolowo (b. 1909)
> Nigerian politician, *Awo: The
> Autobiography of Chief Obafemi
> Awolowo*

Hope is delicate suffering.

> Imamu Amiri Baraka (b. 1934)
> American writer, *Cold, Hurt, and
> Sorrow*

The sharp knife of dawn glitters
  in my hand
but how bare is everything—tall
  tall tree
infinite air, the unrelaxing tension
  of the world
and only hope, hope only, the
  kind eagle soars and wheels in
  flight.

> Martin Carter (b. 1927)
> Guyanan writer and diplomat, "The
> Knife of Dawn"

"Hope" is the thing with
  feathers—
That perches in the soul—
And sings the tune without the
  words—
And never stops—at all—

> Emily Dickinson (1830-1886)
> American poet

A great Hope fell
You heard no noise
The Ruin was within.

> Emily Dickinson (1830-1886)
> American poet

What one hopes for is always better than what one has.

> Ethiopian proverb

Hope can be neither affirmed nor
denied. Hope is like a path in the
countryside: originally there was
no path—yet, as people are walking all the time in the same spot, a
way appears.

> Lu Xun (1881-1936)
> Chinese writer

Guns alone are not the answer. We
must provide hope for young people for better housing, clothing,
and food; and if we do, the radicals
will wither away.

> Ramon Magsaysay (1907-1957)
> Philippine politician, speaking of Huk
> Communist insurgents

He who does not hope to win has
already lost.

> José Joaquín de Olmedo
> (1780-1847)
> Ecuadoran poet

on HUMAN NATURE

A prince who has no pride . . . a
poet who has no jealousy, a trader
who is not a thief, a husband who
is not vindictive, a nobleman who
is not poor, . . . a gambler who is
grateful, . . . a minister who
speaks the truth, a king's son who

is not discourteous. (It would be rare to find.)

Bana (7th century)
Indian poet, *Harshcharita*

How do most people live without any thoughts? There are many people in the world—you must have noticed them in the street—how do they live? How do they get strength to put on their clothes in the morning?

Emily Dickinson (1830–1886)
American poet

The nature of man is evil; what is good in him is artificial.

Hsun-tzu (298–238 B.C.E.)
Chinese philosopher

The mind that cannot bear to see the suffering of others is humanity. It is electricity; it is ether. Everyone has it. This is why it is said that the nature of all men is originally good.

K'ang Yu-wei (1858–1927)
Chinese political philosopher

It is true that water will flow indifferently to east and west, but will it flow equally well up and down? Human nature is disposed toward goodness, just as water tends to flow downwards. There is no water but flows downwards, and no man but shows his tendency to be good. Now, by striking water hard, you may splash it higher than your forehead, and by damming it, you may make it go uphill. But, is that the nature of water? It is external force that causes it to do so. Likewise, if a man is made to do what is not good, his nature is being similarly forced.

Mencius (c. 390–305 B.C.E.)
Chinese philosopher, "Kao-tzu," *Meng-tzu*, pt. 1, ch. 2

When people have peace, they hate it and long for excitement, and when they have excitement, they want peace.

Amos Oz (b. 1939)
Israeli writer

Verily man was created avid of gain; when evil befalls him, apt to grieve; when good befalls him, grudging.

Qur'an (c. 610–656)
sacred book of Islam, 70:19

You take people as far as they will go, not as far as you would like them to go.

Jeanette Rankin (1880–1973)
American feminist and politician

I think that man can live more simply than any other thing, and that this is one of his most striking characteristics. An idea like wanting to live the life of a stone could occur only to a man.

Akiyama Shun (b. 1930)
Japanese writer, "The Simple Life"

When man has freed himself of all his desires, he will also be utterly indifferent to the misery and the grief of men everywhere. . . . To let others live, and not to live oneself, simply violates nature.

Tai Chen (1724–1777)
Chinese philosopher

The world changes, but men are always the same.

Richard Wright (1908–1960)
American writer, *The Outsider*

on HUMAN RIGHTS

The fight is never about grapes or lettuce. It is always about people.

Cesar Chavez (1927-1993)
American labor rights activist, on
activities of the National Farm Workers
Association

Human law may know no distinction among men in respect of rights, but human practice may.

Frederick Douglass (1817-1895)
American abolitionist

In the field of modern cosmology, the first principle is called "the Cosmological Principle." It says that the universe has no center, that it has the same properties throughout. Every place in the universe has, in this sense, equal rights. How can the human race, which has evolved in a universe of such fundamental equality, fail to strive for a society without violence and terror? How can we fail to build a world in which the rights due to every human being from birth are respected?

Fang Lizhe (b. 1936)
Chinese scientist and activist,
acceptance speech upon winning the
1989 Robert F. Kennedy Human Rights
Award

No attempt must be made to encase man, for it is his destiny to be set free.

Frantz Fanon (1925-1961)
Martiniquen writer

Peace will help development. Development will engender peace. They are both causes and effects. They strengthen each other. Their common goal is the reign of human rights.

José Figueres (b. 1906)
Costa Rican soldier and politician

I am not interested in picking up the crumbs of compassion thrown from the table of someone who considers himself my master. I want the full menu of rights.

Desmond Tutu (b. 1931)
South African antiapartheid activist and
religious leader

on HUMANITY

Mankind consists of many classes and many different characters. Some are like rare jewels which one does not sell at any price. There are others so suspect that no one would like to buy them.

'Abd al Hamid (705-750)
Arab writer

People are worms, and even the God who created them is immensely bored with their antics.

Christina Ama Ata Aidoo (b. 1942)
Ghanaian writer, *No Sweetness Here*

For man is but clay and straw, and the god is his builder, and he is tearing down or building up every day.

Amen-em-Opet (c. 1200 B.C.E.)
Egyptian scribe

Look at this wagon. Is it a wheel or a spoke? . . . It is a composite and so is a man.

Buddha (c. 563-483 B.C.E.)
Founder of Buddhism, the sutra of the
"Five Heaps"

The human condition . . . is defined by the aspiration to always supersede oneself, which in turn requires nonconformity.

Pablo Antonio Cuadra (b. 1912)
Nicaraguan poet, "Notes on Culture in the New Nicaragua"

A man is likewise form and expression, a written sign thrown unto boundless matter, an undifferentiated word of what is. I've therefore been created in the image of the inscriptions that, as a child, I used to project unto my bits of bone, stone, wood, and iron, probably even in the image of a single one of their words, a single one of their letters.

Mohammed Dib (b. 1920)
Algerian writer, *My Talisman*

I will establish a savage, "man"
    shall be his name.
Verily, savage-man I will create.
He shall be charged with the
    service of the gods
That they might be at ease!

Enuma elish
an ancient Sumerian creation epic

One could almost say that man gave birth to man in order to destroy himself.

Abellatif Laabi (20th century)
Moroccan writer, translator

The world holds two classes of men—intelligent men without religion and religious men without intelligence.

Abu'l-Ala-Al'Ma'arri (973–1057)
Arab poet

To be a *man* is the most extraordinary thing among the ordinary things of earth.

Eugenio Maria de Hostos
(1839–1903)
Puerto Rican patriot

Man's role is uncertain, undefined, and perhaps unnecessary.

Margaret Mead (1901–1978)
American anthropologist, *Male and Female*

The people turn in allegiance to Humanity, as surely as water flows downward or as a wild animal takes cover in the wilderness.

Mencius (390–305 B.C.E.)
Chinese philosopher

on HUMILITY

Hide the good you do, and make known the good done to you.

'Ali (c. 600–661)
First Imam of the Sh'ia branch of Islam; fourth caliph

Great shame it is to deem of high
    degree
Thyself, or over others reckon
    thee:
Strive to be like the pupil of thine
    eye—
To see all else, but not thyself
    to see.

Ansari (1006–1088)
Persian Sufi poet

The greater you are, the more you must practice humility.

Ben Sira (c. 2nd century B.C.E.)
Hebrew scholar and philosopher, *The Wisdom of Ben Sira*

Use your light, but dim your brightness.

> Lao-tzu (c. 604-531 B.C.E.)
> Chinese philosopher and founder of
> Taoism, *Tao-te-ching*

Be humble, and you will remain
  entire.
Be bent, and you will remain
  straight.
Be vacant, and you will remain
  full.
Be worn, and you will remain
  new.
He who has little will receive.
He who has much will be
  embarrassed.
Therefore the sage keeps to One
  and becomes the standard for
  the world.

> Lao-tzu (c. 604-531 B.C.E.)
> Chinese philosopher and founder of
> Taoism, *Tao-te-ching*

If one avoids haughtiness to the utmost extent and is exceedingly humble, he is termed a saint, and this is the standard of saintliness.

> Maimonides (1135-1204)
> Spanish Hebrew philosopher, *Mishneh
> Torah*

Don't be humble. You're not that great.

> Golda Meir (1898-1978)
> Israeli prime minister

Whoever has in his heart even so much as a rice grain of pride cannot enter into paradise.

> Muhammad (570-632)
> Prophet of Islam

Let not thy heart be puffed up because of thy knowledge; do not be overconfident because thou art a wise man. Take counsel with the ignorant as well as the wise. The full limits of craftsmanship cannot be attained, and there is no craftsman equipped to his full ability.

> Ptah-hotep (c. 2300 B.C.E.)
> Egyptian vizier, *Instruction of Ptah-
> hotep*

Conceal your good deeds as you conceal your evil deeds.

> Rabi'a al-Adawiyya (c. 717-801)
> Iraqi Sufi poet and mystic

God cannot be realized if there is the slightest trace of pride.

> Ramakrishna (1836-1886)
> Indian Hindu mystic

Discard yourself and thereby regain yourself. Spread the trap of humility and ensnare love.

> Rumi (1207-1273)
> Persian Sufi poet

Humility is the embroidery of chiefs.

> Sa'di of Shiraz (c. 1184-1292)
> Persian poet, *Pandnama*

Whoever humbles himself, God elevates him; whoever is proud, God brings him down. Whoever runs after honors, honors run away from him.

> *Talmud*
> (c. late 4th-early 6th century)
> ancient body of Jewish civil and
> canonical law, Erubin 13

The more you forget yourself, the more Jesus will think of you.

> Mother Teresa (b. 1910)
> Yugoslavian missionary, *Life in the
> Spirit*

Humility must always be doing its work like a bee making honey in the hive: without humility all will be lost.

Teresa of Avila (1515-1582)
Spanish nun, "Interior Castle"

on HUMOR

A difference of taste in jokes is a great strain on the affections.

George Eliot (1819-1880)
English writer, *Daniel Deronda*

Humor is laughing at what you haven't got when you ought to have it.

Langston Hughes (1902-1967)
American writer

Wit has truth in it; wisecracking is simply calisthenics with words.

Dorothy Parker (1893-1967)
American writer

He deserves paradise who makes his companions laugh.

Qur'an (c. 610-656)
sacred book of Islam

on HUNGER

I'm hungry, black earth, hungry,
    hear me.
With the black ox I'm hungry
    tonight.
He thinks, and thinking feeds him,
I think, and thinking makes my
    hunger grow.
    I'm hungry, black earth,
    hungry,
        hear me.
    One can't hide it when he's
        hungry.

Fazil Husnu Daglarca (b. 1914)

Turkish poet, "Toprak Ana" ("Mother Earth")

To a man with an empty stomach, food is God.

Mohandas K. Gandhi (1869-1948)
Indian spiritual and political leader

When you have a healthy appetite there is no such thing as bad bread.

Gabriel García Márquez (b. 1928)
Colombian writer, *El Coronel no Tiene quien le Escriba*

Hungry men have no respect for law, authority, or human life.

Marcus Garvey (1887-1940)
American political leader, *Philosophy and Opinion*

It is desirable for a ruler that no man should suffer from cold and hunger under his rule. Man cannot maintain his standard of morals when he has no ordinary means of living.

Kenko Hoshi (14th century)
Japanese Buddhist, *Sinclair, The Cry for Justice*

So long as people, being ill-governed, suffer from hunger, criminals will never disappear.

Kenko Hoshi (14th century)
Japanese Buddhist

When one man has his stomach full, it cannot satisfy every man.

Vai (Liberian) proverb

There is no god like one's
    stomach:
We must sacrifice to it every day.

Yoruba (West African) folk poem

133

When hunger gets inside you, nothing else can.

Yoruba (West African) proverb

on HYPOCRISY

The moment it was certain that the lion had been chained, sufficient words could not be found to damn him.

Madame Celeste Chateaubriand
(c. 19th century)
French salonist, in 1815, referring to the French abandonment of Napoleon once he had been defeated at Waterloo

Like beautiful flowers, full of colors but without scent, are the well-spoken words of the man who does not practice what he preaches.

Dhammapada (c. 3rd century B.C.E.)
collection of ancient Buddhist poems and aphorisms

The well-informed, but dishonest in their hostility and malice, often succeed in passing off lies as truth and in clothing deception in the guise of wisdom.

al-Jahiz (c. 778-869)
Arabic philosopher and writer, *The Exploits of the Turks and the Army of the Khalifate in General*

All the things we did for our
country.
Some of us died,
Some of us gave speeches.

Orhan Veli Kanik (1914-1950)
Turkish poet, "Varan icin" ("For the Homeland")

I always feel that I am bound in an iron chain while a foreman is whipping me on the back. No matter how hard I work, the whip will fall. When I turn my head and ask what are really my faults, the man will clasp his hands and politely shake them and say that I am doing an extremely fine job; that he and I are surely the best of friends; and what a fine day, ha, ha, ha.

Lu Xun (1881-1936)
Chinese writer

The false wise man, like an
ignorant physician,
a man without understanding,
claims to
know about God.
. . . .
He entangles things with
difficulties; he destroys them;
he causes the people to perish;
he mysteriously puts an
end to everything.

Nahuatl (Aztec) writing
from the *Codice Matritense de la Real Academia*

God hates the man who says one thing with his mouth and another with his mind.

Talmud
(late 4th-early 6th century)
ancient body of Jewish civil and canonical law, Pesahim 113b

Those who pretend to know what they don't, will be thought ignorant of even what they know.

Thiruvalluvar (c. 2nd century)
Indian Tamil writer, *Kural*

What is said over the dead lion's body could not be said to him alive.

Zairean proverb

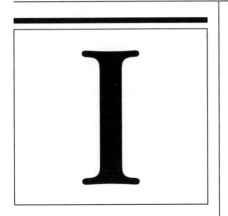

on **IDEALS**

"True men" . . . are strong willed, have dignity in their demeanor, serenity in their expression. They are cool like autumn, warm like spring. Their passions arise like the four seasons, in harmony with the ten thousand creatures, and no one knows their limits.

Chuang-tzu (c. 369-286 B.C.E.)
Chinese Taoist philosopher

The best preacher is the heart; the best teacher, time; the best book, the world; the best friend, God.

Hebrew proverb

Do not feel badly if your kindness is rewarded with ingratitude; it is better to fall from your dream clouds than from a third-story window.

Joaquim Maria Machado de Assis (1839-1908)
Brazilian writer, *Epitaph for a Small Winner*

He alone is entitled to be called a man who possesses a thoughtful nature and feels for others in the same way as he does for his own self; does not fear the unjust, however powerful, but fears the truly virtuous, however weak.

Dayananda Saraswati (1824-1883)
Indian Hindu religious leader and reformer

on **IDEAS**

Government cannot kill the liberty to think. The idea, the thought, lives forever.

Roman Baldorioty de Castro (1822-1887)
Puerto Rican politician

Ideas rise with new mornings but never die.

Frank Marshall Davis (b. 1905)
American writer, "I Sing No New Songs"

You can kill a man, but you can't kill an idea.

Medgar Evers (1926-1963)
American civil rights activist, "Freedom Journal"

A false idea is not only one which is absolutely subjective but one which is absolutely objective.

Aaron David Gordon (1856-1922)
Israeli writer

To make ideas effective, we must be able to fire them off. We must put them into action.

Virginia Woolf (1882-1941)
English writer

on **IDENTITY**

The basic tenet of black consciousness is that the black man must reject all value systems that seek to make him a foreigner in the country of his birth and reduce his basic human dignity.

> Steve Biko (1946-1977)
> South African political activist

A cat goes to a monastery, but she still remains a cat.

> Congo proverb

In the wind that blew last night,
Peach blossoms fell, scattered in
  the garden.
A boy came out with a broom,
Intending to sweep them away.
No, do not sweep them away, no,
  no.
Are fallen flowers not flowers?

> anonymous Korean poet (c. late
> 15th century)

Our wine is bitter, but it is our wine.

> José Martí (1853-1895)
> Cuban patriot

It seems as if
I'll never get beyond
the footprints that I made

> Qernertoq (c. 900-1400)
> Eskimo poet, "The Widow's Song"

Rose is a rose is a rose is a rose.

> Gertrude Stein (1874-1946)
> American writer

on IDEOLOGY

Black cat, white cat. What does it matter, as long as it catches mice?

> Deng Xiaoping (b. 1904)
> Chinese political leader and secretary-
> general of the Communist Party,
> debating the necessity for Communist
> orthodoxy

The thing which seems so glorious when viewed from the heights of the country's cause looks so muddy when seen from the bottom. One begins by getting angry and then feels disgusted.

> Rabindranath Tagore (1861-1941)
> Indian writer and philosopher

Since ideology is part of the human personality, it deserves a place in the kingdom of eternal truths.

> Abraham B. Yehoushua (b. 1936)
> Israeli writer

on IGNORANCE

Wisdom is prevented by ignorance, and delusion is the result.

> *Bhagavad Gita*
> (c. 4th-3rd century B.C.E.)
> teachings of Krishna from the Hindu
> epic, the *Mahabharata*

Ignorance alone is the prime cause of all misery.

> Chandrasekhara Bharati Swamigal
> (d. 1954)
> Hindu sage

Ignorance is the night of the mind, a night without moon or star.

> Confucius (551-479 B.C.E.)
> Chinese philosopher and founder of
> Confucianism, *Analects*

A man who has learned little grows old like an ox: his flesh grows, but not his mind.

> *Dhammapada* (c. 3rd century B.C.E.)
> collection of ancient Buddhist poems
> and aphorisms

Much that we hug today as knowledge is ignorance pure and simple.

. . . It makes the mind wander and even reduces it to a vacuity.

> Mohandas K. Gandhi (1869-1948)
> Indian spiritual and political leader, *The Gandhi Sutras: The Basic Teachings of Mahatma Gandhi*

Nothing in all the world is more dangerous than sincere ignorance and conscientious stupidity.

> Martin Luther King, Jr.
> (1929-1968)
> American civil rights leader, *Strength to Love*

To act without clear understanding, to form habits without investigation, to follow a path all one's life without knowing where it really leads—such is the behavior of the multitude.

> Mencius (c. 390-305 B.C.E.)
> Chinese philosopher, *Meng-tzu*

Man's life is subject to afflictions from ignorance, desire, aversion, ego, and attachment—ignorance being the root cause of all afflictions.

> Patanjali (240-180 B.C.E.)
> Indian philosopher

The world is fettered by the chain forged by superstition and ignorance.

> Dayananda Saraswati (b. 1824)
> Indian philosopher

The ignorant torment themselves more than they do others.

> Thiruvalluvar (c. 2nd century)
> Indian writer, *Kural*

on ILLNESS

The physician who is not wise is himself ill.

> Rasa'il al-Kindi (810-873)
> Arab philosopher and physician

It is not that you become soft [from illness] so much as that the world you live in expands and your awareness of it is enormously enlarged.

> Norman Washington Manley
> (1893-1969)
> Jamaican politician

There is no disease for which Allah has not sent a cure.

> Muhammad (570-632)
> Prophet of Islam

To this fool doctor no man need apply
For treatment if he does not wish to die.
At last to him the Death-Angel appears
Saying, "Buy now the goods you've sold for years!"

> 'Ubayd-i-Zakani (c. 14th century)
> Persian poet

on ILLUSION

Who is this person staring at me so sternly?
The martial bones I bring from a former existence
regret the flesh that covers them.
Once life is over, the body itself will be seen
to have been a deception.

> Qiu Jin (1874-1907)
> Chinese poet and activist, untitled, *Qiu Jin ji*

The truth is that God alone is real and all else unreal. Men, universe, house, children—all these are like the magic of the magician. The magician strikes his wand and says, "Come, delusion! Come, confusion!" Then he says to the audience, "Open the lid of this pot: see the birds fly into the sky." But the magician alone is real and his magic unreal. The unreal exists for a second and then vanishes.

> Ramakrishna (1836–1886)
> Indian Hindu mystic

Now they say that the world is unreal. Of what degree of unreality is it? Is it like that of a son of a barren mother or a flower in the sky—mere words without any reference to facts? Whereas the world is a fact, and not a mere word. The answer is that it is a superimposition on the one Reality, like the appearance of a snake on a coiled rope seen in the dim light.

> Ramana Maharshi (1879–1950)
> Indian Hindu religious leader

on IMAGINATION

A man who has no imagination has no wings.

> Muhammad Ali (b. 1942)
> American athlete

Imagination and fiction make up more than three quarters of our real life.

> Simone Weil (1909–1943)
> French philosopher, *Gravity and Grace*

on IMPERIALISM

All peoples have the right of self-determination.

> Afro-Asian declaration on colonialism
> overwhelmingly approved by the United Nations General Assembly (the United States and eight other nations abstained)

I wish I could bring Stonehenge to Nyasaland to show there was a time when Britain had a savage culture.

> Hastings Banda (b. 1906)
> Malawian politician

I am sending you out against the whites, who have invaded Zululand and driven away our cattle.

> Cetsahwayo (19th century)
> Zulu chief, speech to his mustered men at Ulundi, preparing to face the invading British, whom he defeated

Had there only been the protectorate and colonialism, everything would have been simple. Then my past, our past, would have been simple. No, Mr. Sartre, hell isn't others. It is also in ourselves.

> Driss Chraibi (b. 1926)
> Moroccan writer, on the source of Morocco's problems

Believe me, dear reader, our real national duty . . . is . . . to make Egyptians feel, individually and collectively, that God has created them for glory, not ignominy; strength, and not weakness; sovereignty, and not submission; renown, and not obscurity, and to remove from their hearts the hideous and criminal illusion that they are created from some other clay than Europeans, formed in some other way, and endowed with an intelligence other than theirs.

> Taha Husayn (1891-1973)
> Egyptian writer, *Mustaqbal al-thaqafa* (*The Future of Culture*)

Turk, Persian, Arab
intoxicated with Europe,
And in throat of each,
the fish hook of Europe.

> Muhammad Iqbal (1873-1938)
> Indian poet and philosopher,
> *Javidnama*

God said this is our land, land in which we flourish as a people. . . . We want our cattle to get fat on our land so that our children grow up in prosperity; and we do not want the fat removed to feed others.

> Jomo Kenyatta (1891-1978)
> Kenyan politician

When the missionaries arrived, the Africans had the land and the missionaries had the Bible. They taught us to pray with our eyes closed. When we opened them, they had the land and we had the Bible.

> Jomo Kenyatta (1891-1978)
> Kenyan politican

Listen, cause I'm going to translate the words of the White Man, the Toubab. And when the toubab talks, a nigger like you and me shuts up his mouth, puts off his hat, puts off his shoes, and listens. These words you got to know like the sourates of prayer, like the beads hanging over your favorite lady's ass.

> Ahmadou Kourouma (b. 1927)
> Ivory Coast writer

Being that the idea of getting civilized would never take root in no Black man's head, he has to be taught how to develop, he has to learn how to love money more than the hunt, more than friendship and fraternity, more than his women and children, more than the pardon of Allah.

> Ahmadou Kourouma (b. 1927)
> Ivory Coast writer

You have said that it is me that is killing you: Now here are your masters coming. . . . You will have to pull and shove wagons; but under me you never did this kind of thing.

> Ndebele Lobengula (1870-1896)
> Mashonaland king, last speech to his subjects after the British seized Mashonaland (1896)

America is a colonial power. She has colonized 22 million Afro-Americans by depriving us of first-class citizenship, by depriving us of civil rights, actually by depriving us of human rights.

> Malcolm X (1925-1965)
> American civil rights activist,
> *Malcolm X Speaks*

I have no intention of being an indifferent looker-on if the distant powers have the idea of dividing up Africa, for Ethiopia has been for more than fourteen centuries an island of Christians in the middle of the sea of pagans.

> Menelik (1849-1913)
> Ethiopian emperor, address to European powers (1891) in defiance of Italian colonization

If this [Suez] Canal be made, which nation of Europe should make use of it for their ships? Will it not be the English, in passing from their own country to their Indian empire and back again? And do you not think that when they come to see this beautiful garden of Egypt which is now my own, they will envy me its possession . . . and by using their ships . . . take possession of Egypt as they have done India?

> Muhammed 'Ali (1769-1849)
> Egyptian viceroy, on the proposed Suez Canal, which, once built, resulted in British control of Egypt

The English have come. . . . They have built a fort, they eat my land, and yet they have given me nothing at all.

> Mwanga II (c. 1866-1903)
> Bugandan king, after British arrival (1890)

The British, the Ethiopians, and
  the Italians are squabbling,
The country is snatched and
  divided by whosoever is
  stronger,
The country is sold piece by
  piece without our knowledge,
And for me, all this is the teeth of
  the last days of the world.

> Faarah Nuur (c. 1930)
> Somali clan leader and poet

Small nations are like indecently dressed women. They tempt the evil-minded.

> Julius K. Nyerere (b. 1922)
> Tanzanian politician

You have now become a great people, and we have scarcely a place left to spread our blankets.

> Red Jacket (c. 1758-1830)
> Seneca leader, to missionaries at Seneca, New York (1805)

It is us today. It will be you tomorrow.

> Haile Selassie (1892-1975)
> Ethiopian emperor, speech to the League of Nations

Go back home where you came from. This country is mine, and I intend to stay here and to raise this country full of grown people.

> Sitting Bull (c. 1834-1890)
> Dakota Sioux chief, in the *Report of the Commission of Indian Affairs to the Secretary of State* (1876)

What have we done that the American people want us to stop?

> Sitting Bull (c. 1834-1890)
> Dakota Sioux chief

Brothers! I have listened to a great many talks from our Great Father [President Andrew Jackson]. But they always began and ended in this: "Get a little farther; you are too near me." I have spoken.

> Speckled Snake (c. 19th century)
> Creek chief, speech when the U.S. government was urging the Creeks to move west of the Mississippi River (1829)

The rest of mankind is the carving knife . . . while we are the fish and the meat.

> Sun Yat-sen (1866-1925)
> Chinese military and political leader, on colonialism in China

I am the maker of my own fortune, and Oh! that I could make that of my Red People, and of my country, as great as the conceptions of my mind, when I think of the spirit that rules the universe. I would not then come to Governor Harrison to ask him to tear up the treaty, and to obliterate the landmark, but I would say to him, "Sir, you have the liberty to return to your own country."

Tecumseh (c. 1768-1813)
Shawnee chief

This our fatherland today and
  yesterday
Is pillaged by the foreign
  conquerors
Grown rich out of the spoil of
  nation on nation
Yet I and this whole line of ours
Who are black are left with
  nothing of nothing . . .

Thunder on, engines of the gold
  mines . . .
Roar on, only stop jarring on
  my ears,
I have served the white
  employers well
And now my soul weighs heavily
  on me . . .
Come, release my sleep, to rise
  far off
Far in the ancient birthplace
  of my race.

B. W. Vilakazi (1906-1947)
Zulu writer, "On the Gold Mines"

on **INDIVIDUALITY**

Do not resemble me—
Never be like a musk melon
Cut in two identical halves.

Matsuo Basho (1644-1694)
Japanese poet

Meeting people unlike oneself does not enlarge one's outlook; it only confirms one's idea that one is unique.

Elizabeth Bowen (1899-1973)
Irish writer, *The House in Paris*

It is beneath human dignity to lose one's individuality and become a mere cog in the machine.

Mohandas K. Gandhi (1869-1948)
Indian spiritual and political leader

Nobody walks with another man's gait.

Kikuyu (Kenyan) proverb

It is not necessary for eagles to be crows.

Sitting Bull (c. 1834-1890)
Dakota Sioux chief

on **INFINITY**

What is beyond the mind,
has no boundary,
In it our senses end.

Mira Bai (c. 1520)
Indian Hindu poet

There is a concept which corrupts and upsets all others. I refer not to Evil, whose limited realm is that of ethics; I refer to the infinite.

Jorge Luis Borges (1899-1986)
Argentinian writer, *Labyrinths*

How immense the high sky is!

Nguyen Du (1765-1820)
Vietnamese poet, *The Tale of Kieu*,
xxii, 93

On the seashore of endless worlds children meet.

The infinite sky is motionless
  overhead and the
  restless water is boisterous.
On the seashore of endless worlds
  the children meet
with shouts and dances.

> Rabindranath Tagore (1861–1941)
> Indian writer and philosopher, "On the
> Seashore," *The Crescent Moon*

on INTELLECTUALS

Intellect does not attain its full
force unless it attacks power.

> Madame de Staël (1766–1817)
> French writer, *De la littérature
> considerée dons ses rapports avec les
> institutions sociales (The Influence of
> Literature upon Society)*

Only those who know the supremacy of the intellectual life—the life
which has a seed of ennobling
thought and purpose within it—
can understand the grief of one
who falls from that serene activity
into the absorbing, soul-wasting
struggle with worldly annoyances.

> George Eliot (1819–1880)
> English writer, *Middlemarch*

What I was utterly convinced of,
and still am, is the idea that the
only responsibility the free intellectual has is vis-à-vis himself. He is
not responsible to either a political
party or a ruler.

> Tawfiq al-Hakim (b. 1902)
> Egyptian writer, *al Ta'aduliyya*

Swollen in head, weak in legs;
sharp in tongue, but empty in
belly.

> Mao Zedong (1893–1976)
> Chairman of People's Republic of
> China

Authors and actors and artists and
  such
Never know nothing, and never
  know much.

> Dorothy Parker (1893–1967)
> American writer, "Bohemia," *Sunset
> Gun*

on ISLAM

The first pillar on which the religion of Islam is built is that the idea
of divine unity should burnish the
human mind and cleanse it from
the weakness of illusion. Among
the most important of its bases is
the belief that God is alone in the
disposition of beings, single in the
creation of things which act and
those which are acted upon, and
that it is an obligation to cast aside
all belief that men or inanimate
bodies, whether higher or lower,
have any influence for good or evil
upon creation. . . . It is necessary
to reject any belief that God in the
Highest has appeared or appears in
the garb of humankind or any other
animal, to do good or ill; or that the
holy essence has suffered the extremes of pain or the pains of disease in certain phases, for the
benefit of any created thing.

> Jamal al-Din al-Afghani (1839–1897)
> Egyptian nationalist and religious leader

An Islamic reformation cannot be a
belated and poor copy of the European Christian model. It will have
to be an indigenous and authentically Islamic process if it is to be a
reformation at all.

> Abdullahi Ahmed An-Na'im
> (20th century)
> Sudanese social reformer

There is no end to its [the *Qur'an*'s] miracle; it is ever fresh and new to its reciters.

> Abu Hamid Muhammad al-Ghazali (1058-1111)
> Arab Islamic philosopher and theologian

The best Islam is to feed the hungry and to greet those whom you know—and those whom you do not know.

> Muhammad (570-632)
> Prophet of Islam

There is no God but God, and Muhammad is the Prophet of God.

> Muslim shahada, Islamic confession of faith

Oh you who believe, believe in God and his messenger and the book which he has revealed to his messenger and the book which he revealed before. And whoever disbelieves in God and his angels and his books and his messengers and the last day, he indeed strays far away.

> *Qur'an* (c. 610-656)
> sacred book of Islam, 4:36

Believers, fear God and trust his
  Apostle.
He will grant you a double
  measure of his
mercy; He will guide your steps
  with light
and will forgive you: God is the
  Compassionate,
the Merciful.

> *Qur'an* (c. 610-656)
> sacred book of Islam

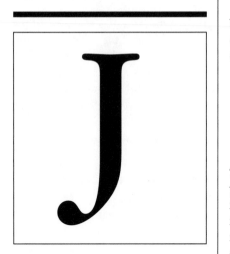

on **JOY**

I love the sound of the distant
   bugle call in the countryside in
   early morning
I love to be pushed in busy
   crowds
I love the sound of gongs and
   trumpets along the streets
I love circus performances
I even wish to die in this moment
   of glorious encounter.

> Ai Qing (b. 1910)
> Chinese poet, "Jintian" ("Today")

Ah-ho, where is your Daddy?
He points to a bird flying in the
   air.
Aha! So I am that flying bird!
Watch me outfly the white clouds,
Watch me race against the
   gleaming sails,
And see who flies the higher,
See who speeds the faster.

> Guo Moruo (1892-1978)
> Chinese writer, *The Goddesses*

What is a long life without joy,
compared with a short but joyful
one?

> Hsiang Hsiu (c. 250)
> Chinese philosopher, "Nan Yang-sheng
> lun" (Criticisms of the Text Concerning
> the Cultivation of Life), *Ch'uan Shang-
> ku San-tai Ch'in Han San-kuo Liu-
> chao wen*

The trick is not how much pain
you feel—but how much joy you
feel. Any idiot can feel pain. Life is
full of excuses to feel pain, excuses
not to live, excuses, excuses, excuses.

> Erica Jong (b. 1942)
> American writer

Occasionally in life there are those
moments of unutterable fulfillment
which cannot be completely explained by those symbols called
words. Their meanings can only be
articulated by the inaudible language of the heart.

> Martin Luther King, Jr.
> (1929-1968)
> American civil rights leader, upon
> receiving the Nobel Peace Prize at
> Oslo, Norway (December 11, 1964)

Men without joy seem like
corpses.

> Kathe Kollwitz (1867-1945)
> East Prussian artist

I have a faithful joy
and a joy that is lost.
One is like a rose,
the other, a thorn.
The one that was stolen
I have not lost.

> Gabriela Mistral (1889-1957)
> Chilean poet, "Richness," *Tala* (*Felling*)

Consider how shameful rejoicing
is,
Since it comes between two bouts
of woe.
You wept when you came into
this world,
And another will mourn you
when you go.

Samuel ha-Nagid (993–1056)
Spanish Hebrew poet, "Two Bouts of
Woe"

on JUDGMENT

Throw sugar to the parrot, but
place carrion before the wolf.

Kasim i Anwar (1356–1433)
Central Asian Herat poet

Do not judge others. Be your own
judge and you will be truly happy.
If you will try to judge others, you
are likely to burn your fingers.

Mohandas K. Gandhi (1869–1948)
Indian spiritual and political leader

A man remains over after death,
and his deeds are placed beside
him in heaps.

Instructions for Meri-ka-Re
(c. 2100 B.C.E.)
guide to personal conduct, behavior,
and social commitment supposedly
given to ancient Egyptian king Meri-ka-
Re by his father

God does not look at your ledger
figures or your wealth; he looks at
your deeds.

Muhammad (570–632)
Prophet of Islam

Gravedigger, tell me the truth

Surely there must be some
tribunal
Or are the worms our judges?

Nicanor Parra (b. 1914)
Chilean poet, *Poemas y antipoems*
(*Poems and Antipoems*)

Sugar and sand may be mixed together, but the ant rejects the sand
and goes off with the sugar grain;
so pious men lift the good from the
bad.

Ramakrishna (1836–1886)
Indian Hindu mystic

Judgment delayed is judgment
voided.

Talmud
(c. late 4th-early 6th century)
ancient body of Jewish civil and
canonical law, Sanhedrin 95

Do not judge your fellow man until
you have stood in his place.

Talmud
(c. late 4th-early 6th century)
ancient body of Jewish civil and
canonical law, Hillel

on JUSTICE

Forget not that the greatest curse
of a man is to remain a slave. Forget not that the grossest crime is to
compromise with injustice and
wrong. Remember the eternal law:
you must give, if you want to get.

Subhas Chandra Bose (1897–1945)
Indian nationalist leader

Justice can never be done in the
midst of injustice.

Simone de Beauvoir (1908–1986)
French writer and philosopher, *The
Second Sex*

145

These are the laws of justice which Hammurapi the able king has established. . . . That the strong may not oppress the weak, to give justice to the orphan and the widow, I have inscribed my precious words on my stele.

> Hammurapi (1792–1750 B.C.E.)
> Babylonian king

We will not be satisfied until justice rolls down like waters and righteousness like a mighty stream.

> Martin Luther King, Jr.
> (1929–1968)
> American civil rights leader, speech in Washington, D.C. (June 15, 1963)

Justice, being destroyed, will destroy; being preserved, will preserve; it must never, therefore, be violated.

> Manu (c. 1200 B.C.E.)
> Indian Hindu poet and ruler

When you cannot be just because of your nature, be so through your pride.

> Eugenio Maria de Hostos
> (1839–1903)
> Puerto Rican patriot

If you wish to know what justice is, let injustice pursue you.

> Eugenio Maria de Hostos
> (1839–1903)
> Puerto Rican patriot

Nature has placed the need to see justice done in some souls, and the need to flout and affront it in others.

> José Martí (1853–1895)
> Cuban patriot, "General Grant"

An unrectified case of injustice has a terrible way of lingering, restlessly, in the social atmosphere like an unfinished question.

> Mary McCarthy (1912–1989)
> American writer and critic, "My Confession," *On the Contrary*

Remember this: you can have justice, or you can have two dollars. But you can't have both.

> Luis Muñoz Marín (b. 1898)
> Puerto Rican politician

It is better to protest than to accept injustice.

> Rosa Parks (b. 1913)
> American civil rights activist

Absolute justice demands that men's incomes and rewards should . . . vary, and that some have more than others—so long as human justice is upheld by the provision of equal opportunity for all.

> Syed Qutb (d. 1966)
> Egyptian fundamentalist Islamic scholar, "Islamic Approach to Social Justice"

Come, let us
With the mangled kind
Make pact, no less
Against the lesser
Leagues of death, and mutilations
 of the mind.
Take justice
In your hands who can
Or dare.

> Wole Soyinka (b. 1934)
> Nigerian writer, "Flowers for My Land," *A Shuttle in the Crypt*

A man should not act as a judge either for someone he loves or for someone he hates. For no man can see the guilt of someone he loves or the good qualities in someone he hates.

Talmud
(c. late 4th-early 6th century)
ancient body of Jewish civil and
canonical law, Tractate Ketubbot

on JUSTIFICATION

How quick come the reasons for approving what we like!

Jane Austen (1775-1817)
English writer, *Persuasion*

When the ape cannot reach the ripe banana with its hand, he says it is sour.

Bambara (West African) proverb

Although bedbugs are unpleasant when they suck your blood, at least they bite you without a word, which is quite straightforward and frank. Mosquitoes are different. Of course, their method of piercing the skin may be considered fairly thoroughgoing; but before biting, they insist on making a long speech, which is irritating. If they are expounding on the reasons that make it right for them to feed on human blood, that is even more irritating. I am glad I do not know their language.

Lu Xun (1881-1936)
Chinese writer

People pretend . . . not to like grapes when they are too high for them to reach.

Marguerite of Navarre (1492-1549)
French writer and religious reformer,
"Novel LI, The Sixth Day," *The
Heptmeron, or Novels of the Queen of
Navarre*

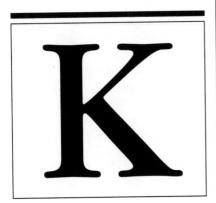

on KILLING

Those birds who are killed in
  skies
through stars, clouds, wind
  and the sun do not testify
against the murderers . . .

> Sherko Bekas (b. 1940)
> Kurdish poet, "The Roots"

A man's head is not like a scallion,
which will grow again if you cut it
off; if you cut it off wrongly, then
even if you want to correct your
error, there is no way of doing it.

> Mao Zedong (1893–1976)
> Chairman of People's Republic of
> China

I do not want them to get used to
shedding blood so young; at their
age they do not know what it
means to be a Muslim or an infidel,
and they will grow accustomed to
trifling with the lives of others.

> Saladin (1137–1193)
> Egyptian and Syrian sultan, when his
> children asked if they might execute a
> prisoner

In killing, I tried to make sure of
  men and myself

my
youthful way of proving was
  studded in colors of blood
but with
the blood of other men I couldn't
  paint away the blue
sky   I
need my own   I got it today . . .

> Tanikawa Shuntaro (b. 1931)
> Japanese poet, in a poem on Billy the
> Kid

on KNOWLEDGE

The thing that's important is that
you never know. You're always sort
of feeling your way.

> Diane Arbus (1923–1971)
> American photographer

Knowledge is wonderful and truth
  serene
But man in their service bleeds.

> Bhartrihari (c. 7th century)
> Indian Hindu poet and philosopher

All who worship ignorance enter
into blind darkness; those who delight in knowledge enter, as it
were, into greater darkness.

> *Brihadaranyaka Upanishad*
> (c. 700 B.C.E.)
> sacred philosophical Hindu literature

Inaction is the master of all knowledge. . . . Be empty: that is all. The
perfect man's use of his mind is
like a mirror. He does not antici-
pate [events], nor does he go
counter to them. He responds, but
he does not retain. Thus he is able
to master things and not be injured
by them.

> Chuang-tzu (c. 369–286 B.C.E.)
> Chinese Taoist philosopher

The essence of knowledge is, having it, to apply it; not having it, to confess your ignorance.

> Confucius (551–479 B.C.E.)
> Chinese philosopher and founder of Confucianism, *Analects*

I am not supposed to be an expert in every field. I am supposed to be an expert in picking experts.

> Moshe Dayan (1915–1981)
> Israeli military and political leader

What novelty is worth the sweet monotony where everything is known, and loved because it is known?

> George Eliot (1819–1880)
> English writer

It is knowledge that ultimately gives salvation.

> Mohandas K. Gandhi (1869–1948)
> Indian spiritual and political leader

Perplexity is the beginning of knowledge.

> Kahlil Gibran (1883–1931)
> Syrian writer, *The Voice of the Master*

My words are very easy to know, and very easy to practice. Yet all men in the world do not know them, nor do they practice them.
It is because they have knowledge, that they do not know me.

> Lao-tzu (c. 604–531 B.C.E.)
> Chinese philosopher and founder of Taoism, *Tao-te-ching*

If you think, "I know well," only slightly do you know!

> *Kena Upanishad* (c. 600–300 B.C.E.)
> sacred philosophical Hindu literature

Seek knowledge from the cradle to the grave.

> Muhammad (570–632)
> Prophet of Islam

Knowledge is the true organ of sight, not the eyes.

> *Panchatantra* (c. 5th century)
> collection of Hindu tales

To teach the evil-natured man knowledge and skill is to put a sword in the hand of a brigand.

> Rumi (1207–1273)
> Persian Sufi poet and mystic

What does it profit you that all the libraries of the world should be yours? Not knowledge but what one does with knowledge is your profit.

> Sa'ib of Tabriz (c. 1601–1677)
> Persian poet

Of what a strange nature is knowledge! It clings to the mind, when it has once seized on it, like a lichen on the rock.

> Mary Shelley (1797–1851)
> English writer, *Frankenstein*

Cooking is impossible without fire, and liberation is impossible without knowledge.

> Shenkara (788–820)
> Indian Hindu philosopher

Know the enemy and know yourself.

> Sun Tzu (c. 335–288 B.C.E.)
> Chinese military leader, *The Art of War*

Knowledge and action are really two words describing the same, one effort.

> Wang Yang-ming (1472–1529)
> Chinese philosopher

Not to know is bad; not to wish to know is worse.

> Wolof (West African) proverb

The power of knowledge can as easily bring progress in good as progress in evil.

> Wu Chih-hui (1864–1954)
> Chinese political theorist

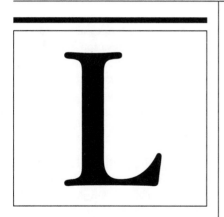

on **THE LAND**

If thou hast sown a seed—have
faith;
Or planted a tree—it will not die.
. . .
Every clod is a rock of strength
to us,
And every foot of soil an ageless
shield.

Levi Ben Amittai (b. 1901)
Israeli poet

And when not a bone or a tooth of
my people survives, you, you will
live on. You, my earth. No one will
conquer you. No one will kill you.

Driss Chraibi (b. 1926)
Moroccan writer

One does not sell the earth upon
which the people walk.

Crazy Horse (1842-1877)
Oglala Sioux chief

You work here [on the farm] simply, without philosophizing; sometimes the work is hard and
crowded with pettiness. But at
times you feel a surge of cosmic ex-

altation, like the clear light of the
heavens. . . . And you, too, seem
to be taking root in the soil which
you are digging, to be nourished
by the rays of the sun, to share life
with the tiniest blade of grass, with
each flower; living in nature's
depths, you seem then to rise and
grow into the vast expanse of the
universe.

Aaron David Gordon (1856-1922)
Israeli writer

Revolution is always based on land.
Revolution is never based on begging somebody for an integrated
cup of coffee.

Malcolm X (1925-1965)
American civil rights activist, *Malcolm
X Speaks*

No tribe has a right to sell, even to
each other, much less to strangers
. . . sell a country! Why not sell the
air, the great sea, as well as the
earth? Did not the Great Spirit
make them all for the use of his
children?

Tecumseh (c. 1768-1813)
Shawnee chief, to Governor W. H.
Harrison, protesting the land sales of
1805-1806

The way, and the only way, to stop
this evil is for all the red men to
unite in claiming a common and
equal right in the land, as it was at
first, and should be yet; for it was
never divided, but belongs to all
for the use of each.

Tecumseh (c. 1768-1813)
Shawnee chief, to Governor W. H.
Harrison at Vincennes, Indiana (1810)

on LANGUAGE

I feel that the English language will be able to carry the weight of my African experience. But it will have to be a new English, still in full communion with its ancestral home but altered to suit new African surroundings.

> Chinua Achebe (b. 1930)
> Nigerian writer

For there are some things
Which can only be said in song
Only in the mother tongue.

> Kobena Eyi Acquah (1884-1954)
> Ghanaian writer, "Ol' Man River"

If language be not in accordance with the truth of things, affairs cannot be carried on to success.

> Confucius (551-479 B.C.E.)
> Chinese philosopher and founder of Confucianism, *Analects*

European languages must not be considered diamonds displayed under a glass ball, dazzling us with their brilliance.

> Cheikh Anta Diop (b. 1923)
> Senegalese scholar

The poet's language is constructed not for the purpose of being understood but to be heard; it is an intermediary language between music and words, yet closer to music than to words.

> Ahmet Hasim (1885-1933)
> Turkish poet

A riot is at bottom the language of the unheard.

> Martin Luther King, Jr.
> (1929-1968)
> American civil rights leader

Words and sentences are produced by the law of causation and are mutually conditioning—they cannot express the highest Reality.

> *Lankavatara Sutra*
> (c. 1st-6th century)
> Buddhist scriptures originally written in Sanskrit

Every language in the world has something beautiful and something ugly about it, for language is nothing more than the expression of the activities, thoughts, and actions of human beings. There is naturally always something to blame and something to praise.

> Ahmad Faris al-Shidyaq (Faryaq)
> (1804-1887)
> Lebanese writer

Our language is primarily for expressing human goodness and beauty.

> Kawabata Yasunari (1899-1972)
> Japanese writer

Language is the mirror of a nation, the image of its civilization, the expression of its society, the picture of its character and peculiarities and the register of all the knowledge, technique, and arts it possesses. It fixes everything than can be expressed in language, everything that can be conceived in the mind or all those ideas which touch upon their sensual life.

> Ibrahim al-Yaziji (1847-1906)
> Lebanese scholar

LAST WORDS

Walk on!

> Buddha (c. 563-483 B.C.E.)
> Founder of Buddhism, last words to his disciples

All my possessions for a moment of time.

> Elizabeth I (1533-1603)
> English queen

Like a fossil tree
Which has borne not one blossom
Sad has been my life
Sadder still to end my days
Leaving no fruit behind me.

> Minamoto no Yorimasa (d. 1180)
> Japanese warrior, poem composed
> seconds before he committed ritual
> suicide. (In doing so, he represented
> the ideal Japanese warrior.)

In the depths of the ocean is our capital.

> Lady Nii (d. 1185)
> Japanese courtier, who dove into the
> ocean with the child emperor after the
> imperial forces lost the sea battle of
> Dannoura

What is the answer? In that case, what is the question?

> Gertrude Stein (1874-1946)
> American writer, response when her
> companion, Alice B. Toklas, asked
> "What is the answer?"

on LAW

To win a cat and lose a cow—the consequence of litigation.

> Chinese proverb

The law . . . has always been my sword and my shield.

> Benito Juárez (1806-1872)
> Mexican revolutionary and political
> leader

It is one thing to legislate and another to apply the laws.

> Benito Juárez (1806-1872)
> Mexican revolutionary and political
> leader

The moment you have protected an individual, you have protected society.

> Kenneth Kaunda (b. 1924)
> Zambian nationalist and politician

It may be true that the law cannot make a man love me, but it can keep him from lynching me, and I think that's pretty important.

> Martin Luther King, Jr.
> (1929-1968)
> American civil rights leader

The more laws and orders are multiplied, the more theft and violence increase.

> Lao-tzu (c. 604-531 B.C.E.)
> Chinese philosopher and founder of
> Taoism, *Tao-te-ching*

In university they don't tell you that the greater part of the law is learning to tolerate fools.

> Doris Lessing (b. 1919)
> English writer, *Martha Quest*

That which is lawful is clear, and that which is unlawful, likewise; but there are certain doubtful things between the two from which it is well to abstain.

> Muhammad (570-632)
> Prophet of Islam

A man's respect for law and order exists in precise relationship to the size of his paycheck.

> Adam Clayton Powell, Jr.
> (1908-1972)
> American politician and civil rights
> leader, *Keep the Faith, Baby!*

By God, he that is the weakest among you shall be in my sight the strongest until his rights have been assured for him; and he who is strongest shall be treated as the weakest until he complies with the law of Islam.

Umar ibn-al-Khattab (c. 581–644)
Arab Islamic leader and second caliph of Islam

Punish severely the light crimes. . . . If light offenses do not occur, serious ones have no chance of coming. This is said to be "ruling the people in a state of law and order."

Shang Yang (d. 338 B.C.E.)
Chinese philosopher and government official

on LAZINESS

The idea of passing one's whole life in moral idleness, and having one's hardest work and duty done by another—whether God or man—is most revolting to us, as it is most degrading to human dignity.

Elena Petrovna Blavatsky (1831–1891)
American spiritualist, *The Key to Theosophy*

Yield not to weaknesses that let the hours
Of duty pass. Though thou art palsied, walk,
And rise, though thou be broken; for thy lot
Is worthlessness, if thou defer resolve
Unto the day of health.

Ibn al'Farid (1181–1235)
Arab poet

Idleness leads to relaxation, sooner or later bringing about ideological and material corruption, accompanied by lack of discipline, anarchy, chaos and defeat.

Samora Machel (1933–1986)
Mozambiquen activist and politician

Clear my feet of indolence,
Keeper of the path of men.

Navajo prayer to the Mountain Spirit

See now, how your companions
lie in drunken slumber
in our land of sweet darkness,
what can they accomplish?
If you intend to make honey,
gather the sweetness from the flowers and make the honey.

Qu Junong (c. 20th century)
Chinese poet

on LEADERSHIP AND LEADERS

Obey me as I obey God and His Messenger; if I disobey them, then you should disobey me.

Abu-Bakr (c. 580–634)
Companion to the Prophet Muhammad and first caliph of Islam

A monarch should be ever intent on conquest; otherwise, his neighbors rise in arms against him.

Akbar (1542–1605)
Mughal Indian emperor

An imbecile can manage his own affairs better than a wise man the affairs of other people.

Arabic proverb

I have always felt it was a handicap for oppressed peoples to depend so largely upon a leader, because unfortunately in our culture, the charismatic leader usually becomes a leader because he has found a spot in the public limelight. It usually means he has been touted through the public media, which means that the media made him, and the media may undo him.

Ella Baker (1903-1986)
American civil rights activist

The movement of history is a race we must win, and the leaders have an important part to play in winning this race. Through their wisdom, patience, and imagination, they can direct the course of events and speed up the pace of evolution.

Habib ibn Ali Bourguiba (b. 1903)
Tunisian politician

It is easy to get a thousand soldiers, but difficult to get a general.

Chinese proverb

A ship with two captains sinks.

Egyptian proverb

Though God hath raised me high, yet this I count the glory of my crown: that I have reigned with your love.

Elizabeth I (1533-1603)
English queen, to a deputation from the House of Commons (1601)

Of myself I must say this, I never was any greedy, scraping grasper, nor a strait fast-holding prince, nor yet a master; my heart was never set on worldly goods, but only for my subjects' good.

Elizabeth I (1533-1603)
English queen, to a deputation from the House of Commons (1601)

Must! Is *must* a word to be addressed to princes? Little man, little man! Thy father, if he had been alive, durst not have used that word.

Elizabeth I (1533-1603)
English queen, to Robert Cecil, from her death bed

How can anybody who is the head of a nation afford not to be a pragmatist?

Indira Gandhi (1917-1984)
Indian prime minister

To me rule [is] not merely a crown or a mace but an honorable service.

Hussein (b. 1935)
Jordanian king

He who finds a new path is a pathfinder, even if the trail has to be found again by others; and he who walks far in advance of his contemporaries is a leader, even though centuries may pass before he is recognized as such and intelligently followed.

Ibn Khaldun (1332-1406)
Arab historian and philosopher

Everyone who leads large masses of people and is excessively idolized by them must be vigorously opposed, however enlightened or holy he may be, irrespective of his office or profession.

K'ang Yu-wei (1858-1927)
Chinese political philosopher

Anyone who wants to be a leader must be the servant, not the boss, of those he wants to serve.

> Aminu Kano (b. 1920)
> Nigerian politician

Of the best rulers
The people (only) know that they exist;
The next best they love and praise;
The next they fear;
And the next they revile.

When they do not command the people's faith,
Some will lose faith in them,
And then they resort to oaths!
But (of the best) when their task is accomplished, their work done,
The people all remark, "We have done it ourselves."

> Lao-tzu (c. 604–531 B.C.E.)
> Chinese philosopher and founder of Taoism

Young people, what need have you to follow the trendy slogans of these intellectual leaders? You ought better to gather some comrades and pool together all your energies; go forward in one common impetus, following what appears to be the path of survival. All together you will never be short of strength. If you encounter a deep forest, you can always hack your way through; you can open up the wilderness; you can dig wells in the desert. Why should you stick to old ruts and beg for guidance of these wretched guides?

> Lu Xun (1881–1936)
> Chinese writer

A leader who doesn't hesitate before he sends his nation into battle is not fit to be a leader.

> Golda Meir (1898–1978)
> Israeli politician

Dogs and pigs in your realm feed on the food of your subjects, but you do not restrain them. People are starving on your roads, but you do not open your granaries. When people die as a result, you say, "It is not my fault; it is a bad year." How is this different from stabbing a man to death and saying, "It is not my fault; it is the sword"? If your majesty would stop putting blame on the year, people throughout the empire would come to you.

> Mencius (c. 390–305 B.C.E.)
> Chinese philosopher, giving advice to a king of the Warring States

A people only become unmanageable when one tries to lead them with a violent love. . . . But if one approaches them with trust and takes them by the hand, if one lures them forward with riches and drives them from behind with just punishment . . . there will not be a single one who will not adapt himself to the ruler.

> Mo-tze (c. 5th century B.C.E.)
> Chinese philosopher

I apply not my lash where my tongue suffices, nor my sword where my whip is enough. And if there be one hair binding me to my fellow men, I let it not break. If they pull, I loosen; and if they loosen, I pull.

> Mu'awiyah (c. 602–680)
> Islamic religious and military leader

If people work together, they must act in an orderly way. If everyone were to do just what he pleased, there would not be much of the tribe left. So someone has to become the leader.

Jawaharlal Nehru (1889-1964)
Indian prime minister

Blindness in a leader is unpardonable.

Jawaharlal Nehru (1889-1964)
Indian prime minister

I have come out of brambles and thorns, paid with my skin to chase the aggressors. I have worn a coat of armor and slept in fields. I have known peril and danger, braved sabers and swords, and swept aside clouds and hurricanes to found the Empire and the price of innumerable difficulties. You who, because of my work, will succeed me, must not seek pleasure.

Nguyen Trai (1380-1442)
Vietnamese poet, advice for the crown prince written in the name of the first Le king

Whether it be to promote a talented man, to receive criticism, to develop policy, or merely to pronounce a single word or make a single gesture, keep the rule of the Golden Mean. . . . To hold in esteem those who possess the virtue of humanity is to be assured of the consent of the people who bear the throne, like the ocean which carries the ship but can also overturn it.

Nguyen Trai (1380-1442)
Vietnamese poet, advice for the crown prince written in the name of the first Le king

Some people have wondered if I didn't have a feeling that I was a man of destiny and that great forces were at work on me. No, I never had that feeling. I was ashamed. I wanted to do what was good rather than what was bad.

U Nu (b. 1907)
Burmese politician and first prime minister of Burma

Governors must never forget that he who is unable to run his own house and family is still less competent to be entrusted with public matters.

Pachacutec Inca Yupanqui
(1438-1471)
Incan ruler

I am here by the will of the Great Spirit, and by his will I am a chief. My heart is red and sweet, and I know it is sweet because whatever passes near me puts out its tongue to me; and yet you men have come here to talk with us, and you say you do not know who I am. I want to tell you that if the Great Spirit has chosen anyone to be the chief of this country, it is myself.

Sitting Bull (c. 1834-1890)
Dakota Sioux chief, to Senator Henry L. Dawes (1883)

It is no easy task to lead men. But it is easy enough to drive them.

Rabindranath Tagore (1861-1941)
Indian writer and philosopher

I never give answers. I lead on from one question to another. That is my leadership.

Rabindranath Tagore (1861-1941)
Indian writer and philosopher

In the beginnings of mankind, probably no one was pleased about becoming king. If someone was unlucky enough to win the hearts of the people, he could not really refuse the throne.

> Teng Mu (1247-1306)
> Chinese writer, "Po-ya ch'in" ("The Lute of Po-ya")

If the ruler claims as his own what people desire, and retains for himself alone what everyone longs for, he teaches the people to steal and deceive by his example.

> Teng Mu (1247-1306)
> Chinese writer, "Po-ya ch'in" ("The Lute of Po-ya")

I don't mind how much my ministers talk—as long as they do what I say.

> Margaret Thatcher (b. 1925)
> English prime minister

It is necessary to a king that he adhere to justice in all his actions, and that he receive into his service ministers who are just and virtuous. . . . If the minister be unjust and cruel, it shall be speedily come to pass that the edifice of his master's power and dominion shall be leveled with the earth.

> Timur (1336-1405)
> Turkic conqueror

I am leader by default, only because nature does not allow a vacuum.

> Desmond Tutu (b. 1931)
> South African antiapartheid activist and religious leader

When his horse is uneasy harnessed to a carriage, a gentleman is not comfortable in it. When the common people are uneasy under a government, a gentleman is not comfortable in his post. . . . It is traditionally said that the ruler is like a boat and the common people are the water. Water supports the boat but may also upset it.

> Xunzi (300-235 B.C.E.)
> Chinese philosopher

You cannot salvage the situation with strong leadership alone. You have to have strong followers to support the leadership
. . . .
You have to have them all with you before you can push a revolution to a successful conclusion.

> Zhou En-lai (1898-1976)
> Chinese revolutionary and prime minister of the People's Republic

The young viper grows as it sits,
Always in a great rage,
With a shield on its knees.

> Zulu poem
> in praise of Shaka, the greatest Zulu king (early 19th century)

on LEARNING AND EDUCATION

Learning is not attained by chance. It must be sought for with ardor and attended to with diligence.

> Abigail Adams (1744-1818)
> American First Lady and feminist

I say most unambiguously that on the Day of Judgement, God will say, "You were the educated. Why did you not stop the ignorant ones from straying into sin?" Thus, on

Judgement Day the educated will be held responsible.

> Sir Sayyid Ahmad Khan
> (1817-1898)
> Indian Islamic reformer and educator

Learn about a pine tree from a pine tree, and about a bamboo plant from a bamboo plant.

> Matsuo Basho (1644-1694)
> Japanese poet

. . . from your youth up cultivate education,
And you will keep on finding wisdom until you are gray.
Approach her like a man who plows and sows,
And wait for her abundant crops.
For in cultivating her, you will toil but little,
And soon you will eat her produce.

> Ben Sira (c. 2nd century B.C.E.)
> Hebrew scholar and philosopher, *The Wisdom of Ben Sira*

I am convinced that we must train not only the head, but the heart and hand as well.

> Madame Chiang Kai-shek (b. 1897)
> Chinese politician, *This Is Our China*

Give a man a fish and you feed him for a day. Teach a man to fish and you feed him for a lifetime.

> Chinese proverb

Learning without thought is useless. Thought without learning is dangerous.

> Confucius (551-479 B.C.E.)
> Chinese philosopher, founder of Confucianism, *Analects*

The children need the bread of the mind.

> Rafael Cordero y Molina
> (1790-1868)
> Puerto Rican educator

There can be no education without leisure; and without leisure, education is worthless.

> Sarah Josepha Hale (1788-1879)
> American writer and editor

Be not strict to the extent of stifling his faculties or lenient to the point of making him enjoy idleness and accustom himself thereto. Straighten him as much as thou canst through kindness and gentleness, but fail not to resort to force and severity should he not respond.

> Harun al-Rashid (763-809)
> Islamic Arab ruler, instructions given to the tutor of his son

The literary and martial arts are, it is unnecessary to say, to be practiced always. The ancient rule declares that letters are the left hand and militarism the right. Neither must be neglected.

> Hojo Soun (c. 1519)
> Japanese samurai, "Twenty-one Articles of Advice" to his son

If you plan for a year, plant a seed. If for ten years, plant a tree. If for a hundred years, teach the people. When you sow a seed once, you will reap a single harvest. When you teach the people, you will reap a hundred harvests.

> Kuan Chung (c. 643-600 B.C.E.)
> *Kuan Tze*

That is what learning is. You suddenly understand something you've understood all of your life, but in a new way.

> Doris Lessing (b. 1919)
> English writer, *The Four-Gated City*

I remember as a young man striving for an education how I walked three kilometers back and forth from the slums . . . to the state university. . . . I would walk that distance under the rain, starved, sleepy, shivering, and with the raindrops mixing with the tears on my cheeks, but I stood it all because as a poor boy, like the children of the countless miserable families in our country today, I also dreamed of a better life for myself.

> Diosdado Macpagal (b. 1910)
> Philippine politician

A segregated school system produces children who, when they graduate, graduate with crippled minds.

> Malcolm X (1925-1965)
> American civil rights activist,
> *Malcolm X Speaks*

Seek learning, though it be as far as China.

> Muhammad (570-632)
> Prophet of Islam

Learning is the best of all wealth; it is easy to carry, thieves cannot steal it, and tyrants cannot seize it; neither fire nor water can destroy it; and far from decreasing, it increases by giving.

> *Naladiyar* (c. 5th-6th century)
> Tamil ethical literature

My education finished 9th July.

Whatever moral good and general knowledge I may have got from it, I have retained no literal rules. I don't believe I can repeat a single line of any language. . . . I regret German very much, French I can read alone, history is still going on, the rules of geography and grammar are tiresome, there is no general word to express the feelings I have always entertained towards arithmetic.

> Beatrix Potter (1866-1943)
> English writer and illustrator, diary
> entry (July 10, 1885)

The first problem for all of us, men and women, is not to learn, but to unlearn.

> Gloria Steinem (b. 1934)
> American feminist, "A New Egalitarian
> Life Style"

He who learns when a child, unto what is he to be compared? Unto ink written upon a new writing sheet; and he who learns when an old man, unto what is he like? Unto ink written on a rubbed writing sheet.

> *Talmud*
> (c. late 4th-early 6th century)
> ancient body of Jewish civil and
> canonical law, Aboth, 4:20

Untilled soil, however fertile it may be, will bear thistles and thorns; and so it is with man's mind.

> Teresa of Avila (1515-1582)
> Spanish nun, "Maxims for Her Nuns"

A university must have a social conscience.

> Desmond Tutu (b. 1931)
> South African antiapartheid activist and
> religious leader

Learning stamps you with its moments. Childhood's learning is made up of moments. It isn't steady. It's a pulse.

> Eudora Welty (b. 1909)
> American writer, *One Writer's Beginnings*

Only that education deserves emphatically to be termed cultivation of the mind which teaches young people how to begin to think.

> Mary Wollstonecraft (1759-1797)
> English feminist, "On National Education," *A Vindication of the Rights of Women*

on LEISURE

Only those who take leisurely what the people of the world are busy about can be busy about what the people of the world take leisurely.

> Chang Ch'ao (c. 1676)
> Chinese writer

Life is short. Work only pleases those who will never understand it. Idleness cannot degrade anybody. It differs greatly from laziness.

> René Maran (1887-1960)
> Martinican writer

on LIBERTY

The most serious problem seems to be that, in itself, political independence is totally inadequate if it is not accompanied by stability and economic security and genuine personal liberty.

> Abu Bakar Tafawa Balewa (1912-1966)
> Nigerian politician

Nature, in truth, endows us at birth with the instinctive desire for liberty; but whether because of negligence, or because of an inclination inherent in humanity, it remains still under the bonds imposed on it.

> Simón Bolívar (1783-1830)
> South American revolutionary leader

The majority of men hold as a truth the humiliating principle that it is harder to maintain the balance of liberty than to endure the weight of tyranny.

> Simón Bolívar (1783-1830)
> South American revolutionary leader

I believe in Liberty for all men: the space to stretch their arms and their souls; the right to breathe and the right to vote, the freedom to choose their friends, enjoy the sunshine, and ride on the railroads, uncursed by color; thinking, dreaming, working as they will in a kingdom of beauty and love.

> W. E. B. Du Bois (1868-1963)
> American writer and educator, *Darkwater: Voices from within the Veil*

The first teacher of nations, the one who produces all the others and whom all the others cannot produce is Liberty!

> Mustafa Fazil (1830-1875)
> Egyptian prince, "Manifeste de la Jeune Turquie," an open letter to the Sultan Abdul 'Aziz, published in *Liberté* (March 24, 1867)

Liberty, oh Liberty, what crimes are committed in thy name!

> Marie Jeanne Roland (1754-1793)
> French revolutionary, before her execution

I have one abiding religion—human liberty.

> Wole Soyinka (b. 1934)
> Nigerian writer

Let us remember that no blessing of God is so sweet as life and liberty. Let us remember that the stature of all mankind is diminished so long as nations or parts of nations are still unfree. Let us remember that the highest purpose of man is the liberation of man from his bonds of fear, his bonds of human degradation, his bonds of poverty—the liberation of man from the physical, spiritual, and intellectual bonds which for too long stunted the development of mankind's majority.

> Achmad Sukarno (1902-1970)
> Indonesian politician

I have never considered that when men have gained their liberty they have the right to live in idleness and create disorder.

> François Dominique Toussaint-
> L'Ouverture (1743-1803)
> Haitian revolutionary leader

There was one of two things I had a right to—liberty or death. If I could not have one, I would have the other, for no man should take me alive. I should fight for my liberty as long as my strength lasted, and when the time came for me to go, the Lord would let them take me.

> Harriet Ross Tubman (1820-1913)
> American abolitionist

on LIES

One falsehood spoils a thousand truths.

> Ashanti (West African) proverb

The whole world is absolutely brought up on lies. We are fed nothing but lies. We begin with lies, and half our lives we live with lies. Most human beings waste some twenty-five to thirty years of their lives before they break through the actual and conventional lies which surround them.

> Isadora Duncan (1877-1927)
> American dancer

Society can only exist on the basis that there is some amount of polished lying and that no one says exactly what he thinks.

> Lin Yutang (1895-1976)
> Chinese writer

Avenging spies pursue men's falsehoods closely.

> *Rig-Veda* (c. 1000 B.C.E.)
> Hindu sacred literature

All warfare is based on deception.

> Sun Tzu (c. 335-288 B.C.E.)
> Chinese military leader, *The Art of War*

This is the punishment of a liar: he is not believed, even when he speaks the truth.

> *Talmud*
> (c. late 4th-early 6th century)
> ancient body of Jewish civil and
> canonical law, Sanhedrin 29

on **LIFE**

For a lifetime people struggle
To prolong their mortal lives.

al-Akhtal (645-713)
Arab Christian poet

The earth is a beehive; we all enter by the same door but live in different cells.

Bantu proverb

Through the years, a man peoples a space with images of provinces, kingdoms, mountains, bays, ships, islands, fishes, rooms, tools, stars, horses, and people. Shortly before his death, he discovers that the patient labyrinth of lines traces the image of his own face.

Jorge Luis Borges (1899-1986)
Argentinian writer

People have to choose something decently constant to depend on, thought Maud Martha. People must have something to lean on. . . . Was, perhaps, the whole life of a man a dedication to this search for something to lean upon, and was, to a great degree, his "happiness" or "unhappiness" written up for him but the demands or limitations of what he chose for that work?
   For work it was. Leaning was a work.

Gwendolyn Brooks (b. 1917)
American writer, *Maud Martha*

It is Heaven's role to declare a man's destiny; it is man's role to shorten or lengthen his days.

Chinese proverb

One must choose in life between boredom and torment.

Madame de Staël (1766-1817)
French writer, letter to Claude Rochet (1800)

Few men reach the other shore. The rest run up and down this side of the torrent.

Dhammapada (c. 3rd century B.C.E.)
collection of ancient Buddhist poems and aphorisms

Me, you—we're no more than travelers.

Mohammed Dib (b. 1920)
Algerian writer

Believe in life! Always human beings will live and progress to greater, broader, and fuller life.

W. E. B. Du Bois (1868-1963)
American writer and educator

A crust of bread and a corner to
   sleep in,
A minute to smile and an hour to
   weep in,
A pint of joy to a peck of trouble,
And never a laugh but the moans
   come double;
   And that is life.

A crust and a corner that love
   makes precious,
With a smile to warm and the
   tears to refresh us;
And joy seems sweeter when
   cares come after,
And a moan is the finest of foils
   for laughter;
   And that is life.

Paul Laurence Dunbar (1872-1906)
American writer, "Life"

163

That . . . is how the world moves: Not like an arrow, but a boomerang.

> Ralph Ellison (1914-1994)
> American writer, *Invisible Man*

Life is but an endless series of experiments.

> Mohandas K. Gandhi (1869-1948)
> Indian spiritual and political leader

Life becomes livable only to the extent that death is treated as a friend, never as an enemy.

> Mohandas K. Gandhi (1869-1948)
> Indian spiritual and political leader

Life/personality must be taken as a total entity. All of your life is all of your life, and no one incident stands alone.

> Nikki Giovanni (b. 1943)
> American writer, *Gemini*

I look back on my life like a good day's work; it was done and I am satisfied with it.

> Grandma Moses (1860-1961)
> American artist

The life of man is long, perhaps
  longer than necessary
Or perhaps it is shorter than
  necessary?

> Nazim Hikmet (1902-1963)
> Turkish poet

Born like a lily in the garden
I grew like a lily
And when the time came,
I withered
And died.

> Inca elegy (15th century)
> thought to be the epitaph of the great

Inca leader Pachacutec Inca Yupanqui (1438-1471)

Life is a struggle and not a matter of privilege. It is nothing but one's knowledge of the temporal and the spiritual world.

> Muhammad Iqbal (1873-1938)
> Indian poet and philosopher

The time of life is borrowed,
in an instant it must be left
  behind.

> Ixtilxochitl (c. 1550)
> Aztec king, *Obras Historicas (History of the Chichimec Nation)*

The light of life is faint. Its presence always draws on procreation.

> Yusuf Al-Khal (b. 1917)
> Lebanese poet and teacher

The end of living is the true enjoyment of it.

> Lin Yutang (1895-1976)
> Chinese writer

Life is too short to make an overserious business out of it.

> Lin Yutang (1895-1976)
> Chinese writer

Life is a gift, given in trust—like a child.

> Anne Morrow Lindbergh (b. 1906)
> American writer and aviator

An atom tossed in a chaos made
Of yeasting worlds, which bubble
  and foam.
Whence have I come?
What would be home?
I hear no answer. I am afraid!

> Amy Lowell (1874-1925)
> American writer, "The Last Quarter of the Moon," *Sword Blades and Poppy Seeds*

Life is seething before your eyes; corner stones collapse, illusions evaporate, truths come tottering like bombs, elements disintegrate demanding new components, new voices destroy the walls of muteness and rise, species amalgamate, forces are set free from their hiding places, and conscience asks its possessor to take a stand; Hold on . . . escape . . . live . . . die . . . complicate yourself . . . renew yourself . . . There is no other way than to wade into the waves of darkness and to swim to the shore of light.

> Naguib Mahfouz (b. 1911)
> Egyptian writer, "Hikaya bila Bidaya wa la Nihaya" ("Stories of Beginnings and Endings")

With flowers you write
Giver of Life.
With songs you give color,
With songs you shade
those who live here on earth.
Later you will erase eagles and tigers.
We exist only in your book
while we are here on earth.

> Mexica song-poem (c. 16th century)

Life is a quest and love a quarrel . . .

> Edna St. Vincent Millay
> (1892-1950)
> American poet, "Weeds," *Second April*

Life has no friend . . .

> Edna St. Vincent Millay
> (1892-1950)
> American poet, "Fatal Interview," *Fatal Interview*

It's not true that life is one damn thing after another—it's one damn thing over and over.

> Edna St. Vincent Millay
> (1892-1950)
> American poet

Where are we going?
We came only to be born.
Our home is beyond:
In the realm of the defleshed ones.

> Nahuatl (Aztec) poem
> in the *Coleccion de Canteres Mexicanos* (c. 1500s)

The phenomena of life may be likened unto a dream, a phantasm, a bubble, a shadow, the glistening dew, or lightning flash, and thus they ought to be contemplated.

> *Prajna-Paramita* (Diamond Sutra)
> (c. 868)
> Buddhist text

Life is indistinct,
A momentary sweeping light or fleeting shadow.
The morning is cool and cold dew freezes,
The tepid sun spreads like a disease
The dew melts—the wonderful mystery of life—
But the stream of inexhaustible treasury of meanings is not seen
And also the least particle in the mighty whirl.
Will you come to grasp, through the cracks, the meaning of all that?

> Qu Qiubai (1899-1935)
> Chinese poet and revolutionary, *Wenji*

Life was meant to be lived, and curiosity must be kept alive. One must never, for whatever reason, turn one's back on life.

Eleanor Roosevelt (1884–1962)
American humanitarian and First Lady

The illusion of art is to make one believe that great literature is very close to life, but the exact opposite is true. Life is amorphous, literature is formal.

Françoise Sagan (b. 1935)
French writer

I want to take my rightful share of life by force, I want to give lavishly, I want love to flow from my heart, to ripen and bear fruit. There are many horizons that must be visited, fruit that must be plucked, books read, and white pages in the scrolls of life in which to inscribe vivid sentences in a bold hand.

al-Tayyib Salih (b. 1929)
Sudanese writer, *Mawsimal-Hijra ila al-Shamal (Season of Migration)*

I shall live because there are a few people I want to stay with for the longest possible time and because I have duties to discharge. It is not my concern whether or not life has meaning.

al-Tayyib Salih (b. 1929)
Sudanese writer, *Mawsimal-Hijra ila al-Shamal (Season of Migration)*

Persons who merely have-a-life customarily move in a dense fluid. That's how they're able to conduct their lives at all. Their living depends on not seeing.

Susan Sontag (b. 1933)
American writer and critic, *Death Kit*

Some say that life has no form, that it is extremely diffuse. I think I can agree with them. . . . A life without conclusions is painful.

Natsume Soseki (1867–1916)
Japanese writer

Life itself is a strange mixture. We have to take it as it is, try to understand it, and then to better it.

Rabindranath Tagore (1861–1941)
Indian writer and philosopher

Life is a sea. We are the ships. Let us go straight to harbor.

Lucie Campbell Williams (1885–1962)
American educator

Life's bare as a bone.

Virginia Woolf (1882–1941)
English writer, "An Unwritten Novel," *Monday or Tuesday*

on LIMITATIONS

Within his own house every beggar is an emperor: do not overstep your own limit and be a king.

Sa'ib of Tabriz (c. 1601–1677)
Persian poet

I do not tell you to detach your heart from the total of world: detach your heart from whatever lies beyond your reach.

Sa'ib of Tabriz (c. 1601–1677)
Persian poet

on LISTENING

Give your ears, hear what is said. . . . At a time when there is a whirlwind of words, they will be a mooring-stake for your tongue.

Amen-em-Opet (c. 1200 B.C.E.)
Egyptian scribe, "Instruction of Amen-em-Opet"

Do you not hear the chirping of the noisy birds? And the churning of the curd by the cowherds' wives to the jingle of the bracelets?

Andal (c. 9th century)
Indian poet

If you love to hear, you will
 receive,
And if you listen, you will be
 wise.

Ben Sira (c. 2nd century B.C.E.)
Hebrew scholar and philosopher, *The Wisdom of Ben Sira*

on LONELINESS

Darkness and a passing word rake me.
I shiver, and so does the great room where the one I want is lying
The night sinks in, the trees are as dead as columns of stone
. . . .
My body is quiet and alone, the tale and time
go stiffly, icily by.

Chairil Anwar (1922–1949)
Indonesian poet, *The Captured and the Freed*

The heaven's blue expanse
 stretched like a curtain
With tiny stars, uncounted
 gleaming pearls;
Winds moving dreamlike in the
 tranquil darkness

And brooding in them still the
 peace of God,
With hints and whispers faint, like
 secret kisses,
With revelation fraught, stirring
 the grass;
And sleep that heals and sleep
 that soothes and comforts—
These are not for me, the outcast,
 not for me . . .

Chiam Nachman Bialik
(1873–1934)
Israeli writer, "Scroll of Fire"

What loneliness is more lonely than distrust?

George Eliot (1819–1880)
English writer, *Middlemarch*

I grow lean
in loneliness
like a water lily
gnawed by a beetle

Kaccipettu Nannakalyar
(3rd century)
Indian Tamil poet, "What She Said"

Loneliness is dangerous . . . because if aloneness does not lead to God, it leads to the devil. It leads to the self.

Joyce Carol Oates (b. 1938)
American writer, "Shame," *The Wheel of Love and Other Stories*

So lonely am I
My body is a floating weed
Severed at the roots
Were there water to entice me
I would follow it, I think.

Ono no Komachi (c. 850)
Japanese poet

Every time I think of living as a member of society, according to the organization of society, I become unpleasantly aware that from first to last man lives his life alone, by himself.

> Akiyama Shun (b. 1930)
> Japanese writer, "The Simple Life"

Tired of humanity and its heritage
Laden with a tiny heart emptied
 of its contents,
We wander each in his own way,
 purposeless and
 helpless. . . .

> Saul Tchernichovsky (1875–1944)
> Israeli poet

Being unwanted, unloved, uncared for, forgotten by everybody, I think that is a much greater hunger, a much greater poverty than the person who has nothing to eat.

> Mother Teresa (b. 1910)
> Yugoslavian missionary

Beyond the curtain of lianas, the
 rain falls ceaselessly.
Nostalgic atmosphere, endless
 night.
I seem to hear the faint sound of
 footsteps;
I am alone . . . unspeakable
 misery . . .

> Vu Hoang-Chuong (b. 1916)
> Vietnamese poet, "Nuages"

on LONGING

It seems to me we can never give up longing and wishing while we are thoroughly alive. There are certain things we feel to be beautiful and good, and we must hunger after them.

> George Eliot (1819–1880)
> English writer

But for my sighs, I should be drowned by my tears; and but for my tears, I should be burned by my sighs.

> Ibn al'Farid (1181–1235)
> Arab poet

Clean is the autumn wind,
Splendid the autumn moon,
The blown leaves are heaped and
 scattered,
The ice-cold raven starts from its
 roost.
Dreaming of you—when shall I
 see you again?
On this night sorrow fills my
 heart.

> Li Po (701–762)
> Chinese poet, "Verses"

I try to forget, but it is in vain.
I try to go, but I have no way.

> Po Chu-i (772–846)
> Chinese poet, "To the Distant One"

. . . The heart was weary with
 dreams,
He was foot-sore with wandering,
 but respite had
 not yet come.
How sweet is rest! But his weary
 heart still pounded
 and pounded.
With longings ungratified . . .

> David Shimoni (b. 1886)
> Israeli poet, "In the Woods of Hedera"

on LOSS

But there is always this feeling of
  having lost something . . .
What is it that you lost?
What is it?

> Bian Zhilin (b. 1910)
> Chinese poet, "Zhongnanhai," *Sanqiu
> cao* (*Leaves of Three Autumns*)

Man, nourished by years and
  women's bodies,
When God despoils you, you
  kneel,
And only the memory of things
Sheds a vain warmth on your
  empty hands.

> Jorge Carrera Andrade (b. 1903)
> Ecuadoran writer, "Nada Nos
> Pertenece" ("Nothing Belongs to Us"),
> *Pais secreto* (*Secret Country*)

An Immortal said: "In playing chess,
there is no infallible way of winning, but there is an infallible way of
not losing." He was asked what this
infallible way could be, and replied:
"It is not to play chess."

> Feng Yulan (1895-1972)
> Chinese scholar

On the one hand, loss implies gain;
on the other hand, gain implies
loss.

> Lao-tzu (c. 604-531 B.C.E.)
> Chinese philosopher and founder of
> Taoism, *Tao-te-ching*

on LOVE

Love is a great beautifier.

> Louisa May Alcott (1832-1888)
> *Little Women*

Love is like a reservoir of
  kindness and pleasure,
like silos and pools during a seige.

> Yehuda Amichai (b. 1924)
> Israeli writer, *Time*

. . . With your sweet smiles
Torture me not!

> Andal (c. 9th century)
> Indian poet

Love's a danger that quickly fades.

> Chairil Anwar (1922-1949)
> Indonesian poet, "Tuti's Ice Cream"

He that is not jealous is not in love.

> Augustine (354-430)
> North African Christian religious leader

Is not general incivility the very essence of love?

> Jane Austen (1775-1817)
> English writer, *Pride and Prejudice*

The face of a lover is an unknown,
precisely because it is invested
with so much of oneself. It is a
mystery, containing, like all myster-
ies, the possibility of torment.

> James Baldwin (1924-1987)
> American writer, *Another Country*

Love builds . . .

> Mary McLeod Bethune
> (1875-1955)
> American educator, *My Last Will and
> Testament*

Remembered she will bring
  remorse,
Seen she makes the mind unclear,
Touched she nearly drives one
  mad,
Why call such a creature dear?

> Bhartrihari (c. 7th century)
> Indian poet and philosopher, *Sringar
> Sataka*

Whoever loves true life, will love true love.

> Elizabeth Barrett Browning
> (1806-1861)
> English poet, *Aurora Leigh*

Love has the sweetness of the future world, of paradise. . . . Great cold and great heat cause the same pain. Great light is to man's eye the same as great darkness. Too much sweetness is as loathsome as bitterness. Hilarious laughter brings tears as much as deep sorrow. The goal of life is love.

> Yehuda Burla (1886-1969)
> Israeli writer, "Without a Star"

Do you know you live in me bit
  by bit
Yet there is such a thing as being
  lovely with you
For instance we drink raki and
  it is
As if a carnation is engulfing us.
. . . .
You are bent on that carnation, I
  take it
And give it to you. You then pass
  it on
To someone else. And a greater
  beauty is reached.

> Edip Cansever (1928-1986)
> Turkish poet, "The Gravitational
> Carnation"

Others, like myself, must have felt their lives crumble away in the course of an existence devoid of love. If I cry, I cry a little for them.

> Andree Chedid (b. 1920)
> Egyptian writer, *From Sleep Unbound*

For times to come, I tell the
  plight

I've earned through loving in excess.

> Beatriz de Dia (c. 1140-1189)
> Provençal troubadour

As love is union, it knows no extremes of distance.

> Juana Ines de la Cruz (1651-1695)
> Mexican nun and poet, "Repuesta a Sor
> Filotea" ("Reply to Sister Phiolotea")

Love is above the laws, above the opinion of men; it is the truth, the flame, the pure element, the primary idea of the moral world.

> Madame de Staël (1766-1817)
> French writer, *Zulma, and Other Tales*

In matters of the heart, nothing is true except the improbable.

> Madame de Staël (1766-1817)
> French writer

I love nothing and that is the true cause of my ennui.

> Marie Anne de Vichy-Chamrond
> (1697-1780)
> French socialite, *Correspondence
> inedite*

Love for the joy of loving, and not for the offerings of someone else's heart.

> Marlene Dietrich (1901-1992)
> American actor

I wanted to escape from love, but didn't know how.

> Ding Ling (c. 1904-1986)
> Chinese writer

I had discovered that love might be a pastime as well as a tragedy, and I gave myself to it with pagan innocence.

> Isadora Duncan (1878-1927)
> American dancer

Love is the subtlest force in the world.

> Mohandas K. Gandhi (1869-1948)
> Indian spiritual and political leader

I love her indifference;
For broader my outlook be
When I find the joy of my heart
So hid from me.

Flasks full of wine in the tavern show,
Few with love of wine to it did ever go;
So the more men in the world you find,
The fewer there are firm of will of mind.

> Mirza Ghalib (1797-1869)
> Indian Urdu poet

He who has loved relates an endless tale.
Here the most eloquent of tongue must fail.

> Hafiz (d. 1389)
> Persian poet

At one glance
I love you
With a thousand hearts.

> Mihri Hatun (d. 1506)
> Turkish writer

Few people know what they mean when they say, "I love you." . . . Well, what does the word *love* mean? It means total interest. I think the reason very few people really fall in love with anyone is they're not willing to pay the price. The price is you have to adjust yourself to them.

> Katharine Hepburn (b. 1909)
> American actor

Only the really plain people know about love—the very fascinating ones try so hard to create an impression that they soon exhaust their talents.

> Katharine Hepburn (b. 1909)
> American actor

That many-faceted thing called love succeeds in building bridges from the loneliness on this shore to the loneliness on the other one. These bridges can be of great beauty, but they are rarely built for eternity, and frequently they cannot tolerate too heavy a burden without collapsing.

> Karen Horney (1885-1952)
> American psychoanalyst, "The Distrust between the Sexes"

Why abandon me?
I can not live any longer.
How could I survive
While enduring misery
As terrible as this.

> Inpumon-in no tayu (c. 1200)
> Japanese poet

To love someone
Who does not return that love
Is like offering prayers
Back behind a starving god
Within a Buddhist temple.

> Kasa no Iratsume (9th century)
> Japanese poet, *Manyo-Shu (Collection of Ten Thousand Leaves)*

Though in this world a hundred tasks thou tryest,
'Tis Love alone which from thyself will save thee.
Even from earthly love thy face avert not,

Since to the Real it may serve to
  raise thee.

> Jami (1414-1492)
> Persian writer

To be in love with someone . . . is
to appropriate as a part of one's
own self—which means that one's
self-regard is doubled.

> Yoshiyuki Junnosake (b. 1924)
> Japanese writer

Love, twin-fuselaged
Sweeps serenely thus
(Weather Report: Unfair)
To passion's terminus.

> P. Lal (b. 1929)
> Indian writer, *Love's the First*

By accident of fortune a man may
rule the world for a time, but by
virtue of love he may rule the
world forever.

> Lao-tzu (c. 604-531 B.C.E.)
> Chinese philosopher and founder of
> Taoism, *Tao-te-ching*

In the evening of life we shall be
judged on love, and not one of us
is going to come off very well, and
were it not for my absolute faith in
the loving forgiveness of my Lord I
could not call on him to come.

> Madeleine L'Engle (b. 1918)
> American writer, *The Irrational Season*

Love is a game—yes?
I think it is a drowning.

> Amy Lowell (1874-1925)
> American writer, "Twenty-four Hokku
> on a Modern Theme," *What's O'Clock*

I have heard much of these lan-
guishing lovers, but I never yet saw
one of them die for love.

> Marguerite of Navarre (1492-1549)
> French writer and religious reformer,
> "Novel VIII, the First Day," *The
> Heptmeron, or Novels of the Queen of
> Navarre*

Nearly all human beings love, but
nearly none know how to love.

> Eugenio Maria de Hostos
> (1839-1903)
> Puerto Rican patriot

Love is the invention of a few high
cultures . . . it is cultural artifact.
To make love the requirement of a
lifelong marriage is exceedingly
difficult, and only a few people can
achieve it. I don't believe in setting
universal standards that a large proportion of people can't reach.

> Margaret Mead (1901-1978)
> American anthropologist

Lovers. Not a soft word, as people
thought, but cruel and tearing.

> Alice Munro (b. 1931)
> Canadian writer, "Something I've Been
> Meaning to Tell You," *Something I've
> Been Meaning to Tell You*

We can only learn to love by loving.

> Iris Murdoch (b. 1919)
> Irish writer, *The Bell*

Love can't always do work. Sometimes it just has to look into the
darkness.

> Iris Murdoch (b. 1919)
> Irish writer, *The Nice and the Good*

What does your mind seek?
Where is your heart?

If you give your heart to each and
  every thing,
you lead it nowhere; you destroy
  your heart.
Can anything be found on earth?

> Nezahualcoyotl (1418-1472)
> Aztec poet, in the *Coleccion de
> Cantares Mexicanos*

In love there are two things: bodies and words.

> Joyce Carol Oates (b. 1938)
> American writer

My love
Is like the grasses
Hidden in the deep mountain:
Though its abundance increases,
There is none that knows.

> Ono no Yoshiki (d. 902)
> Japanese poet, from the *Kokin Shu*
> (compiled 905-922)

By the time you swear you're his,
  Shivering and sighing,
And he vows his passion is
  Infinite, undying—
Lady, make a note of this:
  One of you is lying.

> Dorothy Parker (1893-1967)
> American writer, "Unfortunate
> Coincidence," *Enough Rope*

Scratch a lover, and find a foe!

> Dorothy Parker (1893-1967)
> American writer, "Ballad of Great
> Weariness," *Enough Rope*

Intellect in its effort to explain
Love got stuck in the mud like an
ass. Love alone could explain love
and loving.

> Rumi (1207-1273)
> Persian Sufi poet and mystic

A lover's life lies in death. You shall
not find a heart without losing the
heart.

> Rumi (1207-1273)
> Persian Sufi poet and mystic

Love possesses seven hundred
wings, and each one extends from
the highest heaven to the lowest
earth.

> Rumi (1207-1273)
> Persian Sufi poet and mystic

Where love is absent there can be
no woman.

> George Sand (1804-1876)
> French writer, *Leila*

Let me only glance where you
  are, the voice dies,
  I can say nothing,

but my lips are stricken to
  silence, underneath my
skin the tenuous flame suffuses;
nothing shows in front of my
  eyes, my ears are
  muted in thunder.

And the sweat breaks running
  upon me, fever
shakes my body, paler I turn than
  grass is;
I can feel that I have been
  changed, I feel that
  death has come near me.

> Sappho (c. 610-580 B.C.E.)
> Greek poet

It is better to be loved than feared.

> Senegalese proverb

Nearly all women sleep when
  they are loved.

Maybe the body has to coil again
From its full stretch, maybe the
  drowned brain
Emerges from its Springtide into
  rest
Maybe they bank their ecstasy in
  dreams
Against a future anguish and
  devaluation.

But as the unhurried stars wheel
  overhead
Above a thousand million nests of
  love
One or two women lie and think
  and glow.

> A. J. Seymour (b. 1914)
> Guyanese poet, "Springtide"

I had thought that
This life at least would be one
That went as I wished.
Why then must I give it up
So easily, because of love.

> Sohekimon-in no shosho (c. 1243)
> Japanese poet

At first only your hands came
  between me and loneliness
Then of a sudden the doors were
  opened wide
Then your face and then your
  eyes and then your lips
Then everything came.

> Cemal Sureya (b. 1931)
> Turkish poet, "At First," *Uvercinka*

If love is the answer, could you
please rephrase the question?

> Lily Tomlin (b. 1936)
> American comedian

Love is no fox,
Nor you a bunch of grapes

But unbeknown my heart stole
  out
And plucked you in secret, when
  no one was about.

> Simazaki Toson (1872-1943)
> Japanese writer

When a chap is in love, he will go
out in all kinds of weather to keep
an appointment with his beloved.
Love can be demanding, in fact
more demanding than law. It has
its own imperatives—think of a
mother sitting by the bedside of a
sick child through the night, im-
pelled only by love. Nothing is too
much trouble for love.

> Desmond Tutu (b. 1931)
> South African antiapartheid activist and
> religious leader

My love is like the dark
honeycomb of deep red shadow
which the hermetic pomegranate
produces within its concave walls.

> Xavier Villaurrutia (1903-1950)
> Mexican poet, "Soneto del la granada"
> ("Sonnet to a Pomegranate")

[Love] is like a tree which shows
the first signs of growth when the
shoot blossoms.

> Wang Yang-ming (1472-1529)
> Chinese philosopher, *Wang Wen-ch'eng
> kung ch'uan-shu*

I looked only for a more enduring
Measure of time to receive my
  breath,
When the glittering stars should
  be my eyes,
. . . .
My voice the thunder, suddenly
  breaking

To wake the spring, to wake new
life.
Ah, beyond thought, beyond
compare
Is the inspiration, the power of
love.

    Xu Zhimo (c. 1895-1931)
    Chinese writer

How is love to be explained,
And what does it mean? One
evening
It captivates us with its gentle
sunlight,
Its fluffy clouds, and its plaintive
breeze.

    Xuan Dieu (20th century)
    Vietnamese poet, "Voi vang" ("Why?")

They say: Thou art become mad
with love for thy beloved.
I reply: The savour of life is for
madmen.

    Al-Yafi'i (1299-1367)
    Arab Islamic historian

Love tastes sweet, but only with
bread.

    Yiddish proverb

on LUCK

If Heaven above lets fall a plum,
open your mouth.

    Chinese proverb
    (c. 19th and early 20th century)

The superior man is quiet and
calm, waiting for the appointments
of heaven, while the mean man
walks in dangerous paths, looking
for lucky occurrences.

    Confucius (551-479 B.C.E.)
    Chinese philosopher and founder of
    Confucianism, *Analects*

Old—and so much still to do.
Heaven-and-earth is too vast: drink
up!
With luck even a fool wins glory,
Without it a hero is helpless.

    Dang Dung (18th century)
    Vietnamese patriot, "Regrets"

Is it not our elders who say that all
dogs eat rubbish, but it is the unlucky ones that get caught?

    Peter Enahoro (b. 1935)
    Nigerian journalist

It is in the nature of things that
some people should be unlucky
enough to get their heads chopped
off.

    Lu Xun (1881-1936)
    Chinese writer, "Ah Q chen-chuan"
    ("The True Story of Ah Q")

Foolish are they indeed who trust
to fortune!

    Lady Shikibu Murasaki (978-1030)
    Japanese writer, *The Tale of Genji*

The worst cynicism: a belief in
luck.

    Joyce Carol Oates (b. 1938)
    American writer, *Do With Me What
    You Will*

on LUXURY

Some people think luxury is the
opposite of poverty. It is not. It is
the opposite of vulgarity.

    Coco Chanel (1883-1971)
    French designer

Trust to me, ladies, and do not
envy a splendor which does not
constitute happiness.

    Josephine (1763-1814)
    French empress

on **MADNESS**

There are forty kinds of lunacy, but only one kind of common sense.

Bantu proverb

Each of us keeps, battened down inside himself, a sort of lunatic giant—impossible socially, but full-scale—and it's the knockings and batterings we sometimes hear in each other that keep our intercourse from utter banality.

Elizabeth Bowen (1899-1973)
Irish writer, *The Death of the Heart*

I may be a lunatic, but then, wasn't my lunacy caused by a monster that lurks at the bottom of every human mind? Those who call me a madman and spurn me may become lunatics tomorrow. They harbor the same monster.

Akutagawa Ryunosuke
(1892-1927)
Japanese writer

If I am mad, then who on the face of the earth is sane? If you are sane, then there is no madman in the world.

Sa'ib of Tabriz (c. 1601-1677)
Persian poet

on **MARRIAGE**

I married beneath me—all women do.

Nancy Astor (1879-1964)
English politician

If a woman *doubts* to whether she should accept a man or not, she certainly ought refuse him. If she can hesitate as to "Yes," she ought to say "No," directly.

Jane Austen (1775-1817)
English writer

Those who are outside want to get in, and those who are inside want to get out.

Ch'ien Chung-shu (b. 1910)
Chinese writer, *Fortress Besieged*

Marriage is traditionally the destiny offered to women by society. Most women are married or have been, or plan to be or suffer from not being.

Simone de Beauvoir (1908-1986)
French writer and philosopher, *Le Force de l'Age (The Prime of Life)*

Any intelligent woman who reads the marriage contract, and then goes into it, deserves all the consequences.

Isadora Duncan (1878-1927)
American dancer, *My Life*

She [a wife] should always be cheerful and skillful in her domestic duties, with her household vessels well cleaned and her hand tight on the purse strings.

Laws of Manu (c. 100-200)
ancient Indian text

Women have a mother-nature and a daughter-nature; there are no women with a wife-nature. The quality of wife is an acquired character; it is a combination of mother and daughter.

Lu Xun (1881-1936)
Chinese writer

The wife is half the man, the best
  of friends,
the root of the three ends of life,
and of all that will help him in
  the other world.

Mahabharata
(540 B.C.E.-3rd century C.E.)
Hindu epic

He who is able to get married should; it keeps the eye cast down and keeps a man chaste. He who is unable should take to fasting, which will cool his passion.

Muhammad (570-632)
Prophet of Islam

Let no believing man hate his believing wife; if he is displeased with one trait of her character, let him be pleased with another that is within her.

Muhammad (570-632)
Prophet of Islam

Love thy wife as is fitting. Fill her belly; clothe her back; ointment is the prescription for her body. Make her heart glad as long as thou

livest, for she is a profitable field for her lord.

Ptah-hotep (c. 2300 B.C.E.)
Egyptian vizier, *Instruction of Ptah-hotep*

I saw in this barren garden a picture of life—the life I would live cut off from everything that had delighted me and consoled me in my melancholy childhood. I turned from the window with a heavy heart and avoided the garden for a long, long time.

Huda Shaarawi (1879-1947)
Egyptian feminist, concluding an account of her marriage to her much older and already married cousin

When a man seduces a woman, it should, I think, be termed a *left-handed marriage*.

Mary Wollstonecroft (1759-1797)
English suffragist

on MATERIALISM

The sum total of worldly possessions is nothing but sorrow and evil.

Fakhir al-Din Razi (1149-1209)
Central Asian Islamic philosopher

Do not think you need necessarily have as fine swords and clothing as your neighbor. As long as they are not disreputable, they will do. And if you borrow and so lose your independence, you will be despised.

Hojo Soun (c. 1519)
Japanese samurai, "Twenty-one Articles of Advice" written for his son and regarded as the epitome of martial spirit

Wealth and kinsfolk are as
borrowed things.
All borrowed things must one day
be returned.

> Labid (c. 600)
> Arab poet

Wealth and fame are of dubious
value when we think that life is
like a fleeting dream.

> Li Ju-chen (c. 1763–1830)
> Chinese writer, *Ching-hua yuan*
> *(Flowers in the Mirror)*

Lust for fame and fortune is like an
intoxication. While a man is intoxicated, he doesn't realize it. It's only
after it is all over that he realizes
that everything is like an illusion. If
men could realize this all the time,
there would be much less trouble
on earth, and there would be
much happier people too.

> Li Ju-chen (c. 1763–1830)
> Chinese writer, *Ching-hua yuan*
> *(Flowers in the Mirror)*

Material civilization, nay, even luxury, is necessary to create work for
the poor. Bread! Bread! I do not believe in a God who cannot give me
bread here, giving me eternal bliss
in heaven!

> Vivekananda (1863–1902)
> Indian religious leader

on MEANING

Light floods the room.
Someone asks a question.
But the night arrives on time.

> Teresa Calderon (b. 1955)
> Chilean poet

Gilgamesh, whither are you
wandering?
Life, which you look for, you will
never find.

> *Epic of Gilgamesh* (c. 1760 B.C.E.)
> Sumerian epic poem

Put on clean clothes,
and wash your head and bathe.
Gaze at the child that is holding
your hand,
and let your wife delight in your
embrace.
These things alone are the
concern of men.

> *Epic of Gilgamesh* (c. 1760 B.C.E.)
> Sumerian epic poem

Therefore the universe is the out-
ward visible expression of the
Real, and the Real is the inner unseen reality of the Universe.

> Jami (1414–1492)
> Persian writer

You do not see that the Real is in
your own home,
And you wander from forest to
forest furtively.
Here is the truth!
Go where you will, to Banaras or
to Mathura,
If you do not find go in your own
soul,
The world will be meaningless to
you.

> Kabir (1440–1519)
> Indian Mughal poet and philosopher

When I nourish this great breath
within me, all things are then complete within me.

> Mencius (c. 390–305 B.C.E.)
> Chinese philosopher Meng-tzu,
> referring to *chi*, or great vital spirit
> within

There's something I would like to understand. And I don't think anyone can explain it. . . . There's your life. You begin it, feeling that it's something so precious and rare, so beautiful that it's like a sacred treasure. Now it's over, and it doesn't make any difference to anyone, and it isn't that they are indifferent, it's just that they don't know, they don't know what it means, that treasure of mine, and there's something about it that they should understand. I don't understand it myself, but there's something that should be understood by all of us. Only what is it? What?

Ayn Rand (1905-1982)
American writer, *We the Living*

All that can be spelled out is without importance.

Zhou Zuoren (1885-1968)
Chinese critic and writer

on MEDITATION

If you rest in the stillness like a broken gong, you have already reached heaven, for anger has left you.

Dhammapada (c. 3rd century B.C.E.)
collection of ancient Buddhist poems and aphorisms

Meditation is not a means to an end. It is both the means and the end.

Jiddu Krishnamurti (1895-1986)
Indian philosopher

An hour's meditation is better than a year of adoration.

Muhammad (570-632)
Prophet of Islam

Each soul must meet the morning sun, the new, sweet earth, and the Great Silence alone!

Ohiyesa (1858-1939)
Sioux writer and physician

Close the eye that sees falsely, and open the intellectual eye.

Attributed to Rumi (1207-1273)
Persian Sufi poet and mystic, *Divani Shamsi Tabriz*

on MEMORY

It takes time for the absent to assume their true shape in our thoughts. After death they take on a firmer outline and then cease to change.

Colette (1873-1954)
French writer

Consumed by the agony of
  remembrance
The remembrance of night's
  festive company
The one remaining candle flickers
  and dies.

Mirza Ghalib (1797-1869)
Indian Urdu poet

The heart is a bird that knows
  how to nestle.
And how to love its nest. And
  how to forget.

To forget is to break the ties of
  yesterday,
and to take a great leap, and drop
  into the unknown.

To forget is to let the grass
  overflow, and prefer
to the certain delight, the
  uncertainty to come.

> Luis Llorens Torres (1878–1944)
> Puerto Rican writer, "Psalms"

The memories of long love gather
like drifting snow, poignant as the
mandarin ducks who float side by
side in sleep.

> Lady Shikibu Murasaki (978–1030)
> Japanese writer, *The Tale of Genji*

Who will blow on the embers long
buried, under the cold of forgetful-
ness?

> Jean-Baptiste Mutabaruka (b. 1937)
> Rwandan poet

What are you meditating?
What are you remembering, oh
  my friends?
Meditate no longer!
At our side the beautiful flowers
  bloom;
so does the Giver of Life concede
  pleasure to man.
All of us, if we meditate, if we
  remember
become sad here.

> Nahuatl (Aztec) poem, in the
> *Canteres Mexicanos*

Others may forget you, but not I.
I am haunted by your beautiful
  ghost.

> Yamatohime (c. 671)
> Japanese poet and empress

on MEN

War is thy desert, thy task. Thou
shalt find drink, nourishment, food
to the sun, the lord of the earth.
Thy real home, thy lot is the home
of the sun there in the heavens.
Perhaps thou wilt receive the gift,
perhaps thou will merit death by
the obsidian knife.

> Aztec ritual words, uttered by
> midwives to newborn boys

Probably the only place where a
man can feel really secure is in a
maximum security prison, except
for the imminent threat of release.

> Germaine Greer (b. 1939)
> Australian writer, *The Female Eunuch*

When men talk about defense,
they always claim to be protecting
women and children, but they
never ask the women and children
what they think.

> Patricia Schroeder (b. 1940)
> American politician

on MEN AND WOMEN

The world's male chivalry has
  perished out,
But women are knight-errants to
  the last.

> Elizabeth Barrett Browning
> (1806–1861)
> English poet, *Aurora Leigh*

There is more difference within
the sexes than between them.

> Ivy Compton-Burnett (1892–1969)
> English writer, *Mother and Son*

Love is the whole history of a
woman's life; it is but an episode in
a man's.

> Madame de Staël (1766–1817)
> French writer, *De l'influence des*

passions sur le bonheur des individus et des nations (A Treatise on the Influence of the Passions upon the Happiness of Individuals and of Nations)

Men and women are two locked caskets, of which each contains the key to the other.

Isak Dinesen (1885-1962)
Danish writer

I'm not denyin' the women are foolish: God Almighty made 'em to match the men.

George Eliot (1819-1880)
English writer, *Adam Bede*

Man is not the enemy here, but the fellow victim. The real enemy is women's denigration of themselves.

Betty Friedan (b. 1921)
American feminist

Men and women should live next door and visit each other once in a while.

Katharine Hepburn (b. 1909)
American actor

Woman reaches love through friendship; man reaches friendship through love.

Muhammad Hijazi (20th century)
Iranian writer and politician, *Hazar Sokhan (A Thousand Sayings)*

Women want mediocre men, and men are working to be as mediocre as possible.

Margaret Mead (1901-1978)
American anthropologist

Whether women are better than

men I cannot say—but I can say they are certainly no worse.

Golda Meir (1898-1978)
Israeli prime minister

What is most beautiful in virile men is something feminine; what is most beautiful in feminine women is something masculine.

Susan Sontag (b. 1933)
American writer and critic, "Notes on Camp," *Against Interpretation*

Man is a rough-hewn and woman a finished product.

Rabindranath Tagore (1861-1941)
Indian writer and philosopher

In politics, if you want anything, ask a man; if you want anything done, ask a woman.

Margaret Thatcher (b. 1925)
English prime minister

Women have served all these centuries as looking-glasses possessing the magic and delicious power of reflecting the figure of man at twice its natural size.

Virginia Woolf (1882-1941)
English writer, *A Room of One's Own*

Why are women . . . so much more interesting to men than men are to women?

Virginia Woolf (1882-1941)
English writer, *A Room of One's Own*

on MERCY

He [God] is the Most Merciful of those who show mercy.

Qur'an (c. 610-656)
sacred book of Islam, XII:64

God is merciful to those who are merciful to others.

> *Talmud*
> (c. late 4th–early 6th century)
> ancient body of Jewish civil and
> canonical law, Sifre 117

on MIDDLE AGE

What is an adult? A child blown up by age.

> Simone de Beauvoir (1908–1986)
> French writer and philosopher, *La
> Femme rompue*

I'm my age and I feel glorious.

> Betty Friedan (b. 1921)
> American feminist, *It Changed My Life*

Fear comes with middle age.

> Lillian Hellman (1906–1984)
> American writer

on THE MILITARY

No sword can match dhu-al-Faqar, and no young warrior can compare with 'Ali!

> verse found on many medieval
> Arab swords; refers to 'Ali
> (c. 600–661)
> Arab ruler and religious leader, whose
> exemplary acts led to a chivalry
> movement similar to the much later
> one of medieval Europe

Soldier, you have fallen for this earth
Your fathers may well lean down from heaven to kiss your brow.
You are great, for your blood saves the True Faith
. . . .
If, as you lie swathed in blood under this chandelier,

If I could detain the moonlight by your side
To stay till dawn as guardian of your tomb
If I could charge your chandelier with morning light
And wrap the silken sunset about your wounds—
Still I could not say: "I have done something for your
memory . . . "

> Mehmet Akif Ersoy (1873–1936)
> Turkish poet, "For the Fallen at
> Gallipoli"

The soldiers fight and the kings are heroes.

> Hebrew proverb

The popular masses are like water, and the army is like a fish. How then can it be said that when there is water, a fish will have difficulty in preserving its existence? An army which fails to maintain good discipline gets into opposition with the popular masses, and thus by its own action dries up the water.

> Mao Zedong (1893–1976)
> Chairman of People's Republic of
> China

Having helmets of copper, snouts which are chisels,
Tongues which are awls, hearts which are iron,
Whips which are swords, eating the dew and riding the wind . . .

> Mongols' description of
> themselves, *Secret History of the
> Mongols*

My saddle is my council chamber.

> Saladin (1137–1193)
> Egyptian and Syrian sultan

When we fight, we first use bullets; when the bullets are gone, we use bayonets; when the bayonets are dull, we use the rifle barrel; when this is broken, we use our fists; when our fists are broken, we bite.

Uniform patch of Chinese Warlord Feng Yu-hsaing's Big Sword Unit (Ta-tao-tui) (c. 1917)

One hundred volumes of international law are not the equal of a few cannons; a handful of treaties are not worth a basket of gunpowder. Cannon and gunpowder are not aids for the enforcement of given moral principles, they are implements for the creation of morality where none exists.

Fukuzawa Yukichi (1835-1901)
Japanese reformer

on THE MIND

The mind is everything; what you think, you become.

Buddha (c. 563-483 B.C.E.)
Founder of Buddhism

The mind, by its very nature, persistently tries to live forever, resisting age and attempting to give itself a form. . . . When a person passes his prime and his life begins to lose true vigor and charm, his mind starts functioning as if it were another form of life; it imitates what life does, eventually doing what life cannot do.

Yukio Mishima (1925-1970)
Japanese writer

By the mind one is bound; by the mind one is freed. . . . He who as-

serts with strong conviction: "I am not bound, I am free," becomes free.

Ramakrishna (1836-1886)
Indian mystic, *The Gospel of Ramakrishna*

on MINORITIES

I am visible . . . yet I am invisible. I both blind them with my beak nose and am their blind spot. But I exist, we exist. They'd like to think I have melted in the pot. But I haven't, we haven't.

Gloria Anzaldua (20th century)
American writer, *Borderlands/La Frontera: The New Mestiza*

In every historic catastrophe, in the decay of any nation, there have existed minorities which were there at the time and were not heard; great newspapers closed their doors to them; the great parties mocked them; their great enthusiasms were ironically observed and their solutions, the only ones possible, were ridiculed as impractical.

Eduardo Frei Montalva (b. 1911)
Chilean politician, *Aun es Tiempo (There's Still Time)*

on MODERATION

Only the intelligent can understand what is obvious and what is concealed. Strength may be good or it may be evil. The same is true of weakness. The ideal is moderation. . . . Purify the heart, that is all.

Chou-Tun-I (1017-1073)
Chinese scholar, *The Diagram Explained*

I like to operate like a submarine on sonar. When I am picking up noise from both the left and right, I know my course is correct.

> Gustavo Díaz Ordaz (1911-1979)
> Mexican politician, while campaigning for presidency of Mexico

If one is moderate in developing one's justifiable inclinations, and succeeds in freeing oneself of one's inhibitions, this will not shorten one's life span, but increase it. All of these things can be compared to fire and water: only their excessive use is harmful.

> Ko Hung (283-343)
> Chinese scholar, *Shen-hsien-chuan*

Stretch the bow to the very full,
And you will wish you had
  stopped in time.

> Lao-tzu (c. 604-531 B.C.E.)
> Chinese philosopher and founder of Taoism, *Tao-te-ching*

on MONEY

Let men have attainments that
  shine like the sun
They're but poor abject fellows if
  money they've none.

> *Alf Laila wa Laila (One Thousand and One Nights)* (c. 10th-14th century)

Money is sharper than a sword.

> Ashanti (West African) proverb

Money, it turned out, was exactly like sex, you thought of nothing else if you didn't have it and thought of other things if you did.

> James Baldwin (1924-1987)
> American writer, "The Black Boy Looks at the White Boy," *Nobody Knows My Name*

Let us keep a firm grip upon our money, for without it the whole assembly of virtues are but as blades of grass.

> Bhartrihari (c. 7th century)
> Indian poet and philosopher, *Nita Sataka*

Money is a great dignifier.

> Paul Laurence Dunbar (1872-1906)
> American writer, *The Ordeal at Mt. Hope*

Money kills more people than a club.

> Ibo (West African) proverb

We're a sentimental people. We like a few kind words better than millions of dollars given in a humiliating way.

> Gamel Abdel Nasser (1918-1970)
> Egyptian revolutionary and president, *Realities*, explaining why he was refusing economic assistance from the West

As a cousin of mine once said about money, money is always there but the pockets change; it is not in the same pockets after a change, and that is all there is to say about money.

> Gertrude Stein (1874-1946)
> American writer

Excellent is wisdom when associated with an inheritance.

> *Talmud*
> (c. late 4th-early 6th century)
> ancient body of Jewish civil and canonical law, Kohelet Rabbah 7:11

The whole world, motivated by different reasons and expectations, waited, saying: they who showed Africa and the world the path of manliness and of black redemption, what are they going to do with the beast? They who washed the warrior's spears in the blood of the white profiteers, of all those who had enslaved them to the ministry of the molten beast of silver and gold, what dance are they now going to dance in the arena? . . . But we, the leaders, chose to flirt with the molten god, a blind, deaf monster who has plagued us for hundreds of years.

Ngugi wa Thiong'o (b. 1936)
Kenyan writer, *Petals of Blood*

With your money in your pocket, you are wise and you are handsome and you sing well too.

Yiddish proverb

on MOTHERS AND MOTHERHOOD

Life is nothing but a series of crosses for us mothers.

Colette (1873-1954)
French writer

In the eyes of its mother, every beetle is a gazelle.

Moroccan proverb

In this great house of the Motherland, I am just like any other woman in any other of the innumerable houses of my people. . . .

It's that I so truly feel myself the mother of my people.

Eva Peron (1919-1952)
Argentinian politician

A woman *is* her mother.
That's the main thing.

Anne Sexton (1928-1974)
American poet, "Housewife"

on MUSIC

All music is folk music. I ain't never heard no horse sing a song.

Louis Armstrong (1901-1970)
American musician

Roaming through the jungle of "oohs" and "ahs," searching for a more agreeable noise, I live a life of primitivity with the mind of a child and an unquenchable thirst for sharps and flats.

Duke Ellington (1899-1975)
American musician, *Music Is My Mistress*

Eliminate your consciousness and listen to the sound of music in all the skies.
. . . .
It is thus that people have been moved for thousands of years to produce mysterious sounds

K'ang Yu-wei (1858-1927)
Chinese reformer and political philosopher

on MYSTICISM

I knew that the complete mystic "way" includes both intellectual belief and practical activity; the latter consists in getting rid of the obstacles in the self and in stripping off its base characteristics and vicious morals, so that the heart may attain to freedom from what is not God and to constant recollection of Him.

Abu Hamid Muhammad al-Ghazali (1058–1111)
Arab Islamic philosopher and theologian, *The Deliverer from Error*

Close that gate of thy heart by which otherness enters, for thy heart is My temple. Stand watchful over the closing, and remain in it, until thou meetest.

Niffari (d. 965)
Persian Sufi teacher and writer

There is no real coming and going,
For what is going but coming?

Sa'di of Shiraz (c. 1184–1292)
Persian poet, *Gulistan*

He who does not become an expert in annihilation shall not discover the beautiful face of the bride.

Abu Hasan al-Shadhili (d. 1258)
Arab Sufi leader

on NATIVE AMERICANS

The time is near when our race will become extinct, and nothing left to show the world that we ever did exist.

> Senachwine (c. 1830)
> Potawatomi chief, at a council fire in Indiantown, Illinois (June 1830)

What treaty that the white man ever made with us have they kept? Not one. When I was a boy, the Sioux owned the world; the sun rose and set on their land; they sent ten thousand men to battle. Where are the warriors today? Who slew them? Where are our lands? Who owns them? What white man can say I ever stole his land or a penny of his money? Yet they say I am a thief. What white woman, however lonely, was ever captive or insulted by me? Yet they say I am a bad Indian. What white man has ever seen me drunk? Who has ever come to me hungry and unfed? Who has ever seen me beat my wives or abuse my children? What law have I broken? Is it wrong for me to love my own? Is it wicked for me because my skin is red? Because I am a Sioux; because I was born where my father lived; because I would die for my people and my country?

> Sitting Bull (c. 1834–1890)
> Dakota Sioux chief

Today the children of our public schools are taught more of the history, heroes, legends, and sagas of the old world than of the land of their birth, while they are furnished with little material on the people and institutions that are truly American.

> Luther Standing Bear (1868–1939)
> Sioux writer, letter to Franklin D. Roosevelt (May 2, 1933)

The American Indian is of the soil, for the hand that fashioned the continent also fashioned the man for his surroundings.

> Luther Standing Bear (1868–1939)
> Sioux writer

The old life was attuned to nature's rhythm—bound in mystical ties to the sun, moon and stars; to the waving grasses, flowing streams and whispering winds. It is not a question . . . of the white man "bringing the Indian up to his plane of thought and action." It is rather a case where the white man had better grasp some of the Indian's spiritual strength.

> Luther Standing Bear (1868–1939)
> Sioux writer, "Tragedy of the Sioux"

Where today are the Pequot? Where are the Narragansett, the Mohican, the Pcanet, and other powerful tribes of our people?

They have vanished before the avarice and oppression of the white man, as snow before the summer sun.

> Tecumseh (c. 1768-1813)
> Shawnee chief, to Governor W. H. Harrison, protesting the land sales of 1805-1806

Sleep not longer, O Choctaws and Chickasaws, in false security and delusive hopes. . . . Will not the bones of our dead be plowed up, and their graves turned into plowed fields?

> Tecumseh (c. 1768-1813)
> Shawnee chief, to Governor W. H. Harrison, protesting the land sales of 1805-1806

on NATURE

To sit in the shade on a fine day and look upon verdure is the most perfect refreshment.

> Jane Austen (1775-1817)
> English writer, *Mansfield Park*

The old pond—
A frog leaps in,
and a splash.

> Matsuo Basho (1644-1694)
> Japanese poet

The sea darkens
And a wild duck's call
Is faintly white.

> Matsuo Basho (1644-1694)
> Japanese poet

Limitless stretches the wilderness, lifeless and soundless.
Lost to the end of all time is the jubilant voice of the giants,

Laid into stillness forever the tumult that followed their footsteps;
Where they once trod are now lifted the sandhills and crags of the desert.

> Chiam Nachman Bialik (1873-1934)
> Israeli writer, "The Dead of the Wilderness"

The growing and dying of the moon reminds us of our ignorance, which comes and goes; but when the moon is full, it is as if the eternal light of the Great Spirit were upon the whole world.

> Black Elk (1863-1950)
> Oglala Sioux holy man

Perhaps you have noticed that even in the very lightest breeze you can hear the voice of the cottonwood tree; this we understand is its prayer to the Great Spirit, for not only men, but all things and all beings pray to Him continually in differing ways.

> Black Elk (1863-1950)
> Oglala Sioux holy man

If Nature is against us, we shall fight Nature and make it obey.

> Simón Bolívar (1783-1830)
> South American revolutionary leader

On the temple bell,
Perching, sleeps
The butterfly, oh!

> Taniguchi Buson (1715-1783)
> Japanese painter and poet

The "control of nature" is a phrase conceived in arrogance, born of the Neanderthal age of biology and the convenience of man.

> Rachel Carson (1907-1964)
> American naturalist and writer, *Silent Spring*

All my life through, the new sights of Nature made me rejoice like a child.

> Marie Curie (1867-1934)
> French scientist, *Pierre Curie*

At present, [in the desert] an exasperating clarity reigns. The sky has become less visible than water in a jar. Black peaks, spines of granite, a twisted tree are sculpted in this atmosphere basted with reflections. All that remains: a countryside of imperishable contours.

> Mohammed Dib (b. 1920)
> Algerian writer

Our cup is the full moon; the wine the sun.

> Ibn al'Farid (1181-1235)
> Arab poet

It has been my experience that people who are at cross-purposes with nature are cynical about mankind and ill at ease with themselves.

> Indira Gandhi (1917-1984)
> Indian prime minister

There is something in the decay of nature that awakens thought, even in the most trifling mind.

> Sarah Josepha Hale (1788-1879)
> American writer and editor

Nature is the harmless and kind be-

loved of those who have been disillusioned by other beloveds.

> Muhammad Hijazi (20th century)
> Iranian writer and politician, *Hazar Sokhan (A Thousand Sayings)*

Nature as it is—nature with nothing selected or discarded from it—cannot become a work of art.

> Nagai Kafu (1879-1959)
> Japanese writer

If you were to ask me why I
  dwell among green mountains,
I shall laugh silently; my soul is
  serene.
The peach-blossom follows the
  moving water,
There is another heaven and earth
  beyond the world of men.

> Li Po (701-762)
> Chinese writer, "Conversation in the Mountains"

In nature nothing creates itself and nothing destroys itself.

> Maria Montessori (1870-1952)
> Italian educator, *The Secret of Childhood*

Fragile blades of grass,
Be proud!
Only you so impartially adorn the entire world.

> Ping Hsin (b. 1902)
> Chinese poet, *The Stars*

It seems to me that the earth may be borrowed but not bought. It may be used, but not owned. It gives itself in response to love and tending, offers its seasonal flowering and fruiting. But we are tenants and not possessors, lovers and not masters.

> Marjorie Kinnan Rawlings
> (1896-1953)
> American writer, *Cross Creek*

Only in the plants
the nectars don't darken
a step away from the abyss.
Only in the flowers
the sweetness won't retreat
a step away from death.
For the plants are a different
  nation
from us,
except for the olive trees
which are sad and wise
like people.

> Zelda Shneurson (b. 1913)
> Israeli poet, "Place of Fire"

We did not think of the great open plains, the beautiful rolling hills, and winding streams with tangled growth, as "wild." Only to the white man was nature a "wilderness" and only to him was the land infested with "wild" animals and "savage" people. To us it was tame. Earth was bountiful and we were surrounded with the blessings of the Great Mystery. Not until the hairy man from the east came and with brutal frenzy heaped injustices upon us and the families we loved was it "wild" for us. When the very animals of the forest began fleeing from his approach, then it was that for us the "Wild West" began.

> Luther Standing Bear (1868-1939)
> Sioux writer, *Land of the Spotted Eagle*

A man dies, but not the hills, the grasses, the trees.

> T'ao Ch'ien (365-427)
> Chinese poet

Grass is in my mouth, my throat
grass is on my tongue, my taste,
grass is my love, my touch.
The scent of grass: green,
it is my life, my breath.

> Monika Varma (b. 1916)
> Indian writer

Give me what the tree has and
  what it won't lose
and give me the power to lose
  what the tree has.

> Natan Zach (b. 1930)
> Israeli poet, "Give Me What the Tree Has"

No need for silken string or flute
  of bamboo,
An unsullied music is in the
  streams and hills.
Who would wait for human
  singing
when the clustered trees,
murmur in their sadness for
  themselves.

> Zuo Si (3rd century)
> Chinese poet

on NONCONFORMITY

Assent—and you are sane—
Demure—you're straightaway
  dangerous—
And handled with a Chain—.

> Emily Dickinson (1830-1886)
> American poet

One of the major powers of the muted is to think against the current.

Rachel Blau DuPlessis
(20th century)
American writer

He who prides himself an extraordinary person by his deeds is rejected by the world; he who has independent ideas is hated by the mass.

Shang Yang (d. 338 B.C.E.)
Chinese philosopher, *Shih-chi*

Do the common thing in an uncommon way.

Booker T. Washington (1856–1915)
American educator, *Daily Resolves*

on NONVIOLENCE

Constructive agitation . . . is above all a weapon of peace, a weapon of love, and it is through such a medium that God comes more readily on the side of those who fight in a just cause.

Obafemi Awolowo (b. 1909)
Nigerian politician, presidential address to the Action Group Congress, Lagos (July 12, 1957)

Without knowledge, nonviolence can deteriorate into begging, and history is unmoved by begging. It is only when we stand on the shoulders of the giant of knowledge that we will truly be able to change the course of history. Only with knowledge will we be able to overcome the violence of ignorance at its very roots. Only with

knowledge will we have the compassion necessary to deliver from their folly those with superstitious faith in the omnipotence of violence.

Fang Lizhe (b. 1936)
Chinese scientist and activist, on receiving the 1989 Robert F. Kennedy Human Rights Award

Nonviolence is not a garment to put on and off at will. Its seat is in the heart, and it must be an inseparable part of our very being.

Mohandas K. Gandhi (1869–1948)
Indian spiritual and political leader, *Non-Violence in Peace and War*

It is better to be violent, if there is violence in our hearts, than to put on a cloak of non-violence to cover impotence.

Mohandas K. Gandhi (1869–1948)
Indian spiritual and political leader, *Non-Violence in Peace and War*

Passive resistance is a sport for gentleman (and ladies)—just like the pursuit of war, a heroic enterprise for the ruling classes but a grievous burden on the rest.

Kenneth Kaunda (b. 1924)
Zambian nationalist and politician, *Kaunda on Violence*

I question whether God himself would wish me to hide behind the principles of non-violence while innocent persons were being slaughtered.

Abel Muzorewa (b. 1925)
Zimbabwean minister and politician, *The Observer* (November 5, 1978)

on **OBEDIENCE**

Be obedient to your superior, and your inferior will obey you.

> 'Ali (c. 600–661)
> First Imam of the Sh'ia branch of Islam;
> fourth caliph

Obey what is revealed you from your Lord. God is aware of all you do. And put your trust in Him, for He is your guardian and trustee.

> *Qur'an* (c. 610–656)
> sacred book of Islam, 33:2–3

on **OLD AGE**

Alas, I draw breath heavily
my lungs breathe heavily,
as I call for my song.

When the news arrived of far-off
  friends,
starving for winter game,
I wanted to sing:
. . . .
I forget the fire in my chest,
and the wheeze of my lungs
while I sing,

and I remember the old times
when I was strong.

> Akjartoq (c. 1920)
> Caribou Eskimo poet

Such was my body once. Now it
  is weary and tottering,
the house of many ills, an old
  house with flaking plaster.
Not otherwise is the world of the
  truthful.

> Ambapali (4th century B.C.E.)
> Indian Buddhist poet

What can you expect
from a woman with seventy-seven
  years,
frail as the web of a spider?

> Maryam bint Abi Ya'qub al-Ansari
> (c. 11th century)
> Spanish Arab poet

We have grown so old, old friends
We might never have been so
  young
Though our days were stalks of
  basil
Wet and waving and beaming
We spent long wanting a house
A place of violence and theft
We shall spend longer trying to be
  young
Tinkering with juvenalia
And a steady hole in the scalp.

Youth went out despite
  everything
There should be no cause when
  youth wears out
But death and the mountain.

> Abu al-Athiyah (d. 828)
> Arabic poet

192

Do not treat a man with
   disrespect when he is old,
For some of us are growing old.

> Ben Sira (c. 2nd century B.C.E.)
> Hebrew scholar and philosopher, *The
> Wisdom of Ben Sira*

After the age of 50 we begin to die
little by little in the deaths of
others.

> Julio Cortazar (1914-1984)
> Argentinian writer, *A Certain Lucas*

Old age is better for women than
for men. First of all, they have less
far to fall, since their lives are more
mediocre than those of most men.

> Simone de Beauvoir (1908-1986)
> French writer and philosopher

It is old age, rather than death, that
is to be contrasted with life. Old
age is life's parody, whereas death
transforms life into a destiny: in a
way it reserves it by giving it the
absolute dimension —"As unto
himself eternity changes him at
last." Death does away with time.

> Simone de Beauvoir (1908-1986)
> French writer and philosopher, *The
> Coming of Age*

When you're old, everything you
do is sort of a miracle.

> Millicent Fenwick (1910-1992)
> American politician

My race is run,
And the end has come
Of the mighty trail I blazed:
There lies ahead a darkening sea.
I hear the breakers roar below;
And curling mists, and a numbing
Cold are creeping up, steady

And sure of their helpless prey,
As from here there is no going
   back!

> Mirza Ghalib (1797-1869)
> Indian Urdu poet

But life itself is still
So full of goading excitement!
I alone,
I have only my song,
Though it too is slipping from me.

> Ikinilik (c. 1930)
> Eskimo poet

Who says I am old?
Is an old man like this?
Heart welcomes sweet flowers,
Laughter floats over fragrant cups:
What can I do, what can I say?
My hoary hair floats in the spring
   wind.

> Kim Chong-gu
> (c. 15th-16th century)
> Korean poet

Feeling indisposed towards the
   evening,
I drove up the ancient plains.
The setting sun is unspeakably
   beautiful,
Only it is approaching nightfall.

> Li Shang-yin (812–858)
> Chinese poet, "Rambling at Lo Yu
> Yuan"

"You have grown old, Jamil! Your
   youth is spent!" I say,
Buthaynah, don't say that!
Have you forgotten our days in
   Liwa, and in Dhawi 'l-Ajfur?
. . . And I young and soft-
   skinned, trailing my train behind
   me,

My hair black as the raven's wing,
  perfumed with musk and amber,
That was changed by the
  vicissitudes of time, as you well
  know!
But you! Like the governor's
  pearl, still a young girl,
We were neighbors once, sharing
  the same playground. How did I
  grow old and you did not?

> Jamil bin Ma'mar (c. 600)
> Ummayad love poet; master of the
> tragic 'Udhri love poetry, about which
> it was said: "a people who when they
> love, die."

The struggle tires us, and our hair
is gray.
You and I, old friend, can we just
  watch our efforts being washed
  away?

> Mao Zedong (1893–1976)
> Chairman of People's Republic of
> China, end of a poem Mao Zedong sent
> to Zhou En-lai during Zhou's last year

Disturb me not, O buoyant
  youths!
I of myself must travel on,
And go the road that you must
  tread,
And wait your coming there

> Maori poem (c. 18th century)
> sung by an old man taunted by youths

Old age is like a plane flying
through a storm. Once you're
aboard, there's nothing you can
do. You can't stop the plane; you
can't stop the storm; you can't
stop time. So one might as well accept it calmly, wisely.

> Golda Meir (1898–1978)
> Israeli prime minister

You laugh at me, now that you
  are young,
Because you see me old, and grey-
  haired.
I am an old man, but I have seen
  workmen
Make a coffin and a bier for a
  young lad.

> Samuel ha-Nagid (993–1056)
> Spanish Hebrew poet, "The Old Man's
> Warning"

I look at my shadow over and
  over in the lake;
I see no white face, only the
  white hair,
I have lost my youth, and shall
  never find it again.
Useless to stir the lake-water!

> Po Chu-i (772–846)
> Chinese poet, "Looking in the Lake"

The roots of the aged palm tree exceed those of the young one; the
old have a greater attachment to
the world.

> Sa'ib of Tabriz (c. 1601–1677)
> Persian poet

When a man becomes old, his
greed becomes young: sleep grows
heavy at the time of morning.

> Sa'ib of Tabriz (c. 1601–1677)
> Persian poet

Being over seventy is like being engaged in a war. All our friends are
going or gone and we survive
amongst the dead and dying as on
a battlefield.

> Muriel Spark (b. 1918)
> Scottish writer, *Memento Mori*

My eyes have seen much, but they are not weary. My ears have heard much, but they thirst for more.

Rabindranath Tagore (1861-1941)
Indian writer and philosopher

Sticks in one hand,
Branches in another:
I try to block old age with
bushes,
And frosty hair with sticks.
But white hair came by a short
cut,
Having seen through my devices.

U T'ak (1262-1342)
Korean poet

In late years I desire only peace;
For worldly affairs my heart has
no concern.
I have no long-range plan for my
own care;
All I know is to return to the old
woods,
Where the pine wind blows on
my loosened belt
And the mountain moon shines
on the strung zither.
You ask the law of failure and
success—
"The fisherman's song enters the
riverbank deep."

Wang Wei (699-759)
Chinese poet, "To Sub-prefect Chang"

on OPPRESSION

As long as one people sit on another and are deaf to their cry, so long will understanding and peace elude all of us.

Chinua Achebe (b. 1930)
Nigerian writer

The most potent weapon in the hands of the oppressor is the mind of the oppressed.

Steve Biko (1946-1977)
South African political activist

All oppression creates a state of war.

Simone de Beauvoir (1908-1986)
French writer and philosopher, *The Second Sex*

Oppression costs the oppressor too much if the oppressed stands up and protests. The protest need not be merely physical—the throwing of stones and bullets—if it is mental, spiritual; if it expresses itself in silent, persistent dissatisfaction, the cost to the oppressor is terrific.

W. E. B. Du Bois (1868-1963)
American writer and educator

We shall never secure emancipation from the tyranny of the white oppressor until we have achieved it in our own souls.

W. E. B. Du Bois (1868-1963)
American writer and educator, "Patient Assess," *Crisis*

Why does he harass me? I am not his slave.
I am the slave of the one Creator alone.

Firdausi (c. 955-1020)
Persian poet, *Book of Kings*

Does any man exist whose ideals, tastes, attitudes are so absolutely valid that he has the right to impose them upon others? Does there exist anywhere a type of man, or nation, that dares impose itself as a model to all men?

> Aaron David Gordon (1856–1922)
> Israeli writer

Every pearl in the royal crown is but the crystallized drop of blood fallen from the tearful eyes of the poor peasant.

> Amir Khusrau (1253–1325)
> Indian scholar

Oppressed people cannot remain oppressed forever.

> Martin Luther King, Jr.
> (1929–1968)
> American civil rights leader, "Letter from a Birmingham Jail"

Time is on the side of the oppressed today, it's against the oppressor. Truth is on the side of the oppressed today, it's against the oppressor. You don't need anything else.

> Malcolm X (1925–1965)
> American civil rights activist,
> *Malcolm X Speaks*

From ape to man, the process took
millions of years
from man to ape, will it take so many?
People of the world, come and visit
concentration camps in the heart
of distant jungles!

> Nguyen Chi Thien (b. 1933)
> Vietnamese writer, *Flowers of Hell*

Logic has nothing to do with oppression.

> Gloria Steinem (b. 1934)
> American feminist, "If Men Could Menstruate," *Outrageous Acts and Everyday Rebellions*

We must ask the high cadres . . . When you suppressed the rights of others to express freely their political views, did you secure your own?

> Wei Jingsheng (b. 1950)
> Chinese activist, from the underground periodical *Explorations*

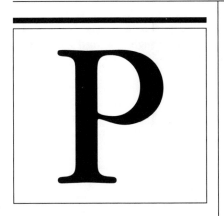

on **PARADOX**

The world is so constructed, that if you wish to enjoy its pleasures, you must also endure its pains. Whether you like it or not, you cannot have one without the other.

Brahmananda (1863-1922)
Hindu Indian philosopher

Three exist where three are not:
  Commoner exists where there is
    no king,
      but a kingdom cannot exist
      where there are no
      commoners;
  Grass exists where there is
    nothing that eats grass,
      but what eats grass cannot
      exist where no grass is;
  Water exists where there is
    nothing that drinks water,
      but what drinks water cannot
      exist where no water is.

Fulani (Nigerian) poem

Where there is no ugliness,
  beauty could not shine
Bitter and sweet, beauty and
  ugliness are foils

and necessary opposites.

Mirza Ghalib (1797-1869)
Indian Urdu poet

The south has a limit and no limit.
The sun is declining when it is at
  high noon.
A creature is dying when it is
  born.

Hui Shi (c. 370-290 B.C.E.)
Chinese philosopher

We pierce doors and windows to
  make a house;
And it is on these spaces where
  there is nothing that the
  usefulness of the house depends,
Therefore just as we take
  advantage of what is, we should
  recognize the usefulness of what
  is not.

Lao-tzu (c. 604-531 B.C.E.)
Chinese philosopher and founder of
Taoism, *Tao-te-ching*

We put thirty spokes together and
  call it a wheel;
But it is on the space where there
  is nothing that the utility of the
  wheel depends.
We turn clay to make a vessel;
But it is on the space where there
  is nothing that the utility of the
  vessel depends.
. . . .
Therefore just as we take
  advantage of what is, we should
  recognize the utility of what is
  not.

Lao-tzu (c. 604-531 B.C.E.)
Chinese philosopher and founder of
Taoism, *Tao-te-ching*

Those who do not know how to weep with their whole heart don't know how to laugh either.

> Golda Meir (1898–1978)
> Israeli prime minister

Be full of sorrow, that you may become full of joy; weep, that you may break into laughter.

> Rumi (1207–1273)
> Persian Sufi poet and mystic

The rose and the thorn, and sorrow and gladness are linked together.

> Sa'di of Shiraz (c. 1184–1292)
> Persian poet

on PASSIVITY

Passivity is fatal to us. Our goal is to make the enemy passive.

> Mao Zedong (1893–1976)
> Chairman of People's Republic of China

Only lies and evil come from letting people off.

> Iris Murdoch (b. 1919)
> Irish writer, *A Severed Head*

on THE PAST

Others fear what the morrow may bring.
I am afraid of what happened yesterday.

> Ansari (1006–1088)
> Persian Sufi poet

The beauty of the past belongs to the past.

> Margaret Bourke-White
> (1906–1971)
> American photojournalist

That past which is so presumptuously brought forward as a precedent for the present was itself founded on some past that went before it.

> Madame de Staël (1766–1817)
> French writer

The Moving Finger writes; and, having writ,
Moves on: nor all thy Piety nor Wit
    Shall lure it back to cancel half
    a Line,
Nor all Thy Tears wash out a
    Word of it.

> Omar Khayyám (c. 1048–1122)
> Persian poet and astronomer

There was a time indeed
they used to shake hands with
    their hearts.

> Gabriel Okara (b. 1921)
> Nigerian writer, "Once Upon a Time"

All men sorrow and lament
Over the spring that is past

> Siro (692–702)
> Korean poet, "Ode to Knight Chukchi"

The past is always with us, for nothing that once was time can ever depart.

> Rabindranath Tagore (1861–1941)
> Indian writer and philosopher

I closed the door on my past, but it crept back in through the window.

> Itamar Yaoz-Kest (b. 1934)
> Israeli writer

on PATIENCE

Whoever knocks persistently, ends
by entering.

> 'Ali (c. 600-661)
> First Imam of the Sh'ia branch of Islam;
> fourth caliph

Be patient with a bad neighbor: he
may move or face misfortune.

> Egyptian proverb

To lose patience is to lose the
battle.

> Mohandas K. Gandhi (1869-1948)
> Indian spiritual and political leader

If, like the prophet Noah, you
   have patience in the distress of
   the flood,
Calamity turns aside, and the
   desire of a thousand years comes
   forth.

> Hafiz (d. 1389)
> Persian poet

Let us proceed with caution, and
concentrating our strength, add to
it daily by winning over to our side
those barons who are vassals of
Shimazu. Then, when Satsuma
stands alone, like a tree shorn of its
leaves and branches, we will attack
and destroy the root.

> Toyotomi Hideyoshi (1536-1591)
> Japanese soldier and ruler, address to
> his generals

The strong, manly ones in life are
those who understand the meaning of the word *patience*. Patience
means restraining one's inclinations. There are seven emotions:
joy, anger, anxiety, love, fear, grief,
and hate; and if a man does not
give way to these, he can be called
patient. I am not as strong as I
might be, but I have long known
and practiced patience.

> Tokugawa Ieyasu (1543-1616)
> Japanese military and political leader,
> instructing his successor

Strength comes from waiting.

> José Martí (1853-1895)
> Cuban patriot

A noble, courageous man is recog-
nizable by the patience he shows
in adversity.

> Pachacutec Inca Yupanqui
> (1438-1471)
> Incan ruler

Some people think that as soon as
you plant a tree, it must bear fruit.
We must allow it to grow a bit.

> Tunku Putra Abdul Rahman
> (b. 1903)
> Malaysian politician

on PATRIOTISM AND NATIONALISM

Sovereignty and the right to rule
cannot be conferred on anyone no
matter who . . . as a result of an academic discussion. Sovereignty is
acquired by force and power and
violence.

> Kemal Ataturk (1881-1938)
> Turkish patriot and political leader

The escapist dream, the desire to
leave, cannot remain the only
theme. The dream must be different . . . no longer a desire to de-

part, but to create a new land inside our land.

Amilcar Cabral (1924–1973)
Guinea-Bissauan nationalist, "Notes sur
la poesie des Iles du Cap Vert," *Unite
et lutte*

We would rather starve than sell our national honor.

Indira Gandhi (1917–1984)
Indian prime minister, *New York Times*
(January 23, 1967)

If the half of my heart is here,
  doctor,
The other half is in China
With the army going down
  towards the Yellow River.
And then every morning, doctor,
Every morning at dawn
My heart is shot in Greece.

Nazim Hikmet (1902–1963)
Turkish poet, "Angina Pectoris"

Everything that exists in those regions, by way of justice, order, freedom and independence, great prosperity and great possessions, is undoubtedly the product of this noble feeling which spurs the members of the nation in their entirety to strive for a common purpose and a single goal.

Mustafa Kamil (1874–1908)
Egyptian nationalist

You're not supposed to be so blind with patriotism that you can't face reality. Wrong is wrong, no matter who does it or who says it.

Malcolm X (1925–1965)
American civil rights activist,
Malcolm X Speaks

All around, vastly and untidily, stretched the country for which he

grieved. He was to give his life for it. But would that great country . . . take the slightest heed of his death? He did not know; and it did not matter. His was a battlefield without glory, a battlefield where none could display the deeds of valor; it was the front line of the spirit.

Yukio Mishima (1925–1970)
Japanese writer

If the People one day desire to live, then fate must needs respond.

Al-Shabbi (1909–1934)
Arab poet

Nationalism cannot flower if it does not grow in the garden of internationalism.

Achmad Sukarno (1902–1970)
Indonesian politician

on PEACE

It is better we disintegrate in peace and not in pieces.

Nnamdi Azikwe (b. 1904)
Nigerian politician

So when in this day I see the leaders of nations again talking peace while preparing for war, I take fearful pause.

Martin Luther King, Jr.
(1929–1968)
American civil rights leader, *Where Do
We Go from Here: Chaos or
Community?*

Give ear. I am the mouth of my nation. When you listen to me, you listen to all the Iroquois. There is no evil in my heart. My song is the song of peace. We have had many war songs in my country, but we have thrown them all away.

Kiosaton (c. 1650)
Iroquois chief, asking French Governor Montmagny for the return of two prisoners (September 1645)

You can't separate peace from freedom, because no one can be at peace unless he has his freedom.

Malcolm X (1925-1965)
American civil rights activist, speech at the Militant Labor Forum Symposium, New York City (January 7, 1965)

It is better to win the peace and to lose the war.

Bob Marley (1945-1981)
Jamaican singer

The only alternative to war is peace and the only road to peace is negotiations.

Golda Meir (1898-1978)
Israeli prime minister

Peace is much more precious than a piece of land.

Anwar Sadat (1918-1981)
Egyptian military and political leader

Peace is in proportion to every pause: observe the difference between to run, to walk, to stand, to sit, to lie, to die.

Sa'ib of Tabriz (c. 1601-1677)
Persian poet

Stability and peace in our land will not come from the barrel of a gun, because peace without justice is an impossibility.

Desmond Tutu (b. 1931)
South African antiapartheid activist and religious leader

Today, as chief
Of the guardians of the seas
Of the land of the dawn,
I gaze up with awe
At the rising sun!

Yamamoto Isokuru (1884-1943)
Japanese Imperial Admiral

We do not want the peace of slaves nor the peace of the grave.

Emiliano Zapata (1879-1919)
Mexican revolutionary

on PERFECTION

Of all religious systems, Islam alone declares that individual perfection is possible in our earthly existence.

Muhammed Asad (1757-1799)
writer, *Islam at the Crossroads*

Perfect happiness is the absence of happiness; perfect glory is the absence of glory.

Chuang-tzu (c. 369-286 B.C.E.)
Chinese Taoist philosopher

Man is perfect only when bestowal and denial, humiliation and honor have become alike in his heart.

Abu 'Uthman al-Hayri (c. 910)
Sufi leader

All things are complete within ourselves.

Mencius (c. 390-305 B.C.E.)
Chinese philosopher

When perfection is unduly increased, it becomes the destroyer of life: the tender branch breaks when it bears too much fruit.

Sa'ib of Tabriz (c. 1601-1677)
Persian poet

If man cannot, what god dare claim perfection?

> Wole Soyinka (b. 1934)
> Nigerian writer, *Ogun Abibiman*

on PERSEVERANCE

Should various misfortunes assail thee, persevere in patience of body, speech, and mind.

> Buddhist scripture
> *The Supreme Path, the Rosary of Precious Gems*

If one concentrates on one thing and does not get away from it . . . he will possess strong, moving power.

> Cheng Yi (1033–1108)
> Chinese scholar, *I-shu*

Our greatest glory is not in never falling but in rising every time we fall.

> Confucius (551–479 B.C.E.)
> Chinese philosopher and founder of Confucianism, *Analects*

Our mountains will always be, our
   rivers will always
   be, our people will always be,
The American invaders defeated,
   we will rebuild our
   land ten times more beautiful.

> Ho Chi Minh (1892–1969)
> Vietnamese political leader, *Prison Diary, Poems*

You will kill ten of our men, and we will kill one of yours; and in the end, it will be you who tire of it.

> Ho Chi Minh (1892–1969)
> Vietnamese political leader, speaking about the Vietnam War

God is with those who patiently persevere.

> *Qur'an* (c. 610–656)
> sacred book of Islam, 8:46

On a charcoal kiln
a vine keeps climbing, while
being burned to death.

> Natsume Soseki (1867–1916)
> Japanese writer

When we undertake a task, we should not falter from first to last until the task is accomplished; if we fail, we should not begrudge our lives as a sacrifice—this is what we mean by loyalty. The ancient teaching of loyalty meant sometimes death.

> Sun Yat-sen (1866-1925)
> Chinese military and political leader

To keep a lamp burning, we have to keep putting oil in it.

> Mother Teresa (b. 1910)
> Yugoslavian missionary

on PERSPECTIVE

Long is the night to him who is awake; long is a mile to him who is tired; and long is life to the fool who does not know the true law.

> *Dhammapada* (c. 3rd century B.C.E.)
> collection of ancient Buddhist poems and aphorisms

How can one grasp the dimensions of a spacious house from the perspective [of a person] sitting in a well?

> Hui-lin (c. 5th century)
> Chinese Buddhist monk and philosopher, *Sung-shu*

When the water surges over the drowning man, then one javelin's length or a thousand are alike.

Abu'l Fadl al-Suqqari al-Marwazi
(c. 9th-10th century)
Persian poet

When a man is in the plains, he sees the lowly grass and the mighty pine tree and says how big is the tree and how small is the grass. But when he ascends the mountain and looks from its high peak to the plain below, the mighty pine tree and the lowly grass blend into one indistinct mass of green. So in the sight of the worldly man there are differences of rank and position, but when the divine sight is opened, there remains no distinction of high and low.

Ramakrishna (1836-1886)
Indian Hindu mystic

Snake's poison is life to the snake; it is in relation to man that it means "death."

Rumi (1207-1273)
Persian Sufi poet and mystic

For the water animals, the ocean is like a garden; for the land animals, it is death and pain.

Rumi (1207-1273)
Persian Sufi poet and mystic

A human feast is an indifferent morsel to a god.

Wole Soyinka (b. 1934)
Nigerian writer

We do not burn the woods to trap a squirrel—

We do not ask the mountain's aid to crack a walnut.

Wole Soyinka (b. 1934)
Nigerian writer

Mountains hide the light of day,
The Yellow River flows into the oceans;
But your view encompasses three hundred miles
By going up one flight of stairs.

Wang Zhi-huan (b. 695)
Chinese poet

I wonder what Heaven must think of the people down here on this small black speck in the universe that is earth, or of all their talk about the last few years—which are no more than a flash compared with eternity—being "a time of emergency." It's really ridiculous.

Yamamoto Isokuru (1884-1943)
Japanese Imperial Admiral

on **PHILOSOPHY**

The noblest in quality and highest in rank of all human activities is philosophy. . . . The philosopher's aim in his theoretical studies is to ascertain the truth; in his practical knowledge, to conduct himself in accordance with that truth.

Rasa'il al-Kindi (810-873)
Arab philosopher and physician

What one decides to do in a crisis depends upon one's philosophy of life, and that philosophy cannot be changed by an incident. If one hasn't any philosophy in a crisis, others make the decision.

Jeanette Rankin (1880-1973)
American feminist and politician

The most disappointing feature of working for a cause is that so few people have a philosophy of life. We used to say, in the suffrage movement, that we could trust the woman who believed in suffrage, but we could never trust the woman who just wanted to vote.

Jeanette Rankin (1880–1973)
American feminist and politician

Philosophy is the friend and milk-sister of religion; thus, injuries from people related to philosophy are the severest injuries [to religion] apart from the enmity, hatred, and quarrels which such [injuries] stir up between the two, which are companions by nature and lovers by essence and instinct.

Abu-l-Walid ibn-Rushd (1126–1198)
Spanish Arab philosopher

on PLACE

The place honors not the man; it is the man who honors the place.

Hebrew proverb

Everything that possesses life dies if it has to live in uncongenial surroundings.

Muhammad Iqbal (1873–1938)
Indian Muslim poet and philosopher

on PLEASURE

Cling to nothing for its loss is pain.

Dhammapada (c. 3rd century B.C.E.)
collection of ancient Buddhist poems
and aphorisms

Life is a curse, and yet in the
world of men

There is a moment of consolation,
a moment of pleasure.
Don't we feel it when we read
Musset's poetry?
Isn't that the feeling when we
listen to Mozart?

Nagai Kafu (1879–1959)
Japanese writer, "Flower of Grass"

I believe that man was created to enjoy himself, indeed, that he can claim it as his legitimate right. In fact, as long as he lives, man cannot help enjoying himself, even if he tries not. . . . Today the average person, when he hears the word *pleasure*, immediately thinks of something immoral. But nothing could be more wrong.

Nagai Kafu (1879–1959)
Japanese writer

Gold in piles, Jade in heaps
—then comes a single day old
death sweeps them all away!
What use are they?
—The cloudless hour, the day
benign, salute with carven cup
and amber wine.
With swaying waists, with flashing
teeth and eyes
—Ah, there's where pleasure truly
lies.

Ma Chih-yuan (1260–1325)
Chinese writer

Banish care. If there be bounds to pleasure, the saddest life must also have an end. Then weave your wreath of flowers, and sing your songs in praise of the all-powerful God; for the glory of this world soon fades away. Rejoice in the green freshness of your spring, for the day will come when you shall sigh for these joys in vain.

> Nezahualcoyotl (1418–1472)
> Mexican ruler

After carrying and collecting like the ant,
Enjoy—before the grave worm devours thee.

> Sa'di of Shiraz (c. 1184–1292)
> Persian poet, *Bustan*

Flowers and fruit are never combined in one place: it is impossible that teeth and delicacies should exist simultaneously.

> Sa'ib of Tabriz (c. 1601–1677)
> Persian poet

Pleasure is the state of being brought about by what you learn;
Learning is the process of entering into experience of this kind of pleasure.
No pleasure, no learning.
No learning, no pleasure.

> Wang Ken (1483–1540)
> Chinese philosopher, "Song of Joy"

on POETRY AND POETS

Poetry, whose material is language, is perhaps the most human and least worldly of the arts, the one in which the end product remains closest to the thought that inspired it.

> Hannah Arendt (1906–1975)
> American philosopher and historian, *The Human Condition*

"Poets are bandleaders who have failed?"
"Something like that."

> Ayi Kwei Armah (b. 1938)
> Ghanaian writer, *The Beautyful Ones Are Not Yet Born*

Poetry creates an abstract world using concrete materials—just like life itself.

> Asaf Halet Celebi (1907–1958)
> Turkish poet

A poem is nothing but a long word made up of syllables joined together. Syllables by themselves have no meaning. It is therefore futile to struggle with meaning in a poem.

> Asaf Halet Celebi (1907–1958)
> Turkish poet

It shall come to pass
That I must search for new songs,
That I must dig in the ruins for new poetry,
That I reject the roses that come from the dictionary;

For roses grow on the arm of the peasant,
In the hand of the worker,
The wound of the fighter,
On the face of the rock.

> Mahmoud Darwish (b. 1942)
> Palestinian poet, *Akhir al-Layl* (*End of the Night*)

The bad poem dies before its author, but the excellent one lives, though its author dies.

> Dibil (d. 872)
> Arab poet

They [poems] take shape in the minds of men and rise up like bubbles from the depths of the sea, bubbles that seek the air to burst into light.

> Eskimo, anonymous (c. 1930)

When poems stop talking about the moon and begin to mention poverty, trade unions, color, color lines and colonies, somebody tells the police.

> Langston Hughes (1902–1967)
> American writer, *My Adventures as a Social Poet*

I chisel the jade, I pour gold in
  the crucible;
Here is my song!
I inlay the emeralds;
Here is my song.

> Ixtilxochitl (c. 1550)
> Aztec king

[Poetry] was invented by primitive man to make it easy to remember the second line; then he found a certain beauty in it.

> Orhan Veli Kanik (1914–1950)
> Turkish poet, *Garip (A Stranger in a Strange Land)*

Poetry is an impassioned testament to man's inner freedom.

> Shiv Kumar (b. 1921)
> Indian writer

A poem is something sacred. Let
  no one
Take it for anything except itself.

> José Martí (1853–1895)
> Cuban patriot, *Poetry Is Sacred*

The poet is an untier of knots, and love without words is a knot, and it drowns.

> Gabriela Mistral (1889–1957)
> Chilean poet

Political poetry is more profoundly emotional than any other—at least as much as love poetry—and cannot be forced because then it becomes vulgar and unacceptable. It is necessary first to pan though all other poetry in order to become a political poet.

> Pablo Neruda (1904–1973)
> Chilean poet and diplomat

All perishes
Only poetry remains.

> Nguyen Chi Thien (b. 1933)
> Vietnamese writer, *Flowers of Hell*

Too much blood has run under
  the bridge
To go on believing
That only one road is right.

In poetry everything is permitted.

With only one condition, of
  course:
You must improve upon the blank
  page.

> Nicanor Parra (b. 1914)
> Chilean poet, "Jovenes"

If the world is drunk and tattered,
I am its disheveled song,
I am the song,
And if the world is a maddened
  dog,
I am the saliva dripping from its
  mouth,
I am the saliva.

I am the man devoured by
  longings
For another incarnation,
Incarnation of man.

> Abraham Schlonski (b. 1900)
> Israeli poet

The poet speaks to all men of that other life of theirs that they have smothered and forgotten.

> Edith Sitwell (1887-1964)
> English writer, *Rhyme and Reason*

[The poets' role is that of] capturing on their instruments the secret stir of life in the air and giving it voice in the music of prophecy.

> Rabindranath Tagore (1861-1941)
> Indian writer and philosopher, during
> lectures in China (1924)

It is poetry which, without exertion, moves heaven and earth, stirs the feelings of gods and spirits invisible to the eye, softens the relations between men and women, calms the hearts of fierce warriors.

> Ki no Tusrayuki (c. 859-945)
> Japanese editor

To be a poet is to shiver with the
  wind,
To dream by moonlight and to
  frolic with the clouds;
To have one's soul pinned to a
  thousand heartstrings,
Or torn apart by a hundred
  different loves.

> Xuan Dieu (20th century)
> Vietnamese poet, "Cam Suc" ("Poetic
> Feeling")

The painter paints, the storyteller
  tells his story, the sculptor
  sculpts
the poet, however, doesn't
  poetize,
he's a mountain by the roadside,
or a tree, or a scent,
something already passed,
  something that was
but won't be again . . .
. . . .
something which leaves behind
something.

> Natan Zach (b. 1930)
> Israeli poet, "The Painter Paints"

on POLICY

People can be depended on to enjoy the results, but they must not be consulted about the beginnings.

> Li Ping (c. 200 B.C.E.)
> Chinese engineer

If we want to work out a policy for the present, we must examine the past and prepare for the future, discard the material and elevate the spirit, rely on the individual and exclude the mass.

> Lu Xun (1881-1936)
> Chinese writer, *Lu Xun Quanji*

The wise man does not try to set up detailed systems. One uses what is right for today to govern the world of today, but this does not mean that it will be right for a later day.

> Wang Fu-chih (1619-1692)
> Chinese philosopher

on POLITICAL MOVEMENTS

A rich man told me recently that a liberal is a man who tells other people what to do with their money.

Imamu Amiri Baraka (b. 1934)
American writer

When a just cause reaches its floodtide . . . whatever stands in the way must fall before its overwhelming power.

Carrie Chapman Catt
(1859–1947)
American suffragist, speech "Is Woman Suffrage Progressing?" at Stockholm, Sweden

Radicalism is a label that is always applied to people who are endeavoring to get freedom.

Marcus Garvey (1887–1940)
American political leader, *Philosophy and Opinions*

A political movement must keep in touch with reality and the prevailing conditions. Long speeches, the shaking of fists, the banging of tables, and strongly worded resolutions out of touch with the objective conditions do not bring about mass action and can do a great deal of harm to the organization and the struggle we serve.

Nelson Mandela (b. 1918)
South African president, "No Easy Walk to Freedom"

All reactionaries are paper tigers.

Mao Zedong (1893–1976)
Chairman of People's Republic of China

I am not a man speaking but a people protesting.

José Martí (1853–1895)
Cuban patriot

Socialism is an attractive goal, but concentration of power is as dangerous as concentration of capital.

Asoka Mehta (b. 1911)
Indian politician

My interest is not in the capture of power, but in the control of power by the people.

Jayaprakash Narayan (1902–1979)
Indian nationalist, at the All India Youth Conference (June 29, 1975)

Democracy and socialism are means to an end, not the end itself.

Jawaharlal Nehru (1889–1964)
Indian prime minister

The forces of a capitalist society, if left unchecked, tend to make the rich richer and the poor poorer.

Jawaharlal Nehru (1889–1964)
Indian prime minister

Today we are passing to our liberation through a desert strewn with bodies and where anguish and pain are devastating us. Many suffer the temptation of those who walked with Moses and wanted to turn back and did not work together. It is the same old story. God, however, wants to save the people by making a new history. . . . History will not fail; God sustains it.

Oscar Romero (1917–1980)
El Salvadorean Catholic archbishop, "The Church and Human Liberation" (March 24, 1980), last sermon before he was killed

Every political good carried to the extreme must be productive of evil.

Mary Wollstonecraft (1759-1797)
English feminist, *The French Revolution*

on POLITICS

The secret of political bargaining is to look more strong than what you really are.

Subhas Chandra Bose (1897-1945)
Indian nationalist leader

If the superior man enters public life, he does not change from what he was in private life.

Chung yung (Doctrine of the Mean)
Confucian text

The pursuit of politics is religion, morality, and poetry all in one.

Madame de Staël (1766-1817)
French writer

The people are aware of how politics affects their daily life. It's the politicians who are behind the times.

Takako Doi (b. 1928)
Japanese politician

Politics is the reflex of the business and industrial world.

Emma Goldman (1869-1940)
American anarchist, "The Tragedy of Women's Emancipation," *Anarchism and Other Essays*

Politics is the profession of those who have neither trade nor art.

Muhammad Hijazi (20th century)
Iranian writer and politician, *Hazar Sokhan (A Thousand Sayings)*

Military action without politics is like a tree without a root.

Ho Chi Minh (1892-1969)
Vietnamese political leader

Politics is war without bloodshed; war is politics with bloodshed.

Mao Zedong (1893-1976)
Chairman of People's Republic of China, *Quotations*

Politics and church are the same. They keep the people in ignorance.

Bob Marley (1945-1981)
Jamaican singer

Politics is a game of worldly people. . . . And instead of the maxim "One should conquer anger by opposing it with tranquility, non-anger," as preached by Buddha, I prefer to rely on the maxim of Sri Krishna: "My response to the devotees is in perfect harmony with the manner of their approach." Both methods are equally honest and righteous, but the one is more suited to this world than the other.

Tilak (1856-1920)
Indian political leader

on POPULAR OPINION

General opinion is the opinion of one or a few for which the public is held responsible.

Muhammad Hijazi (20th century)
Iranian writer and politician, *Hazar Sokhan (A Thousand Sayings)*

It's painful to listen to the news in the morning.

It's painful to listen to the barking of dogs.

> Nizar Qabbani (b. 1932)
> Syrian/Lebanese writer and publisher

"Young man," he said, "go after property. But never show God your nakedness, and never despise the people. The voice of the people is the voice of God."

> Ngugi wa Thiong'o (b. 1936)
> Kenyan writer

How should one live, to please people?
Live lavishly and they laugh at you; live frugally and they despise you.
If you are tall, they call you a giant; if you are short, they call you a dwarf;
If you are fat, they call you a great barrel;
If you are thin, they say you are hanging your backbone out to dry.

> Vietnamese folksong

on POVERTY

Poor is a state of mind you never grow out of, but being broke is just a temporary condition.

> Dick Gregory (b. 1932)
> American civil rights activist, *Nigger*

There is something about poverty that smells like death. Dead dreams dropping off the heart like leaves in a dry season and rotting around the feet; impulses smothered too long in the fetid air of underground caves.

> Zora Neale Hurston
> (1903–1960)
> American writer, *Dust Tracks on a Road*

It's easy to be independent when you've got money. But to be independent when you haven't got a thing—that's the Lord's test.

> Mahalia Jackson (1911–1972)
> American singer, *Movin' On Up*

Always think of the days of scarcity during the days of abundance, so that you will not long for the days of abundance during times of scarcity.

> Li Ju-chen (c. 1763–1830)
> Chinese writer and scholar, *Ching-hua yuan (Flowers in the Mirror)*

The poor attend to their own virtue in solitude.

> Mencius (c. 390–305 B.C.E.)
> Chinese philosopher, *Meng-tzu*

The poor are our brothers and sisters . . . people in the world who need love, who need care, who have to be wanted.

> Mother Teresa (b. 1910)
> Yugoslavian missionary

I believe that honor and money nearly always go together. . . . Seldom or *never* is a poor man honored by the world; however worthy of honor he may be, he is apt rather to be despised by it.

> Teresa of Avila (1515–1582)
> Spanish nun, "Way of Perfection"

When poverty is more disgraceful than even vice, is not morality cut to the quick?

> Mary Wollstonecraft (1759-1797)
> English feminist, "Of the Pernicious Effects which Arise from the Unnatural Distinctions Established in Society," *A Vindication of the Rights of Women*

on POWER

I am more and more convinced that man is a dangerous creature; and that power, whether vested in many or a few, is ever grasping, and like the grave, cries, "Give, give!"

> Abigail Adams (1744-1818)
> American First Lady and feminist, letter to her husband, John Adams (November 27, 1775)

Grass never grows again where my horse has once trodden.

> Attila the Hun (406-453)
> Central Asian ruler and conqueror of Europe

The weight of great power crushes the goodness of the man who rules and the honesty of those who are ruled.

> Roman Baldorioty de Castro (1822-1887)
> Puerto Rican politician

Chairman Mao once said that political power comes from the barrel of a gun. He was only partly right: power that comes from the barrel of a gun can be effective only for a short time. In the end, people's love for truth, justice, freedom, and democracy will triumph. No matter what governments do, the human spirit will always prevail.

> Dalai Lama (b. 1935)
> Tibetan spiritual and political leader

Power concedes nothing without a demand. It never did, and it never will. Find out just what people will submit to, and you have found out the exact amount of injustice and wrong which will be imposed upon them; and these will continue till they have resisted with either words or blows, or with both. The limits of tyrants are prescribed by the endurance of those whom they suppress.

> Frederick Douglass (1817-1895)
> American abolitionist, letter to Gerrit Smith (March 30, 1849)

Influence comes out of the work that you've done and the things you've stood for. Influence and power shouldn't be given to just anybody who wants them.

> Millicent Fenwick (1910-1992)
> American politician

Power is of two kinds: one is obtained by the fear of punishment and the other by acts of love.

> Mohandas K. Gandhi (1869-1948)
> Indian spiritual and political leader

When one reaches absolute power, one loses total contact with reality.

> Gabriel García Márquez (b. 1928)
> Colombian writer

He who is able to conquer others is powerful; he who is able to conquer himself is more powerful.

> Lao-tzu (c. 604-531 B.C.E.)
> Chinese philosopher and founder of Taoism, *Tao-te ching*

211

Power in defense of freedom is greater than power in behalf of tyranny and oppression.

> Malcolm X (1925-1965)
> American civil rights activist, speech in New York City (1965)

Power never takes a back step—only in the face of more power.

> Malcolm X (1925-1965)
> American civil rights activist, *Malcolm X Speaks*

Every Communist must grasp the truth: Political power grows out of the barrel of a gun.

> Mao Zedong (1893-1976)
> First chairman of People's Republic of China

When one by force subdues men, they do not submit to him in heart. They submit because their strength is not adequate to resist.

> Mencius (c. 390-305 B.C.E.)
> Chinese philosopher

He is the best of men who dislikes power.

> Muhammad (570-632)
> Prophet of Islam

To be a complete victim may be another source of power.

> Iris Murdoch (b. 1919)
> Irish writer, *The Unicorn*

Power comes invariably to be usurped by a handful of the most ruthless among the erstwhile revolutionaries when power comes out of the barrel of a gun and the gun is not in the hands of the common people.

> Jayaprakash Narayan (1902-1979)
> Indian nationalist

Power is not merely shouting aloud. Power is to act positively with all the components of power.

> Gamel Abdel Nasser (1918-1970)
> Egyptian revolutionary and president, *The Philosophy of Revolution*

Power immobilizes; it freezes with a single gesture—grandiose, terrible, theatrical, or finally, simply monotonous—the variety which is life.

> Octavio Paz (b. 1914)
> Mexican writer

Our shouting is louder than our actions
Our swords are taller than us.
That is our tragedy.

> Nizar Qabbani (b. 1932)
> Syrian/Lebanese writer and publisher

For whoso desireth power: Lo! all power is with God.

> *Qur'an* (c. 610-656)
> sacred book of Islam, xxxv:10

To achieve . . . you have to know what you're doing, and that's real power.

> Ayn Rand (1905-1982)
> American writer

Who grasps with his fist one who has an arm of steel injures only his own powerless wrist. Wait till inconstant fortune ties his hand, then . . . pick out his brains.

> Sa'di of Shiraz (c. 1184-1292)
> Persian poet, *Gulistan*

Without compulsion, no settlement could be founded. The workers would have no supervisor. The rivers would not bring the overflow.

Sumerian text (c. 3000 B.C.E.)

Power takes as ingratitude the writhing of its victims.

Rabindranath Tagore (1861-1941)
Indian writer and philosopher, *Stray Birds*

Not hammer-strokes, but dance of the water sings pebbles into perfection.

Rabindranath Tagore (1861-1941)
Indian writer and philosopher, *Stray Birds*

The force of arms only reveals man's weakness.

Rabindranath Tagore (1861-1941)
Indian writer and philosopher

Power . . . is the supreme end for all those who have not understood.

Simone Weil (1909-1943)
French philosopher, *Gravity and Grace*

on **PRAYER**

Greed, hate, delusion, rooted in self,
O may they die whenever rooted in me.

Burmese prayer in Pagan pagoda (c. 1140)

Prayer is the little implement
Through which Men reach
Where Presence—is denied them.

Emily Dickinson (1830-1886)
American poet

Prayer is not an old woman's idle amusement. Properly understood and applied, it is the most potent instrument of action.

Mohandas K. Gandhi (1869-1948)
Indian spiritual and political leader,
Non-Violence in Peace and War

Ziyad, the slave of Aiyash, son of Abu Rabi'a said, "I am more afraid of being hindered from prayer than of being denied an answer to my prayer."

al-Jahiz (c. 778-869)
Arab philosopher and writer, *Kitab al-Bayan (The Book of Proof)*

In the secret of night,
my prayer climbs like the liana,
. . . .
My prayer is, and I am not.
It grows, and I perish.
I have only my hard breath,
my reason and my madness.
I cling to the vine of my prayer.
I tend it at the root
of the stalk of night.

Gabriela Mistral (1889-1957)
Chilean poet, "The Liana"

Him to whom you pray is nearer to you than the neck of your camel.

Muhammad (570-632)
Prophet of Islam

My lot is low, my purpose high; but I am confident of one thing, that the God will be gratified to hear me, though fools may laugh.

Tulsidas (1523-1624)
Indian philosopher, *Ramcharitmanas*

on **PREJUDICE**

Race prejudice decreases values, both real estate and human.

W. E. B. Du Bois (1868–1963)
American writer and educator

Give me a prejudice and I will move the world.

Gabriel García Márquez (b. 1928)
Colombian writer

Whoever thinks he is objective must already be half drunk.

Lu Xun (1881–1936)
Chinese writer

The Ku Klux Klan never dies. They just stop wearing sheets because sheets cost too much.

Thurgood Marshall (1908–1993)
American Supreme Court Justice

on **THE PRESENT**

Say not "tomorrow" or "the day after tomorrow": for those that perished, perished because they abode always in their hopes, until the truth came upon them suddenly in their heedlessness; and willful as they were, they were carried to their dark, narrow graves, abandoned by all their kith and kin.

Ibrahim ben Adham (d. 777)
Prince of Balkh and Sufi mystic convert

Happy are those whose life is
  today
and only today
sad are the prophets
and those others whose eyes are
  open to the past.

Blessed are they who neither see
  their painful yesterdays
not their tomorrows filled with
  despair:
They shall rest in peace.

Ayi Kwei Armah (b. 1938)
Ghanaian writer, Ramblers' song,
Fragments

Today's hunger does not share itself with tomorrow's hunger.

Bamabara (West African) proverb

Listen to the Exhortation of the
  Dawn!
Look to this Day!
For it is Life, the very Life of Life.
In its brief course lie all the
Verities and Realities of your
  Existence;
The Bliss of Growth,
The Glory of Action,
The Splendor of Beauty;
For Yesterday is but a Dream,
And Tomorrow is only a Vision:
But Today well lived makes
Every Yesterday a Dream of
  Happiness,
And every Tomorrow a Vision of
  Hope.
Look well therefore to this Day!
Such is the Salutation of the
  Dawn!

Sanskrit poem
"The Salutation of the Dawn"
[attributed by some to Kalidasa (5th
century B.C.E.), Hindu poet]

One person dies at the age of ten, another at the age of one hundred. Perfect saints die, and so do dangerous fools. . . . Once dead, they are molding bones. As molding bones, they are equal. Who can tell the difference between them? Let

us therefore grasp life's moment—
what is the point of worrying
about the time after death?

Yang Tse (420–360 B.C.E.)
Chinese Taoist philosopher, *Lieh-tzu*

on PRIDE

The worst man is the one who sees
himself as the best.

'Ali (c. 600–661)
First Imam of the Sh'ia branch of Islam;
fourth caliph

They came to shoe the Pasha's
horses, so the black beetle
stretched forth its foot.

Arab proverb

There is no cure for the
  misfortune of the proud,
For a wicked plant has taken root
  in him.
An intelligent man's mind can
  understand a proverb;
And a wise man desires a listening
  ear.

Ben Sira (c. 2nd century B.C.E.)
Hebrew scholar and philosopher

You are either alive and proud, or
you are dead, and when you are
dead, you can't care anyway.

Steve Biko (1946–1977)
South African political activist

Pride only goes the length one can
spit.

Congo proverb

I believe in pride of race and lineage and self: in pride of self so
deep as to scorn injustice to other
selves; in pride of lineage so great
as to despise no man's father; in
pride of race so chivalrous as neither to offer bastardy to the weak
nor beg wedlock of the strong,
knowing that men may be brothers
in Christ, even though they be not
brothers-in-law.

W. E. B. Du Bois (1868–1963)
American writer and educator,
Darkwater: Voices from within the Veil

Never bend your head. Always
hold it high. Look the world
straight in the face.

Helen Keller (1880–1968)
American writer and lecturer, to a
five-year-old blind child

Do not turn thy cheek in scorn,
nor walk insolently on the earth;
Allah does not love an arrogant
boaster.

Qur'an (c. 610–656)
sacred text of Islam, 31:18

One in whose head is conceit,
Think not that he will ever listen
  to truth.

Sa'di of Shiraz (c. 1184–1292)
Persian poet, *Bustan*

The proverb runs: How great that
man would be were he not so arrogant.

Talmud
(c. late 4th–early 6th century)
ancient body of Jewish civil and
canonical law, Kallah Rabbati 3

Why was man created on the sixth
day? To teach that if he is ever
swollen with pride, it can be said
to him: A flea came ahead of thee
in creation.

Talmud
(c. late 4th–early 6th century)
ancient body of Jewish civil and
canonical law, Sanhedrin 38a

on PRIORITIES

The hungry man is not in the proper frame of mind to pray. Let him first eat, and then pray.

> Nanak (1469–1539)
> Indian religious leader and founder of Sikhism

One must eat and breathe before concerning himself with politics, social affairs, and culture.

> Park Chung Hee (1917–1979)
> South Korean politician and soldier

on PRISON

Prison is a good place in which to reflect. It was a permanent polishing of my ideas.

> Muhammed Ahmed Ben Bella (b. 1916)
> Algerian revolutionary leader and politician

Every house was festooned with
  flowers and with lanterns.
On the national day, the whole
  country went wild with joy,
But on that very day, I was placed
  in chains and transferred:
The wind remains contrary to the
  flight of the eagle.

> Ho Chi Minh (1892–1969)
> Vietnamese political leader

A prison is never narrow when the imagination can range in it as it will.

> Marguerite of Navarre (1492–1549)
> French writer and religious reformer,
> "Novel XL, the Fourth Day," *The Heptmeron, or Novels of the Queen of Navarre*

The sentence was seven years' hard labor, to be followed by five

in exile. I was not frightened. I was even flattered to get such a long term, which was the first official acknowledgement of my work in the country.

> Irina Ratushinskaya (20th century)
> Russian writer

Sometimes people have sympathized with me because long years of my life were spent in jail and in exile. Well, those years . . . were a mixed experience. I hated them because they separated me from the dearest thing in the world—the struggle of my people for rebirth. At the same time, they were a blessing because I had what is so rare in this world—the opportunity of thinking about basic issues, the opportunity of examining afresh the beliefs I held.

> Achmad Sukarno (1902–1970)
> Indonesian politician

on PROBLEMS

Everything is small at the beginning and then increases, except trouble, which is great at its beginning and then decreases.

> Arab proverb

You're either part of the problem or part of the solution.

> Eldridge Cleaver (b. 1935)
> American civil rights activist,
> *Soul on Ice*

The day the world turns our way, we are great philosophers and can close our eyes to possessions; but the day the world turns against us, we are bawling children, grasping for toys.

Muhammad Hijazi (20th century)
Iranian writer and politician, *Hazar Sokhan* (*A Thousand Sayings*)

He who regards many things easy will find many difficulties. Therefore the sage regards things difficult, and consequently never has difficulties.

Lao-tzu (c. 604–531 B.C.E.)
Chinese philosopher and founder of Taoism, *Tao-te-ching*

You can't solve a problem? Well, get down and investigate the present facts and [the problem's] past history! When you have investigated the problem thoroughly, you will know how to solve it.

Mao Zedong (1893-1976)
Chairman of People's Republic of China

The origin is the lack of mutual love. . . . All the disorders of the world have this cause and this alone.

Mo-tze (c. 5th century B.C.E.)
Chinese philosopher

Crises and deadlocks, when they occur, have at least this advantage: that they force us to think.

Jawaharlal Nehru (1889-1964)
Indian prime minister

Every little thing counts in a crisis.

Jawaharlal Nehru (1889-1964)
Indian prime minister

That which brings misfortune is not big.

Nigerian proverb

The march of good fortune has backward slips: to retreat one or two paces gives wings to the jumper.

Sa'ib of Tabriz (c. 1601-1677)
Persian poet

A thorn can only be extracted if you know where it is.

Rabindranath Tagore (1861-1941)
Indian writer and philosopher

on PROGRESS

We have turned our mud into something useful. We are going to be producing this year about thirteen million clay bricks. . . . All right, we have mud. Make something of the mud. And this is the view I have of our whole region: to take our circumstances as they are and turn them into assets.

Linden Forbes Sampson Burnham (1926-1985)
Guyanese politician

Creation was not finished at the dawn of this earth, but creation continues, and we have a lot to do to make the world a better place.

George Cable Price (b. 1919)
Belizean politician

Always remember that the people are not fighting for ideas, nor for what is in men's minds. The people fight and accept the sacrifices demanded by the struggle in order to gain material advantages, to live better and in peace, to benefit from progress, and for the better future of their children. National liberation, the struggle against colonialism, the construction of peace, progress and independence are hollow words devoid of any significance unless they can be translated into a real improvement of living conditions.

Amilcar Cabral (1924–1973)
Guinea-Bissauan nationalist, *Palavras de orden gerais do Camarada Amilcar Cabral aos responsaveis do partido* (November 1965)

You cannot hope to build a better world without improving the individuals. To that end each of us must work for his own improvement, and at the same time share a general responsibility for all humanity, our particular duty being to aid those to whom we think we can be most useful.

Marie Curie (1867–1934)
French scientist, *Pierre Curie*

We consider progress as legitimate only when it reinforces, rather than undermines, freedom and democracy.

Eduardo Frei Montalva (b. 1911)
Chilean politician

Whenever you take a step forward, you are bound to disturb something. You disturb the air as you go forward, you disturb the dust, the ground. You trample upon things. When a whole society moves forward, this trampling is on a much bigger scale; and each thing that you disturb, each vested interest which you want to remove, stands as an obstacle.

Indira Gandhi (1917–1984)
Indian prime minister, address to United Nations Plenary Session, Conference on the Human

Environment, Stockholm, Sweden (June 14, 1972)

We are moving. We are travelling at a remarkable speed, but we also carry with us our old baggage which is fit for the journey.

Tawfiq al-Hakim (b. 1902)
Egyptian writer, *"Postscript to Food for the Millions"*

Do you suppose mankind has finally understood and learned? Has the time come for mankind, which knew how to spend millions of millions on destruction and enslavement, to learn how to spend it on construction and on making people happy? . . . Do you suppose the air squadrons of today with the white parachutes will be the angels of the sky tomorrow, landing to erase the divisions that the hand of barbarism has placed on earth, beginning long ago, to separate one man from his brother?

Tawfiq al-Hakim (b. 1902)
Egyptian writer, *The Reign of Darkness*

The salvation of the world is attainable, but it is necessary for each of us to set to work with all our strength. If we exert a little more effort, the salvation of the world will come a little sooner. The world is built little by little, a bit at a time. But even this little depends entirely upon the energetic contributions of you and me and the other fellow.

Hu Shih (1891–1962)
Chinese writer, "Shih-yen-chu-i"

There is a spirit and a need and a man at the beginning of every great human advance. Each of these must be right for that particular moment of history, or nothing happens.

> Coretta Scott King (b. 1927)
> American civil rights leader, *My Life with Martin Luther King, Jr.*

To live today and still say "reject the barbarians" and "drive them out of our territory" is certainly superficial and absurd talk.
. . . How can we get along without weapons and techniques? The method of self-strengthening lies in learning what they can do, and in taking over what they rely upon.

> Li Hung-chang (1823–1901)
> Chinese politician

We are still climbing a steep hill. We are far from the top, but we can see the top in the distance.

> Luis Muñoz Marín (b. 1898)
> Puerto Rican politician

We must make progress slowly so as to preserve the progress we have already made.

> Haile Selassie (1892–1975)
> Ethiopian emperor

When old words die out on the tongue, new melodies break forth from the heart; and where the old tracks are lost, new country is revealed with its wonders.

> Rabindranath Tagore (1861–1941)
> Indian writer and philosopher, *Gitanjali*

By habits of thrift and economy, by way of the industrial school and college, we are coming up. We are crawling up, working up, yea, bursting up—often through oppression, unjust discrimination and prejudice—but through them all we are coming up, and with proper habits, intelligence, and property, there is no power on earth than can permanently stay our progress.

> Booker T. Washington (1856–1915)
> American educator, speech at Harvard University (1896)

The history of mankind's battle forward through bloodshed is like the formation of coal, where a great deal of wood is needed to produce a small amount of coal.

> Wen Yiduo (1899–1947)
> Chinese writer

on PROMISES

A promise is a cloud; fulfillment is rain.

> Arab proverb

In your promises cleave to what is right,
And you will be able to fulfill your word.

> Confucius (551–479 B.C.E.)
> Chinese philosopher, founder of Confucianism, *Analects*

If the unemployed could eat plans and promises, they would be able to spend the winter on the Riviera.

> W. E. B. Du Bois (1868–1963)
> American writer and educator, "As the Crow Flies," *Crisis* (January 1931)

Breach of promise is no less an act of insolvency than a refusal to pay one's debt.

Mohandas K. Gandhi (1869–1948)
Indian spiritual and political leader

Good words do not last long unless they amount to something. Words do not pay for my dead people. . . . Good words will not give my people good health and stop them from dying. Good words will not get my people a home where they can live in peace and take care of themselves. I am tired of talk that comes to nothing. It makes my heart sick when I remember all the good words and broken promises.

Chief Joseph (c. 1840–1904)
Nez Percé chief

on **PROPERTY**

Public property has the same standing with me as that of an orphan; if it is much, it must be conserved, and if it is little, it must be used with care.

Abu-Bakr (c. 580–634)
Companion to the Prophet Muhammad
and first caliph of Islam

A life is sacred. Property is intended to serve life, and no matter how much we surround it with rights and respect, it has no personal being. It is part of the earth man walks on; it is not man.

Martin Luther King, Jr.
(1929–1968)
American civil rights leader, *The Trumpet of Conscience*

There is something that governments care for far more than human life, and that is the security of property; and so it is through property that we shall strike the enemy.

Emmeline Pankhurst (1858–1928)
English suffragist, speech (October 17, 1912)

The white people have no right to take the land from the Indians, because they had it first; it is theirs. They may sell, but all must join. Any sale not made by all is not valid. The late sale is bad; it was made by a part only. Part do not know how to sell. It requires all to make a bargain for all. All red men have equal rights to the unoccupied land. The right of occupancy is as good in one place as in another. There cannot be two occupations in the same place; the first excludes all others. It is not so in hunting or traveling; for there, the same ground will serve many, as they may follow each other all day; but the camp is stationary, and that is occupancy. It belongs to the first who sits down on his blanket or skins which he has thrown upon the ground, and till he leaves it, no other has a right.

Tecumseh (c. 1768–1813)
Shawnee chief, in council with
Governor W. H. Harrison at Vincennes,
Indiana (1810)

on **PROVERBS**

Proverbs are the lamp of speech.

Arabic proverb

When the occasion comes, the proverb comes.

Twi (West African) proverb

on **THE PUBLIC**

Blessed are the common people. God loves them; that is why he made millions of them.

> Nnamdi Azikwe (b. 1904)
> Nigerian politician, address at the annual convention of the National Council of Nigeria and the Cameroons, Kaduna Nigeria (April 5, 1948)

In the turbulence of this anxious and active world many people are leading uneventful, lonely lives. To them, dreariness, not disaster, is the enemy. They seldom realize that on their steadfastness, on their ability to withstand the fatigue of dull repetitive work, and on their courage in meeting constant small adversities depend in great measure the happiness and prosperity of the community as a whole. . . . The upward course of a nation's history is due in the long run to the soundness of heart of its average men and women.

> Elizabeth II (b. 1926)
> English queen, radio broadcast, from Sandringham to the Commonwealth (December 25, 1954)

Our nation is founded upon people—if we cannot think how to foster those people, then we ourselves destroy our own foundation.

> K'ang Yu-wei (1858-1927)
> Chinese political philosopher, *Memorial*

The people who fill the modern world are winning the right to live, after a ceaseless struggle. They have a right to poetry, as to everything else, and poetry will address itself to their tastes.

> Orhan Veli Kanik (1914-1950)
> Turkish poet, *Garip (A Stranger in a Strange Land)*

This country [the Philippines] is like a pyramid, like a tower. It is made up of millions of stones. . . . And the foundation stone of this pyramid is the common man.

> Ramon Magsaysay (1907-1957)
> Philippine president

I am alone with the masses.

> Mao Zedong (1893-1976)
> Chairman of People's Republic of China

Great bodies of people are never responsible for what they do.

> Virginia Woolf (1882-1941)
> English writer, *A Room of One's Own*

on **PUNISHMENT**

He who injures or kills another who longs for happiness will not find it for himself.

> *Dhammapada* (c. 3rd century B.C.E.)
> collection of ancient Buddhist poems and aphorisms

Society punishes only the unsuccessful traitor.

> Muhammad Hijazi (20th century)
> Iranian writer and politician, *Hazar Sokhan (A Thousand Sayings)*

He may only chastise who loves.

> Rabindranath Tagore (1861-1941)
> Indian writer and philosopher, "The Judge," *The Crescent Moon*

on QUESTIONS AND ANSWERS

Whenever you do something without asking yourself, "Why am I doing this?"—that is meaningless life. . . . The "why" of life makes it meaningful. . . . Only when an answer is given is one living life as a man.

Hu Shih (1891-1962)
Chinese writer, "Hsin sheng-huo" ("The New Life"), *Hsin sheng-huo tso chi*

There is really nothing more to say—except why. But since why is difficult to handle, one must take refuge in how.

Toni Morrison (b. 1931)
American writer, *The Bluest Eye*

Everyone wants to know why. As if we have answers for everything. In fact, the real great questions always remain unanswered. You do agree with me, don't you?

Yizhar Simlansky (b. 1916)
Israeli writer

There ain't no answer. There ain't going to be any answer. There never has been an answer. That's the answer.

Gertrude Stein (1874-1946)
American writer

Do not question too much, lest your head fall off. In truth, you are questioning too much about a divinity about which further questions cannot be asked.

Brihadaranyaka Upanishad
(c. 600-300 B.C.E.)
sacred philosophical Hindu literature

You ask what is the ultimate
  answer?
It is the song of a fisherman
  sailing back to shore.

Wang Wei (699-759)
Chinese poet

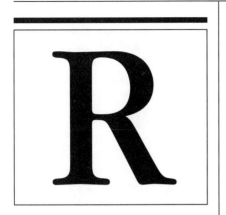

on RACE

The whites have always had the say in America. White people made Jesus white, angels white, the Last Supper white. If I threaten you, I'm blackmailing you. A black cat is bad luck. If you're put out of a club, you're blackballed. Angel's-food cake is white; devil's-food cake is black. Good guys in cowboy movies wear white hats. The bad guys always wore black hats.

> Muhammad Ali (b. 1942)
> American athlete

That is all anyone here ever struggles for: to be nearer the white man. All the shouting against the white man was not hate. It was love. Twisted, but love all the same.

> Ayi Kwei Armah (b. 1938)
> Ghanaian writer, *The Beautyful Ones Are Not Yet Born*

Black! Black! Black! I am proud of being a Negro. Nor have I ever tried to beg tolerance from anyone. Superiority is not proved by color, but by the brain, by educa-

tion, by willpower, by moral courage.

> José Celso Barbosa (1857–1921)
> Puerto Rican politician

I know of no rights of race superior to the rights of humanity.

> Frederick Douglass (1817–1895)
> American abolitionist

Most men in this world are colored. A belief in humanity means a belief in colored men. The future will, in all reasonable possibility, be what colored men make of it.

> W. E. B. Du Bois (1868–1963)
> American writer and educator

Just being a Negro doesn't qualify you to understand the race situation any more than being sick makes you an expert on medicine.

> Dick Gregory (b. 1932)
> American civil rights activist, *Nigger*

I want to be the white man's brother, not his brother-in-law.

> Martin Luther King, Jr.
> (1929–1968)
> American civil rights leader

Men have no special right because they belong to one race or another: the word *man* defines all rights.

> José Martí (1853–1895)
> Cuban patriot, *Mi Raza (My Race)*

Pride of race is the antidote to prejudice.

> Arthur A. Schomburg (1874–1938)
> American educator, *The Negro Digs Up His Past*

We shall be free only together, black and white. We shall survive only together, black and white. We can be human only together, black and white.

> Desmond Tutu (b. 1931)
> South African antiapartheid activist and religious leader

My flock is black, my flock is white. One has got to say to our people, "I love you. I care for you, enormously." And when I care about black liberation, it is because I care about white liberation.

> Desmond Tutu (b. 1931)
> South African antiapartheid activist and religious leader

on RACISM

Sometimes it's [racial prejudice] like a hair across your cheek. You can't see it, you can't find it with your fingers, but you keep brushing at it because the feel of it is irritating.

> Marian Anderson (1902–1993)
> American singer, quoted by Emily Kimbrough, "My Life in a White World"

White folks still in the lead.

> Louis Armstrong (1900–1971)
> American musician

Our dehumanization of the Negro then is indivisible from our dehumanization of ourselves; the loss of our own identity is the price we pay for our annulment of his.

> James Baldwin (1924–1987)
> American writer, *Notes of a Native Son*

The wonder is not that so many Negro boys and girls are ruined but that so many survive.

> James Baldwin (1924–1987)
> American writer, *Notes of a Native Son*

Negro servants have been smuggling odds and ends out of white homes for generations, and white people have been delighted to have them do it, because it has assuaged a dim guilt and testified to the intrinsic superiority of white people.

> James Baldwin (1924–1987)
> American writer, *The Fire Next Time*

The fear I heard in my father's voice . . . when he realized that I really *believed* I could do anything a white boy could do, and had every intention of proving it, was not at all like the fear I heard when one of us was ill or had fallen down the stairs or strayed too far from the house. It was another fear, a fear that the child, in challenging the white world's assumptions, was putting himself in the path of destruction.

> James Baldwin (1924–1987)
> American writer, *The Fire Next Time*

It is a great shock at the age of five or six to find that in a world of Gary Coopers, you are the Indian.

> James Baldwin (1924–1987)
> American writer, Cambridge University speech (1965)

If you are black, the only roads into the mainland of American life are through subservience, cowardice, and loss of manhood. These are white man's roads.

> Imamu Amiri Baraka (b. 1934)
> American writer, "Black Is a Country," *Home*

We are aware that the white man is sitting at our table. We know he has no right to be there; we want to remove him from our table, strip the table of all the trappings put on it by him, decorate it in true African style, settle down and then ask him to join us on our terms if he wishes.

> Steve Biko (1946-1977)
> South African political activist

The natives are unintelligent—
We can't understand their
  language.

> Chinweizu (20th century)
> Nigerian writer and critic

I have no protection at home, or resting place abroad. . . . I am an outcast from the society of my childhood, and an outlaw in the land of my birth. I am a stranger with thee, and a sojourner as all my fathers were.

> Frederick Douglass (1817-1895)
> American abolitionist

Where justice is denied, where poverty is enforced, where ignorance prevails, and where any one class is made to feel that society is in an organized conspiracy to oppress, rob, and degrade them, neither persons nor property will be safe.

> Frederick Douglass (1817-1895)
> American abolitionist, speech on the
> twenty-fourth anniversary of
> Emancipation, Washington, D.C. (April
> 1886)

Cannot the nation that has absorbed ten million foreigners into its political life without catastrophe absorb ten million Negro Americans into that same political life at less cost than their unjust and illegal exclusion will involve?

> W. E. B. Du Bois (1868-1963)
> American writer and educator, "No
> Cowards or Trucklers"

The problem of the twentieth century is the problem of the color line.

> W. E. B. Du Bois (1868-1963)
> American writer and educator, speech
> at the Pan-African Conference (January
> 1900)

If a man calls me a nigger, he is calling me something I am not. The nigger exists only in his own mind; therefore his mind is the nigger. I must feel sorry for such a man.

> Dick Gregory (b. 1932)
> American civil rights activist, *The
> Shadow that Scares Me*

Because my mouth
Is wide with laughter,
You do not hear
My inner cry?
Because my feet
Are gay with dancing,
You do not know
I die?

> Langston Hughes (1902-1967)
> American writer, "In Love with
> Harlem," *Freedomways*

The white Christian church never raised to the heights of Christ. It stayed within the limit of culture.

> Jesse Jackson (b. 1941)
> American civil rights activist and
> politician

When blacks are unemployed, they are considered lazy and apathetic. When whites are unemployed, it's considered a depression.

> Jesse Jackson (b. 1941)
> American civil rights activist and
> politician

We used to be "shiftless and lazy," now we're "fearsome and awesome." I think the black man should take pride in that.

> James Earl Jones (b. 1931)
> American actor

Discrimination is a hellhound that gnaws at Negroes in every waking moment of their lives to remind them that the lie of their inferiority is accepted as truth in the society dominating them.

> Martin Luther King, Jr.
> (1929–1968)
> American civil rights leader, speech to
> the Southern Christian Leadership
> Conference (August 16, 1967)

If our black face, King, displeases your ministers,
Ethiopians do not like the white ones on their males.

> Juan Latino (c. 1573)
> Spanish ex-slave, Latin grammarian,
> and poet

To remain neutral, in a situation where the laws of the land virtually criticized God for having created men of color, was the sort of thing I could not, as a Christian, tolerate.

> Albert John Luthuli (1898–1967)
> South African civil rights activist, on
> receiving the Nobel Peace Prize (1961)

I think the black man in America wants to be recognized as a human being; and it's almost impossible for one who has enslaved another to bring himself to accept the person who used to pull his plow, who used to be an animal, subhuman, who used to be considered as such by him—it's almost impossible for that person in his right mind to accept that person as his equal.

> Malcolm X (1925–1965)
> American civil rights activist, on "The
> Open Mind" television program
> (October 15, 1961)

Racism is a human problem and a crime that is absolutely so ghastly that a person who is fighting racism is well within his rights to fight against it by any means necessary until it is eliminated.

> Malcolm X (1925–1965)
> American civil rights activist, speech
> (December 12, 1964)

They tell us we are all citizens, that we were born in this country. Well, a cat can have kittens in the oven, but that doesn't make them biscuits!

> Malcolm X (1925–1965)
> American civil rights activist

For the white man to ask the black man if he hates him is just like the rapist asking the raped, or the wolf asking the sheep, "Do you hate me?" The white man is in no moral position to accuse anyone else of hate!

> Malcolm X (1925–1965)
> American civil rights activist, *The
> Autobiography of Malcolm X*

Whites tend to regard Africans as a separate breed. They do not look upon them as people with families of their own; they do not realize that they have emotions—that they fall in love like white people do; that they want to be with their wives and children like white people want to be with theirs; that they want to earn enough money to support their families properly, to feed and clothe them and send them to school. And what "house-boy" or "garden-boy" or laborer can ever hope to do this?

Nelson Mandela (b. 1918)
South African president, "Statement during the Rivonia Trial" (April 20, 1964)

Political division, based on color, is entirely artificial; and when it disappears, so will the domination of one color group by another.

Nelson Mandela (b. 1918)
South African president, "Statement during the Rivonia Trial" (April 20, 1964)

Your door is shut against my
    tightened face,
And I am sharp as steel with
    discontent;
But I possess the courage and the
    grace
To bear my anger proudly and
    unbent.
The pavement slabs burn loose
    beneath my feet.

Claude McKay (1890-1948)
American writer, "White Houses"

Maybe the greatest challenge here [in South Africa], even more than the racism, is the *mediocrity*, the *inanity*, that keeps coming at you.

There are various dodges and on-and-off switches one can operate to deal with racism: its stark, visible, etc. mediocrity is sump'n else. I'm learning to keep my cool in its presence, because to rave and rail and shout only breeds ulcers. But damn it, it may be, indeed I believe it *is*, something that one can deal with better than the more complex, barbed-wire tangle the American thing is.

Es'kia Mphahlele (1919-1982)
South African writer and educator, on the now-dismantled racist society, *Exiles and Homecomings*

When the white man wins, it is a battle. When the Indian wins, it is a massacre.

Native American maxim (c. 1880)

I have seen white settlers in Africa who had sworn that they would never sit down to table with those "smelly blacks" sit down quite happily with half-nude tribesmen once a country achieves independence. It is the context of power which changes behavior and transmutes antipathy into sympathy.

Lewis Nkosi (b. 1936)
South African writer, *Home and Exile and Other Selections*

The black man continues on his way. He plods wearily no longer—he is striding freedom road with the knowledge that if he hasn't got the world in a jug, at least he has the stopper in his hand.

Adam Clayton Powell, Jr. (1908-1972)
American politician and civil rights leader, "Black Power: A Form of Godly Power," *Keep the Faith, Baby!*

When you're wrong, you're wrong. But when you're right, you're wrong anyhow.

> Bayard Rustin (1910–1987)
> American civil rights leader, *Down the Line*

For goodness sake, will they hear, will white people hear what we are trying to say? Please, all we are asking you to do is to recognize that we are humans, too.

> Desmond Tutu (b. 1931)
> South African antiapartheid activist and religious leader

We don't want apartheid liberalized. We want it dismantled. You can't improve something that is intrinsically evil.

> Desmond Tutu (b. 1931)
> South African antiapartheid activist and religious leader

Just because I smile and smile
And happiness is my coat . . .
You think that I'm a gatepost
Numb to the stab of pain.

Just because of the laugh on my
  lips
And my eyes lowered in respect
  . . .
You think I'm like a stone
And don't know what it is to die.

> B. W. Vilakazi (1906–1947)
> Zulu writer

Treat us like men, and there is no danger but we will all live in peace and happiness together. For we are not like you, hard hearted, unmerciful, and unforgiving. What a happy country this will be, if the whites will listen.

> David Walker (c. 1800)
> American abolitionist, *Walker's Appeal* (September 28, 1829)

on **REALITY**

People who shut their eyes to reality simply invite their own destruction, and anyone who insists on remaining in a state of innocence long after that innocence is dead turns himself into a monster.

> James Baldwin (1924–1987)
> American writer, *Notes of a Native Son*

Bodies are born from the Quiet
  Nothingness,
Like images in a mirror,
Once we know this essential
  nothingness
We will see Reality.

> Ban-Tinh (19th century)
> Vietnamese poet, "Transcendence"

Reality is not always probable, or likely.

> Jorge Luis Borges (1899–1986)
> Argentinian writer, *Borges on Writing*

Reality favors symmetry.

> Jorge Luis Borges (1899–1986)
> Argentinian writer, *Conversations with Jorge Luis Borges*

Once upon a time, Chuang Chou dreamt that he was a butterfly, fluttering happily like a butterfly. He was conscious only of his happiness as a butterfly, unaware that he was Chuang Chou. Suddenly he awakened, and there he was, veritably Chuang Chou himself. Now he does not know whether the

butterfly is a dream of Chuang
Chou or whether Chuang Chou is
a dream of the butterfly.

>Chuang-tzu (c. 369-286 B.C.E.)
>Chinese Taoist philosopher

Do not be amazed by the true
dragon.

>Dogen (1200-1253)
>Japanese Zen monk, *Fukanzazenji*

Life and death are nothing but the
mind. Years, months, days, and
hours are nothing but the mind.
Dreams, illusions, and mirages are
nothing but the mind. The bubbles
of water and the flames of fire are
nothing but the mind. The flowers
of the spring and the moon of the
autumn are nothing but the mind.
Confusions and dangers are nothing but the mind.

>Dogen (1200-1253)
>Japanese Zen monk, in the *Repository
>of True Buddhist Teachings*

I believe that unarmed truth and
unconditional love will have the final word in reality.

>Martin Luther King, Jr.
>(1929-1968)
>American civil rights leader

Reality is a staircase going neither
up nor down. We don't move, today is today, always is today.

>Octavio Paz (b. 1914)
>Mexican writer and diplomat

The cure for the unpleasant constitution of the world is to ignore it:
Here he is awake who is plunged
in heavy sleep.

>Sa'ib of Tabriz (c. 1601-1677)
>Persian poet

A man weeps on dreaming of the
death of a living friend, and re-
joices on dreaming of a dead friend
come to life; griefs and joys of the
waking state may last longer, but in
eternity these are as unreal as
those of the dreams.

>Shenkara (788-820)
>Indian Hindu philosopher

All is illusion; the Buddha alone is
real.

>Shotoku (572-622)
>Japanese prince

Reality has come to seem more and
more like what we are shown by
cameras.

>Susan Sontag (b. 1933)
>American writer and critic,
>"Photography Unlimited"

The camera makes everyone a
tourist in other people's reality,
and eventually in one's own.

>Susan Sontag (b. 1933)
>American writer and critic, *On
>Photography*

Fetch me the fruit of the banyan
 tree.
Here is one, sir.
Break it . . . What do you see?
Nothing, sir.
My son, what you do not perceive
 is the essence, and in that
 essence
the mighty banyan tree exists. . . .
 That is the true, that is the self,
 and you are that self.

>*Upanishads* (c. 600-300 B.C.E.)
>sacred philosophical Hindu literature

Attachment is a manufacturer of illusions and whoever wants reality ought to be detached.

> Simone Weil (1909-1943)
> French philosopher, *Gravity and Grace*

Distance is the soul of reality.

> Simone Weil (1909-1943)
> French philosopher

A test of what is real is that it is hard and rough. Joys are found in it, not pleasure. What is pleasant belongs to dreams.

> Simone Weil (1909-1943)
> French philosopher, *Gravity and Grace*

The true yogi meditates, realizing
. . . I am a stranger to this world,

there is no one with me!
Just as the spume and the waves
are born of the ocean then melt
  back into it,
so the world is born of me and
  melts back into me.

> *Yoga Darshana Upanishad*
> (c. 14th-15th century)
> texts based on the *Yoga Sutra*

on **REASON**

We cannot escape the clear fact that what is going to win in this world is reason, if this ever becomes a reasonable world.

> W. E. B. Du Bois (1868-1963)
> American writer and educator, speech
> at the Southern Youth Legislature
> (October 20, 1946)

Human reason can reach only to the last point of its own limitations. However great be the effort of moral man, it nonetheless leads him to error.

> Fakhir al-Din Razi (1149-1209)
> Central Asian Islamic philosopher

I'll not listen to reason. Reason always means what someone else has got to say.

> Elizabeth Gaskell (1810-1865)
> English writer, *Cranford*

on **REFORM AND REFORMERS**

How can one not speak about war, poverty, and inequality when people who suffer from these afflictions don't have a voice to speak?

> Isabel Allende (b. 1942)
> Chilean writer

Cautious, careful people, always casting about to preserve their reputation and social standing, never can bring about a reform.

> Susan B. Anthony (1820-1906)
> American suffragist

Pray for the dead and fight like hell for the living.

> Mother Jones (1830-1930)
> American labor activist, in her
> autobiography

An absolutely brainless man might find some nourishment in a dunghill; a brainy man wouldn't pay any attention to the dunghill in the first place. But it takes a half-brainy, half-brainless clod like myself to come up with the idea of improving and preserving the dunghill. Such a man goes over and preaches at the flies that have gathered atop the turds, saying: "Hey, come on! Let's keep this place in better shape!"

Lao She (1899-1966)
Chinese writer

The mistake the world is making with the simple peoples is to try and hurry them into political concepts they don't understand and aren't prepared to cope with. I know. I am a peasant myself. . . . I say, Spit on the big, fancy schemes. I want all the little things first. Then perhaps we can get on to the bigger things.

Ramon Magsaysay (1907-1957)
Philippine politician

I, for one, believe that if you give people a thorough understanding of what confronts them and the basic causes that produce it, they'll create their own program; and when the people create a program, you get action.

Malcolm X (1925-1965)
American civil rights activist

Liberals want to set up social welfare committees to help whites and West Indians love each other in Birmingham. But all such efforts are doomed to failure. For the strong the weak are just too much of a temptation; and in all fairness it seems to me quite wicked for black people to have tempted the powerful with so much powerlessness for so long. The obvious answer is to redress this imbalance in power.

Lewis Nkosi (b. 1936)
South African writer, *Home and Exile and Other Selections*

You have to make more noise than anybody else; you have to make yourself more obtrusive than anybody else; you have to fill all the papers more than anybody else; in fact, you have to be there all the time and see that they do not snow you under, if you are really going to get your reform realized.

Emmeline Pankhurst (1858-1928)
English suffragist, speech (November 13, 1913)

Social change rarely comes about through the efforts of the disenfranchised. The middle class creates social revolutions.

Faye Wattleton (b. 1943)
American social activist

on REGRETS

Always repenting of wrongs done
Will never bring my heart to rest.

Chi K'ang (223-262)
Chinese poet

There's no way to reach the heavenly river.
I've revenged nothing, my hair has turned white.
How many times, in the moonlight, have I sharpened my sword?

Dang Dung (18th century)
Vietnamese patriot, "Regrets"

When death, the great reconciler, has come, it is never our tenderness that we repent of, but our severity.

George Eliot (1819-1880)
English writer

Though I feel bitter
And even though I may cry
How can I complain?
Without being as indifferent
As the moon I saw that night.

> Gofukakausa-in no shosho no
> naishi (c. 1250)
> Japanese poet

Repentance is a gift of God's grace.

> Rabindranath Tagore (1861-1941)
> Indian writer and philosopher

on RELATIONSHIPS

It is not time or opportunity that is to determine intimacy; it is disposition alone. Seven years would be insufficient to make some people acquainted with each other, and seven days are more than enough for others.

> Jane Austen (1775-1817)
> English writer, *Sense and Sensibility*

Harmony between two individuals is never granted—it has to be conquered indefinitely.

> Simone de Beauvoir (1908-1986)
> French writer and philosopher, *Le Force de l'Age*

When a pair of magpies fly
  together
They do not envy the pair of
  pheasants.

> Lady Ho (c. 300 B.C.E.)
> Chinese poet, "A Song of Magpies"

Every human encounter is the external embodiment of an attraction between two magnetic fields. The encounter comes suddenly, unexpectedly. It is a moment of truth. It is a moment of revelation, as when the right ray of sun penetrates through the right window pane, and falls with the right slant on one picture in the museum.

> Amalia Kahana-Carmon
> (20th century)
> Israeli poet

Each attraction, limited as it may appear to be, is a cosmic happening —it occurs within the broader pattern of things, within the endlessly complex structure which underlies our lives.

> Amalia Kahana-Carmon
> (20th century)
> Israeli poet

The most important thing in any relationship is not what you get but what you give.

> Eleanor Roosevelt (1884-1962)
> American humanitarian and First Lady

on RELIGION

Every dictator uses religion as a prop to keep himself in power.

> Benazir Bhutto (b. 1953)
> Pakistani politician

I can say without the slightest hesitation, and yet in all humility, that those who say that religion has nothing to do with politics do not know what religion means.

> Mohandas K. Gandhi (1869-1948)
> Indian spiritual and political leader

Religion is not what is grasped by the brain, but a heart grasp.

> Mohandas K. Gandhi (1869-1948)
> Indian spiritual and political leader

Where there is fear, there is no religion.

Mohandas K. Gandhi (1869-1948)
Indian spiritual and political leader

In the heart of all things, of whatever there is in the universe, dwells the Lord. He alone is the reality.

Isha Upanishad (c. 600-300 B.C.E.)
sacred philosophical Hindu literature

We do not want churches. They will teach us to quarrel about God.

Chief Joseph (c. 1840-1904)
Nez Percé chief

Religion is the frozen thought of men out of which they build temples.

Jiddu Krishnamurti (1895-1986)
Indian philosopher

Man has never been the same since God died.

Edna St. Vincent Millay
(1892-1950)
American poet

Religion is a candle inside a multicolored lantern. Everyone looks through a particular color, but the candle is always there.

Mohammed Naguib (b. 1901)
Egyptian soldier and politician

In the name of religion many great and fine deeds have been performed. In the name of religion also, thousands and millions have been killed, and every possible crime has been committed.

Jawaharlal Nehru (1889-1964)
Indian prime minister

It is strange that anyone should be so foolish as to think that religion and faith can be thrust down a person's throat at the point of the sword or a bayonet.

Jawaharlal Nehru (1889-1964)
Indian prime minister

Often in history we see that religion, which was meant to raise us and make us better and nobler, has made people behave like beasts. Instead of bringing enlightenment of them, it has often tried to keep them in the dark; instead of broadening their minds, it has frequently made them narrow-minded and intolerant of others.

Jawaharlal Nehru (1889-1964)
Indian prime minister

Say: O unbelievers!
I do not worship what you
worship
and you do not worship what I
worship;
and I shall not worship what
you worship
and you will not worship what I
worship.
You have your religion and I have mine.

Qur'an (c. 610-656)
sacred book of Islam

God has granted to every people a prophet in its own tongue.

Qur'an (c. 610-656)
sacred book of Islam

O ye who believe, believe in God and His Apostle and the Book which He hath sent down to His Apostle and the Scripture which He hath sent down formerly. Whosoever denieth God and His Angels and His Books and His Apostles and the Last Day hath strayed far from the Truth.

> *Qur'an* (c. 610-656)
> sacred book of Islam, Sura IV:135, famous sura outlining the credo of Muslims

Who has a better religion than he who submits himself entirely to God, intelligently and knowingly, and follows Abraham's perfect creed?

> *Qur'an* (c. 610-656)
> sacred book of Islam, 4:125

I have not served God from fear of God . . . or love of Paradise . . . but of only for the love of Him and the desire for Him.

> Rabi'a al-Adawiyya (c. 717-801)
> Iraqi Sufi poet and mystic

True religion is a revolutionary force: it is an inveterate enemy of oppression, privilege, and injustice.

> Sarvepalli Radhakrishnan (1888-1975)
> Indian philosopher and politician

Religion is behavior and not mere belief.

> Sarvepalli Radhakrishnan (1888-1975)
> Indian philosopher and politician, *Theosophical Movement*

So many religions, so many paths to reach the one and the same goal.

> Ramakrishna (1836-1886)
> Indian Hindu mystic

So long as the bee is outside the petals of the lotus and has not tasted its honey, it hovers around the flower, emitting its buzzing sound; but when it is inside the flower, it drinks its nectar noiselessly. So long as man quarrels and disputes about doctrines and dogmas, he has not tasted the nectar of true faith; when he tastes it he becomes still.

> Ramakrishna (1836-1886)
> Indian Hindu mystic

You say that you are sent to instruct us how to worship the Great Spirit agreeably to His mind; and, if we do not take hold of the religion which you white people teach, we shall be unhappy hereafter. You say that you are right and we are lost. How do we know this to be true? We understand that your religion is written in a book. If it was intended for us, as well as you, why has not the Great Spirit given to us, and not only to us, but why did He not give to our forefathers the knowledge of that book, with the means of understanding it rightly? We only know what you tell us about it. How shall we know when to believe, being so often deceived by the white people?

Brother, you say there is but one way to worship and serve the Great Spirit. If there is but one religion, why do you white people differ so much about it? Why not all agreed, as you can all read the book?

> Red Jacket (c. 1758-1830)
> Seneca leader, at a council of chiefs of the Six Nations after a white missionary had addressed them (1805)

We are told that your religion was given to your forefathers and has been handed down from father to son. We also have a religion which was given to our forefathers and has been handed down to us, their children. We worship in that way. It teaches us to be thankful for all the favors we receive, to love each other, and to be united. We never quarrel about religion.

> Red Jacket (c. 1758-1830)
> Seneca leader, at a council of chiefs of the Six Nations after a white missionary had addressed them (1805)

All this talk of infidelity and religion finally leads to one place: The dream is the same dream, only the interpretations differ.

> Sa'ib of Tabriz (c. 1601-1677)
> Persian poet

There is only one God,
There is only one devotion,
And there is none but one.

> Sankardeva (1449-1569)
> Indian religious leader

The Path is one for all; the means to reach the Goal must vary with the Pilgrims.

> Tibetan precept
> *The Book of Golden Precepts*

We have to learn yet that all religions, under whatever name they may be called—either Hindu, Buddhist, Mohammedan, or Christian—have the same God: and he who derises any one of these derises his own God.

> Vivekananda (1863-1902)
> Indian Hindu religious leader

I do not believe in a religion that cannot wipe out the widow's tears or bring a piece of bread to the orphan's mouth.

> Vivekananda (1863-1902)
> Indian Hindu religious leader

on **RENEWAL**

Like a cowherd driving his cows to the pastures, old age and death drive men to new life.

> *Dhammapada* (c. 3rd century B.C.E.)
> collection of ancient Buddhist poems and aphorisms

Spring dies, the hundred flowers scatter.
Spring is reborn, the hundred flowers bloom.
It is hard for me to see clearly,
Old age blinks my eyes.
Aren't flowers dead, once spring dies?
Last night, out there in the yard, a plum branch blossomed.

> Man Giac (19th century)
> Vietnamese poet, "Rebirth"

Wounds may be calm, and sorrows be silent
The time of lament and the age of madness are dead
Morning has peered out beyond the peaks.

> Al-Shabbi (1909-1934)
> Arab poet

on **RENUNCIATION**

If you love God, tear out your heart's love of the world.

> 'Ali (c. 600-661)
> First Imam of the Sh'ia branch of Islam; fourth caliph

He knows peace who has forgotten desire.

> *Bhagavad Gita*
> (c. 4th-3rd century B.C.E.)
> teachings of Krishna from the Hindu
> epic, the *Mahabharata*

When he has no lust, no hatred,
A man walks safely among the
  things of lust and hatred.

> *Bhagavad Gita*
> (c. 4th-3rd century B.C.E.)
> teachings of Krishna from the Hindu
> epic, the *Mahabharata*

on RESISTANCE

Let me tell you, world,
I—do—not—believe!
If a thousand challengers lie
  beneath your feet,
Count me as number one
  thousand and one.

I don't believe the sky is blue;
I don't believe in thunder's
  echoes;
I don't believe that dreams are
  false;
I don't believe that death has no
  revenge;

> Bei Dao (b. 1949)
> Chinese poet, "The Answer," *The
> August Sleepwalker*

We did not expect to conquer the whites, no. They had too many horses, too many men. I took up the hatchet, for my part, to revenge the injuries which my people could no longer endure.

> Black Hawk (1767-1838)
> Sauk chief

Our hatred knows no bounds, and the war shall be to the death.

> Simón Bolívar (1783-1830)
> South American revolutionary leader
> called the Liberator of South America,
> proclamation to his army before the
> drive to Caracas (1812)

I am not fighting for my kingdom and wealth now. I am fighting as an ordinary person for my lost freedom, my bruised body, and my outraged daughters.

> Boudicca (1st century)
> British warrior and queen, addressing
> her army before the Icenian revolt in
> the year 61

We are slowly going to appropriate their vigor and then their life. Very slowly. We have time!

> Driss Chraibi (b. 1926)
> Moroccan writer

Retreat itself is often a plan of resistance and may be a precursor of great bravery and sacrifice. Every retreat is not cowardice which implies fear to die.

> Mohandas K. Gandhi (1869-1948)
> Indian spiritual and political leader

Our mountains will always be, our
  rivers will always
  be, our people will always be,
The American invaders defeated,
  we will rebuild our
  land ten times more beautiful.

> Ho Chi Minh (1892-1969)
> Vietnamese political leader

He who allows himself to be arrested for a crime he did not commit will be expelled from the party, but if he resists and comes to us on a stretcher, he is a hero.

Aminu Kano (b. 1920)
Nigerian politican

You tell me: "Sheep will always be sheep. What else can they do but obediently walk in line to the slaughterhouse? As to the pigs, which have to be dragged, which jump, squeal, and try to run away, in the end they cannot escape their fate. Why such desperate efforts? Is it not a sheer waste of energy?"

But this is to say that even when faced with death, one should behave like a sheep; thus the world will be in peace, and everyone will be spared much trouble.

Very well, this is perhaps an excellent solution. However, have you ever considered wild boars? With their tusks they can force even experienced hunters to keep at a distance. Actually, all that an ordinary pig needs to do is to run away from the sty where the swineherd was keeping it locked, and reach the forest—in no time it will grow tusks.

Lu Xun (1881-1936)
Chinese writer

They could not capture me except under a white flag. They cannot hold me except with a chain.

Osceola (c. 1803-1838)
Seminole chief, after being captured while under a flag of truce and imprisoned in Fort Moultrie, Georgia (1838)

Recognize your son by the look in
  his eyes, the authenticity
  of his heart his lineage.
Recognize his comrades recognize
  the fighter and salute in
  the red evening of your age.
The bright dawn of a new day.

Leopold Sedar Senghor (b. 1906)
Senegalese political leader and writer,
"On Appeal from the Race of Sheba—
VII"

Look now, my brother, the white people think we have no brains in our heads, but that they are great and big; and that makes them make war with us. We are but a little handful to what you are; but remember . . . when you hunt for a rattlesnake, you cannot find it, and perhaps it will bite you before you see it.

Shingis (c. 18th century)
Delaware chief, to a Moravian
missionary, Christian Frederic Post,
during the French and Indian War

First kill me before you take possession of my fatherland.

Sitting Bull (c. 1834-1890)
Dakota Sioux chief, statement to war
council, Powder River (1877)

God made me an Indian, but not a reservation Indian.

Sitting Bull (c. 1834-1890)
Dakota Sioux chief

The cougar, the wolf, and the bear will fight for their young. And why not the Indian?

Skolaskin (19th century)
Sanpoil prophet

Now we are weak and many of our people are afraid. But hear me: a single twig breaks, but the bundle of twigs is strong. Someday I will embrace our brother tribes and draw them into a bundle, and together we will win our country back from the whites.

> Tecumseh (c. 1768–1813)
> Shawnee chief

on RESPECT

Show regard for no one at the
  expense of your soul,
And respect no one, to your own
  downfall.

> Ben Sira (c. 2nd century B.C.E.)
> Hebrew scholar and philosopher, *The Wisdom of Ben Sira*

We must respect everyone who lives on this earth, be he French or foreigner. We must treat him as a brother so long as he respects our freedom, our personality, and our dignity.

> Habib ibn Ali Bourguiba (b. 1903)
> Tunisian politician/prime minister and president

Respect yourself, and others will respect you.

> Confucius (551–479 B.C.E.)
> Chinese philosopher and founder of Confucianism, *Analects*

Man does not live by bread alone. Many prefer self-respect to food.

> Mohandas K. Gandhi (1869–1948)
> Indian spiritual and political leader

I am not going to respect . . . gray hairs unless there is wisdom beneath them.

> Mohammed Ali Jinna (1876–1948)
> Pakistani political leader and founder of modern Pakistan

To honor an old man is showing respect to God.

> Muhammad (570–632)
> Prophet of Islam

I had to fight hard against loneliness, abuse, and the knowledge that any mistake I made would be magnified because I was the only black man out there. Many people resented my impatience and honesty, but I never cared about acceptance as much as I cared about respect.

> Jackie Robinson (1919–1972)
> American athlete

We have always felt the sympathy of the world, but we would prefer the respect of the world to sympathy without respect.

> Anwar Sadat (1918–1981)
> Egyptian military and political leader, speech to the People's Assembly, after the first attack of the Yom Kippur War (October 6, 1973)

on RESPONSIBILITY

The responsibility to nightmare is to wake up.

> Michael Harper (b. 1938)
> American poet, *Images of Kin*

You must create your own world. I am responsible for my world.

> Louise Nevelson (1899–1988)
> American artist

Somewhere along the line of development we discover what we really are, and then we make our real decision for which we are responsible. Make that decision primarily for yourself, because you can never really live anyone else's life, not even your own child's. The influence you exert is through your own life and what you become yourself.

> Eleanor Roosevelt (1884-1962)
> American humanitarian and First Lady

When you have once taken up a responsibility, you must see it through.

> Rabindranath Tagore (1861-1941)
> Indian writer and philosopher

on RESTRAINT

Restraint never ruins one's health.

> Mohandas K. Gandhi (1869-1948)
> Indian spiritual and political leader

Restraint does not mean weakness. It does not mean giving in.

> Jawaharlal Nehru (1889-1964)
> Indian prime minister

on REVOLUTION

All the world wondered as they witnessed . . . a people lift themselves from humiliation to the greatest pride.

> Corazon Aquino (b. 1933)
> Philippine politician

Those who are inclined to compromise never make a revolution.

> Kemal Ataturk (1881-1938)
> Turkish patriot and political leader

Cowards and fools call us fools for talking of force when we have nothing in our hands, no guns, not even sharp knives or needles. Don't believe them; they will give you every reason for doing nothing, for just talking about freedom and doing nothing to gain it. I tell you that there will be plenty of weapons in this war. Weapons are not only those you make for yourselves; they are also those which come into your hand without your making them.

> Ba Maw (b. 1893)
> Burmese revolutionary and politician

March swiftly to revenge the dead, to give life to the dying, to free the oppressed, and to give liberty to all.

> Simón Bolívar (1783-1830)
> South American revolutionary leader
> called the Liberator of South America,
> address to the people of New Granada
> (Colombia) (December 15, 1812)

Give me blood, I promise you freedom.

> Subhas Chandra Bose (1897-1945)
> Indian nationalist leader, slogan when
> pulling together an army of liberation

In May the malinches bloom in
  the streets of Managua
But April in Nicaragua is the
  month of death.
In April they killed them.
I was with my comrades in the
  April rising
and I learned how to use a Rising
  machine-gun.

> Ernest Cardenal (20th century)
> Nicaraguan poet, "Hora"

Long live religion! And death to foreigners!

> Rafael Carrera (1814–1865)
> Guatemalan politician, battle cry

were some who ran one way.
were some who ran another way.
were some who did not run at all.
were some who will not run again.
and I was with them all.
when the sun and streets exploded.
and a city of clerks turned a city
  of men!

> Martin Carter (b. 1927)
> Guyanan writer and diplomat, "Jail Me
> Quickly"

A revolution is not a bed of roses. A revolution is a struggle to the death between the future and the past.

> Fidel Castro (b. 1927)
> Cuban revolutionary and politician,
> speech, Havana (January 1961)

It does not matter how small you are if you have faith and a plan of action.

> Fidel Castro (b. 1927)
> Cuban revolutionary and politician

Whoever hesitates while waiting for ideas to triumph among the masses before initiating revolutionary action will never be a revolutionary. Humanity will, of course, change. Human society will, of course, continue to develop—in spite of men and the errors of men. But that is not a revolutionary attitude.

> Fidel Castro (b. 1927)
> Cuban revolutionary and politician
> (1967)

We are working for a revolution. If we do not start it by improving the life of the soldiers, all slogans of reforming and improving society are but empty words.

> Chiang Kai-Shek (1887–1975)
> Chinese military and political leader,
> letter to Zhou En-lai (1925)

Prepare the Way for Heaven!

> Chinese rebel slogan
> from *All Men Are Brothers*, popular
> 13th-century Chinese classic

Any revolution which denies the right to criticize is bound to wallow in stagnation and backwardness.

> Pablo Antonio Cuadra (b. 1912)
> Nicaraguan poet, "Notes on Culture in
> the New Nicaragua," *Vuelta*

A fire had been lit, and it would never be extinguished; its bloody flames would not stop until their sinister glow had been thrown across the entire nation.

> Mohammed Dib (b. 1920)
> Algerian writer

Revolutions are not made with literature. Revolutions equal gunfire.

> François Duvalier (1907–1971)
> Haitian politician, *Papa Doc*

A nonviolent revolution is not a program of seizure of power. It is a program of transformation of relationships, ending in a peaceful transfer of power.

> Mohandas K. Gandhi (1869–1948)
> Indian spiritual and political leader,
> *Non-Violence in Peace and War*

The ultimate end of all revolutionary social change is to establish the sanctity of human life, the dignity of man, the right of every human being to liberty and well-being.

> Emma Goldman (1869–1940)
> American anarchist, *My Further
> Disillusion*

Revolution is the festival of the oppressed.

> Germaine Greer (b. 1939)
> Australian writer

The consequences of militancy do not disappear when the need for militancy is over.

> Germaine Greer (b. 1939)
> Australian writer, *The Female Eunuch*

The question is one of fighting the causes and not just being satisfied with getting rid of the effects.

> Che Guevara (1928–1967)
> Cuban revolutionary

The true revolutionary is guided by feelings of great love.

> Che Guevara (1928–1967)
> Cuban revolutionary

In a revolution one wins or dies.

> Che Guevara (1928–1967)
> Cuban revolutionary

One does not necessarily have to wait for a revolutionary situation: it can be created.

> Che Guevara (1928–1967)
> Cuban revolutionary, *Guerrilla Warfare*

Revolution cleanses men, improving them as the experimental farmer corrects the defects of his plants.

> Che Guevara (1928–1967)
> Cuban revolutionary, *Reminiscences of
> the Cuban Revolutionary War*

Rebels seldom make good revolutionaries, because organized action, even union with other people, is not possible for them.

> Lillian Hellman (1906–1984)
> American writer, *The Listener*

The poor and ignorant and downtrodden of this little Indian town proclaim the future independence of this great nation! Enthusiasm rises to religious heights, and unarmed as they are, they will follow no matter where, and fight and die no matter how.

> Miguel Hildalgo (1753–1811)
> Mexican revolutionary, to the
> townspeople of Guadalupe, at the
> beginning of the Mexican war for
> independence

Colonial atrocities have prepared the soil; it is for socialists to sow the seeds of revolution.

> Ho Chi Minh (1892–1969)
> Vietnamese political leader

Today we should make poems
 including
  iron and steel
And the poet should know how
 to lead
  an attack.

> Ho Chi Minh (1892–1969)
> Vietnamese political leader, on reading
> *Anthology of a Thousand Poets*

I have a government that is organized and ready to go. Your statesmen make eloquent speeches about helping those with self-determination. We are self-determined. Why not help us? Am I any different from Nehru, Quezon—even your George Washington. I, too, want to set my people free.

> Ho Chi Minh (1892-1969)
> Vietnamese political leader, to an American military officer (1945)

Men have always looked before and after, and rebelled against the existing order. But for their divine discontent, men would not have been men, and there would have been no progress in human affairs.

> Kabir (1440-1519)
> Indian Mughal poet and philosopher

In this revolution no plans have been written for retreat.

> Martin Luther King, Jr.
> (1929-1968)
> American civil rights leader

People never move towards revolution; they are pushed towards it by intolerable injustices in the economic and social order under which they live.

> Suzanne LaFollette (1893-1983)
> American feminist and writer, "The Beginnings of Emancipation," *Concerning Women*

Revolution is a bitter thing, mixed with filth and blood, not as lovely or perfect as the poets think. It is eminently down to earth, involving many humble, tiresome tasks, not so romantic as the poets think. . . . So it is easy for all who have romantic dreams about revolution to become disillusioned on closer ac-

quaintance, when a revolution is actually carried out.

> Lu Xun (1881-1936)
> Chinese writer, lecture to the League of Left-Wing Writers (1930)

As long as there shall be stones, the seeds of fire will not die.

> Lu Xun (1881-1936)
> Chinese writer

Revolution, counterrevolution, nonrevolution.
Revolutionaries are massacred by counterrevolutionaries.
Counterrevolutionaries are massacred by revolutionaries. Non-revolutionaries are sometimes taken for revolutionaries, and then they are massacred by counterrevolutionaries, or again they are taken for counterrevolutionaries, and then they are massacred by revolutionaries. . . .
Revolution. To revolutionize; to revolutionize the revolution of revolution; to rev . . .

> Lu Xun (1881-1936)
> Chinese writer

Revolutionary tactics cannot be invented by leaders; they must develop spontaneously—history comes first, leaders' consciousness second.

> Rosa Luxembourg (1871-1919)
> German revolutionary

It's the occasion that makes the revolution.

> Joaquim Maria Machado de Assis (1839-1908)
> Brazilian writer, *Esau and Jacob*

Personalities and fame pass; the revolution must remain.

Samora Machel (1933–1986)
Mozambiquen politician

For the first time in my life, I felt that a wave, a justice was sweeping away a deep-seated decay without any indulgence. I dearly wished that it would keep going without hesitation or deviation, in a spirit of purity forever.

Naguib Mahfouz (b. 1911)
Egyptian writer

Revolutions are never peaceful.

Malcolm X (1925–1965)
American civil rights activist, speech, New York City (December 1963)

Revolutions are never waged singing "We Shall Overcome." Revolutions are based upon bloodshed.

Malcolm X (1925–1965)
American civil rights activist, speech, New York City (April 1964)

The revolutionary war is a war of the masses; it can be waged only by mobilizing the masses and relying on them.

Mao Zedong (1893–1976)
Chairman of People's Republic of China, "Be Concerned with the Well-Being of the Masses"

Revolution is not a dinner party, not an essay, nor a painting, nor a piece of embroidery; it cannot be advanced softly, gradually, carefully, considerately, respectfully, politely, plainly, and modestly.

Mao Zedong (1893–1976)
Chairman of People's Republic of China

Revolutionary war is an antitoxin which not only eliminates the enemy's poison but also purges us of our own filth.

Mao Zedong (1893–1976)
Chairman of People's Republic of China

A revolution does not march a straight line. It wanders where it can, retreats before superior forces, advances wherever it has room, attacks whenever the enemy retreats or bluffs, and above all, is possessed of enormous patience.

Mao Zedong (1893–1976)
Chairman of People's Republic of China

Revolution is a drama of passion. We did not win the people over by appealing to reason but by developing hope, trust, fraternity.

Mao Zedong (1893–1976)
Chairman of People's Republic of China

It takes a revolution to make a solution.

Bob Marley (1945–1981)
Jamaican singer, *To the Point International*

A violent revolution has always brought forth a dictatorship of some kind or the other. . . . After a revolution, a new privileged class of rulers and exploiters grows up in the course of time to which the people at large is once again subject.

Jayaprakash Narayan (1902–1979)
Indian nationalist

Arms of the people! This way!
Menace and siege

Still are wasting the earth, mixing
  it with death,
With the sharpness of goads!
  Salud, salud,
The mothers of the world cry
  salud to you,
The schools cry salud, the old
  carpenters,
Army of the People, they cry
  salud with ears of grain,
. . . .
All that is of the earth and the
  mouth
Of man.

> Pablo Neruda (1904–1973)
> Chilean poet and diplomat, "Oda Solar
> al Ejercito del Pueblo" ("Ode of the
> Sun to the People's Army")

You who demand power!
Do you not know
that
even your greatest demonstration
  of authority
can not take away
the dream of the people?

To suddenly lose a dream
just within grasp,
does not destroy
the will of the people,
but drives it deeper into the
  soul. . . .

> Nyein Chan (20th century)
> Burmese poet, "The Dream of a
> People"

It is the Revolution, the magical
word, the word that is going to
change everything, that is going to
bring us immense delight and a
quick death.

> Octavio Paz (b. 1914)
> Mexican writer, *Labyrinth of Solitude*

No one makes a revolution by himself.

> George Sand (1804–1876)
> French writer

I am fascinated by revolution. I am
completely absorbed by it. I am
crazed, am obsessed by the romanticism. . . . Revolution surges,
flashes, thunders in almost every
corner of the earth. . . . Brothers
and sisters, keep fanning the
flames of the leaping fire. . . . Let
us become logs to feed the flames
of revolution.

> Achmad Sukarno (1902–1970)
> Indonesian politician

Revolution is only truly revolution
if it is a continuous struggle—not
just an external struggle against an
enemy, but an inner struggle, fighting and subduing all negative aspects which hinder or do damage
to the course of the revolution. In
this light, revolution is . . . a
mighty symphony of victory over
the enemy and over oneself.

> Achmad Sukarno (1902–1970)
> Indonesian politician

If the idea of revolution is to win
out, it must be through political
enlightenment. It is useless to try
to impose it by force of arms.

> Sun Yat-sen (1866–1925)
> Chinese military and political leader

A successful rebel is called "emperor;" one who fails is just a
"rebel."

> Teng Mu (1247–1306)
> Chinese writer, "Po-ya ch'in" ("The
> Lute of Po-ya")

To take part in the African revolution, it is not enough to write a revolutionary song. You must fashion the revolution with the people. And if you fashion it with the people, the songs will come by themselves.

> Ahmed Sekou Toure (1922–1984)
> Guinean politician, address to the
> Second Congress of Black Writers and
> Artists (1959)

Our aspirations are higher than the Himalayas. Our pain is as intense as if we had a volcano in us. What we want is the emancipation of India. . . . Are we afraid of your cannon and guns? Arm, brothers, arm!

> Brahmabandhab Upadhyay
> (1861–1907)
> Indian reformer; he wrote this
> declaration of independence in his
> weekly Calcutta paper in 1907, was
> arrested for doing that, and died in
> prison

We vow that we shall fight everlastingly and without respite. When we have nothing else left, we shall arm ourselves with branches. How then can you live among us?

> Anti-French manifesto by
> Vietnamese (1862)

Seek justice from tyrannical governments not with your hat in your hands but with a rifle in your fist.

> Emiliano Zapata (1879–1919)
> Mexican revolutionary

Revolution is a universal rule of evolution. Revolution is a universal principle of the world. Revolution is the essence of the struggle for survival or destruction in a time of transition. . . . Revolution turns slaves into masters.

> Zou Rong (1885–1905)
> Chinese activist, *Gemingjun*

on REWARD

He who wishes to secure the good of others has already secured his own.

> Confucius (551–479 B.C.E.)
> Chinese philosopher and founder of
> Confucianism, *Analects*

Every kind of reward constitutes a degradation of energy.

> Simone Weil (1909–1943)
> French philosopher, *Oppression and
> Liberty*

on RISKS

Does not the history of the world show that there would have been no romance in life if there had been no risks?

> Mohandas K. Gandhi (1869–1948)
> Indian spiritual and political leader

A lot of people refuse to do things because they don't want to go naked. . . . We as black people, we as people, we as the human species have got to get used to the fact we're not going to be right most of the time, not even when our intentions are good. We've got to go naked and see what happens.

> Nikki Giovanni (b. 1943)
> American writer

Deep in the sea are riches beyond
  compare,
But if you seek safety, it is on the
  shore.

> Sa'di of Shiraz (c. 1184–1292)
> Persian poet

Venture all; see what fate brings.

Vietnamese proverb

Only by great risks can great results be achieved.

Xerxes (c. 480 B.C.E.)
Persian King, comment before the
invasion of Greece, which failed

on RULES

Chastity and other such ordinances are laid down by clever weaklings.

*Brhaspati Sutra,
Tattvopaplavasimha (Lion
Assaulting All Philosophical
Principles)* (7th century)
attributed to Carvaka, Indian
philosopher

When a man says, "One must," he should first of all say, "I must." Only then can he say, "You must," and "He must!"

Aaron David Gordon (1856–1922)
Israeli writer

If you're going to play the game properly, you'd better know every rule.

Barbara Jordan (b. 1936)
American politician

on **SACRIFICE**

Offer unto me that which is very dear to thee—which thou holdest most covetable. Infinite are the results of such an offering!

Bhagavad Gita
(4th-3rd century B.C.E.)
teachings of Krishna from the Hindu epic, the *Mahabharata*

The pearl on my beloved's neck,
Afflicted sore the oyster!

Bhartrihari (c. 7th century)
Indian poet and philosopher

We shall not lightly talk about sacrifice until we are driven to the last extremity which makes sacrifice inevitable.

Chiang Kai-Shek (1887-1975)
Chinese military and political leader, speech to the Fifth Congress of the Kuomintang

It was better that a little blood should be shed that much blood should be saved. The blood that was shed was bad blood; the blood that was saved was good blood.

Porfirio Díaz (1830-1915)
Mexican soldier and politician

If we ever get free from all the oppressions and wrongs heaped upon us, we must pay for their removal. We must do this by labor, by suffering, by sacrifice, and, if needs be, by our lives, and the lives of others.

Frederick Douglass (1817-1895)
American abolitionist, letter (March 30, 1849)

People, people
We are not heirs of the dragon,
We are but grass
Growing on ancient and barren ground.
We are poor in money and status
Not in courage nor intelligence.
Facing a long night with no dawn
We offer up the torch of our lives.
. . . .
If I fail
Please don't remove
My lettered headband . . .

Fang Zhou (20th century)
Chinese activist, "The Call (dedicated to the hunger strikers)," honoring the student uprising in Tiananmen Square, China, posted on the wall of the Student Broadcast Station, Beijing University (May 20, 1989)

Martyrdom does not end something; it is only the beginning.

Indira Gandhi (1917-1984)
Indian prime minister

The willing sacrifice of the innocents is the most powerful retort to insolent tyranny that has yet to be conceived by God or man.

Mohandas K. Gandhi (1869-1948)
Indian spiritual and political leader, *Young India*

Self-sacrifice of one innocent man is a million times more potent than the sacrifice of a million men who die in the act of killing others.

> Mohandas K. Gandhi (1869-1948)
> Indian spiritual and political leader

Sacrifice is a state of mind in which our thoughts turn with longing [toward Heaven, the Ancestors]. It is the supreme expression of loyalty, love, and respect.

> Hsun-tzu (298-238 B.C.E.)
> Chinese philosopher

I may be crucified for my beliefs and, if I am, you can say, "He died to make men free."

> Martin Luther King, Jr.
> (1929-1968)
> American civil rights leader, *Why We Can't Wait*

Sacrifice is not something that comes from outside. It is something that comes from inside, being born in our hearts.

> *Li Chi* (200 B.C.E.)
> compilation of Confucian writings

To gain that which is worth having, it may be necessary to lose everything else.

> Bernadette D. McAliskey (b. 1947)
> Irish politician, *The Price of My Soul*

Blood and tears are going to be our lot, whether we like them or not. Our blood and tears will flow; maybe the parched soil of India needs them so that the fine flower of freedom may grow again.

> Jawaharlal Nehru (1889-1964)
> Indian prime minister, press conference (April 1942)

I have given my sweat and my tears,
now take my blood as well, so life can grow.

> Nyein Chan (20th century)
> Burmese poet, "I Am a Child of Burma"

Ye will not attain unto piety until ye spend of that which ye love. And whatsoever ye spend, God is aware thereof.

> *Qur'an* (c. 610-656)
> sacred book of Islam, 3:92

If everyone would refrain from sacrificing even one single hair, and if everyone would refrain from benefitting the world, the world would be in order.

> Yang Tse (420-360 B.C.E.)
> Chinese Taoist philosopher, on the "Yang Tse chapter" of *Leih Tzu* (the *Ch'ung-hsu chih-te chen-ching* [*Pure Classic of the Perfect Virtue of Simplicity and Vacuity*])

The enemies of the country and of freedom of the people have always denounced as bandits those who sacrifice themselves for the noble causes of the people.

> Emiliano Zapata (1879-1919)
> Mexican revolutionary

on SALVATION

Where lies our salvation? You asked.
We do not need any salvation.
Does not our end lie on this beginning shore?

> Kofi Awoonor (b. 1935)
> Ghanaian writer, "Salvation"

For these two paths, light and
dark,
Are held to be eternal for the
world;
By one, man goes to nonreturn,
By the other, he returns again.

> *Bhagavad Gita*
> (c. 4th-3rd century B.C.E.)
> teachings of Krishna from the Hindu
> epic, the *Mahabharata*, 8:26

Thou must redeem us eventually.
Why delay?

> *Talmud*
> (c. late 4th-early 6th century)
> ancient body of Jewish civil and
> canonical law, Midrash Tehillim 87

on SCHOLARS

Originality is the essence of true
scholarship. Creativity is the soul
of the true scholar.

> Nnamdi Azikwe (b. 1904)
> Nigerian politician

The scholar who cherishes the
love of comfort is not fit to be
deemed a scholar.

> Confucius (551-479 B.C.E.)
> Chinese philosopher and founder of
> Confucianism, *Analects*

A man is not learned because he
talks too much.

> *Dhammapada* (c. 3rd century B.C.E.)
> collection of ancient Buddhist poems
> and aphorisms

When you talk with famous scholars, the best thing is to pretend
that occasionally you do not quite
understand them. If you understand too little, you will be despised; if you understand too
much, you will be disliked; if you

just fail occasionally to understand
them, you will suit each other very
well.

> Lu Xun (1881-1936)
> Chinese writer

The worst of scholars is he who
visits princes, and the best of
princes is he who visits scholars.

> Muhammad (570-632)
> Prophet of Islam

The ink of the scholar is more sacred than the blood of the martyr.

> Muhammad (570-632)
> Prophet of Islam

A sage is jealous of another sage,
but not of one unlearned in his
subject.

> *Talmud*
> (late 4th-early 6th century)
> ancient body of Jewish civil and
> canonical law, Abodah Zarakh 55

A scholar takes precedence over a
king of Israel, for if a scholar dies,
there is none to replace him; while
if a king of Israel dies, all Israel are
eligible for kingship.

> *Talmud*
> (late 4th-early 6th century)
> ancient body of Jewish civil and
> canonical law, Horayoth 13a, describing
> the order of precedence in payment of
> ransom, in the event of an abduction

The unlearned lose the power of
clear thinking as they grow old,
but scholars gain in it as their years
advance.

> *Talmud*
> (late 4th-early 6th century)
> ancient body of Jewish civil and
> canonical law, Kinnim

on **SCIENCE AND TECHNOLOGY**

The time that one gains cannot be accumulated in a storehouse; it is contradictory to want to save up existence, which, the fact is, exists only by being spent and there is a good case for showing that airplanes, machines, the telephone, and the radio do not make men of today happier than those of former times.

> Simone de Beauvoir (1908-1986)
> French writer and philosopher, *The Ethics of Ambiguity*

Who can deny that much that passes for science and art today destroys the soul instead of uplifting it and instead of evoking the best in us, panders to our basest passions?

> Mohandas K. Gandhi (1869-1948)
> Indian spiritual and political leader

Science may have found a cure for most evils; but it has found no remedy for the worst of them all—the apathy of human beings.

> Helen Keller (1880-1968)
> American writer and lecturer, *My Religion*

We human beings have not secured happiness; on the contrary, science gives us catastrophes. We are like travelers losing their way in a desert. They see a big black shadow ahead and desperately run to it, thinking it may lead them somewhere. But after running a long way, they no longer see the shadow and fall into the slough of despond. What is that shadow? It is this "Mr. Science."

> Liang Qichao (1808-1883)
> Chinese political theorist

The negative cautions of science are never popular.

> Margaret Mead (1901-1978)
> American anthropologist, *Coming of Age in Samoa*

The phrase "popular science" has in itself a touch of absurdity. That knowledge which is popular is not scientific.

> Maria Mitchell (1818-1889)
> American astronomer

Our scientific world is our world of reasoning. It has its greatness and uses and attractions. We are ready to pay homage due to it. But when it claims to have discovered the real world for us and laughs at the worlds of all simple-minded men, then we must say it is like a general grown intoxicated with his power, usurping the throne of his king.

> Rabindranath Tagore (1861-1941)
> Indian writer and philosopher, *Personality*

Science knows the qualities of electricity, but not its real essence.

> Mahmoud Mohammed Taha (1909-1985)
> Sudanese reformer, *The Second Message of Islam*

You men, let me tell you a secret: God's kingdom has been brought closer by Mwaura's Matatu Matamu Model T Ford. Even the journey to the Devil's place is nothing in

Mwaura's Matatu Matamu Model T
Ford. Get in! Get in!

> Ngugi wa Thiong'o (b. 1936)
> Kenyan writer, comically recording the
> feel of an African marketplace

on THE SEASONS

I will break the back
of this long, midwinter night,
folding it double,
cold beneath my spring quilt,
that I may draw out
the night, should my love return

> Hwang Chin-i (c. 1506-1544)
> Korean poet

Autumn rain, autumn wind, they
make one die of sorrow.

> Qiu Jin (1874-1907)
> Chinese poet and activist, *Qiu Jin ji*

In Winter the bare boughs that
seem to sleep
Work covertly, preparing for their
Spring.

> Rumi (1207-1273)
> Persian Sufi poet and mystic

However far I gaze
Neither cherry blossoms nor
Crimson leaves are in sight.
Only a fisherman's hut on the
shore
In the autumnal evening.

> Fujiwara Teika (1162-1241)
> Japanese poet

Looking about
I see no cherry blossoms
And no crimson leaves
A straw-thatched hut by a bay
In the autumn dusk.

> Fujiwara Teika (1162-1241)
> Japanese poet, *Shin Kokinshu*

on SECRETS

A chicken is hatched even from
such a well-sealed thing as an egg.

> Chinese proverb

Probably one of the most private
things in the world is an egg until
it is broken.

> M. F. K. Fisher (1908-1992)
> American writer, "How Not to Boil an
> Egg," *How to Cook a Wolf*

The hardest thing in the world
Is to reveal a hidden love.

> Ho Shuang-ch'ing (b. 1712)
> Chinese poet, poem set to the tune "A
> Watered Silk Dress"

I warned you
Don't ask for explanations
When you walk with me.

> Lami'a Abbas al-'Imarah
> (20th century)
> Iraqi poet, "The Path of Silence"

I have found a little girl being wiser
than myself. I asked her, "What do
you carry under the cover of your
basket?" Whereupon she answered: "If I had wished everyone
to know what was in it, I would
not have covered it."

> Rabbi Joshua
> in the Talmud (ancient body of Jewish
> civil and canonical law), quoted in *Jews
> and Arabs*, by S. D. Gotein, who
> points out that a similar story occurs in
> Arabic literature, with the questioner
> being the conqueror of Egypt, Amr Ibn
> al As

on SEEING

The secret of seeing is to sail on
solar wind. Hone and spread your
spirit till you yourself are a sail,

whetted, translucent, broadside to
the merest puff.

Annie Dillard (b. 1945)
American writer, *Pilgrim at Tinker
Creek*

The night has given me dark eyes
But I use them to look for light.

Gu Cheng (b. 1957)
Chinese poet

I who am blind can give one hint
to those who are not—one admo-
nition to those who would make
full use of the gift of sight: Use
your eyes as if tomorrow you
would be stricken blind. And the
same method can be applied to the
other senses. Hear the music of
voices, the song of a bird, the
mighty strains of an orchestra, as if
you would be stricken deaf tomorrow. Touch each object you want
to touch as if tomorrow your tac-
tile sense would fail. Smell the per-
fume of the flowers, taste with
relish each morsel, as if tomorrow
you could never smell and taste
again. Make the most of every
sense.

Helen Keller (1880-1968)
American writer and lecturer, blind and
deaf from infancy on

I can see, and that is why I can be
so happy, in what you call the
dark, but which to me is golden. I
can see a God-made world, not a
man-made world.

Helen Keller (1880-1968)
American writer and lecturer, blind and
deaf from infancy on

The world of sight is still limitless.
It is the artist who limits vision to

the cramped dimensions of his
own ego.

Marya Mannes (b. 1904)
American writer, *More in Anger*

Nobody sees a flower—really—it is
so small—we haven't time—and to
see takes time like to have a friend
takes time.

Georgia O'Keeffe (1887-1986)
American artist

on THE SELF

I, who have been so many men in
vain, want to be one man, myself
alone. From out of a whirlwind the
voice of God replied: I am not, either. I dreamed the world the way
you dreamed your work, my Shake-
speare: one of the forms of my
dream was you, who, like me, are
many and one.

Jorge Luis Borges (1899-1986)
Argentinian writer, "Everything and
Nothing"

Torturing, fatiguing, boring
thoughts have been laboriously
turned this way and that since
time immemorial.
What is the point of such
thoughts?
The highest value lies only in the
self.

Chung-ch'ang T'ung (c. 179-219)
Chinese philosopher

My body is white, in shape I am
rounded;
Sometimes I float on the surface,
sometimes I am under water,
Large or small, the hand that
molded me matters little:

I shall always preserve my
vermilion heart.

> Ho Xuan Huong (19th century)
> Vietnamese poet

To search for truth about self is as
valuable as to search for truth in
other areas of life.

> Karen Horney (1885-1952)
> American psychoanalyst, *Self-Analysis*

Here I stand and make
Both myth and reality in my own
  way
And live the violence of my dream
  and of my reality

> Jabra Ibrahim Jabra (b. 1919)
> Palestinian writer, *A Poem Sequence*

Do I not have a self? If not, how do
I have knowledge or affection?
Since I have a self, can that which
penetrates my body as well as the
material force of heaven, the physical substance of earth, and the
breath of man be cut off or not? If
it can be, then one can draw a
knife and cut water to pieces.

> K'ang Yu-wei (1858-1927)
> Chinese political philosopher, *Mengt-
> tzu wei* (*Esoteric Meanings of
> Mencius*)

In ourselves we harbor the intu-
ition of another evolution, of other
possibilities of life.

> Abellatif Laabi (20th century)
> Moroccan writer

When God wishes well unto His
servant, He causes him to see the
faults of his soul.

> Muhammad (570-632)
> Prophet of Islam

I who wanted to speak of the
  century
we are all wrapped up in,
within my book still being born,
everywhere I found myself
while events escaped me.
. . . .
over and over I spoke of myself
and what is worse
I painted myself
on top of each event.

> Pablo Neruda (1904-1973)
> Chilean poet and diplomat

The word which can never die on
this earth, for it is the heart of it
and the meaning and the glory.
The sacred word: EGO.

> Ayn Rand (1905-1982)
> American writer, *Anthem*

You have mourned over others;
now sit down for a while and
weep over your own self.

> Rumi (1207-1273)
> Persian Sufi poet and mystic

The old religions said that he was
an atheist who did not believe in
God. The new religion says that he
is the atheist who does not believe
in himself.

> Vivekananda (1863-1902)
> Indian religious leader

Our own self is the measuring
square, and the world or the state
are the squares to be measured
with it. When we apply our measuring square, we should notice
that the incorrectness of the
squares means that our measuring
square is incorrect. We therefore
have to correct this measuring

square of ours, rather than look for correctness in the squares.

Wang Ken (1483-1540)
Chinese philosopher, *Wang Hsin-chai hsien-sheng i-chi*

on SELF-DESCRIPTION

. . . the scourge of God sent to men as a punishment for their sins.

Chingiz (Genghis) Khan
(c. 1162-1227)
Mongol conqueror, reported to have described himself thusly at the capture of Bukhara

He is this sort of man: so intent upon enlightening those eager for knowledge that he forgets to eat, and so happy in doing so that he forgets his sorrows, and does not realize that old age is creeping up on him.

Confucius (551-479 B.C.E.)
Chinese philosopher and founder of Confucianism, *Analects*, depiction of himself when asked how he should be described by one of his students

Labeled a delinquent. That's the only kind of label I want to be crucified under.

Dazai Osamu (1909-1948)
Japanese writer, *The Setting Sun*

on SELF-DISCIPLINE

He who conquers one passion, conquers many; and he who conquers many, conquers one.

Akaranga Sutra
Jain scripture, I.i.4

The man of least capacity is the one who shows himself incapable of self-correction.

'Ali (c. 600-661)
First Imam of the Sh'ia branch of Islam; fourth caliph

He who has conquered himself by the Self, he is a friend of himself; but he whose self is unconquered, his self acts as his own enemy like an external foe.

Bhagavad Gita
(c. 4th-3rd century B.C.E.)
teachings of Krishna from the Hindu epic, the *Mahabharata*

Valor is the conquest of one's own self.

Bhagavad Gita
(c. 4th-3rd century B.C.E.)
teachings of Krishna from the Hindu epic, the *Mahabharata*

Those indeed are conquerors who, as I have now, have conquered the intoxications (the mental intoxications arising from ignorance, sensuality, or craving after future life). Evil dispositions have ceased in me; therefore it is I that am conqueror!

attributed to Buddha
(c. 563-483 B.C.E.)
founder of Buddhism

Fools of poor understanding have themselves for their greatest enemies, for they do evil deeds which bear bitter fruits.

Dhammapada (c. 3rd century B.C.E.)
collection of ancient Buddhist poems and aphorisms, 5:66

The conquest of oneself is better than the conquest of all others.

> *Dhammapada* (c. 3rd century B.C.E.)
> collection of ancient Buddhist poems
> and aphorisms

Who but the self can be master of the self? With self well controlled, another master is hard to find.

> *Dhammapada* (c. 3rd century B.C.E.)
> collection of ancient Buddhist poems
> and aphorisms

When heat and cold have become the same, and greed and desire but useless terms, and you yourself are like wax resolved in the flame, then smooth enough you will find the rest of your life.

> Hamzah of Barus
> Malaysian writer, *Sha'ir Dagang*

He who conquers others is
  strong.
He who conquers himself is
  mighty.

> Lao-tzu (c. 604–531 B.C.E.)
> Chinese philosopher and founder of
> Taoism, *Tao-te-ching*

Let a wise man, like a driver of horses, exert diligence in restraint of his senses, straying among seductive sensual objects.

> *Manava-dharma-sastra*
> Vedic legislation, II:88

When you have an itch, you
  scratch.
But not to itch at all
Is better than any amount of
  scratching.

> Nagarjuna (100–165)
> Indian philosopher

It is always more difficult to fight one's own failings than the power of an adversary.

> Jawaharlal Nehru (1889–1964)
> Indian prime minister

'Tis easy to break an idol, very easy: to regard the self as easy to subdue is folly, folly.

> Rumi (1207–1273)
> Persian Sufi poet and mystic

on SELF-ESTEEM

Some men, like spaniels, will only fawn the more when repulsed, but will pay little heed to a friendly caress.

> Abd-el-Kader (1078–1166)
> Persian Sufi leader

If you have no confidence in self, you are twice defeated in the race of life. With confidence, you have won even before you have started.

> Marcus Garvey (1887–1940)
> American political leader, *Philosophy and Opinions*

Beware of allowing a tactless word, a rebuttal, a rejection to obliterate the whole sky.

> Anaïs Nin (1903–1977)
> American writer

No one can make you feel inferior without your consent.

> Eleanor Roosevelt (1884–1962)
> American humanitarian and First Lady

He who despises himself esteems himself as a self-despiser.

> Susan Sontag (b. 1933)
> American writer and critic, *Death Kit*

If my homely speech and poor wit are subjects for their laugh, good that they laugh, but for no fault of mine.

> Tulsidas (1523–1624)
> Indian philosopher, *Ramcharitmanas*

Him who is this person in the mirror—him indeed I reverence.

> *Upanishads* (c. 600–300 B.C.E.)
> sacred philosophical Hindu literature, Kaushitaki

on **SELF-IDENTITY**

It's impossible to get out of your own skin into somebody else's. . . . Somebody else's tragedy is not your own.

> Diane Arbus (1923–1971)
> American photographer

We've all got an identity. You can't avoid it. It's what's left when you take everything else away.

> Diane Arbus (1923–1971)
> American photographer

Any life, no matter how long and complex it may be, is made up of a *single moment*—the moment in which a man finds out, once and for all, who he is.

> Jorge Luis Borges (1899–1986)
> Argentinian writer

First,
erase your name,
unravel your years,
destroy your surroundings,
uproot what you seem,
and who remains standing?
Then,
rewrite your name, restore your
 age,

rebuild your house,
pursue your path,
and then,
endlessly,
start over, all over again.

> Andree Chedid (b. 1920)
> Egyptian writer

on **SELFISHNESS**

Selfishness must always be forgiven . . . because there is no hope of a cure.

> Jane Austen (1775–1817)
> English writer, *Mansfield Park*

Every ignoramus imagines that all that exists, exists with a view to his individual sake; it is as if there were nothing that exists except him. And if something happens to him that is contrary to what he wishes, he makes the trenchant judgement that all that exists is an evil.

> Maimonides (1135–1204)
> Spanish Hebrew philosopher, *Guide of the Perplexed*

on **SELF-KNOWLEDGE**

Recover the source of all strength in yourself, and all else will be added to you . . . political freedom, the mastery of human thought, the hegemony of the world.

> Aurobindo Ghose (1872–1950)
> Indian political leader and Hindu philosopher

Seek not the depths of your knowledge with staff or sounding line. For self is a sea boundless and measureless.

> Kahlil Gibran (1883–1931)
> Syrian writer, *The Prophet*

The greatest calamity that befalls the heedless is that they are ignorant of their own faults: for anyone who is ignorant here shall also be ignorant hereafter: "*Those who are blind in this world shall be blind in the next world*" (Qur'an, xvii.72).

al-Hujwiri (c. 11th-12th century)
Sufi teacher

To recognize oneself is to reach the Almighty.

Raidas (15th century)
Indian mystic and religious leader

We are "influenced" by something which is close and similar to the roots of our soul. Real influence is that which helps us be ourselves, that which elicits the hidden, the deepest secrets in ourselves.

Yizhar Simlansky (b. 1916)
Israeli writer

on SELF-PITY

Never feel self-pity, the most destructive emotion there is. How awful to be caught up in the terrible squirrel cage of self.

Millicent Fenwick (1910-1992)
American politician

All black people who are even minimally conscious, black people who have ever experienced Europe's technological power crusading in the vanguard of a civilizing mission, have profound feelings of inferiority and bitterly regret the fact that the Industrial Revolution did not agreeably commence in Da-

homey or Dakar. Nothing is achieved by concealing this fact.

Lewis Nkosi (b. 1936)
South African writer, *Home and Exile and Other Selections*

I never complained of the vicissitudes of fortune, nor suffered my face to be overcast that the revolution of the heavens, except once, when my feet were bare, and I had not the means of obtaining shoes. I came to the chief of Kufah in a state of much dejection, and saw there a man who had no feet. I returned thanks to God and acknowledged his mercies, and endured my want of shoes with patience, and exclaimed,

"Roast fowl to him that's sated will seem less
Upon the board than leaves of garden cress.
While, in the sight of helpless poverty,
Boiled turnip will a roasted pullet be."

Sa'di of Shiraz (c. 1184-1292)
Persian poet, *Gulistan*

The weeping of the candle is not in mourning for the moth: the dawn is at hand, and it is thinking of its own dark night.

Sa'ib of Tabriz (c. 1601-1677)
Persian poet

on SELF-PRESERVATION

To protect myself from the rear, I have to stand slantwise.

Lu Xun (1881-1936)
Chinese writer

The nature of a panther is that he never attacks. But if anyone attacks or backs into a corner, the panther comes up to wipe that aggressor or that attacker out.

> Huey Newton (1942–1989)
> American civil rights activist

on SELF-RELIANCE

Woman must not depend upon the protection of man, but must be taught to protect herself.

> Susan B. Anthony (1820–1906)
> American suffragist

Though God creates the mother, and the breast, and the milk, the children must draw for themselves their mother's milk.

> Nasir-i-Khusraw (1004–1061)
> Persian writer, *Safar-Nama*
> (*Narrative of Travels*)

No nation respects a beggar.

> Elijah Muhammad (1897–1975)
> American religious leader

All I steal is room for a hut,
All I need I steal,
Wind blows in, sweeps my floor,
Moon at the door is my lamp.
. . . .
I lean on a tree, happy in the
  shade:
Lonely, but glad to be alone.

> Nguyen Trai (1380–1442)
> Vietnamese poet, "Stolen from Nature"

God changes not what is in a people, until they change what is in themselves.

> *Qur'an* (c. 610–656)
> sacred book of Islam, sura xiii: 10

Be nobody's darling.

> Alice Walker (b. 1944)
> American writer, "Be Nobody's
> Darling," *Revolutionary Petunias and
> Other Poems*

The accumulated experience of history teaches us that, when no one looks after the people, the people take care of themselves; and when the people take care of themselves, it is no river that runs along in its riverbed, but a deluge that inundates.

> Rafael Enriquez de Zayas
> (1848–1932)
> Mexican writer, *Porfirio Diaz, la
> evolucion de su vidao*

on SENSUALITY

When men no pleasure feel nor
  pain,
A state of stupid torpor gain;
They then have reached
  perfection, rise
To heaven, so say the would-be
  wise.
But should not trees—if this be
  true—
And boulders gain perfection too?
For they are calm and torpid, feel
Nor pain nor pleasure, woe nor
  weal;
They dread no want, they seek no
  ease,
Like self-tormenting devotees.

> *Mahabharata* (540–300 B.C.E.)
> Hindu epic

Deliverance is not for me in
  renunciation . . .
No, I will never shut the doors of
  my senses.

The delights of sight and hearing
and touch
  will bear thy delight.

Rabindranath Tagore (1861-1941)
Indian writer and philosopher,
Gitanjali

on SEX

Water I give him in my hands
and he seems to drink fire;
and I appear to offer him
all the glass of my body.

Delmira Augustini (1886-1914)
Uruguayan poet

It doesn't matter what you do in
the bedroom as long as you don't
do it on the street and frighten the
horses.

Mrs. Patrick Campbell (1865-1940)
English actress

Her hand, my hand
Have touched for a long time;
Her lips, my lips,
When shall we have enough?

Guo Moruo (1892-1978)
Chinese writer, *The Vase*

Whatever else can be said about
sex, it cannot be called a dignified
performance.

Helen Lawrenson (1907-1982)
American writer and editor

The fly runs toward the fire or
lamp, thinking that it is a flower,
and gets burnt up. Even so, the
passionate man runs towards a
false beautiful form, thinking that
he can obtain real happiness, and
gets burnt up in the fire of lust.

Sivananda Sarasvati (1887-1963)
Indian religious leader

I let down my silken hair
Over my shoulders
And open my thighs
Over my lover.

Tzu Yeh (c. 3rd-4th century)
Chinese poet, "Song"

My arms grow beautiful
in the coupling
and grow lean
as they come away
What shall I make of this?

Venmanipputi (c. 1st-3rd century)
Indian Tamil poet, "What She Said to
Her Girlfriend"

on SHAME

Where there is no shame, there is
no honor.

Congo proverb

You have already beaten him—you
struck him where every human
worthy of the name is most vulner-
able. You have shamed him before
his friends and before the world,
and in doing that you have hurt
him far more than you could by
any bodily punishment.

Ousmane Sembane (b. 1923)
Senegalese writer, *God's Bit of Wood*

It's far better to make people angry
than to make them ashamed.

Rabindranath Tagore (1861-1941)
Indian writer and philosopher

on SILENCE

Silence is the door of consent.

Berber proverb

Blessed is the man who, having nothing to say, abstains from giving us wordy evidence of the fact.

> George Eliot (1819–1880)
> English writer, *Impressions of Theophratus Such*

Silence is also speech.

> Fulfulde (West African) proverb

Never forget that when we are silent, we are one. And when we speak, we are two.

> Indira Gandhi (1917–1984)
> Indian prime minister

Silence is a fence around wisdom.

> Hebrew proverb

You can't improve on saying nothing.

> Golda Meir (1898–1978)
> Israeli prime minister

Nothing is so good for an ignorant man as silence, and if he knew this, he would no longer be ignorant.

> Sa'di of Shiraz (c. 1184–1292)
> Persian poet, *Gulistan*

To the seeker after pearls, silence is a speaking argument, for no breath comes forth from the diver of the sea.

> Sa'ib of Tabriz (c. 1601–1677)
> Persian poet

Man goes into the noisy crowd to drown his own clamor of silence.

> Rabindranath Tagore (1861–1941)
> Indian writer and philosopher

Respect my silence.

> Derek Walcott (b. 1930)
> West Indian poet, "A Patriot to Patriots"

on SIN

Not to commit faults counts for more than to do good.

> 'Ali (c. 600–661)
> First Imam of the Sh'ia branch of Islam; fourth caliph

Q. What is the most harmful sin?
A. The sin thou dost not know to be a sin.

> al-Antaki (d. 830)
> Sufi leader

All sins are committed in secrecy. The moment we realize that God witnesses even our thoughts, we shall be free.

> Mohandas K. Gandhi (1869–1948)
> Indian spiritual and political leader

Anything that's natural can't be sinful—it may be inconvenient, but it's not sinful.

> Madeleine L'Engle (b. 1918)
> American writer

By Him Who holds my soul, if ye did not sin, verily would God do away with you, and bring forth a people who sin and who ask forgiveness of God, and them would He forgive.

> Muhammad (570–632)
> Prophet of Islam

When God loves a man, sin shall not harm him.

> Muhammad (570–632)
> Prophet of Islam

Whatever of good befalleth thee, it is from God, and whatever of ill befalleth thee, it is from thyself.

> *Qur'an* (c. 610–656)
> sacred book of Islam, iv:79

Shall I tell you upon whom the
devils descend?
They descend upon every sinful,
lying person.

> *Qur'an* (c. 610-656)
> sacred book of Islam, 26:221-22

Forsake the outwardness of sin and
the inwardness thereof. Lo! those
who garner sin will be awarded
that which they have earned.

> *Qur'an* (c. 610-656)
> sacred book of Islam, VI:120

If ever we have any sin
committed
Against the gods, or friend, or
house's chieftain,
Of such may now our hymn be
expiation.
O heaven and earth, from
dreadful darkness save us.

> *Rig-Veda* (c. 1000 B.C.E.)
> Hindu sacred literature

The rosary in the hand, repentance
on the lips, and the heart full of
sinful longings—sin itself laughs at
our repentance!

> Sa'ib of Tabriz (c. 1601-1677)
> Persian poet

Sin begins in thought, which is the
intimation of conscience. So, if the
conscience holds sin, then its
thoughts shall be evil.

> Mahmoud Mohammed Taha
> (1909-1985)
> Sudanese Islamic reformer, *The Second
> Message of Islam*

Rabbi Akiba said: "In the beginning, sin is like a thread of a spider's web; but in the end, it
becomes like the cable of a ship."

> *Talmud*
> (c. late 4th-early 6th century)
> ancient body of Jewish civil and
> canonical law, Bereshit Rabbah 22:6

It is true that we cannot be free
from sin, but at least let our sins
not always be the same.

> Teresa of Avila (1515-1582)
> Spanish nun, "Conception of Love
> of God"

on SLAVERY

The sky is dark. But to understand
something is to give light. Those
who deny liberty to the slaves may
have white skins, but their consciences are blacker than the skin
of the Negro.

> Roman Baldorioty de Castro
> (1822-1887)
> Puerto Rican politician

We do not give [slaves] what is
more important than food or clothing or kindness. We do not give
them freedom.

> Segundo Ruiz Belvis (1829-1867)
> Puerto Rican lawyer

Slavery is the offspring of darkness.

> Simón Bolívar (1783-1830)
> South American revolutionary leader
> called the Liberator of South America

Must I dwell in slavery's night
And all pleasure take its flight
Far beyond my feeble sight,
Forever?

> Juana Ines de la Cruz (1651-1695)
> Mexican nun and poet, "The Slave's
> Complaint"

I hear the mournful wail of millions!

Frederick Douglass (1817-1895)
American abolitionist

Slaves are generally expected to sing as well as to work.

Frederick Douglass (1817-1895)
American abolitionist, *Autobiography*

No man can put a chain about the ankle of his fellow man without at last finding the other end fastened about his own neck.

Frederick Douglass (1817-1895)
American abolitionist

The sunlight that has brought life and healing to you has brought [slave] stripes and death to me. This Fourth of July is yours, not mine.

Frederick Douglass (1817-1895)
American abolitionist

Raphael painted, Luther preached, Corneille wrote, and Milton sang; and through it all, for four hundred years, the dark captives wound to the sea amid the bleaching bones of the dead; for four hundred years the sharks followed the scurrying ships; for four hundred years America was strewn with the living and dying millions of a transplanted race; for four hundred years Ethiopia stretched forth her hands unto God.

W. E. B. Du Bois (1868-1963)
American writer and educator

I know why the caged bird sings, ah me,

. . . .

It is not a carol of joy or glee,
But a prayer that he sends from
his heart's deep core,
But a plea . . .

Paul Laurence Dunbar (1872-1906)
American poet, "Sympathy"

The moment the slave resolves that he will no longer be a slave, his fetters fall. He frees himself and shows the way to others. Freedom and slavery are mental states.

Mohandas K. Gandhi (1869-1948)
Indian spiritual and political leader,
Non-Violence in Peace and War

Slavery time was tough, boss. You just don't know how tough it was.

Tines Kendricks (c. 19th century)
American ex-slave

A nation may lose its liberties and be a century in finding it out. Where is the American liberty? . . . In its far-reaching and broad sweep, slavery has stricken down the freedom of us all.

John Mercer Langston (1829-1897)
American politician

Slavery has as many shapes among us as there are things we need.

Eugenio Maria de Hostos
(1839-1903)
Puerto Rican patriot

It isn't those who are taken by force, put in chains, and sold as slaves who are the real slaves; it is those who will accept it, morally and physically.

Ousmane Sembane (b. 1923)
Senegalese writer

I was born in slavery, but I received from nature the soul of a free man.

François Dominique
Toussaint-L'Ouverture (1743–1803)
Haitian revolutionary leader

Man alone can enslave man.

Simone Weil (1909-1943)
French philosopher, *Oppression and Liberty*

Am I African? What would my feelings be when I looked into the black face of the African, feeling that maybe his great-great-great-grandfather had sold my great-great-great-grandfather into slavery?

Richard Wright (1908-1960)
American writer, *On Visiting Africa*

I want to die a slave to principles, not to men.

Emiliano Zapata (1879-1919)
Mexican revolutionary

on SLEEP

Sleep is as powerful as a sultan.

Egyptian proverb

Sleep has no master.

Jamaican proverb

Sleep is the brother of death.

Muhammad (570-632)
Prophet of Islam

on SNOBS AND SNOBBERY

There is no rationale that defends it and no attack that dissolves it.

Maya Angelou (b. 1928)
American writer

A friend told me
he'd risen above jazz.
I leave him there.

Michael Harper (b. 1938)
American poet, *Images of Kin*

on SOCIETY

Misery is evil; quarreling, a misfortune. There is only one possibility of avoiding both: a clear division of society. [Otherwise] the strong tyrannize the weak, the intelligent frighten the stupid, the inferior resist the superior, and the young mock the old.

Hsun-tzu (298–238 B.C.E.)
Chinese philosopher, "A Wealthy State"

We should not expect people to be good, but should make it impossible for them to be bad.

Lin Yutang (1895-1976)
Chinese writer, "Han Fei as a Cure for Modern China"

I am weary of elbowing my way
    along the path to glory and profit.
I delight in the company of
    chrysanthemums and pine trees,
    of the wind and the moon.
I allowed myself to put a foot
    inside the circle of the madding
    crowd.
And when I suddenly think of it,
    I shudder indescribably.

Nguyen Cong Tru (1773-1858)
Vietnamese poet

We praise like frogs,
Swear like frogs,
Turn midgets into heroes,
and heroes into scum:
We never stop and think.

Nizar Qabbani (b. 1932)
Syrian/Lebanese writer and publisher

Class war is not the cause of social progress; it is a disease developed in the course of social progress. The cause of the disease is the inability to subsist, and the result of the disease is war.

Sun Yat-sen (1866–1925)
Chinese military and political leader

There may be many who will gladly face death in the battlefield, but few who will face a hostile society.

Thiruvalluvar (c. 2nd century)
Indian Tamil writer, *Kural*

In all things that are purely social we can be as separate as the fingers, yet one as the hand in all things essential to mutual progress.

Booker T. Washington (1856–1915)
American educator

No human emotion can transcend the social conditions around it.

Zhang Jie (b. 1937)
Chinese writer

on SOLITUDE

Here I am, a wild beast
cut off from his companions.

Chairil Anwar (1922–1949)
Indonesian poet

Whoever fears to be alone and craves for men's society is far from salvation.

Attar (d. 1229)
Persian poet

There are sores which slowly erode the mind in solitude like a kind of canker.

Sadiq Hidayat (1903–1951)
Persian writer, *Buf-i Kur* (The Blind Owl)

I retired as deep as I could into the depths of my own being, like an animal that hides itself in a cave in the wintertime. I heard other people's voices with my ears; my own, I heard in my throat. The solitude that surrounded me was like the deep, dense night of eternity, that night of dense, clinging, contagious darkness which awaits the moment it will descend upon silent cities full of dreams of lust and rancor.

Sadiq Hidayat (1903–1951)
Persian writer, *Buf-i Kur* (The Blind Owl)

But understand that I want to remain alone, truly alone, so I can precede my face, my voice, my hell without anyone telling me which is the best path, without anyone laughing at the giant's wings and the dwarf's legs that impede my gait.

Abellatif Laabi (20th century)
Moroccan writer

My body is a prisoner
In this room above the misty
River, the jade green river,
That is the only companion
of my endless days.

Li Ch'ing-chao (1084–1151)
Chinese poet

Under the eaves, I find a place
and sleep alone,
And waking, I see the bed half-filled with the moon.

Po Chu-i (772–846)
Chinese poet, "Lonely Night in Early Autumn"

The bitter pinecone may be eaten,
The mist on high give
nourishment.
The whole world takes to go-and-
getting;
My way alone is difficult.

> Tu Fu (712–770)
> Chinese poet, "The Empty Purse"

on SORROW

Life has an end; only sorrow is endless.

> Chong Ch'ol (1537–1594)
> Korean poet and government official,
> "Hymn of Constancy"

Rather than calling this diary a record of my life, it's more accurate
to regard it as the sum of all my
tears.

> Ding Ling (1904–1986)
> Chinese writer, "Miss Sophia's Diary"

There is no sorrow I have thought
more about than that—to love
what is great, and try to reach it,
and yet to fail.

> George Eliot (1819–1880)
> English writer

Misery is a communicable disease.

> Martha Graham (1894–1991)
> American dancer

Sorrow shatters my heart;
And men distress it with blame,
Because it follows love.

> Moses ibn Ezra (1070–1139)
> Spanish Hebrew poet, "Sorrow Shatters
> My Heart"

You went away from my heart
And I held on, loving you
But your tear stains spread

And spread, till the tears
Became a lake, and the lake
Engulfed my heart
That night, as I slept, I drowned
In my heart.

> Shiraishi Kazuko (b. 1931)
> Japanese poet, "Lake," *Tonight Is Nasty*

Sorrow is tranquility remembered
in emotion.

> Dorothy Parker (1893–1967)
> American writer, *Sentiment*

Sadness is twilight's kiss on earth.

> Wole Soyinka (b. 1934)
> Nigerian writer

To me she was as cold as the moon
at dawn; and, since I have left her,
the dawn is the sight I find most
sad.

> Mibu-no Tadamine (c. 905)
> Japanese poet, *Waga*

It isn't lightning, or the beating of
rain,
I'm simply sad, night after night.

> Tran Te Xuong (1869–1907)
> Vietnamese poet, "Night Sadness"

on THE SOUL

Invest in the human soul. Who
knows, it might be a diamond in
the rough.

> Mary McLeod Bethune
> (1875–1955)
> American educator

It is not born,
it does not die;
having been,
it will never not be;
unborn, enduring,
constant, and primordial,

it is not killed
when the body is killed.

> *Bhagavad Gita*
> (c. 4th-3rd century B.C.E.)
> teachings of Krishna from the Hindu
> epic, the *Mahabharata,* Krishna
> answering the leader of one army,
> Arjuna, who asked why he should fight

There is a Light that shines beyond all things on earth, beyond us all, beyond the heavens, beyond the highest, the very highest heavens. This is the Light that shines in our heart.

> *Chandogya Upanishad*
> (c. 7th-8th century B.C.E.)
> sacred philosophical Hindu literature

Our souls and our bodies are two different worlds.

> Fakhir al-Din Razi (1149-1209)
> Central Asian Islamic philosopher

The soul should be examined in the light of other souls.

> Aaron David Gordon (1856-1922)
> Israeli writer

The soul of the slave, the soul of the "little man," is as dear to me as the soul of the great.

> Aaron David Gordon (1856-1922)
> Israeli writer

When a man offers you his soul, do you give him change?

> Luis Muñoz Marín (b. 1898)
> Puerto Rican politician

The soul after death goes nowhere where it has not been from the very beginning, nor does it become other than that which it has always been, the one eternal omnipresent.

> Yajnavalkya (4th century B.C.E.)
> Indian philosopher

on SPEECH

The less said the better.

> Jane Austen (1775-1817)
> English writer, *Sense and Sensibility*

A chattering bird builds no nest.

> Cameroon (West African) proverb

Once you have spoken, even the swiftest horses cannot retract your words.

> Chinese proverb

Explain yourself without gestures. The moment you gesticulate, you look common.

> Colette (1873-1954)
> French writer

Better than a thousand meaningless words is one word of sense, which brings the hearer peace.

> *Dhammapada* (c. 3rd century B.C.E.)
> collection of ancient Buddhist poems
> and aphorisms

Too many words are fit for a beast of burden.

> Yunus Emre (c. 1321)
> Turkish poet

The music of life is in danger of being lost in the music of the voice.

> Mohandas K. Gandhi (1869-1948)
> Indian spiritual and political leader

All is never said.

> Ibo (Nigerian) proverb

Words are sweet, but they never take the place of food.

> Ibo (Nigerian) proverb.

Speech is not what one should desire to understand. One should know the speaker.

> *Kaushitaki Upanishad*
> (c. 600–300 B.C.E.)
> sacred philosophical Hindu literature

My voice is the only material thing in which I can still reveal myself. Go ahead and cut off the hand or the testicles of a voice. Try to find the head of a voice, the orifice through which it passes, or even the breasts to which you can attach the clips of your electrodes. Nothing. Resonant tooth.

> Abellatif Laabi (20th century)
> Moroccan writer

Keep your mouth shut, and close up the doors of sight and sound, and as long as you live you will have no vexation. But open your mouth, or become inquisitive, and you will be in trouble all your life long.

> Lao-tzu (c. 604–531 B.C.E.)
> Chinese philosopher and founder of Taoism, *Tao-te-ching*

Be a craftsman in speech, so that thou mayest be strong; for the tongue is a sword to a man, and speech is more valorous than any fighting.

> Meri-ka-Re (c. 2100 B.C.E.)
> Egyptian king

Speech is our second possession, after the soul—and perhaps we have no other possession in this world.

> Gabriela Mistral (1889–1957)
> Chilean poet/diplomat

He who holds his tongue will be saved.

> Muhammad (570–632)
> Prophet of Islam

The more we say, the more there remains to be said.

> Nanak (1469–1539)
> Indian religious leader and founder of Sikhism

In saying what is obvious, never choose cunning. Yelling works better.

> Cynthia Ozick (b. 1931)
> American writer, "We Are the Crazy Lady and Other Feisty Feminist Fables"

Place a padlock on your throat and hide the key.

> Rumi (1207–1273)
> Persian Sufi poet and mystic

Ten doors are opened if one door be shut: the finger is the interpreter of the dumb man's tongue.

> Sa'ib of Tabriz (c. 1601–1677)
> Persian poet and poet in the court of Shah Jahan of India

Mark my words: It is through the ears you can touch a man to pleasure or rage. Let the spirit which dwells there hear good things, and it will fill the body with delight; let it hear bad, and it will swell with fury.

> Xerxes (c. 480 B.C.E.)
> Persian king

on SPIRIT

There is in this world no such force as the force of a man determined to rise. The human soul cannot be permanently chained.

W. E. B. Du Bois (1868–1963)
American writer and educator

There are many people like me who believe firmly, if somewhat incoherently, that pockets on this planet are filled with what humans have left behind them, both good and evil, and that any such spiritual accumulation can stay there forever, past definition of such a stern word.

M. F. K. Fisher (1908–1992)
American writer, *A Considerable Town*

Qi is like water, and words are like objects floating on the water. When the water reaches a sufficient level, the objects, small and big, can freely move; such is the relation between qi and words. When qi is at its fullness, both the amplitude and the sound of the sentences reach a perfect pitch.

Han Yu (768–824)
Chinese poet

It is the mind that makes the body.

Sojourner Truth (c. 1797–1883)
American abolitionist

on SPIRITUALITY

I have now reigned above fifty years in victory and peace, beloved by my subjects, dreaded by my enemies, and respected by my allies. Riches and honors, power and pleasure have waited on my call,

nor does any earthly blessing appear to be wanting for my felicity. In this situation I have diligently numbered the days of pure and genuine happiness which have fallen to my lot. They amount to fourteen. O man, place not thy confidence in this present world.

'Abd-ar-Rahman (891–961)
Islamic ruler of Spanish Córdoba

And he who would be a friend with God must remain alone, or make the whole world his friend.

Mohandas K. Gandhi (1869–1948)
Indian spiritual and political leader

Remember it is the heart and not the body, which strives to draw near to God. By *heart* I do not mean the flesh perceived by the senses, but that secret thing which is sometimes expressed by spirit, and sometimes by soul.

Abu Hamid Muhammad al-Ghazali
(1058–1111)
Arab Islamic philosopher and theologian

I hear people are going about saying I am a saint, and others saying that I am impious. I prefer those who call me impious; and so does God. . . . They call me a saint because they respect me; but the others call me impious out of zeal for their religion. A man who is zealous for his religion is dearer to me, and dearer to God also, than a man who venerates a creature.

al-Hallaj (d. 922)
Persian Sufi mystic

Neither time nor space exists for the man who knows the eternal.

Space and time are real for the man who is yet imperfect, and space is divided for him into dimensions; time, into past, present, and future.

Jiddu Krishnamurti (1895-1986)
Indian philosopher

on **STRATEGY**

Wait not while your foe fits arrow to bowstring when you can send your own arrow into him.

Babur (1483-1530)
First Mughal emperor of India,
Babur-nama

The fundamental principle of revolutionary wars: strike to win; strike only when success is certain; if not, then don't strike.

Vo Nguyen Giap (b. 1912)
Vietnamese military leader, *People's War, People's Army*

If we have to fight, we shall fight. You will kill ten of our men, and we will kill one of yours, and in the end it will be you who will tire of it.

Ho Chi Minh (1892-1969)
Vietnamese political leader, to French negotiators

What is basic guerilla strategy? Guerilla strategy must be based primarily on alertness, mobility, and attack. It must be adjusted to the enemy situation, the terrain, the existing lines of communication, the relative strengths, the weather, and the situation of the people.

Mao Zedong (1893-1976)
Chairman of People's Republic of China

When guerillas engage a stronger enemy, they withdraw when he advances, harass him when he stops, strike him when he is weary, pursue him when he withdraws.

Mao Zedong (1893-1976)
Chairman of People's Republic of China

There is in guerilla warfare no such thing as a decisive battle.

Mao Zedong (1893-1976)
Chairman of People's Republic of China

We should support whatever the enemy opposes and oppose whatever the enemy supports.

Mao Zedong (1893-1976)
Chairman of People's Republic of China

Do not press an enemy at bay. Prince Fu Ch'ai said: "Wild beasts, when at bay, fight desperately. How much more is this true of men! If they know there is no alternative, they will fight to the death."

Sun Tzu (335-288 B.C.E.)
Chinese military leader, *The Art of War*

Let your plans be dark and impenetrable as the night, and when you move, fall like a thunderbolt.

Sun Tzu (335-288 B.C.E.)
Chinese military leader, *The Art of War*

Attack the enemy's strategy.

Sun Tzu (335-288 B.C.E.)
Chinese military leader, *The Art of War*

Those skilled in war bring the enemy to the field of battle and are not brought there by him.

Sun Tzu (335-288 B.C.E.)
Chinese military leader, *The Art of War*

on STRENGTH

If you are to be leaders, teachers, and guides among your people, you must have strength. No people can be fed, no people can be built up on flowers.

> Alexander Crummell (1819–1898)
> American minister and writer

The most important thing is to be strong. With strength, one can conquer others, and to conquer others gives one virtue.

> Mao Zedong (1893–1976)
> Chairman of People's Republic of China

There are two ways of exerting one's strength: one is pushing down, the other is pulling up.

> Booker T. Washington (1856–1915)
> American educator

on STRIFE

Why really, the land spins around as does a potter's wheel.

> Ipu-wer (c. 2000 B.C.E.)
> Ancient Egyptian prophet

Since all are brothers in the
world,
Why is there such constant
turmoil?

> Meiji (1852–1912)
> Japanese emperor
> This poem was read by his grandson, Japanese emperor Hirohito, expressing misgivings about growing militarism at a conference in 1941, two months before Pearl Harbor.

Men will take up weapons of warfare, so that the land lives in confusion. Men will make arrows of metal, beg for the bread of blood, and laugh with the laughter of sickness.

> Nefer-rohu (c. 2200 B.C.E.)
> Egyptian prophet

on STRIVING

It is good to preserve the name, wealth, and honors you inherit, but it is better in every way if you yourself create a position and a name. The first requires good sense, but the second demands willpower and great virtue.

> Roman Baldorioty de Castro
> (1822–1887)
> Puerto Rican politician

O it was the heart like this tiny
  star near to the sorrows
straining against the whole world
  and the long twilight
spark of man's dream conquering
  the night
moving in darkness stubborn and
  fierce
till leaves of sunset change from
  green to blue
and shadows grow like giants
  everywhere.

> Martin Carter (b. 1927)
> Guyanan writer and diplomat, "I Come from the Nigger Yard"

A life without fighting is a dead sea in the universal organism.

> Joaquim Maria Machado de Assis
> (1839–1908)
> Brazilian writer, *Epitaph for a Small Winner*

When have you seen in the whole world

Who ever once acquired pleasure
  without pain?
Who, in attaining all his desires,
Has remained at his height of
  perfection?

> Sa'di of Shiraz (c. 1184–1292)
> Persian poet, *Gulistan*

I do not know anyone who has got
to the top without hard work. That
is the recipe. It will not always get
you to the top, but should get you
pretty near.

> Margaret Thatcher (b. 1925)
> English prime minister

Better the arrow that missed the
lion than the one that killed a rabbit.

> Thiruvalluvar (c. 2nd century)
> Indian Tamil writer, *Kural* (also known
> as the *Tamil Veda*)

Before proceeding, one must reach.

> Wolof (West African) proverb

on SUCCESS

The penalty of success is to be
bored by people who used to snub
you.

> Nancy Astor (1879–1964)
> English politician

You need the knack of being obse-
quious to your superiors and ingra-
tiating to everyone else.
Is the smell of fleshpots so greatly
preferable? For to strive for the fra-
grance of good reputation and
merit entails much suffering.

> Cao Ba-Quat (1809–1854)
> Vietnamese poet, "Tai tu da cung phu"
> ("Song of the Gifted Man Sunk in
> Abject Poverty")

All real success springs from that
inward might which we exert
upon society.

> Alexander Crummell (1819–1898)
> American minister and writer

Success is counted sweetest
By those who ne'er succeed.

> Emily Dickinson (1830–1886)
> American poet

If there is no struggle, there is no
progress. Those who profess to favor freedom, and yet deprecate agitation, are men who want crops
without plowing up the ground.
They want rain without thunder
and lightning. . . . Men may not
get all they pay for in this world;
but they must certainly pay for all
they get.

> Frederick Douglass (1817–1895)
> American abolitionist

It's them as take advantage that get
advantage i' this world.

> George Eliot (1819–1880)
> English writer, *Adam Bede*

To have realized your dream makes
you feel lost.

> Oriana Fallaci (b. 1930)
> Italian journalist, *Letter to a Child
> Never Born*

Heroes are made in the hour of defeat. Success is, therefore, well described as a series of glorious
defeats.

> Mohandas K. Gandhi (1869–1948)
> Indian spiritual and political leader

The worst of men is he whose to-day falls short of his yesterday.

> Al Hariri (1054-1122)
> Arab poet

Success and failure are not true opposites and they're not even in the same class; they're not even a couch and a chair.

> Lillian Hellman (1906-1984)
> American writer, *The Listener*

You can be up to your boobies in white satin, with gardenias in your hair and no sugar cane for miles, but you can still be working on a plantation.

> Billie Holiday (1915-1959)
> American singer, *Lady Sings the Blues*

The small man is one who throws away his opportunities, whereas great deeds are accomplished through utilizing the mistakes [of others] and inflexibly following them up.

> Li Ssu (c. 280-208 B.C.E.)
> Chinese official and writer

The real demon is success—the anxieties engendered by this quest are relentless, degrading, corroding. What is worse, there is no end to this escalation of desire.

> Marya Mannes (b. 1904)
> American writer, "The Roots of Anxiety in Modern Women"

A man can make what he wants of himself if he truly believes that he must be ready for hard work and many heartbreaks along the way.

> Thurgood Marshall (1908-1993)
> American jurist

Success often comes to those who dare and act; it seldom goes to the timid who are ever afraid of the consequences.

> Jawaharlal Nehru (1889-1964)
> Indian prime minister

Those who are prepared to die for any cause are seldom defeated.

> Jawaharlal Nehru (1889-1964)
> Indian prime minister

As in the case in all branches of art, success depends in a very large measure upon individual initiative and exertion, and cannot be achieved except by dint of hard work.

> Anna Pavlova (1881-1931)
> Russian dancer

What is the use of acquiring one's heart's desire if one cannot handle and gloat over it, show it to one's friends, and gather an anthology of envy and admiration?

> Dorothy L. Sayers (1893-1957)
> English writer

Put your heart, mind, intellect, and soul even to your smallest acts. This is the secret of success.

> Sivananda Sarasvati (1887-1963)
> Indian religious leader, "Exponent of Japa"

Define the limits of your vision:
Having this, you will not be
  poorer
Than a man who rules a
  dukedom.

> Su Shih (1036-1101)
> Chinese government official and writer

An intelligent and prudent person attending to Dharma (duty), artha (wealth) and Kama (love) also without becoming the slave of his passions obtains success in everything that he may undertake.

Vatsyayana
(late 4th-early 5th century)
Indian Hindu philosopher, *Kama Sutras*

I have learned that success is to be measured not so much by the position that one has reached in life as by the obstacles which he has overcome while trying to succeed.

Booker T. Washington (1856-1915)
American educator, *Up from Slavery*

on SUFFERING

Those to whom love draws nigh are the most severely tested.

Attar (d. 1229)
Persian poet

The world is afflicted with death and decay; therefore, the wise do not grieve, knowing the terms of the world.

Buddhaghosa ("Voice of the Buddha") (c. 5th century)
Indian scholar

Without the bitterest suffering, we cannot rise above others.

Chinese proverb

The Four Noble Truths: Suffering, the origins of suffering, the cessation of suffering, and the Noble Eightfold Path which leads to the cessation of suffering.

Dhammapada (c. 3rd century B.C.E.)
collection of ancient Buddhist poems and aphorisms

True suffering does not know itself and never calculates.

Mohandas K. Gandhi (1869-1948)
Indian spiritual and political leader

When a man suffers, let him examine his deeds.

Talmud
(c. late 4th-early 6th century)
ancient body of Jewish civil and canonical law, Berakhoth 54

on SUFISM

To lay aside what you have in your head, and to give away what you have in your hands, and not to flinch from whatever befalls you.

Abu Sa'id (967-1049)
Persian mystic and poet, definition of Sufism

The whole of existence is imagination within imagination, while true Being is God alone.

Ibn 'Arabi (1165-1240)
Arab Sufi philosopher and poet

You are asleep, and your vision is a dream.
All you are seeing is a mirage.
When you wake up on the morn of the last day
You will know all this to be Fancy's illusion;
When you have ceased to see double,
Earth and Heaven will become transformed;
When the real sun unveils his face to you,
The moon, the stars, and Venus will disappear;
If a ray shines on the hard rock

Like a wool of many colors, it drops to pieces.

> Sa'di of Shiraz (c. 1184–1292)
> Persian poet, *Gulistan*

The Phantasmal is the Bridge to the Real.

> Sufi saying

on SURVIVAL

Often my creative life has seemed like a long tunnel, dark and damp. And sometimes I wondered whether I could live through it.

But I did.

> Ai Qing (b. 1910)
> Chinese poet, who suffered under Maoist rule

Every live thing is a survivor on a kind of extended emergency bivouac.

> Annie Dillard (b. 1945)
> American writer, *Pilgrim at Tinker Creek*

The human community is evolving. . . . We can survive anything you care to mention. We are supremely equipped to survive, to adapt and even in the long run to start thinking.

> Doris Lessing (b. 1919)
> English writer

I don't know how to fight. All I know is how to stay alive.

> Alice Walker (b. 1944)
> American writer, *The Color Purple*

on SYMBOLS

The power of a thing or an act is in the meaning and the understanding.

> Black Elk (1863–1950)
> Oglala Sioux holy man

In symbols there is a meaning that words cannot define.

> Ibn al'Farid (1181–1235)
> Arab poet

Doest not thou know that the light of the sun is the reflection of the Sun beyond the veil?

> Rumi (1207–1273)
> Persian Sufi poet and mystic

on TALENT

I believe talent is like electricity. We do not understand electricity. We use it. Electricity makes no judgement. You can plug into it, and light up a lamp, keep a heart pump going . . . or you can electrocute a person with it. . . . I think talent is like that.

Maya Angelou (b. 1928)
American writer

Everyone has talent. What is rare is the courage to follow the talent to the dark place where it leads.

Erica Jong (b. 1942)
American writer, "The Artist as Housewife: The Housewife as Artist"

God has given each normal person a capacity to achieve some end. True, some are endowed with more talent than others, but God has left none of us talentless.

Martin Luther King, Jr.
(1929-1968)
American civil rights leader

on TAOISM (DAOISM)

The Portal of God is nonexistence.

Chuang-tzu (c. 369-286 B.C.E.)
Chinese Taoist philosopher

The Great Way is simple
yet few know its origin
follow your desires without recrimination
adapt to things without praising them.

Chung-ch'ang T'ung (c. 179-219)
Chinese philosopher, *Ch'uan Han San-kuo Chin Nan-pei-ch'ao shih*

Before heaven and earth were produced,
There was Something, without form and yet all complete,
Silent! Empty!
Sufficient unto itself! Unchanging!
Moving everywhere but never exhausted!
This indeed might well be the mother of all below heaven.

Lao-tzu (c. 604-531 B.C.E.)
Chinese philosopher and founder of Taoism, *Tao-te-ching*

Act nonaction; undertake no undertaking; taste the tasteless.

Lao-tzu (c. 604-531 B.C.E.)
Chinese philosopher and founder of Taoism, *Tao-te-ching*

Banish wisdom, throw away knowledge,
and the people will benefit a hundredfold!
Banish "humanity," throw away righteousness,
and the people will become conscientious and full of love!
Banish skill, throw away profit

and thieves and robbers will disappear!

> Lao-tzu (c. 604–531 B.C.E.)
> Chinese philosopher and founder of Taoism, *Tao-te-ching*

on TEACHING

I cut the tree and my calloused hand carves it, but someone more able than I must finish it with beauty and brilliance.

> Rafael Cordero y Molina
> (1790–1868)
> Puerto Rican educator

It would be a greater pity to prostitute the lessons of wisdom to rascals incapable of understanding and appreciating them; there is no file that can clean iron of its rust after the rust has eaten through.

> Lokman (c. 1100 B.C.E.)
> Ethiopian fabulist

Just as a person is commanded to honor and revere his father, so he is under an obligation to honor and revere his teacher, even to a greater extent than his father; for his father gave him life in this world, while his teacher instructs him in wisdom, secures for him life in the world to come.

> Maimonides (1135–1204)
> Spanish Hebrew philosopher, *Misneh Torah*

Iron was black and sheenless, but cleansing and polishing washed away its blackness.

> Rumi (1207–1273)
> Persian Sufi poet and mystic

A teacher who teaches less than his fellow instructors should be dismissed. The other teachers will become more diligent both out of fear and out of gratitude.

> *Talmud*
> (c. late 4th–early 6th century)
> ancient body of Jewish civil and canonical law, Baba Batra, 21a

on THOUGHT

All that we are is the result of what we have thought; it is founded on our thoughts and made up of our thoughts. If a man speak or act with an evil thought, suffering follows him as a wheel follows the hoof of the beast that draws the cart.

> *Dhammapada* (c. 3rd century B.C.E.)
> collection of ancient Buddhist poems and aphorisms, "The Twin Verses"

The kingdoms and the crowns which the Moslems have lost in the course of history are far less important than the kingdom of the free and searching mind which they have lost in the process of intellectual stagnation.

> Mohammed Ayub Khan
> (1907–1970)
> Pakistani politician

After my death, my thought will still smile at every mystery from which the cover has been ripped. . . . Like a blue shadow it will wander at night in the pale light of the moon, when loving lads kiss the eyes of tired maidens.

> Zalman Shneour (b. 1887)
> Israeli poet

Too much awareness is a sickness;
It keeps me awake all night.

> Yi Cho-nyon (1269-1343)
> Korean poet

on TIME

Oh! how the hours hasten to change into days, the days into months, the months into years, and those into life's annihilation!

> 'Ali (c. 600-661)
> First Imam of the Sh'ia branch of Islam;
> fourth caliph

Tonight I think again
of many days that are sacrificed
for one night of love.
Of the waste and the fruit of the
   waste,
of plenty and of fire.
And how painlessly—time.

> Yehuda Amichai (b. 1924)
> Israeli writer

Time is the substance I am made of. Time is a river which sweeps me along, but I am the river; it is a tiger which destroys me, but I am the tiger; it is a fire which consumes me, but I am the fire. The world, unfortunately, is real; I, unfortunately, am Borges.

> Jorge Luis Borges (1899-1986)
> Argentinian writer, "The New
> Refutation of Time"

There is no time for cut-and-dried monotony. There is time for work. And time for love. That leaves no other time!

> Coco Chanel (1883-1971)
> French designer

An inch of time is an inch of gold. But an inch of gold cannot buy an inch of time.

> Chinese proverb

Men see only the present; Heaven sees the future.

> Chinese proverb

As the herdsman drives cattle by the rod to the pen, so does time drive man to death.

> *Dhammapada* (c. 3rd century B.C.E.)
> collection of ancient Buddhist poems
> and aphorisms

Who is moving in the distance?
It is the clock's pendulum,
Hired by the god of death
To measure life.

> Gu Cheng (b. 1957)
> Chinese poet

Mountains are steadfast but the
   mountain streams
Go by, go by
And yesterdays are like the
   rushing streams,
They fly, they fly,
And the great heroes, famous for
   a day,
They die, they die.

> Hwang Chin-i (c. 1506-1544)
> Korean poet

Man in the midst of the world is
   like a weaver,
And his days are but a thread.
Alas, the day that his web is
   finished
There is no more hope for his life.

> Moses ibn Ezra (1070-1139)
> Spanish Hebrew poet, "Man"

277

From your past emerges the present, and from the present is born your future.

> Muhammad Iqbal (1873-1938)
> Indian poet and philosopher

O, how strange are the deserted campsites and their long-gone inhabitants!
And how strangely time changes all!
The camel of youth walks slowly now; its once quick pace is gone; it is bored with traveling.

> Jarir (653-732)
> Umayyad Islamic poet

It is the strangely irrational notion that there is something in the very flow of time that will inevitably cure all ills. Actually time is neutral. It can be used either destructively or constructively. I am coming to feel that the people of ill will have not used time much more effectively than the people of good will.

> Martin Luther King, Jr.
> (1929-1968)
> American civil rights leader, "Letter from a Birmingham Jail"

We must use time creatively, and forever realize that the time is always ripe to do right.

> Martin Luther King, Jr.
> (1929-1968)
> American civil rights leader, "Letter from a Birmingham Jail"

We kill time; time buries us.

> Joaquim Maria Machado de Assis
> (1839-1908)
> Brazilian writer, *Epitaph for a Small Winner*

Time ripens all beings by itself, in itself. But no one here on earth knows one whom time has fully ripened.

> *Mahabharata* (540-300 B.C.E.)
> Hindu epic

I must govern the clock, not be governed by it.

> Golda Meir (1898-1978)
> Israeli politician

There are thirty-six thousand days
To a life
And I have wasted sixteen thousand
On nothing.
Please tell God to set back his clock.

> Nguyen Cong Tru (1773-1858)
> Vietnamese poet, "Fleeting Life"

Wasting time is an unbearable punishment.

> Quin Guanshu (b. 1929)
> Chinese scientist

And God had him die for a hundred years and then revived him and said: "How long have you been here?"
"A day or part of a day," he answered.

> *Qur'an* (c. 610-656)
> sacred book of Islam, II:261

The feeling of Sunday is the same everywhere, heavy, melancholy, standing still. Like when they say, "As it was in the beginning, is now and ever shall be, world without end."

> Jean Rhys (1894-1979)
> British novelist, *Voyage in the Dark*

The Past, the Future, O dear, is from you; you should regard both these as one.

> Rumi (1207-1273)
> Persian Sufi poet and mystic

Time has lost its shoes here
it stood still.

> Fadwa Tuqan (b. 1917)
> Palestinian poet, "From behind the Bars"

on TOLERANCE

It is forbidden to decry other sects; the true believer gives honor to whatever in them is worthy of honor.

> Asoka (273-232 B.C.E.)
> Indian king, decree to his subjects

The highest result of education is tolerance.

> Helen Keller (1880-1968)
> American writer and lecturer

on TRADITION

For tradition to be alive it has to be allowed to be a fountain of power for things undreamt of, things to come.

> Jabra Ibrahim Jabra (b. 1919)
> Palestinian writer, "The Rebels, the Committed and the Other: Transitions in Arabic Poetry Today" *Middle East Forum*

Some people imagine that by returning to tradition, you will renew it. This is not true, for by returning to tradition, you renew nothing. But by setting out from it and adding to it, you renew its power, because only by addition

can you prepare the future path for the living sap within it.

> Jabra Ibrahim Jabra (b. 1919)
> Palestinian writer

My hope is that tradition should be the sap of progress.

> Enrique A. Laguerre (b. 1906)
> Puerto Rican writer, *Cauce sin río*

I am the East.
I have philosophies, I have religions, who
would exchange them for airplanes?

> Ameen Rihani (1876-1940)
> Syrian-American poet

on TRANSCENDENCE

Since sorrow follows joy
As autumn does the spring
Man must transcend the joys
Of earth, which sorrows bring.

> Mirza Ghalib (1797-1869)
> Indian Urdu poet

It has been preached in every country, taught everywhere, but only believed in by a few, because until we get the experience ourselves, we cannot believe in it.

> Vivekananda (1863-1902)
> Indian Hindu religious leader

on TRANSIENCE

Thou hast seen Alp Arslan's head in pride exalted to the sky; Come to Mrev, and see how lowly in the dust that head doth lie!

> epitaph of conqueror Alp Arslan (1029-1072)
> a leader of the Seljuqs, who conquered and ruled much of the Middle East

The idol of yesterday is the demon of today, ruthlessly trodden in the dust.

> Surendranath Banerjea
> (1848–1925)
> Indian political leader

There are many mountain peaks which man has ascended. But the men who did so are gone, yet the peaks remain.

> Fakhir al-Din Razi (1149–1209)
> Central Asian Islamic philosopher

The sound of the bell of Gionshoja echoes the impermanence of all things. The hue of the flowers of the teak tree declares that they who flourish must be brought low. Yea, the proud ones are but for a moment, like an evening dream in springtime. The mighty are destroyed at the last; they are but as dust before the wind.

> *Heike Monogatari*
> greatest chronicle of the Japanese samurai

When the body is burnt, it
  becometh ashes,
When it is not burnt, a host of
  worms eat it up.
A soft clay vessel will break when
  water is put into it, such
  is the nature of the body.

> Kabir (1440–1519)
> Indian Mughal poet and philosopher

In the face of approaching death, from which there is no escape, is there any consolation in this incomprehensible life other than to sing about this momentary pleasure?

> Nagai Kafu (1879–1959)
> Japanese writer, *Sneers*

O you, foolish man, don't you realize that your sojourn here on earth is but for a glance, after which you return to the real world, the world in which you stay for ever and ever? Verily, you are nothing but a passer-by, following the will of your Creator—the mighty, the majestic.

> Rasa'il al-Kindi (810–873)
> Arab philosopher and physician

Prosperity and glory will all come to an end, just like the spring flowers that quickly wither away. When I chance to have them, I do not rejoice; nor do I grieve when I lose them.

> Ko Hung (283–343)
> Chinese scholar

All but God is vain,
Every delight, inevitably, must
  vanish.

> Labid (c. 600)
> Arab poet

Must the poetry of everything
  vanish
Or can my life ever condense it?

> Pablo Neruda (1904–1973)
> Chilean poet and diplomat, "Barrio sin luz" ("Lightless Suburb"),
> *Crepusculario*

Truly do we live on earth?
Not forever on earth; only a little
  while here.
Although it be jade, it will be
  broken,
Although it be gold, it is crushed,
Although it be quetzal feather, it is
  torn asunder.

Not forever on earth; only a little
while here.

> attributed to Nezahualcoyotl
> (1418-1472)
> Aztec ruler, in the *Coleccion de
> Canteres Mexicanos*

It is not true, it is not true
that we come to this earth to live.
We come only to sleep, only to
dream.
Our body is a flower.
As grass becomes green in the
springtime,
so our hearts will open, and give
forth buds,
and then they wither.
So did Tochihuitzin say.

> attributed to Nezahualcoyotl
> (1402-1472)
> Aztec ruler, in the *Coleccion de
> Canteres Mexicanos*

Everyone that is thereon will pass
away;
There remaineth but the
countenance of thy Lord of
Might and Glory.

> *Qur'an* (c. 610-656)
> sacred book of Islam

Inscriptions on metal and stone,
however permanent they may
seem, will some day pass away.
Thus I would rather shine as do
the sun and the moon,
and become as old as heaven and
earth.

> Ts'ao Chih (192-232)
> Chinese writer, "Yuan-yu" ("Journey to
> the Faraway")

The great glories of this world pass
away in the twinkling of an eye.

> T'u Lung (c. 1592)
> Chinese poet

A body is like lightning, gone in a
moment, back to Nothingness.
As spring flowers are dead in the
fall.
Forget about this growing and
dying, it is all irrelevant.
Life's motions are like dew on the
grass.

> Van-Hanh (d. 1018)
> Vietnamese poet, "Man's Body"

Nothing lives long
Only the earth and the mountains.

> White Antelope (d. 1864)
> Southern Cheyenne chief, last stanza of
> death song, sung as he was carrying a
> white flag and an American flag,
> approaching U.S. army lines, and was
> shot

on TRAVEL

There is no happiness for the man
who does not travel. Living in the
society of men, the best man becomes a sinner. For Indra is the
friend of the traveller. Therefore
wander!

> *Aitareya Upanishad* (c. 600 B.C.E.)
> sacred philosophical Hindu literature

When I saw the world full of
constraints,
Terror sent me riding on an
endless journey.

> al-Akhtal (645-713)
> Arab Christian poet

You cannot travel on the path before you have become the Path
itself.

> Buddha (c. 563-483 B.C.E.)
> Founder of Buddhism

Why do people so love to wander?
I think the civilized parts of the

World will suffice for me in the future.

Mary Cassatt (1844–1926)
American artist

Only the air-spirits know
What lies beyond the hills,
Yet I urge my team farther on
Drive on and on
On and on!

Eskimo poem (20th century)

A good traveler is one who does not know where he is going to, and a perfect traveler does not know where he came from.

Lin Yutang (1895–1976)
Chinese writer

I arrive where an unknown earth
  is under my feet.
I arrive where a new sky is above
  me,
I arrive at this land
A resting place for me.
O spirit of the earth! The stranger
  humbly offers his heart as food
  for thee.

purportedly chanted by the leader
of the Maoris
upon landfall at their new homeland,
Te Aotearoa (the Long White Cloud),
New Zealand

Become placeless, for to change this place of water and clay is but to move from one prison to another.

Sa'ib of Tabriz (c. 1601–1677)
Persian poet

It is said: "When a mountain is piled up, the first basket of earth is the beginning of the end . . . and when one travels, the first step is the beginning of the arrival."

Seng-chao (384–414)
Chinese monk and philosopher

The first thing you have to do is to travel, away from this city in which you live, so that you can see with your own eyes what you can never see in your own country and hear with your own ears what you have never before heard; and in order to learn in what conditions peoples, other than your own people, live . . . ; so that you may learn what their character is, and what their faith and their politics are. After this you can compare what is good with us and what is not good with us.

Ahmad Faris al-Shidyaq
(1804–1887)
Lebanese writer

How can you be satisfied with yourself if you leave this world without having seen it, although you were in a position to see it? Has not Al-Mutanabbi said: "I consider nothing more shameful for a man to give up when he is capable of running the course."

Ahmad Faris al-Shidyaq
(1804–1887)
Lebanese writer

Now faintly the falling sun
Shines on my traveler's robes.
As I move onward, so does the
  scenery change:
Suddenly I feel as though under
  another sky.
I meet fresh people.
I do not know when I shall see
  my native home.
. . . .

O, from the ancient days always
there have been travelers.
So why should I grieve?

Tu Fu (712-770)
Chinese poet, "Chengtu"

A traveler's thoughts in the night
Wander in a thousand miles of
dreams.

Wang Wei (699-759)
Chinese poet, "Seeking a Mooring"

To be a stranger in a strange land:
Whenever one feasts, one thinks
of one's brother twice as much
as before,
There where my brother far away
is ascending,
The dogwood is flowering, and a
man is missed.

Wang Wei (699-759)
Chinese poet, "Thinking of My Brother
in Shantung on the Ninth Day of the
Ninth Moon"

on TRUST

You shake man's hand, you no
shake his heart.

Jamaican proverb

Trust only him who doubts.

Lu Xun (1881-1936)
Chinese writer

Mistrust begets mistrust, and suspicion begets suspicion. It may have been permissible in the days of conventional weapons for nations to live in a perpetual atmosphere of suspicion and mistrust. But in the nuclear age such a concept is obsolete. We cannot afford to live in mistrust of our neighbors. We have to learn to live with them in

mutual trust and confidence; and where this happy state of affairs has not existed in the past, someone has to break the ice. For trust also begets trust, and confidence begets confidence.

U Nu (b. 1907)
Burmese politician and first prime
minister of Burma

on TRUTH

Every truth in this round world has its opposite somewhere.

Ba Maw (b. 1893)
Burmese revolutionary leader and
politician

We must prepare and study truth under every aspect, endeavoring to ignore nothing, if we do not wish to fall into the abyss of the unknown when the hour shall strike.

Elena Petrovna Blavatsky
(1831-1891)
American spiritualist

No one is right.
The labyrinth, without a doubt,
does not lead to the Minotaur.

Teresa Calderon (b. 1955)
Chilean poet, "Deducciones"
("Deductions")

Nothing is absolute.
There's no need, nevertheless,
to be very sure about things.
It seems enough to know how to
name them
or somehow babble them into
existence.

Teresa Calderon (b. 1955)
Chilean poet, "Nunca Supe" ("I Never
Realized")

The slogan "all men are equal before the truth" is a bourgeois slogan that absolutely denies the fact that truth has a class-character.

> Communist Party of China, *May 16 Circular*

Absolute truth is indestructible. Being indestructible, it is eternal. Being eternal, it is self-existent. Being self-existent, it is infinite. Being infinite, it is vast and deep. Being vast and deep, it is transcendental and intelligent.

> Confucius (551–479 B.C.E.)
> Chinese philosopher and founder of Confucianism, *Analects*

It is man that makes truth great, not truth that makes man great.

> Confucius (551–479 B.C.E.)
> Chinese philosopher and founder of Confucianism, *Analects*

Those who know the truth are not equal to those who love it.

> Confucius (551–479 B.C.E.)
> Chinese philosopher and founder of Confucianism, *Analects*

Hypocrisy, false labels, can create slogans but no poems; propaganda but not life: there are no roots, there are no realities to nurture creative work.

> Pablo Antonio Cuadra (b. 1912)
> Nicaraguan poet, "Notes on Culture in the New Nicaragua," *Vuelta*

This empty world may change
But Reality is the same.
It has never been easy to know
But Truth shines everywhere.

> Cuu-Chi (19th century)
> Vietnamese poet, "Truth Is One"

They who know truth in truth, and untruth in untruth, arrive at truth, and follow true desires.

> *Dhammapada* (c. 3rd century B.C.E.)
> collection of ancient Buddhist poems and aphorisms, I.12

Truth is such a rare thing, it is delightful to tell it.

> Emily Dickinson (1830–1886)
> American poet

The simplest truths often meet the sternest resistance and are slowest in getting general acceptance.

> Frederick Douglass (1817–1895)
> American abolitionist, "The Women's Suffrage Movement," *The New National Era*

Truth has rough flavors if we bite it through.

> George Eliot (1819–1880)
> English writer, *Armgart*, scene 2

Truth and morning become light with time.

> Ethiopian proverb

Although man passes his whole life investigating what is truth, his entire conclusion may be summed as follows: "It is said . . . " Or sometimes: "They have said . . . "

> Fakhir al-Din Razi (1149–1209)
> Central Asian Islamic philosopher

In the dictionary of the seeker of truth there is no such thing as being "not successful." He is or should be an irrepressible optimist because of his immovable faith in the ultimate victory of Truth, which is God.

> Mohandas K. Gandhi (1869–1948)
> Indian spiritual and political leader

Truth is superior to man's wisdom.

Mohandas K. Gandhi (1869-1948)
Indian spiritual and political leader

Persecution cannot harm him who stands by Truth. Did not Socrates fall proudly a victim in body? Was not Paul stoned for the sake of the Truth? It is our inner selves that hurt us when we disobey it, and it kills us when we betray it.

Kahlil Gibran (1883-1931)
Syrian writer, *The Secrets of the Heart*

Truth is heavy; therefore, few care to carry it.

Hebrew proverb

Truth made you a traitor as it often does in a time of scoundrels.

Lillian Hellman (1906-1984)
American writer, *Scoundrel Time*

The knowledge that mankind needs is not the way or principle which has an absolute existence, but the particular truths for here and now and for particular individuals. Absolute truth is imaginary, abstract, vague, without evidence, and cannot be demonstrated.

Hu Shih (1891-1962)
Chinese writer

Does man possess any truth?
If not, our song is no longer true.
Is anything stable and lasting?
What reaches its aim?

Huehuetlatolli
Nahuatl (Aztec) discourses of the elders

Children say that people are hung sometimes for speaking the truth.

Joan of Arc (c. 1412-1431)
French religious and military leader, defense given at her tribunal

We should never be ashamed to approve truth or acquire it, no matter what its source might be, even if it might have come from foreign peoples and alien nations far removed from us. To him who seeks truth, no other object is higher in value. Neither should truth be underrated, nor its exponent belittled. For indeed, truth abases none and ennobles all.

Rasa'il al-Kindi (810-873)
Arab philosopher and physician

Truth sounds paradoxical!

Lao-tzu (c. 604-531 B.C.E.)
Chinese philosopher and founder of Taoism, *Character of Tao*

Truth is on the side of the oppressed.

Malcolm X (1925-1965)
American civil rights activist

Speaking the truth to the unjust is the best of holy wars.

Muhammad (570-632)
Prophet of Islam

It is better to understand a part of truth and apply it to our lives than to understand nothing at all and flounder helplessly in a vain attempt to pierce the mystery of existence.

Jawaharlal Nehru (1889-1964)
Indian prime minister

One day Soshi was walking on the bank of a river with a friend. "How delightfully the fishes are enjoying themselves in the water!" exclaimed Soshi. His friend spake to him thus: "You are not a fish; how do you know that the fishes are enjoying themselves?" "You are not myself," returned Soshi; "how do you know that I do not know that the fishes are enjoying themselves?"

> Kakuzo Okakura (1862–1913)
> Japanese art critic and philosopher

Truth, like beauty, is neither created nor lost.

> Nicanor Parra (b. 1914)
> Chilean poet, *Poemas y antipoems*
> *(Poems and Antipoems)*

Do not veil the truth with falsehood, nor conceal the truth knowingly.

> *Qur'an* (c. 610–656)
> sacred book of Islam, 2:42

It is He who hath appointed the sun for brightness and the moon for a light, and hath ordained her stations that ye may learn the number of years and the reckoning of time. God hath not created all this but for the truth. He maketh His signs clear to those who understand.

> *Qur'an* (c. 610–656)
> sacred book of Islam, 10

I think if the people in this country can be reached with the truth, their judgement will be in favor of the many, as against the privileged few.

> Eleanor Roosevelt (1884–1962)
> American humanitarian and First Lady

Seek for the truth from the heart which is empty of thought.

> Sa'ib of Tabriz (c. 1601–1677)
> Persian poet, in a play on words from a pupil's absurd line: Seek for the bottleless wine from the wineless bottle.

To be outspoken is easy when you do not wait to speak the complete truth.

> Rabindranath Tagore (1861–1941)
> Indian writer and philosopher, *Stray Birds*

Truth reveals itself in beauty.

> Rabindranath Tagore (1861–1941)
> Indian writer and philosopher

Of course it's the same old story. Truth usually is the same old story.

> Margaret Thatcher (b. 1925)
> English prime minister

Truth burns up error.

> Sojourner Truth (1797–1883)
> American abolitionist

The truths that seem most truthful, if you look at them from all sides, if you look at them close up, turn out to be either half truths or lies.

> Mario Vargas Llosa (b. 1936)
> Peruvian writer, *Who Killed Palimino Molero?*

If you do not tell the truth about yourself, you cannot tell it about other people.

> Virginia Woolf (1882–1941)
> English writer, *The Moment and Other Essays*

on **TYRANNY AND TYRANTS**

You cannot run faster than a bullet.

Idi Amin (b. 1925)
Ugandan dictator

I would not oppose your firing on
the people
If they had committed some truly
unpardonable crime;
Otherwise your gun barrels
will weep,
Your bullets too, your bullets
will cry.
When you train your eyes through
the gun sights
Look over as well at the people's
eyes;
Then resolve anew whom you
should,
Should really be aiming at.

Anonymous poem
dedicated to the People's Liberation
Army and read over the loudspeakers
during the student uprising in
Tiananmen Square, China (1989)

If when I die, I am still a dictator, I
will certainly go down into the
oblivion of all dictators. If, on the
other hand, I succeed in establishing a truly stable foundation for a
democratic government, I will live
forever in every home in China.

Chiang Kai-shek (1887-1975)
Chinese military and political leader

They who study mankind with a
whip in their hands will always go
wrong.

Frederick Douglass (1817-1895)
American abolitionist, speech in
Geneva, New York (August 1, 1860)

The tyrant is only the slave turned
inside out.

Egyptian proverb

The most horrible thing is not a
government that stages public ex-
ecutions, but a government that secretly disposes of its victims.

Lu Xun (1881-1936)
Chinese writer

A tyrant does not remain in the
world;
But the curse on him abides
forever!

Sa'di of Shiraz (c. 1184-1292)
Persian poet, *Gulistan*

The more complete the despotism,
the more smoothly all things move
on the surface.

Elizabeth Cady Stanton
(1815-1902)
American suffragist, *History of Woman
Suffrage*

When you stop a dictator, there are
always risks. But there are greater
risks in not stopping a dictator.

Margaret Thatcher (b. 1925)
English prime minister, on the Falkland
Islands War with Argentina (1982)

on UNCERTAINTY

The Creator knows whom he will give,
But whom he will give does not know.

> Ibo (Nigerian) prayer

The appalling uncertainty of man's existence is haltingly underscored by the momentous certainty of the phenomenon of death.

> William R. Tolbert, Jr. (1913–1980)
> Liberian politician, inaugural speech.
> The government he represented was overthrown by a coup, with numerous executions.

on UNDERSTANDING

Oh, that I only knew that these things are well-pleasing to a god! Who can understand the counsel of the gods in the midst of heaven?

> Babylonian lament (c. 1000 B.C.E.)

Be steadfast in your understanding,
And let what you say be one.
Be quick to hear,
And make your reply with patience.
If you possess understanding, answer your neighbor,
But if you do not have it, keep your hand over your mouth!
Both glory and disgrace come from speaking,
And a man's tongue is his downfall.

> Ben Sira (c. 2nd century B.C.E.)
> Hebrew scholar and philosopher,
> *The Wisdom of Ben Sira*

Believe nothing, O monks, merely because you have been told it . . . or because it is traditional, or because you yourselves have imagined it. Do not believe what your teacher tells you merely out of respect for the teacher. But whatsoever, after due examination and analysis, you find to be conducive to the good, the benefit, the welfare of all beings—that doctrine believe and cling to, and take it as your guide.

> attributed to Buddha
> (c. 563–483 B.C.E.)
> Founder of Buddhism

Great understanding is broad and unhurried; little understanding is cramped and busy.

> Chuang-tzu (c. 369–286 B.C.E.)
> Chinese Taoist philosopher

Knowing is many-sided,
Moving, nonmoving, all are equal.

> Cuu-Chi (19th century)
> Vietnamese poet, "Truth Is One"

What I've learnt I don't understand

And what I don't understand I grasp it *only when it's too late.*

Mahmoud Darwish (b. 1942)
Palestinian poet

Herein lies the tragedy of the age: not that men are poor—all men know something of poverty. Not that men are wicked—who is good? Not that men are ignorant— what is truth? Nay, but that men know so little of men.

W. E. B. Du Bois (1868-1963)
American writer and educator, *The Souls of Black Folk*

Anger and intolerance are the twin enemies of correct understanding.

Mohandas K. Gandhi (1869-1948)
Indian spiritual and political leader

Through what is near, one understands what is far away.

Hsun-tzu (298-238 B.C.E.)
Chinese philosopher

To lay hold of the mean without taking into account the occasion is like grasping one thing only.

Mencius (c. 390-305 B.C.E.)
Chinese philosopher, *Meng-tzu*

What you cannot explain in terms of symbols is lost forever like blind totems and ruins in an old man's face.

Pritish Nandy (b. 1947)
Indian poet

The wave is ignorant of the true nature of the sea: how can the temporal comprehend the eternal?

Sa'ib of Tabriz (c. 1601-1677)
Persian poet

The stupid don't even understand something that happened long ago, the wise understand it before it develops.

Shang Yang (d. 338 B.C.E.)
Chinese philosopher, *Shih-chi*

To understand is hard. Once one understands, action is easy.

Sun Yat-sen (1866-1925)
Chinese military and political leader

The way of heaven is far away from us; only the way of man is close. Since we do not reach heaven, how could we succeed in understanding it?

Tso-Chuan (c. 524 B.C.E.)
Chinese philosopher

on UNITY

Sticks in a bundle are unbreakable.

Bondei (Kenyan) proverb

I believe in the essential unity of man, and for that matter, of all lives. Therefore, I believe that if one man gains spiritually, the whole world gains with him, and if one man falls, the whole world falls to that extent.

Mohandas K. Gandhi (1869-1948)
Indian spiritual and political leader

Being that I am a man, I would be uncompassionate to flee from men, and not to share their griefs and miseries. . . . Being that I was born on the earth, then mankind in the ten thousand countries of the earth are all my brothers [literally, of the same womb] of different bodily types. Being that I have knowledge of them, then I have love [ch'in] for them.

> K'ang Yu-wei (1858–1927)
> Chinese political philosopher

Unity cannot be taken for granted.

> Jomo Kenyatta (1891–1978)
> Kenyan political leader, founder of modern Kenya

Unity and victory are synonymous.

> Samora Machel (1933–1986)
> Mozambiquen activist and politician

Gnats an elephant can quell if they,
unite against their foe, so huge and grim.
And ants collected in one huge array,
though fierce a lion be, will vanquish him.

> Sa'di of Shiraz (c. 1184–1292)
> Persian poet, *Gulistan*

The civilization of the twentieth century cannot be universal except by being a dynamic synthesis of all the cultural values of all civilizations. It will be monstrous unless it is seasoned with the salt of negritude, for it will be without the savor of humanity.

> Leopold Sedar Senghor (b. 1906)
> Senegalese political leader and writer

Men of little ability, too,
By depending upon the great, may prosper:
A drop of water is a little thing,

But when will it dry away if united to a lake?

> *Subhashita Ratna Nidhi (Precious Treasury of Elegant Sayings)*
> (c. 13th century)
> Tibetan sayings, attributed to Grand Lama of Saskya, stanza 173

Unity in variety is the plan of the universe.

> Vivekananda (1863–1902)
> Indian religious leader

on THE UNIVERSE

In everything that moves through the universe, I see my own body, and in everything that governs the universe, my own soul.

> Chang Tsai (1021–1077)
> Chinese philosopher, *The Western Inscription*

The primordial breath is my skiff,
the gentle breeze my rudder,
I float in greatest purity
and take my delight in the entire cosmos.

> Chung-ch'ang T'ung (c. 179–219)
> Chinese philosopher, *Ch'uan Han San-kuo Chin Nan-pei-ch'ao shih*

The universe is illusion merely, not one speck of it real, and we are not only its victims, falling always into or smashed by a planet slung by the sun—but also its captives, bound by the mineral-made ropes of our senses.

> Annie Dillard (b. 1945)
> American writer, *Holy the Firm*

Our sun is but one star floating like an insect in the river,
Like a grain of sand in the Ganges;

Huge white stars with
  temperatures of myriad degrees,
Endlessly distant, are still its
  neighbors.
They help me onward with their
  dazzling light
As I roam afar and loudly sing.

K'ang Yu-wei (1858–1927)
Chinese political philosopher, *Kang
Nabai zhutian jiang*, based on Hasian
Kung-chuan, "K'ang Yu-wei's Excursion
into Science"

The sun sinks beyond the
  mountains
The Yellow River flows into the
  ocean
However, if you wish to see much
  more,
Climb one more story!

Wang Zhi-huan (c. 695)
Chinese poet

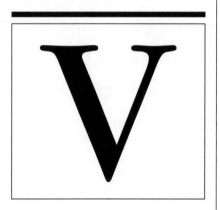

on **VANITY**

Vanity working on a weak head produces every sort of mischief.

Jane Austen (1775-1817)
English writer, *Emma*

She wanted to be the reason for everything and so was the cause of nothing.

Djuna Barnes (1892-1982)
American writer, *Nightwood*

In my opinion, better far it be
To destroy vanity within my life
Than to destroy my life in vanity.

Juana Ines de la Cruz (1651-1695)
Mexican nun and poet, "Oh World, Why Do You Thus Pursue Me"

Beware of over-great pleasure in being popular or even beloved.

Margaret Fuller (1810-1850)
American writer and critic, letter to her brother (December 20, 1840)

Vanity is the beginning of corruption.

Joaquim Maria Machado de Assis (1839-1908)
Brazilian writer, *Dom Casmurro*

Praise shames me, for I secretly beg for it.

Rabindranath Tagore (1861-1941)
Indian writer and philosopher, *Stray Birds*

on **VICE**

Crime and vice generally require darkness for prowling. They disappear when light plays upon them.

Mohandas K. Gandhi (1869-1948)
Indian spiritual and political leader

Iniquity, committed in this world, produces not fruit immediately, but, like the earth, in due season, and advancing by little and little, it eradicates the man who committed it.

Manu (c. 1200 B.C.E.)
Indian Hindu poet and ruler

The inhabitant of the soul of the universe is never seen; its voice alone is heard. All we know is that it has a gentle voice, like a woman, a voice so fine and gentle that even children cannot become afraid. And what it says is: *Sila ersinarsinivdluge*—"Be not afraid of the universe."

Najgneq (c. 1920)
Alaskan shaman

The most malignant of enemies is the lust which abides within.

Sa'di of Shiraz (c. 1184-1292)
Persian poet

Tea, wine and women:
My three perpetual plagues.
I must forebear.
I might be able to give up tea,

maybe,
And even wine.

> Tran Te Xuong (1869–1907)
> Vietnamese poet, "Women"

Remember, earthly life is comparable with vanities. So do not be deceived by earthly life, and do not be led astray by deception against God. Take warning from those that passed away before you. And be serious and forget not, for you are not forgotten.

> 'Uthman (d. 656)
> Arab Islamic leader and third caliph of Islam

on VICTORY

A nation which makes the final sacrifice for life and freedom does not get beaten.

> Kemal Ataturk (1881–1938)
> Turkish patriot and political leader

That is what always happens: we never know whether we are victors or whether we are defeated.

> Jorge Luis Borges (1899–1986)
> Argentinian writer, *Borges on Writing*

The greatest pleasure is to vanquish your enemies, to chase them before you, to rob them of their wealth, to see their near and dear bathed in tears, to ride their horses and sleep on the white bellies of their wives and daughters.

> Chingiz (Genghis) Khan
> (c. 1162–1227)
> Mongol conqueror, to his generals after invading Russia (1224)

Victory breeds hatred, for the conquered is unhappy. The calm one is he who has given up both victory and defeat.

> *Dhammapada* (c. 3rd century B.C.E.)
> collection of ancient Buddhist poems and aphorisms

I glory in conflict that I may hereafter exult in victory.

> Frederick Douglass (1817–1895)
> American abolitionist

The fundamental principle is that no battle, combat, or skirmish is to be fought unless it will be won.

> Che Guevara (1928–1967)
> Cuban revolutionary

Although our fight will be long and hard, our people are resolved to fight till final victory.

> Ho Chi Minh (1892–1969)
> Vietnamese political leader

Sometimes it's worse to win a fight than to lose.

> Billie Holiday (1915–1959)
> American singer, *Lady Sings the Blues*

It is true we have won all our wars, but we have paid for them. We don't want victories anymore.

> Golda Meir (1898–1978)
> Israeli prime minister

We do not rejoice in victories. We rejoice when a new kind of cotton is grown and when strawberries bloom in Israel.

> Golda Meir (1898–1978)
> Israeli prime minister

Thus we may know that there are five essentials for victory: (1) He will win who knows when to fight and when not to fight. (2) He will win who knows how to handle both superior and inferior forces. (3) He will win whose army is animated by the same spirit throughout all the ranks. (4) He will win who, prepared himself, waits to take the enemy, unprepared. (5) He will win who has military capacity and is not interfered with by his sovereign. Victory lies in the knowledge of these five points.

> Sun Tzu (c. 335-288 B.C.E.)
> Chinese military leader, *The Art of War*

To win, one must be big enough to see the worth in others, big enough to cheer when others score.

> Lucie Campbell Williams
> (1885-1962)
> American educator

He has annihilated the enemies! Where shall he now make war? He has vanquished all the kings! Where shall he now make war?

> "Great Song" of Zulu King Shaka's regiments (1787-1828)

on VIOLENCE

Violence never settles anything right: apart from injuring your own soul, it injures the best cause. It lingers on long after the object of hate has disappeared from the scene to plague the lives of those who have employed it against their foes.

> Obafemi Awolowo (b. 1909)
> Nigerian politician

Violence is as American as cherry pie.

> Stokely Carmichael (b. 1941)
> American civil rights activist, *Black Power*

If the motive is good, and there are no other possibilities, then seen most deeply it [violence] is nonviolence, because its aim is to help others.

> Dalai Lama (b. 1935)
> Tibetan spiritual and political leader

If I die a violent death, as some fear and a few are plotting, I know that the violence will be in the thought and the action of the assassins, not in my dying.

> Indira Gandhi (1917-1984)
> Indian prime minister, handwritten statement discovered after she was killed by her bodyguards

It is organized violence on top which creates individual violence at the bottom.

> Emma Goldman (1869-1940)
> American anarchist, statement to the jury (June 15, 1917)

The power which establishes a state is violence; the power which maintains it is violence; the power which eventually overthrows it is violence.

> Kenneth Kaunda (b. 1924)
> Zambian nationalist and politician, *Kaunda on Violence*

[Man] has now reached the day when violence toward another human being must become as abhorrent as eating another's flesh.

> Martin Luther King, Jr.
> (1929-1968)
> American civil rights leader, *Why We Can't Wait*

If violence is wrong in America, violence is wrong abroad. If it is wrong to be violent defending black women and black children and black babies and black men, then it is wrong for America to draft us and make us violent abroad in defense of her. And if it is right for America to draft us and make us violent abroad in defense of her, then it is right for you and me to do whatever is necessary to defend our own people right here in this country.

> Malcolm X (1925-1965)
> American civil rights activist

Violence represents the worst kind of conformism.

> Mario Vargas Llosa (b. 1936)
> Peruvian writer

on VIRTUE

Nobody is more dangerous than he who imagines himself pure in heart; for purity, by definition, is unassailable.

> James Baldwin (1924-1987)
> American writer, *Nobody Knows My Name*

Five things constitute perfect virtue: gravity, magnanimity, earnestness, sincerity, kindness.

> Confucius (551-479 B.C.E.)
> Chinese philosopher and founder of Confucianism, *Analects*

Is there anyone who exerts himself even for a single day to achieve humanity? I have not seen any who had not the strength to achieve it.

> Confucius (551-479 B.C.E.)
> Chinese philosopher and founder of Confucianism, *Analects*

The superior man thinks always of virtue; the common man thinks of comfort.

> Confucius (551-479 B.C.E.)
> Chinese philosopher and founder of Confucianism, *Analects*

So far as the human mind can shake off selfishness and act from a sacred regard to truth, justice and duty, so far will men not only be virtuous, but fearless in virtue.

> Sarah Josepha Hale (1788-1879)
> American writer and editor, "The Apparition," *Sketches of American Character*

The Desert people are closer to being good than settled people because they are closer to the First State and are more removed from all the evil habits that have infected the heart of the settlers.

> Ibn Khaldun (1332-1406)
> Arab historian and philosopher, *Al Muqaddimah* (the introduction to his history of the world)

Remain in the company of saints, though you get but chaff to eat.

> Kabir (1440-1519)
> Indian Mughal poet and philosopher, *Sakhi*

Is the reward of excellence aught save excellence?

> *Qur'an* (c. 610-656)
> sacred book of Islam, LIX:18

The preservation or loss of a nation depends upon the depth or shallowness of its virtue, not upon its strength or weakness.

Su Shih (1036–1101)
Chinese government official and writer

Elegance is inferior to virtue.

Mary Wollstonecraft (1759–1797)
English suffragist, *A Vindication of the Rights of Women*

on **WAITING**

The days go by
Eternity does not come nor the
  miracle.

The days go by
The ship does not approach
The sea does not turn into flower
  or belfry
The fall is not revealed.
. . . .
The days go by
And the sound of the moon is not
  heard.

> Vicente Huidobro (1893-1948)
> Chilean writer, "Tiempo de Espera"
> ("Time of Waiting")

If you wait for tomorrow, tomorrow comes. If you don't wait for
tomorrow, tomorrow comes.

> Malinke (West African) proverb

on **WAR**

After a war life catches
desperately at passing
hints of normalcy like
vines entwining a hollow

twig.

> Chinua Achebe (b. 1930)
> Nigerian writer, "After a War,"
> *Christmas in Biafra and Other Poems*

I am become death—the shatterer
of worlds.

> *Bhagavad Gita*
> (c. 4th-3th century B.C.E.)
> teachings of Krishna from the Hindu
> epic, the *Mahabharata*

War lives on despotism and is not
waged with God's love.

> Simón Bolívar (1783-1830)
> South American revolutionary leader
> called the Liberator of South America

To lead an uninstructed people to
war is to throw them away.

> Confucius (551-479 B.C.E.)
> Chinese philosopher and founder of
> Confucianism, *Analects*

Ho-ka hey! It is a good day to fight!
It is a good day to die! Strong
hearts, brave hearts to the front!
Weak hearts and cowards to the
rear!

> Crazy Horse (1842-1877)
> Oglala Sioux chief, to his troops (June
> 25, 1876), the morning before the
> Battle of Little Bighorn

Suppose our war is ended here,
  my friend,
Say we are discharged and back in
  the village again.
How can a man return to his
  mother,
His face smeared with a dismal
  stain?
That there is no way out changes
nothing.

Thank heaven, we shunned the
  lowliness we disdain.
Answer me, did all these heroes
Sacrifice their lives in vain?

> Fazil Husnu Daglarca (b. 1914)
> Turkish poet, "Sehitlerle Oluler"
> ("Martyrs and Corpses")

When war blows dustily over the
  earth
It is women who suffer:
Oh Heaven, so blue, so high,
Who shall we blame?

> Dang Tran Con (1710-1745)
> Vietnamese poet, "Lament of a
> Warrior's Wife"

What difference does it make to
the dead, the orphans, and the
homeless, whether the mad destruction is wrought under the
name of totalitarianism or the holy
name of liberty and democracy?

> Mohandas K. Gandhi (1869-1948)
> Indian spiritual and political leader,
> *Non-Violence in Peace and War*

If they are to fight, they are too
few; if they are to die, they are too
many.

> Hendrick (c. 1750)
> Mohawk chief, about his warriors at
> the Battle of Lake George (1755)

We love peace, but we are not
afraid of war.

> Ho Chi Minh (1892-1969)
> Vietnamese political leader

"To war!" is only two words, yet
few of us have really thought
through their meaning.

> Hu Shih (1891-1962)
> Chinese writer in *The Independent
> Critic*

We will drink from his skull,
We will adorn ourselves with his
  teeth
With his bones we will make
  flutes.

> Incan war song (c. 1550)
> recounted by Spanish contemporary
> Guaman Poma

If truth be not glorified and ele-
vated by our sword, going to war is
not good for our community.

> Muhammad Iqbal (1873-1938)
> Indian poet and philosopher

It is indeed difficult to insure triumph when it depends on the success of bayonets, for war is always
a hazard.

> Benito Juárez (1806-1872)
> Mexican revolutionary and politician

War is just like bush-clearing—the
moment you stop, the jungle
comes back even thicker, but for a
little while you can plant and grow
a crop in the ground you have won
at such a terrible cost.

> Kenneth Kaunda (b. 1924)
> Zambian nationalist and politician,
> *Kaunda on Violence*

Even though I am a military man, I
don't think we can win the heart
of the people just with a gun, but
only by giving them a better way of
life. That is obvious.

> Nguyen Cao Ky (b. 1930)
> South Vietnamese politician and soldier

On the field of battle men grapple
  each other and die,
The horses of the fallen utter
  lament to heaven,
Ravens and kites peck men's guts,

And flying away, hang them on
the boughs of dead trees.
So men are smeared on the desert
grass,
And the generals return empty-
handed.
Know that weapons of war are
utterly evil—
The virtuous man uses them only
when he must.

Li Po (701-762)
Chinese poet, "Fighting on the South
Frontier"

The first law of war is to preserve
ourselves and destroy the enemy.

Mao Zedong (1893-1976)
Chairman of People's Republic of
China

History shows that wars are divided into two kinds—just and unjust. All wars that are progressive
are just, and all wars that impede
progress are unjust.

Mao Zedong (1893-1976)
Chairman of People's Republic of
China

As far as world war goes, there are
really only two possibilities: either
war provokes revolution, or revolution averts war.

Mao Zedong (1893-1976)
Chairman of People's Republic of
China

The main form of struggle is war;
the main form of organization is
the army. . . . Without armed
struggle there would be no place
for the proletariat, there will be no
place for the people, there will be
no place for the Communist Party,

and there will be no victory in revolution.

Mao Zedong (1893-1976)
Chairman of People's Republic of
China, *Twenty-five Years of the
Chinese Liberation Army, Peking*

Enemy advances, we retreat; enemy halts, we harass; enemy tires,
we attack; enemy retreats, we
pursue.

Mao Zedong (1893-1976)
Chairman of People's Republic of
China

War can be abolished only through
war; and in order to get rid of the
gun, it is necessary to take up the
gun.

Mao Zedong (1893-1976)
Chairman of People's Republic of
China "Problems of War and Strategy"

The dagger plunged in the name of
Freedom is plunged into the breast
of Freedom.

José Martí (1853-1895)
Cuban patriot, *Granos de oro:
pensamientos seleccionados en las
Obras de Jose Marti*

We don't want wars even when we
win.

Golda Meir (1898-1978)
Israeli prime minister

We have always said that in our
war with the Arabs we had a secret
weapon—no alternative.

Golda Meir (1898-1978)
Israeli prime minister

War is at first like a young girl
With whom every man desires to
flirt.
And at the last it is an old woman.

All who meet her feel grieved and hurt.

> Samuel ha-Nagid (993–1056)
> Spanish Hebrew poet, "War"

People do not want words. They want the sound of battle.

> Gamel Abdel Nasser (1918–1970)
> Egyptian revolutionary and president

We have to go along a road covered with blood. We have no other alternative. For us it is a matter of life or death, a matter of living or existing. We have to be ready to face the challenges that await us.

> Gamel Abdel Nasser (1918–1970)
> Egyptian revolutionary and president

The clutch
flaming in the smoking wreckage,
crushed limbs
and fractured plates
and broken breasts and shattered
 bones:
bones, and limbs, and plates
and the same, after-all:
cartilages and sockets
disjoint at the joint,
even before the attack of
 harmation.
Look!
at your blood ablaze in the shred
 of blades.

> Pol Ndu (b. 1940)
> Nigerian poet, "July 66," on the Biafran (Nigerian Secessionist) War

For several endless days
bitterness and hatred poured
through cascading muskets of
 destruction.

> Pol Ndu (b. 1940)
> Nigerian poet, "July 66," on the Biafran (Nigerian Secessionist) War

I sit and sew—a useless task it
 seems,
My hands grown tired, my head
 weighed down with dreams—
The panoply of war, the martial
 tread of men,
Grim-faced, stern-eyed, gazing
 beyond the ken
Of lesser souls, whose eyes have
 not seen Death,
Nor learned to hold their lives but
 as a breath—
But—I must sit and sew.

> Alice Dunbar Nelson (1875–1935)
> American writer, "I Sit and Sew"

. . . In war, human lives are like
 dust
as bullets and arrows fly with
 death.
The wandering ghosts, the lost
 souls,
make the scene still more
 mournful.
There were children, just tiny
 things,
born in a bad time, separated
 from their parents.
No one was there to hold them
 close.
Heart-rending were their infant
 cries.

> Nguyen Du (1765–1820)
> Vietnamese poet, "Calling the Wandering Souls"

We tell our children that the bombs cannot kill everyone, that they must not be afraid. . . . We know our sacrifice is necessary. If the bombs do not fall on you, they fall on friends. We accept fate. We are calm. It is useless to be a pessimist. Some day we will win a beautiful life, if not for ourselves, then for our children.

Nguyen Thi Binh (b. 1930)
Vietnamese politician

You can no more win a war than you can win an earthquake.

Jeanette Rankin (1880–1973)
American feminist and politician

Rapidity is the essence of war.

Sun Tzu (c. 335–288 B.C.E.)
Chinese military leader, *The Art of War*

Place your army in deadly peril, and it will survive; plunge it into desperate straits, and it will come off in safety.

Sun Tzu (c. 335–288 B.C.E.)
Chinese military leader, *The Art of War*

There is no instance of a country having benefited from prolonged warfare.

Sun Tzu (c. 335–288 B.C.E.)
Chinese military leader, *The Art of War*

As water has no constant form, there are in war no constant conditions.

Sun Tzu (c. 335–288 B.C.E.)
Chinese military leader, *The Art of War*

Blue is the smoke of war, white the bones of men.

Tu Fu (712-770)
Chinese poet

The God of War
He kills on the right and destroys
   on the left
He kills on the left and destroys
   on the right.

Yoruba (West African) poem

By valor alone, by the force of arms only, can wars be brought to a close.

Zenobia of Palmyra (240–300)
Palmyran queen and military leader,
letter to the Roman emperor Aurelian
Augustus

on WATER

The old pond, ah!
A frog jumps in:
The water's sound.

Matsuo Basho (1644–1694)
Japanese poet

When we use the water in the sweat lodge, we should think of Wakan-Tanka who is always flowing, giving His power and life to everything; we should even be as water, which is lower than all things, yet stronger even than the rocks.

Black Elk (1863–1950)
Oglala Sioux holy man

My first idea of movement, of the dance, certainly came from the rhythm of the waves.

Isadora Duncan (1878–1927)
American dancer, *My Life*

O masculine sea, feminine sea,
   mad sea,
Delirious sea, surrounding sea of
   Iku.

Hawaiian song
one ending of the cycle of Pele and
Hiiakau, pre-1800

The white sea, the rough sea
The sea with the swamping
   breakers . . .

The sacred ocean,
Sea of the bleached skull . . .

> Hawaiian song
> *O Kane, O Lono of the Blue Sea*,
> pre-1800

The highest good is like that of the water. The goodness of water is that it benefits the ten thousand creatures, yet itself does not scramble, but is content with the places that all men disdain.

> Lao-tzu (c. 604–531 B.C.E.)
> Chinese philosopher and founder of Taoism

on WEALTH

There is a great deal of truth in Andrew Carnegie's remark: "The man who dies rich, dies disgraced." I should add: The man who lives rich, lives disgraced.

> Muhammad Aga Khan III
> (1877–1957)
> Mohammedan leader, *The Memoirs of Aga Khan: World Enough and Time*

Beware of Kashmi [Goddess of Wealth], my son! She is fickle and her ways are but little understood. When acquired, she is hard to keep. Even though held fast by the cords of heroism, she escapes. . . . She does not regard race, she does not follow the fortune of a family, does not consider character, does not count intelligence, does not court righteousness, does not honor generosity.

> Bana (7th century)
> Indian poet

[Wealth] dwells on the edge of a sword, as if perpetually engaged in learning cruelty.

> Bana (7th century)
> Indian poet

One cannot say one controls a country if one does not control its wealth.

> José Celso Barbosa (1857–1921)
> Puerto Rican politician

A poor man is honored for his
  knowledge,
And a rich man is honored for his
  wealth.
If a man is honored in poverty,
  how much more will he be in
  wealth?
And if a man is dishonored when
  he is rich, how much more will
  he be when he is poor?

> Ben Sira (c. 2nd century B.C.E.)
> Hebrew scholar and philosopher, *The Wisdom of Ben Sira*

A man's increase in worldly
  wealth does ofttimes loss betide,
And all his pains, save virtue's
  gains, but swell the debit side.

> Abu'l-Fath al-Busti (d. 1009)
> Persian poet

Men should beware of coveting riches; when riches come through covetousness, Heaven's calamities follow.

> Chinese proverb

If the search for riches were sure to be successful, though I should become a groom with whip in hand to get them, I would do so.

>   Confucius (551-479 B.C.E.)
>   Chinese philosopher and founder of
>   Confucianism, *Analects*

Reverse cannot befall that find
 Prosperity
Whose sources are interior.
As soon Adversity
A diamond overtake.

>   Emily Dickinson (1830-1886)
>   American poet

He who is kind and helpful to his neighbors, he will find that God will increase his wealth.

>   Fakhir al-Din Razi (1149-1209)
>   Central Asian Islamic philosopher

Increases of material comforts, it may be generally laid down, do not in any way whatsoever conduce to moral growth.

>   Mohandas K. Gandhi (1869-1948)
>   Indian spiritual and political leader

As the bee collecteth honey with
 great zest, so the fool
collecteth wealth.

>   Kabir (1440-1519)
>   Indian Mughal poet and philosopher

He who has little will receive.
He who has much will be
 embarrassed.

>   Lao-tzu (c. 604-531 B.C.E.)
>   Chinese philosopher and founder of
>   Taoism

Riches are not from an abundance of worldly goods, but from a contented mind.

>   Muhammad (570-632)
>   Prophet of Islam

Superabundance is not far from want.

>   Nigerian proverb

A man's respect for law and order exists in precise relationship to the size of his paycheck.

>   Adam Clayton Powell, Jr.
>   (1908-1972)
>   American politician and civil rights
>   leader, "Black Power: A Form of Godly
>   Power," *Keep the Faith, Baby!*

The material things which ye are given are but the conveniences of this life and the glitter thereof; but that which is with God is better and more enduring: Will ye not then be wise?

>   *Qur'an (c. 610-656)*
>   sacred book of Islam, xxviii:60

Wealth is the product of man's capacity to think.

>   Ayn Rand (1905-1982)
>   American writer

For riches are like chariot wheels
 revolving:
Now to one man they come, now
 to another.

>   *Rig-Veda* (c. 1500 B.C.E.)
>   sacred Hindu literature

Thou, lord of all prosperity,
Best wielder of the golden ax,
Make wealth easy for us to gain.

>   *Rig-Veda* (c. 1500 B.C.E.)
>   sacred Hindu literature

I would rather be gifted with wealth, so long as it is accompanied by wisdom and moderation, than with boldness and immoderation.

Saladin (1137-1193)
Egyptian and Syrian sultan

A miser utilizes his wealth to the same extent as a wanderer his own shadow.

Satavahana Hala (2nd century)
Indian king and poet, *Gatha Saptasati*

When you are rich, people come to meet you and people see you to your door; when you are penniless, you may go out early and come home late, and nobody cares a hoot.

Vietnamese proverb

on WILDERNESS

The countryside liberates its own distant points. Everywhere else, distance is a living relationship. Here, no such thing. No relationship, no lasting exchange. It only exists in and for itself, knowing only itself, and you reach the boundary of your powerlessness, of human powerlessness.

Mohammed Dib (b. 1920)
Algerian writer

Vast landscapes bring men to a
  halt,
Then men become aware of being
  surrounded
by profuse remotenesses
They are always
Remotenesses that make men
  men.

. . . .

Occasionally man cannot exceed
  the place
that transgresses every
  remoteness,
Without being seen anymore
Man at such times becomes the
  landscape.

Tanikawa Shuntaro (b. 1931)
Japanese poet, *Rokujuni no sonetto*
(Sixty-two Sonnets)

I was born on the prairie, where the wind blew free and there was nothing to break the light of the sun. I was born where there were no enclosures and where everything drew a free breath. I want to die there, and not within walls.

Ten Bears (c. 1800-1872)
Yamparika Comanche negotiator

on WILL

The general of a large army may be defeated, but you cannot defeat the determined mind of a peasant.

Confucius (551-479 B.C.E.)
Chinese philosopher and founder of
Confucianism, *Analects*

If we develop the force of will, we shall find that we do not need the force of arms.

Mohandas K. Gandhi (1869-1948)
Indian spiritual and political leader

Strength does not come from physical capacity. It comes from an indomitable will.

Mohandas K. Gandhi (1869-1948)
Indian spiritual and political leader

Willpower should be understood to be the strength of mind which makes it capable of meeting suc-

304

cess or failure with equanimity. . . . Success develops arrogance, and the man's spiritual progress is thus arrested. Failure, on the other hand, is beneficial, inasmuch as it opens the eyes of the man to his limitations and prepares him to surrender himself. Self-surrender is synonymous with eternal happiness. Therefore, one should try to gain the equipoise of mind under all circumstances: that is will-power.

Ramana Maharshi (1879-1950)
Indian Hindu religious leader

on WISDOM

Those who know the world live alone.

'Ali (c. 600-661)
First Imam of the Sh'ia branch of Islam; fourth caliph

In seeking wisdom, thou art wise; in imagining that thou hast attained it, thou art a fool.

attributed to Ben Sira
(c. 2nd century B.C.E.)
Hebrew scholar and philosopher

All wisdom comes from the Lord,
And remains with him forever.
The sand of the seas, and the drops of rain,
And the days of eternity—who can count them?
The height of the heavens, and the breadth of the earth,
And the deep, and wisdom—who can track them out?
Wisdom was created before them all,

And sound intelligence from eternity.

Ben Sira (c. 2nd century B.C.E.)
Hebrew scholar and philosopher, *The Wisdom of Ben Sira*

Wisdom makes her sons exalted,
And lays hold of those who seek her.
Whoever loves her, loves life,
And those who seek her early will be filled with joy.

Ben Sira (c. 2nd century B.C.E.)
Hebrew scholar and philosopher, *The Wisdom of Ben Sira*

The truly wise mourn not either for the dead or for the living.

Bhagavad Gita
(c. 4th-3rd century B.C.E.)
teachings of Krishna from the Hindu epic, the *Mahabharata*, 2:11

He whose mind is not troubled in sorrow and has no desire in pleasure, his passion, fear, and anger departed, he is called a steady-minded sage.

Bhagavad Gita
(c. 4th-3rd century B.C.E.)
teachings of Krishna from the Hindu epic, the *Mahabharata*, 2:56

There is no purifier in this world equal to wisdom.

Bhagavad Gita
(c. 4th-3rd century B.C.E.)
teachings of Krishna from the Hindu epic, the *Mahabharata*, 4:38

If one extends knowledge to the utmost, one will have wisdom. Having wisdom, one can then make choices.

Cheng Yi (1033-1108)
Chinese scholar, *I-shu*

Wisdom is nothing but sincerity.

> Chou-Tun-I (1017-1073)
> Chinese scholar, *The Diagram
> Explained*

Great wisdom is generous; petty wisdom is contentious.

> Chuang-tzu (c. 369-286 B.C.E.)
> Chinese Taoist philosopher, *On
> Leveling All Things*

Just as the paths of the birds or the fish are invisible, so is the path of the possessors of wisdom.

> *Dhammapada* (c. 3rd century B.C.E.)
> collection of ancient Buddhist poems
> and aphorisms, Arahantavaggo

Just as solid rocks are not shaken by the wind, so wise men are not moved by either blame or praise.

> *Dhammapada* (c. 3rd century B.C.E.)
> collection of ancient Buddhist poems
> and aphorisms, Panditavaggo

It is unwise to be too sure of one's own wisdom. It is healthy to be reminded that the strongest might weaken and the wisest might err.

> Mohandas K. Gandhi (1869-1948)
> Indian spiritual and political leader

One wise man is better than forty fools; one moon sheds more light than myriads of stars.

> *Hitopadesha* (c. 3rd-4th century)
> Indian moral tales and aphorisms

[The sage] knows that luxuriant fragrances harm [human] nature; therefore, he avoids them and pays no more attention to them. It is not that he still desires them and then curbs those desires. [No], he keeps these things outside, so that his heart cannot remain enchained.

> Hsi K'ang (223-262)
> Chinese philosopher, "Yang-sheng lun"
> ("The Cultivation of Life"), *Hsi Chung-
> san chi*

[The sage] forgets joy and can therefore become joyful; he loses his life and can thereby preserve his body.

> Hsi K'ang (223-262)
> Chinese philosopher, "Yang-sheng lun"
> ("The Cultivation of Life"), *Hsi Chung-
> san chi*

Those who seek the truth by means of intellect and learning only get further and further away from it. Not till your thoughts cease all their branching here and there, not till you abandon all thoughts of seeking for something, not till your mind is motionless as wood or stone will you be on the right road to the Gate.

> Huang Po (c. 850)
> Chinese Zen Buddhist leader

Good and learned friends, perfect wisdom is inherent in all people. It is only because they are deluded in their minds that they cannot attain enlightenment by themselves. They must seek the help of good and learned friends of high standing to show them the way.

> Hui Neng (638-713)
> Chinese Buddhist leader, *The Platform
> Scripture*

Wisdom is the finest beauty of a
  person.
Money does not prevent you from
  becoming blind.

Money does not prevent you from
becoming mad.
Money does not prevent you from
becoming lame.
You may be ill in any part of your
body,
So it is better for you to go and
think again
And to select wisdom . . .

Ifa (Yoruban) oracle poem

He who knows others is learned;
he who knows himself is wise.

Lao-tzu (c. 604–531 B.C.E.)
Chinese philosopher and founder of
Taoism, *Character of Tao*

Great wisdom consists in not demanding too much of human
nature, and yet not altogether
spoiling it by indulgence.

Lin Yutang (1895–1976)
Chinese writer

Train thou thy son to be a docile
man,
Whose wisdom is agreeable to the
great;
Let him direct his mouth by what
is said,
Docility his wisdom doth
discover;
Conduct in him grows perfect day
by day,
While error casts the unteachable
away;
The ignorant and fool will be
thrown over,
But knowledge shall lift up the
scholar's head.

Ptah-hotep (c. 2300 B.C.E.)
Egyptian vizier, "On Home Education"

Friendship of the wise is good; a
wise enemy is better than a foolish
friend.

Rumi (1207–1273)
Persian Sufi poet and mystic

Each one must learn for himself
the highest wisdom. It cannot be
taught in words. . . . Men who
work cannot dream, and wisdom
comes to us in dreams.

Smohalla (c. 1815–1907)
Wanapam (Native American) prophet

Seven characteristics distinguish
the wise: he does not speak in the
presence of one wiser than himself, does not interrupt, is not
hasty to answer, asks and answers
the point, talks about first things
first and about last things last, ad-
mits when he does not know, and
acknowledges the truth.

Talmud
(c. late 4th–early 6th century)
ancient body of Jewish civil and
canonical law, Aboth 5.7

on WOMEN

The only question left to be settled
now is: Are women persons?

Susan B. Anthony (1820–1906)
American suffragist

All the privilege I claim for my own
sex . . . is that of loving longest,
when existence or hope is gone.

Jane Austen (1775–1817)
English writer, *Persuasion*

Nine times out of ten, a woman
had better show more affection
than she feels.

Jane Austen (1775–1817)
English writer

307

Indeed, we men said: "Bloody, painful are the words of the women."

> *Florentine Codex* (c. 1550)
> collection of Aztec writings

Is there a heart that girls cannot
subdue
When they walk like swans, their
bangles jingling,
Their girdles tinkling, their anklets
jangling,
And their eyes like those of deer
Glance, frank but timid?

> Bhartrihari (c. 7th century)
> Indian poet and philosopher, the
> *Sringar Sataka*

Intimacies between women often go backwards, beginning in revelations and ending in small talk without the loss of esteem.

> Elizabeth Bowen (1899–1973)
> Irish writer, *The Death of the Heart*

  Most illogical
Irrational nature of our
  womanhood,
That blushes one way, feels
  another way,
And prays, perhaps another!

> Elizabeth Barrett Browning
> (1806–1861)
> English poet, *Aurora Leigh*

Of my two "handicaps," being female put many more obstacles in my path than being black.

> Shirley Chisholm (b. 1924)
> American politician, *Unbought and Unbossed*

The American woman's inequality with men is proved by her defiant attitude.

> Simone de Beauvoir (1908–1986)
> French writer and philosopher,
> *America Day by Day*

One is not born a woman—one becomes one.

> Simone de Beauvoir (1908–1986)
> French writer and philosopher

The happiest women, like the happiest nations, have no history.

> George Eliot (1819-1880)
> English writer, *The Mill on the Floss*

It has been women who have breathed gentleness and care into the harsh progress of mankind.

> Elizabeth II (b. 1926)
> English queen

Toughness doesn't have to come in a pinstripe suit.

> Dianne Feinstein (b. 1933)
> American politician

If . . . the fundamental human drive is not the urge for pleasure or the satisfaction of biological needs, but the need to grow and to realize one's full potential, their [American housewives'] comfortable, empty, purposeless days are indeed cause for a nameless terror.

> Betty Friedan (b. 1921)
> American feminist, *The Feminine Mystique*

Of all the evils for which man has made himself responsible, none is so degrading, so shocking, or so brutal as his abuse of the better half of humanity; to me, the female sex is not the weaker sex.

> Mohandas K. Gandhi (1869–1948)
> Indian spiritual and political leader

If she [woman] is weak in striking, she is strong in suffering.

> Mohandas K. Gandhi (1869–1948)
> Indian spiritual and political leader

It is not that women are really smaller-minded, weaker-minded, more timid and vacillating; but that whosoever, man or woman, lives always in a small, dark place, is always guarded, protected, directed, and restrained will become inevitably narrowed and weakened by it. The woman is narrowed by the home, and the man is narrowed by the woman.

> Charlotte Perkins Gilman
> (1860–1935)
> American writer

It would not be going too far to assert that . . . conflict confronts every woman who ventures upon a career of her own and who is . . . unwilling to pay for her daring with the renunciation of her femininity.

> Karen Horney (1885–1952)
> American psychoanalyst, "The Overvaluation of Love"

Women forget all those things they don't want to remember, and remember everything they don't want to forget.

> Zora Neale Hurston (1903–1960)
> American writer, *Their Eyes Were Watching God*

Men have callously and unscrupulously repressed women, restrained them, deceived them, shut them up, imprisoned them, and bound them. . . . And yet . . . those whom we call good men, righteous men, have been accustomed to the sight of such things, have sat and looked and considered them to be matters of course.

> K'ang Yu-wei (1858–1927)
> Chinese political philosopher, *Datongshu*

She was like the sun, making red, in her rising,
The clouds of dawn with the flame of her light.

> Judah ha-Levi (c. 1075–1141)
> Spanish Hebrew poet and theologian

Where women are honored, there the gods delight; where they are not honored, there all acts become fruitless.

> *Laws of Manu* (c. 100–200)
> ancient Indian text

For a woman is the everlasting field
in which the self is born.

> *Mahabharata* (540–300 B.C.E.)
> Hindu epic

To be successful, a woman has to be much better at her job than a man.

> Golda Meir (1898–1978)
> Israeli prime minister

A woman's mind, since it is tied down by her womb, cannot leave the body as a man's mind can. . . . A woman has two nerve centers controlling her mind—the brain and the womb. The two always function so close together that her mind, caught between them, cannot depart from her body.

> Yukio Mishima (1925–1970)
> Japanese writer

Verily, the best of women are those who are content with little.

> Muhammad (570–632)
> Prophet of Islam

Prince, a precept I'd leave for you,
Coined in Eden, existing yet:
Skirt the parlor, and shun the zoo—
Women and elephants never forget.

> Dorothy Parker (1893–1967)
> American writer, *Ballad of Unfortunate Mammals*

I always say it was great for God to send his only son, but I'm waiting for him to send his only daughter. Then things will really be great.

> Candace Pert (b. 1947)
> American biochemist

Sun and moon have no light left, earth is dark;
Our women's world is sunk so deep, who can help us?
Jewelry sold to pay this trip across the seas,
Cut off from my family I leave my native land.
Unbinding my feet, I clean out a thousand years of poison,
With heated heart arouse all women's spirits.
Alas, this delicate kerchief here

Is half stained with blood, and half with tears.

> Qiu Jin (1874–1907)
> Chinese poet and activist, "Regrets: Lines Written En Route to Japan," *Qiu Jin ji*

Womanhood is the great fact in her life; wifehood and motherhood are but incidental relations.

> Elizabeth Cady Stanton (1815–1902)
> American suffragist, *History of Woman Suffrage*

Today a woman without a man is like a fish without a bicycle.

> Gloria Steinem (b. 1934)
> American feminist

Some of us are becoming the men we wanted to marry.

> Gloria Steinem (b. 1934)
> American feminist

Dat man over dar say dat womin needs to be helped into carriages, and lifted over ditches, and to hab de best place everywhar. Nobody eber helps me into carriages, or ober mud-puddles, or gibs me any best place! And a'n't I a woman? Look at me! Look at my arm! [and she bared her right arm to the shoulder, showing her powerful muscles]. I have ploughed and planted and gathered into barns, and no man could head me! And a'n't I a woman? I could work as much and eat as much as a man— when I could get it—and bear de lash as well! And a'n't I a woman? I have borne thirteen chillern and seen 'em mos' all sold off to slavery, and when I cried out with my mother's grief, none but Jesus heard me! And a'n't I a woman?

Sojourner Truth (c. 1797-1883)
American abolitionist

Women and revolution! What tragic, unsung epics of courage lie silent in the world's history.

Yang Ping (b. 1908)
Chinese writer, "Fragment from a Lost Diary"

A beautiful woman who is pleasing to men is good only for frightening fish when she falls into the water.

Zen proverb

on WORDS

It is with a word as with an arrow: once let it loose, and it does not return.

Abd-el-Kader (1078-1166)
Persian Sufi leader

I will scrape and dig into *every word* as far as I can get, right down to the essence of the word, to the substance of the image.

Chairil Anwar (1922-1949)
Indonesian poet

Without knowing the force of words, it is impossible to know men.

Confucius (551-479 B.C.E.)
Chinese philosopher and founder of Confucianism, *Analects*

Your words are the seed, your
soul is the farmer, the world is
your field:
Let the farmer look to the sowing,
that the soil may abundance yield.

Nasir-i-Khusraw (c. 1004-1061)
Persian writer, *Diwan*

It seems to me that the spoken and written word are signs of failure. Whoever is truly measuring himself against fate has no time for such things. As to those who are strong and winning, most of the time they keep silent. Consider, for instance, the eagle when it swoops upon a rabbit: it is the rabbit that squeals, not the eagle.

Lu Xun (1881-1936)
Chinese writer

Words cannot describe
everything.
The heart's message cannot be
delivered in words.
If one receives words literally, he
will be lost.
If he tries to explain with words,
he will not attain
enlightenment in this life.

Mu-mon Gensen (1322-1390)
Japanese Buddhist monk, *The Gateless Gate*

Slogans are apt to petrify man's thinking . . . every slogan, every word almost, that is used by the socialist, the communist, the capitalist. People hardly think nowadays. They throw words at each other.

Jawaharlal Nehru (1889-1964)
Indian politician

What of spoken words? Spoken words are living things like cocoabeans packed with life. And like cocoa-beans they grow and give life. . . . They will enter some insides, remain there and grow like the corn blooming on the alluvial sod at the riverside.

> Gabriel Okara (b. 1921)
> Nigerian writer, *The Voice* (This book is an early attempt to merge English and African language structure in prose form.)

The word is a bouncing ball
The ruler throws from his
  balcony.
. . . .
The word has been a shot of
  morphine.
Rulers calm their people with
  speeches.

> Nizar Qabbani (b. 1932)
> Syrian/Lebanese writer and publisher

"I am ashamed of my emptiness,"
  said the Word to the Work.
"I know how poor I am when I
  see you," said the Work to the
  Word.

> Rabindranath Tagore (1861-1941)
> Indian poet and philosopher, *Stray Birds*

on WORK

There is a dialectical relation between one's life and one's work. The former obviously influences the latter, but one's work also becomes an influence on one's life. It is a two way affair, a mysterious process where what we call life and what we call creation merge, and do not merge, cross feed each other.

> Etel Adnan (b. 1925)
> Lebanese writer

I pray every single second of my life—not on my knees but with my work. . . . Work and worship are one with me.

> Susan B. Anthony (1820-1906)
> American suffragist

Work is good, provided you do not forget to live.

> Bantu proverb

The path of wisdom is for the meditative, and the path of work is for the active.

> *Bhagavad Gita*
> (c. 4th-3rd century B.C.E.)
> teachings of Krishna from the Hindu epic, the *Mahabharata*, 3:3

To know how to do something well is to enjoy it.

> Pearl S. Buck (1892-1973)
> American writer, *The Joy of Children*

To labor without ceasing all one's life, and then, without living to enjoy the fruit, worn out with labor, to depart, one knows not whither—is not this a just cause for grief?

> Chuang-tzu (c. 369-286 B.C.E.)
> Chinese Taoist philosopher

The return from your work must be the satisfaction which that work brings you and the world's need of that work. With this, life is heaven, or as near heaven as you can get. Without this—with work which you despise, which bores you and which the world does not need—this life is hell.

> W. E. B. Du Bois (1868-1963)
> American writer and educator, speech (March 2, 1958)

The satisfaction with your work, even at best, will never be complete, since nothing on earth can be perfect. The forward pace of the world which you are pushing will be painfully slow. But what of that: the difference between a hundred and a thousand years is less than you now think. But doing what must be done—that is eternal, even when it walks with poverty.

W. E. B. Du Bois (1868-1963)
American writer and educator, speaking about the civil rights movement

May not men earn their bread by intellectual labor? No, the needs of the body must be supplied by the body.

Mohandas K. Gandhi (1869-1948)
Indian spiritual and political leader

We must put work in the center of our aspirations; we must build all our edifices on this foundation. If work becomes our ideal, or, rather, if we bring the ideal of work into functioning, we shall be cured of the plague that has seized us, we shall be able to bridge the gap between us and nature.

Aaron David Gordon (1856-1922)
Israeli writer

The reward of work is to come, whereas the endurance of the labor is immediate.

al-Jahiz (c. 778-869)
Islamic philosopher and writer, *The Exploits of the Turks and the Army of the Khalifate in General*

Many people may think that, now there is Uhuru, now I can see the sun of freedom shining, richness will pour down like manna from heaven. I tell you there will be nothing from Heaven. We must all work hard, with our hands, to save ourselves from poverty, ignorance, and disease.

Jomo Kenyatta (1891-1978)
Kenyan politician, Independence Day message (1963)

To deny a man a job is to say that a man has no right to exist.

Martin Luther King, Jr.
(1929-1968)
American civil rights leader

The term *dignity of labor* is certainly not applicable to those people who talk but don't do a bit of physical work.

Li Dazhao (1888-1927)
Chinese political theorist

The world is like a great empty dream.
Why should one toil away one's life?

Li Po (701-762)
Chinese poet

Do something useful and you will have everything you want. Doors are shut for those who are dull and lazy; life is secure for those who obey the law of work.

José Martí (1853-1895)
Cuban patriot

Those who earn an honest living are the beloved of God.

Muhammad (570-632)
Prophet of Islam

No one eats better food than that which he eats from the work of his hands.

> Muhammad (570–632)
> Prophet of Islam, *Hadith*

Say: O my people! Work according to your power. Lo! I too am working. Thus ye will come to know for which of us will be the happy sequel. Lo! the wrong-doers will not be successful.

> *Qur'an* (c. 610–656)
> sacred book of Islam, vi:135

I'm in no soft, smooth
  comfortable world,
I'm perched in no glory and
  splendor;
I'm in a smoke-filled somber
  factory
Casting my iron flower in the
  forge, flames around me.

> Qu Qiubai (1899–1935)
> Chinese poet and revolutionary, *Wenji*

Nothing ever comes to one, that is worth having, except as a result of hard work.

> Booker T. Washington (1856–1915)
> American educator, *Up from Slavery*

No race can prosper till it learns that there is as much dignity in tilling a field as in writing a poem.

> Booker T. Washington (1856–1915)
> American educator

Work is the medicine for poverty.

> Yoruba (West African) proverb

on **THE WORLD**

The difference [between the East and the West] is part of the law of opposites which keeps our world balanced and right, and something in it goes wrong anytime we meddle with that law by expecting those on the other side of the globe to walk or live or think generally in the way we do. When those on one side try to do this sort of thing, it is really they who are standing on their heads, and not anyone else.

> Ba Maw (b. 1893)
> Burmese revolutionary leader and politician

The whole world is run on bluff.

> Marcus Garvey (1887–1940)
> American political leader, *Philosophy and Opinions*

Only today do I realize that this world in which I have moved about for half a lifetime has been for over four thousand years a man-eating world.

> Lu Xun (1881–1936)
> Chinese writer, "K'uang-jen jih-chi" ("A Madman's Diary")

Of late, the factual world has been buried under agnosticism, and its mystery has deepened as human society has come to cover a wider territory. Usually the statements of people who have witnessed the same incident contradict one another. An extraordinary incident that shocks the whole society always contains an eternal mystery.

> Yukio Mishima (1925–1970)
> Japanese writer

Of the enemies of the soul—the world, the devil, the flesh—the *world* is the most serious and the most dangerous.

> Gabriela Mistral (1889-1957)
> Chilean poet

Four things support the world: the learning of the wise, the justice of the great, the prayers of the good, and the valor of the brave.

> Muhammad (570-632)
> Prophet of Islam

The world is a dense forest
Spread with the fetters of illusion
And like a deer I ramble in it
The snares and attachments have
  caught me
While like a hunter destiny
  pursues me.

> Sankardeva (1449-1569)
> Indian religious leader

The world exists on three things: truth, justice, and peace.

> *Talmud*
> (c. late 4th-early 6th century)
> ancient body of Jewish civil and
> canonical law, Aboth 1:18

on WORLDLINESS

Heaven is found in eating delicious food, keeping company with young women, wearing fine clothes, perfumes, garlands. . . . Hell is found in the troubles caused by enemies, weapons, diseases. . . . Moksha [liberation] is death.

> *Brhaspati Sutra* (7th century)
> attributed to Carvaka, the legendary
> founder of Carvakaism, an Indian
> materialistic philosophy opposed to the
> more spiritual Hindu philosophers

The waves of human passion rise and fall; worldly things are as transitory as passing clouds.

> Cao Ba-Quat (1809-1854)
> Vietnamese poet, "Tai tu da cung phu"
> ("Song of the Gifted Man Sunk in
> Abject Poverty")

All that is worldly can be transcended: one can reflect on all things between heaven and earth from a higher vantage point. The demands of the present are neglected, life becomes eternal. Coming to heaven, one enters a sphere beyond space and time. Why then should one aspire to being received by king and emperors?

> Chung-ch'ang T'ung (c. 179-219)
> Chinese philosopher, "Lo-chih-luh"
> ("Desire for Joy")

The comfort of the life of the world is but little in the Hereafter.

> *Qur'an* (c. 610-656)
> sacred book of Islam, IX:38

Again, the worldly man is like a snake trying to swallow a mole. The snake can neither swallow the mole nor give it up.

> Ramakrishna (1836-1886)
> Indian Hindu mystic

on WORSHIP

Even if the most wicked worships Me with undivided devotion, he should be regarded as good, for he is rightly resolved.

Very soon he becomes a righteous soul and attains to eternal peace. Know thou, O son of Kunti, that my devotee never perishes.

Bhagavad Gita
(c. 4th–3rd century B.C.E.)
teachings of Krishna from the Hindu
epic, the *Mahabharata*, 9:30-31

Those who, murmuring against it, do not follow my doctrine, deluded in all knowledge, you must know they are lost, the fools.

Bhagavad Gita
(c. 4th–3rd century B.C.E.)
teachings of Krishna from the Hindu
epic, the *Mahabharata*, 3:32

Love of God hath so absorbed me that neither love nor hate of any other thing remains in my heart.

Rabi'a al-Adawiyya (c. 717-801)
Iraqi Sufi poet and mystic

My Lord
if I worship Thee from fear of
  Hell
burn me in Hell

and if I worship Thee from hope
  of Paradise
exclude me thence

but if I worship Thee
for Thine own sake alone
do not withhold from me Thine
  External Beauty.

Rabi'a al-Adawiyya (c. 717-801)
Iraqi Sufi poet and mystic, "Two
Prayers"

My love for God leaves no room for hating Satan.

Rabi'a al-Adawiyya (c. 717-801)
Iraqi Sufi poet and mystic

Two ways I love Thee: selfishly,
And next, as worthy is of Thee.
'Tis selfish love that I do naught
Save think on Thee with every
  thought.
'Tis purest love when Thou dost
  raise
The veil to my adoring gaze.
Not mine the praise in that or this:
Thine is the praise in both, I wish.

Rabi'a al-Adawiyya (c. 717-801)
Iraqi Sufi poet and mystic

He is truly a religious man who professes what he believes and practices what he enjoins.

Sarvepalli Radhakrishnan
(1888-1975)
Indian philosopher and politician

Leave this chanting and singing
  and telling
thy beads! Whom dost thou
  worship in this lonely
dark corner of a temple? Open
  thine eyes and see,
thy God is not before thee.
He is there where the tiller is
  tilling the hard
ground and the pathmaker is
  breaking stones.
He is with them in sun and in
  shower.

Rabindranath Tagore (1861-1941)
Indian writer and philosopher,
Sadhana

He who knows the precepts by heart, but fails to practice them, is like one who lights a lamp and then shuts his eyes.

Tibetan doctrine

on WRITERS AND WRITING

People create stories create people; or rather stories create people create stories.

Chinua Achebe (b. 1930)
Nigerian writer

An African writer who really wants to interpret the African scene has to write in three dimensions at once. There is the private life, the social life, and what you may call the supernatural.

Elechi Amadi (b. 1934)
Nigerian writer

I like to think of myself as a painter or composer using words in the place of pictures and musical symbols. . . . In my ideal novel, the reader should feel a sense of aesthetic satisfaction that he cannot quite explain—the same feeling he gets when he listens to a beautiful symphony.

Elechi Amadi (b. 1934)
Nigerian writer

A story is not only meaning, it's music as well.

Aharon Appelfeld (b. 1932)
Israeli writer

A writer should have another lifetime to see whether he is appreciated.

Jorge Luis Borges (1899–1986)
Argentinian writer, *Conversations with Jorge Luis Borges*

Every novel is an ideal plane inserted into the realm of reality.

Jorge Luis Borges (1899–1986)
Argentinian writer, *Labyrinths*

If a writer disbelieves what he is writing, then he can hardly expect his reader to believe it.

Jorge Luis Borges (1899–1986)
Argentinian writer

A writer needs loneliness, and he gets his share of it. He needs love, and he gets shared and also unshared love. In fact, he needs the universe. To be a writer is, in a sense, to be a daydreamer—to be living a kind of double life.

Jorge Luis Borges (1899–1986)
Argentinian writer, *Borges on Writing*

What a writer wants to do is not what he does.

Jorge Luis Borges (1899–1986)
Argentinian writer, *The Listener*

The history of catastrophe requires such a literature to hold a broken mirror up to broken nature.

Edward Kamau Brathwaite
(b. 1930)
Barbadian poet

I write nothing in this life because I do not want to spend today remembering whatever good I did yesterday.

Rafael Cordero y Molina
(1790–1868)
Puerto Rican educator

Writing is a trade . . . which is learned by writing.

Simone de Beauvoir (1908–1986)
French writer and philosopher, *La Force de l'age*

317

There is one last thing to remember: writers are always selling somebody out.

> Joan Didion (b. 1934)
> American writer, *Slouching Towards Bethlehem*

As for writing, I sometimes feel that it would not be much of a loss if we gave it up entirely. We write, some people read, time passes, and there is no effect whatsoever. What is the meaning of it, then, except we've gotten paid for it?

> Ding Ling (c. 1904-1986)
> Chinese writer, *Shanghai, Spring 1930*

Writers should be read—but neither seen nor heard.

> Daphne du Maurier (1907-1989)
> English writer

Because I had loved so deeply,
  Because I had loved so long,
God in his great compassion
  Gave me the gift of song.

> Paul Laurence Dunbar (1872-1906)
> American writer, "Compensation"

Life can't ever really defeat a writer who is in love with writing, for life itself is a writer's lover until death—fascinating, cruel, lavish, warm, cold, treacherous, constant.

> Edna Ferber (1885-1968)
> American writer

The poem or the story or the novel must follow a certain line. It is a kind of party line, even though what is in question is not a political party; but it is, in the true sense of the word, a party line.

> Nadine Gordimer (b. 1923)
> South African writer

I want to paint windows all over the earth and let eyes accustomed to darkness grow accustomed to light.

> Gu Cheng (b. 1957)
> Chinese poet, "I Am a Willful Child"

If a writer does not have the courage to reveal the dark diseases of society, does not have the courage to participate positively in solving the crucial problems of people's lives, and does not have the courage to attack all the deformed, sick, black things, then can he be called a writer?

> Huang Quiyun (b. 1939)
> Chinese writer, during the "Hundred Flowers" period, when Mao Zedong called for greater artistic freedom, then retracted that stance

Some of today's writers—or, I should say, the great majority of them—are inclined to shun tales that present imaginings, labeling them all as "fabrications." Yet has there been any poet or man of letters, ancient or modern, who did not make free use of his imagination? Would a writer, even a naturalistic writer, be able to present truth if he were lacking in imagination? . . . The artist justifies his existence only when he can transform his imagination into truth.

> Tanizaki Jun'ichiro (1886-1965)
> Japanese writer

Reading, contemplation, and observation are the three things a novelist should not neglect at any time.

> Nagai Kafu (1879-1959)
> Japanese writer, "How to Write a Novel"

Everything that I have said can be ascribed to morbid elucubrations, hysteria, and poorly controlled dreams.

Mohammed Khair-Eddine (b. 1941)
Moroccan writer

All books are either dreams or swords,
You can cut, or you can drug, with words.

Amy Lowell (1874-1925)
American writer, "Sword Blades and Poppy Seeds," *Sword Blades and Poppy Seeds*

It seems to me that the polemics aimed at the vices of an era should drop out of sight at the same time as their targets. My writings can be compared with the white corpuscles that form a scab over a wound: as long as they do not eliminate themselves of their own accord, it is a sign that the infection remains active.

Lu Xun (1881-1936)
Chinese writer

I live with the people I create, and it has always made my essential loneliness less keen.

Carson McCullers (1917-1967)
American writer, *The Square Root of Wonderful*

A person who publishes a book appears willfully in public with his pants down.

Edna St. Vincent Millay (1892-1950)
American poet

In all ages, literature aims at an interpretation of the universe and a deep perception of humanity by means of language.

Yukio Mishima (1925-1970)
Japanese writer

Man's wisdom is at the tip of his pen,
His intelligence is in his writing.
His pen can raise a man to the rank
That the scepter accords to a king.

Samuel ha-Nagid (993-1056)
Spanish Hebrew poet, "The Power of the Pen"

A writer is, in the end, not his books but his myth—and that myth is in the keeping of others.

V. S. Naipaul (b. 1932)
West Indian writer

I have never thought of my life as divided between poetry and politics.

Pablo Neruda (1904-1973)
Chilean poet and diplomat

The poet . . . gives a gallery of ghosts shaken by fire and the darkness of his times. Perhaps I did not live in myself; perhaps I lived the life of others. . . . This is a life made up of other lives, for a poet has many lives.

Pablo Neruda (1904-1973)
Chilean poet and diplomat, *Memoirs*

The typewriter separated me from a deeper intimacy with poetry, and my hand brought me closer to that intimacy again.

Pablo Neruda (1904-1973)
Chilean poet and diplomat

The role of the writer is not to say what we can all say, but what we are unable to say.

> Anaïs Nin (1903–1977)
> American writer, *The Diary of Anaïs Nin*

Every writer has a vision. Otherwise, I do not see what he is doing writing.

> Lewis Nkosi (b. 1936)
> South African writer

When a book leaves your hands, it belongs to God. He may use it to save a few words, or to try a few others, but I think that for the writer to worry is to take over God's business.

> Flannery O'Connor (1925–1964)
> American writer, *The Habit of Being*

A writer needs people around him. He needs live struggles of active life. Contrary to popular mythology, a novel is not a product of the imaginative feats of a single individual but the work of many hands and tongues. A writer just takes down notes dictated to him by life among the people. . . . I love to hear the voices of the people working on the land, forging metal in a factory, telling anecdotes in crowded matatus and buses, gyrating their hips in a crowded bar before a jukebox of a live band. . . . I need the vibrant voices of beautiful women: their touch, their sighs, their tears, their laughter. I like the presence of children prancing about, fighting, laughing, crying. I need life to write about life.

> Ngugi wa Thiong'o (b. 1936)
> Kenyan writer, *Detained*

Literature must be an analysis of experience and a synthesis of the findings into a unity.

> Rebecca West (1892–1983)
> English writer, *Ending in Earnest*

All desire to practice the art of a writer has left me. . . . It's not the writing but the architecture that strains. If I write this paragraph, then there is the next and then the next.

> Virginia Woolf (1882–1941)
> English writer

Fiction, imaginative work that is, is not dropped like a pebble upon the ground, as science may be; fiction is like a spider's web, attached ever so lightly perhaps, but still attached to life at all four corners.

> Virginia Woolf (1882–1941)
> English writer, *A Room of One's Own*

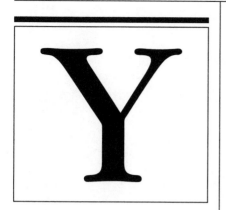

on YOUTH

Youth is something very new: twenty years ago no one mentioned it.

Coco Chanel (1883-1971)
French designer, *Coco Chanel: Her Life, Her Secrets*

On the neck of the young man sparkles no gem so gracious as enterprise.

Hafiz (d. 1389)
Persian poet

Youth condemns; maturity condones.

Amy Lowell (1874-1925)
American writer, *Tendencies in Modern American Poetry*

The young cannot teach tradition to the old.

Yoruba (West African) proverb

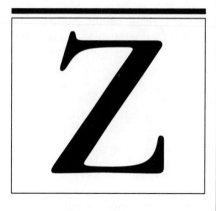

on ZEN

The body of Buddha is
  everywhere,
Does the Goddess of Mercy live in
  the eastern sea?
Every green mountain is a place
  of awakening;
Why must you seek Mount
  Potalaka?

> Baeg Un (1299-1375)
> Korean Zen Buddhist monk, "To A
> Friend Seeking Potalaka"

Do away with mental deliberation
and cognition, and simply go on
sitting.

> Dogen (1200-1253)
> Japanese Zen monk

Biographical Index

Understanding the Biographical Index

We tried as much as possible to render foreign names in the forms familiar to Western readers. This makes the book easier to understand—but possibly confusing to those who have encountered other modes of transliteration or other names. Here are our basic guidelines.

Chinese names. We chose the transliteration by which people are best known in the West. We used the Wade-Giles system or its variants for classical Chinese names, but the pinyin system used in modern China (but not Taiwan) for recent Chinese names. For a few figures, such as Confucius, we used the Latinized form by which they became famous in the West centuries ago.

Pronunciation marks. Arabic, Vietnamese, and other languages appear or are transliterated by scholars with diacritical marks that are unfamiliar to most Western readers. We chose not to use them.

Alphabetization. Names are alphabetized by the first letter of the name by which the person is generally known. The major exception is Arabs whose names begin with "al-," meaning "the." Following convention, we have ignored the "al-" in alphabetization. Remember that in many cultures family names appear before given names, the reverse of the Western form.

Pseudonyms. We listed people known primarily by their pseudonyms or married names under those assumed names. When a figure changed names, we chose the name under which he or she is best known. In such cases, we included the person's other names in their biographies.

A

'Abd al-'Aziz b. Sulayman
(d. 767)
Sufi poet
(Abu al-Rasibi)
Sufi ascetic; contemporary of famous Sufi poet and saint Rabi'a.

on death, page 57

'Abd al Hamid (705–750)
Arabic writer
('Abd al Hamid bin Yahya bin Said)
Founder of Arabic epistolary style; at first an itinerant pedagogue, later employed under the Umayyads as a secretary. A principal assistant to Caliph Marwan, with whom he apparently died at Busir.

on humanity, page 130

Abd-el-Kader (1078–1166)
Persian Sufi leader
('Abd al-Qadir al-Jilani)
From Baghdad; founder of the Qadiriya, the first large Sufi order; known for his influence and the devotion he inspired in his followers.

on death, page 57
on self-esteem, page 255
on words, page 311

'Abd-ar-Rahman (891–961)
('Abd-al-Rahman)
Islamic ruler of Spanish Córdoba
Began rule in Córdoba, Islamic Spain, in 912; named himself caliph in 929. Campaigned against the Fatimids and kings of León and Navarre, leading the Umayyad emirate to the height of its power.

on homesickness, page 126–127
on spirituality, page 268

Muhammad 'Abduh
(1849–1905)
Egyptian reformer
One of the most important Islamic figures of the nineteenth century; founder of Islamic modernism; sought to reform Al-Azhar University; argued for Islamic receptivity to Western science and for a return to Islamic purity.

on experience, page 85
on God, page 108

Abu al-Athiyah (d. 828)
Arabic poet
Prominent poet of the Umayyad dynasty; famous for ascetic views, gloomy outlook, and use of the *Hadith (Sayings of the Prophet Muhammad)* in his poetry.

on old age, page 192

Abu-Bakr (c. 580–634)
Companion to the Prophet Muhammad and first caliph of Islam
One of the first converts to Islam; father-in-law to Muhammad; elected *khalifat rasul Allah* (successor of the messenger of God); became first caliph of Islam, or leader of the Muslim community, upon Muhammad's death.

on advice, page 6
on leadership and leaders, page 154
on property, page 220

Abu Sa'id (967–1049)
Persian Sufi leader and poet
(Abu Sa'id ibn Abi 'l-Kahyr)
First Sufi to draw up a basic monastic rule for his disciples; first master of theosophic verse; popularized the quatrain as a means of conveying religious, philosophic, and mystic thoughts; also considered to have influenced later Sufi poets by establishing typical elements and images of mystic poems.

on God, page 111–112
on Sufism, page 273

Bella Abzug (b. 1920)
American politician
Initially gained fame as a lawyer defending individuals accused of un-American activities during the 1950s; involved in peace movement; founder of Women Strike for Peace (1961) and the National Women's Political Caucus. Elected to Congress (1971), where her rhetorical style earned her the nickname "Battling Bella."

on feminism, page 94

Chinua Achebe (b. 1930)
Nigerian writer
(Albert Chinualmogo)
Novelist, poet, and essayist considered a leading writer of African literature; highly successful first novel *Things Fall Apart*, about the Ibo tribe, has now been translated into forty different languages; known for addressing political subjects.

on caution, page 33
on grieving, page 119

on language, page 152
on oppression, page 195
on war, page 297
on writers and writing,
page 317

Kobena Eyi Acquah
(1884–1954)
Ghanaian writer
Poet, novelist, and Fante language scholar; wrote poetry in Fante; one novel (published posthumously) in English; possibly best known as editor of the *Fante Grammar of Function*, for use in schools of the former Gold Coast.

on language, page 152

Abigail Adams (1744–1818)
American First Lady and feminist
Wife of second U.S. president, John A. Adams, and mother of sixth U.S. president, John Quincy Adams; prolific letter writer and early feminist; in letters to her husband during the Continental Congress, often described her concerns about women's rights under the new republic.

on feminism, page 94
on learning and education,
page 158
on power, page 211

Jane Addams (1860–1935)
American social worker
Worked for social justice for immigrants, women, children, and African Americans; advocated fair housing and factory inspections; founded social settlement Hull House in Chicago, 1889; first woman president of National Conference of Social Work, 1910;

founder of National Federation of Settlements; helped found American Civil Liberties Union, 1920; president of the Women's International League for Peace and Freedom, 1919-1935; cowinner of Nobel Peace Prize, 1931.

on civilization, page 42

Ibrahim ben Adham (d. 777)
Prince of Balkh and Sufi mystic
   convert
Prince who became an ascetic Sufi convert; figures in numerous Sufi legends apparently patterned after the story of Buddha.

on the present, page 214

Etel Adnan (b. 1925)
Lebanese writer
Poet, prose writer, painter; born in Beirut, but left Lebanon in 1976; currently lives in Paris and the United States; often includes visual elements such as signs or arrows in her writings.

on adolescence, page 4
on work, page 312

Jamal al-Din al-Afghani
(1839-1897)
Islamic teacher and Egyptian
   nationalist
Early advocate of pan-Islamism; born in Iran, but claimed to have been born in Afghanistan to make his background more acceptable to Sunni disciples; traveled extensively; sought to revive Islam as a political force. Invited to Iran by the shah; later fell out of favor, was forced to take sanctuary in a

mosque, and was eventually removed by the shah's troops to Iraq. Leader of antigovernment protest resulting in the Iranian Constitutional Revolution in the early 1900s; major influence on Egyptian Nationalist Party of Mustafa Kamil.

on Islam, page 142

Muhammad Aga Khan III
(1877-1957)
Islamic leader
Born in Karachi; became leader of Isma'ili sect of Islam in 1985. Known as energetic and enlightened leader; established Aligarh University (1910); worked for British in both world wars; president of League of Nations assembly (1937).

on wealth, page 302

Luis Aguillar (b. 1926)
Cuban educator and writer
Critic of oppression and censorship in modern Cuba; supporter of the Cuban revolution against Batista; former member of the Revolutionary Institute of Culture; resigned as a protest against trial of Cuban revolutionary hero Hubert Matos; emigrated to United States.

on conformity, page 47

Sir Sayyid Ahmad Khan
(1817-1898)
Indian Islamic reformer and
   educator
(Syed Ahmed Khan)
Formed school (which later became a college) teaching modern Western thought along with tradi-

tional Islamic learnings; promoted Muslim interests.

> on learning and education,
> page 158–159

Ai Qing (b. 1910)
Chinese poet
(Ai Ching; pseudonym of Jiang Haicheng)
Known for socially conscious works; first collection of poetry, *Ta-yen-ho*, brought fame; joined Communists at Yenan (1941), became associate editor of the Communist *People's Literature* journal, and campaigned for Communist control of literature. In later years, became victim of Mao's Anti-Rightist campaign during the "Hundred Flowers" period (1956–1957); accused of being a revisionist, was sent to state farm in desert area of Zinjiang for "rehabilitation." Returned to Beijing in 1975; works published again in 1978.

> on joy, page 144
> on survival, page 274

Christina Ama Ata Aidoo
(b. 1942)
Ghanaian writer
Novelist, playwright, short story writer, and professor of literature; writes in English. Considered one of Ghana's leading literary figures.

> on children and childhood,
> page 37
> on humanity, page 130

Akbar (1542–1605)
Mughal emperor of India
(Akbar the Great; Jalal-ud-Din Muhammad)
Conqueror of Malwa, Raiputaana, Gujrat, Bengal, Afghanistan, Kashmir, Sindh, Qandahar, and Ahmadnagar, making him ruler of northern India. Known for his reforms, including abolition of slavery, *sati* (immolation of a widow with her dead husband), and legalized polygamy; tax reforms; and legalization of marriage for widows.

> on government, page 114
> on leadership and leaders,
> page 154

al-Akhtal (645–713)
Arab Christian poet
(Ghiyath ibn Ghawth al-Alchtal)
Called "the poet of the Umayyads," the first Muslim Arab dynasty; unlike many others of the period, he (along with Jarir and al-Farazdaq) broke with traditional style and developed an original voice, chiefly by using obscenities and manipulating the short ghazal (lyric poem) form.

> on life, page 163
> on travel, page 281

Akjartoq (c. 1920)
Caribou Eskimo poet
Included in collection of Eskimo songs gathered in the first quarter of the twentieth century by explorer Knud Rasmussen; poetry describes role of women in Eskimo society.

> on old age, page 192

Muhyi al-Din ibn al-'Arabi. *See* Ibn 'Arabi

Nobuko Albery (b. 1940)
Japanese writer
(Nobuko Morris)
Japanese-born novelist and historian; moved to and wrote in Monaco. Married to theatrical producer Sir Donald Albery.

on beginnings, page 23

Louisa May Alcott (1832–1888)
American writer
Author of children's classic *Little Women*, based largely on her own experiences; subsequently wrote sequels and related works; daughter of Bronson Alcott, transcendentalist and teacher.

on genius, page 106
on love, page 169

Aleek-chea-ahoosh. *See* Plenty Coups

'Ali (c. 600–661)
First Imam of the Sh'ia branch of Islam; fourth caliph
('Ali ibn Abi Talib)
Cousin and son-in-law of Muhammad; led split from 'Uthman over interpretation of the Qur'an; elected fourth caliph after death of 'Uthman; was opposed by Syrian governor Mu 'awiya.

on behavior, page 24
on charity, page 37
on epitaphs, page 79
on familiarity, page 89
on friendship, page 103
on gifts and giving, page 107
on God, page 108
on gossip, page 113
on haste, page 122
on humility, page 131
on obedience, page 192

on patience, page 199
on pride, page 215
on renunciation, page 235
on self-discipline, page 254
on sin, page 260
on time, page 277
on wisdom, page 305

Muhammad Ali (b. 1942)
American athlete
(Cassius Clay)
Three-time world heavyweight boxing champion; retired in 1981; one of the most recognized names in sports around the world.

on imagination, page 138
on race, page 223

Isabel Allende (b. 1942)
Chilean writer
Won acclaim for her first novel, *The House of the Spirits*. Born in Lima, Peru; goddaughter and niece of former president Salvador Allende; forced into exile with her family upon the 1973 overthrow of Chile's coalition government by a military junta.

on reform and reformers,
page 230

Elechi Amadi (b. 1934)
Nigerian writer
Novelist, playwright, teacher. Along with Wole Soyinka and Chinua Achebe, considered a premier African writer; known for focus on African atmosphere, typically centering around traditional African society before colonial rule and showing no political slant. Famous particularly for loose trilogy of village life comprising his first

novel, *The Concubine*; *The Great Ponds*; and *The Slave*.

on writers and writing, page 317

Ambapali (4th century B.C.E.)
Indian Buddhist poet
Called "the Mary Magdalene of Buddhism"; initially a courtesan who became a disciple of the Buddha and gave him a garden in which to establish a retreat.

on old age, page 192

Amen-em-Opet (c. 1200 B.C.E.)
Egyptian scribe
Known as the "Truly Silent One of Abydos"; chiefly famous due to the "Instruction of Amen-em-Opet" (attributed to him but actual author questionable), a book of instruction, giving advice from father to son on behavior, deportment, and the like.

on humanity, page 130
on listening, page 166–167

Yehuda Amichai (b. 1924)
Israeli writer
Bavarian-born novelist, poet, and short story writer. Joined British Army in 1942 and served in Middle East until 1946; also joined the Palmach and fought on the front in Israel's War of Independence. Works influenced by his orthodox upbringing and war experience; known for simple style and personal nature of topics.

on love, page 169
on time, page 277

Idi Amin (b. 1925)
Ugandan dictator
Established military dictatorship (1971), after having been commander-in-chief of the army and air force; infamous for the atrocities under his regime, including killing his opponents, expelling Ugandan Asians, taking over foreign-owned businesses. Defeated in his 1978 attempt to annex a portion of Tanzania; fled Uganda (1978).

on tyranny and tyrants, page 287

Levi Ben Amittai (b. 1901)
Israeli poet
Born in White Russia; settled in Palestine (1920). Poetry celebrates simple agrarian life, in keeping with views of early Zionist pioneers.

on the land, page 151

Abdullahi Ahmed An-Na'im (20th century)
Sudanese rights activist
Noted Islamic reformer; disciple of Sudanese reformer M. M. Taha; executive director of Africa Watch.

on Islam, page 142

Marian Anderson (1902–1993)
American singer
First African American singer to perform at the New York Metropolitan Opera; United Nations delegate (1958); winner of Presidential Medal for Freedom (1963).

on racism, page 224

Corrine Andrews. *See* Rebecca West

Maya Angelou (b. 1928)
American writer
Poet, memoirist, and actress; toured Europe as cast member of *Porgy and Bess*, and sang in New York nightclubs. Joined Harlem Writers Guild; edited *African Review* in Ghana; has held faculty positions at various U.S. universities. Best known for multivolume memoir, *I Know Why the Caged Bird Sings*; U.S. inaugural poet (1992).

on adolescence, page 4-5
on snobs and snobbery,
page 263
on talent, page 275

Ansari (1006-1088)
Persian Sufi poet
(Abu Isma'il Abd'allah bin Abu Mansur Muhammad)
Claimed to have been descended from Muhammad's companion Abu Ayyub; known for mystical verses, especially *Munajat (Supplications)*.

on humility, page 131
on the past, page 198

Maryam bint Abi Ya'qub al-Ansari (c. 11th century)
Spanish Arab poet
Born to noble family of Umayyad Spain.

on old age, page 192

Andal (c. 9th century)
Indian Tamil poet
Devotee of Krishna; one of the "Alvar," a group of twelve Tamil poets of the period; considered an incarnation of Devi.

on listening, page 167
on love, page 169

al-Antaki (d. 830)
Sufi leader
(Ahmad bin 'Asim)
Early Sufi from Antioch; died in Damascus.

on sin, page 260

Katherine Anthony (1877-1965)
American writer and educator
Known particularly for biographies, such as those on Dolley Madison and Susan B. Anthony; propounded theory of biographer as melder of novelist's, scholar's, and historian's skills.

on biography, page 25

Susan B. Anthony (1820-1906)
American suffragist
Leader of the American women's suffrage movement; also involved in temperance and abolitionist movements. Founded National Woman Suffrage Association with Elizabeth Cady Stanton (1869), International Council of Women (1888), and International Woman Suffrage Alliance (1904).

on failure, page 87
on feminism, page 94-95
on reform and reformers,
page 230
on self-reliance, page 258
on women, page 307
on work, page 312

Chairil Anwar (1922-1949)
Indonesian poet
Considered premier poet of Indonesian language. Member of the "Generation of 45," a group responsible for vitalization of Indonesian language in literature. Work rooted

in Indonesian cultural traditions but also shows influence of Western poetic forms and sensibilities.

on art and artists, page 18
on heaven, page 123
on loneliness, page 167
on love, page 169
on solitude, page 264
on words, page 311

Kasim i Anwar (1356–1433)
Central Asian (Herat) poet
(pseudonym of Mu'in al Din 'Ali Husayn Sarabi Tabrizi)
Mystic of Safawid dynasty.

on judgment, page 145

Gloria Anzaldua (20th century)
American writer
Work generally explored feminist themes.

on feminism, page 96
on minorities, page 183

Aharon Appelfeld (b. 1932)
Israeli writer
Bukovnia-born novelist and short story writer. Many works focus on anti-Semitism and the pre-World War II Jewish community.

on art and artists, page 18
on belief, page 24
on writers and writing,
page 317

Corazon Aquino (b. 1933)
Philippine politician
Widow of politician Benigno S. Aquino, President Ferdinand Marcos's chief opponent and challenger, who was assassinated in 1983. Protested February 1986 presidential election; led a campaign

and garnered wide popular support; was elected president in 1986.

on honesty, page 127
on revolution, page 239

Jacobo Arbenz (1913–1971)
Guatemalan politician
Soldier, reformer, and politician. As president of Guatemala, emphasized land reform; cooperation with indigenous Communists led to his overthrow (organized by the CIA) in 1954.

on dignity, page 71

Diane Arbus (1923–1971)
American photographer
Famous for documentary photographs, especially of subjects such as circus freaks, twins, and midgets; work marked by a stark style, irony, and psychological effect. Received Guggenheim Fellowship (1963, 1966). Committed suicide in 1971.

on knowledge, page 148
on self-identity, page 256

Hannah Arendt (1906–1975)
American philosopher and
historian
German-born; fled the Nazis in 1940 and settled in the United States. A leading political theorist; held academic positions; served as editor-in-chief at Schocken Books. While subjects of her works tend to be theoretical, they are widely read outside of strictly academic circles. Most famous for *Origins of Totalitarianism* and *The Human Condition*.

on poetry and poets, page 205

Ayi Kwei Armah (b. 1938)
Ghanaian writer
Novelist, short story writer, poet, journalist known for anticolonialist views (against both white and black colonialism); major figure in development of contemporary African literature.

    on corruption, page 51-52
    on greed, page 118
    on hope, page 127
    on poetry and poets, page 205
    on the present, page 214
    on race, page 223

Louis Armstrong (1900-1971)
American musician
(Satchmo)
Jazz trumpeter and singer, also appeared in numerous films. Set innovative standards in early jazz; moved out of collective improvisation into virtuoso deliveries, for which he became famous.

    on music, page 185
    on racism, page 224

Muhammed Asad (1757-1799)
Islamic writer
(pseudonym Ghalib)
Qualified for the civil service, but decided to renounce the world and become a dervish; eventually became *shaykh* (leader) of ancient monastery at Gatala.

    on perfection, page 201

Muhammad Husan Askari
(d. 1974)
Pakistani writer
Prominent literary critic; argued that Pakistani literature should reflect general Islamic themes.

    on anger, page 16

Asoka (273-232 B.C.E.)
Indian king
Ruler of Magadha, Maurya dynasty; established Buddhism as India's state religion.

    on conquest, page 48-49
    on tolerance, page 279

Nancy Astor (1879-1964)
English politician
Born in United States; married to William Waldorf Astor; succeeded husband as Conservative member of Parliament (1919); first woman with seat in House of Commons.

    on marriage, page 176
    on success, page 271

Kemal Ataturk (1881-1938)
Turkish patriot and political leader
(Mustafa Kemal Ataturk)
Led Turkish nationalist movement; general in World War I; helped defeat Allied attack on Turkey; later defeated joint Greek-Allied force. Elected first president of the Turkish Republic (1923-1938); known for far-reaching reforms and advocacy of modernization; considered the father of modern Turkey.

    on patriotism and nationalism, page 199
    on revolution, page 239
    on victory, page 293

Attar (d. 1229)
Persian poet
(Farid al-Din)
Mystic who wrote only on reli-

gious subjects; one of the most prolific authors in Persian literature.

  on fear, page 93
  on solitude, page 264
  on suffering, page 273

Attila the Hun (406–453)
Central Asian ruler and conqueror
  of Europe
Became king of the Huns in 434; eventually controlled territory extending from Germany to the frontiers of China. Defeated during his seige of Gaul, but attacked Italy; only the intercession of Pope Leo I (and large bribes) saved Rome.

  on power, page 211

Averroes. *See* Abu-l-walid ibn-Rushd

Augustine (354–430)
North African Christian religious
  leader
Born in Numidia (modern Tunisia); became bishop of Hippo in 396. Famous for his *Confessions* (400) and the twenty-two-volume *City of God* (412–427). Known as Saint Augustine of Hippo.

  on love, page 169

Delmira Augustini (1886–1914)
Uruguayan poet
Considered among the most important female writers of early twentieth-century Latin America; well known for combining the intellectual with the erotic.

  on sex, page 259

Nizamuddin Aulia (1234–1325)
Indian Muslim religious leader
Born in Uttar Pradesh; grew up in poverty; later attained great fame and devotion as religious sage; a disciple of Bakhtiar Kaki and of Khwaja Moinuddin Chishti; became leader of Chishti mystics, group which reached its height under his influence after being opened to people of all classes.

  on charity, page 37

Jane Austen (1775–1817)
English writer
Famous chiefly for six novels, four of which (*Sense and Sensibility*, *Pride and Prejudice*, *Mansfield Park*, and *Emma*) were first published anonymously; two (*Persuasion*, *Northanger Abbey*), posthumously.

  on complaint, page 46
  on gossip, page 113
  on haste, page 122
  on justification, page 147
  on love, page 169
  on marriage, page 176
  on nature, page 188
  on relationships, page 232
  on selfishness, page 256
  on speech, page 266
  on vanity, page 292
  on women, page 307

Obafemi Awolowo (b. 1909)
Nigerian politician
Leader of the Action Group political party; former premier of the western region of Nigeria; also lawyer and educator.

  on diplomacy, page 71
  on hope, page 128

on nonviolence, page 191
on violence, page 294

Kofi Awoonor (b. 1935)
Ghanaian writer
(George Awoonor-Williams)
Poet, novelist, critic, and playwright. Professor of English literature at the University of Ghana; founded the Ghana Playhouse and managed Ghana's film industry. Left Ghana for London (1967), then the United States, where he became a professor of comparative literature. Returned to Ghana (1975), where he was arrested for supposed political offenses; released upon worldwide appeal. Works often concern the traditional Ewe culture, and relationship between African oral traditions and the European written ones; best-known works include *Night of My Blood* and *The Breast of the Earth*.

on beginnings, page 23
on birth, page 25
on freedom, page 100
on salvation, page 248

Mohammed Ayub Khan
(1907–1970)
Pakistani military and political
    leader
First Pakistani commander-in-chief; field marshal. Forced President Iskander Mirza to place Pakistan under martial law, then exiled Mirza in a bloodless coup; became president in 1958; stabilized economy and established political autocracy. Facing opposition from both left and right, was

forced out of office in 1969; martial law reinstated.

on thought, page 276

Salah al-Din al-Ayyubi. *See*
Saladin

Abu 'I Kalam Azad (1888–1958)
Indian politician and Muslim
    theologian
Reviver of Muslim thought in India.

on faith, page 87

Nnamdi Azikwe (b. 1904)
Nigerian politician
Patriot active in nationalist movement; became president of the National Council of Nigeria and the Cameroons, vice-president of the Nigerian National Democratic party, member of the House of Assembly, prime minister of the eastern region, and governor-general of Nigeria. Elected first president of the Nigerian republic in 1963; suspended from office during military uprising in 1966.

on peace, page 200
on the public, page 221
on scholars, page 249

B

Mallam Ba (c. 1920)
Malian writer
Theologian, writer, and scholar; called "the sage of Bameko" (the major city in Mali). Work focuses on Islamic philosophy and African

religions (including those of the Bambara and Fulani peoples).

on happiness, page 121

Ba Maw (b. 1893)
Burmese revolutionary leader and politician
Lawyer; defended leaders of peasant rebellion; first prime minister of Burma (1937–1939); first head of state of independent Burma.

on revolution, page 239
on truth, page 283
on the world, page 314

Babur (1483–1530)
First Mughal emperor of India
(Zahir al-Din Muhammad; Babar; Babur the Conqueror)
Invaded India in 1526, and began establishing the Mughal empire; first Mughal emperor known for religious tolerance and interest in the arts.

on anxiety, page 16
on decisions, page 63
on strategy, page 269

Baeg Un (1299–1375)
Korean Zen Buddhist monk
Introduced the Chinese sect Im Je (Lin-chi in Chinese) to Korea. This sect advocated nonattachment to both material as well as spiritual goals, the ideal being a human free of all obsessions.

on Zen, page 322

Joan Baez (b. 1941)
American singer and activist
Singer, songwriter, and human rights activist; founder of Institute for the Study of Non-violence.

on choice, page 39

Mira Bai (c. 1520)
Indian Hindu poet
Princess, and Hindu saint, religious teacher, and poet.

on Buddhism, page 31
on infinity, page 141

Augusta Baker (b. 1913)
American librarian
Former slave; worked in variety of positions with American Library Association; writer and lecturer on children and books; known for work in literacy, civil rights, and African folklore.

on culture, page 55

Ella Baker (1903–1986)
American civil rights activist
Founding member of the Young Negroes Cooperative League, Student Non-violent Coordinating Committee (SNCC), and the Mississippi Freedom Democratic Party of the 1960s.

on leadership and leaders, page 155

Roman Baldorioty de Castro (1822–1887)
Puerto Rican politician
A leader of the Autonomist Party (against Spanish colonial rule); arrested in 1887 for his views; health was broken by the imprisonment; died shortly after release. Also

known as a social progressive, abolitionist, and educational reformer.

> on ideas, page 135
> on power, page 211
> on slavery, page 261
> on striving, page 270

James Baldwin (1924-1987)
American writer
Novelist, essayist, playwright, and civil rights activist. Grew up in a poor section of Harlem, New York; worked in Paris and New York.

> on African Americans, page 7
> on the Americas, page 13
> on anger, page 16
> on children and childhood, page 37
> on convictions, page 50
> on death, page 57
> on dependence, page 68
> on freedom, page 100
> on generations, page 106
> on ghettos, page 107
> on hate, page 122
> on help, page 124
> on history, page 125
> on love, page 169
> on money, page 184
> on racism, page 224
> on reality, page 228
> on virtue, page 295

Abu Bakar Tafawa Balewa (1912-1966)
Nigerian government official
Held numerous government positions, including minister of works, minister of transport, and premier; assassinated in 1966 military uprising.

> on government, page 114
> on liberty, page 161

Bana (7th century)
Indian poet
Sanskrit epic poet, known for prose romances.

> on human nature, page 128-129
> on wealth, page 302

Hastings Banda (b. 1906)
Malawi political leader
Leader of the Malawi African Congress; minister of national resources (1961); prime minister (1963); president of the Malawi republic (formerly Nyasaland) (1966); life president (1971) whose early liberalism has increasingly given way to totalitarianism.

> on imperialism, page 138

Jatindranath Banerjea (1877-1930)
Indian nationalist
Religious leader.

> on God, page 108

Surendranath Banerjea (1848-1925)
Indian politician
Indian nationalist; founder of the Calcutta Indian Association (1876); editor of the *Bengali* (1879-1921); initiator of the Indian National Congress; member of the Central Legislature; eventually broke with the congress due to its extremist slant.

> on transience, page 280

Ban-Tinh (19th century)
Vietnamese poet

> on reality, page 228

Cao Ba-Quat (1809–1854)
Vietnamese poet
A leading poet of his era; a civil servant; executed for role in Le Duy-Cu's revolt against the Hue court.

on success, page 271
on worldliness, page 315

Imamu Amiri Baraka (b. 1934)
American writer
(Leroi Jones)
Poet, novelist, and dramatist. Advocated black self-awareness and nationalism; later, Maoism-Marxism.

on African Americans, page 7
on God, page 108
on hope, page 128
on political movements,
   page 208
on racism, page 224

José Celso Barbosa (1857–1921)
Puerto Rican politician
Member of Baldorioty's Autonomist Party (against Spanish colonial rule); pro-United States. After Spanish American War, became a senator; actively sought social legislation to aid the poor; most famous for drafting the Puerto Rican Bill of Rights.

on race, page 223
on wealth, page 302

Djuna Barnes (1892–1982)
American writer
Novelist, poet, illustrator, and dramatist; critically acclaimed, although not widely read. Began as magazine illustrator and reporter; switched to short stories and one-act plays, many of which she illustrated; most famous for *Nightwood.*

on vanity, page 292

Matsuo Basho (1644–1694)
Japanese poet
A master of haiku; his poems and commentary highly influential; wrote many poems about identifying self with the creative spirit of nature. Born to a samurai family, took the name *Basho* from a kind of native banana tree. Tried to alleviate anxiety and depression by studying Zen Buddhism, but never became a monk. Traveled extensively and wrote famous travel book *The Narrow Road to the Deep North.*

on aging, page 10
on brotherhood and sisterhood,
   page 29
on individuality, page 141
on learning and education,
   page 159
on nature, page 188
on water, page 301

Babikir Badri (1861–1954)
Sudanese scholar
Began as soldier in army of the Mahdi, an Islamic holy man. Became an educational pioneer in education for women; known for modern, progressive views.

on fate, page 91

Bei Dao (b. 1949)
Chinese poet
(Zhao Zhenkai)
Innovative poet best known for

applying cinematic montage techniques to his work.

on heroes, page 124
on resistance, page 236

Sherko Bekas (b. 1940)
Kurdish poet
Born in southern Kurdistan, Iraq; son of poet; first collection of poems published in 1968; work often revolves around need for Kurdish independence. Nationalist involved in Kurdish national liberation movement. Since 1987, has lived and worked in Sweden.

on freedom, page 100–101
on killing, page 148

Segundo Ruiz Belvis
(1829–1867)
Puerto Rican lawyer
Commissioner to the Spanish government in Madrid when Puerto Rico was under Spanish rule. Active abolitionist; in 1867 presented his famous *Informe* (*Report*), detailing and condemning slavery in Puerto Rico; exiled for his views.

on slavery, page 261

Sylvain Bemba (b. 1932)
Congolese writer
Noted short story writer, journalist.

on adaptability, page 4

Muhammed Ahmed Ben Bella
(b. 1916)
Algerian revolutionary and
  politician
A founder of the National Liberation Front (FLN), which fought long war for independence from the French, declared president after independence; deposed in 1965.

on prison, page 216

Ben Sira (2nd century B.C.E.)
Hebrew scholar and philosopher
(Simeon ben Jeshua ben Eleazer ben Sira)
Noted sage and aphorist; author of *The Wisdom of Ben Sira* (c. 180 B.C.E.; also called *Ecclesiasticus* and part of the Apocrypha); contains psalms as well as poems on daily life, conduct, and historical events.

on acceptance, page 1
on anger, page 16
on character, page 35
on charity, page 37
on children and childhood,
  page 37–38
on death, page 57
on friendship, page 103–104
on gifts and giving, page 107
on the golden rule, page 112
on humility, page 131
on learning and education,
  page 159
on listening, page 167
on old age, page 193
on pride, page 215
on respect, page 238
on understanding, page 288
on wealth, page 302
on wisdom, page 305

Mary McLeod Bethune
(1875–1955)
American educator
Founder of the Bethune-Cookman College, co-founder of the National

Association of Colored Women's Clubs.

on African Americans,
page 8
on love, page 169
on the soul, page 265

Yahya Kemal Beyath
(1884–1958)
Turkish poet
Neoclassical poet who imitated the masters of Ottoman and Persian traditions; best-known poems capture scenes of Istanbul.

on death, page 57

Bhartrihari (c. 7th century)
Indian Hindu poet and
philosopher
Famous for his three *satakas* ("centuries") of stanzas setting forth rules of conduct, love, and renunciation.

on aging, page 10
on fools and foolishness, page 99
on knowledge, page 148
on love, page 169
on money, page 184
on sacrifice, page 247
on women, page 308

Bhoja (995–1055)
Indian poet
King of Dharanagari, poet, and dramatist. In Hindu tradition, represents the ideal prince.

on death, page 58
on duty, page 75

Benazir Bhutto (b. 1953)
Pakistani politician
Daughter of former prime minister

Sulfikar Ali Bhutto; during exile in England, coleader of Pakistan People's Party, opposing General Zia ul-Haq; returned to Pakistan (1986) and spearheaded campaign for open elections; elected prime minister (1988); lost office, then was reelected prime minister (1993).

on bravery, page 28
on history, page 125
on religion, page 232

Chiam Nachman Bialik
(1873–1934)
Israeli writer
Considered a major contributor to the Hebrew literary renaissance.

on loneliness, page 167
on nature, page 188

Bian Zhilin (b. 1910)
Chinese poet
One of the early modernists in Chinese literature.

on loss, page 169

Steve Biko (1946–1977)
South African political activist
Founder and leader of the black consciousness movement; honorary president of the Black People's Convention (an umbrella group of over seventy black organizations). Highly popular, he was served with police orders restricting his movements, freedom of speech, and freedom of association; detained four times by police; died while in police custody, allegedly because of beatings by police.

on civil rights, page 40
on equality, page 80
on identity, page 135–136

on oppression, page 195
on pride, page 215
on racism, page 225

Bishr al Hafifi (767–842)
Persian Sufi ascetic
Al Hafifi means "the barefooted";
apparently Bishr took his appella-
tion seriously. Born near Merv
(Marw) in Iran; originally part of a
bandit gang. Converted to Sufism;
vowed to lead an exemplary, ascetic life and did so; sometimes
was near starvation; lived near
Baghdad.

on action, page 2

Nathan Bistritzki (b. 1895)
Israeli writer
Zionist writer who explored ten-
sions of the third *aliyah* (return to
Israel); followed a psychoanalytic
style popular in the period.

on friendship, page 104
on generations, page 106

Black Elk (1863–1950)
Oglala Sioux holy man
(Hehaka Sapa)
As a youth, participated in the Bat-
tle of Little Big Horn; later joined
Chief Sitting Bull in Canadian exile.
By 1930 was the last living human
who understood Sioux metaphys-
ics; his teachings were collected in
Black Elk Speaks and by anthro-
pologist J. E. Brown.

on death, page 58
on defeat, page 64–65
on nature, page 188
on symbols, page 274
on water, page 301

Black Hawk (1767–1838)
Sauk chief
(Makataimeshekiakiak)
Leader of the Sauks (Sacs) and
Foxes in the Black Hawk War of
1832, defending the Mississippi re-
gion from white settlers.

on brotherhood and sisterhood,
page 29
on defeat, page 65
on resistance, page 236

Elena Petrovna Blavatsky
(1831–1891)
American spiritualist
Russian-born founder of the Theo-
sophical Society; her supposed
psychic powers were debunked by
the Society for Psychical Research,
but she retained a large following,
including writer Annie Besant.

on laziness, page 154
on truth, page 283

Karen Blixen. *See* Isak Dineson

Louise Bogan (1897–1970)
American poet
Literary critic and winner of the
Bollingen Prize in poetry (1954).

on art and artists, page 18

Simón Bolívar (1783–1830)
South American revolutionary
leader called the Liberator of
South America
Venezuelan-born; raised an army in
1813 to fight the Spaniards; in
1821, became president of Colombia (consisting of modern-day
Venezuela, Colombia, and New
Granada); freed Ecuador (1822)
and Peru (1824); named perpetual

protector of upper Peru, which was renamed Bolivia; retired from office in 1830 after facing dissension in 1829, when Venezuela separated from Colombia.

on democracy, page 66
on failure, page 87
on freedom, page 101
on government, page 114
on liberty, page 161
on nature, page 188
on resistance, page 236
on revolution, page 239
on slavery, page 261
on war, page 297

Maria-Luisa Bombal
(1910–1980)
Chilean writer
Novelist, short story writer, and essayist; upon publication of first novel, *La ultima niebla* (*The final mist*), was acknowledged as one of the leading members of the avant-garde literary movement; wrote numerous other novels, essays, and short stories. Work shows conservative feminist ideology prevalent among upper-class Latin Americans in the 1930s and 1940s; later work explores female archetypes.

on happiness, page 121

Jorge Luis Borges (1899–1986)
Argentinian writer
Poet and short story writer well known for fantasy elements in his works; first book of poems, *Fervor de Buenos Aires;* followed this with numerous collections of poetry and short stories; became director of the National Library (1955) after going blind; one of most famous works is *Labyrinths;*

had enormous impact on world literature, as well as Latin American literature.

on critics and criticism, page 55
on desire, page 69
on enemies, page 77
on experience, page 85
on graves and graveyards, page 117
on infinity, page 141
on life, page 163
on reality, page 228
on the self, page 252
on self-identity, page 256
on time, page 277
on victory, page 293
on writers and writing, page 317

Subhas Chandra Bose
(1897–1945)
Indian nationalist leader
Campaigned actively for complete Indian independence; president of the All-India Congress (1938); an Axis supporter in World War II, became commander-in-chief of the Japanese-backed Indian National Army; believed killed in Formosa.

on justice, page 145
on politics, page 209
on revolution, page 239

Boudicca (1st century)
British warrior and queen
(Boadicea)
Led revolt of the Iceni against Roman colonies Camulodunum (Colchester), Londinium (London), and Verulamium (St. Albans); eventually was defeated by Roman governor in Britain, Suetonius Paulinus, in the Midlands; was said to have

committed suicide by taking poison, rather than surrendering.

on resistance, page 236

Habib ibn Ali Bourguiba
(b. 1903)
Tunisian politician
Tunisian nationalist; became first prime minister of Tunisia; president (1957); president for life (1975); faced growing opposition from Muslim fundamentalists; deposed by his prime minister in 1987.

on leadership and leaders,
page 156
on respect, page 238

Margaret Bourke-White
(1906-1971)
American photographer and writer
Journalist; noted as one of the first female war correspondents.

on the past, page 198

Elizabeth Bowen (1899-1973)
Irish writer
(née Dorothea Cole)
Novelist, short story writer, and literary critic; known for exploring moral dilemmas in her work; wrote over seventy short stories, ten novels, and numerous nonfiction works.

on art and artists, page 18
on children and childhood,
page 38
on despair, page 70
on experience, page 86
on individuality, page 141
on madness, page 176
on women, page 308

Brahmananda (1863-1922)
Hindu Indian philosopher
Disciple and transmitter of teachings of Sri Ramakrishna.

on paradox, page 197

Edward Kamau Brathwaite
(b. 1930)
Barbadian poet
Famed epic poet; focus on the black diaspora; best known for a trilogy, *The Arrivants*, about the privations of black people transported from Africa to the West Indies; one of the best-known Caribbean writers.

on writers and writing,
page 317

Osborne Henry Kwesi Brew
(b. 1928)
Ghanaian diplomat and poet
Known for poetry emphasizing the value of the individual.

on change, page 34

Fanny Brice (1891-1951)
American comedian and singer
One of the first famous female comics; performed in New York's popular Yiddish theater; became nationally known as star of Ziegfeld Follies and of various films.

on honesty, page 127

Gwendolyn Brooks (b. 1917)
American writer
Poet and novelist known for her strong voice and social observation; much of work centers around the African American experience in America; as such, considered to

have foreshadowed later African American writers' works (such as Imamu Amiri Baraka's); won Pulitzer Prize for *Annie Allen*, her second book of poems; well known for her novel *Maud Martha*.

on life, page 163

Charlotte Brontë (1816–1855)
English writer
Sister of writers Anne and Emily Brontë; after boarding-school and home studies, worked as governess and teacher; returned home in 1845; orchestrated publication of book of poetry with sisters; began writing intensively; *Jane Eyre* published in 1847 to immediate success; married father's curate in 1854; died the next year during pregnancy.

on caution, page 33

Elizabeth Barrett Browning
(1806–1861)
English poet
Wife of poet Robert Browning; childhood marked by intellectual precociousness; read Homer in original at age 10, wrote epic on Battle of Marathon at age 14; first published work was *Essay on Mind, and Other Poems* at age 19. At age 15 became semi-invalid after spinal injury. Married poet Robert Browning in 1846; traveled to Italy; formed literary circle; published numerous poems and collections; most famous works include *Sonnets from the Portuguese* and *Aurora Leigh*.

on art and artists, page 18

on beauty, page 22
on blessings, page 26
on books and reading, page 27
on conformity, page 47
on decisions, page 63
on freedom, page 101
on genius, page 106
on grieving, page 119
on history, page 125
on love, page 170
on men and women, page 180
on women, page 308

Pearl S. Buck (1892–1973)
American writer
Raised in China, returned to China in adulthood to work as a missionary; 1938 winner of Nobel Prize in literature for novel *The Good Earth*, substantially based on her knowledge of China.

on children and childhood,
  page 38
on freedom, page 101
on work, page 312

Buddha (c. 563–483 B.C.E.)
Founder of Buddhism
(Prince Siddhartha Gautama)
Buddha means "The Enlightened One"; son of a prince in a region north of Benares, forsook courtly life at age 30 for ascetic life; after years of self-mortification, received enlightenment, according to tradition, under a bodhi tree in Bihar; for the next forty years he taught what he had learned, that existence is suffering, and that enlightenment comes from following path of contemplation and recognizing the underlying unity of life.

on belief, page 24–25
on eternity, page 81

on good and evil,
  page 112–113
on humanity, page 130
on last words, page 152
on the mind, page 183
on self-discipline, page 254
on travel, page 281
on understanding, page 288

Buddhaghosa (c. 5th century)
Indian Buddhist scholar
Called "Voice of the Buddha"; well
known for *Visuddhimagga* (*The
Path of Purity*), a collection of
Buddhist doctrines.

on suffering, page 273

Yehuda Burla (1886–1969)
Israeli writer
Among the first modern novelists
of the Sephardim (Jews of Middle
Eastern background), about whom
he wrote.

on fate, page 91
on love, page 170

**Linden Forbes Sampson
Burnham** (1926–1985)
Guyanese politician
Cofounded the Marxist-Leninist
People's Progressive Party (PPP)
(1949) and the more moderate socialist People's National Congress
(1957). Prime minister of Guyana
(1964); led Guyana to independence (1966); became president
through elections marked by wide-
spread complaints of rigging (1968
and 1973); became executive president under a new constitution
(1980); died while in office.

on progress, page 217

Taniguchi Buson (1715–1783)
Japanese painter and poet
(Yosa Buson)
Paintings followed the Naga
school; his poetry, the school of
haiku master Basho.

on grieving, page 119
on nature, page 188

Abu'l-Fath al-Busti (d. 1009)
Persian poet
Poet of the Ghaznawi period; well-
known for Arabic verse and prose
composition, especially his skillful
word-play; in law, followed Shafi'
school; abducted by Subuktigin, father of Sultan Mahmud; became
secretary to Sultan Mahmud; died
in exile in Bukhara. Most famous
works still recited by professional
storytellers.

on anger, page 16
on fate, page 91
on wealth, page 302

C

George Cable Price (b. 1919)
Belizean politician
Head of the People's United Party;
prime minister in 1981 and 1989.

on cooperation, page 51
on progress, page 217

Amilcar Cabral (1924–1973)
Guinea-Bissauan nationalist
Considered in the 1960s and 1970s
a leading African revolutionary the-
oretician; head of the Guinea-
Bissauan nationalist movement
(PAIGC); led Guinea-Bissau to inde-

pendence from the Portuguese; later assassinated by rebels purportedly backed by the Portuguese.

> on patriotism and nationalism, page 199-200
>
> on progress, page 217-218

Teresa Calderon (b. 1955)
Chilean poet
Common themes include tension between past and future, and unsolvable problems in human relationships; received prize in Gabriela Mistral poetry competition (1982).

> on meaning, page 178
>
> on truth, page 283

Mrs. Patrick Campbell (1865-1940)
English actress
(née Beatrice Stella Tanner)
London and Paris educated; made first stage appearance in Liverpool (1888); became famous for variety of roles; role of Eliza Doolittle in *Pygmalion* written for her by George Bernard Shaw; first appeared as Eliza in 1914; known for correspondence with Shaw.

> on sex, page 259

Cannonchet (c. 1630-1676)
Narragansett chief
Leader during King Philip's War of 1675-1676 against white settlement; defeated, but escaped to attack again; finally captured, sentenced to death, shot; his head was sent to Hartford, Connecticut, as a trophy.

> on death, page 58

Edip Cansever (1928-1986)
Turkish poet
One of modern Turkey's leading poets; recipient of Turkish Language Society Poetry Prize.

> on love, page 170

Ernest Cardenal (20th century)
Nicaraguan poet
Involved in revolutionary politics; became monk, then ordained priest; set up small religious community on remote island, Lake Nicaragua; famous works include *Hora*, *Epigrams*; poetry covers wide range, from love poems to political satire.

> on revolution, page 239

Stokely Carmichael (b. 1941)
(Kwame Toure)
American political activist
Trinidad-born; joined civil rights movement as college student; became field organizer and, later, chair for Student Nonviolent Coordinating Committee (SNCC) (1966-1967). Launched black power movement (1966), explained in *Black Power: The Politics of Liberation in America* (1967; with Charles Hamilton); advocated armed revolution; initially worked with Black Panthers, but broke from party in 1969; moved to Guinea (1969), worked for Pan-Africa movement, and changed name.

> on change, page 34
>
> on violence, page 294

Rafael Carrera (1814-1865)
Guatemalan politician
Noted for populist views; sup-

ported colonial rule, but strongly defended the indigenous community.

on revolution, page 240

Jorge Carrera Andrade
(b. 1903)
Ecuadoran writer
Poet, essayist, and diplomat. Served in consular service in Japan and China; representative to UNESCO. Considered one of Ecuador's premier contemporary poets; known for mastery of metaphor.

on loss, page 169

Rachel Carson (1907–1964)
American naturalist and writer
Famous for nonfiction works *The Sea Around Us*, about the danger of marine pollution, and *Silent Spring*, about the danger of pesticides; works were largely responsible for increasing concern about pollution and resulting legislation controlling it.

on nature, page 188–189

Martin Carter (b. 1927)
Guyanan writer and diplomat
Known as the major voice of radicalism in Caribbean poetry; born in Georgetown, British Guiana (now Guyana); educated at Queen's College; worked as clerk in civil service for four years; forced to resign due to political activities; later became United Nations representative for Guyana.

on hope, page 128
on revolution, page 240
on striving, page 270

Rosalynn Smith Carter
(b. 1927)
American First Lady and
 humanitarian
Married to President Jimmy Carter; works with civil rights and humanitarian organizations, such as Habitat for Humanity.

on goals, page 107

Mary Cassatt (1844–1926)
American artist
Attended Pennsylvania Academy of Fine Arts, but left to study in Paris; exhibited in Paris under name May Stevenson (1872–1873); invited by Degas to join impressionists (1877); left impressionists with Degas in 1882; work became more formal; continued to work until developed cataracts in both eyes (1912).

on art and artists, page 18
on travel, page 281–282

Fidel Castro (b. 1927)
Cuban revolutionary and political
 leader
Led uprising against Cuban President Batista; named prime minister in 1959; established Marxist-Leninist program to govern Cuba; replaced U.S. economic dominance of Cuba with dependence on the Soviet Union and other communist countries; became president of the nonaligned countries' movement in 1979; with fall of Soviet Union, his government weakened.

on contradictions, page 50
on revolution, page 240

Carrie Chapman Catt
(1859-1947)
American suffragist
Journalist; president of National Woman Suffrage Association (1900-1904 and 1915-1947); founded League of Women Voters (1919).

> on causes, page 33
> on political movements,
>   page 208

Asaf Halet Celebi (1907-1958)
Turkish poet
Famous for iconoclastic surreal poetry; an innovator in modern Turkish literature.

> on poetry and poets, page 205

Aime Cesair (b. 1913)
Martiniquen writer
Poet and playwright; one of most famous writers in Third World; involved in anticolonialist movement.

> on culture, page 55-56

Cetsahwayo (19th century)
Zulu chief

> on imperialism, page 138

Chandrasekhara Bharati Swamigal (d. 1954)
Hindu sage
(Sankaracharya of Srngeri)
Vedanta philosopher and teacher; member of school of Sankaran Advaita.

> on ignorance, page 136

Coco Chanel (1883-1971)
French designer
Revolutionized women's fashions by dispensing with corsets and restrictive cuts, and by introducing such breakthroughs as the chemise dress and the collarless cardigan jacket; known also for "little black dresses," costume jewelry, and perfumes, including Chanel No. 5.

> on goals, page 108
> on luxury, page 175
> on time, page 277
> on youth, page 321

Chang Ch'ao (c. 1676)
Chinese writer

> on leisure, page 161

Chang Tsai (1021-1077)
Chinese philosopher
Neo-Confucianist philosopher; writer of the *Western Inscription*, a key writing of Sung dynasty China; propounds universal (in addition to filial) love to the central concept of Ren (Jen); advocated study of the physical sciences.

> on brotherhood and sisterhood,
>   page 29
> on Confucianism, page 48
> on the universe, page 290

Chao Meng-fu (1254-1322)
Chinese painter
President of the Han-lin Academy (Chinese body of scholars); noted for scholarship and calligraphy. His wife, the Lady Kwan (Guan), was also a distinguished painter.

> on adaptability, page 4

Madame Celeste Chateaubriand
(c. 19th century)
French salonist
> on hypocrisy, page 134

Gadadhar Chattonpadhyaya.
See Ramakrishna

Cesar Chavez (1927–1993)
American labor rights activist
National Farm Workers Association head; worked on behalf of migrant farm workers; began by helping Mexican Americans with immigration authorities, welfare boards and police; organized grape strike from 1965 to 1970; advocated nonviolence; often called "the Messiah of the Mexican American civil rights movement."
> on human rights, page 130

Andree Chedid (b. 1920)
Egyptian writer
Poet, novelist, and short story writer; lives in France; named to French Legion of Honor for her writing.
> on art and artists, page 18
> on love, page 170
> on self-identity, page 256

Cheng Yi (1033–1108)
Chinese scholar
Founded School of Law and Principles, which followed Confucianist and rationalist precepts.
> on evil, page 83
> on perseverance, page 202
> on wisdom, page 305

Chi K'ang (223–262)
Chinese poet
(Qigong)
Taoist poet.
> on regrets, page 231

Chiang Kai-shek (1887–1975)
Chinese military and political leader
Anti-Communist Chinese nationalist leader; commander of Kuomintang army (1926); president of Republic of China (1928–1931); head of the executive branch (1935–1945). When Kuomintang fell after Communist advances, withdrew to Formosa (now Taiwan) and held title of president of the Republic of China.
> on revolution, page 240
> on sacrifice, page 247
> on tyranny and tyrants,
>   page 287

Madame Chiang Kai-shek
(b. 1901)
Chinese politician
(Mayling Soong)
Sociologist, reformer, and educator; married to Chinese nationalist leader Chiang Kai-shek. Active politician; strongly affected U.S. policy on China in the 1940s and 1950s. Wrote sociological works on China.
> on government, page 114
> on learning and education,
>   page 159

Ch'ien Chung-shu (b. 1910)
Chinese writer
Novelist; short story writer, essayist; born in Wunsi, Kiangsu province; graduated Beijing University

(1933); wed writer Yang Ciang; taught in many universities; vice president of the Academy of Social Sciences.

on marriage, page 176

Chin 'gak (1178–1234)
Korean poet and official
Served as national preceptor in Korean government.

on Buddhism, page 31

Chingiz (Genghis) Khan
(c. 1162–1227)
Mongol conqueror
One of the greatest conquerors in world history; conquered China, Korea, and other areas in Asia; eventually governed area over four thousand miles across.

on action, page 2
on self-description, page 254
on victory, page 293

Albert Chinualmogo. *See* Chinua Achebe

Chinweizu (20th century)
Nigerian writer and critic
Known for his poetry, critical essays, and work compiling African writers; associate professor at San Jose State University in the 70s; has written number of works including the historical study, *The West and the Rest of Us.*

on racism, page 225

Shirley Chisholm (b. 1924)
American politician
Born in Brooklyn; first African American woman elected to Congress; received master's degree in child education from Columbia University; ran nursery school; directed child-care centers; elected to New York State Assembly; elected to U.S. House of Representatives (1968); unsuccessfully campaigned for Democratic nomination for president (1972); known for legislative positions on women's rights, civil rights, and improvement of inner-city conditions.

on duty, page 75
on ethics and morality,
  page 82
on women, page 308

Chong Ch'ol (1537–1594)
Korean poet and government
  official
Governor of Kangwon province; second state counselor under King Sonjo; suffered many exiles during a particularly turbulent career as a government servant; as poet, known for moral verses and ones on such topics as wine, music and love.

on sorrow, page 265

Cho'oe Ch'i-won (c. 857)
Korean poet and politician
Considered the most renowned scholar, politician, and poet of Silla.

on departures, page 68
on home, page 126
on homesickness, page 127

Chou Shu-jen. *See* Lu Xen

Chou-Tun-I (1017–1073)
Chinese official and scholar
Known as Philosopher Chou,

ranked among the top two in literary repute among Sung dynasty philosophers; known as leader of a brilliant set of followers.

>on moderation, page 183
>on wisdom, page 306

Driss Chraibi (b. 1926)
Moroccan writer
Literary innovator; best-known member of the "Generation of 54" (group of young novelists who revolutionized Moroccan literature); first novel, *Le Passe Simple*, was banned in Morocco until 1977, but influence was widely felt. Controversial for refusal to blame problems of contemporary Morocco on colonialism alone.

>on imperialism, page 138
>on the land, page 151
>on resistance, page 236

Agatha Christie (1891-1976)
English writer
Began publishing detective stories in 1920; first novel, *The Mysterious Affair at Styles* immediately successful; joined second husband, archeologist Max Mallowan, on archeological excavations; wrote over seventy novels, plus short stories and plays; known for characters such as Hercule Poirot and Miss Marple.

>on beginnings, page 23
>on genius, page 106-107
>on habit, page 121

Chuang-tzu (c. 369-286 B.C.E.)
Chinese Taoist philosopher
Lived hermit's life, yet famous for his ideas; leading exponent of Taoism; reportedly was offered the prime ministership by the King of Wei, but turned it down, saying: "I prefer the enjoyment of my own free will."

>on contentment, page 49-50
>on creation, page 53
>on death, page 58
>on dreams, page 73
>on familiarity, page 89
>on fate, page 91-92
>on fools and foolishness, page 99
>on happiness, page 121
>on ideals, page 135
>on knowledge, page 148
>on perfection, page 201
>on reality, page 228-229
>on Taoism, page 275
>on understanding, page 288
>on wisdom, page 306
>on work, page 312

Chu Hsi (1130-1200)
Chinese philosopher
Leading Neo-Confucian philosopher and official; key formulator of Neo-Confucian theory; as such, considered the most notable philosopher of his time and largely responsible for preserving the Confucian tradition in the face of the highly popular Buddhist and Taoist teachings; known for his commentaries on the Four Books (the major Confucian texts).

>on anger, page 16

Chu Ui-sik (1675-1720)
Korean poet
Poet known for his "sijo," the most popular and elastic form of Korean poetry.

>on change, page 34

Ch'u Yuan (c. 300 B.C.E.)
Chinese writer
Nobleman and poet; minister to King Huai of Chu dynasty; ultimately banished; killed himself in exile. Attributed author of *Li Sao* (*Encountering Sorrow*), although modern scholars have questioned this.

on fate, page 91

Chung-ch'ang T'ung (c. 179-219)
Chinese philosopher
Government official and Confucian philosopher; author of the *Chang Yang*, a critical study of the political situation during the late Han dynasty, along with proposed changes to make a better society.

on the self, page 252
on Taoism, page 275
on the universe, page 290
on worldliness, page 315

Cassius Clay. *See* Muhammad Ali

Eldridge Cleaver (b. 1935)
American civil rights activist
Leader of the Black Panther movement. Lived in Algeria in exile; ultimately returned to United States and became advocate of capitalism.

on the Americas, page 13
on enemies, page 77
on hate, page 122
on problems, page 216

Colette (1873-1954)
French writer
Novelist and memoirist; famous for bohemian life; first books, the *Claudine* series, published under name of her husband, Willy; after 1906 divorce, worked in acting troupes, as mime and music hall dancer; gained notoriety for lesbian affair; famous for works on love, nature, and animals, and ability to capture emotions of young girls and aging women; most famous works include *Cheri* and *Gigi*.

on acting and actors, page 1
on familiarity, page 89
on happiness, page 121
on memory, page 179
on mothers and motherhood, page 185
on speech, page 266

Ivy Compton-Burnett (1892-1969)
English writer
Had difficult childhood—governess to eleven siblings, two brothers (including favorite) died, two youngest sisters committed suicide; this background influenced work, marked by themes of parental tyranny, misery, and greed.

on men and women, page 180

Confucius (551-479 B.C.E.)
Chinese philosopher and founder of Confucianism
(K'ung Fu Tzu)
Born of poor but aristocratic parents; joined Chinese civil service and rose to rank of minister in Chinese state of Lu; jealousy of peers caused breach with ruler, left service and became wandering sage. Returned to Lu in 485 and devoted remaining years to teaching; after his death, disciples collected his

writings but probably made extensive changes. Basic tenets include promotion of moral (versus religious) values—especially benevolence (*jen,* or *ren*), reciprocity (*shu*) and filial piety (*hsiao*, or *xiao*)—and emphasis on social control and obligation to society. Until recently, Confucianism was China's state religion; it is still a powerful force, especially among Chinese living overseas.

on advice, page 6
on boldness, page 26
on caution, page 33
on character, page 35
on Confucianism, page 48
on cowardice, page 52
on death, page 59
on emotions, page 77
on error, page 81
on ethics and morality, page 82
on fault, page 93
on the golden rule, page 112
on government, page 114-115
on happiness, page 121
on ignorance, page 136
on knowledge, page 149
on language, page 152
on learning and education,
 page 159
on luck, page 175
on perseverance, page 202
on promises, page 219
on respect, page 238
on reward, page 245
on scholars, page 249
on self-description, page 254
on truth, page 284
on virtue, page 295
on war, page 297
on wealth, page 302-303
on will, page 304
on words, page 311

Rafael Cordero y Molina
(1790-1868)
Puerto Rican educator
Worked to end educational discrimination, especially based on race and monetary status; founded an open-admissions school, which he supported partly by making shoes; called El Maestro (Teacher).

on learning and education,
 page 159
on teaching, page 276
on writers and writing,
 page 317

Julio Cortazar (1914-1984)
Argentinian writer
One of the best-known Spanish-American writers outside of Spanish-speaking world; most famous works include *Hopscotch* and "Blow-Up" (from *Blow-Up and Other Stories*), both made into films.

on heaven, page 123
on old age, page 193

Crazy Horse (1842-1877)
Oglala Sioux chief
(Tashonka Yotanka)
Chief of the Oglala tribe of Sioux; a principal leader of the 1876-1877 Sioux uprising, in which he led the Sioux in the Battle of Little Bighorn, defeating U.S. General Custer. Surrendered in 1877; was killed resisting imprisonment.

on the land, page 152
on war, page 297

Crowfoot (c. 1836-1890)
Blackfoot chief
(Isapo-Muxika)
Most influential chief of the Black-

foot (Native American) confederacy; noted peacemaker in tribal disputes.

on death, page 59

Alexander Crummell
(1819–1898)
American minister and writer
Essayist; Episcopal minister; leading abolitionist; part of the "Back to Africa" movement of 1850s; advocated black colonialism.

on strength, page 270
on success, page 271

Pablo Antonio Cuadra (b. 1912)
Nicaraguan poet
Poet, journalist, and editor; early member of "Vangardia," Nicaraguan literary movement; poetry focuses on the nation and its people.

on censorship, page 34
on humanity, page 131
on revolution, page 240
on truth, page 284

Marie Curie (1867–1934)
French scientist
Polish-born; isolated radium and polonium; joint winner of Nobel Prize for physics (1903); winner of Nobel Prize for chemistry (1911); married to scientist Pierre Curie.

on fear, page 93
on goals, page 108
on nature, page 189
on progress, page 218

Cuu-Chi (19th century)
Vietnamese poet

on truth, page 284
on understanding, page 288

D

Fazil Husnu Daglarca (b. 1914)
Turkish poet
Called Turkey's leading living poet; best known for socially conscious poetry; winner of Golden Wreath, Poet of the Year at Rotterdam International Gathering (1977).

on death, page 59
on hunger, page 133
on war, page 297–298

Dalai Lama (b. 1935)
Tibetan spiritual and political leader
(Tenzin Gyatso)
Leader of Tibetan Buddhism; temporal head of Tibet. As young leader, sought to compromise with China's Mao Zedong, then resisted increasing Chinese encroachment; led his government into exile in India during Chinese invasion. Seeks nonviolent solution to Chinese control; strong proponent for self-government of Tibet and for nonviolence in world disputes. Winner of Nobel Prize for peace (1989).

on cooperation, page 51
on death, page 59
on forgiveness, page 100
on power, page 211
on violence, page 294

Dang Dung (18th century)
Vietnamese patriot
Supported cause of pretender to the throne Tran Quy Khoang; when captured, drowned himself to avoid imprisonment by the Chi-

nese; left behind one poem, "Regrets."

on luck, page 175

on regrets, page 231

Dang Tran Con (1710–1745)
Vietnamese poet
One of Vietnam's most popular traditional poets, especially for "Chin phu ngam khuc" ("Tale of the Soldier's Wife") written in classical Chinese.

on war, page 298

Mahmoud Darwish (b. 1942)
Palestinian poet
Born in al-Barweh; worked as journalist in Haifa; left Israel in 1971 for Lebanon; in 1982, left for Paris, where he edits the magazine *Al Karmal*.

on poetry and poets, page 205
on understanding, page 289

Narendeanath Datta. *See*
Vivekananda

Bette Davis (1908–1989)
American actor
Nominated ten times for an Academy Award; won for *Dangerous* (1935) and *Jezebel* (1938).

on acting and actors, page 1

Frank Marshall Davis (b. 1905)
American writer
Poet and journalist; helped start *Atlanta Daily World* (1931); worked with the Associated Negro Press; best known for free-verse poems, many with socially minded themes.

on ideas, page 135

Moshe Dayan (1915–1981)
Israeli military and political leader
Founder of Haganah underground militia; served in British Army in World War II; held variety of government posts, including member of the Knesset, minister of agriculture, minister of defense, and foreign minister. Resigned in protest of Begin administration's stance regarding negotiations for Palestinian autonomy in Israeli-occupied West Bank and Gaza Strip.

on knowledge, page 149

Marie-Françoise de Beauveau (1711–1786)
French courtier
(Marquise of Boufflers)
Wrote poetry, epigrams, and letters. Noted for her sophistication. As mistress of the exiled Polish king Stanislas, his minister of state, and his minister of finance simultaneously, was called Dame de Volupté (Lady of Pleasure).

on envy and jealousy, page 79

Simone de Beauvoir (1908–1986)
French writer and philosopher
Novelist and essayist; existentialist and feminist; known for groundbreaking study of women's status, *The Second Sex*, and for relationship with philosopher Jean Paul Sartre.

on feminism, page 95
on freedom, page 101
on genius, page 107
on justice, page 145
on marriage, page 176
on middle age, page 182
on old age, page 193

on oppression, page 195
on relationships, page 232
on science and technology,
page 250
on women, page 308
on writers and writing,
page 317

Beatriz de Dia (c. 1140–1189)
Provençal troubadour
Most famous female troubadour;
little known of her life beyond a
few remaining songs that she apparently wrote.

on love, page 170

Juana Ines de la Cruz
(1651–1695)
Mexican nun and poet
One of the first major literary figures in the New World; called the
Tenth Muse and the Mexican Nun.

on fame, page 88
on gifts and giving, page 107
on love, page 170
on slavery, page 261
on vanity, page 292

Bernardo De Montegudo
(1785–1825)
Latin American political leader
Protégé of José de San Martín, who
helped win independence for Argentina, Chile, and Peru; propagandist for Pan-Americanism.

on the Americas, page 13

Marquise de Pompadour
(1721–1746)
French salonist
Mistress of Louis XV of France; patron of the arts.

on consequences, page 49

Noemia de Sousa (b. 1927)
Mozambiquen poet
(pseudonym Vera Micaia)
Poet of the Negritude movement;
currently writing in France.

on ancestors and ancestry,
page 15

Madame de Staël (1766–1817)
French writer
(Anne Maria Louis Germaine
Necker, Baroness de Staël-
Holstein)
Novelist and literary critic; known
for her salons, which attracted intelligentsia of the period.

on afterlife, page 9
on character, page 35–36
on death, page 59
on ethics and morality, page 82
on genius, page 107
on happiness, page 121
on intellectuals, page 142
on life, page 163
on love, page 170
on men and women,
page 180–181
on the past, page 198
on politics, page 209

Deng Xiaoping (b. 1904)
(Teng Hsiao-peng)
Chinese political leader and
secretary-general of the
Communist Party
Began as early Communist revolutionary; quickly rose to high positions. Long associated with the
right wing, or more pragmatic faction of the Communist Party; periodically suffered from this
association. During the Chinese
Cultural Revolution (1966–1969),
branded as a counterrevolutionary

and sentenced to internal exile; rescued by patron Zhou En-lai. After Zhou and Mao died, became de facto leader of China; promoted extensive economic liberalization and limited political reform; most recently, supported crackdown on democratic rights movements. Currently in semiretirement, but still widely acknowledged as "power behind the throne."

on ideology, page 137

Jean Hackques Dessalines

(1749–1806)

Haitian revolutionary and ruler

Noted for boldness during Haitian revolt against the French, at one point fighting his way out from a 12,000-troop French siege with only six hundred men. As emperor, became a tyrannical ruler; assassinated by one of his officers.

on freedom, page 101

Marie Anne de Vichy-Chamrond (1697–1780)

French socialite

on faith, page 87
on love, page 170

Bernadette Devlin. *See* Bernadette D. McAliskey

Porfirio Díaz (1830–1915)

Mexican soldier and politician

Hero of the War of Reform and the war against the French; president of Mexico (1877–1880 and 1884–1911); fell from power during Mexican revolution (1911).

on sacrifice, page 247

Gustavo Díaz Ordaz

(1911–1979)

Mexican politician

Held variety of positions, including president (1964–1970).

on moderation, page 184

Mohammed Dib (b. 1920)

Algerian writer

Poet, short story writer, and playwright; founded French-language Algerian literature in 1950s; during World War II worked as interpreter for Allied Forces in North Africa; published first novel *La Grand Maison* (1952); sided with nationalist forces in Algerian War of Independence; was deposed and exiled to France (1959); opted for life of solitude.

on books and reading, page 27
on dignity, page 71
on humanity, page 131
on life, page 163
on nature, page 189
on revolution, page 240
on wilderness, page 304

Dibil (d. 872)

Arab poet

Arab leader of "New Poets," who revolted against classical Arab poetry, which centered on nomadic desert life; used rich classical allusions; wrote short, often obscene poems; genius was widely recognized.

on poetry and poets, page 205

Emily Dickinson (1830–1886)

American poet

Led a secluded life; all but unpublished during her lifetime; poetry noted for spare, insightful, sometimes mystical nature.

on ancestors and ancestry,
   page 15
on beauty, page 22
on compassion, page 44
on death, page 59
on despair, page 70
on faith, page 87–88
on friendship, page 104
on happiness, page 121
on hope, page 128
on human nature, page 129
on nonconformity, page 190
on prayer, page 213
on success, page 271
on truth, page 284
on wealth, page 303

Joan Didion (b. 1935)
American writer
Journalist, screenwriter, essayist, and novelist; novels known for laconic style and explorations of modern American psyche; most famous works include novels *Play It As It Lays* and *The White Album*, and essay collection *Slouching towards Bethlehem*; married to writer John Gregory Dunne.

on dreams, page 73
on writers and writing,
   page 318

Doan Thi Diem (c. 1705)
Vietnamese poet
Well known in Vietnam for adaptations of classical Chinese poetry into Vietnamese.

on farewells, page 90

Marlene Dietrich (1901–1992)
American actor
German-born; film actress and cab-

aret performer; best known for films directed by Josef Von Sternberg, such as *Morocco, Blond Venus*, and *The Devil Is a Woman*.

on love, page 170

Annie Dillard (b. 1945)
American writer
Poet and novelist; winner of 1975 Pulitzer Prize.

on seeing, page 251–252
on survival, page 274
on the universe, page 290

Abu al'Fadl Ja'far al-Dimishqi
(c. 9th century)
Arabic writer
Prose writer; known for his business book *The Beauties of Commerce*.

on business, page 31–32

Farrid al-Din. *See* Attar

Jalil al-Din. *See* Rumi

Isak Dinesen (1885–1962)
Danish writer
(Karen Blixen)
Novelist, short story writer, and essayist. For many years, lived in East Africa (now Kenya), where she gained much inspiration, expressed most notably in book *Out of Africa*.

on achievement, page 1
on the future, page 105
on men and women, page 181

Ding Ling (c. 1904–1986)
Chinese writer
Novelist and short story writer; one of China's most influential

and controversial writers. Political activist; as reform-minded writer, was first forced into exile by right-wing Kuomintang (Nationalist) government; later, was target of left-wing Communist government in antirightist campaign of 1957. Stopped writing for publication; later, resumed career after being rehabilitated by government in 1979.

on advice, page 6
on enemies, page 77
on feminism, page 95
on forgiveness, page 100
on happiness, page 122
on love, page 170
on sorrow, page 265
on writers and writing,
    page 318

Cheikh Anta Diop (b. 1923)
Senegalese scholar
Leading African intellectual; known for his work in African history and culture; one of the leaders of the Negritude Movement; currently a director of the research department of IFAN (Institut Fondamental de l'Afrique Noir) in Dakar.

on language, page 153

Dogen (1200-1253)
Japanese Zen monk
Master of the Soto Zen school of Japanese Buddhism; advocated religion of practical simplicity, absolute faith, and individual spiritual awakening.

on reality, page 229
on Zen, page 322

Takako Doi (b. 1928)
Japanese politician
Japanese Socialist Party leader; one of Japan's leading female politicians; studied law and had post at Dashisha University; entered House of Representatives (1969); deputy leader of Socialist Party (1983-1986); became leader of party in 1986.

on politics, page 209

Frederick Douglass (1817-1895)
American abolitionist
Born into slavery, escaped, changed his name, and moved to Massachusetts, where became an agent for Massachusetts Anti-Slavery Society; known for stirring, eloquent speeches. Later, journalist and U.S. diplomat.

on African Americans, page 8
on civil rights, page 40
on equality, page 80
on freedom, page 101
on human rights, page 130
on power, page 211
on race, page 223
on racism, page 225
on sacrifice, page 247
on slavery, page 262
on success, page 271
on truth, page 284
on tyranny and tyrants,
    page 287
on victory, page 293

W. E. B. Du Bois (1868-1963)
American writer and educator
(William Edward Burghardt
Du Bois)
Born in Massachusetts; received doctorate from Harvard; became

professor of economics and history at Atlanta University (1897–1910); cofounder of National Association for the Advancement of Colored People (1909); editor of NAACP magazine, *Crisis* (1910–34). Known for numerous works, many centering on issues of slavery, civil rights, and problems facing African Americans; most famous include *The Souls of Black Folk*, *The Gift of Black Folk*, *Color and Democracy*; lectured extensively. In later years, advocated radical black movement; joined the Communist party (1961); moved to Ghana and became naturalized citizen shortly before his death.

on African Americans, page 8
on the Americas, page 13
on boldness, page 26–27
on business, page 32
on civil rights, page 40
on democracy, page 66
on farewells, page 90
on freedom, page 101
on liberty, page 161
on life, page 163
on oppression, page 195
on prejudice, page 214
on pride, page 215
on promises, page 219
on race, page 223
on racism, page 225
on reason, page 230
on slavery, page 262
on spirit, page 268
on understanding, page 289
on work, page 312–313

Amandine Aurore Lucile Dudevant. *See* George Sand

Daphne du Maurier

(1907–1989)
British writer
Novelist and short story writer; daughter of actor Gerald du Maurier. Wrote chiefly romantic suspense and mystery; noted for gothic style; best-known works include *Rebecca*, *Jamaica Inn*, and *My Cousin Rachel*.

on writers and writing, page 318

Rachel Blau DuPlessis

(20th century)
American writer
Critic and professor; professor of English at Temple University.

on nonconformity, page 191

Paul Laurence Dunbar

(1872–1906)
American poet
Son of former slaves; best known for lyrical poetry; worked as elevator operator until his genius was recognized (his poetry was submitted sub rosa to a literary meeting); promising career was cut short by depression and alcoholism; most famous works were *Lyrics of a Lowly Life* and *The Sport of Gods*.

on death, page 59–60
on life, page 163
on money, page 184
on slavery, page 262
on writers and writing, page 318

Isadora Duncan (1878–1927)

American dancer
Dancer, choreographer, and

teacher; instituted new style of modern dance.

on art and artists, page 18
on lies, page 162
on love, page 170
on marriage, page 176
on water, page 301

François Duvalier (1907–1971)
Haitian politician
("Papa Doc")
Absolute dictator; earliest positions in the field of medicine, in which he trained; was director of public health service (1946); minister of health (1949); opposed government after 1950 military coup; was elected president by a landslide in 1957. As dictator, famed and feared for his dreaded secret police, the Tonton Macoutes; succeeded by his son, Jean Claude.

on revolution, page 240

Faisal al-Duwish (c. 1930)
Arabian religious leader
Fundamentalist Muslim, early ally of King 'Abd Aziz ibn Saud, who unified Arabia under his rule; later fought against ibn Saud.

on charity, page 37

E

Amelia Earhart (1898–1937)
American aviator
Writer and social worker; first woman to make solo transpacific and transatlantic flights, and to receive Distinguished Flying Cross;

believed killed when plane crashed in the Pacific.

on bravery, page 28

Charles Alexander Eastman.
See Ohiyesa

Lady Eguchi (c. 890)
Japanese writer
Works collected in famous anthology *Kokin Shu* (compiled 905–922).

on departures, page 68

George Eliot (1819–1880)
English novelist
(Mary Ann Evans)
Considered a leading English novelist, particularly for her portrayals of working and agrarian classes. Took charge of household at age sixteen, upon mother's death; educated at home; after father's death in 1849, traveled abroad, then returned to England; became writer, then assistant editor for *Westminster Review*. Wrote first story in 1856, published in 1857; first novel, *Adam Bede*, immediately successful; *The Mill on the Floss* and *Silas Marner* also popular; wrote poems and more novels, including *Middlemarch* and *Daniel Deronda*.

on bravery, page 28
on envy and jealousy, page 79
on error, page 81
on expectations, page 85
on fame, page 89
on fools and foolishness, page 99
on gifts and giving, page 107
on happiness, page 122
on humor, page 133
on intellectuals, page 142

on knowledge, page 149
on loneliness, page 167
on longing, page 168
on men and women, page 181
on regrets, page 231
on silence, page 260
on sorrow, page 265
on success, page 271
on truth, page 284
on women, page 308

Elizabeth I (1533-1603)
English queen
Daughter of Henry VIII and Anne Boleyn; assumed throne in 1588.

last words, page 153
on leadership and leaders, page 155

Elizabeth II (b. 1926)
English queen
Born in London; proclaimed queen upon death of George VI, her father (1952); crowned a year later.

on the public, page 221
on women, page 308

Duke Ellington (1899-1975)
American musician
Pianist, composer, and bandleader; as leading jazz composer, wrote over two thousand pieces. Only formal music education was early childhood piano lessons; had long-standing engagement at Harlem nightspot, the Cotton Club. Famous for such standards as "Sophisticated Lady" and "Mood Indigo."

on music, page 185

Ralph Ellison (1914-1994)
American writer
One of most influential African American writers, critics, and essayists; most famous for his single novel, *Invisible Man*, which won National Book Award (1953). Initially intended to be musician; majored in music at Tuskegee Institute; was jazz trumpeter before established as writer. Was encouraged to write by author Richard Wright. Held numerous academic positions, including Albert Schweitzer Professor of the Humanities at New York University (1970-1979); also wrote two books of essays, *Shadow and Act* and *Going to the Territory*.

on the Americas, page 13
on life, page 164

Yunus Emre (c. 1321)
Turkish poet
Most renowned poet of Anatolian Turkish folk poetry; wrote in simple, forceful, direct style; work aimed at rural masses; also wrote many devotional hymns.

on cooperation, page 51
on speech, page 266

Peter Enahoro (b. 1935)
Nigerian journalist
Journalist, author, editor, and publisher; began career as publicity officer in Nigerian government. Became journalist; rose to editorship of *Daily Times* of Nigeria. In 1966, went into exile in England, where edited *Africa Magazine*; returned to Nigeria to edit *Africa Now* magazine.

on delusion, page 66
on luck, page 175

Mehmet Akif Ersoy (1873–1936)
Turkish poet
Championed Islam as force against Western imperialism; best at depicting common people in everyday life. Two stanzas of one of his poems comprise the Turkish national anthem.

on the military, page 182

Mary Ann Evans. *See* George Eliot

Medgar Evers (1926–1963)
American civil rights activist
African American born in Mississippi. As successful insurance salesman, was shocked at poverty of rural African Americans he met; quit to become full-time chapter organizer and field secretary for the National Association for the Advancement of Colored People in Mississippi; investigated murders of various African Americans; first major civil rights leader to be assassinated; his murderer was not convicted until 1994.

on ideas, page 135

F

Fakhir al-Din Razi (1149–1209)
Central Asian Islamic philosopher
One of most famous Islamic theologians; born in Rayy. After failing at alchemy, traveled to India; settled in Herat (in present-day Afghanistan). At first poor, soon came into great wealth, and was surrounded by disciples; famous for clear thinking; was frequently visited and asked opinions on numerous topics; wrote vast number of works, mostly supporting orthodox Sunni branch of Islam.

on fame, page 89
on materialism, page 177
on reason, page 230
on the soul, page 266
on transience, page 280
on truth, page 284
on wealth, page 303

Oriana Fallaci (b. 1930)
Italian journalist
Became reporter at age sixteen; first became known doing celebrity interviews for *L'Europeo* magazine (1955–1975); covered Vietnam War (1967–1968) and wrote memoir about it, *Nothing, and So Be It*; famous for interviews with such political leaders as Henry Kissinger and Yasir Arafat.

on equality, page 80
on fame, page 89
on success, page 271

Fang Lizhe (b. 1936)
Chinese scientist and activist
Astrophysicist known for strong political stances; sometimes called the "Chinese Sakharov." Opposed Maoism beginning in the 1950s; periodically ousted from Communist Party (1957, 1966, 1987). During 1980s thaw, appointed to prominent academic positions, including vice-chancellor of Keda, University of Science and Technology of Hefei (Anhi Province); dismissed from job under accusations of having encouraged student prodemocracy protests. In 1989, first dissident to appeal directly to

Deng Xiaoping (urged release of political prisoners); won 1989 Robert F. Kennedy Human Rights Award; went into exile in United States.

  on human rights, page 130
  on nonviolence, page 191

Fang Zhou (20th century)
Chinese political activist
Participated in Chinese students' strike for democracy at Tiananmen Square (1989); wrote poem dedicated to hunger strikers and posted it on wall of Student Broadcast Station at Beijing University.

  on sacrifice, page 247

Frantz Fanon (1925–1961)
Martiniquen writer
Educated in France; received medical degree, specialized in psychiatry; work chiefly about the harmful effect of white colonization on blacks; most famous works were *Black Skins, White Masks* and *The Wretched of the Earth.*

  on human rights, page 130

Ibn al'Farid (1181–1235)
Arab poet
Lived and wrote in Cairo, Egypt; considered one of greatest mystical poets.

  on laziness, page 154
  on longing, page 168
  on nature, page 189
  on symbols, page 274

Faryaq. *See* Ahmad Faris al-Shidyaq

Mustafa Fazil (1830–1875)
Egyptian prince
Grandson of Muhammed 'Ali; went to Istanbul at early age; held several high political offices; political views considered too liberal; exiled to Paris in 1866.

  on government, page 115
  on liberty, page 161–162

Dianne Feinstein (b. 1933)
American politician
Mayor of San Francisco; elected senator from California (1992).

  on women, page 308

Feng Yulan (1895–1972)
Chinese scholar
Philosopher and historian of philosophy; highly influential; known for analysis of traditional Chinese philosophies; works known in both China and the West; after establishment of Communist republic, became well known for witty scientific articles and autobiographical writings.

  on loss, page 169

Millicent Fenwick (1910–1992)
American politician
Member of New Jersey State General Assembly; member of U.S. House of Representatives (Republican, New Jersey) from 1975 to 1982; famous for outspokenness.

  on behavior, page 24
  on feminism, page 95
  on government, page 115
  on old age, page 193
  on power, page 211
  on self-pity, page 257

Edna Ferber (1885-1968)
American writer
Prolific novelist, short story writer, and playwright; born in Kalamazoo, Michigan. Most famous fiction works are *So Big*, which won Pulitzer Prize; *Show Boat*, basis of musical play and film by same title; *Cimarron*; and *Saratoga Trunk*. With George S. Kaufman, wrote such popular plays as *Dinner at Eight* and *Stage Door*.

on writers and writing, page 318

José Figueres (b. 1906)
Costa Rican soldier and politician
Soldier and planter; revolted against dictatorial president and undemocratic traditions; was architect of liberal democracy in Costa Rica. Elected president (1953); abolished the army (one of the few leaders in the world to have ever done so); promoted significant social reforms; reelected in 1970.

on human rights, page 130

Firdausi (c. 955-1020)
(pen name of Abu'l Kasim Mansur)
Persian poet, born in Khorason, famous for writing the *Book of Kings* (*Shah Nama*), an epic of actual events and Persian mythology.

on oppression, page 195

Dorothy Canfield Fisher
(1879-1958)
American writer
Works include novels, textbooks, essays, etc.; most revolve around need for self-confidence and the strength of the American heritage; they often depict Vermont (her home); best known for children's book *Understood Betsy*.

on freedom, page 101

M. F. K. Fisher (1908-1992)
American writer
Well known for writings on food and travel; best-known work is *How to Cook a Wolf*.

on secrets, page 251
on spirit, page 268

Ella Fitzgerald (b. 1918)
American singer
Raised in Yonkers, New York, orphanage; at age sixteen, entered talent contest and caught attention of bandleader Chick Webb; joined Webb's band as singer and headed it for two years after his death (1939); became well known as cabaret singer during the 1940s; developed "scat-singing" technique, using voice as instrument during jazz improvisations.

on behavior, page 24

John Hope Franklin (b. 1915)
American educator and historian
African American scholar and activist for human rights and equality; member of the U.S. Commission for UNESCO; board member of the American Council on Human Rights.

on African Americans, page 8

Eduardo Frei Montalva
(b. 1911)
Chilean politician
Known as a reformer; studied at Catholic University in Santiago, where later became a professor. Became minister of roads and public works (1945); elected president (1965).

on minorities, page 183
on progress, page 218

Betty Friedan (b. 1921)
American feminist
Called "mother of the new feminist movement;" wrote *The Feminine Mystique* (1963), which largely precipitated birth of women's liberation movement. Organized National Organization for Women (NOW) (1966) and served as first president (1967-1970); cofounded National Women's Political Caucus (1971); convened International Feminist Conference (1973); cofounded First Women's Bank (1973).

on action, page 2
on dependence, page 68
on feminism, page 95
on men and women, page 181
on middle age, page 182
on women, page 308

Athol Fugard (b. 1932)
South African playwright
Playwright and theater director; plays, set in contemporary South Africa, show bleakness of life under apartheid; some works censored by government authorities.

Recently has moved away from strictly South African themes.

on hate, page 123

Margaret Fuller (1810-1850)
American writer and critic
Social critic, educator, and editor known for feminist views.

on vanity, page 292

G

Indira Gandhi (1917-1984)
Indian prime minister
First woman prime minister of India; daughter of India's first prime minister, Jawaharlal Nehru. Presided over India's development into a modern power and resisted separatist tendencies within India. In 1975, was convicted of election malpractices; in response, declared a state of emergency and strictly curtailed democratic freedoms; eventually acquitted of charges. Reelected in 1980, but assassinated by members of her Sikh bodyguard during that term.

on bravery, page 28-29
on defeat, page 65
on diplomacy, page 71
on leadership and leaders, page 155
on nature, page 189
on patriotism and nationalism, page 200
on progress, page 218
on sacrifice, page 247
on silence, page 260
on violence, page 294

Mohandas K. Gandhi
(1869–1948)
Indian spiritual and political
  leader

Known as Mahatma ("Great Soul");
pioneered nonviolent resistance;
regarded as great politician and
moral teacher; even his enemies
conceded his personal honesty and
integrity. Born in Porbandar, Ka-
thiawar, British India; he initially
followed a "typical" career path of
an educated middle-class Indian,
studying law in London, returning
to set up a lucrative law practice in
Bombay. In 1893, gave up practice
to live in British South Africa,
where opposed discrimination
against Indians. Returned to India
in 1914; became involved in *Swa-
raj* (home rule) movement. Led
nonviolent civil disobedience
movements against British rule; arrested many times; gained respect
worldwide, including many of his
British official enemies. By late
1930s and early 1940s, led (with
Nehru and Jinnah) negotiations for
eventual independence; by 1947,
was more concerned with communal strife in India; argued unsuccessfully against partitioning of
India into Muslim Pakistan and India, but successfully for end to discrimination against "outcastes"
(those lowest in the Hindu caste
system). Was assassinated in 1948
by a Hindu fanatic. Autobiography,
*The Story of My Experiment with
Truth*, details uniquely candid,
spiritual approach to life.

on slavery, page 262
on speech, page 266
on spirituality, page 268
on success, page 271
on suffering, page 273
on truth, page 284-285
on understanding, page 289
on unity, page 289
on vice, page 292
on war, page 298
on wealth, page 303
on will, page 304
on wisdom, page 306
on women, page 308-309
on work, page 313

Bal Gangalhar. *See* Tilak

Gabriel García Márquez
(b. 1928)
Colombian writer
Novelist and short story writer;
one of Latin America's (and the
world's) best-known writers.
Known for lyrical, fantastic style,
with "magic realism"; best known
for *One Hundred Years of Solitude.* Received Nobel Prize for literature (1982).

on books and reading, page 28
on expectations, page 85
on fame, page 89
on hunger, page 133
on power, page 211
on prejudice, page 214

Marcus Garvey (1887-1940)
American political leader
Controversial black leader;
preached self-sufficiency; led a
"Back to Africa" movement, arguing that freedom and self-sufficiency would come with return to
the black homeland.

on convictions, page 50

on enemies, page 78
on hunger, page 133
on political movements,
  page 208
on self-esteem, page 255
on the world, page 314

Elizabeth Gaskell (1810-1865)
English writer
Married a Unitarian minister from
Manchester, which gave her an opportunity to study working-class
people; in 1848, published first
book anonymously, followed by
succession of novels, as well as
study of Charlotte Brontë.

on reason, page 230

Imomotimi Gbaingbain. *See*
  Gabriel Okara

Genghis Khan. *See* Chingiz Khan

Geronimo (1829-1909)
Apache chief
(Gokhlayeh)
Chiricahua Apache born in Ari-
zona; led his people in series of up-
risings against whites (so-called
Apache Wars of 1880s); eventually
captured by General George Cook.
Escaped, but then surrendered; retired to farming in Oklahoma with
remnants of his people. Dictated
his autobiography, *Geronimo, His
Own Story,* in 1906.

on adaptability, page 4
on defeat, page 65

Mirza Ghalib (1797-1869)
Indian Urdu poet
(Asad Allah Beg Khan)
Resident poet of the Indian Mughal
court.

on danger, page 57

on love, page 171
on memory, page 179
on old age, page 193
on paradox, page 197
on transcendence, page 279

Abu Hamid Muhammad al-Ghazali (1058–1111)
Arab Islamic philosopher and
   theologian
Professor of philosophy at Niza-
miyah College, Baghdad; became
Sufi mystic after a breakdown and
speech impediment that inhibited
his ability to lecture; writings aim
for reconciliation between philosophy and Islamic dogma.

on fools and foolishness,
   page 99
on God, page 109
on good and evil, page 113
on Islam, page 143
on mysticism, page 185–186
on spirituality, page 268

Aurobindo Ghose (1872–1950)
Indian political leader and Hindu
   philosopher
(Sri Aurobindo)
Considered one of greatest mystic
philosophers of modern India; opposed Shankara's views on Vedanta
philosophy; promoted "internal
yoga" as discipline.

on freedom, page 102
on self-knowledge, page 256

Vo Nguyen Giap (b. 1912)
Vietnamese military leader
Studied law at Hanoi University;
joined Communist Party; trained in
China. Led Viet Minh army against
French occupiers, culminating in
victory at Dien Bien Phu (1954),
which signaled end of French rule
in North Vietnam. Later, as vice
premier and defense minister of
North Vietnam, masterminded attack that resulted in conquest of
South Vietnam.

on strategy, page 269

Kahlil Gibran (1883–1931)
Syrian/Lebanese writer
Novelist, poet, essayist, and artist.
Although resident of New York
City from 1912 on, influenced Ara-
bic literature; works are mystical
and religious.

on children and childhood,
   page 38
on government, page 115
on knowledge, page 150
on self-knowledge, page 256
on truth, page 285

Charlotte Perkins Gilman
(1860–1935)
American writer
Feminist and economist; met social
worker Jane Addams at 1895 California Women's Conference; attended International Social and
Labor Congress in London (1896);
wrote *Women and Economics*,
breakthrough work attacking
women's financial dependency;
also known for other works advocating women's assertiveness.

on women, page 309

Nikki Giovanni (b. 1943)
American writer
Considered a leading voice in Afri-
can American literature.

on life, page 164
on risks, page 245

Françoise Giroud (b. 1916)
Swiss/French politician and
    journalist
Minister of Women; cofounder of
Elle and *L'Express* magazines.

on feminism, page 95

**Gofukakausa-in no shosho no
naishi** (c. 1250)
Japanese poet
Daughter of poet and painter
Fujiwara no Nobuzane; sisters also
poets; died not long before her father; had forty-four poems in imperial anthologies.

on regrets, page 232

Gokhlayeh. *See* Geronimo

Emma Goldman (1869–1940)
American anarchist
Known as "Red Emma"; born in
Lithuania; immigrated to United
States in 1885. Joined anarchists in
agitating against execution of four
anarchists involved in so-called
Haymarket bomb-throwing incident. Active in labor rights; became internationally famous for
fiery rhetoric; eventually deported
to Soviet Union (whose government she opposed); returned to
United States in 1924.

on feminism, page 95
on politics, page 209
on revolution, page 241
on violence, page 294

Gonardiya. *See* Patanjali

Nadine Gordimer (b. 1923)
South African writer
Short story writer, novelist, and

playwright; born in Transvaal;
works center around social cruelty
and hypocrisy in South Africa, and
problems between the races; because of topics, works were
banned in South Africa; widely
read worldwide; winner of Nobel
Prize for literature (1991).

on beauty, page 22
on censorship, page 34
on change, page 34
on writers and writing,
    page 318

Aaron David Gordon
(1856–1922)
Israeli writer
As prophet of Second and Third
Aliyoth, had great influence over
both Israeli life and literature; influence began at end of Second
Aliyah; many of his thoughts and
beliefs formed foundation for Third
Aliyah; synthesized such ideals as
individual freedom, creativity, love
of nature, and honor in work.

on ideas, page 135
on the land, page 151
on oppression, page 195–196
on rules, page 246
on the soul, page 266
on work, page 313

Elizabeth Goudge (1900–1984)
English writer
Novelist; incorporates fantasy elements in stories of family life and
love.

on acting and actors, page 1–2

Yakuba Gowon (b. 1934)
Nigerian political leader
As army general, took over govern-

ment and became president (1966), a leader during bloody Biafran war, in which Ibo peoples sought independence from Nigerian federal government; deposed in 1975.

on government, page 115

Martha Graham (1894-1991)
American dancer
Dancer and choreographer; founder of Martha Graham Dance Company; innovator of modern dance; received Presidential Medal of Freedom (1976).

on sorrow, page 265

Grandma Moses (1860-1961)
American artist
(née Anna Mary Robertson)
American painter; became famous in later years; known for primitive style.

on life, page 164

Germaine Greer (b. 1939)
Australian writer
Feminist author; most famous for writing *The Female Eunuch*; recent work includes *The Change: Women, Aging, and the Menopause*.

on family, page 90
on feminism, page 95-96
on men, page 180
on revolution, page 241

Dick Gregory (b. 1932)
American civil rights activist
African American activist and comedian; ran for president; in later years became active as a nutritionist.

on the Americas, page 13

on poverty, page 210
on race, page 223
on racism, page 225

Sarah Moore Grimké
(1792-1873)
American abolitionist
Teacher and early advocate of women's rights. Born in South Carolina; moved to Philadelphia in 1821 because of antislavery beliefs; became Quaker (1823); launched abolitionist campaign; with sister Angelina, became first women lecturers for American Anti-Slavery Society; retired in 1867.

on feminism, page 96

Gu Cheng (b. 1957)
Chinese poet
Known for modernist disjunctive style and willingness to challenge Communist literary orthodoxy.

on art and artists, page 18-19
on enemies, page 78
on seeing, page 252
on time, page 277
on writers and writing,
page 318

Che Guevara (1928-1967)
Cuban revolutionary
Born in Argentina; graduated in medicine from University of Buenos Aires; joined Castro's revolutionary movement in Mexico. Active in Cuba's revolution; held variety of government positions; led guerilla movements in South America; killed in those efforts. In 1960s, became folk hero of New Left; his books, *Guerilla Warfare* and *Reminiscences of the Cuban*

Revolutionary War, were widely quoted.

on action, page 2
on adventure, page 5
on revolution, page 241
on victory, page 293

Guo Moruo (1892-1978)
Chinese writer
(pseudonym of Guo Kaizhen or Kuo K'ai-chen)
Poet, essayist, historian, playwright, and translator; considered a leading literary figure of Communist China; friend of Mao Zedong; work reflects social and political orientation; one of the key figures in the creation of a modern Chinese literature. Held numerous political and cultural positions, including president of Chinese Academy of Sciences; during Cultural Revolution, claimed to have ideological shortcomings and admitted his books should be burned; however, was not purged, as many other contemporaries were; instead retained positions and continued writing.

on joy, page 145
on sex, page 259

H

Hafiz (d. 1389)
Persian poet
(Shamsu'd Din Muhammad Hafiz)
Considered the greatest lyrical poet in Iran; born in Shiraz; nicknamed "Chagarlab" (Sugar Lips) by contemporaries for sensuality of his poetry, which focused on such

subjects as love, flowers, and wine. As Sufi, wrote poetry that can be understood on another, more esoteric and religious level as well. Tomb is still site of pilgrimages in Iran.

on God, page 109
on love, page 171
on patience, page 199
on youth, page 321

Oscar Hahn (b. 1938)
Chilean poet
First important poem written at age seventeen, on bombing of Hiroshima; published first book of poems in 1961; combines elements of Spanish Golden Age and everyday Chilean life. Taught in Africa until 1973; later moved to United States.

on children and childhood, page 38

Tawfiq al-Hakim (b. 1902)
Egyptian writer
Dramatist, novelist, essayist, and civil servant. Literary pioneer; considered founder of Egypt's contemporary dramatic tradition; member of Arabic Language Academy; winner of numerous writing awards. Studied in France; also wrote in French.

on art and artists, page 19
on creativity, page 54
on intellectuals, page 142
on progress, page 218

Hakuin (1685-1768)
Japanese Zen master
Member of Rinzai school of Japanese Buddhism; devoted to popu-

larizing Zen Buddhism; also renowned painter.

on death, page 60

Clara Hale (1905-1992)
American social worker
Founder of Hale House, a home for children, in Harlem.

on children and childhood, page 38

Sarah Josepha Hale
(1788-1879)
American writer and editor
First U.S. female magazine editor; ran private school from her home (1806-1811); upon death of husband in 1822, opened shop and began publishing poetry and novels; edited *Ladies' Magazine* (1828), which was bought by publisher Louis Godey and changed to *Godey Lady's Book* (1837), one of most popular women's magazines of the time; as editor of *Godey's*, expressed conservative feminist views in articles and editorials.

on family, page 90
on learning and education, page 159
on nature, page 189
on virtue, page 295

al-Hallaj (d. 922)
Persian Sufi mystic
(Al-Husayn ibn Mansur al-Hallaj)
Executed for heresy by Caliph Muqtadir for proclaiming the so-called Doctrine of Identity—he reportedly shouted, "I am the Truth" (i.e., God is within).

on spirituality, page 268

Hammurapi (1792-1750 B.C.E.)
Babylonian king
(Hammurabi)
Sixth king of Amorite dynasty in Babylon, modern-day Iraq; extended Babylonian empire; known for efficient administration. A tablet inscribed with the Code of Hammurapi, Babylonian law code, shows an advanced legal system.

on crime, page 54-55
on justice, page 146

Han Fei-tzu (c. 280-233 B.C.E.)
Chinese philosopher
Government official; disciple of Xun Zi (Hsun Tzu); commentator on the Dao De Jing (Tao Te Ching), the naturalist work of Chinese religion and philosophy. As official envoy, was falsely accused of treason and forced to commit suicide.

on effort, page 76
on happiness, page 122

Han Wenju (c. 1900)
Chinese activist and writer
Studied with scholar Kang Yuwei; a Macao-based organizer of abortive 1900 uprising against Manchu (Ching dynasty) rule; urged revolutionary attack on imperial autocracy.

on government, page 115-116

Han Yu (768-824)
Chinese poet
Confucian thinker; official during later, strife-filled years of Tang dynasty. Leader of Ku wen (Gu wen), or old prose movement, which favored move away from ornate

prose and return to simple, direct prose.

on spirit, page 268

Handhala of Badghis
(c. 7th century)
Persian poet
Wrote during Tahirid and Saffarid periods; works among few of the time that are preserved; known for *Diwan of Handhala of Badghis*; influenced other poets, including Ahmad of Khujistan.

on boldness, page 27

Abu Hanifah (d. 767)
Arab-Persian Islamic jurist
First, and probably the most important, legal scholar of Islam. Founded first and largest school of Islamic jurisprudence (the 'Iraq school), which is technically still adhered to by half of all Sunni Muslims; notable for its tolerance and emphasis on juridical speculation. Grandson of a Persian slave; merchant by profession. Passed insights orally; one disciple, abu-Yusuf, wrote his views in the *Kitab al-Kharaj*.

on faith, page 88

Manhar-ul-Haque (1866-1921)
Bengali lawyer
President of Muslim League; promoted rights of Muslims in British-ruled India.

on diversity, page 72

Al Hariri (1054-1122)
Arab poet
Native of Basra (Iraq); an official (chief of intelligence) with enough leisure to participate actively in literary affairs; his *Makamat*, or *Sessions*, were contemporaneously considered classics; much transcribed and translated into Hebrew, Persian, and Syriac; although modern scholars consider much of his work derivative and overly flowery.

on success, page 272

Michael Harper (b. 1938)
American poet
Born in Brooklyn; traveled extensively; works influenced by travel, other cultures, family, and racial history; winner of various prizes and awards, including Guggenheim (1976).

on responsibility, page 238
on snobs and snobbery,
page 263

Simazaki Haruki. *See* Simazaki Toson

Harun al-Rashid (763-809)
Islamic Arab ruler
Fifth caliph of the Abbasid dynasty; quelled unrest in the Arab empire; ruled at the peak of his dynasty's power, wealth, and culture. Fame is due primarily to his mention in some tales of the *Arabian Nights*; his dividing the empire among his three sons contributed to the ultimate dissolution of the empire.

on learning and education,
page 159

Ahmet Hasim (1885-1933)
Turkish poet
Heavily influenced by French symbolists; poems noted for strong im-

agery and mood of spiritual exile; considered influential to neosurrealist movement of 1950s.

on generations, page 106
on language, page 153

Shaykh Muhammad 'Abdille Hasan (20th century)
Somali nationalist
Fought British and Italian colonizers from 1900 to 1920; regarded as founder of Somali nationalism.

on anger, page 16

Abul Hassan. *See* Amir Khusrau

Mihri Hatun (d. 1506)
Turkish writer
First prominent poet of Ottoman (Turkish) Empire; member of intellectual circle centered around Prince Ahmad.

on love, page 171

Abu 'Uthman al-Hayri (c. 910)
Sufi leader
(Abu 'Uthman al-Hayri al-Nisaburi)
Considered one of the greatest leaders of his time; established Sufism in Nishapur; introduced strict system of education for his disciples.

on perfection, page 201

Lillian Hellman (1906–1984)
American writer
Playwright and memoirist; found success with first play, *The Children's Hour*, which addressed topic of homosexuality; other works similarly controversial. Companion of novelist Dashiell Hammett; visited Spain during Civil War, and Russia in 1944; famous for stance when questioned by U.S. House Committee on Un-American Activities; later works primarily autobiographical, such as *Pentimento* and *Scoundrel Time*.

on fame, page 89
on middle age, page 182
on revolution, page 241
on success, page 272
on truth, page 285

Hendrick (c. 1750)
Mohawk chief
Reluctantly joined with British in French and Indian War; fought alongside Colonel Ephraim Williams at Battle of Lake George, 1755.

on war, page 298

Katharine Hepburn (b. 1909)
American actor
Began film career in 1932; won Academy Award four times (1933, 1967, 1968, 1982); known for her roles in comedies such as *Bringing Up Baby* and *The Philadelphia Story*, and dramas such as *The African Queen*, *The Lion in Winter*, and *On Golden Pond*.

on acting and actors, page 2
on love, page 171
on men and women, page 181

Sadiq Hidayat (1903–1951)
Persian writer
Essayist and short story writer; considered father of the Persian short story. Member of the old Qajar nobility; killed himself in Paris in 1951.

on character, page 36

on death, page 60
on dignity, page 71
on solitude, page 264

Toyotomi Hideyoshi
(1536-1591)
Japanese soldier and ruler
Warlord who united all of Japan (1590); attempted to invade Korea, planning to go on to China and become overlord over both, but failed.

on patience, page 199

Muhammad Hijazi
(20th century)
Iranian writer and politician
Senator; perhaps best known for sayings and proverbs; influenced by traditional wisdom of ancient Iran, Sufism, Greek philosophy, and French rationalism.

on advice, page 6
on cleverness, page 43
on death, page 60
on flattery, page 98-99
on happiness, page 122
on men and women, page 181
on nature, page 189
on politics, page 209
on popular opinion, page 209
on problems, page 216-217
on punishment, page 221

Nazim Hikmet (1902-1963)
Turkish poet
Playwright, novelist, and best-known Turkish poet; controversial for socially engaged poetry, introduction of free verse, and his pro-Communist political views; most famous work is *The Epic of Sheik Bedreddin*. Praised by European and American poets, was viewed with suspicion by Turkish government; arrested in 1938; released in 1950; moved to Soviet Union.

on creation, page 53
on death, page 60
on defeat, page 65
on goals, page 108
on life, page 164
on patriotism and nationalism, page 200

Miguel Hildalgo (1753-1811)
Mexican revolutionary
As priest, rang church bells to promote revolution against Spanish rule; with army of eighty thousand, marched on Mexico City; eventually was captured and shot; known as prime instigator of Mexican independence.

on action, page 2-3
on revolution, page 241

Rolando Hinojosa-Smith
(b. 1929)
American writer
Internationally known poet and educator; work reflects Chicano background; professor at University of Texas; best known for *Klail City y sus alrededores*.

on change, page 34

Lady Ho (c. 300 B.C.E.)
Chinese poet
Wife of Han P'in, retainer of Duke Yuan of Sung; forced to marry Duke when husband was arrested by him; wrote poem "The Song of Magpies"; committed suicide.

on relationships, page 232

Ho Chi Minh (1892–1969)
Vietnamese political leader
(Nguyen Ai Quoc)
A founder of the Communist Party of Vietnam, founded in France in 1918; sought recognition from victorious Allies during Versailles Treaty negotiations, but was ignored. Became head of Viet Minh movement, which sought Vietnam's independence from France; became prime minister (1953) and president (1954) of North Vietnam; devoted remainder of life to seeking reunification of North with South, under his Communist rule. Also wrote poetry.

Ho Nansorhon (1563–1589)
Korean poet
Sister of novelist Ho Kyun.

Ho Shuang-ch'ing (b. 1712)
Chinese poet

Hojo Soun (c. 1519)
Japanese samurai
Samurai known for "Twenty-one Articles of Advice," addressed to his son and regarded as epitome of martial spirit.

Billie Holiday (1915–1959)
American singer
Famous singer; toured with Benny Goodman, Count Basie, Artie Shaw, and other Big Band greats; also appeared in such films as *Symphony in Black*.

Honen (1133–1212)
Japanese Buddhist leader
(Honen Shonin)
Founder of Jodo school of Japanese Buddhism.

Benjamin L. Hooks (b. 1925)
American civil rights activist
Lawyer, businessman, and minister; formerly executive director of National Association for the Advancement of Colored People.

Karen Horney (1885–1952)
American psychoanalyst
German-born neo-Freudian; emphasized environmental and cultural influences in development of neuroses; opposed antifeminist slant of strict Freudianism; taught at Berlin Psychoanalyst Institute (1918–1932); moved to United States (1932); after publishing critique of Freudianism, *New Ways in Psychoanalysis*, was expelled from New York Psychoanalytic Institute (1941); founded Asso-

ciation for the Advancement of Psychoanalysis.

on action, page 3
on anxiety, page 17
on love, page 171
on the self, page 253
on women, page 309

James Africanus Horton
(1835–1883)
British physician
Development economist and physician; first practiced in Britain; served twenty years in West Africa as one of few black officers in British Army; stimulated development of mineral resources in Ghana; opened development bank in Sierra Leone.

on civilization, page 42
on government, page 116

Felix Houphouet-Boigny
(b. 1905)
Ivory Coast political leader
Wealthy planter and physician; led anticolonialist party; sought and won independence from the French; as leader, promoted conservative probusiness and pro-French policies, which brought relative prosperity to the country.

on the Americas, page 13

Hsiang Hsiu (c. 250)
Chinese philosopher
Government official in third-century China; staunch Confucianist; attempted to incorporate Taoism into Confucianism.

on joy, page 145

Hsi K'ang (223–262)
Chinese philosopher
One of "Seven Sages of the Bamboo Grove," philosophers of early third-century; through works, explored ways of avoiding old age and death.

on beauty, page 22
on wisdom, page 306

Hsin Ch'i-chi (1140–1207)
Chinese poet
Served as an official of southern Sung dynasty; also known as a composer and poet.

on aging, page 11

Hsun-tzu (298–238 B.C.E.)
Chinese philosopher
(Xun zi; Hsun Ching [Xun Ching]) Confucian philosopher; diametrically opposed to philosophy of Mencius; emphasized that human nature is originally evil and that social control is vital. Disciples aided in unification of China in 221 B.C.E. under tyrannical Chin dynasty.

on concentration, page 46
on effort, page 76
on equality, page 80
on human nature, page 129
on sacrifice, page 248
on society, page 263
on understanding, page 289

Hui Shi (c. 370–290 B.C.E.)
Chinese philosopher
Founder of School of Names (also called School of Logicians, or Dialecticians); philosophy emphasized changeability and relativity of reality.

on death, page 60
on paradox, page 197

Huai Nan Tzu (c. 122 B.C.E.)
Chinese scholar
Prince in Han dynasty; attributed author of *The Book of the Prince of Huai Nan*, an early Taoist work.

   on appearances, page 17
   on desire, page 69

Huang Po (c. 850)
Chinese Zen Buddhist leader
A leading Chinese Zen (Chan) master; teacher of Dhyana Buddhism; best known for teachings called *The Zen Teaching of Huang Po*, collected by P'ei Hsiu of the Tang dynasty.

   on effort, page 76
   on wisdom, page 306

Huang Quiyun (b. 1939)
Chinese writer
Active during "Hundred Flowers" period of late 1950s, when Mao Zedong called for greater freedom in literature; works centered around social ills.

   on writers and writing,
      page 318

Arianna Stassinopoulos Huffington (b. 1950)
Greek writer
Well known for her controversial biographies, especially *Picasso: Creator and Destroyer,* as well as one on opera diva Maria Callas; first book published at age 23; married to congressman; also has a cable talk show; most recently has focused on spirituality; recent work *The Fourth Instinct* explores Americans' need for a spiritual transformation of their lives.

   on creativity, page 54

Langston Hughes (1902–1967)
American writer
Poet, short story writer, playwright, anthologist, translator, and editor. Leading figure in "Black Renaissance" in American literature. Spent time in Paris, Russia, and Far East; worked as war correspondent during Spanish Civil War; spent last thirty years of life in New York City. Also wrote radio and television scripts, and lyrics for over forty popular songs. Known for strong socio-political protest and civil rights activism.

   on democracy, page 66–67
   on dreams, page 73
   on ghettos, page 107
   on humor, page 133
   on poetry and poets, page 206
   on racism, page 225

Hui-lin (c. 5th century)
Chinese Buddhist monk
Religious leader, scholar, and writer; wrote about karma and reincarnation.

   on perspective, page 202

Hui Neng (638–713)
Chinese Buddhist leader
Sixth patriarch of Chinese Zen Buddhism; founded "abrupt teaching" school of Buddhism (tunchiao); popularized Zen in China by relating it to Taoism; believed to have written only Chinese work that was later given status of sutra, The Platform Sutra.

   on Buddhism, page 31
   on wisdom, page 306

Vicente Huidobro (1893–1948)
Chilean writer
Avant-garde poet, dramatist, essayist, and novelist. Contributor to French poet Apollinaire's *Nord-Sud*; pioneer of "new" poetry. Born into upper-class family; raised by Jesuits; later made complete break with family. Considered one of most important and influential voices of twentieth-century Spanish American poetry.

on waiting, page 297

al-Hujwiri (c. 11th–12th century)
Sufi teacher
('Ali ben 'Uthman al-Jullabi al-Hujwiri)
Sufi scholar, teacher, and writer; born in Afghanistan; best known for his *Kasuf ul-Mahjub* (*The Unveiling of the Veiled*).

on self-knowledge, page 257

Ho Xuan Huong (19th century)
Vietnamese poet
Well known for early feminist and sexual allusions; sometimes praised highly, sometimes considered pornographic; little known of her background and life.

on the self, page 253

Zora Neale Hurston
(1903–1960)
American writer
Novelist and short story writer; one of best-known African American writers of her time; known for capturing the black experience; one of first writers to incorporate folk images and speech; considered spiritual ancestor of contemporary African American women writers.

on African Americans, page 8
on fools and foolishness,
    page 99
on poverty, page 210
on women, page 309

Taha Husayn (1891–1973)
Egyptian writer
Novelist, literary critic, and short story writer; called "the leader of the modernists." Dean of Faculty of Letters, University of Cairo; head of Farouk I University in Alexandria. Wrote controversial work on Jahili (pre-Islamic) literature; famous especially for autobiography, *Al-Ayyam* (*The Days*), in which he discusses his early blindness and creation of a sensibility dictated by sound rather than sight.

on imperialism, page 138–139

Hu Shih (1891–1962)
Chinese writer
Influential modern philosopher; leading figure in Chinese thought and writing; known as literary reformer.

on honesty, page 127
on progress, page 218
on questions and answers,
    page 222
on truth, page 285
on war, page 298

Hussein (b. 1935)
Jordanian king
(Hussein ibn Talal)
Great-grandson of Hussein ibn Ali, cousin of King Faisal II of Iraq; king of Jordan since 1953, succeeding his father, who was deposed due to

mental illness; known for middle-of-the-road leadership, maintaining a balance between Arab nationalism and Western influences.

on honesty, page 127
on leadership and leaders, page 155

Hwang Chin-i (c. 1506-1544)
Korean poet
Considered Korea's greatest female poet; work often focused on mutability of love; known for use of symbolism, strong emotion, and flowing rhythms.

on the seasons, page 251
on time, page 277

I

Ibn 'Arabi (1165-1240)
Arab Sufi philosopher and poet
(Muhyi al-Din ibn al-'Arabi)
Born in Arab Spain; settled in Baghdad. Wrote prodigiously, chiefly on Sufi mysticism; influenced Persian Sufi poet Rumi, as well as Turkish poets, and possibly Western ones such as Dante. Advocated pantheistic theology; known for diverging from traditional Islamic tenet that there is only one God, and instead declaring that there is *nothing* but God.

on Sufism, page 273

Ibn 'Ata'allah (c. 1252-1309)
(al-Iskandari)
Egyptian Sufi leader
Organizer and most famous member of Shadhilyah sect; emphasized

that adherents could forgo monastic life and participate in secular life; wrote the *Hakim (Sayings)*, which popularized Sufism.

on desire, page 69

Moses ibn Ezra (1070-1139)
Spanish Hebrew poet
A leading Hebrew poet of his time; as youth, wrote secular poems; when older, focused on religious poetry.

on aging, page 11
on graves and graveyards, page 117
on sorrow, page 265
on time, page 277

Ibn Hazm (994-1064)
Arab Spanish poet and philosopher
(Abu Muhammad 'Ali bin Ahmad bin Sa'id)
Worked in Arab Andalusian region of Spain; best known for tract on courtly love, *Tauq al-Hamanah*. Religious literalist; viewed scriptures as ultimate authority.

on evil, page 83

Ibn Khaldun (1332-1406)
Arab historian and philosopher
('Abd al Rahman ibn Khaldun)
A leading Islamic philosopher; born in Tunis; after holding various political positions in Spain, left politics (1375) and went to Cairo. Became professor; best known as historian, especially for history of the Arabs, *Kitab al-ibar*, and *al-Muqaddimah (Introduction [to History])*, outlining his theory of history, in which nomadic cultures

attain civilization, reach their peak, fall victim to their own success, then are destroyed by another nomadic culture.

> on history, page 125
> on leadership and leaders, page 155
> on virtue, page 295

Pahn Huy Ich (c. 1750)
Vietnamese poet
Well known in Vietnam for adaptations of classical Chinese poetry into Vietnamese.

> on farewells, page 90

Yusuf Idris (b. 1927)
Egyptian writer
Short story writer, dramatist, novelist, and essayist for newspaper *Al-Ahram*; known for incorporation of surreal and absurd in his work.

> on dignity, page 71

Tokugawa Ieyasu (1543–1616)
Japanese military and political leader
Founder of Tokugawa shogunate, which lasted until 1867; one of three unifiers of Japan; chose as headquarters fishing village of Edo, which grew to become Tokyo. As ruler, known for administrative ability; established military government; enforced four social classes (samurai, farmer, artisan, merchant).

> on patience, page 199

Ikinilik (c. 1930)
Eskimo poet
Hunter; wrote of seasonal pattern of activities; works are both self-

reflective and introspective; depicts physical life and expresses wonderment at natural world; work included in collection of Eskimo songs gathered in first quarter of twentieth century by explorer Knud Rasmussen.

> on old age, page 193

Lami'a Abbas al-'Imarah
(20th century)
Iraqi poet
Work tends to focus on emotions, the inner life.

> on secrets, page 251

Inpumon-in no tayu (c. 1200)
Japanese poet
Lady-in-waiting to Princess Koshi (1147–1214); active in court poetry circles; became nun in 1192.

> on love, page 171

Ipu-wer (c. 2000 B.C.E.)
Ancient Egyptian prophet
Considered by later Egyptians to be a prophet during First Intermediate period (c. 2000 B.C.E.), a period marked by civil strife and collapse of powerful Old Kingdom.

> on strife, page 270

Muhammad Iqbal (1873–1938)
Indian Muslim poet and philosopher
A leading Indian Muslim thinker; championed Muslim cause in India. Born in Sialkot (now Pakistan); studied law in England. Considered spiritual father of modern Pakistan. Wrote in Persian, Urdu, and English; regarded as premier Urdu poet of the twentieth century.

on adventure, page 5
on bravery, page 29
on civilization, page 42
on Communism, page 43
on conduct, page 46
on corruption, page 52
on democracy, page 67
on enemies, page 78
on freedom, page 102
on God, page 109
on history, page 125
on imperialism, page 139
on life, page 164
on place, page 204
on time, page 278
on war, page 298

Kasa no Iratsume (9th century)
Japanese poet
Prominent female poet in her time;
lover of equally famous poet
Otomo no Yakamochi.

on love, page 171

Isapo-Muxika. *See* Crowfoot

al-Iskandari. *See* Ibn 'Ata'allah

Iskander Mirza (b. 1899)
Pakistani politician
President of Pakistan; forced by
General Mohammed Ayub Khan to
place country under martial law;
removed from office in bloodless
coup led by Ayub Khan (1958).

on democracy, page 67

Tatanka Iyotake. *See* Sitting Bull

Ixtilxochitl (c. 1550)
Aztec king
Spokesman for Texcoco; wrote
two of most famous Aztec collections, *Relaciones* and *Historia*

Chichimeca, explaining Aztec history and customs.

on life, page 164
on poetry and poets, page 206

J

Jabra Ibrahim Jabra (b. 1919)
Palestinian writer
Novelist, poet, painter, and critic; a
leading voice in Palestinian literature; lives in exile from homeland;
in writings, reminisces about childhood in homeland; expresses dissatisfaction with Arab inability to
rectify Palestinian situation.

on the self, page 253
on tradition, page 279

Jesse Jackson (b. 1941)
American civil rights activist and
politician
Minister and civil rights leader;
worked with Martin Luther King,
Jr. Founded Operation PUSH (People United to Save Humanity),
designed to encourage African
American economic independence, increase pride in heritage.
As politician, put together so-called
Rainbow Coalition of minority social and political groups; ran for
president in 1984 and 1988.

on the Americas, page 14
on books and reading, page 28
on racism, page 225-226

Mahalia Jackson (1911-1972)
American singer
Considered one of world's finest

gospel singers; three-time Grammy Award winner (1961, 1962, 1976).

on poverty, page 210

Nur Jahan (c. 1646)
Indian poet and empress
Wife of Emperor Jehan-gir.

on grieving, page 119

al-Jahiz (c. 778-869)
Islamic philosopher and writer
(Abu 'Uthman amr ibn Bahr al-Jahiz)
Considered a premier Islamic thinker and writer of his time; largely credited for raising the level of Arabic writing; founded elegant, ornamental style of writing, eventually called "adab" literature. Best-known books include *Kitab al-Hayawan* (*Book of Animals*) and *Kitab al-Bayan* (*Book of Proof*), and for major book on rhetoric. Also known for interest in and writings on science; had a rationalist sect named after him.

on death, page 60
on diplomacy, page 71
on familiarity, page 89
on hypocrisy, page 134
on prayer, page 213
on work, page 313

Jami (1414-1492)
Persian writer
Poet, prose writer, religious leader, and mystic. Often called last great classical poet of Persia; member of Naqshbandi order of Sufis; known for book on Sufi biographies, but best known for poetry in range of styles; prolific writer; was widely imitated during his time.

on faith, page 88
on God, page 109
on love, page 171-172
on meaning, page 178

Nabil Janabi (20th century)
Iraqi poet
Known for social criticism and writings against Iraqi government. Imprisoned for criticism of Iraqi government's repression of Kurdish independence movement; upon release, was harassed for lack of support of the war with Iran; now lives in Great Britain.

on freedom, page 102

Jarir (653-732)
Umayyad Islamic poet
Best known for love poems, considered among the finest of Umayyad dynasty Arab poetry.

on time, page 278

Jeanne, Marquise de Pompadour. *See* Marquise de Pompadour

Dai Jian (20th century)
Chinese poet
on grieving, page 119

Jiang Haicheng. *See* Ai Qing

Mohammed Ali Jinna
(1876-1948)
Pakistani political leader, father of modern Pakistan
Born in Karachi; worked as lawyer in Bombay; elected to Viceroy's legislative council; member of Indian National Congress. Became prime mover in India's All Muslim League; opposed Gandhi's policy

of nonviolence and resigned from Congress. At London Round Table Conference (1931), advocated "fourteen points" safeguarding Muslim minorities; eventually advocated separate state for Muslims. Upon creation of Pakistan, became first governor general; called "Quaid-i-Azam" (Great Leader).

on respect, page 238

Fatima Jinna (1893–1967)
Pakistani politician
Sister of politician Mohammed Ali Jinna; organized women in support of All-India Muslim League. Ran against Ayub Khan for president of Pakistan; lost by small margin.

on decisions, page 63–64
on effort, page 76

Joan of Arc (c. 1412–1431)
French religious and military
leader
(Jeanne d'Arc)
Aided French dauphin in his quest for the throne; claimed divine guidance in this task; involved in numerous military conflicts (1429–1430); eventually caught, charged with witchcraft and heresy, and burned at the stake; after revision of trial, innocence proclaimed (1456). Canonized in 1920.

on truth, page 285

James Earl Jones (b. 1931)
American actor
Stage and screen actor. Born in Mississippi, graduated from University of Michigan with degree in drama. First professional role in *Wedding in Japan*; acted in various Shake-

spearean plays. First major film role in *The Great White Hope,* about boxing champion Jack Johnson, propelled him to stardom and critical acclaim. Winner of numerous awards, including Obie, Tony, Emmy, and nomination for Academy Award.

on racism, page 226

Leroi Jones. *See* Imamu Amiri Baraka

Mother Jones (1830–1930)
(Mary Harris Jones)
American labor activist
Born Mary Harris in Ireland; moved to United States in 1835; became teacher, then dressmaker; married member of Iron Molders Union (1861); husband and four children died in Memphis yellow fever epidemic; returned to dressmaking business, which was later destroyed by the 1871 Chicago fire; began attending meetings at Knights of Labor hall; by 1890s, was organizer for United Mine Workers of America (UMWA); worked extensively in western Virginia; active in Colorado coal miners' strikes (1903–1904); strong fighter for worker's rights; publicized evils of child labor.

on feminism, page 96
on reform and reformers, page 230

Erica Jong (b. 1942)
American writer
Novelist and poet known for innovative style and attention to feminist issues; most famous work is *Fear of Flying;* active in fight for

authors' rights; head of Authors' Guild.

on advice, page 6
on joy, page 145
on talent, page 275

Barbara Jordan (b. 1936)
American politician
Member of U.S. House of Representatives (1973-1978) (Democrat, Texas); first woman and first African American to give keynote address at Democratic National Convention (1976).

on effort, page 76
on rules, page 246

Chief Joseph (c. 1840-1904)
Nez Percé chief
Native American leader during Nez Percé War of 1877; fought against relocation of his people; initially advocated peace, but later turned to violence as last resort; led 1,700-mile flight to join Sitting Bull in Canada, but was stopped 30 miles short of the border (1877); met with President McKinley and Theodore Roosevelt; advocated Native Americans' rights to education.

on defeat, page 65
on freedom, page 102
on promises, page 220
on religion, page 233

Josephine (1763-1814)
French empress
Wife of Napoleon I; accompanied Napoleon during his Italian campaign, but soon returned to Paris; became social leader; upon dissolution of her marriage in 1809, retained title of empress.

on luxury, page 175

Benito Juárez (1806-1872)
Mexican revolutionary and political leader
Key figure in Mexican independence; successfully revolted against Santa Anna (1855); held various government positions; eventually led revolt against President Ignacio Comonfort; after three years of civil war, became president (1861-1872); died in office.

on enemies, page 78
on history, page 125
on law, page 153
on war, page 298

Tanizaki Jun'ichiro (1886-1965)
Japanese writer
Novelist and essayist; a leading Japanese writer of his time, particularly of those publishing in Meiji era (before 1912); work considered innovative; popular with Western readers.

on art and artists, page 19
on evil, page 83
on writers and writing, page 318

Yoshiyuki Junnosake (b. 1924)
Japanese writer
Novelist and short story writer; highly popular in Japan and abroad; known for independent voice and sensual slant; winner of Akutagawa Prize (1954) and Shinchosa Literary Prize (1965), among others.

on love, page 172

K

Kabir (1440–1519)
Indian Mughal poet and
  philosopher
Religious philosopher; known for
mystical poetry. Although claimed
to have faith in both the Hindu
Rama-Visnu and the Islamic Allah,
rejected both the Veda and the
Qur'an and taught his own philosophy; known for collection of ser-
mons called the *Bijak*.

  on conduct, page 47
  on faith, page 88
  on fate, page 92
  on meaning, page 178
  on revolution, page 242
  on transience, page 280
  on virtue, page 295
  on wealth, page 303

Muhammad ben Kafif
(c. 8th century)
Arab Sufi poet
(Abu 'Abdullah Muhammad
ben Kafif)
One of more influential Sufis of his
time; known for mystical verses.

  on faith, page 88

Nagai Kafu (1879–1959)
Japanese writer
Novelist, editor, and critic; considered one of Japan's leading literary
figures. As professor of French literature at Keio University, considered a leading expert on Western
naturalistic realism; work influenced by French realists. As editor,
published new writers, including
Tanizaki Jun'ichiro; believed literature should examine life's realities;

stressed observation skills and
truthfulness in transmittal of emotions and experiences.

  on beauty, page 22
  on compassion, page 45
  on nature, page 189
  on pleasure, page 204
  on transience, page 280
  on writers and writing,
    page 318

Amalia Kahana-Carmon
(20th century)
Israeli poet
Often described as the "Israeli Virginia Woolf"; although belongs to
the age group of the Palmach generation of the fifties, work is classi-
fied as part of the later "New
Wave" writing; with A. B. Yeho-
shua one of Israel's premier poets.

  on books and reading, page 28
  on relationships, page 232

Jacob Kahan (b. 1881)
Israeli poet
Work considered influential to
other Israeli writers; known for romantic style, imagistic descrip-
tions, and optimistic viewpoints;
renowned for poems about the
fighters for freedom.

  on eternity, page 81

Al Kali (901–967)
Arab philosopher and philologist
(Abu 'Ali al Baghdad al Kali)
Considered first notable Islamic
philosopher; as only Islamic philos-
opher of Arab descent at the time,
was called the "Philosopher of the
Arabs." Advocated neo-Platonism;

believed religious revelation and philosophy could coexist.

on ability, page 1

Mustafa Kamil (1874-1908)
Egyptian nationalist
Charismatic leader of nationalist movement; formed Nationalist Party in 1907 with Muhammad Farid.

on patriotism and nationalism, page 200

K'ang Yu-wei (1858-1927)
Chinese reformer and philosopher
Political philosopher; leader of reform movement of late Ch'ing dynasty; famous for book outlining utopian ideals, *Ta T'ung Shu (Book of Great Unity)*.

on brotherhood and sisterhood, page 29-30
on competition, page 45
on existence, page 85
on feminism, page 96
on human nature, page 129
on leadership and leaders, page 155
on music, page 185
on the public, page 221
on the self, page 253
on unity, page 289-290
on the universe, page 290-291
on women, page 309

Orhan Veli Kanik (1914-1950)
Turkish poet
Highly popular in Turkey; key figure in Turkish literary movement for modernism; focused on writing about and for the common person.

on hypocrisy, page 134
on poetry and poets, page 206
on the public, page 221

Aminu Kano (b. 1920)
Nigerian politician
Revolutionary and reformer; member of the Hausa-Fulani peoples; began career as militant who sought to remove both British and feudal elements of autocratic kingdoms from Nigerian society. In 1950s, raised political army, the Northern Elements Progressive Unio. After independence, held variety of positions—member of Nigerian parliament, minister of health, and delegate to United Nations.

on action, page 3
on change, page 34
on decisions, page 64
on freedom, page 102
on government, page 116
on leadership and leaders, page 156
on resistance, page 236-237

Husayn Wa'idh Kashifi
(15th century)
Islamic poet
Writer of *Anwar-i Suhayl*, a Persian version of the famous Indian work *Kalila and Dimna*, tales of wisdom that were translated into many Indian and Middle Eastern languages.

on grieving, page 119-120

Kenneth Kaunda (b. 1924)
Zambian nationalist and politician
Leading figure in move for Zambian independence; founded Zambian African National Congress (1958); he was imprisoned, and the movement was banned. Elected president of United National Independent Party (1960); actively involved in

fight for independence; became prime minister of Rhodesia (1964). Upon Zambian independence (October 1964), became first president of Zambia; resigned after economic policies failed.

on law, page 153
on nonviolence, page 191
on violence, page 294
on war, page 298

Shiraishi Kazuko (b. 1931)
Japanese poet
Born in Vancouver; considered a leading female poet of postwar Japan.

on sorrow, page 265

Helen Keller (1880–1968)
American writer and lecturer
Blind and deaf after illness at nineteen months; student of Anne Sullivan; became famous for overcoming her disabilities; wrote numerous books, including *The Story of My Life* (1902); lectured widely; received Presidential Medal of Freedom (1964).

on adventure, page 5
on adversity, page 5
on character, page 36
on duty, page 75
on pride, page 215
on science and technology, page 250
on seeing, page 252
on tolerance, page 279

Minnie Kellogg (1880–1949)
Iroquois leader
Founding member of American Indian Association; believed Native

Americans should preserve traditional values.

on culture, page 56

Tines Kendricks
(c. 19th century)
American ex-slave
on slavery, page 262

Kenko Hoshi (14th century)
Japanese Buddhist
Originally an official in Imperial Guard; converted to Buddhism; retired to contemplative life near Kyoto.

on beginnings, page 23
on hunger, page 133

Jomo Kenyatta (1891–1978)
Kenyan political leader and founder of modern Kenya
Orphan educated at mission school; became active in Kenyan nationalist movement; served as president of Pan African Federation with Nkrumah. Member of nationalist extremist Kenya African Union; headed Mau Mau guerilla group, for which eventually sentenced to seven years' hard labor. Upon release in 1958, reentered politics; became president of KANU Party; member of parliament (1961); prime minister (1963); first president of Republic of Kenya (1964).

on goals, page 108
on imperialism, page 139
on unity, page 290
on work, page 313

Keorapetse Kgositsile (b. 1938)
South African poet
African by birth, but much of work

focuses on blacks in the United States; promotes black brotherhood—regardless of nationality—and celebrates black liberation.

on bravery, page 29

Mohammed Khair-Eddine
(b. 1941)
Moroccan writer
Poet and novelist; avant-garde works rebel against traditional Moroccan values; known personally as one who rebelled against his family, government, and people; advocates destruction of old order to start anew.

on ancestors and ancestry, page 15
on writers and writing, page 319

Yusuf Al-Khal (b. 1917)
Lebanese poet
Taught in Lebanon; founded *Shi'r (Poetry)* magazine; also ran an art gallery; translated major English language poets such as Frost, Eliot, and Whitman into Arabic.

on life, page 164

Omar Khayyám (c. 1048–1122)
Persian poet and astronomer
Famed as one of greatest composers of *rubáiyát*, or quatrains; also mathematician; known for scientific achievements in his own land. Born in Nishapur; after education, went to Samarkand, where wrote important work on algebra; Seljuq sultan became his patron, inviting him to make astronomical calculations for reform of calendar, and to work on observatory in Isfahan. Later became court astrologer. Lit-

erary work remained largely unrecognized until Edward Fitzgerald translated and arranged the quatrains into the *Rubáiyát of Omar Khayyám* (1859), which eventually gained worldwide attention.

on death, page 61
on drinking, page 74
on the past, page 198

Ayatollah Khomeini
(1902–1989)
Iranian Sh'ia Muslim and political leader
(Ruholla Mussavi)
As opponent to Shah Mohammed Reza Pahlavi's pro-Western leanings, exiled to Turkey, Paris, and Iraq (1964). Upon collapse of shah's government, returned to Iran and became head of state (1979); spearheaded Iranian return to strict Islamic traditions and principles, termed the "Islamic Revolution."

on government, page 116

Amir Khusrau (1253–1325)
Indian scholar and poet
(Abul Hassan; Yaminuddin)
Librarian and court poet to seven kings of Delhi; known for lyric poems; protege of Nizamuddin Aulia; generally wrote on historical topics.

on oppression, page 196

Nasir-i-Khusraw (1004–1061)
Persian writer
(Abu Mu'ini'd-Din Nasir-i-Khusraw al-Qubadiyani al-Marwazi)
Poet, essayist, missionary, traveler, and Isma'ili Muslim propagandist.

Famous for religious odes and travel prose pieces. Known also for legends attached to his name, partially due to the pseudo-autobiography of him that appears as preface to one of his works, the *Diwan* (collected poems), actual biography pieced together from his *Safar-nama* (*Narrative of His Travels*). Other famous works include *Raw-shan'i-nama* (*Book of Light*) and *Sa'adat-nama* (*Book of Felicity*).

on danger, page 57
on failure, page 87
on self-reliance, page 258
on words, page 311

John Oliver Killens (b. 1916)
American writer
Novelist, essayist, and screenwriter; writer-in-residence at universities, including Columbia University; works often focus on African American experience; addresses civil rights issues; espouses support for black aesthetics.

on civil rights, page 40-41
on conformity, page 47

Kim Chong-gu
(c. 15th-16th century)
Korean poet
Widely read during reign of the Korean tyrant Yonsangun.

on old age, page 193

Rasa'il al-Kindi (810-873)
Arab philosopher and physician
First Islamic philosopher to develop doctrine of the Spirit (or the Mind); first physician to apply

mathematics to medicine, as in measuring doses; astronomer.

on illness, page 138
on philosophy, page 203
on transience, page 280
on truth, page 285

Billie Jean King (b. 1943)
American athlete
Tennis player; major figure in women's professional sports; winner of nineteen Wimbledon titles; founder of World Tennis Team; cofounder of Virginia Slims Pro Tennis Tour.

on ambition, page 12

Coretta Scott King (b. 1927)
American civil rights leader
Widow of civil rights leader Martin Luther King, Jr.; after his assassination, became prominent figure in civil rights movement; founding president of Martin Luther King, Jr., Center for Nonviolent Social Change.

on progress, page 219

Martin Luther King, Jr.
(1929-1968)
American civil rights leader
Clergyman and major civil rights leader; advocated nonviolence; organized numerous civil rights boycotts and marches, including Montgomery, Alabama bus boycott (1956) and the March on Washington D.C. (1963). Well known for oratory skill. Assassinated in Memphis, Tennessee.

on African Americans, page 8
on belief, page 25
on brotherhood and sisterhood, page 30
on Christianity, page 39
on civil rights, page 41

on conformity, page 47
on creativity, page 54
on dreams, page 73
on evil, page 83
on good and evil, page 113
on hate, page 123
on ignorance, page 137
on joy, page 144
on justice, page 146
on language, page 152
on law, page 153
on oppression, page 196
on peace, page 200
on property, page 220
on race, page 223
on racism, page 226
on reality, page 229
on revolution, page 242
on sacrifice, page 248
on talent, page 275
on time, page 278
on violence, page 294-295
on work, page 313

Kiosaton (c. 1650)
Iroquois chief
Native American leader known for speech before French Governor Montmagny, pleading for release of Iroquois prisoners ambushed in 1645.

on peace, page 200-201

Ko Hung (283-343)
Chinese scholar
Military officer and military councilor to governor of Kuang-chou. Known chiefly for *Autobiography*; retained belief in Confucianism, but also followed Taoist teachings and used drugs in effort to attain spiritual freedom.

on belief, page 25
on fate, page 92

on moderation, page 184
on transience, page 280

Kathe Kollwitz (1867-1945)
East Prussian artist
Painter, sculptor, and graphic artist. Often described as expressionist, but considered herself outside of modern art trends; work tends to be political or social commentary, with often tragic subjects. First female member of Prussian Academy of the Arts (1919); expelled from the academy by Nazis (1933).

on death, page 61
on joy, page 144

Takamura Kotaro (1883-1956)
Japanese artist and poet
Sculptor, poet, and painter. Proponent of "new style" poetry and free verse; considered himself more of a sculptor than a writer.

on ancestors and ancestry,
    page 15

Ahmadou Kourouma (b. 1927)
Ivory Coast writer
Novelist; known for blending Western genres with African thinking; *Les soleils des independances* (*The Suns of Independence*) considered best Ivory Coast novel; work addresses disaffection with independence.

on imperialism, page 139

Abba Kovner (b. 1918)
Israeli poet
Born in Crimea; chiefly symbolist poet; awarded Israel Prize for Literature (1970).

on experience, page 86

V. K. Krishna Menon (b. 1897)
Indian politician
Born in Calicut, Malabar; moved to Great Britain in 1924. Became secretary of India League; advocated anticolonialism and Indian nationalism. Became Indian high commissioner (in London) when India became a dominion (1947); head of Indian delegation to United Nations (1952), where led Asian "uncommitted" bloc; formulated plan concerning nationalization of Suez Canal (1956); as defense minister (1957-1962), faced conflict with Great Britain over Kashmir.

on diplomacy, page 72

Jiddu Krishnamurti
(1895-1986)
Indian philosopher
Born in Madras; educated in England by spiritualist Annie Besant, founder of Order of the Star in the East, who named him the Messiah in 1925; known for emphasis on personal experience; eventually dissolved the order and traveled extensively, advocating tolerance of race, religion, and nationality.

on meditation, page 179
on religion, page 233
on spirituality, page 268-269

Kuan Chung (643-600 B.C.E.)
Chinese philosopher
Adviser to Duke Huan of Ch'i; well known for anecdotes about him collected in seventh chapter of Taoist philosophy book, the *Lieh-tzu*.

on learning and education,
page 159

Shiv Kumar (b. 1921)
Indian writer
Poet, novelist, short story writer, essayist, and editor. Considered major Anglo-Indian poet, even though first work published in 1970; poetry marked by ironic humor, depiction of physical experience, especially sex, and examination of East and West.

on poetry and poets, page 206

Joseph Camillo Kumbirai
(1922-1986)
Zimbabwean writer
Poet, priest, teacher, and critic; one of most prolific Shona poets; wrote during both colonial and independence eras; earlier work focuses on Roman Catholicism; later works center around political themes; synthesized traditional didactic *nhango* poetry with lyric poetry.

on God, page 109-110

Mazisi Kumene (b. 1932)
South African writer
Zulu poet and playwright; writes in both English and Zulu; considered a leading African poet.

on destruction, page 70

K'ung Fu Tzu. *See* Confucius

Kuo K'ai-chen. *See* Guo Moruo

Akira Kurosawa (b. 1910)
Japanese film director
A leading Japanese film director; has written twenty screenplays filmed by other directors; reputation as a perfectionist; most fa-

mous films include *Rashomon, The Seven Samurai* (remade as *The Magnificent Seven* in the U.S.), *Yojimbo,* and *Ran;* losing eyesight, but still involved in film making—most recently, *Dreams;* received special Academy Award for lifetime achievement (1990).

on art and artists, page 19

Nguyen Cao Ky (b. 1930)
South Vietnamese politician and
  soldier
Air Force officer; educated in Hanoi under French administration; commanded Ton Son Nhut Air Force Base; prime minister of South Vietnam; vice president (1967-1971). After fall of South Vietnam to Communists, immigrated to United States (1975); currently owns liquor store.

on war, page 298

L

Abellatif Laabi (20th century)
Moroccan writer
Poet, short story writer, and playwright. Founded literary review *Souffles* (1966); major force in Maghrebi (North African) literature; translated many works from Arabic literature into French. Also known for cultural activism; spent eight years in prison for his views; main themes of works are chaos and rebirth.

on humanity, page 131
on the self, page 253
on solitude, page 264
on speech, page 267

Labid (c. 600)
Arab poet
Considered one of finest pre-Islamic Bedouin poets; works included in *Mu'allaqat (Suspended Ones)* anthology, so-called because as winners in an annual poetry competition, their odes were supposedly written in gold and suspended for all to read.

on materialism, page 178
on transience, page 280

Suzanne LaFollette (1893-1983)
American feminist and writer
Editor and prose writer; with Susan B. Anthony and Elizabeth Cady Stanton, leader of the early U.S. feminist movement.

on equality, page 80
on feminism, page 96
on freedom, page 102
on revolution, page 242

Enrique A. Laguerre (b. 1906)
Puerto Rican writer
Novelist, short story writer, poet, and journalist.

on civilization, page 42
on tradition, page 279

P. Lal (b. 1929)
Indian writer
Poet, essayist, editor, and translator; considered a leading figure in Indo-English literature; avant-garde publisher; known as innovator and Orientalist.

on love, page 172

John Mercer Langston
(1829-1897)
American politician
Born on Virginia plantation, son of the master; became lawyer; held

wide range of political and educational positions, from city council member to dean of Howard University's law school. Eventually became first African American elected to public office in United States, as member of U.S. House of Representatives. Active in civil rights organizations, such as the National Equal Rights League and Negro National Labor Union.

on slavery, page 262

Lao She (1899-1966)
Chinese writer
(psuedonym of Shu Ch'ing-Ch'in or Shu She-Yu)
Novelist, short story writer, and dramatist; famous for works focusing on the underprivileged; committed suicide in early days of the Cultural Revolution.

on reform and reformers, page 230-231

Lao-tzu (c. 604-531 B.C.E.)
Chinese philosopher and founder of Taoism
Author of the *Tao-te-ching* (*Way of the Power*), chief work of Taoism; little known about his life; advocated detachment, simplicity, and self-sufficiency; taught that humans should recognize their instinctive unity with nature.

on action, page 3
on beauty, page 22
on charity, page 37
on conquest, page 48
on desire, page 69
on enemies, page 78
on eternity, page 82
on good and evil, page 113
on greed, page 118

on humility, page 132
on knowledge, page 149
on law, page 153
on leadership and leaders, page 156
on loss, page 169
on love, page 172
on moderation, page 184
on paradox, page 197
on power, page 211
on problems, page 217
on self-discipline, page 255
on speech, page 267
on Taoism, page 275-276
on truth, page 285
on water, page 302
on wealth, page 303
on wisdom, page 307

Juan Latino (c. 1573)
Spanish ex-slave, Latin grammarian, and poet

on racism, page 226

Helen Lawrenson (1907-1982)
American writer and editor
Magazine editor and writer.

on sex, page 259

Lee Kuan Yew (b. 1923)
Singaporean prime minister
British educated; led Singapore out of union with Malaysia into modern, independent nation-state; became prime minister; recently criticized as excessively authoritarian.

on freedom, page 102

Madeleine L'Engle (b. 1918)
American writer
Novelist and children's book writer; won Newbery Award

(1963) for her children's classic, *A Wrinkle in Time*.

> on love, page 173
> on sin, page 260

Doris Lessing (b. 1919)
English writer
Novelist, short story writer, and critic; raised in southern Rhodesia (now Zimbabwe). Works generally revolve around female protagonist; addresses humans' urge toward self-destruction; most famous works include *The Grass is Singing* and *The Golden Notebook*.

> on law, page 154
> on learning and education, page 160
> on survival, page 274

Judah ha-Levi (c. 1075–1141)
Spanish Hebrew poet and
   theologian
(Yehuda ha-Levi; Yehuda Halevi) Considered finest Hebrew poet of Middle Ages; developed new genre of poetry in writing about need for a return to Zion. Well known for defense of Judaism, the *Kuzari*.

> on books and reading, page 28
> on women, page 309

Liang Qichao (1808–1883)
Chinese political theorist
Intellectual leader; active participant in government; proponent of constitutional monarchy.

> on government, page 116
> on science and technology, page 250

Li Ch'ing-chao (1084–1151)
Chinese poet
Considered one of greatest female Chinese poets.

> on solitude, page 264

Li Dazhao (1888–1927)
Chinese political theorist
Advocated Marxist socialism; cofounded Chinese Communist Party; executed by Manchurian warlord Zhang Zuolin.

> on brotherhood and sisterhood, page 30
> on ethics and morality, page 82
> on work, page 313

Li Hung-chang (1823–1901)
Chinese politician
General and official in Ching dynasty; advocated modernization; became one of most powerful government officials; rose to prominence fighting the Niam rebels (1860s); held range of positions; implemented numerous programs strengthening China; improved educational reform; developed railways and telegraph lines.

> on progress, page 219

Li Ju-chen (c. 1763–1830)
Chinese writer and scholar
Famous for single novel, *Chinghua yuan*, a major work of Chin dynasty fiction, considered radically feminist.

> on materialism, page 178
> on poverty, page 210

Li Ping (c. 200 B.C.E.)
Chinese engineer
Hydraulic engineer who first

tamed the Yellow River; Chin dynasty provincial governor.

on policy, page 207

Li Po (701-762)
Chinese poet
Along with Tu Fu, regarded as the greatest poet of pre-twentieth-century China; most poetry is calm, sunny, often playful and hyperbolic, spontaneous. Born in Szechuan; traveled extensively, at least partly due to troubles with the government.

on drinking, page 74
on longing, page 168
on nature, page 189
on war, page 298-299
on work, page 313

Li Shang-yin (c. 812-858)
Chinese writer
Considered one of greatest Tang dynasty poets; well known for poems on clandestine love, with many allusions.

on old age, page 193

Li Ssu (c. 280-208 B.C.E.)
Chinese government official
Chief minister during Chin dynasty; as advisor to emperor, attained title of retainer; believed responsible for the suicide of the emperor's heir.

on success, page 272

Lin Yutang (1895-1976)
Chinese writer
Philologist and professor; wrote on wide range of subjects; one of better-known Chinese writers in English-speaking world.

on contentment, page 50
on failure, page 87
on happiness, page 122
on lies, page 162
on life, page 164
on society, page 263
on travel, page 282
on wisdom, page 307

Anne Morrow Lindbergh (b. 1906)
American writer and aviator
Poet and memoirist; married aviator Charles A. Lindbergh; after marriage, learned to fly; assisted husband in charting international air routes later used for commercial air travel; best known for *Gift from the Sea* and *The Unicorn and Other Poems*.

on life, page 166

Liu Shih-p'ei (1884-1919)
Chinese writer
Anarchist based in Tokyo; advocated women's integral role in revolution; espoused highly radical views; went underground with wife, anarchist and editor Ho Chen; bribed by governor of Kiangsu and Kiangnan to spy on subversive organizations.

on dependence, page 69

Luis Llorens Torres (1878-1944)
Puerto Rican writer
Poet, essayist, critic, playwright, and politician; often wrote on patriotic themes.

on the future, page 105
on memory, page 179-180

Ndebele Lobengula (1870–1896)
Mashonaland king
King of area now in Zimbabwe and South Africa; ruler when British seized area.

on imperialism, page 139

Lokman (c. 1100 B.C.E.)
Ethiopian fabulist
Known for proverbs and fables; considered by some to be the Islamic equivalent of King Solomon; quoted in the Qur'an.

on children and childhood, page 38
on conduct, page 47
on teaching, page 276

Amy Lowell (1874–1925)
American writer
Poet, essayist, and translator; major figure in imagist movement; advocated strong, unsentimental style in verse; although best known for poetry, also wrote essays and a biography of Keats; translated Chinese works; won Pulitzer Prize (1926).

on the Americas, page 14
on art and artists, page 19
on beauty, page 22
on books and reading, page 28
on life, page 164
on love, page 172
on writers and writing, page 319
on youth, page 321

Lu Xun (1881–1936)
Chinese writer
(pseudonym of Chou Shu-jen)
Literary innovator; considered premier writer of his time; proponent of literary realism written in vernacular rather than classical style;

most famous work is *Ah Q chen chuan (The True Story of Ah Q)*.

on boldness, page 27
on causes, page 33
on creativity, page 54
on dreams, page 73
on fame, page 89
on the future, page 105
on greatness, page 117
on heroes, page 124
on hope, page 128
on hypocrisy, page 134
on justification, page 147
on leadership and leaders, page 156
on luck, page 175
on marriage, page 177
on policy, page 207
on prejudice, page 214
on resistance, page 237
on revolution, page 242
on scholars, page 249
on self-preservation, page 257
on trust, page 283
on tyranny and tyrants, page 287
on words, page 311
on the world, page 314
on writers and writing, page 319

Lu Yu (1125–1209)
Chinese writer
One of the premier (and most prolific) Sung dynasty poets; failed bureaucrat who retired to rustic life; wrote polemics on "barbarian" Jurchen invaders in North China and the joys of rural life.

on drinking, page 74

Clare Booth Luce (1903–1987)
American diplomat and politician
Member of U.S. House of Representatives (1943–1947) (Republican, Connecticut); U.S. ambassador to

Italy (1953–1957); received Presidential Medal of Freedom (1983).

on bravery, page 29
on enemies, page 78

Albert John Luthuli
(1898–1967)
South African human rights
    activist
Former Zulu chief; worked against apartheid in South Africa; president of African National Congress (1950s); recipient of Nobel Peace Prize (1961).

on racism, page 226

Rosa Luxembourg (1871–1919)
German revolutionary
Socialist activist, writer, and founder of German Communist Party; studied philosophy and law in Zurich; cofounded Social Democratic Party of Poland (1893); lived in France and Berlin; returned to Poland and organized workers' revolts; broke with German Socialist Party when it supported war in 1914; spent four years in prison, where organized Spartacus League, a radical group; part of abortive Spartacus uprising (1919); arrested and killed.

on revolution, page 242

Ly Tru'ong. *See* Man Giac

M

Abu'l-Ala-Al'Ma'arri (973–1057)
Arab poet
Wrote on wide range of subjects, including life and death, philoso-
phy, religion, and society; ascetic who preferred hermit's life; went blind at an early age, but still managed to complete education; sought fortune in Baghdad, but failed; spent last half of life writing, teaching, and studying; best known for *Meditations.*

on humanity, page 131

Ma Chih-yuan (1260–1325)
Chinese writer
Poet and playwright; a leading writer of Yuan dynasty. Served in Kiangsi provincial government; did not achieve fame or fortune; found peace in nature and poetry; play *Autumn in the Han Palace* is considered his greatest work.

on aging, page 11
on pleasure, page 204

Joaquim Maria Machado de Assis (1839–1908)
Brazilian writer
Poet and novelist known for cynical outlook; considered a leading Brazilian writer of his time.

on death, page 61
on generations, page 106
on ideals, page 135
on revolution, page 242
on striving, page 270
on time, page 278
on vanity, page 292

Samora Machel (1933–1986)
Mozambiquen activist and
    politician
Involved in fight for Mozambiquen independence; joined Frelimo independence movement; led Mozambiquens to independence

from Portugal (1975); became president; died in plane crash (1986).

on laziness, page 154
on revolution, page 243
on unity, page 290

Diosdado Macpagal (b. 1910)
Philippine politician
Called "Honest Dadang," "Honest Mac," and the "Poor Man's Best Friend"; won over voters with stories about his rags-to-riches story; elected fifth president of Republic of the Philippines (1961); abolished import and exchange controls, and economic trouble followed; was defeated in 1965 by Ferdinand Marcos; was also poet.

on learning and education, page 160

Grigor Magistros (990–1058)
Armenian scholar and public official
Linguist, writer, scholar, and official; served as governor-general of province of Edessa; named a duke by Byzantine Emperor Constantine I. Poetry shows both Homeric Greek and contemporary Arabic influences; most famous for long narrative work on biblical events.

on effort, page 76

Ramon Magsaysay (1907–1957)
Philippine political leader
Held numerous government positions; as secretary of defense, defeated Communist Huk rebellion; president (1953–1957).

on Communism, page 43–44
on democracy, page 67

on hope, page 128
on the public, page 221
on reform and reformers, page 231

Naguib Mahfouz (b. 1911)
Egyptian writer
Novelist; called variously the "Dickens of the Cairo cafés" and "the Balzac of Egypt" because of story-telling ability, rich characterizations, and prolific output. Leading works include *The Cairo Trilogy* (1956–1957) and the controversial *The Children of Geblawi* (1961); won Nobel Prize for literature (1988).

on art and artists, page 19
on change, page 34
on fear, page 93
on graves and graveyards, page 117
on life, page 165
on revolution, page 243

Maimonides (1135–1204)
Spanish Hebrew philosopher
(Moses ben Maimon)
Born in Spain; immigrated to Egypt. Leading intellectual figure of medieval Judaism; became physician to Saladin, sultan of Egypt, and head of Jewish community. Advocated reconciliation between strict rabbinical Judaism and Aristotelian philosophy; wrote chiefly in Arabic.

on books and reading, page 28
on God, page 110
on humility, page 132
on selfishness, page 256
on teaching, page 276

Makataimeshekiakiak. *See* Black
Hawk

Miriam Makeba (b. 1932)
South African singer and political
activist
Performer and activist known for
political stances; sometimes called
"Mama Africa."

on aging, page 11

Malcolm X (1925–1965)
American civil rights activist
(Malcolm Little; El-Hajj Malik
el-Shabazz)
Born Malcolm Little in Omaha, Nebraska, the son of a Baptist minister; in early years, was arrested for
burglary; in prison, converted to
Islam of the Nation of Islam sect.
Upon release, took the name Malcolm X and promoted Nation of
Islam and black nationalist causes;
initially opposed to integration.
Views changed after the *hijira* (pilgrimage to Mecca), where he was
struck by ideas of Islamic brotherhood. In 1964, founded Organization of Afro-American Unity, which
promoted many orthodox Muslim
beliefs, along with antiracism and
anticolonialism. Wrote *The Autobiography of Malcolm X* with Alex
Haley. Assassinated in New York;
influence increased after his death.

on African Americans,
page 8–9
on the Americas, page 14
on books and reading, page 28
on brotherhood and sisterhood,
page 30
on civil rights, page 41
on enemies, page 78
on freedom, page 102
on gratitude, page 116

on imperialism, page 139
on the land, page 151
on learning and education,
page 160
on oppression, page 196
on patriotism and nationalism,
page 200
on peace, page 201
on power, page 212
on racism, page 226
on reform and reformers,
page 231
on revolution, page 243
on truth, page 285
on violence, page 295

Jamil bin Ma'mar (c. 600)
Islamic poet
Ummayad Islamic master of tragic
'Udhri love poetry.

on old age, page 193–194

Man Giac (19th century)
Vietnamese poet
(Ly Tru'ong)
Son of Vietnamese government of-
ficial; leader of monastery of Gao
Nguya.

on renewal, page 235

Nelson Mandela (b. 1918)
South African president
A leader in antiapartheid movement; led three-day strike in 1961;
sentenced to life imprisonment
(1964); released (1990) to head African National Congress and lead
South Africa to multiethnic policy;
won election to presidency in
1994.

on freedom, page 102
on political movements,
page 208
on racism, page 227

Norman Washington Manley
(1893–1969)
Jamaican politician
Born in Kingston; became lawyer; first received attention in 1938 for successful defense of his cousin and political opponent Alexander Bustamenta, a trade unionist, against charges of sedition; same year founded the People's National Party; became prime minister of Jamaica seven years before country achieved full independence.

on illness, page 137

Marya Mannes (b. 1904)
American writer
Novelist, essayist, social critic, and poet; sharply attacks materialism; work has received mixed reviews.

on seeing, page 252
on success, page 272

Manu (c. 1200 B.C.E.)
Indian Hindu poet and ruler
Possibly legendary figure; considered the father of humankind in some texts and the first king in others; several widely read texts have been attributed to him, including *Manvasrautasutra*.

on justice, page 147
on vice, page 292

Mao Zedong (1893–1976)
Chairman of People's Republic of China
First chairman of People's Republic of China; revolutionary called the "Great Helmsman." Son of peasants; went to University of Peking (Beijeng) (1918); discovered works of Karl Marx and Friedrich Engels.

Helped found Chinese Communist Party (CCP) (1921); set up "people's republic" (a soviet) in Jiangxi (southeastern China) (1931–1934); attacked by Chiang Kai-shek's forces; forced to undertake two-year "Long March" to Shaanxi province (northwestern China); during this time, elected CCP chairman (1935); from new base in Yanan, developed philosophy emphasizing reeducation and "rectification." Directed rural-based guerilla warfare to resist Japanese attacks (1937, 1945), and eventually to overthrow Chiang Kai-shek's nationalist government; founded People's Republic (1949); resigned chairmanship of republic (1959); remained chairman of CCP's Central Committee. Faced dwindling influence due to failure of the Great Leap Forward (1958–1960), an attempt to improve China industrially and agriculturally through use of huge communes; rebounded during the Cultural Revolution (1966–1969), a campaign against "revisionist forces," resulting in many deaths and political chaos; lost political clout in later years, when health deteriorated; famous for his "Little Red Book," also known as "The Sayings of Chairman Mao."

on ability, page 1
on beginnings, page 24
on Communism, page 44
on contradictions, page 50
on enemies, page 78
on experience, page 86
on history, page 125
on intellectuals, page 142
on killing, page 148
on the military, page 182

on old age, page 194
on passivity, page 198
on political movements,
    page 208
on politics, page 209
on power, page 212
on problems, page 217
on the public, page 221
on revolution, page 243
on strategy, page 269
on strength, page 270
on war, page 299

René Maran (1887–1960)
Martinican writer
Poet, novelist, and biographer;
most famous for *Batouala*, the first
book by a black writer on blacks
written for Western literature; criticized French colonialism, but some
felt it also presented Africans as
overly primitive.

on leisure, page 161

Marguerite of Navarre
(1492–1549)
French writer and religious
    reformer
Poet, scholar, and patron of the
arts; sometimes called "the Tenth
Muse" or "the Pearl"; supporter of
Protestantism; author of tales and
of dramatic and religious poems.

on enemies, page 78
on evil, page 83–84
on justification, page 148
on love, page 172
on prison, page 216

Eugenio Maria de Hostos
(1839–1903)
Puerto Rican patriot
Writer and sociologist; opposed
slavery; traveled extensively; in

Puerto Rico, organized Lega de Pa-
triotes Puertorriqueños (League of
Puerto Rican Patriots); worked for
Puerto Rican independence, but efforts failed in his lifetime; many
sayings still quoted in Puerto Rico.

on character, page 36
on civilization, page 42
on feminism, page 96
on good and evil, page 113
on humanity, page 131
on justice, page 146
on love, page 172
on slavery, page 262

Bob Marley (1945–1981)
Jamaican singer
Pioneer of reggae movement;
songs reflect social problems of Jamaica.

on peace, page 201
on politics, page 209
on revolution, page 243

Thurgood Marshall (1908–1993)
American jurist
Chief of legal staff of the National
Association for the Advancement
of Colored People; spearheaded efforts that culminated in landmark
school desegregation case, Brown
v. Board of Education (1954); Solic-
itor General of the United States;
First African American to serve as
Supreme Court justice.

on prejudice, page 214
on success, page 272

José Martí (1853–1895)
Cuban patriot
Fought for Cuban independence;
exiled; wrote chiefly in New York.
Founded Cuban Revolutionary

Party (1892); killed by Spanish after landing in Cuba to lead revolt.

on the Americas, page 14
on bravery, page 29
on identity, page 136
on justice, page 146
on patience, page 199
on poetry and poets, page 206
on political movements,
    page 208
on race, page 223
on war, page 299
on work, page 313

**Abu Mu'ini'd-Din Nasir-i-
Khusraw al-Qubadiyani al-
Marwazi.** *See* Nasir-i-Khusraw

**Abu'l Fadl al-Suqqari
al-Marwazi** (c. 9th–10th century)
Persian poet
Noted for translating Persian proverbs into Arabic; united proverbs into traditional Persian poem form, the *mathnawi.*

on perspective, page 203

Matilda of Magdeburg. *See*
Mechtild of Magdeburg

Abu'l A'la Mawdudi (1903–1979)
Pakistani Islamic leader
Founder of Djamaliti Islami, fundamentalist Islamic group in Pakistan.

on democracy, page 67
on government, page 116

Mayling Soong. *See* Madame
Chiang Kai-shek

Bernadette D. McAliskey
(b. 1947)
Irish politician
(née Bernadette Devlin)
Northern Ireland activist and political leader; youngest member of the British House of Commons. Activist while in college; worked with Civil Rights Association (1966–1969); opposed British presence in Northern Ireland; as a militant independent socialist, elected to House of Commons (1969-1974); arrested during Londonderry riot of August 1969 and sent to prison for four months. After leaving Parliament, remained active in politics; founding member of Irish Republican Socialist Party (1975).

on sacrifice, page 248

Mary McCarthy (1912-1989)
American writer and critic
Novelist, essayist, social critic, and editor. Book reviewer for *Nation* and *New Republic*; editor and critic for *Partisan Review*; famous for novel *The Group,* as well as critical essays; had longstanding feud with writer Lillian Hellman.

on the Americas, page 14
on children and childhood,
    page 38
on justice, page 146

Carson McCullers (1917-1967)
American writer
Novelist, short story writer, and playwright. Known for developing style of writing termed "Southern Gothic"; work marked by unusual characters; most famous works include *The Heart Is a Lonely Hunter, The Member of the Wed-*

ding, and *The Ballad of the Sad Café and Other Stories.*

  on writers and writing,
    page 319

Claude McKay (1890–1948)
American writer
Jamaican-born poet and novelist; one of most outspoken members of the Harlem Renaissance group of African American writers; known for protest poems; traveled extensively; most famous for his poetry collection *Harlem Shadows.*

  on dignity, page 71
  on racism, page 227

Margaret Mead (1901–1978)
American anthropologist
Writer and museum curator; especially known for her groundbreaking *Coming of Age in Samoa.* Proponent of theory that personality is formed through cultural conditioning, rather than heredity alone; accessible style popularized anthropology and other social sciences. Received Presidential Medal of Freedom (1979).

  on aging, page 11
  on causes, page 33
  on diversity, page 72
  on evil, page 84
  on friendship, page 104
  on humanity, page 131
  on love, page 173
  on men and women, page 181
  on science and technology,
    page 250

Mehmet 'Ali. *See* Muhammed 'Ali

Asoka Mehta (b. 1911)
Indian politician
Political activist and socialist involved in struggle for Indian independence and in labor activities; founded Indian Socialist Party (1954); held various political positions; opted for career in academics as party declined in strength and popularity.

  on political movements,
    page 208

Golda Meir (1898–1978)
Israeli prime minister
Immigrated to Palestine from Milwaukee, Wisconsin; became involved in Israeli government, beginning with work for the Histdarut (Federation of Labor); active in fight for state of Israel. Minister of labor (1949–1956); minister of foreign affairs (1956–1966); first female prime minister of Israel (1969–1974); known for her initial diplomatic efforts in approaching Arab and Israeli problems.

  on choice, page 39
  on feminism, page 96
  on guilt, page 120
  on humility, page 132
  on leadership and leaders,
    page 156
  on men and women, page 181
  on old age, page 194
  on paradox, page 198
  on peace, page 201
  on silence, page 260
  on time, page 278
  on victory, page 293
  on war, page 299
  on women, page 309

Cecilia Meireles (1901–1964)
Brazilian poet
Considered one of premier poets in Portuguese language; known for classical lyricism; nominated twice for the Nobel Prize in literature.

on dreams, page 73

Mencius (c. 390–305 B.C.E.)
Chinese philosopher
(Meng-tzu; Meng K'o; Meng-zi)
Considered a cofounder of Confucianism; developed and popularized Confucianism. Born in Tsou a century after death of Confucius; aristocrat and teacher, hoped to find ruler to back his ideas; traveled for forty years searching for this ruler, but failed. Minister in state of Ch'i; later retired from public life and turned to full-time teaching; focused on need for humanitarianism and justice for the common people; advocated social and political reform. After his death, pupils compiled his teachings and sayings into *The Book of Meng-tzu* (also called *The Works of Mencius*).

on character, page 36
on the classes, page 43
on compassion, page 45
on greatness, page 118
on heaven, page 123
on human nature, page 129
on humanity, page 131
on ignorance, page 137
on leadership and leaders, page 156
on meaning, page 178
on perfection, page 201
on poverty, page 210
on power, page 212
on understanding, page 289

Miguel M. Mendez (b. 1930)
American writer
Novelist; a leading voice in Chicano literature; promotes political, social, and linguistic awareness for Chicanos; uses mixture of English and Spanish in works.

on history, page 125

Menelik (1849–1913)
Ethiopian emperor
Considered one of Ethiopia's greatest rulers; born Sahel Mariam, heir to throne of Shoa kingdom, in central Ethiopia; proclaimed king of Shoa (1865); built kingdom into one of strongest powers in country; received arms from European imperialists; proclaimed himself emperor (1889). As emperor, defeated Italian imperialists (1895); obtained international recognition for Ethiopia's independence; laid groundwork for modern administration and government.

on enemies, page 78
on imperialism, page 139

Meng-tzu. *See* Mencius

Meri-ka-Re (c. 2100 B.C.E.)
Egyptian king
King of Ancient Egypt during first intermediate period, time of social equalitarianism. Supposedly received from his father, a Herakleopolitan king, "Instruction to Meri-ka-Re," guide to personal conduct and behavior, and social commitment.

on judgment, page 145
on speech, page 267

Mechthild of Magdeburg
(1210–1297)
German mystic
(Matilda of Magdeburg)
Religious mystic and writer; either a Benedictine or a Cistercian nun; writings center around divine love and mystical religious experience.

on hell, page 124

Vera Micaia. *See* Noemia de Sousa

Barbara Ann Mikulski (b. 1936)
American politician
Elected to U.S. House of Representatives (1977), Senate (1986).

on the Americas, page 14

Edna St. Vincent Millay
(1892–1950)
American writer
Poet and playwright; most popular in her own time; participated in Algonquin Round Table literary group; won Pulitzer Prize for *The Harp Weaver and Other Poems* (1923).

on aging, page 11
on beauty, page 22
on life, page 166
on religion, page 233
on writers and writing,
page 319

Minamoto no Yorimasa
(d. 1180)
Japanese warrior
Composed famous poem seconds before committing suicide; in so doing, represented the ideal Japanese warrior.

last words, page 154

Yukio Mishima (1925–1970)
Japanese writer
(Mishima Yukio)
Novelist and short story writer. Considered more than just a writer, but also a thinker whose works, often philosophical novels, expressed his personal philosophy. Known for ultrapatriotic views and adherence to samurai tradition; supported militarism; committed ritual suicide (*seppuku*).

on children and childhood,
page 39
on Christianity, page 40
on creativity, page 54
on the mind, page 183
on patriotism and nationalism,
page 200
on women, page 310
on the world, page 314
on writers and writing,
page 319

Gabriela Mistral (1889–1957)
Chilean poet
Teacher and diplomat. Held various positions in international education and culture; Chilean consul in Italy; received Nobel Prize in literature (1945).

on children and childhood,
page 39
on death, page 61
on joy, page 145
on poetry and poets, page 206
on prayer, page 213
on speech, page 267
on the world, page 314–315

Maria Mitchell (1818–1889)
American astronomer
First U.S. female astronomer; discovered new comet (1847); first fe-

male member of American Academy of Arts and Sciences.

on science and technology, page 250

Jessica Mitford (b. 1917)
American writer
Born in England; sister of writer Nancy Mitford; social critic; known for investigative studies of various subjects, including *The American Way of Death*.

on crime, page 55

Nancy Mitford (1904-1973)
English writer
Novelist and biographer; sister of writer Jessica Mitford. Known for witty novels such as *Love in a Cold Climate* and, later, extensive biographies such as *Madame de Pompadour* and *Frederick the Great*.

on the classes, page 43

Mo-tze (c. 5th century B.C.E.)
Chinese philosopher
(Mo Ti; Mo Tzu; Mo Zi)
Advocated universal love as solution to both personal and political problems; official in state of Sung.

on brotherhood and sisterhood, page 30
on leadership and leaders, page 156
on problems, page 217

Maria Montessori (1870-1952)
Italian educator
Originator of Montessori method of education; first woman in Italy to earn medical degree; educa-

tional system based on freedom of expression.

on nature, page 189

Cherrie Moraga (b. 1952)
American writer and activist
Feminist and human rights activist; work shows influence of Chicana background.

on feminism, page 96

Nobuko Morris. *See* Nobuko Albery

Toni Morrison (b. 1931)
American writer
Novelist and memoirist; works capture African American experience and speech cadences; received Pulitzer Prize (1987); first African American to receive Nobel Prize in literature (1993).

on questions and answers, page 222

Lucretia Mott (1793-1880)
American abolitionist and suffragist
Quaker minister; incorporated theories of Quakerism with her social activism; deeply involved in anti-slavery movement and women's rights movement.

on feminism, page 96

Es'kia Mphahlele (1919-1982)
South African writer and educator
Known for unpopular antinegritude stance; exiled himself from South Africa.

on racism, page 227

Mu'awiyah (c. 602–680)
Islamic religious and military
leader
(ibn-abi-Suf)
Islamic innovator; reorganized
army; founder of dynasty in Syria;
expanded Arab control into North
Africa; first Umayyad Caliph of Islam.

Muhammad (570–632)
Prophet of Islam
Founder of Islam; considered by
Muslims the "Seal of the
Prophets" (i.e., receiver of the final and perfect revelation from
God). Born in Mecca to poor family of tribe of Quaraysh, hereditary guardians of the shrine in
Mecca; orphaned at age six and
raised by uncle, Abu Talib; initially
worked as trader. Began receiving
revelations from God (c. 610),
commanding that idols of the
shrine be destroyed and that the
rich give to the poor; belief got
some support, but many opponents; reduced to poverty by time
wife and uncle died. Began gathering followers; immigrated to
Yathrib to arbitrate in feuds; migration (called the "Hegira") considered traditional beginning of
Muslim era. Name of town
changed to Medina; led followers
to war with enemies of Islam; by
629, was leader of Mecca and recognized as the "Messenger of
God"; by 630 controlled most of
Arabia. In 632 made last pilgrimage, died shortly thereafter in the
home of one of his wives, Aisha,
daughter of his devoted follower
Abu Bakr, who succeeded him.

Elijah Muhammad (1897–1975)
Founder of the Black Muslims
(now called the American Muslim
Nation)
Follower of and assistant to Wali-
Farad, founder of Nation of Islam

in Detroit; became leader of movement upon Farad's death; called himself the "Messenger of Allah"; advocated separate, autonomous state for African Americans; directed Black Muslim movement.

on self-reliance, page 258

Muhammed 'Ali (1769–1849)
Egyptian viceroy
(Mehmet 'Ali)
Born in Albania; as officer, first sent to Egypt as part of Turkish-Albanian force during 1798 French invasion; after French pullout, supported Egyptian rulers against ruling Mamluks; proclaimed viceroy (1805). As viceroy, oversaw defeat of Mamluks, creation of regular army, and irrigation improvements; created dynasty, with help of adopted son, Ibrahim Pasha. Annexed portions of Arabia, Nubia, and the Sudan; occupied parts of the Morea and Crete; conquered Syria (which he evacuated later). Dynasty he created lasted until 1953.

on imperialism, page 141

Al-Mumazzaq al-'Abdi (c. 600)
pre-Islamic Arab poet
One of the first Arabian poets to denounce worldliness.

on advice, page 6–7

Mu-mon Gensen (1322–1390)
Japanese Buddhist monk
Member of Buddhist Renzai sect; founder of the Hoko-ji in Shizouka.

on dreams, page 73
on words, page 311

Luis Muñoz Marín (b. 1898)
Puerto Rican politician
Advocate of Puerto Rican self-government; involved in foundation of Popular Democrats Party; served various governmental positions, including senator; elected first governor of Puerto Rico (1948); known for social and economic reforms.

on democracy, page 67
on effort, page 77
on justice, page 146
on progress, page 219
on the soul, page 266

Alice Munro (b. 1931)
Canadian writer
Short story writer; known for work centering around woman protagonist.

on love, page 174

Lady Shikibu Murasaki
(978–1030)
Japanese writer
Novelist, poet, diarist, and lady-in-waiting to Empress Akiko. Famous for *The Tale of Genji* (c. 1008), often considered the world's first novel.

on luck, page 175
on memory, page 180

Iris Murdoch (b. 1919)
Irish writer
Novelist, essayist, and philosopher; first works in philosophy; later, explored philosophic ideas in novels; works typically deal with nature of freedom and love; often incorporates gothic elements; known for wit, imagination, and comic inventiveness.

on love, page 174
on passivity, page 198

on power, page 212

al Mutanabbi (915-965)
Arab poet
(abu al Tayyib Ahman ibn-Husayn)
Poet of the Hamdanid dynasty; still one of most widely quoted poets in Islamic world.

on boldness, page 27

Jean-Baptiste Mutabaruka (b. 1937)
Rwandan poet
Born to traditional Tutsi family; although educated in Catholic schools, maintained interest in traditional Tutsi religious ideas, rituals, and customs, and incorporated these in works.

on memory, page 180

Al-Mu'tamid (d. 1095)
Arab Spanish ruler
Muslim ruler well known for hedonism and love of poetry; royal court in Seville was center for literati. United Cordoba with his kingdom; eventually, was deposed and deported to Tangier, Morocco, where he died.

on grieving, page 119

'Abdiliaahi Muuse (c. 1890-1966)
Somali sage
Qur'anic scholar of Habar Yunis clan; known for wisdom and piety; in teachings, emphasized goodwill and cooperation.

on cooperation, page 51
on fools and foolishness,
   page 100

Abel Muzorewa (b. 1925)
Zimbabwean minister and
   politician
Methodist minister; bishop of Rhodesia (1968). Cofounded African National Council, political group opposing Rhodesian Front government's agreement with British; became head of nationalist movement; elected Zimbabwe's first African prime minister. Party eventually lost favor to Robert Mugabe's Patriotic Front Party; voted out of office; public sentiment turned against him because of past collaboration with white regime.

on nonviolence, page 191

Mwanga II (c. 1866-1903)
Bugandan king
Succeeded father (1884); faced dissension due to religious factions (Catholic, Protestant, Muslim); ruled during period of killings and purges; ousted by united forces of all three religious factions; regained throne after four-year civil war; led rebellion to drive British out of Buganda (1894); deposed, captured (1898), and exiled to Seychelles Islands.

on imperialism, page 141

N

Malla Naga *See* Vatsyayana

Nagarjuna (100-165)
Indian Buddhist philosopher
Founder of Middle Doctrine school

(Madhymika), a chief school of Mahayana Buddhism.

> on existence, page 85
> on fools and foolishness, page 100
> on self-discipline, page 255

Samuel ha-Nagid (993–1056)
Spanish Hebrew poet
(Ismail ibn Nagrel'a)
One of first Hebrew poets to write secular verse; ushered in Golden Age of Hebrew literature and arts. Served as vizier of Granada; also known as a scholar and military commander; one of the most highly placed Jews in Muslim Spain.

> on adversity, page 5
> on joy, page 145
> on old age, page 194
> on war, page 299–300
> on writers and writing, page 319

Mohammed Naguib (b. 1901)
Egyptian soldier and political leader
Prime minister (1952); president (1953); ousted by Abdel-Nasser (1954); led Free Officers group, which, with Nasser, ousted King Farouk.

> on religion, page 233

V. S. Naipaul (b. 1932)
West Indian writer
Novelist and memoirist of Indian descent, educated in Britain; won John Llewellyn Prize for first novel.

> on writers and writing, page 319

Najgneq (c. 1920)
Eskimo shaman
Work included in collection of Eskimo songs gathered in first quarter of twentieth century by explorer Knud Rasmussen.

> on vice, page 292

Nanak (1469–1539)
Indian religious leader and founder of Sikhism
(Guru Nanak)
Born a Hindu; traveled to both Hindu and Muslim centers in quest of spiritual truth; eventually evolved his own religion, Sikhism, in many ways a blend of Islamic and Brahman beliefs.

> on God, page 110
> on priorities, page 215
> on speech, page 267

Pritish Nandy (b. 1947)
Indian poet
Works marked by irony, and blend of Indian, Christian, and classic imagery; influenced more by Spanish-language poets than by English-language ones; often addresses social ills and atrocities; blends contemporary with traditional Indian values.

> on death, page 61
> on understanding, page 289

Kaccipettu Nannakalyar
(3rd century)
Indian Tamil poet
Classic Tamil-language poet; work included in the *Kuruntokaj*, one of earliest of eight anthologies of classic Tamil literature dating from

first to third centuries B.C.E.; little known about her life.

on loneliness, page 167

Shiga Naoya (1883-1971)
Japanese writer
Novelist and short story writer; known for "egocentric" slant—focusing on the protagonists of his works, called "I-novels"; added postscripts to his works, explaining his intent.

on art and artists, page 19-20
on evil, page 84

Jayaprakash Narayan
(1902-1979)
Indian nationalist
Fought for Indian independence; espoused radical socialist ideals; declined Nehru's offer to join government; later, worked against Indira Gandhi.

on Communism, page 44
on political movements, page 208
on power, page 212
on revolution, page 243

Gamel Abdel Nasser
(1918-1970)
Egyptian revolutionary and president
(Jamal 'Abd Al Nasir)
One of most important Arab leaders of twentieth century; as head of Free Officers, planned ouster of King Farouk; became president of United Arab Republic (Egypt); as charismatic leader and reformer, presided over very cen-

tralized and undemocratic state; advocated Arab nationalism.

on action, page 3
on cooperation, page 51
on fate, page 92
on heroes, page 124
on money, page 184
on power, page 212
on war, page 300

Pol Ndu (b. 1940)
Nigerian poet
Professor; first published in *Black Orpheus* magazine; included in numerous anthologies; most famous for "Ritual Dance."

on war, page 300

Nefer-rohu (c. 2200 B.C.E.)
Egyptian prophet
Said to be a prophet during the first intermediate period of ancient Egypt, an unstable period marked by influx of Asians into the area, and political turmoil; existing writings speak against collapse of values of the time and the breakdown of the previously strong central government of an all-powerful god-king, and warned of potential for complete disaster.

on strife, page 270

Jawaharlal Nehru (1889-1964)
Indian prime minister
One of India's most influential figures; first prime minister of independent India; initially, member of Gandhi's nonviolent party. As prime minister, held neutral position between Eastern Communist

and Western capitalist blocs; promoted industrialization.

on action, page 3
on adventure, page 5
on boasting, page 26
on causes, page 33
on civilization, page 42
on culture, page 56
on democracy, page 67
epitaph, page 79-80
on the future, page 105
on the golden rule, page 112
on history, page 126
on leadership and leaders,
    page 157
on political movements,
    page 208
on problems, page 217
on religion, page 233
on restraint, page 239
on sacrifice, page 248
on self-discipline, page 255
on success, page 272
on truth, page 285
on words, page 311

Alice Dunbar Nelson
(1875-1935)
American writer
Poet, teacher, journalist, and political and social activist; pioneer in the black short story; first African American woman to serve on Delaware's Republican State Committee.

on war, page 300

Pablo Neruda (1904-1973)
Chilean poet and diplomat
Latin America's leading contemporary poet. Joined Communist Party and was elected to senate (1945); when party was outlawed, traveled abroad until 1952. Consul in Madrid, Calcutta, Rangoon, and Mexico; Chilean ambassador in Paris. Known for mix of poetic and unpoetic, surrealistic tone merged with realistic; received Nobel Prize in literature (1971).

on despair, page 70
on poetry and poets, page 206
on revolution, page 243-244
on the self, page 253
on transience, page 280
on writers and writing,
    page 319

Louise Nevelson (1899-1988)
American artist
Born in Kiev, Russia; sculptor known for large-scale works using wood.

on feminism, page 96
on responsibility, page 238

Huey Newton (1942-1989)
American civil rights activist
Cofounder of the Black Panther party; after arrest and imprisonment for voluntary manslaughter of a police officer, advocated more mainstream approach for Panthers; became drug and alcohol abuser; killed by gunshot.

on self-preservation, page 258

Nezahualcoyotl (1418-1472)
Mexican ruler and poet-king of Texcoco
One of foremost Aztec rulers; much modern knowledge of Aztecs based on his writings.

on love, page 172-173
on pleasure, page 204-205
on transience, page 280-281

Nguyen Ai Quoc. *See* Ho Chi Minh

Nguyen Chi Thien (b. 1933)
Vietnamese writer
Novelist and short story writer; a leading Vietnamese writer; wrote collection of "prison songs" (1979); jailed for protests involving artists who advocated art for art's sake and expressed weariness for war.

> on oppression, page 196
> on poetry and poets, page 206

Nguyen Du (1765–1820)
Vietnamese poet
Writer and interpreter of "Kim Van Kieu" ("The Song of Kieu"), one of best-known traditional Vietnamese poems, considered to be Vietnam's national poem.

> on failure, page 87
> on farewells, page 90–91
> on the future, page 105
> on infinity, page 141
> on war, page 300

Nguyen Gia Thieu (1741–1798)
Vietnamese poet
Buddhist and Taoist scholar; most famous for lyric poems, especially "Cung oan ngam khjuc" ("The Complaint of the Royal Concubine").

> on beauty, page 22–23

Nguyen Khac Hieu. *See* Tan Da

Nguyen Khuyen (1835–1909)
Vietnamese poet
Public servant; known for use of symbolism and allegory, and pointed criticism of collaborationists and decline in values.

> on drinking, page 74

Nguyen Trai (1380–1442)
Vietnamese poet
Involved in fight for national independence under Le Loi; later executed when fell into disfavor; now recognized as a leading figure in Vietnamese history and literature.

> on leadership and leaders, page 157
> on self-reliance, page 258

Nguyen Cong Tru (1773–1858)
Vietnamese poet
Served King Minh Mang and Thieu Tri; poetry reflects dichotomy between duty and hedonism.

> on society, page 263
> on time, page 278

Nguyen Thi Binh (b. 1930)
Vietnamese politician
Foreign minister of South Vietnamese National Liberation Front (indigenous resistance to South Vietnamese government); after North Vietnam's invasion of South Vietnam, lost influence.

> on war, page 300–301

Nguyen Vy (d. 1975)
Vietnamese poet
Formed Bach-nga (The Swan) literary group in Hanoi (1936); from 1963–1965, one of most active and prolific poets in Vietnam.

> on grieving, page 119

Niffari (c. 965)
Persian Sufi teacher and writer
(Muhammad ibn 'Abd al-Jabbar al-Niffari)
Prominent Sufi theorist; famous for writing the *Mawaqit* and *Mukhatabat*, which influenced later Sufis; promoted theory of prayer as divine gift, a means to grace given by God; in this, his ideas parallel those of Christian mystics.

on mysticism, page 186

Florence Nightingale
(1820–1910)
English nurse and writer
Founder of nursing profession and pioneer in hospital care; called "Lady with the Lamp"; first female recipient of British Order of Merit.

on duty, page 75

Lady Nii (d. 1185)
Japanese courtier
Courtier to Japanese Imperial family; famous for loyalty, which led her to dive into the ocean with the child Emperor after the Imperial forces lost the sea battle of Dannoura.

last words, page 154

Anaïs Nin (1903–1977)
American writer
French-born diarist, novelist, and short story writer. Most noted for extensive diaries, which some claim are untrue, that lend insight into bohemian world of 1920s and 1930s.

on adolescence, page 5
on art and artists, page 20
on death, page 61

on self-esteem, page 255
on writers and writing, page 320

Lewis Nkosi (b. 1936)
South African writer
Playwright, short story writer, editor, and critic; a leading figure in African literature; exiled from South Africa; currently, editor and writer in London.

on God, page 110
on racism, page 227
on reform and reformers, page 231
on self-pity, page 257
on writers and writing, page 320

Kwame Nkrumah (1909–1972)
Ghanaian politician and revolutionary leader
Called the "Gandhi of Africa" for nationalistic fervor, leadership against white domination of Africa. Leader of movement liberating Gold Coast from British rule; first president of Ghana republic; overthrown by military coup (1966). Took asylum in Guinea, where he became co-head of state.

on government, page 116

U Nu (b. 1907)
Burmese politician and first prime minister of Burma
(Thakin Nu)
Nationalist; teacher who joined Dobhama Asiayone (Our Burma) nationalist organization (c. 1930s); imprisoned by British at beginning of World War II; released to work in nationalist government, considered a puppet government (1942); formed Anti-Fascist People's Free-

dom League (1945), which collaborated with British against Japanese; when Burma declared independent (1948), became country's first prime minister; toppled by General Ne Win (1962) and imprisoned until 1966; in exile in Thailand and India, organized opposition forces; returned to Burma (1980); still working for nationalism; cofounded National League for Democracy (1988).

> on the Americas, page 14
> on leadership and leaders,
>   page 157
> on trust, page 283

dhu-al-Nun al Misri (d. 860)
Egyptian Sufi leader
Considered by many Sufis the originator of their doctrine, particularly in its ascetic form (although Ma'ruf al-Kharkhi, who died in 815, was perhaps the first Sufi mystic); contended that true knowledge of God is obtainable only by ecstasy; considered asceticism way instrumental in finding such a path; called by followers a *qutb*, or pillar of the universe; ideas show influence of Hellenistic thought; died in al-Jizah (Giza). dhu-al-Nun was by one account also fascinated by artifacts of the ancient Egyptian culture surrounding him; he often wandered around them, attempting to understand the myriad hieroglyphs and unlock their messages.

> on faith, page 88
> on greatness, page 118

Faarah Nuur (c. 1930)
Somali clan leader and poet
Leader of Arab clan, a section of

the Isoaq; played major role in releasing his clanspeople from dominant 'Iidegale clan; one of first anti-imperialist Somalian poets.

> on imperialism, page 140

Nyein Chan (20th century)
Burmese poet
Writes pseudonymously; work attacks military government; edited collection of poems *Voices from the Jungle: Burmese Youth in Transition* (1989), published in Japan.

> on revolution, page 244
> on sacrifice, page 248

Julius K. Nyerere (b. 1922)
Tanzanian nationalist and political
  leader
Led nationalist movement in colonial Tanganyika; formed Tanganyika African National Union; when country gained independence, became first prime minister (1961); declared president when country declared a republic (1962); considered one of Africa's most influential leaders; known for courage and innovation; early critic of Ugandan leader Idi Amin; army ousted Amin; retired from politics in 1985.

> on freedom, page 102
> on home, page 126
> on imperialism, page 140

O

Joyce Carol Oates (b. 1938)
American writer
Novelist, short story writer, and essayist; winner National Book

Award (1969) for *Them;* other works include *You Must Remember This* and *On Boxing.*

on loneliness, page 167
on love, page 173
on luck, page 175

Flannery O'Connor
(1925-1964)
American writer
Short story writer and novelist known for black-humored stories of the South, where she grew up; work also reflects Catholic background; received National Book Award; famous works include novel *Wise Blood* and short story collection *A Good Man Is Hard to Find.*

on writers and writing,
page 320

Sandra Day O'Connor (b. 1930)
American jurist
First female U.S. Supreme Court justice (1981-); appointed as conservative, but has had liberal opinions on some cases.

on feminism, page 96-97

Grace Ogot (b. 1930)
Kenyan writer
Novelist, short story writer, and children's book writer. First novel centered around rural Kenyan life; short stories and children's books known for mythic quality.

on death, page 62

Ohiyesa (1858-1939)
Sioux writer and physician
(Charles Alexander Eastman)
Lobbyist for Sioux in Washington, D.C.; cofounded Boy Scouts of America; prolific writer and lecturer on Indian affairs.

on meditation, page 179

Gabriel Okara (b. 1921)
Nigerian writer
(Imomotimi Gbaingbain)
Poet, novelist, short story writer, and civil servant; one of leading African poets writing in English; works known for mystical quality and capturing of African speech patterns in English.

on advice, page 7
on the past, page 198
on words, page 311-312

Kakuzo Okakura (1862-1913)
Japanese art critic and
philosopher
(pen name Tenshin)
Known for his attempts to protect and restore traditional Japanese art forms.

on adaptability, page 4
on truth, page 285-286

Georgia O'Keeffe (1887-1986)
American artist
Best known works include stark paintings of flowers and desert scenes; companion of photographer Albert Stieglitz; received Presidential Medal of Freedom (1977).

on biography, page 25
on seeing, page 252

Old Tassell (18th century)
Cherokee chief
During his lifetime, spoke against the encroachment of white settlers on ancestral lands.

on customs, page 56

Ono no Komachi (c. 850)
Japanese poet
Daughter of Yoshisada, Lord of Dewa; famed for her beauty; work collected in poetry anthology, *Kokin Shu* (compiled 905–922).

on loneliness, page 167

Ono no Yoshiki (d. 902)
Japanese poet
Work collected in poetry anthology, *Kokin Shu* (compiled 905–922).

on love, page 173

José Joaquín de Olmedo (1780–1847)
Ecuadoran poet
Classical stylist; devoted life to revolution against Spain and organization of newly independent republic; best known for ode in praise of Simon Bolívar.

on hope, page 128

Raisa Davydovna Orlova (1917–1964)
Soviet/German writer
Diplomat, editor, literary critic.

on belief, page 25

José Clemente Orozco (1883–1949)
Mexican painter
Leading twentieth-century muralist in world; known for political commentary in works.

on boldness, page 27

Dazai Osamu (1909–1948)
Japanese writer
Autobiographical novelist and short story writer; one of Japan's most famous modern writers, not only for writings, but for tumultuous, sometimes dissolute life, which included expulsion from a wealthy family, affairs, and several suicide attempts, the last being successful.

on art and artists, page 20
on self-description, page 254

Osceola (c. 1803–1838)
Seminole chief
Born a Creek to a half-breed father; immigrated to Florida (c. 1817); prominent leader of the Second Seminole War of 1835–1842; taken prisoner while under flag of truce; died of an illness at Fort Moultrie, Georgia.

on resistance, page 237

Amos Oz (b. 1939)
Israeli writer
Essayist and novelist; noted for examination of Israeli life; also peace activist. Has won numerous awards for literary brilliance, including German Publishers Peace Prize (1992).

on the future, page 105
on human nature, page 129

Cynthia Ozick (b. 1931)
American writer
Novelist and short story writer; often focuses on Jewish culture; considered to have contributed greatly to rebirth of short story in U.S. literature by incorporating novelistic elements such as social density and philosophic viewpoints.

on speech, page 267

P

Pachacutec Inca Yupanqui
(1438–1471)
Incan ruler
Incan emperor; extended empire to southern Peru and to Ecuador.

on envy and jealousy, page 79
on leadership and leaders,
page 158
on patience, page 199

Herberto Padilla (20th century)
Cuban poet
Considered Cuba's greatest living poet; now living in exile in the United States; works known for lyricism.

on crime, page 54

Christabel Pankhurst
(1880–1958)
English suffragist
Daughter of suffragist Emmeline Pankhurst; also writer and evangelist; with her mother, founded militant Women's Social and Political Union; arrested several times for suffragist demonstrations; faced conspiracy charges (1912); escaped to Paris; later became religious lecturer and writer (1920).

on feminism, page 97

Emmeline Pankhurst
(1858–1928)
English suffragist
Early advocate of women's rights; a leader of British suffragist movement; mother of suffragist Christabel Pankhurst; with daughter, founded militant Women's So-

cial and Political Union; known for oratorical skills; arrested numerous times; held hunger strikes in prison.

on feminism, page 97
on property, page 220
on reform and reformers,
page 231

Park Chung Hee (1917–1979)
South Korean politician and
soldier
Led coup overthrowing second Republic; president (1963–1979); declared martial law and gave himself unlimited power; assassinated.

on priorities, page 216

Dorothy Parker (1893–1967)
American writer
Poet, short story writer, and screenplay writer; best known for epigrams; chief female member of Algonquin Round Table; famed for sharp wit.

on art and artists, page 20
on behavior, page 24
on humor, page 133
on intellectuals, page 143
on love, page 173
on sorrow, page 265
on women, page 310

Rosa Parks (b. 1913)
American civil rights activist
Called "Mother of the Civil Rights Movement"; started Montgomery bus boycott by refusing to move to back of bus.

on civil rights, page 41
on justice, page 146

Nicanor Parra (b. 1914)
Chilean poet
Professor; specializes in "anti-poetry," initially developed as response against Pablo Neruda's surrealism and against traditional lyric poetry; considered literary innovator.

on judgment, page 145
on poetry and poets, page 206
on truth, page 286

Parra-Wa-Samen. *See* Ten Bears

Patanjali (240–180 B.C.E.)
Indian philosopher
(Gonardiya)
Writer of *Yoga-Sutras*, codifying yoga philosophy, an effort to attain perfection through physical movement and psychic control; highly influential in Indian thought and philosophy for centuries.

on ignorance, page 138

Anna Pavlova (1881–1931)
Russian dancer
Ballet dancer known for innovative, emotional style; famed for "Dying Swan" dance.

on success, page 272

Octavio Paz (b. 1914)
Mexican writer and diplomat
Critic, social philosopher; fought for Republicans in Spanish Civil War; ambassador to India (c. 1960s); best known as literary innovator incorporating the metaphysical into poetry; famous for *Labyrinth of Solitude*, examining Mexican culture; *Postdata*, written after student massacre and related

events; emigrated to Great Britain (1968).

on art and artists, page 20
on creativity, page 54
on critics and criticism, page 55
on death, page 62
on democracy, page 67
on power, page 212
on reality, page 229
on revolution, page 244

Eva Peron (1919–1952)
Argentinean politician
Born to humble family; popular stage and screen performer; married president Juan Peron. Soon after marriage, husband was ousted from office and arrested; she convinced unions to strike for his release; aided his comeback to power through speeches; especially known for appealing to *descamisados* (poor classes) by exploiting her humble background. Ran for vice president (1951), but opposed by army; husband elected president (1952); suffered from ill health; husband deposed three years after her death.

on convictions, page 50
on mothers and motherhood, page 185

Candace Pert (b. 1947)
American biochemist
Discovered opiate receptor at age twenty-six, while pharmacology graduate student at Johns Hopkins University (1973); breakthrough led to later discovery of body's natural opiates and ushered in new era in neuroscience. Joined Biological Psychiatry Branch of National

Institute of Mental Health; known
for research on workings of human
mind.

    on women, page 310

Kata Szidonia Petroczi
(1662–1708)
Hungarian poet
Born in Hungary; brought up in Poland after mother died and father
indicted; work usually religious,
often revolving around personal
sorrows and troubles of her homeland.

    on despair, page 70

Souvana Phouma (1901–1984)
Laotian politician
Premier and prince; as leader of
neutralist government in Laos,
gradually became embroiled in
Indo-Chinese-Vietnamese war; lost
effective power with withdrawal
of U.S. support in 1975.

    on Communism, page 44

Mavis Bryant Pierce
(1811–1874)
Seneca leader
Native American activist; worked
to preserve Iroquois lands.

    on home, page 126

Ping Hsin (b. 1902)
Chinese poet
Also short story writer; she was
one of the best known Chinese
writers of the 1920s. Influenced by
Rabindranath Tagore; followed philosophy of "all-embracing love."

    on nature, page 189

Plenty Coups (1848–1932)
Crow chief
(Aleek-chea-ahoosh)
Native American friend to the
whites; represented the Crow in
negotiations with Northern Pacific
Railroad.

    on defeat, page 66

Po Chu-i (772–846)
Chinese poet
One of most prolific Tang dynasty
poets; best known for long narrative poems; style marked by simplicity.

    on longing, page 168
    on old age, page 194
    on solitude, page 264

Katherine Anne Porter
(1894–1980)
American writer
Novelist and short story writer;
best known for *Ship of Fools;* won
Pulitzer Prize and National Book
Award for *Collected Short Stories*.

    on danger, page 57
    on death, page 62

Beatrix Potter (1866–1943)
English writer and illustrator
Wrote highly popular children's
books, with characters such as Peter Rabbit.

    on learning and education,
    page 160

Adam Clayton Powell, Jr.
(1908–1972)
American politician and civil
rights leader
Member of U.S. House of Representatives; pastor of Harlem's Abys-

sinian Baptist church; key civil rights leader in 1960s.

on convictions, page 50–51
on decisions, page 64
on equality, page 80
on honesty, page 127
on law, page 153
on racism, page 227
on wealth, page 303

Mañuel Gonzalez Prada
(1848-1918)
Peruvian poet and political activist
Called "Maestro" by students for attacks on academicism, traditionalism, and colonialism. Published poems attacking political corruption; helped form Union Nacional, political party to promote progressivism (1891); self-exiled to Paris for seventeen years after agitation-caused assassination of Ecuadoran dictator, Garcia Moreno; returned to Lima (1898) and leadership of party for short time; known for famous speech to Baker's Union (1905), pleading for understanding between intellectuals and workers.

on generations, page 106

Ptah-hotep (c. 2300 B.C.E.)
Egyptian vizier
Said to be adviser to king during Old Kingdom; known for *Instruction of Ptah-hotep*, advice written for his son; considered key document in understanding Old Kingdom civilization; advocated individual voluntarism; demonstrated personal aggressiveness of the age.

on evil, page 84

on greed, page 118
on humility, page 132
on marriage, page 177
on wisdom, page 307

Q

Nizar Qabbani (b. 1932)
Syrian/Lebanese writer and publisher
Born in Syria; diplomat; moved to Lebanon, where founded publishing firm; wrote over twenty-five poetry collections and an autobiography.

on emotions, page 77
on enemies, page 78
on generations, page 106
on popular opinion,
    page 209–210
on power, page 212
on society, page 263
on words, page 312

Imru' al-Qays (c. 540)
Pre-Islamic Arab poet
Wrote profound, contemplative *qasidahs*, or laments; later life spent in illness and destitution.

on death, page 62
on fate, page 92

Qernertoq (c. 900–1400)
Eskimo poet
Copper Eskimo of the Musk Ox Folk; work included in collection of Eskimo songs gathered in first quarter of twentieth century by explorer Knud Rasmussen.

on identity, page 137

Qigong. *See* Chi K'ang

Qiu Jin (1874-1907)
Chinese poet and activist
Left husband and children and went to Japan (1904); spoke out against traditional practices toward women such as footbinding and arranged marriages; returned to China (1906); founded *Chinese Women's Journal*; worked for women's reform; advocated revolutionary ideals.

Qu Junong (c. 20th century)
Chinese poet
Uncle of poet and activist Qu Qiubai.

al-Qushayri (c. 1047)
Arab Sufi leader and writer
Famous for *Risala*, considered the most widely read summary of early Sufism.

Qu Qiubai (1899-1935)
Chinese poet and revolutionary
Poet, activist, and revolutionary; traveled in post-Bolshevik Russia; in poetry, advocated revolutionary ideals; head of Chinese Communist Party (1927-1928); captured and executed by Kuomintang forces.

Quin Guanshu (b. 1929)
Chinese scientist
Botanist and writer.

Syed Qutb (d. 1966)
Egyptian fundamentalist Islamic scholar
Leader of Muslim Brotherhood, a fundamentalist Islamic group opposed to secular rule; executed by Gamal Abdel Nasser, Egyptian president.

R

Rabi'a al-Adawiyya (c. 717-801)
Iraqi Sufi poet and mystic
(Rabi'a the Mystic)
Muslim saint; died in Jerusalem; tomb was object of pilgrimages during Middle Ages; known for poetry on divine love and other religious topics.

Sarvepalli Radhakrishnan (1888-1975)
Indian philosopher and political leader
Born in Madras; professor and lecturer; wrote number of scholarly works on philosophy, including *An Idealist View of Life*. As statesman, held numerous positions, including member of Committee of Intellectual Cooperation at League of Nations (1931-1939); chief Indian

delegate to UNESCO (1949); member of Indian Assembly (1947); first Indian ambassador to Russia (1949); vice-president of India (1952-1962); president (1962-1967).

on ethics and morality,
    page 82-83
on God, page 111
on heroes, page 124-125
on religion, page 234
on worship, page 316

Tunku Putra Abdul Rahman
(b. 1903)
Malaysian politician
Prime minister; presided over decolonization of Malaysia from British; noted for sound leadership and ability to reduce tensions between Malaysia's Chinese and Malay ethnic groups.

on patience, page 199

'Abd-al-Rahman (d. 1709)
Indian Sufi writer
(Rahman Baba)
Sufi mystic of Chisti order; considered best Indo-Pakistani mystical poet of his time; work has uniquely sad, ascetic quality.

on homesickness,
    page 126-127

Raidas (15th century)
Indian Hindu mystic and religious
    leader
(Ravidas; Rohidas)
Founder of Hindu sect in Varansi; opposed by many Brahmins because was low-caste leather worker; had many followers, including Princess Mira Bai; known

for devotional verses and avatars; forty-one of his hymns included in Sikh scripture, *Adi Granth*.

on equality, page 80
on God, page 111
on self-knowledge, page 257

Ramakrishna (1836-1886)
Indian Hindu mystic
(Gadadhar Chattonpadhyaya)
Born in Bengali; leading Tantrist teacher; learned from gurus in different schools; evolved theory that all religions are different paths to same goal; known as a charismatic teacher; taught Swami Vivekananda.

on advice, page 7
on desire, page 69
on equality, page 80-81
on experience, page 86
on God, page 111
on habit, page 121
on humility, page 132
on illusion, page 138
on judgment, page 145
on the mind, page 183
on perspective, page 203
on religion, page 234
on worldliness, page 315

Ramana Maharshi (1879-1950)
Indian Hindu religious leader
Hindu sage; moved to holy mountain Arunachala (in Tiruvannamalai) at age seventeen because of religious experience; spent rest of life there; shunned publicity and lived in caves until later in life, when allowed followers to build ashram at base of mountain. Known for teaching method of intellectual penetration, using "cave

of the heart" to attain self-knowledge.

on illusion, page 138
on will, page 304-305

Ayn Rand (1905-1982)
American writer
(née Alissa Rosenbaum)
Novelist, screenwriter, and philosopher; born Alissa Rosenbaum in St. Petersburg, Russia; moved to New York (1926); developed philosophy of "objectivism" through her works—initially, in novels, such as *The Fountainhead* and *Atlas Shrugged* and later, in nonfiction works; as objectivist, advocated self-actualization; anticollectivist and procapitalist.

on adaptability, page 4
on advice, page 7
on greatness, page 118
on happiness, page 122
on heroes, page 125
on meaning, page 179
on power, page 212
on the self, page 253
on wealth, page 303

Jeanette Rankin (1880-1973)
American feminist and politician
First female member of U.S. House of Representatives (1917-1919) (Republican, Montana); first winner of National Organization of Women's Susan B. Anthony Award.

on action, page 3
on feminism, page 97
on human nature, page 129
on philosophy, page 203-204
on war, page 301

K. Nagieswara Rao (1867-1938)
Indian political leader and writer
Involved with and wrote on social, religious, and political reform; advocated change of caste system in favor of "untouchables," who occupied the bottom tier; held various political positions; also known for cultural and literary revival of Andra; editor and publisher of literary journal.

on art and artists, page 20

Abu al-Rasibi. *See* 'Abd al-'Aziz b. Sulayman

Irina Ratushinskaya
(20th century)
Russian writer
Poet and prose writer; dissident during Soviet regime; imprisoned for political beliefs and writings.

on prison, page 216

Marjorie Kinnan Rawlings
(1896-1953)
American writer
Solitude-loving, bought orange grove in Florida called Cross Creek, about which she wrote in *Cross Creek*, considered a pastoral classic; wrote Pulitzer Prize-winning novel *The Yearling*; works typically explore both cruel and benign sides of nature.

on beauty, page 23
on nature, page 189-190

Red Jacket (c. 1758-1830)
Seneca leader
(Sasgoyewatha)
Advocated adherence to traditional Iroquois customs; fought conver-

sion of Native Americans to Christianity.

    on God, page 111
    on imperialism, page 140
    on religion, page 234-235

Willis Reed (b. 1942)
American athlete
Basketball player, coach, and executive; New York Knicks player and coach; twice named most valuable player in NBA playoffs (1970, 1973); New York Nets coach.

    on ambition, page 13

Jean Rhys (1894-1979)
English writer
Dominica-born novelist and dancer; received Royal Society of Literature award; early works focus on bohemian society in 1920s and 1930s Europe; best known for novel, *The Wide Sargasso Sea*.

    on time, page 278

Ameen Rihani (1876-1940)
Syrian-American poet
Moved from Syria to New York; wrote in Arabic and English. Strongly influenced modern Arabic poetry; revived concept of poet as visionary; introduced free verse, prose poems, and modern metaphors to Arabic poetry.

    on tradition, page 279

Luis Muñoz Rivera (1859-1916)
Puerto Rican journalist and
    politician
Founded newspaper *La Democracia*; campaigned for Puerto Ri-

can independence; held range of government positions.

    on bravery, page 29
    on goals, page 108

Paul Robeson (1898-1976)
American actor
Actor, singer, and political activist; studied law and admitted to American bar before beginning acting career. First appeared on U.S. stage in 1921; popular as singer and actor; a leading actor of his time; acclaimed for lead role in *Othello*, and for roles in musical *Show Boat* and plays by Eugene O'Neill. Blacklisted for Communist beliefs; lived for a time in self-imposed exile in Europe.

    on freedom, page 103

Jackie Robinson (1919-1972)
American athlete
First athlete to break color barrier in major league baseball as star player for Brooklyn Dodgers; rookie of the year (1947); most valuable player (1949); elected to National Baseball Hall of Fame (1962).

    on respect, page 238

Marie Jeanne Roland
(1754-1793)
French revolutionary
Political activist; social figure; executed by Jacobins.

    on liberty, page 161

Oscar Romero (1917-1980)
El Salvadoran Catholic archbishop
Leader of El Salvador's Catholic Archdiocese; shot while celebrat-

ing high mass in San Salvador's cathedral.

on political movements,
page 208

Carlos P. Romulo (b. 1899)
Philippine diplomat and soldier
Premier diplomat of Philippines; served in World War II under U.S. General Douglas MacArthur; ambassador to United States; led Philippine Foreign Ministry. First Filipino to win Pulitzer Prize, for reports on Japanese invasion of Southeast Asia during World War II.

on equality, page 81

Eleanor Roosevelt (1884-1962)
American humanitarian and First
 Lady
Writer; married to President Franklin D. Roosevelt; U.S. delegate to United Nations (1945-1953, 1967); received U.N. prize (1968).

on achievement, page 1
on afterlife, page 10
on democracy, page 67
on fear, page 93
on the future, page 105
on life, page 165-166
on relationships, page 232
on responsibility, page 239
on self-esteem, page 255
on truth, page 286

Wendy Rose (b. 1948)
American writer
Hopi poet and anthropologist; published ten books of poetry, as well as anthropological studies; teaches in American Indian Studies program at Fresno City College. Books

include *Hopi Roadrunner Dancing* and *The Halfbreed Chronicles.*

on ancestors and ancestry,
page 15

Rumi (1207-1273)
Persian Sufi poet
(Jalil al-Din)
One of most influential Sufi writers and leaders; known for mystic verses; founder of Mevlevi Order of dervishes. Born in Balkh; father was Sufi and famous preacher; family went into exile in Anatolia, where spent rest of his life. Upon meeting wandering dervish Shams al-Din of Tabriz, renounced Islamic religious sciences, founded Mevlevi order of dervishes. Most famous works include *Divan-i Shams-i Tabriz*, a group of *ghazals* (lyric poems), and *Masnavi*, a long religious poem that Persians call the "Persian Qur'an."

on adversity, page 6
on change, page 35
on character, page 36
on death, page 62
on desire, page 69
on drinking, page 74
on envy and jealousy, page 79
epitaph, page 80
on evil, page 84
on experience, page 86
on flattery, page 99
on greed, page 118
on happiness, page 122
on humility, page 132
on knowledge, page 149
on love, page 173
on meditation, page 179
on paradox, page 198
on perspective, page 203
on the seasons, page 251

on the self, page 253
on self-discipline, page 255
on speech, page 267
on symbols, page 274
on teaching, page 276
on time, page 279
on wisdom, page 307

Abu-l-Walid ibn-Rushd
(1126–1198)
Spanish Arabic philosopher
(Averroes)
A jurist, medical writer, and philosopher, ibn-Rushd (known as Averroes in the West) is most famous for his summaries and commentaries on the works of Aristotle, repudiating the ideas of al-Ghazali and defending original Aristotelean thought. Indicted for irreligiousness in 1195, exiled, then accorded a sinecure from an Islamic prince in Morocco, where he died; his writings stimulated many Westerners, including Roger Bacon, as well as Arabs, although to a lesser degree.

on philosophy, page 204

Bayard Rustin (1910–1987)
American civil rights leader
Organizer of 1953 Montgomery, Alabama bus boycott; planner of 1963 March on Washington. Labor organizer.

on civil rights, page 42
on racism, page 228

Al-Salib ibn Ruzziq (1101–1161)
Egyptian poet and politician
on death, page 62

Ryokan (1758–1831)
Japanese Zen monk and poet
Poet of late Edo period; monk of Soto school; lived as recluse most of life; prolific writer, leaving over 1,400 Japanese poems (*waka*), 400 Chinese poems (*kanshi*), and numerous haiku.

on concentration, page 46

Akutagawa Ryunosuke
(1892–1927)
Japanese writer
Novelist and essayist; works focus on basic problems of art and artist; struggle to prove human nobility.

on madness, page 176

Tamura Ryuichi (b. 1923)
Japanese poet
Leading representative of "Waste Land" group, the first important poetic school in postwar Japan.

on creativity, page 54

S

Anwar Sadat (1918–1981)
Egyptian military and political
  leader
(Muhammed Anwar Al-Sadat)
Born in Tala district to Egyptian-Sudanese family; commissioned in army (1938); advocated overthrow of British-dominated monarchy; imprisoned during World War II for contacts with Germans; with other officers, organized coup ousting King Farouk (1952); worked under Gamel Abdel Nasser, as co-vice-

president (with three others) (1964-1967), only vice president (1969-1970); held strong nationalistic and anti-Communistic views; became president in 1970 upon death of Nasser; especially known for negotiations with Israel, culminating in Camp David talks with Israeli Prime Minister Begin and U.S. President Jimmy Carter (1976); only Arab leader to sign peace treaty with Israel at the time; cowinner of Nobel Price for peace, with Begin (1978); faced opposition from other Arab leaders; assassinated by Muslim fundamentalists (1981).

Sa'di of Shiraz (c. 1184-1292)
Persian poet
(al-Din Mahmud; Shabistari)
Descendent of 'Ali (son-in law of Muhammad, fourth caliph of Islam); traveled extensively; was abducted by Crusaders in Jerusalem, but later ransomed. Considered greatest didactic poet of Persia; wrote wide range of poetry and prose, in both Arabic and Persian. Most famous for *Gulistan* (*Rose Garden*), a loosely woven work of both prose and verse, and *Bustan* (*Orchid Garden*), a long verse work, more religious in nature.

Françoise Sagan (b. 1935)
French writer
Novelist and short story writer; most famous for short works focusing on psychological themes, such as *Bonjour Tristesse*.

Bernardino de Sahagún
(c. 16th century)
Spanish historian
Franciscan missionary; recorded Aztec thought and ways of living, systems of merchant groups, and so on; collected in *Historia general de las cosas de Nueva España*, a leading source of Aztec customs.

Sa'ib of Tabriz (c. 1601–1677)
Persian poet
(Mirza Muhammad Ali Sa'ib of
Tabriz)
Poet in court of Shah Jahan of
India; considered last great Persian poet; known for originality
and wit; compiled anthology of
best verses of his predecessors;
especially famous for *ghazals*, or
odes.

Saladin (1137–1193)
Egyptian and Syrian sultan
(Salah al-Din al-Ayyubi)
One of most famous Muslim heroes; attempted to push Christians
out of Jerusalem; captured Jerusalem (1187); negotiated truce with
Crusaders (1192).

al-Tayyib Salih (b. 1929)
Sudanese writer
Short story writer and novelist;
known for blending traditional and
modern elements in his work;
among his best-known novels is
Season of Migration to the North.

Ghada Samman (b. 1942)
Syrian writer
Essayist, short story writer, and
novelist; early works focus on feminist themes; after the Six-Day War
and Lebanese civil war, changed to
focus on surrealistic nightmare
world born of warfare.

George Sand (1804–1876)
French writer
(pseudonym of Amandine Aurore
Lucile Dudevant)
Novelist known as much for unconventional lifestyle as for works;
had affairs with such men as writer
Alfred de Mussett and composer
Frederic Chopin; writing focused
on unconventional love, free of
class and social barriers.

Margaret Sanger (1883–1966)
American social activist
Writer, editor, and nurse. Founder
of birth control movement in

United States; opened first U.S. birth control clinic in Brooklyn, New York (1916); organized first birth control conference (1921); founder and first president of Planned Parenthood Federation of America.

on consequences, page 49
on diplomacy, page 72

Sankardeva (1449-1569)
Indian religious leader
Poet, philosopher, and mystic; founded Visnu sect of Mahapurusiya; active in social work; wrote dramas and composed songs.

on religion, page 235
on the world, page 315

Santi-deva (7th century)
Indian Buddhist philosopher
Follower of Nagarjun's Madhyamika school of Mahayana Buddhism; guru at Nalanda Buddhist university and monastery in Bihar, India.

on desire, page 69-70
on the golden rule, page 112

Hehaka Sapa. *See* Black Elk

Sappho (c. 610-580 B.C.E.)
Greek poet
First lyric poet; considered greatest female poet of antiquity; called the "Tenth Muse" and the "Pierien Bee." Born on island of Lesbos; went into exile to Sicily; returned to Mityele, where she married and had a daughter. Believed to have taught women and girls, and to have been a lesbian, as love poems

appear to have been written to women. Known for passionate lyricism and grace; only two odes found in full, but numerous fragments found in Egypt.

on love, page 173

Dayananda Saraswati (1824-1883)
Indian philosopher
Revivalist; advocated return to ancient ideals.

on God, page 112
on hypocrisy, page 135
on ignorance, page 137

Domingo Faustino Sarmiento (1811-1888)
Argentinian political leader
President of Argentina (1868); considered one of Argentina's greatest leaders; pursued unpopular Paraguayan war; strong advocate of education.

on government, page 116

Sasgoyewatha. *See* Red Jacket

Satavahana Hala
(1st-2nd century)
Indian king and poet
Seventeenth king of Satavahana Andhra dynasty; poet in Maharastri; believed to be author of *Saptasati* (*Sattasa*), collection of erotic poems.

on wealth, page 304

Ibn Saud (1880-1953)
Saudi Arabian king
(Abd al-Aziz Ibn Abd' al Rahman Aal ibn Saud)
Considered leading Arab ruler of his time; born in Riyadh; went into

exile with his family to Kuwait; succeeded his father as king (1901); led group to reclaim family domain from Rashidi rulers; accomplished this with British recognition (1927). Changed title from sultan of Nejd to king of Hejaz and Nejd (1927), to king of Saudi Arabia (1932); made lands safe for Muslim pilgrimages to Mecca. When oil discovered in 1938, granted major concessions to American oil companies; maintained neutrality in World War II, although friendly to Allies; succeeded by his son.

on advice, page 7
on character, page 37

Dorothy L. Sayers (1893-1957)
English novelist
Famous for mystery novels, featuring Lord Peter Wimsey character; translator of Dante.

on feminism, page 97
on success, page 272

Tawfiq Sayigh (1923-1971)
Iraqi poet
Born in Syria; leading figure in Palestinian poetry; exiled from homeland; much of his work contains childhood memories and criticizes world for remaining silent about Palestinians' plight.

on home, page 126

Abraham Schlonski (b. 1900)
Israeli poet
Poet of Third Aliyah; influenced by Russian contemporaries; work describes revolution and pogroms in Ukraine, as well as work of early

settlers in Israel; known for striking imagery.

on poetry and poets, page 206-207

Arthur A. Schomburg
(1874-1938)
American educator
African American educator and administrator; founded Negro Society for Social Research. Owned extensive private collection focusing on African Americans and others of African descent; this collection was initial basis for Schomburg Center for Research in Black Culture, New York City.

on African Americans, page 9
on race, page 223

Patricia Schroeder (b. 1940)
American politician
Lawyer; member of U.S. House of Representatives (1973-); proponent of women's rights, civil rights, and arms control.

on men, page 180

Seathl (c. 1788-1866)
Dwamish chief
(Seattle)
Native American leader who signed 1855 treaty with governor of Washington territory; remained at peace with whites even through Yakima War of 1855-1856; authenticity of some famous sayings attributed to him recently questioned.

on death, page 62

Haile Selassie (1892-1975)
Ethiopian emperor
(Tafari Makonnen; Ras Tafari)
Called "Lion of Judah"; emancipated slaves in Ethiopia and led

troops against Italian invasion; returned to power (1941); set up National Assembly; overthrown by coup in 1974.

on action, page 3
on civilization, page 42
on compassion, page 45
on equality, page 81
on imperialism, page 140
on progress, page 219

Ousmane Sembane (b. 1923)
Senegalese writer
Filmmaker, short story writer, and novelist; one of best-known African writers outside of Africa; his first novel, *Le docker noir* (*The Black Docker*), was based on his experiences as a dockworker in Marseilles; works following that, including *O pays, mon beau peuple* (*O My Country, My Beautiful People!*), *Les bouts de bois de Dieu* (*God's Bits of Wood*), and *L'harmattan* (*The Storm*), have been widely translated in Europe and the United States.

on shame, page 259
on slavery, page 262

Senachwine (c. 1830)
Potawatomi chief
Native American leader known for antiwar sentiments; advocated nonviolence consistent with religious beliefs, and acceptance of eventual extinction of Native Americans.

on Native Americans, page 187

Seng-chao (384–414)
Chinese Buddhist monk and philosopher
First Chinese philosopher to systemize Buddhist thought; focused on notion of abolition of time; Taoist and Buddhist; combined Chinese and Indian Buddhist thought.

on change, page 35
on travel, page 282

Leopold Sedar Senghor
(b. 1906)
Senegalese political leader and writer
Poet and essayist; founder of political group Bloc Democratique Sengalais; elected president of Senegal (1960).

on ancestors and ancestry, page 15
on culture, page 56
on hell, page 124
on resistance, page 237
on unity, page 290

Seng-ts'an (c. 520–606)
Chinese Buddhist monk
Third patriarch in Dhyana school of Chinese Buddhism; many legends but few facts about his life; supposedly feigned mental illness to avoid execution during Buddhist persecution; went into hiding for ten years; believed to have written *Hsin-hsin-ming*, one of earliest Chinese Zen texts.

on Buddhism, page 31

Elizabeth Seton (1774–1821)
American nun
First canonized American saint; founded Sisters of Charity of St. Joseph; founded first charitable organization in New York, the Society for Relief of Poor Widows and Children.

on adversity, page 6

Anne Sexton (1928–1974)
American poet
Claimed she had "no visible education"; studied under confessional poet Robert Lowell at Boston University; works highly personal and confessional poetry, explore experience of being a woman; known as one of the most embarrassingly honest poets of the confessional school; received Pulitzer Prize (1967); elected Fellow of the Royal Society of Literature in London (1968); committed suicide.

on mothers and motherhood,
page 185

A. J. Seymour (b. 1914)
Guyanese poet
Editor, critic, lecturer; usually writes about love and emotions; known for encouragement of other writers.

on love, page 173–174

Huda Shaarawi (1879–1947)
Egyptian feminist
A leading Arab feminist; member of last generation to reach maturity while harem system still prevailing; leader of first Egyptian women's nationalist demonstration (1919); president of Wafdist Women's Central Committee, the women's nationalist organization; founder and president of Egyptian Feminist Union (1923–1947); president of Arab Feminist Union (1945–1947); founded two publications; vice-president of International Alliance of Women for Suffrage and Equal Citizenship (1935).

on marriage, page 177

Al-Shabbi (1909–1934)
Arab poet
(Abu al-Qasim al Shabbi)
Considered among the most brilliant Arab poets of North Africa; born in Tunis; influenced by the romanticism of the Syro-American poets.

on patriotism and nationalism,
page 200
on renewal, page 235

Abu Hasan al-Shadhili (d. 1258)
Islamic Arab Sufi leader
Founded Shadhilyah Sufi sect in 1227 in Tunis; after a vision, traveled to Egypt, where the sect flourished.

on mysticism, page 186

al-Shafi'i (767–820)
Arab Islamic jurist
Founded Islamic Shaf'ite school of law; school is midway between conservatism and acceptance of religious speculation; his approach still widely practiced in Egypt, Arabia, India, and other nations; worked in Cairo and Baghdad.

on argument, page 17

Idries Shah (b. 1924)
Indian Sufi mystic and writer
Popularizer of Sufi (mystical Islamic) tenets. Born in Simla, India; studied in various Sufi schools in Near and Middle East; author of over thirty works on Sufism and philosophy; director of Institute for Cultural Research; fellow of British Royal Society of the Arts; winner of Cambridge Poetry Gold Medal.

on delusion, page 66

Shang Yang (d. 338 B.C.E.)
Chinese philosopher and
  government official
Chin dynasty official; founded
harsh legalist school; advocated
strict regimentation for citizens,
much like modern police state.

  on law, page 154
  on nonconformity,
    page 191
  on understanding, page 289

Ntozake Shange (b. 1949)
American writer
Poet and playwright; best known
work is *For Colored Girls Who
Have Considered Suicide When
the Rainbow Is Enuf.*

  on ghettos, page 107

Ali Shariati (1933-1977)
Iranian scholar
Islamic theorist; advocated Islamic
humanism, "Islamic Protestantism,"
which in his view would bring a
new Renaissance.

  on brotherhood and sisterhood,
    page 30

Mary Shelley (1797-1851)
English writer
(née Wollstonecraft)
Novelist; daughter of suffragist
Mary Wollstonecraft and political
philosopher William Godwin; wife
of poet Percy Bysshe Shelley; best
known for *Frankenstein.*

  on death, page 62
  on guilt, page 120
  on knowledge, page 149

Shenkara (788-820)
Indian Hindu philosopher
(Sankara; Shamkara;
Shankaracharya)
Considered one of greatest Indian
thinkers; leader of one of the most
famous Vedanta schools; born into
orthodox Brahmin family; traveled
widely through India; founded four
monasteries; promoted nondual-
ism in Vedanta philosophy; wrote
commentaries on *Upanishads,
Brahma Sutra,* and *Bhagavad-
gita,* exploring their nondualistic
elements; sometimes called the
"Thomas Aquinas of Hinduism."

  on knowledge, page 149
  on reality, page 229

Ahmad Faris al-Shidyaq
(1804-1887)
Lebanese writer
(Faryaq)
Called the "Arab Voltaire"; traveled
extensively, primarily in Europe;
wrote numerous travel books and
a biography. Works reflect self-
critical nature as well as sense of
humor about himself.

  on customs, page 56
  on language, page 152
  on travel, page 282

Yoshida Shigeru (1878-1967)
Japanese politician
Prime minister of Japan for five
terms (1946-1954); prior to this,
served in range of government positions; helped draft Japan's final
offer to United States before they
went to war; helped set up meeting between General Douglas Mac-
Arthur and Emperor Hirohito that
helped preserve imperial govern-

ment; president of dominant Liberal Party (1946) and, thus, prime minister of Japan; as prime minister, oversaw occupation policy revision; removed from office in 1954.

on diplomacy, page 72

David Shimoni (b. 1886)
Israeli poet
Known for works embodying spirit of early settlers in Israel.

on longing, page 168

Shingis (c. 18th century)
Delaware chief
Native American leader during French and Indian War; forced into alliance with French by Chief Pontiac.

on resistance, page 237

Zalman Shneour (b. 1887)
Israeli poet
Self-taught; termed an "urban poet" due to focus on cities, urban lifestyles; a key member of literary renaissance in Israeli writing.

on thought, page 276

Zelda Shneurson (b. 1913)
Israeli poet
Known for introducing awareness of God and ecstatic religious viewpoint into her work.

on nature, page 190

Shotoku (572–622)
Japanese prince
Son of emperor Yonen; attempted to develop Buddhism in Japan.

on reality, page 229

Shu Ch'ing-Ch'in. *See* Lao She

Shullushoma (c. 19th century)
Chickasaw chief
Native American leader; met with Secretary of War John C. Calhoun; held that white men were as "savage" as Native Americans.

on civilization, page 42–43

Akiyama Shun (b. 1930)
Japanese writer
Short story writer and novelist; work reflects two driving forces in his life—fear of society and desire to live a simple "ideal" life; works include *The Inner Man*.

on human nature, page 129
on loneliness, page 168

Tanikawa Shuntaro (b. 1931)
Japanese poet
Member of "Teki" group, second important poetic movement in postwar Japan.

on aging, page 12
on killing, page 148
on wilderness, page 304

Prince Siddhartha Guatama.
See Buddha

Norodom Sihanouk (b. 1922)
Cambodian ruler
Became king at age eighteen (1940); obtained independence from France (1953); abdicated from throne, but was named chief of state a few years later (1960); overthrown in 1970; five years later, became chief of state again; overthrown (1976) and placed un-

der house arrest; released; reinstated to office (1993).

on Communism, page 44

Yizhar Simlansky (b. 1916)
Israeli writer
(S. Yizhar)
Novelist and short story writer; literary innovator; work revolves around settler's lives.

on questions and answers, page 222
on self-knowledge, page 257

Siro (692-702)
Korean poet
Works among few surviving early Korean ones; was a dependent of Knight Taemara, who saved him from labor camp.

on the past, page 198

Sitting Bull (c. 1834-1890)
Dakota Sioux chief
(Tatanka Iyotake)
Native American principal chief and medicine man; led warrior society at age twenty-two; War of the Black Hills (1876-1877); allied with Crazy Horse and his warriors; fled to Canada, but faced with starvation, returned to United States and surrendered (1881); toured with Buffalo Bill's Wild West Show (1886); disgusted, he returned to a North Dakota reservation (1887); resisted further land cession and break-up of Sioux nation; was killed on reservation by army officer during attempt to arrest Sitting Bull over Indians performing the Ghost Dance.

on defeat, page 66
on imperialism, page 140

on individuality, page 141
on leadership and leaders, page 157
on Native Americans, page 187
on resistance, page 237

Edith Sitwell (1887-1964)
English writer
Poet and prose writer; member of well-known literary family, including brothers Osbert and Sacheverell; switched from light verse to religious poetry; known as eccentric wit.

on poetry and poets, page 207

Sivananda Sarasvati
(1887-1963)
Indian religious leader
Founder of Divine Life Society, and University at the Forest; advocated a simplistic Vedanta-oriented philosophy; dismissed by many as overly simplistic.

on sex, page 259
on success, page 272

Skolaskin (19th century)
Sanpoil prophet
Native American from upper Columbia; turned down British peace overtures during 1855-1858 Indian war.

on resistance, page 237

James McCune Smith
(1813-1864)
American physician and writer
Received medical degree from University of Glasgow, Scotland; returned to United States to practice medicine; African American anti-slavery essays and other prose pieces.

on freedom, page 103

Smohalla (c. 1815–1907)
Wanapam prophet
Native American founder of the
Dreamer religion; lived in Pacific
Northwest; spurned whites' peace
advances.

on brotherhood and sisterhood,
page 30
on wisdom, page 307

Sohekimon-in no shosho
(c. 1243)
Japanese poet
Used ironic proselike style. Daughter of poet Fujiwara no Nobuzane;
consort of Emperor Gohinkawa.

on love, page 174

Song Hon (1535–1598)
Korean poet
Prolific producer of *sijo*—the most
popular, elastic, and mnemonic poetic form of Korea.

on aging, page 12

Songjong (1457–1494)
Korean king
Ninth king of Yi dynasty; poet; renowned for his love of simple life
(literally tilling fields himself) and
his endowments for education.

on departures, page 68

Susan Sontag (b. 1933)
American writer and critic
Essayist, filmmaker, novelist, and
critic; best known for incisive critical essays, such as those written in
1960s, exposing "camp" radicalism
and trends; writer of experimental
fiction; best-known works include
collection of essays *On Photography* and *Illness as Metaphor*.

on aging, page 12

on ambition, page 13
on art and artists, page 20–21
on books and reading, page 28
on change, page 35
on critics and criticism,
page 55
on existence, page 85
on life, page 166
on men and women, page 181
on reality, page 229
on self-esteem, page 255

Mayling Soong. *See* Madame
Chiang Kai-shek

Natsume Soseki (1867–1916)
Japanese writer
Novelist, essayist, and professor; as
professor, explored Western literary theory; Western influence apparent in his works; known for
attempts to answer questions on
nature of literature; works often
examine relationship between art
and nature; later works favor expression of law of nature through
specific, realistic terms rather than
universal or abstract ones.

on art and artists, page 21
on consequences, page 49
on creativity, page 54
on life, page 166
on perseverance, page 202

Wole Soyinka (b. 1934)
Nigerian writer
Dramatist, poet, novelist, essayist,
and translator; one of most innovative and renowned African writers;
received Nobel Prize for literature
(1986); works often focus on difficulties arising from clash between
tradition and modernism in Africa;
first novel, *The Interpreters*, con-

sidered first truly modern African novel; other works include plays *The Trial of Brother Jeno* and *Kongi's Harvest*, and novel *Season of Anomy*; currently dramatic arts department head at Ife University.

on ancestors and ancestry,
  page 15-16
on evil, page 84
on justice, page 146
on liberty, page 162
on perfection, page 202
on perspective, page 203
on sorrow, page 265

Muriel Spark (b. 1918)
Scottish writer
Novelist, poet, and critic; best known for novel *The Prime of Miss Jean Brodie*.

on old age, page 194

Speckled Snake
(c. 19th century)
Creek chief
Native American leader who believed whites were hypocritical; tried to convince his people to avoid treaties and other overtures from whites.

on imperialism, page 140

Luther Standing Bear
(1868-1939)
Sioux writer
Leading Native American writer of his time; remains one of best-known voices in Native American literature; advocated traditional values.

on ancestors and ancestry,
  page 15
on diversity, page 72

on Native Americans, page 187
on nature, page 190

Elizabeth Cady Stanton
(1815-1902)
American suffragist
Early leader of U.S. women's suffragist movement, with Susan B. Anthony and Suzanne LaFollette; co-organizer of first women's rights convention in Seneca Falls, New York (1848); edited militant feminist periodical *Revolution*; president of National Woman Suffrage Association (1868-1870); abolitionist.

on feminism, page 97
on tyranny and tyrants,
  page 287
on women, page 310

Gertrude Stein (1874-1946)
American writer
Influenced contemporary artists; applied theories of abstract art to writing; best-known works include *The Autobiography of Alice B. Toklas* and *The World Is Round*.

on conformity, page 48
on familiarity, page 90
on generations, page 106
on identity, page 136
last words, page 153
on money, page 184
on questions and answers,
  page 222

Gloria Steinem (b. 1934)
American feminist
One of leading feminists in contemporary United States; founder of Women's Political Caucus

(1971), Women's Action Alliance (1971), and *Ms.* magazine (1972).

on learning and education, page 160
on oppression, page 196
on women, page 310

Su Shih (1036–1101)
Chinese government official and writer
(pseudonym Su Tung p'o)
Poet, philosopher, calligrapher, and painter. Governor of Hangzhou (1089–1091).

on success, page 272
on virtue, page 296

Achmad Sukarno (1902–1970)
Indonesian politician
Involved in Indonesia's movement for independence; first president of Indonesian republic (1945).

on diversity, page 72
on fear, page 93
on liberty, page 162
on patriotism and nationalism, page 200
on prison, page 216
on revolution, page 244

Munawwar Sumadih
(20th century)
Tunisian poet
Typically wrote in free verse; prominent spokesman for younger generation of his time; espoused nationalism and expressed strong feeling for those fighting in Algeria.

on evil, page 84

Sun Tzu (c. 335–288 B.C.E.)
Chinese military leader
Military theorist; author of *The Art of War*, considered a classic of strat-

egy and warfare and admired by such diverse military men and traditions as Napoleon, Mao Zedong, and the U.S. National War College; author himself is little known.

on enemies, page 79
on knowledge, page 149
on lies, page 162
on strategy, page 269
on victory, page 293–294
on war, page 301

Sun Yat-sen (1866–1925)
Chinese military and political leader
(Sun Wen; Sun Zhong Shan)
Known as father of his country; founded the Kuomintang; led Republican Revolution. Born in Canton; studied medicine in Hong Kong. Founded New China Party; led abortive uprising against Manchus (1895); studied in Japan, the United States, and Britain, campaigning for support of overseas Chinese against the Manchu (Ch'ing) dynasty. Won victory against Manchus (1911); became provisional president when China proclaimed republic (1912); was defeated by northern warlord Yuan Shih kai; forced into exile. Returned to China, where elected president of a southern republic (1923). Aided by Chiang Kai-shek, founded Whampoa Military Academy. Died in Peking (Beijing) while trying to negotiate for a united China; three years later Chiang succeeded. Wrote *The Three Principles of the People*, which called for social reform and democracy.

on imperialism, page 140
on perseverance, page 202

on revolution, page 244
on society, page 264
on understanding, page 289

Cemal Sureya (b. 1931)
Turkish poet
Champion of obscurantist verse; aimed to go beyond surrealism by achieving total meaninglessness in poetry.

on change, page 35
on love, page 174

D. T. Suzuki (1870-1966)
Japanese Buddhist scholar
One of best-known contemporary philosophers of Zen and interpreters of Zen in the West; focused on intellectual interpretation of Zen.

on creation, page 53
on experience, page 86

T

Mibu-no Tadamine (c. 905)
Japanese poet
Wrote traditional poetry called *waka* or *waga*; with three other women compiled the *Kokinshu* collection of poems for the Emperor Diago.

on sorrow, page 265

Ras Tafari. *See* Haile Selassie

Rabindranath Tagore
(1861-1941)
Indian writer and philosopher
One of India's most influential thinkers; composer and painter. Born in Calcutta, son of a wealthy family; published first book of po-

etry at age seventeen; studied law in England; returned to India, where he managed family estates, and began collecting Hindu legends and stories. Founded communal school with mission of blending Eastern and Western thought (1901). Major works include *The Crescent Moon*, a book of poems about childhood; a play, *Chitra*; *Binodini*, one of first modern novels of India; and *The Religion of Man*. Received Nobel Prize for literature (1913); knighted by the British in 1915, but resigned his knighthood shortly thereafter in protest of British policy in India.

on achievement, page 1
on adventure, page 5
on afterlife, page 10
on blame, page 26
on boasting, page 26
on boldness, page 27
on bravery, page 29
on children and childhood, page 39
on death, page 62
on decisions, page 64
on error, page 81
on ethics and morality, page 83
on existence, page 85
on freedom, page 103
on good and evil, page 113
on greed, page 118-119
on ideology, 136
on infinity, page 141-142
on leadership and leaders, page 157
on life, page 166
on men and women, page 181
on old age, page 195
on the past, page 198
on poetry and poets, page 207
on power, page 213
on problems, page 217

on progress, page 219
on punishment, page 221
on regrets, page 232
on responsibility, page 239
on science and technology,
  page 250
on sensuality, page 258-259
on shame, page 259
on silence, page 260
on truth, page 286
on vanity, page 292
on words, page 312
on worship, page 316

Mahmoud Mohammed Taha
(1909-1985)
Sudanese Muslim reformer
Renowned for his reformist project; executed by Sudanese authorities due to his opposition to Sharia.
on fear, page 93
on science and technology,
  page 250
on sin, page 261

Tai Chen (1724-1777)
Chinese philosopher
A leading philosopher of Ch'ing dynasty; wrote essays on math and phonology.
on human nature, page 129

Aisha al-Taimuriya (1840-1902)
Egyptian poet
Daughter of ruling Turkish aristocracy.
on feminism, page 97

Tamerlane. *See* Timur

Tan Da (c. 1930)
Vietnamese poet
(Nguyen Khac Hieu)
Considered greatest Vietnamese poet of his time; dominated literary scene; noted for use of imagery and rhythm.
on drinking, page 74
on farewells, page 91

T'ao Ch'ien (365-427)
Chinese poet
Chin dynasty poet known for simple, direct style. Official during tumultuous era known as Six Dynasties; subsequently retired to life of seclusion.
on anxiety, page 17
on death, page 63
on fate, page 92
on nature, page 190

Muhammed Taqi (d. 835)
Arab religious leader
An imam of Sh'ia branch of Islam; born in Medina; mausoleum is in Kazmein; considered a deeply religious sage.
on fear, page 94.
on fools and foolishness,
  page 100
on greed, page 119

Saul Tchernichovsky
(1875-1944)
Israeli poet
Born in Russian; leading Israeli poet of his time; called the "Greek poet in modern Hebrew literature" or "the poet of paganism" because of his subject matter and style.
on children and childhood,
  page 39
on loneliness, page 168

Tecumseh (c. 1768-1813)
Shawnee chief
(Tecumtha; Tekamthi)
Organized Native American con-

federation; led Tecumseh's Rebellion of 1809–1811; fought with British in War of 1812.

on Christianity, page 40
on imperialism, page 140–141
on the land, page 151
on Native Americans,
    page 187–188
on property, page 220
on resistance, page 238

Fujiwara Teika (1162–1241)
Japanese poet
Often wrote about nature; chiefly produced *waka* poetry, a form similar to Chinese poetics.

on the seasons, page 251

Ten Bears (c. 1800–1872)
Yamparika Comanche
    spokesperson
(Parra-Wa-Samen)
Famed for his eloquence; was rejected by his people due to his negotiations with whites.

on defeat, page 66
on wilderness, page 304

Teng Mu (1247–1306)
Chinese writer
Poet and editor; especially noted for editorship of *An Illustrated Account of the Grotto Heavens of Mt. Ta-ti*, a work on spiritual traditions of area surrounding the central shrine of Sung dynasty emperors.

on leadership and leaders,
    page 158
on revolution, page 244

Tenji Shinshi no Ason (c. 1243)
Japanese poet
Had thirty-three poems included in

the imperial anthologies. Daughter of the poet Shinkan.

on change, page 35

Tenshin. *See* Kakuzo Okakura

Tenzin Gyatso. *See* Dalai Lama

Mother Teresa (b. 1910)
Yugoslavian missionary
Roman Catholic nun who founded Missionaries of Charity; received India's Order of the Lotus for charitable work with India's poor; first recipient of John XXIII Peace Prize; recipient Nobel Peace Prize (1979).

on failure, page 87
on greatness, page 118
on humility, page 132
on loneliness, page 168
on perseverance, page 202
on poverty, page 210

Teresa of Avila (1515–1582)
Spanish nun
Founded nine convents; Carmelite-order reformer; copatron saint of Spain; poet.

on advice, page 7
on conduct, page 47
on good and evil, page 113
on humility, page 133
on learning and education,
    page 160
on poverty, page 210
on sin, page 261

U Thant (1909–1974)
Burmese diplomat
Secretary general of United Nations (1961–1971); major diplo-

matic force during Cuban missile crisis (1962–1963).

on cooperation, page 51

Margaret Thatcher (b. 1925)
English prime minister
Tory politician known for conservative views; held variety of government positions, including minister of education and science (1970–1974); and first female British prime minister (1979–1990).

on convictions, page 51
on leadership and leaders,
page 158
on men and women, page 181
on striving, page page 271
on truth, page 286
on tyranny and tyrants,
page 287

The Lu (c. 1930)
Vietnamese writer
Poet and playwright; member of Tu-luc group and leader of New Poetry movement of 1930s; wrote new-style poems termed *May van tho* (new rhymes), marked by French influence and flexible writing style to allow for more self-expression.

on beauty, page 23

Ngugi wa Thiong'o (b. 1936)
Kenyan novelist
Leading figure in Kenyan literature; anti-imperialistic focus—writes of ordinary native people deprived of their land by white settlers; stresses fusion of old and new, traditional and Western, so Africans can progress politically while retaining their cultural identity.

on Christianity, page 40
on despair, page 70

on money, page 185
on popular opinion,
page 210
on science and technology,
page 250–251
on writers and writing,
page 320

Thiruvalluvar (c. 2nd century)
Indian Tamil writer
(Valluvar)
Little known about life; believed that he lived in Madras; best known for his *Thirukural* (or *Kural*), a three-part work written in a classical verse form (distich) and dealing with morals, wisdom, duty, love, and money.

on conformity, page 48
on cowardice, page 52
on fools and foolishness,
page 100
on friendship, page 104
on gossip, page 114
on hypocrisy, page 134
on ignorance, page 138
on society, page 264
on striving, page 271

Tilak (1856–1920)
Indian political leader
(Bal Gangalhar)
Editor of two newspapers and writer. Brahmin who rebelled against British rule; called "Lokamanya" (honored by the people); founded Indian Home Rule League (1914); introduced passive resistance methods in Indian nationalist movement.

on politics, page 209

Timur (1336–1405)
Turkish conqueror
(Tamerlane; Timur-i-Lang)
Born in Kash; called "Lame Timur"

because of injuries he received in wars that resulted in his dominance of Transoxiana (1360-1370); led armies of Turks and Mongols; conquered Persia (1392-1396) and northern India (1398); defeated Ottomans and Mamluks (1402); died trying to conquer China.

on leadership and leaders, page 158

William R. Tolbert, Jr.

(1913-1980)
Liberian politician
Born to a leading farming family; active in both Baptist church and politics; vice-president for 6 four-year terms (1951-1971); assumed presidency after death of President Tubman (1971); elected president (1975); promoted national unity; launched educational and economic reforms; established diplomatic ties with Communist countries; president of OAU (1979); when economy faltered, faced rising opposition; killed during coup.

on uncertainty, page 288

Lily Tomlin (b. 1936)

American comedian
Famous for many characters in comedic sketches; actor in television, movies, Broadway; made start on television series *Laugh-In*.

on love, page 174

Omar Torrijos (1929-1981)

Panamanian military and political leader
Brigadier general; chief of government; anti-American leftist re-former. Established a dictatorship (1968-1981); provided enough social welfare and reform to become popular; negotiated treaty for transfer of Panama Canal control from United States to Panama.

on Communism, page 44

Simazaki Toson (1872-1943)

Japanese writer
(pseudonym of Simazaki Haruki)
Novelist and poet; born in provinces to an established rural family; educated at private university in Tokyo. Member of naturalist school; influenced by Protestant religion; known for his *Before the Dawn (Yoakemae)*, considered one of Japan's greatest epic novels.

on love, page 174

Ahmed Sekou Toure

(1922-1984)
Guinean politician
Union activist; led French West African independence movement; cofounded Rassamblement Democratique Africain; led general strike (1953); advocated federal form of government and total independence; first president of independent Guinea (1958); criticized colonialism and advocated pan-Africanism; liberalized socialist-oriented economy; reestablished diplomatic ties with France; imprisoned opponents and purged suspected traitors.

on revolution, page 245

Kwame Toure. *See* Stokely Carmichael

445

François Dominique Toussaint-L'Ouverture (1743–1803)
Haitian revolutionary leader
Called "Liberator of Haiti"; actively involved in all phases of Haitian independence movement; led slave insurrection (1791); became leader of French republicans and forced British to leave (1799); won civil war, became leader of entire island (1801); after resisting Napoleon's efforts to reestablish slavery, was defeated by French forces; charged with conspiracy; died in French prison.

on family, page 90
on liberty, page 163
on slavery, page 263

Tran Te Xuong (1869–1907)
Vietnamese poet
Known for satirical works.

on sorrow, page 265
on vice, page 292–293

Sojourner Truth (c. 1797–1883)
American abolitionist
African American former slave; became evangelist; changed name to Sojourner Truth and became ardent abolitionist and women's suffragist; traveled and preached nationwide. Worked with biographer Olive Gilbert on *The Narrative of Sojourner Truth*; appointed counselor to the freedman of Washington by Abraham Lincoln; retired in 1875.

on feminism, page 97–98
on spirit, page 268
on truth, page 286
on women, page 310–311

Ts'ai Yen (c. 3rd century)
Chinese poet
Daughter of scholar, became renowned scholar in her own right; considered first great woman poet of China. Captured by the Huns; became concubine of a Hun chieftain and bore him two sons; later ransomed; married a Chinese officer, but left her sons behind; some of her work is believed written about her sons.

on homesickness, page 127

Tsali (d. 1838)
Cherokee warrior
Leader of resistance movement against Cherokees' removal by whites; honored as Native American martyr.

on death, page 63

Ts'ao Chih (192–232)
Chinese writer
Nephew of Ts'ao Pi, first emperor of Wei dynasty; regarded as a premier poet of his era; poetry characterized by brooding melancholy.

on transience, page 281

Tso Ssu (c. 3rd century)
Chinese poet
on concentration, page 46

Tsung Ping (375–443)
Chinese philosopher
Buddhist writer; argued against Confucianism; works focused on infinitude of life and the relative insignificance of the present.

on generations, page 106

Tu Fu (712–770)
Chinese poet
Along with Li Po, considered best poet of premodern China; poetry is considered innovative, dense; late-blooming official (entered civil service at age 45); suffered from court politics; finally left service and spent the remainder of his life wandering. Unlike Li Po, known for his conformity to the dictates of style.

on solitude, page 265
on travel, page 282–283
on war, page 301

T'u Lung (c. 1592)
Chinese poet
Scholar; famous for "The Travels of Mingliaotzu," espousing carefree philosophy of life, and love of truth and freedom.

on transience, page 281

Harriet Tubman (1820–1913)
American abolitionist
Escaped Maryland plantation where she was a slave. Conductor for the Underground Railroad; traveled South to help over three hundred slaves escape North; called the "Moses of her people." During Civil War, served as a nurse and Union spy.

on liberty, page 161

Tulsidas (1523–1624)
Indian philosopher
Plays, poetry, and other works influenced Hindu devotionalism; reinterpreted the *Ramayana.*

on prayer, page 213
on self-esteem, page 256

Fadwa Tuqan (b. 1917)
Palestinian poet
Poet of the West Bank; considered a leading Palestinian poet; early work focused on love; her later work was concerned with issues of Palestinian quest for a homeland.

on time, page 279

Hassan al-Turabi (b. 1930)
Sudanese politician
Islamic fundamentalist leader of National Islamic Front, which formed after a split with the Muslim Brotherhood; entered into coalition government as a minister of justice (1988); supported a coup against the government to form a new, completely fundamentalist government.

on government, page 116

Ki no Tusrayuki (c. 859–945)
Japanese editor
Writer; edited *Kokin wakashu (Anthology of Poems Old and New)*, published in 905.

on poetry and poets, page 207

Desmond Tutu (b. 1931)
South African antiapartheid
  activist and religious leader
Schoolmaster; Anglican priest (1960); bishop of Diocese of Johannesburg (1984); archbishop of Capetown (1986); antiapartheid leader who advocates nonviolence; awarded Nobel Peace Prize (1984).

on brotherhood and sisterhood,
  page 31
on history, page 126
on human rights, page 130

on leadership and leaders,
  page 158
on learning and education,
  page 160
on love, page 174
on peace, page 201
on race, page 224
on racism, page 228

Tzu Yeh (c. 3rd–4th century)
Chinese poet
Forty-two poems in collection *Tzu Yeh ko* (*Songs of Tzu Yeh*) attributed to Tzu Yeh, a young female poet, but little known about her. Attribution believed false; instead she is believed to have written the original poem and melody, but the bulk of *Tzu Yeh* are folk songs from Wu; style of *Tzu Yeh* imitated by other poets, including Li Po.

on sex, page 259

U

U T'ak (1262–1342)
Korean poet
Metaphysician; writer of first extant *sijo*, the most popular form of Korean poetry.

on old age, page 195

Obiora Udechukwu
(20th century)
Nigerian poet
Work drawn from Ibo folk tales; maintained mystery of the legends, while eliminating comedic and romantic elements; work expresses journey of pain.

on destruction, page 70

Umar ibn-al-Khattab
(c. 581–644)
Arab Islamic leader and second
  caliph of Islam
Founder of Muslim Arab empire; father-in-law of Muhammad. Said to have instituted such far-reaching practices as prayers during month of Ramadan, obligatory pilgrimages (*hajj*), and the Hijarah as commencement of the Muslim era; assassinated.

on law, page 154

Brahmabandhab Upadhyay
(1861–1907)
Indian reformer
An associate of Surendranath Banerjea and Ananada Bose; active in various progressive movements; cofounded *Twentieth Century* magazine (1901) and *Sandhya Daily News* (1904), in which he printed anticolonialist tracts; arrested for sedition; became ill and died in jail.

on revolution, page 245

Rodolfo Usigli (1905–1979)
Mexican writer
Playwright; focused on social and political satire, abnormal psychology, and Mexican history; best known Mexican playwright abroad.

on acting and actors, page 2

'Uthman (d. 656)
Arab Islamic leader and third
  caliph of Islam
Twelve-year reign as third caliph of Islam (644–656); oversaw expansion of Islamic empire to North

Africa and Persia; was later killed by mutineers.

on vice, page 293

Uyesugi Kenshin (1530–1578)
Japanese military leader
Master of powerful Uyesugi family; opponent of Oda Nobunaga (a feudal lord who overthrew the ruling Shogun and attempted to unite Japan); as general, died before decisive battle with Nobunaga's forces.

on death, page 63

V

Valluvar. *See* Thiruvalluvar

Van-Hanh (d. 1018)
Vietnamese poet
Buddhist monk with decisive influence at court; served as king's trusted adviser and diplomat.

on transience, page 281

Varahamihira (505–587)
Indian astronomer
Court astronomer for Vikramaditya; wrote several books.

on equality, page 81

Mario Vargas Llosa (b. 1936)
Peruvian writer
Novelist, critic, essayist, and short story writer. Considered Peru's greatest living writer and one of the leading novelists writing in Spanish; called a critical neorealist; works tend to expose philosophi-

cal uncertainties and the decay of values. Ran for president.

on the Americas, page 14
on art and artists, page 21
on democracy, page 67–68
on truth, page 286
on violence, page 295

Monika Varma (b. 1916)
Indian writer
Poet, critic, and translator; poetry based on classical Indian philosophy; shows influence of Christian mystic saints and expresses love of her land.

on nature, page 190

Vatsyayana
(late 4th–early 5th century)
Indian philosopher
(Malla Naga)
Hindu scholar; presumed author of the *Kama Sutra*.

on success, page 272–273

Venmanipputi
(c. 1st–3rd century)
Indian Tamil poet
Tamil poet.

on sex, page 259

B. W. Vilakazi (1906–1947)
Zulu writer
Poet and novelist; first published writer of Western-influenced poetry in Zulu; famous for breakthrough works written in Zulu.

on imperialism, page 141
on racism, page 228

Xavier Villaurrutia (1903–1950)
Mexican poet
In 1920s and 1930s, collaborated

in various avant-garde movements to revitalize Mexican literature; literature professor at University of Mexico.

on love, page 174

Vivekananda (1863–1902)
Indian religious leader
(Narendeanath Datta)
Vedantist evangelist; most important disciple of religious teacher Ramakrishna. Brought thoughts of Ramakrishna to United States; founded Ramakrishna Order (1887); established Vedanta Society in New York; traveled extensively through Europe and the United States; returned to India (1900) and devoted himself to Ramakrishna Mission for remainder of life.

on experience, page 86
on freedom, page 103
on materialism, page 178
on religion, page 235
on the self, page 253
on transcendence, page 279
on unity, page 290

Vu Hoang-Chuong (b. 1916)
Vietnamese poet
Best known for blend of classical and modern styles.

on loneliness, page 168

W

Derek Walcott (b. 1930)
West Indian writer
Poet and dramatist born in Trinidad; known for intense symbolic imagination, both personal and Caribbean; considered most important West Indian poet and playwright writing in English today; received Nobel Prize for literature (1992).

on evil, page 84
on silence, page 260

Alice Walker (b. 1944)
American writer
Novelist and poet; one of most popular contemporary African American writers; influenced by southern speech patterns and tradition of storytelling; won American Book Award and Pulitzer Prize for *The Color Purple*.

on acceptance, page 1
on feminism, page 98
on self-reliance, page 258
on survival, page 274

David Walker (c. 1800)
American abolitionist
African American, born free in Wilmington, North Carolina, was disgusted by slavery surrounding him; moved to Boston, where he opened a secondhand clothing store and began agitating against slavery. Published *Walker's Appeal*, one of greatest and most influential abolitionist pamphlets.

on racism, page 228

Yona Wallach (b. 1946)
Israeli poet
One of Israel's leading women poets.

on death, page 63

Fats Waller (1904-1943)
American musician
Composer, pianist, and singer; influential in 1930s jazz.

on critics and criticism,
page 55

Wang Fu-chih (1619-1692)
Chinese philosopher
A major thinker in seventeenth-century China; neo-Confucianist historian.

on policy, page 207

Wang Hui-yueh (c. 1850),
Chinese philosopher
Wrote treatises during the "Heavenly Kingdom of Highest Peace" (T'ai-p'ing t'ien-kuo), theocratic "dynasty" proclaimed in 1851 by Hung Hsiu-ch'uan; attempted to fuse Confucian and Christian tenets.

on brotherhood and sisterhood,
page 31

Wang Hsun (c. 13th century)
Chinese philosopher
Works influenced Chen-chin, second son of Khubilai Khan and heir apparent to Mongol dynasty.

on good and evil, page 113

Wang Ken (1483-1540)
Chinese philosopher
Founder of "T'ai-chou" school of thought; famous for "Treatise on the Kingly Way"; had reputation as a "democrat" or "leftist."

on pleasure, page 205
on the self, page 253-254

Wang Wei (699-759)
Chinese poet
Also artist and musician; along with Li Po and Tu Fu, one of the leading poets of so-called High T'ang (height of the T'ang dynasty); devout Buddhist whose philosophy is reflected in his work.

on Buddhism, page 31
on old age, page 195
on questions and answers,
page 222
on travel, page 283

Wang Yang-ming (1472-1529)
Chinese philosopher
Ming dynasty official; foremost philosopher of his time; neo-Confucianist; founded school of "idealism." Taught that cultivation of intuitive knowledge led to understanding of Confucian truths, not to study of the Confucian classics; stance has caused later scholars to consider him greatly responsible for the decline of Confucian standards and subsequent collapse of the Ming dynasty.

on action, page 3
on afterlife, page 10
on knowledge, page 151
on love, page 174

Wang Yu-p'u (c. 18th century)
Chinese government official
Salt commissioner; lectured the populace on the sacred edict of Sheng-tso (1662-1722) and Emperor Shih-tsung (1723-1735), using examples from everyday life; words later published, providing codes of behavior and reflecting how government affected people's lives.

on competition, page 45-46

451

Wang Zhi-huan (b. 695)
Chinese poet
Early Tang dynasty poet; laid foundation for new movement in Chinese literature, which culminated in the more direct, less "literary" Tang poetry.

Booker T. Washington
(1856-1915)
American educator
Born a slave in Virginia; educated at Hampton Institute; became teacher and writer; in writing and lectures, addressed problems of African Americans; became head of Alabama-based Tuskegee Institute (1881), designed to train African Americans for trades and professions; advocated moderate civil rights stance; most famous work is *Up from Slavery*.

Faye Wattleton (b. 1943)
American social activist
Head of Planned Parenthood (1978-1990).

Beatrice Webb (1858-1943)
British economist
Sociologist; socialist; coauthored numerous works on labor, history, and economics; cofounded Fabian Society (1883); founded London School of Economics; cofounded *New Statesman* (1913).

Wei Jingsheng (b. 1950)
Chinese prodemocracy activist
Famous for "The Fifth Modernization" (i.e., democracy); dissident, former Red Guard member; sentenced to life in prison for involvement in protests against the government; released in 1993.

Simone Weil (1909-1943)
French philosopher
Revolutionary, poet, journalist, playwright, and scholar; active in the French Resistance during World War II; known for her social philosophy; works, often having mystic slant include *Waiting for God* and *Gravity and Grace*.

Ezer Weizman (b. 1924)
Israeli military and political leader
Born in Palestine; nephew of Chaim Weizman, first president of State of Israel. Pilot in British army;

a founder of the Israeli Air Force; general (1959); Air Force commander for eight years. Held various positions in government, including minister of transport; defense minister (1977) and advocate of negotiations with Palestine Liberation Organization. Founded new party, Yahad (Together); member of inner political cabinet of Prime Minister Peres; elected president.

on emotions, page 77

Eudora Welty (b. 1909)
American writer
Novelist and short story writer; known for rich evocation of the South in her work; best known for short stories; received Pulitzer Prize (1973) for novel *The Optimist's Daughter*; received Presidential Medal of Freedom (1980).

on learning and education, page 161

Wen Yiduo (1899-1947)
Chinese writer
Poet, scholar, and critic; stressed artist's responsibility to society; joined Democratic League; was assassinated.

on beauty, page 23
on progress, page 219

Rebecca West (1892-1983)
English writer
(née Cecily Isabel Andrews Fairfield; Corrine Andrews)
Companion of writer H. G. Wells. Novelist, critic, and journalist; adopted the name of a character in

Henrik Ibsen's play *Romesholm*; novels include *The Return of the Soldier* and *The Thinking Reed*. Her nonfiction analysis of the causes of World War II, *Black Lamb and Grey Falcon*, is considered her greatest work.

on biography, page 25
on feminism, page 98
on history, page 126
on writers and writing, page 320

White Antelope (d. 1864)
Southern Cheyenne chief
Native American leader who advocated peace with the whites.

on transience, page 281

Albery A. Whitman (1851-1902)
American poet
Financial agent and Methodist minister. First book, *Not a Man and Yet a Man,* dealt with status of African Americans in the United States.

on adversity, page 6
on complaint, page 46

Roy Wilkins (1901-1981)
American civil rights leader
Lifetime career with National Association for the Advancement of Colored People (NAACP); began work with NAACP while college student; edited NAACP publication *Crisis* (1934-1949); worked in various NAACP positions; head of NAACP (1955-1977); known for effective, middle-of-the-road leadership.

on civil rights, page 42

Lucie Campbell Williams
(1885–1962)
American educator
Forty-three-year career in teaching; musician, evangelist, and public speaker. Spent most of teaching career in Memphis public school system; wrote over 100 songs, many on religious topics; appointed to the National Education Association.

    on life, page 166
    on victory, page 294

Mary Wollstonecraft
(1759–1797)
English feminist
One of earliest and most influential European women's rights activists; mother of writer Mary Shelley.

    on feminism, page 98
    on learning and education, page 161
    on marriage, page 177
    on political movements, page 209
    on poverty, page 211
    on virtue, page 296

Virginia Woolf (1882–1941)
English writer
Novelist, essayist, and literary critic; member of influential Bloomsbury group of artists and writers. Best known for her novels, including *Mrs. Dalloway*, *To the Lighthouse*, and *The Waves*.

    on aging, page 12
    on argument, page 17
    on art and artists, page 21
    on boldness, page 27
    on critics and criticism, page 55
    on feminism, page 98

    on ideas, page 135
    on life, page 166
    on men and women, page 181
    on the public, page 221
    on truth, page 286
    on writers and writing, page 320

Richard Wright (1908–1960)
American writer
Novelist, essayist, poet, dramatist, and short story writer; advocated racial tolerance; presented harsh realities of racism; famed for novel *Native Son*, one of the strongest works on the plight of African Americans.

    on freedom, page 103
    on human nature, page 129
    on slavery, page 263

Wu Chih-hui (1864–1954)
Chinese political theorist
Leader of new anarchist group in modern China; educated in Japan; worked as journalist; advocated anarchism; lived in Paris; believed European culture superior to Chinese culture.

    on knowledge, page 150

X

Xerxes (c. 480 B.C.E.)
Persian king
King of Persia (486–465 B.C.E.); fought against rebelling Egyptians in his empire, then followed his father's footsteps in attempting to subdue Greece. Repelled; remaining reign was peaceful; murdered

by Artabanus, captain of the guards.

on risks, page 246
on speech, page 267

Xu Zhimo (c. 1895-1931)
Chinese writer
Nature poet; anti-Communist; lived in United States and London; killed in a plane crash.

on love, page 174-175

Xuan Dieu (20th century)
Vietnamese poet
A leader of "New Poetry School" in Vietnam; member of Tu-luc Van Doan (Independent Literary Group); later poetry has been written according to Communist Party dictates.

on love, page 175
on poetry and poets, page 207

Xunzi (300-235 B.C.E.)
Chinese philosopher
Opposed doctrine of Mencius (Meng-tzu); advocated strict Confucian philosophy (Rujia).

on leadership and leaders, page 158

Y

Al-Yafi'i (1299-1367)
Arab Islamic historian
Born in Yemen; chronicler of Islamic theory and practice.

on love, page 175

Yajnavalkya (4th century B.C.E.)
Indian philosopher
Buddhist monk; many Vedic texts attributed to him; also known for his treatise on law.

on the soul, page 266

Yakamochi (717-785)
Japanese poet
Believed to have compiled the *Man'yashu*, a poetry anthology in which 481 of his works appear.

on dreams, page 73-74

Yamamoto Isokuru (1884-1943)
Japanese Imperial Admiral
Educated at naval academy at Etajima; after being wounded in Russo-Japanese War (1904-1905), adopted by the Yamamoto family; studied at Harvard; held range of positions, including naval attache to Japanese embassy in the United States (1926-1928), vice-navy minister (1936-1939); admiral (1940), and commander-in-chief of the combined fleet (1939-1943). Initially opposed to Japan entering World War II, planned and directed attack on Pearl Harbor (1941); after forces defeated in battle of Midway (1942), was killed when plane was shot down over Solomon Islands.

on the Americas, page 15
on peace, page 201
on perspective, page 203

Yamatohime (c. 671)
Japanese poet and empress
Poet; wife of Emperor Tanji.

on memory, page 180

Yaminuddin. *See* Amir Khusrau

Yang Ping (b. 1908)
Chinese writer
Political activist, editor, and journalist.

　on women, page 311

Yang Tse (420–360 B.C.E.)
Chinese Taoist philosopher
Taoist proponent of the school of hedonism, one of the so-called Hundred Schools of Chinese philosophy; his theories later integrated into mainstream Taoism.

　on afterlife, page 10
　on the present, page 214–215
　on sacrifice, page 248

Itamar Yaoz-Kest (b. 1934)
Israeli writer
Hungarian-born poet, novelist, short story writer, and editor.

　on art and artists, page 21
　on emotions, page 77
　on the past, page 198

Kawabata Yasunari (1899–1972)
Japanese writer
Poet, critic, and columnist; best-known member of the Shinkan-kaku-ha (New Sensibility) group; influenced by French surrealistic poetry; a leading discoverer of new talent in Japan.

　on language, page 152

Ibrahim al-Yaziji (1847–1906)
Lebanese scholar
Contributed to Arab renaissance of late nineteenth century; called one of the "humanists of Beirut"; advocated attention to academics, modernization of Arabic language.

　on language, page 152

Abraham B. Yehoushua (b. 1936)
Israeli writer
Short story writer and essayist; lecturer and dean of students at University of Haifa; active member of Labor Party.

　on ideology, page 136

Yi Cho-nyon (1269–1343)
Korean poet
Court official; tried to advise his king to work for people's welfare; when his points were rejected, resigned in protest.

　on thought, page 277

Yi Myong-han (1595–1645)
Korean poet
Works marked by subtlety and lyricism. Senior academician and minister of personnel.

　on dreams, page 74

Yi T'aek (1651–1719)
Korean poet
Member of Sijo school, which produced the most popular form of Korean poetry; also a naval officer.

　on equality, page 81

S. Yizhar. *See* Yizhar Simlansky

Tashonka Yotanka. *See* Crazy Horse.

Andrew Young (b. 1932)
American civil rights activist and politician
Colleague of Martin Luther King, Jr.; ambassador to United Nations; mayor of Atlanta.

　on business, page 32

Fukuzawa Yukichi (1835–1901)
Japanese reformer
A key Meiji reformer, a movement that destroyed the previous feudal system in Japan; argued for adoption of Western science and civilization in Japan; member of Japan's first mission to the United States; wrote his impressions of the West in the best-seller *Conditions in the West*; wrote thirty volumes of wit.

on the military, page 183

Natan Zach (b. 1930)
Israeli poet
Born in Germany; largely responsible for liberating Israeli poetry from traditionalism.

on nature, page 190
on poetry and poets, page 207

'Ubayd-i-Zakani
(c. 14th century)
Persian poet
Poet during reign of Timur; wrote humorous verse, with rich use of epigrams and metaphors.

on illness, page 137

Emiliano Zapata (1879–1919)
Mexican revolutionary
Led first major agrarian revolution of twentieth century; became a guerilla and was killed in an ambush; a legendary figure in Mexican history.

on freedom, page 103
on peace, page 201
on revolution, page 245

on sacrifice, page 248
on slavery, page 263

Zarathustra. *See* Zoroaster

Rafael Enriquez de Zayas
(1848–1932)
Mexican writer
Born in Vera Cruz; lawyer; worked at numerous magazines and newspapers. Best known for epic poem "Juarez," as well as other works about the heroes of 1862 who fought against French occupation. Wrote historical novels and biographies, including one on Benito Juarez.

on self-reliance, page 258

Zenobia of Palmyra (240–300)
Palmyran queen and military leader
Queen of Palmyra (in what is now Syria); married to Odenathus, lord of the city and later governor of the east. Upon his death by murder (c. 267), she led army in war of expansion; conquered Egypt (269) and most of the eastern provinces in Asia Minor (270). Named her son eastern emperor; defeated and captured by the Roman emperor Aurelian (272); blamed war on her secretary to spare her own life; was taken to Rome and given land near Tivoli, where she lived comfortably until her death.

on war, page 301

Zhang Jie (b. 1937)
Chinese writer
Novelist, short story writer, and essayist; one of China's leading fe-

male writers; currently in voluntary exile in the United States.

on freedom, page 103
on society, page 264

Zhao Zhenkai. *See* Bei Dao

Zhou Zuoren (1885–1968)
Chinese critic and writer
Poet and novelist; wrote in Western style; greatly influenced development of literature in Baihua.

on meaning, page 179

Zhou En-lai (1898–1976)
Chinese revolutionary and prime
minister of the People's
Republic
Born to mandarin family in Jaingu province near Shanghai; educated at American missionary college, and in Japan and Paris. Founding member of Chinese Communist Party (CCP). Began organizing Communist cells in Shanghai; supported Mao Zedong as party leader (1935); liaison officer between CCP and Nationalist government led by Chiang Kai'shek (1937–1946); prime minister (1949–1976); foreign minister (1949–1958). As prime minister, involved in Great Leap Forward (1958–1960) and Cultural Revolution (1966–1969); developed "Four Modernizations" program (1975); advocated detente with the United States in early 1970s.

on despair, page 70
on diplomacy, page 72
on leadership and leaders,
  page 158

Zoroaster (c. 630–553 B.C.E.)
Prophet of the ancient Iranian
  religion of Zoroastrianism
(Zarathustra; Zaradusht)
Founder of Zoroastrianism; taught that the world and history reflect the fight between Ormuzd (the creator, or good) and Ahriman (the devil, or bad), resulting in the banishment of evil and the victory of good. Biographical facts about his life based on the one written record of him in the sacred book of Zoroastrianism, the *Avesta*. As chieftain, fought against Turanian and Vedic aggressors on political, military, and theological fronts in defense of a holy agricultural state.

on action, page 3

Zou Rong (1885–1905)
Chinese activist
Revolutionist and writer arrested for writing an anti-Manchu pamphlet; died in prison.

on revolution, page 245

Paul Zoungrana (b. 1917)
Upper Voltan religious leader
Educated in Catholic schools; archbishop of Ougadougou; cardinal (1965).

on culture, page 56

Zuo Si (3rd century)
Chinese poet
on nature, page 190

Bibliography

The following list encompasses most of the books, articles, and essays that we used to compile *The Whole World Book of Quotations*. When quotations are in translation, we tried to include the translators' names. We urge readers to go beyond reading the quotations in this book to reading some of the complete works. As we found, a few brief quotations do not do justice to many of the great thoughts or writings that are incorporated in this listing.

Achebe, Chinua. *Christmas in Biafra and Other Poems*. New York: Doubleday, 1973.

Adams, Russell L. *Great Negroes, Past and Present*. Chicago: Afro-American, 1969.

Aidoo, Ama Ata. *No Sweetness Here*. New York: Dearborn Trade, 1988.

Albery, Nobuko. *The House of Kanze*. New York: Simon & Schuster, 1986.

Alcott, Louisa May. *Little Women*. New York: Knopf, 1988.

Allen, W. E. D. *Russian Embassies to the Georgian Kings*. Cambridge, England: Hakluytr Society, University Press, 1970.

al-Tayib Salih. *Season of Migration to the North*. Trans. Denys Johnson-Davies. London: Heinemann Education Books, African Writers Series, 1970.

'Ali [Ali ibn Abi Talib]. *Maxims of 'Ali*. Trans. Mehdi Nokosteen. Boulder: Col.: Este Es Press, 1973.

Andrzejewski, B. W., and I. M. Lewis. *Somali Poetry: An Introduction*. London: Oxford University Press, 1964.

Anzaldua, Gloria. *Borderlands/La Frontera: The New Mestiza*. San Francisco: Spinsters/Aunt Lute, 1987.

Arberry, A. J. *Sufism: An Account of the Mystics of Islam*. London: Allen & Unwin, 1950.

Armah, Ayi Kwei. *The Beautyful Ones Are Not Yet Born*. London: Heinemann, 1969, reset 1975.

———. *Fragments*. London: Heinemann, 1974.

Armstrong, Virginia Irving. *I Have Spoken*. Chicago: Swallow Press, 1971.

Austen, Jane. *Mansfield Park*. New York: Oxford University Press, 1988.

———. *Persuasion*. Anstey, Leicestershire: F. A. Thorpe, 1990.

———. *Pride and Prejudice*. Boston: G. K. Hall, 1980.

————. *Sense and Sensibility*. Cutchogue, N.Y.: Buccaneer Books, 1985.

Awoonor, Kofi. *Rediscovery and Other Poems*. Evanston, Ill.: Northwestern University Press, 1964.

Badran, Margot, and Miriam Cooke, eds. and trans. *Opening the Gates: A Century of Arab Feminist Writing*. Bloomington: Indiana University Press, 1990.

Bailey, Bernadine. *Famous Latin American Liberators*. New York: Dodd, Mead, 1960.

Balaban, John. *Remembering Heaven's Face*. New York: Simon & Schuster, 1991.

Baldwin, James. "Fifth Avenue Uptown." *Esquire*, July 1960.

————. *The Fire Next Time*. New York: Dial Press, 1963.

————. *Nobody Knows My Name*. New York: Dial Press, 1961.

————. *Notes of a Native Son*. Boston: Beacon Press, 1955.

Bankier, Joanna, Deirdre Lashgari, and Doris Earnshaw. *Women Poets of the World*. Trans. Jonathan Crewe, Eloah F. Giacomelli, Hannah Hoffman, Elene Margot Kolb, Richard Lattimore, Henry Wadsworth Longfellow, Raymond Oliver, and Margaret Smith. New York: Macmillan, 1983.

Jones, Leroi [Imamu Amiri Baraka]. *Home*. New York: Morrow, 1966.

Bargad, Warren, and Stanley F. Chyet, eds. and trans. *Israeli Poetry: A Contemporary Anthology*. Bloomington: Indiana University Press, 1986.

Barksdale, Richard, and Kenneth Kinnamon. *Black Writers of America*. New York: Macmillan, 1972.

Barnes, Djuna. *Nightwood*. New York: New Directions, 1946.

Barnstone, Aliki, and Willis Barnstone, eds. *A Book of Women Poets*. New York: Schocken, 1980.

Basham, A. L., ed. and trans. *The Wonder That Was India*. Taplinger, 1968.

Bauer, W. *China and the Search for Happiness*. New York: Seabury Press, 1976.

Beard, John R. *Toussaint L'Ouverture*. 1863. Reprint, Freeport, N.Y.: Books for Libraries Press, 1971.

Beauvoir, Simone de. *America Day by Day*. Trans. Patrick Dudley. New York: Grove Press, 1953.

————. *The Blood of Others*. New York: Pantheon Books, 1983.

————. *The Second Sex*. Trans. H. M. Parshley. New York: Knopf, 1952.

Bedri, Babikr. *Memoirs.* Vol. 1. Trans. Yousef Bedri and George Scott. New York: Oxford University Press, 1969.

Beeston, A. F. L., T. M. Johnstone, R. B. Serjeant, and G. R. Smith, eds. *Arabic Literature to the End of the Umayyad Period*. London: Cambridge University Press, 1983.

Bei Dao. *The August Sleepwalker*. San Francisco: New Directions, 1988.

Ben Amittai, Levi. *The Palestine Review*. Jerusalem, 1937.

Bennett, Lerone, Jr. *Before the Mayflower: A History of the Negro in America 1619–1964*. Rev. ed. Baltimore: Penguin Books, 1966.

Bhutto, Benazir. *Daughter of the East*. New York: Sands Trade, 1989.

Birch, Cyril, ed. *Anthology of Chinese Literature,* Vol. 2. New York: Grove Press, 1972.

Blavatsky, Elena Petrovna. *The Key to Theosophy*. Los Angeles: Theosophy, 1962.

Bodde, Derek. *China's First Unifier*. Leiden, Netherlands: E. J. Brill, 1938. Reprint, Hong Kong: Hong Kong University Press, 1967.

Bogan, Louise. *A Poet's Alphabet*. New York: McGraw-Hill, 1970.

Borges, Jorge Luis. *Other Inquisitions*. Buenos Aires: Emece, 1960.

Boullata, Issa J., ed. *Critical Perspectives on Modern Arabic Literature*. Washington, D.C.: Three Continents, 1980.

Bourne, Richard. *Political Leaders of Latin America*. New York: Knopf, 1970.

Bradford, Sarah Elizabeth Hopkins. *Harriet, the Moses of Her People*. New York: Peter Smith, 1961.

Brawley, Benjamin. *The Negro Genius*. New York: Biblo & Tannen, 1966.

Brown, Joseph Epes, ed. and rec. *The Sacred Pipe, Black Elk's Account of the Seven Rites of the Oglala Sioux*. Norman University of Oklahoma Press, 1953.

Browne, Lewis, ed. *The Wisdom of Israel*. New York: Modern Library, 1945.

Browning, Elizabeth Barrett. *Aurora Leigh*. Chicago: Cassandra Editions, 1979.

Buck, Pearl S. *The Child Who Never Grew*. John Day, 1950.

———. *What America Means to Me*. Salem, N.H.: Ayer, 1943.

Burgin, Richard. *Conversations with Jorge Luis Borges*. New York: Holt, Rinehart & Winston, 1969.

Butterfield, Fox. *China, Alive in the Bitter Sea*. New York: Time Books, 1982.

Bynner, Witter, and Kiang Kang-hu. *The Jade Mountain*. New York: Knopf, 1929. Reprint, New York: Doubleday, 1964.

Carter, Martin Wylde. *Poems of Resistance from British Guiana*. London: Lawrence & Wishart, 1954.

Carter, Rosalynn Smith, and Jimmy Carter. *Everything to Gain*. New York: Random House, 1987.

Chabal, Patrick. *Amilcar Cabral: Revolutionary Leadership and People's War*. New York: Cambridge University Press, 1983.

Chamberline, Hope. *A Minority of Members (Women in the United States Congress)*. New York: Praeger, 1973.

Chan Wing-tsit. *A Sourcebook in Chinese Philosophy*. Princeton, N.J.: Princeton University Press, 1963.

Chapman, Abraham, ed. *Black Voices: An Anthology of Afro-American Literature*. New York: Mentor/New American Library, 1968.

461

Ch'ien Chung-Shu. *Wei-ch'eng*. Shanghai: Aurora Press, 1947. *A Fortress Beseiged*. Bloomington: Indiana University Press, 1979.

Ching, Julia. *To Acquire Wisdom: The Way of Wang Yang-ming*. New York: Columbia University Press, 1976.

Chisholm, Shirley. *Unbought and Unbossed*. Boston: Houghton Mifflin, 1970.

Chow Tse-Tsung. *The May Fourth Movement: Intellectual Revolution in Modern China*. Cambridge, Mass.: Harvard University Press, 1960.

Christian, Barbara. *Black Women Novelists*. Westport, Conn.: Greenwood Press, 1980.

Christie, Agatha. *Witness for the Prosecution*. New York: Dodd, Mead, 1985.

Chuang-tzu. *Chuang Tzu: Basic Writings*. Trans. Burton Watson. New York: Columbia University Press, 1964.

―――. *Chuang-tzu, Mystic, Moralist and Social Reformer*. Trans. Herbert A. Giles. London: Quaritch, 1889.

―――. *Chuang Tzu: A New Selected Translation (with an Exposition of the Philosophy of Kuo Hsiang)*. Trans. Yu-lan Fung. Shanghai: Commercial Press, 1933. Reprint: New York: Paragon, 1964.

Clarke, John Henrick. *Malcolm X: The Man and His Time*. New York: Macmillan, 1969.

Cleaver, Eldridge. *Soul on Ice*. New York: McGraw-Hill, 1968.

Clendinnen, Inga. *Aztecs: An interpretation*. Cambridge, England: Cambridge University Press, 1991.

Confucius. *The Analects*. London: Oxford University Press, 1937.

―――. *The Analects of Confucius*. Trans. Arthur Waley. London: Allen & Unwin, 1938.

―――. *The Wisdom of Confucius*. Trans. Lin Yutang. New York: Random House, 1938.

Conze, Edward, ed. *Buddhist Texts through the Ages*. Oxford: Bruno Cassirer, 1954.

Cope, J., and U. Krige, eds. *The Penguin Book of South African Verse*. Harmondsworth, U.K.: Penguin, 1968.

Cope, J., trans. *Izibongo*. Oxford, U.K.: Clarendon Press, 1968.

Cortazar, Julio. *A Certain Lucas*. New York: Knopf, 1984.

―――. *Hopscotch*. Trans. Gregory Rabassa. New York: Pantheon Books, 1987.

Cosman, Carol, Joan Keefe, and Kathleen Weaver, eds. *The Penguin Book of Woman Poets*. Trans. Peter H. Lee. New York: Penguin Books, 1978.

Crawford, D. *Thinking Black*. New York: Negro Universities Press, 1969.

Curie, Marie. *Pierre Curie*. Trans. Charlotte and Vernon Kellogg. New York: Macmillan, 1923.

Dalai Lama. *Freedom in Exile*. New York: HarperCollins, 1990.

Davis, A. R., ed. *The Penguin Book of Chinese Verse*. Trans. Robert Kotewall and Normal L. Smith. London: Penguin, 1962.

Dalgado, Abelardo. *Twenty-five Pieces of a Chicano Mind*. Denver: Barrio, 1970.

Devlin, Bernadette. *The Price of My Soul*. New York: Knopf, 1969.

Dib, Mohammed. *Le Metier a tisser*. Paris: Editions de Seuil, 1957.

Didion, Joan. *The Book of Common Prayer*. New York: Simon & Schuster, 1977.

Diederich, Bernard, and Al Burt. *Papa Doc: Haiti and Its Dictator*. Princeton, N.J.: Wiener, 1991.

Di Giovanni, Norman Thomas, Daniel Halpern, and Frank McShane, eds. *Borges on Writing*. New York: Dutton, 1973.

Dillard, Annie. *Holy the Firm*. Boston: Hall, 1977.

———. *Pilgrim at Tinker Creek*. New York: Harper & Row, 1985.

Ding Ling. *I Myself Am a Woman: Selected Writings of Ding Ling*. Ed. Rani E. Barlow and Gary J. Biorge. Boston: Beacon Press, 1989.

Douglass, Frederick. *My Bondage and My Freedom*. Chicago: Johnson, 1970.

———. "The Women's Suffrage Movement." *New National Era*, October 6, 1870.

Du Bois, Shirley Graham. *His Day Is Marching On: A Memoir of W. E. B. Du Bois*. New York: Lippincott, 1971.

Du Bois, W. E. B. *The Gift of Black Folk*. Boston: Stratford, 1924. Reprint, New York: Kraus, 1975.

———. "As the Crow Flies." *Crisis*, January 1931.

———. "Freedom to Learn." *Midwest Journal*, Winter 1949.

———. *The Nation*, January 25, 1958.

———. "Our Own Consent." *Crisis,* January, 1913.

———. "Patient Assess." *Crisis*, March 1930.

Duke, Michael S. *The Iron Horse*. Salt Lake City: Peregrine Smith Books, 1989.

Dunbar, Paul Laurence. *Complete Poems*. New York: Dodd, Mead, 1913.

Duncan, Isadora. *My Life*. New York: Bonie & Liveright, 1927.

Durand, M. M., and Nguyen Tran Huan. *Introduction to Vietnamese Literature*. New York: Columbia University Press, 1985.

Eastman, Charles Alexander. *The Soul of an Indian*. New York: Houghton Mifflin, 1911.

Ebrey, P. B., ed. *Chinese Civilization and Society*. New York: Free Press, 1981.

Eddy, G. S., and Kirby Page. *Makers of Freedom*. 1926. Reprint, Freeport, N.Y.: Books for Libraries Press, 1953.

Elijah, Muhammad. *Message to the Black Man in America*. Chicago: Muhammad Mosque of Islam, 1965.

Eliot, George. *Adam Bede*.

————. *Daniel Deronda*. Gloucester, Mass.: P. Smith, 1973.

————. *Middlemarch*. New York: Modern Library, 1984.

————. *Silas Marner*. Baltimore, Md.: Penguin Books, 1967.

Ellington, Duke. *Music Is My Mistress*. New York: Doubleday, 1973.

Enana, M. A. *Ibn Khaldun: His Life and Work*. Chicago: Kazi, 1974.

Erfos, Israel, ed. *Chiam Nachman Bialik*. New York: Histadruth Iurith of America, 1948.

Fallaci, Oriana. *Letter to a Child Never Born*. New York: Simon & Schuster, 1976.

Fanon, Frantz. *Black Skin, White Masks*. Trans. Charles Lam Markman. New York: Grove Press, 1967.

Feinstein, Alan. *African Revolutionary*. New York: Quadrangle Books, 1973.

Fernes, Elizabeth Warnock. *Women and the Family in the Middle East*. Austin: University of Texas Press, 1985.

Finnegan, Ruth, ed. *A World Treasury of Oral Poetry*. Bloomington: Indiana University Press, 1978.

Fisher, Dorothy Canfield. *Seasoned Timber*. New York: Harcourt, Brace, 1939.

Flynn, J. J. *Negroes of Achievement in Modern America*. New York: Dodd, Mead, 1970.

Foner, Phillip S. *The Life and Writings of Frederick Douglass*. New York: Citadel Press, 1964.

Friedan, Betty. *The Feminine Mystique*. New York: Dell, 1984.

Fuchs, Esther, ed. and trans. *Encounters with Israeli Authors*. Marblehead, Mass.: Micah, 1982.

Fung Yu-Luan. *A History of Chinese Philosophy*. Trans. Derek Bodde. Princeton, N.J.: Princeton University Press, 1953.

Fyfe, Christopher. *Africanus Horton: West African Scientist and Patriot*. New York: Oxford University Press, 1972.

Galik, Marian. *The Genesis of Modern Chinese Literary Criticism*. Trans. Peter Tkac. Totowa, N.J.: Rowman & Littlefield, 1980.

Gandhi, Indira. *Indira Gandhi: Speeches and Writings*. New York: Harper & Row, 1975.

Gandhi, Mohandas K. *Epigrams from Gandhiji*. Ed. S. R. Tikekar. New Delhi: Publications Division, Ministry of Information and Broadcasting, Government of India, 1971.

————. Selected Writing of Mahatma Gandhi. Ed. Ronald Duncan. Boston: Beacon Press, 1951.

Gardiner, Alan. *Egypt of the Pharaohs*. London: Oxford University Press, 1961.

Garvey, Marcus Moziah. *Philosophy and Opinions*. New York: Arno Press, 1968.

Gazarian-Gautiea, Marie-Lise. *Interviews with Latin American Writers*. Normal, Ill.: Dalkey Archive Press, 1992.

Galb, Arthur, Marion Siegel, and A. M. Rosenthal. *New York Times Great Lives of the Twentieth Century*. New York: Times Books, 1988.

Ghose, Sankar. *Leaders of Modern India*. New Delhi, India: Allie, 1980.

Gibney, Frank. *The Pacific Century*. New York: Scribner's, 1992.

Gibran, Khalil. *The Voice of the Master*. Trans. Anthony R. Ferris. New York: Citadel Press, 1958.

Giles, Herbert A. *Gems of Chinese Literature—Prose*. Shanghai: Kelly & Walsh, 1923. Reprint: New York: Paragon, 1964.

Giovanni, Nikki. *Gemini*. Indianapolis, Ind.: Bobbs-Merrill, 1971.

Gordimer, Nadine. *The Late Bourgeois World*. New York: Viking Penguin, 1983.

Golding, Claud. *Great Names in History*. Freeport, N.Y.: Books for Libraries Press, 1935.

Goldman, Emma. *Anarchism and Other Essays*. New York: Dover, 1969.

———. *My Further Disillusionment in Russia*. New York: Crowell, 1970.

Greer, Germaine. *The Female Eunuch*. New York: McGraw-Hill, 1971.

Gregory, Dick, and James R. McGraw. *The Shadow That Scares Me*. Garden City, N.Y.: Doubleday, 1968.

Greider, Jerome B. *Hu Shih and the Chinese Renaissance*. Cambridge, Mass.: Harvard University Press, 1970.

Greider, Jerome B. *Intellectuals and the State in Modern China*. New York: Free Press, 1981.

Grover, Verinder, ed. *Political Thinkers of Modern India*. New Delhi: Deep & Deep, 1990.

al-Hakim, Tawfiq. *Plays, Prefaces and Postscripts. Vol. 2, Theater of Society*. Trans. W. M. Hutchins, with A. I. Abdulai and M. B. Lawain. Washington, D.C.: Three Continents Press, 1981.

Hale, Sarah Josepha. *Sketches of All Distinguished Women*. New York: Harper & Brothers, 1870.

Halman, Talat Sait, ed. *Contemporary Turkish Literature: Fiction and Poetry*. Trans. Taner Baybars, Bernard Lewis, and Ali Yunus. Teaneck, N.J.: Fairleigh Dickinson University Press, 1982.

Hanna, W. A. *Eight Nation Makers*. New York: St. Martin's Press, 1964.

Helms, Christine M. *The Cohesion of Saudi Arabia*. Baltimore, Md.: Johns Hopkins University Press, 1981.

Henderson, J. D., and L. R. Henderson. *Ten Notable Women of Latin America*. Chicago: Nelson Hall, 1978.

Herold, J. Christopher. *Mistress to an Age: A Life of Madame de Staël*. Indianapolis, Ind.: Charter Books, 1958.

Hicks, Roger, and Ngakpa Cogyam. *Great Ocean*. New York: Penguin Books, 1990.

Hitti, Philip K. *History of Syria*. New York: St. Martin's Press, 1957.

———. *Makers of Arab History*. New York: St. Martin's Press, 1968.

Holliday, Billie. *Lady Sings the Blues*. New York: Doubleday, 1965.

Hottinger, A. *The Arabs*. Los Angeles: University of California Press, 1963.

Hourani, Albert. *Arabic Thought in the Liberal Age, 1798–1939*. London: Oxford University Press, 1970.

Hsun Tzu. *The Works of Hsuntze*. Trans. Homer H. Dubs. London: Probsthain, 1928.

Hu Shih and Lin Yutang. *China's Own Critics*. New York: Paragon Books, 1969.

Hualing Nieh, ed. *Literature of the Hundred Flowers*. New York: Columbia University Press, 1981.

Hughes, Langston. *Selected Poems*. New York: Knopf, 1959.

Humphries, Christmas, ed. *The Wisdom of Buddhism*. London: Curzon, 1979.

Idris, Yusuf. *The Cheapest Nights: Short Stories*. Washington, D.C.: Three Continents, 1991.

Irfani, Kawaja Abdul Hamid. *The Sayings of Rumi and Iqbal*. Sialkot: Bazm-e-Rumi, 1976.

Isaacs, Harold, ed. *Straw Sandals: Chinese Short Stories*. Cambridge, Mass.: MIT Press, 1974.

James, Edward T., ed. *Notable American Women*. Cambridge, Mass.: Belknap Press, 1971.

James, Muriel. *Hearts on Fire*. Los Angeles: Tarcher, 1991.

Johns, C. H. W. *Babylonian and Assyrian Laws, Contracts, and Letters*. New York: Scribner's, 1904.

Johnson, Thomas H., ed. *Emily Dickinson: An Interpretive Biography*. Cambridge, Mass.: Belknap Press, 1955.

Johnston, C. H. L. *Famous Indian Chiefs*. 1909. Reprint, Freeport, N.Y.: Books for Libraries Press, 1971.

Jong, Erica. *Fear of Flying*. New York: NAL Dutton, 1974.

———. *How to Save Your Own Life*. New York: Holt, Rinehart & Winston, 1977.

Josephson, Hannah. *Jeannette Rankin: First Lady in Congress*. Indianapolis, Ind.: Bobbs-Merrill, 1974.

Jurji, E. J. *Illumination in Islamic Mysticism*. Princeton, 1938.

K'ang Yu-wei. *Ta t'ung shu: The One World Philosophy of K'ang Yu-wei.* Trans. Laurence G. Thompson. London: Allen & Unwin, 1958.

Katz, Naomi, and Nancy Milton, eds. *Fragment from a Lost Diary and Other Stories.* New York: Pantheon Books, 1973.

Kellogg, Laura C. "Some Facts and Figures on Indian Education." *Quarterly Journal*, April 15, 1913.

Kgositsile, Keorapetse (William). *My Name Is Afrika.* Garden City, N.Y.: Doubleday, 1971.

Khouri, Mounah, and Hamid Algar, eds. *An Anthology of Modern Arabic Poetry.* University of California Press, 1974.

King, Billie Jean, with Kim Chapin. *Billie Jean.* New York: Harper & Row, 1974.

King, Corretta Scott. *My Life with Martin Luther King, Jr.* New York: Holt, Rinehart & Winston, 1969.

King, Martin Luther, Jr. *Strength to Love.* New York: Harper & Row, 1963.

———. *Why We Can't Wait.* New York: Harper & Row, 1964.

Knipe, David M. *Hinduism.* San Francisco: HarperCollins, 1991.

Kollwitz, Hans, ed. *Diaries and Letters of Kathe Kollwitz.* Chicago: Northwestern University Press, 1955.

Konworthy, L., and E. Ferrari. *Leaders of New Nations.* Garden City, N.Y.: Doubleday, 1959 and 1968.

Kravitz, Nathaniel. *Three Thousand Years of Hebrew Literature.* Chicago: Swallow Press, 1972.

Krishnamurti, Jiddu. *From Darkness to Light.* New York: Harper & Row, 1980.

———. *Meditations.* San Francisco: Harper & Row, 1979.

Kritzeck, James, ed. *Anthology of Islamic Literature.* New York: Holt, 1964.

———. *Modern Islamic Literature.* Trans. Bahram Jamalpur, A. Q. Niaz, Burton Raffel, and Nordin Salam. New York: Holt, Rinehart and Winston, 1970.

Kuang-ming Wu. *Chuang Tzu: World Philosophy at Play.* New York: Cross Roads, 1982.

Kurkjian, Vahan M. *A History of Armenia.* New York: Armenian General Benevolent Union, 1958.

La Follette, Suzanne. *Concerning Women.* Salem, N.H.: Ayer, 1972.

Lal, P. *Love's the First.* Calcutta: Writer's Workshop, 1962.

La Mashairi, Kusanyiko. *Anthology of Swahili Poetry.* East Africa: Heinemann, 1973.

Lamson, Peggy. *In the Vanguard.* Boston: Houghton Mifflin, 1979.

Lansing, M. F. *Liberators and Heroes of the West Indian Islands.* Boston: Page, 1953.

Lao-tzu. *The Canon of Reason and Virtue: Lao-tse's Tao Teh King*. La Salle, Ill.: Open Court, 1927.

———. *The Way and Its Power: A Study of the Tao Te Ching*. Trans. Arthur Waley. London: Allen & Unwin, 1934.

———. *The Way of Lao-Tzu*. Trans. Wing-tsit Chan. Indianapolis, Ind.: Bobbs-Merrill, 1963.

Laqueur, Walter, and Barry Rubin, eds. *The Human Rights Reader*. New York: New American Library, 1979, 1989.

Lee, Leo Ou-fan. *The Romantic Generation of Chinese Writers*. Cambridge, Mass.: Books Demand, 1973.

Lee, Peter H., ed. *Anthology of Korean Literature*. Honolulu: University Press of Hawaii, 1981.

———. *Modern Korean Literature*. Honolulu: University Press of Hawaii, 1990.

Legge, J. D. *Sukarno: A Political Biography*. New York: Praeger, 1972.

Legge, James. *The Chinese Classics, with a Translation, Critical and Exegetical Notes, Prolegomena, and Copious Indexes*. Taipei, China: Southern Materials Center, 1985.

———. *The Texts of Taoism*. New York: Julian Press, 1959.

Lengyel, E. *From Prison to Power*. Chicago: Follett, 1964.

Lerner, Gerda. *Black Women in White America: A Documentary History*. New York: Vintage Books, 1973.

Lessing, Doris. *Martha Quest*. New York: New American Library, 1964.

———. *A Man and Two Women*. New York: Simon & Schuster, 1984.

Leviant, Curt, ed. *Masterpieces of Hebrew Literature*. New York: KTAV, 1969.

Leys, Simon. *The Burning Forest*. New York: Holt, Rinehart & Winston, 1991.

Li Po. *The Works of Li Po*. Trans. Shigeyoshi Obata. New York: Dutton, 1922. Reprint, New York: Paragon, 1964.

Lin, Nancy T., trans. *In Quest: Poems of Chou En-lai*. Calif.: Joint, 1979.

Lin Yutang. *The Importance of Living*. London: Heinemann, 1951.

———. *My Country and My People*. London: Heinemann, 1936–51.

———, ed. *The Wisdom of China and India*. Trans. Swami Paramananda. New York: Random House, 1942.

Lindsay, Jack. *The Troubadors and Their World of the Twelfth and Thirteenth Centuries*. London: Muller, 1976.

Liu Wu-chi. *An Introduction to Chinese Literature*. Bloomington: Indiana University Press, 1966.

Lowell, Amy. *Sword Blades and Poppy Seeds*. New York: AMS Press, 1981.

———. *What's O'Clock*. New York: Houghton Mifflin, 1925.

Lowenstein, Tom, and Knud Rasmussen, eds. and trans. *Eskimo Poems of Canada and Greenland*. Pittsburgh, Pa.: University of Pittsburgh Press, 1973.

Lu Xun. *Selected Works*. Trans. Uang Hsien-yi and Gladys Yang. Beijing: Foreign Languages Press, 1980.

Lyell, William A. *Lu Hsun's Vision of Reality*. Berkeley: University of California Press, 1976.

McCarthy, Mary. *On the Contrary*. New York: Farrar, Straus & Cudahy, 1961.

McCullers, Carson. *The Square Root of Wonderful*. Boston: Houghton Mifflin, 1958.

Machado de Assis, Joaquim Maria. *Esau and Jacob*. Berkeley, Calif.: University of California Press, 1965.

Magner, J. A. *Men of Mexico*. 1942. Reprint, New York: Books for Libraries Press, 1968.

Makeba, Miriam, with James Hall. *Makeba, My Story*. New York: New American Library, 1987.

Malcolm X. *Malcolm X Speaks*. Ed. George Breitman. New York: Grove Press, 1965.

―――. "Racism: The Cancer That Is Destroying America." *Egyptian Gazette*, August 25, 1964.

Malcolm X with Alex Haley. *Autobiography of Malcolm X*. New York: Grove Press, 1965.

Mannes, Marya. *More in Anger*. Philadelphia: Lippincott, 1958.

Martí, José. *Inside the Monster: Writings on the United States and American Imperialism*. Trans. Elinor Randall. New York: Monthly Review Press, 1975.

Martinez, Al. *Profiles of Hispano-American Lives*. New York: New American Library, 1974.

Mascaro, Juan, trans. *The Upanishads*. London: Penguin Classics, 1965.

Mead, Margaret. *Coming of Age in Samoa*. New York: Morrow, 1961.

―――. *Male and Female*. New York: Morrow, 1967.

―――. *Sex and Temperament in Three Primitive Societies*. New York: Morrow, 1963.

Mencius. *The Book of Mencius*. Trans. Lionel Giles. London: Murray, 1942.

―――. *Mencius*. Trans. W. A. C. H. Dobson. Toronto: University of Toronto Press, 1963.

―――. *Mencius*. Trans. D. C. Lau. London: Penguin Classics, 1970.

Mendez, Miguel M. *Peregrinos de Aztlan*. Tucson, Ariz.: Editorial Peregrinos, 1974.

Mezey, Robert, ed. *Poems from the Hebrew*. Trans. David Goldstein and Robert Mezey. New York: Crowell, 1973.

Millay, Edna St. Vincent. *Second April*. New York: Harper, 1950.

Miller, Barbara Stoler, trans. *The Bhagavad-Gita: Krishna's Counsel in Time of War*. New York: Bantam Books, 1986.

Mishima, Yukio. *Confessions of a Mask*. Barcelona: Planeta, 1979.

Mishima, Yukio, and Geoffrey Bownas. *New Writing in Japan*. Baltimore, Md.: Penguin Books, 1972.

Mitford, Jessica. *Kind and Unusual Punishment*. New York: Vintage Books, 1973.

Mo Tzu. *The Ethical and Political Works of Motse*. Trans. Y. P. Mei. London: Probsthain, 1929.

Montessori, Maria. *The Secret of Childhood*. Trans. M. Joseph Costelloe. Notre Dame, Ind.: Fides, 1966.

Moore, Gerald, and Ulli Beier, eds. *The Penguin Book of Modern African Poetry*. London: Penguin, 1963.

Moraga, Cherrie. *This Bridge Called My Back*. Latham, N.Y.: Kitchen Table, 1984.

Morris, Colin M., ed. *The Riddle of Violence/Kenneth Kaunda*. San Francisco: Harper & Row, 1981.

Morrison, James Dalton, ed. *Masterpieces of Religious Verse*. New York: Harper & Row, 1948.

Morse, H. B. *The Chronicles of the East India Company Trading to China, 1635–1834*. Cambridge, Mass.: Harvard University Press, 1926.

Moses, Anna Mary Robertson [Grandma Moses]. *Grandma Moses: My Life's History*. New York: Harper, 1952.

Moses, L. G., and R. Wilson, eds. *Indian Lives: Essays on Nineteenth- and Twentieth-Century Native American Leaders*. Albuquerque: University of New Mexico Press, 1985.

Mottahedeh, Roy. *The Mantle of the Prophet*. New York: Simon & Schuster, 1985.

Mu Fu-sheng. *The Wilting of the Hundred Flowers*. New York: Praeger, 1963.

Muller, F. Max, ed. *The Sacred Books of the East.*, Vol. 22. Trans. Hermann Jacobi. Oxford, England: Clarendon Press, 1884.

Munro, Alice. *Something I've Been Meaning to Tell You*. New York: McGraw-Hill Ryerson, 1974.

Murasaki, Lady. *The Tale of Genji*. Trans. Arthur Waley. Boston: Houghton Mifflin, 1929.

Murdoch, Iris. *The Bell*. New York: Viking Press, 1958.

———. *The Nice and the Good*. New York: Viking Press, 1968.

———. *The Unicorn*. New York: Penguin Books, 1963.

Nasser, Gamal Abdel. *The Philosophy of the Revolution*. Washington, D.C.: Public Affairs Press, 1955.

Nauman, St. Elmo, Jr. *Dictionary of Asian Philosophies*. New York: Philosophical Library.

Neruda, Pablo. *World's End*. Buenos Aires: Editorial Losada, 1969.

———. *Petals of Blood*. London: Heinemann, 1977.

Nguyen Khac Vien. *Tradition and Revolution in Vietnam*. Washington, D.C.: Indochina Research Center, 1974.

Nicholson, Reynold A., trans. *Translations of Eastern Poetry and Prose*. New York: Greenwood Press, 1969.

Nies, Judith. *Seven Women: Portraits from the American Radical Tradition*. New York: Viking Press, 1977.

Nin, Anaïs. *Diary*. New York: Swallow Press, 1966.

Nixon, Julie Eisenhower. *Special People*. New York: Simon & Schuster, 1977.

Nixon, Richard. *Leaders*. New York: Warner Books, 1982.

Oates, Jean. *Babylon*. London: Thames & Hudson, 1986.

Oates, Joyce Carole. "What Is the Connection between Men and Women?" *Mademoiselle*, February 1970.

O'Conner, Flannery. *The Habit of Being*. New York: Farrar, Straus & Giroux, 1979.

O'Keeffe, Georgia. *Georgia O'Keeffe*. New York: Penguin Books, 1975.

Olds, L. C. *All under the Heavens*. Vermont: Vermont Printing, 1977.

Ostle, Robin, ed. *Modern Literature in the Near and Middle East, 1850-1970*. New York: Routledge, 1991.

Padilla, Herberto. *Selected Poems of Herberto Padilla*. Ed. Frank Calzon, Laura Yimayo, and Maria Luisa Alvarez. Washington, D.C.: Georgetown University Press.

Parker, Dorothy. *Sunset Gun*. New York: Liveright, 1928.

Paz, Octavio. *Labyrinth of Solitude*. Trans. Lysander Kemp. New York: Grove Press, 1961.

———. *One Earth, Four or Five Worlds*. New York: Harcourt Brace Jovanovich, 1985.

Peden, Margaret Sayers. *A Woman of Genius: The Intellectual Autobiography of Sor Juana Ines de la Cruz*. Salisbury, Conn.: Lime Rock Press, 1982.

Pekarik, Andrew J., ed. and trans. *The Thirty-six Immortal Women Poets*. New York: Braziller, with New York Public Library, 1991.

Pickthall, Marmaduke, trans. *The Koran*. New York: Knopf, 1993.

Plimpton, George, ed. *Writers at Work: The Paris Review Interviews*. New York: Penguin Books, 1976-1977, 1981, 1984, 1986, 1988.

Powell, Adam Clayton, Jr. *Keep the Faith, Baby*. New York: Trident Press, 1967.

———. *Marching Blacks*. New York: Dial Press, 1973.

Preston, Harriet Waters, ed. *The Complete Poetical Works of Elizabeth Barrett Browning*. Boston: Houghton Mifflin, 1900.

Price, Don C. *Russia and the Roots of the Chinese Revolution*. Cambridge, Mass.: Harvard University Press, 1974.

Raffel, Burton, ed. and trans. *From the Vietnamese: Ten Centuries of Poetry*. Trans. Nguyen Ngoc Bieh. New York: October House, 1968.

Rahula, Walpola. *What the Buddha Taught*. New York: Grove Weidenfeld, 1959, 1974.

Ramakrishna, Sri. *The Gospel of Sri Ramakrishna*. Trans. Swami Hikhilananda. New York: Ramakrishna Vivekananda Center, 1942.

Ramanujan, A. K., ed. and trans. *Interior Landscapes: Love Poems from a Classical Tamil Anthology*. Bloomington: Indiana University Press, 1967.

Rand, Ayn. *Anthem*. New York: NAL Dutton, 1946.

———. *Atlas Shrugged*. New York: New American Library, 1957.

———. *The Fountainhead*. New York: New American Library, 1943.

———. *We, the Living*. New York: Random House, 1936.

Rao, P. Rajeswar. *The Great Indian Patriots*. New Delhi: Mittak, 1991.

Rexroth, Kenneth, ed. and trans. *Love and the Turning Year: One Hundred More Poems from the Chinese*. New York: New Directions, 1970.

———. *One Hundred More Poems from the Japanese*. San Francisco: New Directions, 1974.

———. *One Hundred Poems from the Japanese*. New York: New Directions, 1964.

Rexroth, Kenneth, and Ling Chung, eds. and trans. *The Orchid Boat: Women Poets of China*. New York: McGraw-Hill, 1972.

Richardson, B., and W. A. Fabey. *Great Black Americans*. New York: Crowell, 1976.

Rihani, Ameen. *Ibn Sa'oud of Arabia: His People and His Land*. London: Constable, 1928.

Robeson, Paul. *Here I Stand*. Boston: Beacon Press, 1971.

Roosevelt, Eleanor. "Let Us Have Faith in Democracy." *Land Policy Review*, January 1942.

———. *This I Remember*. New York: Harper & Row, 1963.

Rossabi, Morris. *Khublai Khan: His Life and Times*. Los Angeles: University of California Press, 1988.

Ruby, Robert H., and John A. Brown. *Dream Prophets of the Columbia Plateau: Smohalla and Skolaskin*. Norman: University of Oklahoma Press, 1989.

Rustin, Bayard. *Down the Line*. Chicago: Quadrangle Books, 1971.

———. "From Protest to Politics." *Commentary*, February 1965.

Sa'di. *The Gulistan*. Trans. Edward B. Eastwick. England: Octagon Press, 1979.

———. *The Gulistan*. Trans. Edward Rehatsek. New York: Capricorn Books, 1966.

Sahgal, Nayantara. *Indira Gandhi—Her Road to Power*. New York: Ungar, 1982.

Sand, George. *Lelia*. Bloomington: Indiana University Press, 1978.

Sandars, N. K., trans. *The Epic of Gilgamesh*. London: Penguin Classics, 1960.

Sanger, Margaret. *Women and the New Race*. New York: Brentano's, 1920.

Schwartz, Leo W., ed. *A Treasury of Jewish Literature*. New York: Jewish Publication Society, 1937.

Sealy, T. *Sealy's Caribbean Leaders*. Kingston, Jamaica: Eagle Merchant Bank of Jamaica, 1991.

Sen, N. B., comp. *Wit and Wisdom of Gandhi, Nehru, Tagore*. New Delhi: New Book Society of India, 1968.

Senghor, Leopold Sedar. *Selected Poems*. Trans. John Reed and Clive Wake. New York: Atheneum, 1964.

Sergeant, Howard, ed. *Poetry from Africa*. Oxford: Pergamon Press, 1968.

Seymour, A. J. *New Writing in the Caribbean*. Guyana: Guyana Lithographic, 1972.

———. *Tomorrow Belongs to the People*. n.p., 1975.

Shah, Idries. *The Sufis*. New York: Doubleday, 1964.

Shawcross, William. *Sideshow*. New York: Simon & Schuster, 1978.

Shelley, Mary. *Frankenstein (or, the Modern Prometheus)*. New York: Modern Library, 1984.

Sherfan, Andrew Dib, ed. *A Third Treasury of Khalil Gibran*. Secaucus, N.J.: Carol, 1974.

Sheridan, James E. *Chinese Warlord: The Career of Feng Yu-hsiang*. Stanford, Calif.: Stanford University Press, 1966.

Siu, Helen F., and Zelda Stern, eds. *Mao's Harvest: Voices from China's New Generation*. New York: Oxford University Press, 1983.

Slade, Ruth M. *King Leopold's Congo*. Westport, Conn.: Greenwood Press, 1962.

Smith, Margaret. *Rabi'a the Mystic and Her Fellow Saints in Islam*. Cambridge, U.K.: Cambridge University Press, 1928.

Snow, Helen Foster. *Women in Modern China*. The Hague: Mouton, 1967.

Sontag, Susan. *Against Interpretation*. New York: Farrar, Straus & Giroux, 1966.

———. *The Benefactor*. New York: Farrar, Straus & Giroux, 1963.

———. *Death Kit*. New York: Farrar, Straus & Giroux, 1967.

———. "The Double Standard of Aging." *Saturday Review*, October 1972.

———. "Photography Unlimited." *New York Review of Books*, 1977.

Soustelle, Jacques. *Daily Life of the Aztecs on the Eve of the Spanish Conquest*. Menlo Park, Calif.: Stanford University Press, 1961.

Soyinka, Wole. *A Shuttle in the Crypt*. London: Eyre Methuen-Rex Collings, 1972.

Spence, Jonathan D. *The Gate of Heavenly Peace*. New York: Viking Press, 1981.

Spicehandler, Ezra, ed. *New Writing in Israel*. Trans. Marcia Falk, Leonore Gordon, and Shirley Kaufman. New York: Schocken Books, 1976.

Staël, Germaine de. *The Influence of Literature upon Society*. Paris: Larousse, 1935.

Standing Bear, Luther. *Luther of the Spotted Eagle*. Lincoln: University of Nebraska Press, 1978.

Stanton, Elizabeth Cady, Susan B. Anthony, and Matilda Joslyn Gage, eds. *History of Woman Suffrage*. New York: Arno Press, 1969.

Stassinopoulos, Ariana. *The Female Woman*. New York: Random House, 1973.

Steinem, Gloria. "A New Egalitarian Life Style." *New York Times*, August 26, 1971.

———. *Outrageous Acts and Every Day Rebellions*. New York: Holt, Rinehart & Winston, 1983.

Stineman, Esther. *American Political Women*. Littleton, Colo.: Libraries Unlimited, 1980.

Sun Tzu Wu. *The Art of War*. Trans. Lionel Giles. London: Luzac, 1910.

al-Suhrawardy, Allama Sir Abdulla Al-Mamun. *The Sayings of Muhammad*. New York: Citadel Press/Carol Publishing, 1990.

Suzuki, D. T. *Manual of Zen Buddhism*. London: Rider, 1950.

———. *Zen and Japanese Culture*. London: Routledge & Kegan Paul, 1959.

Swann, Brian, and Arnold Krupat, ed. *I Tell You Now: Autobiographical Essays by Native American Writers*. Lincoln: University of Nebraska, 1987.

Tanaka, Yukiko, ed. *To Live and to Write: Selections by Japanese Women Writers, 1913-1938*. Seattle: Seal Press, 1987.

T'ao Ch'ien. *The Poems of T'ao Ch'ien*. Ed. and trans. Lily Pao-hu Chang and Marjorie Sinclair. Honolulu: University of Hawaii Press, 1953.

Tate, Claudia, ed. *Black Women Writers at Work*. New York: Continuum, 1984.

Ngugi wa Thiong'o. *Barrel of a Pen: Resistance to Repression in Neo-Colonial Kenya*. Trenton, N.J.: Africa World Press, 1983.

Tu Fu. *Tu Fu, Selected Poems*. Trans. Rewi Alley. Beijing: Foreign Language Press, 1962.

Tu Fu, and William Hung. *Tu Fu, China's Greatest Poet*. Cambridge, Mass.: Harvard University Press, 1952.

Tuck, J. Nelson, and Norma C. Vergara. *Heroes of Puerto Rico*. New York: Fleet Press, 1969.

Turner, Frederick, ed. *The Portable North American Indian Reader*. New York: Viking Press, 1974.

Tutu, Desmond. *The Words of Desmond Tutu*. London: Hadder & Stoughton, 1989.

Ueda, Makato. *Modern Japanese Writers and the Nature of Literature*. Stanford, Calif.: Stanford University Press, 1976.

Untermeyer, L. *Makers of the Modern World*. New York: Simon & Schuster, 1955.

Vargas Llosa, Mario. "Latin America: The Democratic Option." *Harper's*, June 1987.

Varma, Om Parkash, ed. *Three Hundred Thirty-three Great Indians*. New Delhi: Carma, 1963.

Venkataraman, T. N., ed. *Talks with Sri Ramana Maharshi*. Tiruvannamalai, S. India, 1955.

Venter, Al J. *Black Leaders of Southern Africa*. Pretoria: Sista Publications, 1976.

Verma, H. N., and Amrit Verma. *One Hundred Great Indians through the Ages*. New Delhi: Great Indian Publishers, n.d.

Vilanueva, Tino. *Hay Otra Voz Poems*. New York: Editorial Mensaje, 1972.

Waley, Arthur. *Chinese Poems*. London: Allen & Unwin, 1946.

————. ed. and trans. *One Hundred and Seventy Chinese Poems*. New York: Knopf, 1919, 1947.

Walker, Alice. *The Color Purple*. New York: Harcourt Brace Jovanovich, 1982.

Wallenrod, Reuban. *The Literature of Modern Israel*. New York: Abelard Schuman, 1956.

Walsh, Thomas, ed. *The Catholic Anthology*. New York: Macmillan, 1932.

Wang Wei. *Poems by Wang Wei*. Ed. and trans. Chang-Yin-nan and Lewis C. Walmsley. Rutland, Vt.: Tuttle, 1958.

Washington, William M., ed. *Miss Lucie Speaks*. Nashville, Tenn.: n.p., 1971.

Watson, Forbes. "Mary Cassatt." *Arts Weekly*, 1932.

Weil, Simone. *Oppression and Liberty*. Trans. Arthur Wills and John Petrie. Amherst: University of Massachusetts Press, 1973.

Weinstein, Martin E. *The Human Face of Japan's Leadership*. New York: Praeger, 1989.

White, Steven F., ed. *Poets of Chile: A Bilingual Anthology, 1965–1985*. Greensboro, N.C.: Unicorn Press, 1986.

Wilgus, A. C., ed. *Makers of Democracy in Latin America*. New York: Cooper Square, 1968.

Wilson, John A. *The Culture of Ancient Egypt*. Chicago: University of Chicago Press, 1951.

Wing-Tsit Chan, trans. *A Source Book in Chinese Philosophy*. Princeton, N.J.: Princeton University Press, 1963.

Wingate, F. R. *Mahdism and the Egyptian Sudan*. London: F. Cass, 1993.

Wolf, Eric R. *Peasant Wars of the Twentieth Century*. New York: Harper & Row, 1969.

475

Wollstonecraft, Mary. *A Vindication of the Rights of Woman*. New York: Norton, 1988.

Woods, Donald. *Biko*. New York: Holt, 1991.

Woolf, Virginia. *The Moment and Other Essays*. New York: Harcourt Brace, 1948.

————. *A Room of One's Own*. New York: Harcourt Brace Jovanovich, 1981.

Wright, Harold P. *Manyo-Shui (Collection of Ten Thousand Leaves)*. Woodstock, N.Y.: Overlook Press, 1986.

Yates, Donald A., and James E. Irby, eds. and trans. *Labyrinths: Selected Stories and Other Writings*. New York: New Directions, 1964.